The Private Side
of
American History

Readings in Everyday Life

Third Edition

Since **2** 1865

Third Edition

16 00

The Private Side
of
American History

Readings in Everyday Life

Edited by
Thomas R. Frazier
*The Bernard M. Baruch College
of The City University of New York*

Since **2** 1865

Harcourt Brace Jovanovich, Inc.
*New York / San Diego / Chicago / San Francisco / Atlanta
London / Sydney / Toronto*

ISBN: 0–15–571967–X

Library of Congress Catalog Card Number: 82–84356

Printed in the United States of America

Cover: Detail from the above painting, *Tenement Flats*, by Millard Sheets, 1934, oil on canvas, 40¼ x 50¼ inches. National Museum of American Art (formerly the National Collection of Fine Arts), Smithsonian Institution; transfer from the National Park Service.

Picture Credits

6 The Great Northern Railway. **34** Cook Collection, Valentine Museum, Richmond, Virginia. **60** Brown Brothers. **86** The Bettmann Archive. **114** Jacob A. Riis Collection, Museum of the City of New York. **136** Brown Brothers. **156** Brown Brothers. **172** Brown Brothers. **206** United States Weather Bureau. **234** Photo by Elliott Erwitt, © Magnum Photos, Inc. **246** The Bettmann Archive. **278** UPI. **314** Photo courtesy of Herbert Gans. **344** George Gardner. **372** Donald Miller from Monkmeyer Press Photo Service. **404** © Suzanne Arms/Jeroboam, Inc.

Preface

Most studies of history concentrate on public figures and public affairs, the events and people that most historians consider important and influential. What tends to be left out in these traditional presentations is the ordinary, day-to-day life of most of the members of the given society—that is, the "private side" of history. This phrase is meant to suggest not events hidden from public view but, rather, personal incidents and the attitudes of ordinary people—especially their responses to the policies of the dominant power in their society.

This Third Edition of *The Private Side of American History* continues and expands on the themes of the first two editions. The essays collected here present a sampling of the varied attitudes, life-styles, living arrangements, and cultural conflicts that have affected the American people. The selections deal both with the mainstream culture and with cultural groups considered deviant by the mainstream. Portrayed here are people—rich and poor, black and white, male and female, old and young—as they go about their daily tasks trying to provide for themselves a satisfactory way of life. New topics covered in this Third Edition include the settlement of the Great Plains, the formation of an all-black community, the expansion of women's employment opportunities, the political power of conservative religion, the structure of a high school education, the struggle of farmers against ecological disaster, the impact on society of returning war veterans, the plight of undocumented workers, and the influence of television on perceptions of social reality.

This portrayal is necessarily incomplete, for only an encyclopedic work could encompass the complexities of everyday life throughout American history. But it is hoped that the essays presented here will give the reader a taste of the manifold cultures found within American society today and in the past.

The sixteen selections, arranged in roughly chronological order, are grouped into four sections, each of which concludes with an annotated bibliography. The headnote accompanying each selection attempts to place the subject matter in its historical context. A brief introduction to the volume describes the major areas that should be considered in a historical survey of everyday life.

For assistance in the preparation of this revision I would like to thank Drake Bush, my new editor at Harcourt Brace Jovanovich, and my former editors, William J. Wisneski and Thomas A. Williamson, who suggested the theme of the original edition and provided support and encouragement. For scholarly assistance I would like to express my appreciation to the following colleagues: Paul S. Boyer, University of Wisconsin—Madison; Timothy H. Breen, Northwestern University; Joseph R. Conlin, California State University, Chico; Ronald K. Hambleton, University of Massachusetts—Amherst, David Nasaw, City University of New York, College of Staten Island; Daniel T. Rodgers, Princeton University, Terry P. Wilson, University of California, Berkeley; and Virginia Yans-McLaughlin, Rutgers University.

Thomas R. Frazier

Contents

1900–1930
The Early Twentieth Century

1930–1960
Depression, War, and After

1960–Present
Contemporary Society

Topical Table of Contents

Sex, the Home, and the Family

Violence and
War

Social
Control

The Private Side of American History

Readings in Everyday Life

Third Edition

Since **2** 1865

Introduction

In recent years the traditional presentation of American history in schools and colleges has come under criticism. The growth of various liberation movements in the 1960s has led to a rewriting of many history texts to include material on blacks, American Indians, white ethnic groups, and women, among others. New Left historiography has brought about a reconsideration of economic and class interests both domestically and in foreign policy. A third area in which the historical record has been remiss is the one represented by the essays reprinted in this volume—the realm of the everyday life of the American people, the private side of American history. The traditional emphasis on public events has resulted in an historical record that fails to provide sufficient insight into the role of ordinary people in the development of our culture and society. Their feelings, the ways in which they responded or reacted to public events, the hopes, desires, and needs that have been the basis of their response are now recognized by many American historians as a legitimate and important area of historical concern.

In attempting to understand and write about the everyday life of ordinary people, it has been necessary for historians to draw on the theoretical and methodological approaches of the social sciences. Several of the selections in this volume, in fact, have been written by professional sociologists and anthropologists. Historians are only just beginning to apply to recent American history the new historiographical approach so well represented in the third edition of Volume I of *The Private Side of American History*, which treats America's early growth.

This second volume is concerned not so much with a growing America as with the attempts to build a national culture based on "traditional American values" in the face of serious challenges by different groups who have little desire to participate in such a value system at the expense of their own culture and perceived past. The consensus on the national culture so sought has proved to be extremely fragile and ultimately incapable of being sustained. When history is viewed from the perspective of the "movers and shakers" of the nation, as it has been in the traditional textbooks, the consensus appears to have been established. When the everyday life of the American people is examined, however, the fragility of the consensus is clear. While the people may appear quietly to acquiesce in the dominant culture of the society, they go right on living their lives, often outside its stated values.

In this volume we will examine the attempts to establish a cultural consensus and will look at those who try to pattern their lives after its perceived values. We will look more often, however, at those who live by a different set of norms, those whose continued existence challenges the dominant culture and who, ultimately, refuse to abide by the rules of what has been called "the American way of life." The groups dealt with in this volume fall, for the most part, then, into the category of those left out of or briefly mentioned in, the traditional texts: women, poor people, ethnic minorities, the young, and the old, among others. But the focus here is not on the causes of their oppression or the conflicts in which they engage in their attempts to come to grips with the dominant power in our society. We concentrate, rather, on the effects of their oppression and the adaptations and adjustments they have made in their attempts to live as fully as possible under often difficult circumstances. Throughout the nation's history, the majority of the people in the United States have lived outside the dominant culture; so we are, in fact, exploring here the private lives of most Americans.

What we are concerned with, then, are the things that most Americans do most of the time—the day-to-day activities and experiences that concern and shape the individual and, thus, are factors in shaping American society. This "private side" of American history is revealed by studying those areas of concern common to the majority of people throughout history.

The quality of individual life is determined largely by such basic factors as work, education, family relationships, and stage in the life cycle. By examining what work people do, how they feel about what they do, what its effect is on them, and whether or not it does what they expect it to—to provide them with a living—we can see the effect employment, or lack of it, has on society as a whole. We need also to understand the impact that the various sources of education in our society—schools, mass media, advertising, family and peer group interaction, and religious institutions, among others—have on the total development of the individual. Because, traditionally, the family has been one of the major forces shaping an individual's life, we must look at the family structure in the United States and see how changes in the structure affect the lives of all of its members. We should also note the impact of changes in the society on the various members of the family in their relationships with each other.

Religion is another important part of American life. The religious institutions have been a major force in the establishing of societal norms, and religious ideas have often been influential in forming counter-norms and in providing emotional support for those outside the mainstream of American culture. So, an understanding of the roles religion has played in the cultural development of America is necessary to our study.

Also important are those areas of concern that, for the most part, are even less directly governed by the individual. Included here are such factors as the effect of drought; violence, war and its aftermath; governmental policy; and social control. We can examine how the people of the United States have dealt with these crucial and, in some cases, ultimate questions. We will observe the impact of ecological disaster on critical segments of the population. We will explore both personal and institutional violence. We will look at the contradictory influence governmental decisions have on the lives of the young and on war veterans. We will also examine the means society uses to shape the individual's behavior to the desired norm. Here we will consider how the dominant society attempts to assimilate or govern the groups it considers deviant; the actions "deviant" groups take to maintain their distinctiveness—and the price they pay for their efforts; and, of particular importance, the way certain institutions such as schools and churches operate directly or indirectly as agents of social control. The areas of concern considered here by no means exhaust the possible categories for the study of everyday life, but they are at least suggestive of the kinds of experiences that must be covered in exploring the private side of American history.

In this volume, each section contains at least one selection that attempts to delineate the norms or activities of one segment of the dominant culture. The other selections describe behavior or attitudes that deviate from the traditional norms. The volume begins with an essay that explores the settlement of the Great Plains. This restatement of the classic pattern of town settlement and land speculation describes the last phase of the conquest of the American landscape by the Euro-Americans. The values expressed in this enterprise still operate, but the arena of their implementation has shifted to metropolitan areas. Other essays in this section deal with the attempt of freed slaves to form a community independent of the dominant white culture, technological advances which have both expanded and restricted areas of female employment in the work force, and the attempt of the traditional elite to escape from a changing society by withdrawing into restricted enclaves where they need associate only with others of their own class.

In the next section, we see the struggles of European immigrants to find their place in American life—the first selection deals with childhood, adolescence, and young adulthood among the Jews of New York City's lower East Side, and the second with the struggle of immigrant mill workers to achieve a decent standard of living in the face of oppressive working conditions. The third selection explores the conflict between conservative Protestantism and the perceived threat to the truth of "God's Word" by scientific education. The concluding essay in this section describes the functions of public education in a business society.

The first essay in the third section shows how poor conservation methods combined with adverse weather conditions led to the Dust Bowl of the 1930s. Also, we see how the dominant society dealt with two of its prominent racial and ethnic minorities—blacks and chicanos. Also included in this section is an essay on the returning veterans of the Second World War showing how a governmental policy made their reentry into American life more equitable than has been the case after other wars.

The last section opens with an analysis of the quality of suburban life, a mode of existence chosen by a majority of the American people at the present time. In contrast to the contentment expressed by the suburbanites, the next selection examines the powerful and persistent counter-culture movement that affected so many Americans, particularly adolescents and young adults, in the late 1960s. The third selection deals with the problems facing an increasingly disadvantaged segment of American society—the working-class family. Finally, we take a look at the influence of television and how it contributes to Americans' conceptions of social reality.

This volume provides but a sampling of the enormous variety of life-styles and life experiences of the groups and individuals who make up what we call the American nation. The editor has attempted to acquaint the student with the possibility of better understanding the history of the United States through a study of the many different ways in which people have shaped their lives in order that they might live with as much of their essential humanity intact as possible. For many this has been an extremely difficult task because of the structural disorders in American society. Only if these disorders are seen for what they are, however, and seriously challenged, will the private lives of the American people improve in significant ways.

The Gilded Age

1865–1900

A railroad construction crew in the Montana territory, 1887

The Great Plains—
Homesteads
and Prairie Junctions

RICHARD LINGEMAN

By the middle of the nineteenth century the railroad was in the process of transforming patterns of population settlement in the United States. Nowhere was this more evident than on the Great Plains. This vast unsettled area, from Oklahoma on the south up through the Dakotas, had for years been referred to as the Great American Desert. These millions of acres of treeless, waterless, flat or rolling prairie land were covered with thick turf grasses and inhospitable to the kind of agricultural settlement that predominated further east. The Great Plains were seen as something to cross on the way to the bonanzas of the far west.

The completion of the transcontinental railroad in the 1860s, however, changed all that. The forbidding prairie began to fill up with people who sought one or both of the two great goals of American life—land and/or commercial success. Town settlement in the United States represented the commercial drive of the American people. Agriculture here had not developed, as it had in other countries, around rural villages, except in early New England. American farmers tended to live on and cultivate individual crop lands, and farm families tended to live in isolation from one another and from community life. Towns, on the other hand, had almost solely a trading function. While the few large cities could indulge themselves with cultural, political, and industrial pursuits, the towns were there almost entirely to provide the surrounding agricultural area with goods and services not available on the isolated farms.

The location of towns, prior to the last half of the nineteenth century, was often at the whim of the founders of the community. Where possible, they were located along navigable waters or as stations along a developing network of primitive roadways. Successful towns were those which were able to build and maintain trade routes both with the surrounding farm land and larger commercial centers from which and to which industrial and agricultural goods were shipped in the furtherance of trade.

The coming of the railroad to the Great Plains, however, changed the pattern of town settlement. In the chapter reprinted below from his book on the history of small towns in the United States, Richard Lingeman describes the new process. While previously the railroads tended to follow the already settled towns, henceforth the towns would follow the railroads. Using the vast acreage of public lands provided to the railroad companies to finance their operation, the companies established towns at their convenience, not at the convenience of the growing farm population. Towns lived and died according to the way the railroad treated them.

The other major factor influencing the settlement of the plains was the series of homestead acts passed by the federal and state governments. These acts provided cheap or even free land to settlers who were willing to live and work there. The purpose of the homestead legislation was to encourage settlement in the less fertile and more isolated areas of the plains. It was thought that this settlement would increase the prosperity of the region and the nation through an increase in agricultural productivity and trade. What may not have been foreseen was the way land speculators took advantage of the homestead acts to increase their holdings.

Life on the homesteads of the Great Plains has been dealt with in classic works of American literature. The back-breaking work and depressing isolation seems to have taken a particularly heavy toll on women. But the desire for land continued to drive families to the plains, in spite of the physically and psychologically hostile environment encountered there. Cycles of fertility and drought, the recurrence of tornadoes and dust storms, were not enough to preclude settlement. And the towns prospered or faltered according to the health of the surrounding agricultural areas.

Today, with the diminishing importance of the railroad, many previously prosperous towns have virtually disappeared. The increased mechanization of agriculture has led to a declining farm population that is still, however, dependent ultimately on the weather for success or failure. The small commercial town has become an anachronism in American life. Increasingly, agricultural freight is shipped by truck on interstate highways, and the population continues to shift toward the metropolitan regions. Soon the prosperous and vital small town will remain only as a memory, a cultural artifact from an earlier time. And its loss will be mourned by those who look back nostalgically to a time when the small town served as a symbol for the "traditional" American way of life.

The original cattle ranchers belonged to a pastoral era, when the land was free to all and its riches for the taking. Many ranchers acceded to the farmers when the railroads came through; some even platted a town on their spreads, sold off the land, became president and chief stockholder of the town bank, and lived out their days in quiet respectability as the town's leading citizen. Their lives, as Walter Prescott Webb pointed out, had spanned the entire history of the cattle kingdom. Yet before the rancher and the miner there were others—the fur trappers, the mountain men who blazed the trails of the West, living off the land in their own style. And before them, of course, the Indians, who created a colorful, nomadic culture around the buffalo—a culture that died when the buffalo was killed off, and the hunters driven farther and farther off their hunting lands and herded onto reservations. All of these inhabitants lived in a state of closeness with the Plains, exploiting the varied wealth that nature had placed there millennia ago.

The mountain men were inveterate loners, living a half-Indian existence and scorning civilization. They were obviously not town planters and avoided human society for months on end. Yet they had their own form of community—the trappers' rendezvous, the gatherings of trappers bringing their pelts to sell to the fur traders, an occasion for orgiastic drinking and wenching. The itinerant traders gave way to the trading posts, often small forts run by private individuals where the trappers and the Indians traded their furs for civilized goods. Sometimes these forts grew into towns, especially if they were on a trading route—some of the scattered military posts the United States set up across its new empire did likewise. Non-gold-seeking settlers headed for the Northwest via the Oregon Trail in the 1840s, and a few intrepid men who had preceded them set up forts and trading posts to temporarily house them when they arrived. The gold frontier stimulated more settlement, and the need for communication back east grew. The freight companies had been in the West almost from the beginning, starting with the Santa Fe Trail expeditions to Mexican territory. They continued at great hazard and difficulty to bring supplies out, aided by government subsidies. Stage lines and the brief-lived pony express brought mail and passengers to the new settlers and carried the gold and silver from the mines. And along these stage routes were small stations that sometimes grew into towns. All of these modes of transportation had their day and played their part, but it was the coming of the railroad after the Civil War that opened up the West to agriculture and mass settlement; for it was the railroad that forged ties of steel between the West and the urban centers of the East, which provided a market for the West's produce. The coming of the railroad also heralded the introduction of the industrial age to the West, in the form of mass-produced technologies, without which agriculture on the Great Plains would have been impossible. So, unlike the reign of the mountain men and the forty-niners and the cattlemen, the conquest of the Great Plains by the farmers was a product of industrialization.

In the Middle West the towns preceded the railroads. But in the Far West the railroads preceded the towns. In the Middle West towns grew up along trails and wilderness roads and rivers, streams, and canals, and then wherever a town boomer decided to create one. But the railroads did not become an economic force until the 1850s, and so they connected already existing towns. The harbingers of the future were those first railroad towns laid out by the Illinois Central in the 1850s. With its 2,573,800 acres of land, the Illinois Central was the biggest land baron in the state, causing a British visitor to say, "This is not a railroad company, *it is a land company.*"[1] It was good rich, prairie land, worth twice as much, one of the Central's founders estimated, as all the farmland in Ohio. And Illinois grew so fast that the price of this land exceeded the railroad proprietors' wildest dreams. Between 1854 and 1857, the company sold half its land for over $15 million, at an average price of $13 an acre. In the middle of the alternate, six-square-mile checkerboard sections interspersed with sections of public-domain land on each side of its right-of-way running the length of the state, the Central strung a series of monotonously laid-out towns, and gave them names that ran in alphabetical order. Thus it profited several times over—from the sale of the land and from the produce the farmers to whom it had sold the land brought to the towns it had platted and shipped on the trains it owned at freight rates it fixed noncompetitively. Owning a railroad was a license to print money, in short—or so it seemed at the time.

The railroad and right-of-way acts of the 1850s set the direction of the postwar railroad boom. The big difference was that the West afforded opportunities for plunder that made Illinois look like small potatoes. Eventually the western railroads would be given more than ninety million acres of good western land, with the four largest (Union Pacific, Southern or Central Pacific, Northern Pacific, and Santa Fe) receiving over eighty-eight million of those acres.

The misuse of government monetary subsidies by railroad managements through devices such as the Crédit Mobilier of America, the construction company that reaped profits of 100 percent, was a national scandal of the Gilded Age. The land grants to the western railroads were also criticized as a great land grab, directed toward enriching the railroad entrepreneurs while removing public lands from the reach of the common man. There is a great deal of truth to this, although the argument can be made that, given the decision to entrust railroad building to private enterprise, the public-lands subsidy represented a transfer of the enormous risks involved in building transcontinental railroads from the government, which could ill afford them, to private contractors, who were "paid" in land that had cost the government nothing. Finally, even more tellingly criticized was the tremendous waste involved in the construction of the western railroads because of the haste with which they were laid down, necessitating that most of them be completely rebuilt as little as fifteen years after they were completed. Add to this waste the excessive debt structure erected upon the railroads, the governmental graft that they encouraged, the subsidies from state and local governments that were never redeemed (which placed an onerous burden of interest charges on the taxpayers), and the anarchically competing railroad systems that burgeoned and collapsed into bankruptcy in the nineties.

---

[1] Quoted in T. H. Watkins and Charles Watson, Jr., *The Land No One Knows* (San Francisco: Sierra Club Books, 1975), p. 75.

Yet the driving of the Golden Spike on May 10, 1869 at Promontory, Utah—the junction of the Union Pacific and Central Pacific railroads— was an event of immense symbolic importance. This jointure of the Atlantic and Pacific coasts by a frail-seeming pair of tracks crossing vast plains, deserts, and mountains meant to the people that the American East and West were at last one; the Civil War had preserved the constitutional union and now the transcontinental railroad had forged a geographical union across the continent to the shores of the Pacific. Little wonder that there was national jubilation on the day of the ceremony.

The railroads laid 22,885 miles of track in the West between 1865 and 1873—32 percent of the mileage in the entire country—at a cost of $1.2 billion (an amount equal to about half the national debt as it stood in 1873, still swollen by the costs of the Civil War). Most of these lines were extended in section after section of track across uninhabited lands by the straightest route possible, with no population centers to detour them. Unlike the East and the Middle West, where tangled skeins of railroads, financed by small companies, joined up towns and consolidated into larger systems that were merged with trunk lines linking the heartland with the coast, in the Far West the trunk lines were put down first, in a single giant stride that took from eight to fifteen years of effort, with the only witnesses the grim-visaged Indians. The capital this great effort demanded was colossal, the return low once it was completed; in 1873 the return on investment in the West was about 2 percent compared with 6 percent in the East. Poor's *Manual of Railroads of the United States* for 1873–74 explained the reason for the disparity: there was "an excess of mileage to population"[2] in the West. Because of overconstruction the annual earnings of western railroads declined from $12,615,846 in 1869 to $11,402,161 in 1872. Poor called for a stop to this "suicidal" policy which was "working more mischief to the railroad interests of the country than all other causes combined."[3] Undoubtedly, the burst of railroad building overcommitted western financiers such as Jay Gould and was the main cause of the panic of 1873.

The panic slowed down but did not stop the railroads' growth, and it may have stepped up immigration by the unemployed. This was all to the good for the railroads, who desperately needed people in their empty domains. As one executive capsulized it, "No people, no trains." To get these people the railroads found themselves cast by history in a major role in the West's settlement. They fell heir to the role of organizing parties of settlers, transporting them to their home sites, and distributing land among them—roles previously played by the New England colonies and the land companies and town boomers of the Middle West. They too organized themselves into land companies to sell off their lands on attractive terms to settlers. They laid out towns along their rights-of-way; they subsidized immigration societies that propagandized the virtues of the West to settlers, and put out the guides advising them where to go, what to bring; and they ran immigrants' trains with special reduced fares.

---

[2]Quoted in Walter Prescott Webb, *The Great Plains* (New York: Grossett & Dunlap, 1973), p. 278.
[3]Ibid.

The first settlers after the war came by covered wagon, of course, often a long line of them abreast (rather than single file, because of the dust) sweeping across the level prairies. The lure that brought them was land, but what set off this migration from past ones was that *some* of the land was free. For with the withdrawal of the South from the Union, Congress was able at last to pass a real free-land act—the Homestead Act of 1862. The act provided that, upon payment of a small entry fee, a settler could take up as much as 160 acres of land for his own use. If he erected a dwelling on this land and lived there for five years, the land was his for nothing; if he wished to exercise preemption rights he could, after six months, buy the land at $1.25 an acre. That was the act in essence; it was later subjected to numerous amendments, with variances for mineral, timber, and desert land, large parcels reserved for the states to sell, as well as other laws requiring irrigation, out-and-out payment, or other preconditions for occupancy.

The law was imperfectly administered by inadequate personnel who were often corrupt; it was evaded widely by ranchers and others who needed larger acreage to profitably graze their animals and who hired dummy entrymen to claim land for them. At most the act affected about 80–100 million acres out of the nearly 500 million acres of western land open to settlement. Between 1862 and 1882, 552,112 homestead entries were filed, but only 194,488 of these claims were "proved up" either by the claimant fulfilling the five-year residency requirement or paying the preemption rate of $1.25 an acre outright. The rest of the land—more than two thirds of it—went to speculators or large owners. And so the act that seemed to fulfill at last the Jeffersonian dream of a nation of small holders; of which Abraham Lincoln said: "I am in favor of settling the wild lands into small parcels so that every poor man may have a home,"[4] and which Horace Greeley called "a reform calculated to diminish sensibly the number of paupers and idlers and increase the proportion of working, independent, self-subsisting farmers in the land evermore,"[5] was at best only a partial success.

Yet, this "common man's land law" did stir the yearnings of thousands of immigrants—the tenant farmers and renters of the Middle West, the incorrigibly restless who always saw hope just over the horizon, the Civil War veterans with their land warrants looking for a new start, the landless sons of farmers, and the urban proletariat seeking escape from the satanic mills (a small number, actually; the immigration was twenty times as great from the country to the cities than the other way), and the foreign immigrants who may have been handworkers (tailors, locksmiths, carpenters, fishermen) rather than farmers in the old country but who all single-mindedly equated the New World's promise with a plot of land, free and clear and theirs alone.

The Homestead Act was a greater boon to the early settlers than to the later ones. The best land was the rich black soil of the prairie plains east of the 98th meridian. Although it had some timbered areas, this land was

[4]Quoted in Watkins and Watson, *The Land No One Knows*, p. 51.
[5]Ibid.

mainly treeless, level as a billiard table, its sticky black loam inviting to the plough. Rainfall was adequate and corn, wheat, or almost any other crop the farmer put in would thrive. (The relative abundance of rainfall demarcated the region from the more arid High Plains west of the parallel.)

The men in Congress who had passed the Homestead Act had based their estimates of farm size on the experience of the Middle West, where 160 acres of land—a quarter section—was more than adequate and indeed abundant. Thus plots of 80 and even 40 acres were permitted to be registered. These sizes would provide a living for a man and a small family and were the most workable size in terms of labor and machinery available to the ordinary homesteader. Larger farms were often taken up in part for speculation and not worked in their entirety. The level prairie land did, however, favor largescale mechanized farming, and so in the treeless parts of Indiana, Illinois, and Iowa, known as the Grand Prairie, large numbers of "bonanza" farms worked by laborers or tenants appeared. Still, in the immediate postwar period there was opportunity for the small farmer, for he could take up the land and, without the need for clearing out the stumps, put in a crop.

Consequently, rural life in the prairie region lost some of the pioneer diversions that arose out of cooperative labors. The prairie farmers lived lives of lonely toil, unlivened by the social sharing, the mutual help, the common bonds of being in the same boat. They worked hard, made money (some of them), and lived the boring, unimaginative lives chronicled by Hamlin Garland in his novels, stories, poems, and sketches. Garland wrote of the "main-travelled road" that provided a title for one of his books of short stories, which "has a dull little town at one end and a home of toil at the other."[6] Walter Prescott Webb observed that Garland and others who wrote of the prairie agricultural regions became realists, pointing up the grim side of life, the narrow, provincial cast of mind that dominated. The chroniclers of the Plains—the Wild West—on the other hand, emphasized romance, unpredictability, extremes of nobility and evil. The romance of the Wild West missed, of course, the grimness of life there, but the life that Garland saw had all color and romance leached out of it. The pain and dreariness and loneliness of prairie life demanded to be told, as though eastern readers must be deliberately disabused of any sentimentality they might have about the region. The Far West, on the other hand, inspired novels steeped in color, exoticism, adventure. The Far West literature was the literature of the frontier and the cattle kingdom and the mining camps while that of the Prairie Plains was the literature of the farms and "dull little towns"—the literature of the ordinary, of monotonous hardship, of a milieu from which many Americans, like the authors, had escaped with relief and loathing (yet with a residue of nostalgia and inarticulated loss).

Those prosperous small farms of the Prairie Plains were by no means within the reach of all. Much of the best land (the now familiar story) was taken by absentee speculators or large landholders. This was possible because large areas of public-domain land were assigned to the railroads, or to the states for resale, or kept off the market by the U. S. government to prevent

---

[6]Quoted in Webb, *The Great Plains*, p. 473.

speculators from buying it up. This land was often ultimately sold for prices beyond the reach of the immigrant.

Further, as mechanization increased productivity, the small farm of around a hundred acres was becoming less competitive with the larger farm. The census figures from 1880 on showed a steady decline in farms of fewer than one hundred acres. There was a growing trend toward tenancy among two groups—the small farmer who lacked the capital to buy up good land and the former smallholder who had lost his farm because he could not meet the payments to the bank or loan shark or simply could not make a go of his land. The smallholders had to struggle to keep their heads above water. Those without enough money to buy land were forced to work as farm laborers, while others rented; but farm workers tended to be an itinerant proletariat, unable to save enough to buy their own farms, while the tenants often had to deal with harsh landlords who took their entire crops in payment of rent, then threw them off the land. Other tenants had it better, but still they were often in a situation of being required to make their own improvements of the property and once they did so, finding that the owner has raised their rent because the farm had become more valuable. These landless farmers—who numbered from 25 to 40 percent of the total in some areas—had shallow economic roots and were prone to have another go farther west rather than eventually buy and work a profitable farm where the good land was.

Indeed, the railroads in their proselytizing for new settlers did not ignore this landless tenant class. In 1879 the Burlington Railroad, a big holder of Nebraska land, took out ads in Illinois papers urging young men to come west: "Life is too short to be wasted on a rented farm."[7] The Santa Fe also advertised its lands in Kansas, claiming that there were "no lands owned by speculations"[8] in its grant. That was only partly true for the speculators had already bought up the railroad lands in eastern Kansas, where the best soil was; one of these buyers was a foreign-born landlord whose large holdings in Illinois had made him the focal point of the tenant agitation. In Ford County, Illinois, which had the largest amount of tenancy and tenant unrest, as early as 1872 the people began organizing homesteading groups, which migrated to Kansas.

So the Prairie Plains—the richest agricultural region in the entire country—were soon filled up and developed or held by speculators. Consequently, the homesteaders' march was quickly pushed farther west, across the 98th meridian and into the High Plains. The High Plains area was flat and treeless and had a semiarid climate, with annual rainfall averaging from twenty-five inches in the east to fifteen inches or below in desert regions. This vast area comprised most of North and South Dakota, Kansas, Nebraska, Oklahoma, western Texas, eastern Montana, Wyoming, and Colorado and a thin slice of New Mexico. The eastern parts of many of the states the 98th meridian crossed were good farming regions; but generally

---

[7]Quoted in Paul Gates, *Landlords and Tenants on the Prairie Frontier* (Ithaca, N.Y.: Cornell University Press, 1973), p. 286.
[8]Ibid.

the meridian marked the beginning of a significant decline in rainfall. This semiaridity made farming in the region precarious—subject to the vicissitudes of alternating adequate rainfall and drought. There were other hostile environmental factors in the region—high winds, extremes of climate with frigid winters and burning summers, plagues of insects, shallowness of the soil, toughness of the matted grass, and absence of trees except in river bottomland. The exiguousness of this land made new demands of those who settled there—in some ways a revolutionary way of life, as Webb claimed in his classic study *The Great Plains.* If the plains brought out resourcefulness and innovation, they put such a high price on success that a cruel toll was exacted from the many unable to meet this price. The area that represented the last dream of the landless, of those seeking a new life, turned into a nightmare for many. Here there were no hostile Indians to unite against, no forests to clear away in cooperative labor— here the enemy was implacable Nature and a cruel isolation that turned many inward and set them down the route to madness.

Until the railroads began their drumbeating, the Plains had no propagandists to sing its praises. Far from being another Garden of the Universe, on most American maps through the 1850s it was identified as the Great American Desert. Explorers over the course of centuries had found it an inhospitable place, with little promise for farming. Some thinkers decided its hostility to settlement was a good thing: The G. A. D. would serve as a barrier to curb the native restlessness of Americans, thus stopping emigration once and for all. Of course, some saw the beauties of the prairie—the endless rolling grass like a great green ocean; the bright-hued flowers which grew up in riotous colors after the rains; the overarching blue dome of sky. Others noted its utility for grazing—a prediction that the Coronados of the cattle country took up when they staked out their Kingdom after the Civil War. Brigham Young was alerted to the potential of the Salt Lake area by John C. Frémont's reports. But given the agricultural methods of the day and the experience with the forested lands and rich soil east of the Mississippi, few envisioned the area patchworked with farms. The essentially agrarian mind-set of the day lacked a sense of how industrialization would revolutionize farming. The railroad technocrats and robber barons supplied the cutting edge of this industrial vision, motivated by the need for people and profits, capable of bringing to bear all the latest technologies against the enemy, Nature. Fittingly, the railroad men, who had forced their rails across this hostile land, were the first believers in its future. They had to believe, for they needed people, towns, farm produce; inexorably committed to growth, groaning under crushing debt, they knew a Plains devoted to cattle was not enough. A few Abilenes and Dodge Cities located on a few trunk lines sufficed to handle the cattle trade; but large-scale freight and passenger operations shuttling from east to west required a population base—people growing grain, people consuming the manufactured products of the East, people living in towns and on farms. In their briskly efficient vision, they divided the land into a great checkerboard of sections extending out from twenty to one hundred miles on either side of their right-of-way. These squares had to be sold off for farms and towns if any immediate profit was to be made from the land alone; after that, would come the steady, long-range return from freight.*

Without the railroads the people would have probably come anyway, only more slowly. Certainly the promise of the Homestead Act and the increase in immigration from Europe were sufficient to insure that. The early wagonborne settlers confronted a prospect that affirmed the Great American Desert appellation, but still they came, their very innocence of what they would find perhaps their strongest impetus. The new settlers saw an endless vista, a horizon unbroken by trees and overhead a burning sun in a vast cloudless sky. An eerie stillness surrounded them; it was due to the absense of any birds on the Plains. There were few game animals, other than the herds of buffalo (gone by the 1880s), but an overplenitude, it seemed, of dangerous rattlesnakes. The lost babe in the woods of the early colonists' tales had his or her counterpart in the child of the wagon train who wandered off in the tall bluestem prairie grass and was not seen again until winter when the grass was withered by frost and the pathetic little corpse was found, dead of a rattler's bite or starvation. In the monotonous vastness of it all, one could easily lose one's bearings, for there were no landmarks, no trees, no rocks—it was especially easy to become confused at night or on a cloudy day, when there was no sun to point out east and west.

One of the most terrifying hazards of the plains was prairie fires, set by lightning or perhaps a campfire. These would sweep over an area, driving all the animals before them and leaving bare, black stubble. Such a burned-over area was one woman's most vivid memory of her arrival at her new home in Adams County, Nebraska:

> I shall never forget the black prairie as I saw it in 1872, just after a prairie fire had swept over it. To me, coming from southern Michigan with her clover fields, large houses and larger barns, trees, hills, and running streams, the vast stretches of black prairie never ending—no north, south, east, or west—dotted over with tiny unpainted houses— no I can't say barns—but shacks for a cow, and perhaps a yoke of oxen—that picture struck such a homesick feeling in my soul it took years to efface.[9]

Even the crude shacks relieving the emptiness of the land were rare at first, because there were no trees and imported lumber was prohibitively expensive. Most of the settlers either made dugouts in the sparse hills or, more frequently, employed the native building material—the sod of the plains matted with the tough wiry roots of the grass. To quarry this

*The railroads bear a substantial share of the blame for the uncertainties of farming and town-planting on the Plains. They sought to settle a large population scattered on small farms, producing for the urban market back east. Thus, the farmers were more vulnerable to economic cycles, and towns lacked industry and marketing relations with the farmers. The farms themselves were isolated economic units, each in competition with its neighbors. See *Garden in the Grasslands*, David M. Emmons (Lincoln: University of Nebraska Press, 1971.).

[9]Quoted in Dorothy Weyer Creigh, *Adams County* (Hastings, Neb.: Adams County-Hastings Centennial Commission, 1972), p. 10.

"Nebraska marble," the settler hired a man with a grasshopper plough to cut foot-wide strips of soil. Rectangles two feet long were then cut from these strips. A clearing sixteen by twenty-four feet was made, and the pieces of sod were piled up on top of one another around its outline, making walls two feet thick and still covered with grass. Space for a door and a window would be left open, and a ridgepole laid along the top of the peaked roof, with brush for rafters and more sod placed on top to make a roof. The naturally insulated sod house—or "soddie"—was cool in summer and warm in winter, and since it was built low to the ground, it was resistant to tornados. And it cost nothing to build. It was also dark inside, and its roof leaked so that the dirt floor became a bog when it rained. Displaced snakes and mice would crawl out of the sod unless the builder had taken care to chink their holes when he removed the sod.

One sees contemporary photographs of the soddies with families seated outside squinting in the bright sun, the farmer often standing squarely by his plough, the tool of his trade, and a weapon of his survival like a Kentucky woodsman's long rifle. In the windows were often potted geraniums or begonias which the women had brought, as slips, from back east, the only reminder of the homes they had left, undoubtedly with considerable regret, to live on this godforsaken prairie. The chroniclers of the Plains have shown how hard the life was on a woman (with the significant exception of Willa Cather, who extolled the strength of pioneer women in characters like Alexandra Bergson in *O Pioneers* and Antonia Shimerda in *My Ántonia*).

The classic figure of the suffering woman of the Great Plains is Beret, the Norwegian immigrant in Ole Rölvaag's saga of life in the Dakotas, *Giants in the Earth* (a novel based closely on immigrant accounts). While her husband, Per Hansa, a robust, genial, optimistic man, revels in his new farm and builds it into a profitable enterprise, despite vicissitudes of drought, blizzard, and plagues of grasshoppers, Beret slowly is driven mad—not just by the harshness of life, the lack of amenities, the emptiness of the vistas—but by a sense of some profound guilt that haunts her. There was something unwholesome about life there, Beret found; the absence of civilization made her vulnerable to her inner demons. She is gripped suddenly by an unnameable fear: *"Something was about to go wrong."* She views the flat, empty land and thinks, "Why, there isn't even a thing that one can *hide behind!*"[10] She grows worse until a preacher comes to the small settlement, starts a church, is kind to her, and succeeds in exorcising her oppressive sense of looming evil. But her sanity is won at the cost of becoming a religious fanatic. In the depths of a raging blizzard, when one of their neighbors is dying, she develops an *idée fixe* that he must have a minister; she nags Per Hansa until he fatalistically sets out in the storm to find a preacher; he never comes back. His body is discovered the following spring, sheltering by a haystack: "His face was ashen and drawn. His eyes were set towards the west."[11]

Rölvaag pits the Old World superstitions and guilts, as well as the deep ties to the little villages with their rhythms and community, against the

[10]O. E. Rölvaag, *Giants in the Earth* (New York: Harper & Row, 1955), p. 474.
[11]Ibid, p. 475.

pioneer's westering urge. Beret has brought a heavy baggage of sin, like her father's old trunk which she cherishes and plans to use for her coffin. Her guilt transforms the vast indifferent land into an ominous presence. The guilt she feels—what Per Hansa cannot understand—is for the hubris that leads a man to cast off the settled ways of the village back in Norway and go forth into the wild godless land, beyond the reach of custom and tradition. It is the woman, with her conservative, old-country notions, who brakes Per Hansa's dream. He is the optimist, oriented in the future, a pragmatist. For the man, then, the Plains represented freedom, opportunity, and a rejection of the old ways, and Beret, as Rölvaag depicts her, must instinctively fight this and hate it until her hate seeps into her own system, poisoning her.

Webb considers the tragedy of women of the Plains and concludes that the region "exerted a peculiarly appalling affect on women" if the fictional characterizations were any indication, and his own upbringing convinces him there is much truth to the fiction. "Imagine a sensitive woman set down on an arid plain to live in a dugout or a pole pen with a dirt floor, without furniture, music, or pictures, with the bare necessities of life! . . . The wind, the sand, the drought, the unmitigated sun, and the boundless expanse of a horizon on which danced fantastic images conjured up by the mirages, seemed to overwhelm the women with a sense of desolation, insecurity and futility, which they did not feel when surrounded with hills and green trees."[12]

Webb is not saying that women were spiritually inferior or hinting at darker psychopathologies as Rölvaag does; rather he is describing the result of the social role of many women of the day, who were conditioned to finding meaning in keeping a home, who were used to the amenities and the "finer things." When such accoutrements of civilization as they had known it were absent, many women had trouble adjusting. Fortunate were those who at least had other women to commiserate with. Mary Ballon, who kept a boarding house while her husband prospected in California in 1852, described in a letter to her son back east how she and the few other women in a little mining town longed for home: "I would not advise any Lady to come out here and suffer the toil and fatigue that I have suffered . . . Clark Simmon's wife says if she was safe in the States she would not care if she had one cent. She came in here last night and said, 'Oh dear I am so homesick that I must die' and then again my other associate came in with tears in her eyes and said she had cried all day, she said if she had as good [i.e. bad] a home as I had got she would not stay twenty-five minutes in California."[13]

Whatever the causes, the fact remains that most women courageously survived the grim life in the lonely sod huts. Elinore Pruitt Stewart, a young widow, went west in 1909, determined to homestead. With the help and advice of the Wyoming rancher, whom she worked for as housekeeper and then married, she proved up her claim. In one of her letters published in *Harper's Magazine*, she avers that she is "very enthusiastic about women

[12]Webb, *The Great Plains*, p. 506.
[13]Christiane Fischer, editor, *Women in the American West 1849–1900* (Hamden, Conn., the Shoe String Press, 1977), p. 44.

homesteading. It really requires less strength and labor to satisfy a large family than it does to go out to wash"[14] (she had been a "washlady" in Denver before moving to Wyoming). But she added that "temperament has much to do with success . . . and persons afraid of coyotes and work and loneliness had better let ranching alone."[15] Later, when towns grew up, with opportunities to pursue their own interests, rather than laboring unremittingly for their husbands' dreams, they blossomed—like those slips of flowers they had carried west. In the rough mining and cow towns, "respectable" women were often put on a pedestal and given deference and protection because they were so scarce; at the same time, the truly independent women were in the shady part of society for the most part— the madams, actresses, and roughneck females of the West who kicked the traces of Victorian gentility and managed to become financially successful and even win the grudging respect, if not social acceptance, of their fellow townspeople. The western woman was still, on the whole, a more independent, self-reliant article than her sisters back east, and in the freer air of the region various women's causes, ranging from prohibition—a preeminently women's cause on the frontier—to voting rights, flourished. When the Nineteenth Amendment to the Constitution, giving women the right to vote, was ratified in 1920, only two states east of the Mississippi (New York and Michigan) had woman's suffrage laws while thirteen states west of the 98th meridian had given women the vote—Wyoming had granted it as early as 1869 and Colorado in 1893.

Women did not play a leading role in founding towns on the Plains; it was men who platted the towns, laid them out, sold the real estate, built the buildings. But the acute loneliness of Plains life and the absence of amenities for her and her children surely made many a woman a staunch backer of urban as opposed to rural life, yearning for a town nearby, not to live in, but for the trading, the schools, churches, and above all the sociability as an antidote to loneliness.

Many settlers came in groups to begin with—family groups, neighborhood groups, groups from the same town, and, of course, ethnic groups of foreign immigrants from the same village in the old country. Some of the groups formed the nuclei of towns; they made up a little settlement on adjacent claims and claimed town status themselves or, by their presence, encouraged a promoter to come in and plant one nearby. The small party of Norwegians in *Giants in the Earth* clung together in their adjoining homesteads and organized schools and a township government with a justice of the peace as more settlers joined them. On the farthest outposts of the frontier, a group of wagons on the distant eastern horizon was a welcome sight and any company was welcome. And, if the newcomers took up homesteads, it was proof that the country was "settling up"—that it was becoming a going proposition. The appearance of the railroad in the area was an even more welcome harbinger. These settlers were not the kind of loners who fled as soon as a neighboring chimney sent a plume of smoke up against the big sky; for a complex of reasons, beyond relieving

[14]Elinore Pruitt Stewart, *Letters of a Woman Homesteader* (Lincoln, Neb.: University of Nebraska Press, Bison Books, 1961), p. 214.

[15]Ibid, p. 215.

the monotonous isolation of their life, they longed for a crossroads, a group of houses, a post office, a store or two, a depot—a village with a name, a bare minimal urban presence. This yearning stemmed from their cultural heritage, their origins in some town back east or the Old World. But most of all, a town was a guarantor that this wilderness, a wilderness not of trees but of empty spaces, was surrendering to civilization and progress.

There is a section in Rölvaag's novel when the settlement is plunged into great excitement by the arrival of five wagons carrying Norwegians. Per Hansa, the area's most effective booster, is away, but Tonseten makes a passionate plea to convince them to stay. When the newcomers jibe at the lack of trees, he tells them that a lack of trees is a positive virtue—it makes the ploughing easier, makes it possible to plant for yourself the size of wood lot you need, and so on, forgetting the cold winters when the only fuel was twisted strands of dried grass. After painting the future of his own region—the churches, schools, and town that would grow up—Tonseten warns them against going elsewhere: "Suppose they went to a place where no one had come yet? Couldn't they understand that all of Dakota Territory would never be peopled? Why, there weren't enough folks in the whole world for that, and never would be either! . . . Or if they should be so unfortunate as to choose a location where no one followed after? . . . What then?"[16] Tonseten is a gifted booster; the people decide to stay. And eventually, one fine day, "a strange monster came writhing westward over the prairie, from Worthington to Luverne; it was the greatest and the most memorable event that had yet happened in these parts. . . . People felt that day a joy that almost frightened them; for it seemed now that all their troubles were over, that there could be no more hardships to contend with."[17] Such optimism, at the mere coming of the railroad, was obviously a bit steep; still Rölvaag has captured the yearning of early settlers for neighbors and for a town and a train which would bring them the goods of civilization.

For those who had none, the desire for the railroad paralleled, became indistinguishable from, the need for neighbors. Promoters, aware of this need and the possibility of profiting from it, were not long in appearing on the scene. These individuals often represented smaller companies and promised a spur line between the settlement and the main trunk line, thus insuring that it would grow into a town. Naturally, the settlers would be required to subscribe to the railroad's stock. In short it was the same game that the local railroads had played back in the Middle West, a game that had the power of making or breaking a town. Wherever a group of shacks or soddies clustered together and called itself a town, wherever a county had been organized, the railroad promoters were not far behind.

State governments too were hit up for their share, and here the lobbyists working the legislature spread out the bribes with a lavish hand. The Union Pacific, for example, doled out four hundred thousand dollars between 1866 and 1872, while the Central Pacific spread around a half a million dollars annually between 1875 and 1885. That these systematic

---

[16]Rölvaag, *Giants in the Earth*, p. 158–59.
[17]Ibid, p. 387.

lobbying campaigns paid off is obvious from the rich returns in state land grants the railroads raked in. Frederick A. Cleveland and Fred W. Powell calculated that the railroads were granted "one fourth of the whole area of Minnesota and Washington; one fifth of Wisconsin, Iowa, Kansas, North Dakota, and Montana; one seventh of Nebraska; one eighth of California; and one ninth of Louisiana." Congressional land grants between 1862 and 1872 handed over more than 200 million acres of public-domain land to railroad companies.

Land, of course, was not cash in hand, nor was it sufficient to pay off the railroads' costs. The land was converted into ready cash by the device of floating land bonds—bonds with the land as collateral. Other capital was raised by mortgages on equipment, and other bonds and stocks. Union Pacific issued bonds with a par value of $110 million—for which they received only $74 million in cash, because investors considered railroads a very risky investment with a low return. In addition the U.S. government lent the roads $64 million, most of this to the Union Pacific and the Central Pacific. This amount—plus $114 million in accumulated interest—was almost miraculously paid off in the 1890s. Total land sales, one estimate has it, brought the railroads $440 million by 1940. At any rate, the railroad promotors managed to enrich themselves personally by stock watering or forming construction companies, billing their own railroads exorbitantly and skimming off fat profits, rather than by profits from operations.

The desperation with which the western towns sought railroads was probably far more intense than the competition in the Middle West. A couple of examples will suffice to show how much of their resources some towns and cities were willing to pledge. In 1872 Los Angeles was handed a take-it-or-leave-it demand for six hundred thousand dollars by the Southern Pacific and paid up; this was the equivalent of a one-hundred-dollar assessment on every man, woman, or child then living in Los Angeles County. In 1880 Superior, Minnesota, turned over one third of its "lands, premises and real estate,"[18] as well as right-of-way land, to induce the Northern Pacific to pass through. In Nebraska, where settlement was thin, forty-three counties between 1867 and 1892 made a total of $5 million in subscriptions to railroad companies, some of which never laid any track. That comes to more than one hundred thousand dollars a county, a considerable burden of debt on a populace of newly-arrived settlers, many of whom had little money. Yet without the railroad their areas' economic potential could not begin to be realized. Without towns nearby, farmers were isolated from their markets, and had no idea of the going prices for their grain. If there were no competing lines in their area, the local dealers who bought their grain and shipped it to market had to pay inflated shipping costs, meaning they paid the farmer that much less for his crop. Nor could the town merchants survive without a railroad, for the farmers would be compelled to take their grain and do their shopping where the depot was.

---

[18]Thomas C. Cochran and William Miller, *The Age of Enterprise* (New York, Harper & Row, 1961), p. 132.

In Adams County, which began to fill up in 1870, the Burlington and the Union Pacific had large land grants. The Burlington, or its agents, had energetically promoted the virtues of Adams County in Michigan, and many people from that state, especially Civil War veterans, emigrated. The railroad carried them by train to the end of the line, after which the passengers debarked and walked to the first town in the county, Juniata. The railroad had planned Juniata as its first depot in the new county, and to get it underway had brought four settlers to the location where Juniata was to be. The four men took out four adjoining homesteads in their own names and built the requisite dwellings on each of the adjoining corners, using wood that the railroad had furnished. A railroad surveyor then laid out the town's streets, and when the first settlers received their patents from the government, they sold the land to the railroad, with two of the men receiving one quarter of the town lots in payment for their services as group leaders. The Burlington also drilled a well for the settlers.

Juniata grew and became the first county seat of Adams County. Meanwhile, in 1872 a representative of the St. Joseph and Denver City Railroad, which ran north-south, asked the county commissioners to authorize seventy-five thousand dollars in bonds so that it could lay tracks through the county, making a junction with the Burlington at Juniata. The taxpayers voted the proposition down; many felt that the St. Joseph and Denver City would have to come through the county anyhow, bonds or no. They were only half right; the railroad did lay tracks through the county by the end of the year, but it made the junction with the Burlington at a point several miles east of Juniata, where there was a cluster of three or four houses. This settlement was christened Hastings, after Major Thomas del Monte Hastings, a railroad construction engineer. The custom of naming a town— or even its streets—after a railroad employee was common enough, but the name was also chosen because it started with "h," and like the Burlington (and the Illinois central before it), the St. Joseph and Denver City was naming the supply stations at the end of each completed section in alphabetical sequence—thus, Hastings was the end of the sequence running Alexandria, Belvidere, Carleton, Davenport, Edgar, Fairfield, and Glenville. Juniata, named after the river in Pennsylvania, followed Archer, Burks, Crete, Dorchester, Exeter, Fairmont, Grafton, Harvard, and Inland and was succeeded in its turn by Kenesaw, which was founded in 1872.

As the county was settled, every new town was founded by one of the railroads. There was Prosser, laid out by the Missouri Pacific in 1887, on land purchased from a homesteader by railroad agents who passed themselves off as representatives of eastern capitalists looking for cheap land for sheep grazing. The Missouri Pacific was the recipient of a $175,000 subsidy from the county, which Juniata (by now more wary about railroads' locations) almost did not support until it received assurances that Prosser would not be located too close to it. The town was named after the superintendent of the construction crew that laid the track, and its streets were named for his children. The town reached its peak in the early 1900s when it had a grain elevator, a roundhouse, stockyards, a state bank, and other small businesses. Thirty years later the bank was merged with one in Hastings, other businesses moved out, and the Missouri Pacific tore down its depot and roundhouse and took up its tracks, leaving only a tiny village. The railroad gave and the railroad—and time—took away.

Then there was Hansen, a top on the Grand Island and St. Joseph, successor to the St. Joseph and Denver City. It was founded in 1879 and named for a civil engineer working on the railroad at the time. Since its biggest business was a blacksmith's shop, one could have predicted the future of Hansen. When the automobile came, it dwindled away to some homes and grain elevators serving the area's farmers. The railroad remained but trains made only irregular freight stops.

The four men who preempted the land for Kenesaw and sold out to the railroad promptly moved away, leaving an empty town. Others came, however, and the town did well. Before the turn of the century, it boasted a general store, a hotel, a grain business, two lumberyards, two hardware stores, a billiard parlor, a restaurant, a physician, a newspaper, and a bank. In its heyday, Kenesaw had a municipal electric plant, an opera house, and two hotels, and four westbound passenger trains and three eastbound stopped daily, plus many freight trains. The Ray Bash Players gave regular performances, and Walter Schultz's Kenesaw motion picture theater was another favorite entertainment; Schultz was famous in the area as the inventor of "Walt's Disc Talking Equipment Company," which was sold to buyers as far away as Mexico and Puerto Rico. Hit hard by the Depression in 1930, Kenesaw survived as a village of seven hundred or so souls, thanks in part to federal relief projects. In the 1960s, eighty new homes went up, and town businesses such as the Kenesaw Cafe and Supper Club, Larmore's Jack and Jill Grocer, the Silver Dollar Tavern, the Holiday Coin Laundromat, Sharon's Beauty Shop, Sheila's Beauty Shop, Shurigar Brothers Land Leveling, Custom Combining and Grain Drying, Beals Care Home and the Jackson Funeral Home prospered. But while once a considerable railroad yard bisected the center of the town and the Burlington employed forty men in the town, now only one passenger train a day ran through, no boarding.

So it went. Towns and villages, all drawing sustenance from the umbilical railroad. Most of those that lived by the railroad, died, or rather stagnated, by it. With the coming of the automobile, the towns no longer served as trading centers for the surrounding farms; the farmers drove to the county seat or the city, and the trains no longer stopped at crossroads to pick up farmers—or the towns they had gone to, for that matter. The one exception was the town of Hastings, for on that fateful day when the people of Juniata voted down the bond issue for the St. Joseph and Denver City, Hastings was on its way. Two other railroads later came in, making Hastings a small but considerable terminus. Feeling its oats, it began to petition for the transfer of the county seat from Juniata. There ensued several years of petitions and votes, with the Juniata townspeople staving off the challenge by every legal means. So many such battles were going on in Nebraska at the time, as town fortunes ebbed and flooded with the locations of the railroads, that the Nebraska legislature passed a law requiring a petition of three fifths of the voters in the last election; if this was achieved then a general referendum on the question was held. Juniata first sought to gain approval for an allocation of funds to build a courthouse, on the theory that such a commitment would strengthen its hold on the seat, but a Hastings partisan at the meeting jumped on his horse, rode to Hastings, and galloped back in the van of an army of Hastings men. According to the county historian, they came "in wagons, on horses, on whatever conveyances they could muster [and] some brought shotguns, revolvers and other weapons with which to defend what they considered to be their rights."[19]

The county commissioner adjourned the meeting but later accepted a bid for construction of the courthouse in Juniata, at which point the one Hastings man on the scene, A. E. Cramer, the county clerk, protested that the procedure was illegal and refused to put his official seal on the document. The commissioners promptly declared the office of county clerk vacant. Cramer took it to court, and the judge ultimately ruled in his favor. Another petition was got up by the Hastings forces, who, while the Juniata-dominated county commissioners stalled, kept adding names with such vigor that when the commissioners finally got round to the petition they suggested that some of the signatures must be invalid, inasmuch as their total number exceeded the entire population of the county.

Finally, an election was held in 1877. Poll watchers from Hastings were posted in Juniata and vice versa. Crowds of angry men milled about in both places, and in Juniata the local partisans attacked and drove away the Hastings men, who were convoying a poll watcher. The poll-watcher—the same Mr. Cramer who as county clerk had fought off the Juniata courthouse—quickly realized that the Hastings escort was badly outnumbered. He hightailed it back to Hastings, leaving the victors busily augmenting Juniata's vote total. When Cramer arrived home, he found that word had preceded him on the telegraph, and a mob of Hastings men armed with "whips, clubs, scythes" and other weapons had already mobilized. The Hastings army, led by Cramer, returned to Juniata and successfully retook the polls from Juniata.

The upshot of the victory was that Cramer and another Hastings loyalist were allowed to supervise the Juniata vote count. The ballots had been made up in rolls, with perforations around each one so that it could be torn off and given to the voter. The poll watchers noted that in some cases the voters had not even observed the nicety of tearing off individual ballots, so that long, unseparated strips of pro-Juniata votes festooned the ballot boxes.

When the votes were at last tabulated, Hastings was adjudged the winner by a comfortable margin. Juniata promptly cried foul, and the court appointed a referee to supervise the recount. The referee found irregularities on both sides (including long strips of unseparated pro-Hastings votes) but decided that more Juniata votes were tainted by fraud. As a result, although Hasting's final vote was decreased, its margin of victory was increased.

This did not end the melodrama. On the day the judge announced the referee's decision, a Hastings man was dispatched to Juniata to secure the county records; he was accompanied by a cowboy named Smith, "a thorough westerner and an excellent shot with the revolver,"[20] who happened to be working at the local livery stable. The two men entered Juniata at dusk, when the local folk were eating supper. They quickly proceeded to

[19]Quoted in Creigh, *Adams County*, p. 907.
[20]Ibid, p. 909.

the office of the county clerk, still Hastings's man in Juniata, A. E. Cramer, who had all the records piled on his desk ready to go. The Hastings emissaries swooped them up, stacked them in the wagon, and sped off for home, while the burghers of Juniata were obviously chewing their suppers.

Later, Hastings also added the county jail to its booty. A Juniata townsman recalled the bitter gall of that moment:

> The rapid growth of Hastings took from Juniata the county seat, and along with it the only building we had that in any way suggested that we were the honest legitimate county seat of Adams county. It was the Adams county jail. Such an addition to our town! About as large as a good-sized dry good box, but our hopes were built on nothing less than that every man, woman and child in Hastings would find in it an abiding place. So with wrath in our heart, and tears in our eyes, we watched it disappear toward the east, and poor Juniata was no more the metropolis of Adams county.[21]

Diminutive as it was, the jail was sturdily built and considered impervious to jailbreaks. The small wooden building that had served as the county courthouse was another matter, though; the Hastings people let Juniata keep that. The county treasurer, a Juniata man, moved the building to his own yard, where it stayed, a reminder of the town's glory days, along with the town windmill, the wooden bandstand at the downtown intersection and the public bell in front of J. J. Williams's restaurant, which served both to call people to meals and as a fire alarm.

With the capture of the county seat and the completion of the railroads, Hastings enjoyed a rapid growth, from a population of zero in 1870 to more than 3,000 in 1878, while the entire county was increasing from 19 to 10,235. Immigration was to be even greater in the next decade, as more railroads came in to carry the immigrants and rainfall increased abnormally throughout the Plains area, creating the illusion that this condition was permanent. The early settlers of the seventies might have raised a note of caution out of their own harsh experiences. Adams County had better agricultural conditions than most, with reasonably good rain, a considerable pool of underground water, and fertile soil. The first settlers sought out a conjunction of fertile soil, level land, and water for their homesteads, with land along the Blue River especially prized. But by 1873 more than half the land of the county—and all the best land—was taken up, leaving less desirable locations for the rest.

In 1873 the people got their first taste of Plains weather when on Easter Sunday a blizzard struck. It had been a warm, sunny day, and indeed spring had arrived so early that many farmers already had their crops in; however, since the winter had been unusually dry, the ground was hard, and birds ate most of the seeds. Then at about four o'clock an eerie stillness settled in, as though the whole world was holding its breath. Huge, churning clouds billowed up on the horizon to the northeast, while in the southwestern sky an inky blackness appeared. The silence grew more ominous, and people sensed something bad was coming. A roar was heard growing

[21]Ibid., p. 910.

louder and louder until it was like a thousand freight trains. The two storms, barreling in from opposite directions, collided above Adams County and the sky became a maelstrom of the elements. The wind snatched up trees, barns, and houses and hurled them about; the air was thick with dust and the roar was deafening. The heavy winds were followed by snow, and although the temperature never went below freezing, the wind was so fierce that a few hours' exposure to it meant death. Some people did die, others huddled in their flimsily built houses and soddies. The soddies survived but many wooden houses were blown away. One family, just recently arrived, had thrown up a temporary shack, twelve by sixteen feet. When the storm came, seven of them crowded in to wait it out; later they brought in their four horses: "Their tails were a foot in diameter, filled with snow so firmly packed that it was a difficult task to remove it. Every muscle in their bodies quivered like a man shaking with the ague. They were so hungry that they soon began gnawing at the 2 × 4 scantling in front of them. To prevent this we had to fill the scantlings with shingle nails."[22] The family survived in their little shack—probably because they were in a relatively protected area. By Wednesday afternoon the storm finally abated, but many settlers had lost not only their crops but the animals upon which they depended for food. Cattle starved because the snow had covered the buffalo grass in the draws where they fed.

The following year another kind of blizzard struck—a blizzard of grasshoppers. This biblical horde waited until the end of July, when the wheat was waving thick and green in the fields, and the new settlers watched proudly as the wind sent shimmering silver waves across it. Then seething masses of black clouds blotted out the sun. The clouds were alive— as swarming, shrilling, ravening mass of insects which descended upon the grain. In forty-eight hours it was over, not a green thing was left standing. They even ate green paint, later legends had it. The fish in the streams and the fowl in the barnyards had gorged on the insects so that their flesh tasted of it for weeks. So severe were the effects of the grasshopper plague that local relief societies were organized to help the destitute. Congress appropriated $180,000, allowed homesteaders to delay their loan payments, and temporarily waived the requirement that they must occupy their claims continuously. In many areas the grasshoppers deposited their eggs in the soil; their progeny were back the following year, eating the seed corn as soon as it had been planted.

The tide of immigration was slowed but not stopped by these disasters. Many settlers stuck it out. They had no choice, having sold everything to come; they were situational optimists with a pragmatic faith that their situation would improve in time. They had engaged in a radical leap, and were loathe to admit defeat, to skulk back to their hometowns, tails between their legs, to hear the "I-told-you so's" of friends and relatives. They had a stubborn pride—and also fancied a visit to the homeplace in a state of greater prosperity than when they left. They continued to write cheerful letters to their friends back east, and the immigration societies kept up their propaganda din. The claims in their brochures were moderated, but,

---

[22]Ibid., p. 1013.

as Walter Prescott Webb remarks about a similarly subdued description of the cattle industry during the boom of the 1880s, it was "the sort of moderation that makes the thing discussed more desirable."[23] It was the last great American land rush, and its numbers were swelled by the European immigrants arriving at Ellis Island. Recruited both at home and abroad by the railroads, the immigrants were assisted from their point of embarkation by the railroads, herded onto special immigrants' trains, and sold land on "easy" credit terms by the railroads once they arrived west. Gone were the great lumbering, jouncing covered wagons, replaced by the speed and efficiency of the railroad cars, on which people were human freight. *Harper's Magazine* christened the immigrant cars "the Modern Ship of the Plains" and described a typical one:

> An immigrant sleeper is now used, which is constructed with sections on each side of the aisle, each section containing two double berths. The berths are made with slats of hard wood running longitudinally; there is no upholstery in the car, and no bedding supplied, and after the car is vacated the hose can be turned in upon it, and all the woodwork thoroughly cleansed. The immigrants usually carry with them enough blankets and wraps to make them tolerably comfortable in their berths; a cooking stove is provided in one end of the car, on which the occupants can cook their food, and even the long transcontinental journeys of the immigrants are now made without hardship.[24]

Whether it was truly without hardship, the journey was undoubtedly a long one for people who probably had few "blankets and wraps" to make them "tolerably comfortable," and who had just arrived in a strange land.

Another special accommodation for immigrants was the zulu car—a freight car with bunks and a stove, in which a single family or small group traveled with all their possessions stored alongside them in the car. The traffic in people and their goods was so much a part of the railroad's business that as late as 1972 the Burlington and Northern (formerly the Burlington and Missouri) Railroad's schedule of freight charges still listed "emigrant movables," which included not only household goods but also agricultural implements and even livestock. For the immigrants, train travel had not only the advantages of special low rates and greater speed, it also enabled them to bring with them all the goods and equipment necessary for starting a new life, without having to buy the extra equipment needed for wagon travel.

One of the largest groups of foreign immigrants to come to Adams County, Nebraska, was the German-Russians; though these immigrants had cultural problems of assimilation unique to themselves, their story is similar to those of many other foreign ethnic groups who went west. (Foreigners played a larger role in the early settlement of the West than is commonly realized. In the early 1870s three of ten westerners were foreign-born. More than half the men in Utah, Nevada, Arizona, Idaho, and California were immigrants. After 1880, however, cities exercised a stronger

---

[23]Webb, *The Great Plains*, p. 235.
[24]Quoted in Creigh, *Adams County*, p. 359–60.

lure, and the proportion of foreign-born fell to one in twenty. The great majority of them threw off their ethnic identification much more rapidly than their compatriots in the cities.) The German-Russians' story also shows how farflung were the railroads' efforts to attract settlers. The German-Russians came from the Ukraine and Crimea; they were Germans who had migrated to Russia in the early 1800s, settling at first along the Volga, north of the Black Sea. With the upwelling of nationalism under Czar Alexander II from 1868 on, the expatriated Germans lost their former special privileges under Russian law and began to consider emigrating. Alert American railroads and steamship lines spotted the opportunities for revenue this group offered and began cultivating them. The Burlington and Missouri transported a delegation of German-Russians to Nebraska, where they were lectured on the virtues of the state and the ease with which they could purchase railroad land. The delegation returned to Russia, and by 1876 the first German-Russians began arriving in Hastings. One man, Pastor Neumann, a prominent American Lutheran but also an agent for the railroads, was an influential force in settling the early immigrants on the journey to America. He traveled up and down the Ukraine, speaking to the German-Russians in their home villages, urging them to make the move. Neumann met one party (they often traveled in communal groups, and many were Mennonites) in New York and sent them on to Dorchester, Wisconsin; at some point in their journey they were met by Burlington representatives, who offered them free passage to Lincoln, Nebraska, on the theory that if one group settled there, then other German-Russians would follow. In preparation for these later groups, the railroad built immigrant hostels in Lincoln and Sutton. These served as halfway houses for new arrivals until they could find land or jobs. Since the majority did not have enough money to buy land, they often ended up working for the railroad during the period it was pushing its tracks westward. Still another effort by the Burlington involved persuading already arrived German-Americans to write their friends back in the old country and tell them of the glories of Nebraska; the railroad provided them with a circular to send along entitled *An unseren Verwandten und Freunde im Russland (To Our Relatives and Friends in Russia).*

These efforts paid off, and an ever-increasing number of German-Russians—mainly Protestants from the Volga region—came to the town of Hastings in the 1880s. The attitude of some of the native Americans in the town toward the arrivals was perhaps summed up by a news item in the Hastings *Gazette Journal* in 1886; "A carload of Russians was unloaded today."[25] The reference might as easily have been to cattle, and there was no further identification of the individuals who came, where they went, or how many of them there were. Like other immigrant groups, the German-Russians met prejudice; in the town they were commonly referred to as "Rooshians"—until World War I when their German heritage was suddenly recollected and they became the object of anti-German hysteria. Some Hastings people did help, though; a member of one immigrant party recalled that a lumberyard gave them boards to build shacks with and

[25]Ibid., p. 348.

that the mayor of the town visited them and sent them food. The mayor was Jacob Fisher, an immigrant from Germany.

Because of the common language, the German-Americans provided more help than others in the town, but the German-Russians gradually formed their own self-help organizations, centered around their churches. The majority, who had no money with which to purchase farms, worked for the railroads and in the town's brick and cigar factories. They all lived on the south or "wrong" side of the Burlington tracks, and even their ghetto was subdivided, with immigrants from Norka living on one side of Burlington Avenue and those from Frank on the other. In Hastings they served their time as a low-wage labor pool. Many men worked for fifteen dollars a week in factories or, with their families, as migrant workers in the beet fields. Perhaps the greatest contribution the German-Russian wheat farmers from the Steppes made to the Plains was their introduction in the 1880s of hard red or winter wheat, which they had smuggled in in their luggage and which was admirably suited to the Plains environment because, being ready for harvest in the spring, it did not depend upon the uncertain summer rain to bring it to maturity.

Some 115,000 German-Russian immigrants came to the United States between 1873 and 1914, and another 150,000 to western Canada—a majority of them frugal-living Mennonites. Most came to Nebraska in the 1880s, as did the other foreign immigrants—Germans, Irish, and Scandinavians in the main. In the seventies it had been the American-born, from Illinois, Iowa, Michigan, and New England. The Hastings newspaper had remarked in 1878 that "the B & M aims to put a settler on every 80 acres in Southern Nebraska,"[26] and by the end of the 1880s they—and whoever else was responsible—had probably accomplished this. By 1890 there was little good land left to be homesteaded in the eastern part of the Great Plains. In that year the director of the Bureau of the Census announced that the frontier was over: "The unsettled area had been so broken into by isolated bodies of settlement that there can hardly be said to be a frontier line."[27]

Actually, good land remained farther west and in Oklahoma and four times as many acres were taken up by homesteaders after 1890 than before. But the tide of humanity had washed over the Great Plains until it lapped the foot of the Rockies; the land that had been leapfrogged by the Oregon parties and the forty-niners was now engrossed by the later arrivals. Between 1870 and 1890, 430 million acres of the Great Plains to the 100th meridian had been claimed by various parties and 225 million were under cultivation. (Only 80 million acres of the West's land had gone directly to homesteaders under the Homestead Act of 1862, however.) By 1880 Kansas had 850,000 people and Nebraska 450,000; by 1885, 550,000 people lived in the Dakota Territory east of the Missouri—an increase of 400 percent over five years. Smaller numbers had moved into eastern Wyoming and Montana, where the cattle kings put up a determined resistance in the famous, if exaggerated, "range wars."

[26]Ibid., p. 16.
[27]Quoted in Ray Allen Billington, *The Westward Movement in the United States* (New York: Van Nostrand Reinhold, 1959), p. 86.

The last frontier in the classic meaning of the term was the region to the south known as Indian Territory. Here, by treaty, lived twenty-two tribes that had been driven off their lands both east of the Mississippi and in the southern plains. Their treaties with the U.S. government had granted them the right to live there "as long as the grass shall grow and the waters flow," or words to that effect, a legal phraseology popular in broken treaties with the Indians. Will Rogers, the vaudeville satirist who had Cherokee blood, was later to write of this treaty: "They sent the Indians to Oklahoma. They had a treaty that said, 'You shall have this land as long as grass grows and water flows.' It was not only a good rhyme but looked like a good treaty, and it was till they struck oil. Then the government took it away from us again. They said the treaty refers to 'water and grass; it don't say anything about oil.' "[28]

Actually, Rogers may have been telescoping history, because the first interest in the land came before oil was discovered there. In 1880, caught up in the homesteading fever, a group of frontiersmen began making forays into Indian Territory and more specifically into the triangle of two million acres of unassigned land known as the Oklahoma District. These men were lawless types who styled themselves "boomers." The army tried to chase out the renegades, but it was an impossible job keeping up with them. Further, in the manifest-destiny spirit of the times, congressmen took up their cause, asking rhetorically how good red-blooded Americans could be denied this land in favor of a few scrawny redskins living under some sort of outmoded treaty. Why, it was a waste of good land to keep it out of the hands of white men who knew how to make it worth something. Bowing to the popular mood, Congress sold out the Indians once again and passed an act opening up the Oklahoma District to homesteaders. The president set the date of entry for noon, April 22, 1889.

In the few months remaining before the day, thousands of people gathered along the borders of the district, joining the boomers already there. Temporary towns had sprung up all along the border. They had names such as Beaver City and Purcell and populations up to fifteen thousand, yet there was not a permanent building in any of them, with the exception of the single plastered house where the railroad agent lived. The inhabitants lived in dugouts, sod houses, shacks, and tents; many of them were dressed like Indians, an observer noted, because "clothing is the most difficult thing to obtain."[29] Soldiers patrolled the border, trying to keep back the gun-jumpers. It was estimated that nearly one hundred thousand people were poised at the border.

At last the day arrived. A young man named Hamilton Wicks participated in the rush and set down his experiences for *Cosmopolitan* soon afterward. Observing from a more detached vantage point, aboard a chartered train bound for Guthrie, the nascent capital of the district, Wicks saw all manner of people edging up to the starting line. There was a "tatterdemalion group, consisting of a shaggy-bearded man, a slatternly-looking woman, and several girls and boys, faithful images of their par-

[28]Richard M. Ketchum, *Will Rogers* (New York: American Heritage Publishing Company, 1973), p. 12.

[29]Quoted in Billington, *Westward Movement*, p. 178.

ents, in shabby attire, usually with a dog and a coop of chickens" sitting in their covered wagon. Nearby he saw "a couple of flashy real-estate men from Wichita . . . driving a spanking span of bays, with an equipage looking for all the world as though it had just come from a fashionable livery stable." Others proceeded forward in all manner of vehicles, horses and on foot. "The whole procession marched, rode, or drove, as on some gala occasion, with smiling faces and waving hands. Every one imagined that Eldorado was just ahead."[30] All lined up as the hour of noon approached, while a troop of cavalry restrained them with difficulty. At least a bugle sounded, and with a great shout of exultation, the crowd rushed headlong toward the promised land.

Wick's train kept pace and then outdistanced the rest with a rush down the last grade and across the bridge near the Cimarron River, where the town site of Guthrie swung into view. The town—the first, perhaps, of many American towns to bestow on itself the proud sobriquet "Magic City"—had already been roughly laid out. There was a water tank, a station, a Wells Fargo office and, the cynosure of all desires, the Government Land Office, a hastily erected structure twenty by forty feet, where land claims would be filed. As soon as the train stopped, Wicks bundled his blankets out the car window and jumped after them. He joined the thousands of others milling and rushing about, all bent on claiming a valuable town lot. Since there were no markers, it was difficult to tell where the best spots would be—whether one had a desirable corner lot or merely a less valuable section of street. The object of this surreal game was to select one's lot and then, before anyone else, drive a stake and erect some sort of dwelling, in conformity with the Homestead Act. Wicks scuttled about until he saw a man who looked like one of the deputies posted on the site to keep order. The man had taken advantage of his assignment to stake an early claim. Playing a hunch, Wicks asked him if the spot he was standing on might perchance be a street. "Yes," the deputy replied. "We are laying off four corner lots right here for a lumber yard." "Is this the corner where I stand?" Wicks pursued. "Yes," the deputy said, beginning to catch Wicks's drift and eyeing him ominously. Jamming his stake in the ground with his heel, Wicks shouted, "Then I claim this corner lot! I propose to have one lot at all hazards on this town site, and you will have to limit yourself to three, in this location at least." An "angry altercation" followed, but Wicks stuck by his claim and buttressed it by sticking a folding cot into the ground and draping it with a blanket. "Thus I had a claim that was unjumpable because of substantial improvements," Wicks noted.[31]

His brother later arrived by train with a proper tent and other equipment. They hired a man to plough around their corner lot and set up their tent. Feeling secure at last, Wicks strolled around the new town. Ten thousand people had squatted upon that square mile of prairie within the space of an afternoon, and the array of white tents looked as if "a vast flock of huge-white-winged birds had just settled down upon the hillsides and in the valleys. Here indeed was *a city laid out and* populated in half a day."[32]

[30]Ibid., p. 180.
[31]Ibid., p. 183.
[32]Ibid., p. 184.

Soon thousands of campfires were winking in the dark bowl of the prairie, and "there arose from this huge camp a subdued hum declaring that this almost innumerable multitude of the brave and self-reliant men had come to stay and work, and build in that distant Western wilderness a city that should forever be a trophy to American enterprise and daring."[33]

For all the frenetic excitement of that day and the acquisitive emotions aroused, not a single killing or serious fight took place in Guthrie, even though many were armed. Wicks himself speaks of the people rushing about, "each solely dependent on his own efforts, and animated by a spirit of fair play and good humor."[34] It was a spirited race to drive one's stake in first, and the losers acceded more or less graciously to a prior claim. Disputed claims were often resolved by a flip of a coin. And as for those luckless ones who landed in a place that turned out to be the middle of a street (it was rather like playing chess on a board without squares), they accepted the luck of the draw with a shrug.

Thirty-six hours later, the citizens of the new town of Guthrie, who hailed from thirty-two states, three territories, and a half a dozen foreign countries, and few of whom knew each other, formed themselves into an electorate and chose a mayor and a five-member city council, adopted a city charter, and authorized the first tax, a simple head tax. Within a week, permanent buildings were going up and church services were being held. The West had seen many forms of innovative social organizations among those who settled there, but Guthrie represented the first "instant city." Or perhaps not so novel, after all, being the latest in a western lineage that went back to the ex-Revolutionary War soldiers in Marietta, Ohio, nailing their by-laws to a tree—or even further to the Pilgrims drawing up their Compact in the tossing *Mayflower.*

[33]Ibid.
[34]Ibid., p. 183.

Cotton remained the primary cash crop in the South after the Civil War

The Freedpeople
Form a Community:
Promised Land, S.C.

ELIZABETH RAUH BETHEL

Even though the passage of the Thirteenth Amendment to the Constitution guaranteed the freedom of the former slaves, the future for the freedpeople was anything but clear. During slavery times their lives were stunted by oppressive laws and customs. Having been barred by law from free access to traditional institutions such as legal marriage, they entered upon freedom with many almost insurmountable handicaps. Most had little or no education, had to seek normalization of family relationships, had been trained only to perform unskilled agricultural labor, and had to face continued onslaughts of discrimination and prejudice from their former overlords. In their favor was their eager enthusiasm to enjoy the benefits of their newly free condition, strong ties of kinship, the consolation and hope provided by an active religious life, and the willingness to work hard and long to free themselves from dependence on their former masters. For a few years during Reconstruction they also had the aid and support of such federal agencies as the Freedman's Bureau, which tried to assist them in adapting to the new situation in which they found themselves.

The leaders of the defeated Confederacy assumed that, even though legal slavery was gone, the traditional racial pattern of southern life would continue. Afro-Americans would constitute a dependent caste, existing to serve the needs of the dominant white society. In order to ensure that this condition would continue, southern states began in 1865 to pass black codes, systems of law which would replace the customs of slavery with a legally determined caste system. While Radical Reconstruction was able to eliminate many of the more oppressively discriminatory racial laws, it could not change the intent of the southern whites to maintain the racial barriers.

The former slaves reacted in various ways to the new situation. Many tried to exercise their new freedom by moving away from their former owners' homes, but still found themselves engaged in unskilled farm labor. Some who had developed artisan's skills during slavery were able to establish themselves as independent craftsmen. A few, whether through luck, enterprise, or skill, were able to achieve the elusive goal of almost all freedpeople—land ownership. The freedpeople and their friends realized that without economic independence, legal freedom would mean little. The way to economic independence in the South seemed to be through land ownership; the envisioned "forty acres and a mule" expressed this desire.

In the early days of Reconstruction, some plantations in the South were turned over to the freedpeople to farm. The lack of clear land titles and the hostility of governments both North and South to land reform, however, led to a restoration of most of those plantations to their former owners or their sale at public auction. If land was to be owned by freedpeople, it would have to be bought by them. This fact alone prevented land ownership for the masses of Afro-Americans. In some cases, however, land ownership for freedpeople was made possible by the policies of Reconstruction state governments. Such a case is described in this selection reprinted from a book by Elizabeth Rauh Bethel, a sociologist at Lander College.

Professor Bethel's book describes not only the results of land ownership by freedpeople, but also a particular variety of community formation. Some blacks in the South decided that the only way to survive in a hostile white environment was to have as little contact with that environment as possible, and so organized all-black towns and farm communities. Several of these towns have survived up to the present time, although they can not be said to have prospered. Still, for black people of the rural South, survival itself can be seen as a kind of prosperity. And those black communities such as Promised Land, South Carolina, Mound Bayou, Mississippi, and Boley, Oklahoma, that have survived reflect the determination of their inhabitants to live as fully as possible in a world which has denied them full partnership. The strands of kinship, religion, mutual aid, and hard work mesh in the effort to form and maintain a community life which has, for a century or more, expressed the determination of the freedpeople and their descendants to live free and independent.

*For Sale: The homestead, grist mill, and 2742 acres of farmland from
the estate of Samuel Marshall, six miles from Abbeville. Contact estate
executors, S. S. Marshall and J. W. W. Marshall.*
Abbeville, South Carolina *Press*
12 November 1869

DR. MARSHALL'S FARM

P romised Land was from the outset an artifact of Reconstruction
politics. Its origins, as well, lie in the hopes, the dreams, and the struggles
of four million Negroes, for the meaning of freedom was early defined in
terms of land for most emancipated Negroes. In South Carolina, perhaps
more intensely than any of the other southern states, the thirst for land
was acute. It was a possibility sparked first by General William T. Sherman's military actions along the Sea Islands, then dashed as quickly as it
was born in the distant arena of Washington politics. Still, the desire for
land remained a goal not readily abandoned by the state's freedpeople,
and they implemented a plan to achieve that goal at the first opportunity.
Their chance came at the 1868 South Carolina Constitutional Convention.

South Carolina was among the southern states which refused to ratify
the Fourteenth Amendment to the Constitution, the amendment which
established the citizenship of the freedmen. Like her recalcitrant neighbors, the state was then placed under military government, as outlined by
the Military Reconstruction Act of 1867. Among the mandates of that federal legislation was a requirement that each of the states in question draft
a new state constitution which incorporated the principles of the Fourteenth Amendment. Only after such new constitutions were completed and
implemented were the separate states of the defeated Confederacy eligible
for readmission to the Union.

The representatives to these constitutional conventions were selected
by a revolutionary electorate, one which included all adult male Negroes.
Registration for the elections was handled by the Army with some informal
assistance by "that God-forsaken institution, the Freedman's Bureau."[1] Only

---

[1]Abbeville, South Carolina *Press*, 6 July 1866 (hereinafter cited as *AP*). *Press* editor Hugh
Wilson had no affection or toleration for things northern. He consistently wrote editorials
which decried Negro suffrage, charged that the Union League was dominated by "artful
and designing demagogues" (*Press*, 19 April 1867), and dismissed Negroes who affiliated
with the Republicans and/or the League as "ignorant and deluded." The political polari-
zation was clearly and concisely illustrated by one banner headline in the *Press* which
declared: "THIS IS A WHITE MAN'S COUNTRY AND MUST BE RULED BY WHITE MEN,"
17 April 1868. Despite *AP* claims to white rule, however, less than 60 percent of the registered
white electorate cast a ballot in the 1867 election. They were overwhelmed by an 85 percent
participation rate among the state's 81,000 registered Negro voters. Joel Williamson, *After
Slavery, The Negro in South Carolina During Reconstruction, 1861–1877* (Chapel Hill, N.C.,
1965), p. 343, summarized Negro political participation between 1868 and 1878 by noting
that "the overwhelming majority of adult, male Negroes exercised their suffrage in the

"The Freedpeople Form a Community: Promised Land, S.C." From *Promisedland: A Century
of Life in a Negro Community*, by Elizabeth Rauh Bethel (Philadelphia: Temple University
Press, 1981), pp. 17–40. Copyright © 1981 by Temple University.

South Carolina among the ten states of the former Confederacy elected a Negro majority to its convention. The instrument those representatives drafted called for four major social and political reforms in state government: a statewide system of free common schools; universal manhood suffrage; a jury law which included the Negro electorate in county pools of qualified jurors; and a land redistribution system designed to benefit the state's landless population, primarily the freedmen.

White response to the new constitution and the social reforms which it outlined was predictably vitriolic. It was condemned by one white newspaper as "the work of sixty-odd Negroes, many of them ignorant and depraved." The authors were publicly ridiculed as representing "the maddest, most unscrupulous, and infamous revolution in history."[2] Despite this and similar vilification, the constitution was ratified in the 1868 referendum, an election boycotted by many white voters and dominated by South Carolina's 81,000 newly enfranchised Negroes, who cast their votes overwhelmingly with the Republicans and for the new constitution.

That same election selected representatives to the state legislature charged with implementing the constitutional reforms. That body, like the constitutional convention, was constituted with a Negro majority; and it moved immediately to establish a common school system and land redistribution program. The freedmen were already registered, and the new jury pools remained the prerogative of the individual counties. The 1868 election also was notable for the numerous attacks and "outrages" which occurred against the more politically active freedmen. Among those Negroes assaulted, beaten, shot, and lynched during the pre-election campaign months were four men who subsequently bought small farms from the Land Commission and settled at Promised Land. Like other freedmen in South Carolina, their open involvement in the state's Republican political machinery led to personal violence.

Wilson Nash was the first of the future Promised Land residents to encounter white brutality and retaliation for his political activities.[3] Nash

---

Republican direction at every opportunity." Negro and Republican domination of the state's political machinery persisted until the 1876 general elections; and throughout the period of Republican rule there was violent, militant, and persistent objection to the regime by native white Democrats.

[2]Fairfield, South Carolina *Herald*, 29 April 1868; W. E. B. DuBois, *Black Reconstruction in America* (1935; reprinted., New York, 1973), p. 429. Francis B. Simpkins and Robert H. Woody, *South Carolina During Reconstruction* (Chapel Hill, N.C., 1932), pp. 93–94, judged the 1868 constitution, in retrospect, as "embodying some of the best legal principles of the age . . . as good as any other constitution the state has ever had, or as most American states had at that time." Despite the prevailing white belief that the constitutional convention was dominated by unlettered Negroes, many Negro representatives to the convention were involved in the teaching profession through their participation in the Freedman's Bureau schools throughout the state, and and equal number were ministers by profession. Williamson, *After Slavery*, p. 365 ff provides a detailed analysis of the convention's composition. See also Emily Bellinger Reynolds and Joan Reynolds Faunt, *Biographical Directory of the Senate of the State of South Carolina, 1776–1964* (Columbia, S.C., 1964), for additional information.

[3]Wilson Nash and his family were enumerated in the 1880 Household Census Manuscripts, Smithville Enumeration District, Abbeville County, S.C. His political activities and involvements were reported in the *AP*, 11 September 1868. The attack was described in Bureau of

was nominated by the Republicans as their candidate for Abbeville County's seat in the state legislature at the August 1868 county convention. In October of that year, less than two weeks before the general election, Nash was attacked and shot in the leg by two unidentified white assailants. The "outrage" took place in the barn on his rented farm, not far from Dr. Marshall's farm on Curltail Creek. Wilson Nash was thirty-three years old in 1868, married, and the father of three small children. He had moved from "up around Cokesbury" within Abbeville County, shortly after emancipation to the rented land further west. Within months after the Nash family was settled on their farm, Wilson Nash joined the many Negroes who affiliated with the Republicans, an alliance probably instigated and encouraged by Republican promises of land to the freedmen. The extent of Nash's involvement with local politics was apparent in his nomination for public office; and this same nomination brought him to the forefront of county Negro leadership and to the attention of local whites.

After the attack Nash sent his wife and young children to a neighbor's home, where he probably believed they would be safe. He then mounted his mule and fled his farm, leaving behind thirty bushels of recently harvested corn. Whether Nash also left behind a cotton crop is unknown. It was the unprotected corn crop that worried him as much as his concern for his own safety. He rode his mule into Abbeville and there sought refuge at the local Freedman's Bureau office where he reported the attack to the local bureau agent and requested military protection for his family and his corn crop. Captain W. F. DeKnight was sympathetic to Nash's plight but was powerless to assist or protect him. DeKnight had no authority in civil matters such as this, and the men who held that power generally ignored such assaults on Negroes.[4] The Nash incident was typical and followed a familiar pattern. The assailants remained unidentified, unapprehended, and unpunished. The attack achieved the desired end, however, for Nash withdrew his name from the slate of legislative candidates. For him there were other considerations which took priority over politics.

Violence against the freedmen of Abbeville County, as elsewhere in the state, continued that fall and escalated as the 1868 election day neared.

Refugees, Freedmen, and Abandoned Lands, Letters Received (hereafter cited as Bureau Letters), vol. 6–8, DeKnight to Headquarters, 30 October 1868, South Carolina Department of Archives and History (hereafter cited as SCDAH).

[4]See especially Bureau Letters, DeKnight to Headquarters, 5, 7, 8, 12, 16, 19, and 21 September and 2 and 7 October 1868. The frustration and anger accumulated since emancipation erupted in a series of violent interracial attacks in Abbeville during the fall 1868. Freedman David Jones was shot. Freedman Manfield Calhoun was lynched. Justice of the Peace J. S. Chipley, a white Democrat, refused to act on either incident and was removed from office. Wyatt Aiken, a white planter and prominent county Democrat, delivered a speech in the Abbeville city square "calculated to incite the crowd and create a disturbance in general" according to DeKnight. Freedmen George Matthews and Jeff Buchannan were shot in separate incidents, and two other Negroes were beaten in the city square. In his reports to district headquarters DeKnight declared that the condition of the county's freedmen was "worse than bondage . . . crimes were increasing daily. The freedmen are safe nowhere." As the local situation worsened and violence prevailed DeKnight wrote with increasing frustration, asking his superiors "Is there no help or protection for the freedpeople?" Indeed, there was little of either in Abbeville in the 1860's.

The victims had in common an involvement with the Republicans, and there was little distinction made between direct and indirect partisan activity. Politically visible Negroes were open targets. Shortly after the Nash shooting young Willis Smith was assaulted, yet another victim of Reconstruction violence. Smith was still a teenager and too young to vote in the elections, but his age afforded him no immunity. He was a known member of the Union League, the most radical and secret of the political organizations which attracted freedmen. While attending a dance one evening, Smith and four other League members were dragged outside the dance hall and brutally beaten by four white men whose identities were hidden by hoods.[5] This attack, too, was an act of political vengeance. It was, as well, one of the earliest Ku Klux Klan appearances in Abbeville. Like other crimes committed against politically active Negroes, this one remained unsolved.

On election day freedmen Washington Green and Allen Goode were precinct managers at the White Hall polling place, near the southern edge of the Marshall land. Their position was a political appointment of some prestige, their reward for affiliation with and loyalty to the Republican cause. The appointment brought them, like Wilson Nash and Willis Smith, to the attention of local whites. On election day the voting proceeded without incident until midday, when two white men attempted to block Negroes from entering the polling site. A scuffle ensued as Green and Goode, acting in their capacity as voting officials, tried to bring the matter to a halt and were shot by the white men.[6] One freedman was killed, two others injured, in the incident which also went unsolved. In none of the attacks were the assailants ever apprehended. Within twenty-four months all four men— Wilson Nash, Willis Smith, Washington Green, and Allen Goode—bought farms at Promised Land.

Despite the violence which surrounded the 1868 elections, the Republicans carried the whole of the state. White Democrats refused to support

[5]The Union League was first organized in Pekin, Illinois on 25 June 1862 as a grass roots home militia. At the close of the war the League, with extensive lodges already established throughout the North, moved south and served as the propaganda machine for the Republican party. It organized newly enfranchised Negroes into viable voting blocs. Meetings were cloaked in a web of secrecy, and members were frequently supplied with arms and drilled as militia units. By 1866 the League was well established in South Carolina and by 1867 had captured the majority of the Negro vote in that state. It was this organization that evoked the Ku Klux Klan attacks during Reconstruction, although by 1870 the League's political potency was greatly diminished. See Austin Marcus Drumm, "The Union League in the Carolinas" (Ph.D. diss., University of North Carolina at Chapel Hill, 1955). A recounting of the attack on Willis Smith is contained in U.S., Congress, House, *Report of the Joint Committee to Inquire into the Condition of Affairs of the Late Insurrectionary States*, H. Rep. 22, 42 Cong., 2d sess., 1871–1872, vol. V, pp. 1564–1566.

[6]Bureau of Refugees, Freedmen, and Abandoned Lands, Reports, Orders and Circulars, DeKnight to Headquarters, 8 November 1868, SCDAH. One Negro was killed in the incident and four others injured. The politicization of freedmen during Reconstruction elicited violence and strained race relations throughout the South. Charles Nesbitt, "Rural Acreage in Promise Land, Tennessee," in Leo McGee and Robert Boone, eds., *The Black Rural Landowner— Endangered Species* (Greenwood, Conn, 1979), pp. 67–81, reported similar interracial tensions resulting from local freedmen's political involvement for the same period. In the Tennessee community Negro voters refused to approach polling places unarmed or alone.

an election they deemed illegal, and they intimidated the newly enfranchised Negro electorate at every opportunity. The freedmen, nevertheless, flocked to the polls in an unprecedented exercise of their new franchise and sent a body of legislative representatives to the state capital of Columbia who were wholly committed to the mandates and reforms of the new constitution. Among the first legislative acts was one which formalized the land redistribution program through the creation of the South Carolina Land Commission.[7]

The Land Commission program, as designed by the legislature, was financed through the public sale of state bonds. The capital generated from the bond sales was used to purchase privately owned plantation tracts which were then subdivided and resold to freedmen through long-term (ten years), low-interest (7 percent per annum) loans. The bulk of the commission's transactions occurred along the coastal areas of the state where land was readily available. The labor and financial problems of the rice planters of the low-country were generally more acute than those of the up-country cotton planters. As a result, they were more eager to dispose of a portion of the landholdings at a reasonable price, and their motives for their dealings with the Land Commission were primarily pecuniary.

Piedmont planters were not so motivated. Many were able to salvage their production by negotiating sharecropping and tenant arrangements. Most operated on a smaller scale than the low-country planters and were less dependent on gang labor arrangements. As a consequence, few were as financially pressed as their low-country counterparts, and land was less available for purchase by the Land Commission in the Piedmont region. With only 9 percent of the commission purchases lying in the up-country, the Marshall lands were the exception rather than the rule.

The Marshall sons first advertised the land for sale in 1865. These lands, like others at the eastern edge of the Cotton Belt, were exhausted from generations of cultivation and attendant soil erosion; and for such worn out land the price was greatly inflated. Additionally, two successive years of crop failures, low cotton prices, and a general lack of capital discouraged serious planters from purchasing the lands. The sons then advertised the tract for rent, but the land stood idle. The family wanted to dispose of the land in a single transaction rather than subdivide it, and Dr. Marshall's farm was no competition for the less expensive and more fertile land to the west that was opened for settlement after the war. In 1869 the two sons once again advertised the land for sale, but conditions in Abbeville County were not improved for farmers, and no private buyer came forth.[8]

---

[7]For an excellent history of the commission's operations see: Carol R. Bleser, *The Promised Land, A History of the South Carolina Land Commission* (Columbia, S.C., 1969).

[8]The death of the family patriarch, Samuel Marshall, prompted several attempts to dispose of the property. Neither of Marshall's sons was interested in farming. One was a physician in the village of Greenwood, the other a merchant in Abbeville. The first advertisement for the land appeared in the *AP*, 10 November 1865. A second notice appeared 30 October 1868. At that time the family sought to rent the property. The final attempt to dispose of the land publicly was made through the 12 November 1869 advertisement. The Marshall family was

Having exhausted the possibilities for negotiating a private sale, the family considered alternative prospects for the disposition of a farm that was of little use to them. James L. Orr, a moderate Democrat, former governor (1865 to 1868), and family son-in-law, served as negotiator when the tract was offered to the Land Commission at the grossly inflated price of ten dollars an acre. Equivalent land in Abbeville County was selling for as little as two dollars an acre, and the commission rejected the offer. Political promises took precedence over financial considerations when the commission's regional agent wrote the Land Commission's Advisory Board that "if the land is not bought the (Republican) party is lost in this district."[9] Upon receipt of his advice the commission immediately met the Marshall family's ten dollar an acre price. By January 1870 the land was subdivided into fifty small farms, averaging slightly less than fifty acres each, which were publicly offered for sale to Negro as well as white buyers.

The Marshall Tract was located in the central sector of old Abbeville County and was easily accessible to most of the freedmen who were to make the lands their home.[10] Situated in the western portion of the state,

---

typical of many white landowners in their response to the post-1865 economic and social conditions. Faced with the dissolution of their traditional labor force, some planters simply abandoned agriculture and attempted to sell their land. For most the attempt was ineffective. Economic conditions precluded advantageous land transactions for sellers; land prices plunged as a function of oversupply. By 1868, however, the Freedman's Bureau was established in the up-country; and the Marshall family's attempt to rent their land was consistent with prevailing trends. The Bureau at that time was supervising a number of "gang-type" labor arrangements in the county, one indication that large-scale cultivation of entire plantations had resumed. See: Bureau of Refugees, Freedmen, and Abandoned Lands, Labor Contracts for Abbeville County, 1865–1868, SCDAH. One disadvantage the Marshall family faced in utilizing such labor was that their land was only partially cleared; and, with the established pattern of wages paid not in cash but in crop shares, generally one-third, most freedmen were probably reluctant to work the Marshall land. Additionally, the family lacked a supervisor. Thus, although the Marshalls faced typical problems with regard to their land, the solution derived was atypical; and the disposition of the land followed an unusual route. See especially Joel Williamson, *After Slavery*, pp. 99 ff, for a cogent discussion of the state's labor problems during Reconstruction.

[9]J. Hollinshead to Governor Robert K. Scott, 3 November 1869, Governor Scott's Papers, SCDAH. It was the conflict between sound economic policy and political expediency that finally led to the corruption of the land redistribution program. In his 1871 Governor's Message Scott urged that the Land Commission pursue the business of subdivision and resale as speedily as possible and that the prices be established at a fixed rate. Only a few months later the fraudulent nature of the commission's operations was exposed to an enraged white public. See *AP*, 3 January 1872, for one example of press coverage of the "outrageous and enormous swindle" in which "hundreds of thousands of dollars of the public funds have been wasted with no other result than to enrich a number of rapacious plunderers at the expense of the Public Treasury." Of course, the article failed to note that, while there was certainly fraudulent manipulation of public monies, there was also one positive aspect of the program, the advancement of Negro landownership.

[10]A distinction is made here between "old" Abbeville County, a geographical and political unit which disappeared after 1897, and the contemporary county lines. In 1897 portions of Abbeville, Laurens, and Edgefield counties were partitioned to create Greenwood County. In that partitioning a portion of the Abbeville-Greenwood county line was drawn directly through the Promised Land community in such a way that the Negro population there was distributed rather evenly between two voting precincts, an obvious instance of nineteenth-century gerrymandering.

the tract was approximately sixty miles northwest of Augusta, Georgia, one hundred and fifty miles northeast of Atlanta, and the same distance northwest of Charleston. It would attract few freedmen from the urban areas. Two roads intersected within the lands. One, running north to south, linked those who soon settled there with the county seat of Abbeville to the north and the Phoenix community, a tiny settlement composed primarily of white small-scale farmers approximately eighteen miles to the south. Called New Cut Road, Five Notch Road, and later White Hall Road, the dirt wagon route was used primarily for travel to Abbeville. The east-west road, which would much later be converted to a state highway, was the more heavily traveled of the two and linked the cluster of farms to the village of Greenwood, six miles to the east, and the small settlement of Verdery, three miles to the west. Beyond Verdery, which served for a time as a stagecoach stop on the long trip between Greenville and Augusta, lay the Savannah River. The road was used regularly by a variety of peddlers and salesmen who included the Negro farmers on their routes as soon as families began to move onto the farms. Despite the decidedly rural setting, the families who bought land there were not isolated. A regular stream of travelers brought them news of events from well beyond their limited geography and helped them maintain touch with a broader scope of activities and ideas than their environment might have predicted.

The Marshall Tract had only one natural boundary to delineate the perimeter of Negro-owned farms, Curltail Creek on the north. Other less distinctive markers were devised as the farms were settled, to distinguish the area from surrounding white-owned lands. Extending south from White Hall Road, "below the cemetery, south of the railroad about a mile" a small lane intersected the larger road. This was Rabbit Track Road, and it marked the southern edge of Negro-owned lands. To the east the boundary was marked by another dirt lane called Lorenzo Road, little more than a trail which led to the Seaboard Railroad flag stop. Between the crossroads and Verdery to the west, "the edge of the old Darraugh place" established the western perimeter. In all, the tract encompassed slightly more than four square miles of earth.[11]

The farms on the Marshall Tract were no bargain for the Negroes who bought them. The land was only partially cleared and ready for cultivation, and that which was free of pine trees and underbrush was badly eroded. There was little to recommend the land to cotton farming. Crop failures in 1868 and 1869 severely limited the local economy, which further reduced

[11]There is not complete agreement among former and present Promised Land residents regarding the boundaries of the community. Some prefer to exclude Moragne Town in their discussions and ascribe to that area an independent identity. Others disagree as to the southern boundary and do not generally recognize portions of the landholdings south of the east-west road, which merged into the White Hall area during the nineteenth century. This is an important point in the status differences which emerged during the years following settlement, and residents often described one or another of the families in terms of both the location of their homes—"not *really* in Promiseland"—and in terms of their church attendance—"but they went to Mt. Zion." Interview with James Evert Turner, 27 September 1979, Chicago, Ill. I have taken a broader view and defined Promised Land as all land encompassed by the original Marshall Tract and owned by Negroes. In this view Moragne Town is a subset of the community rather than an independent entity and is discussed in terms of status rather than geographical distinctions.

the possibilities for small farmers working on badly depleted soil. There was little credit available to Abbeville farmers, white or black; and farming lacked not only an unqualified promise of financial gain but even the possibility of breaking even at harvest. Still, it was not the fertility of the soil or the possibility of economic profit that attracted the freedmen to those farms. The single opportunity for landownership, a status which for most Negroes in 1870 symbolized the essence of their freedom, was the prime attraction for the freedmen who bought farms from the subdivided Marshall Tract.

Most of the Negroes who settled the farms knew the area and local conditions well. Many were native to Abbeville County. In addition to Wilson Nash, the Moragne family and their in-laws, the Turners, the Pinckneys, the Letmans, and the Williamses were also natives of Abbeville, from "down over by Bordeaux" in the southwestern rim of the county which borders Georgia. Others came to their new farms from "Dark Corner, over by McCormick," and another nearby Negro settlement, Pettigrew Station—both in Abbeville County. The Redd family lived in Newberry, South Carolina before they bought their farm; and James and Hannah Fields came to Promised Land from the state capital, Columbia, eighty miles to the east.

Many of the settlers from Abbeville County shared their names with prominent white families—Moragne, Burt, Marshall, Pressley, Frazier, and Pinckney. Their claims to heritage were diverse. One recalled "my grandaddy was a white man from England," and others remembered slavery times to their children in terms of white fathers who "didn't allow nobody to mess with the colored boys of his." Others dismissed the past and told their grandchildren that "some things is best forgot." A few were so fair skinned that "they could have passed for white if they wanted to," while others who bought farms from the Land Commission "was so black there wasn't no doubt about who their daddy was."[12]

After emancipation many of these former bondsmen stayed in their old neighborhoods, farming in much the same way as they had during slavery times. Some "worked for the marsters at daytime and for theyselves at night" in an early Piedmont version of sharecropping. Old Samuel Marshall was one former slave owner who retained many of his bondsmen as laborers by assuring them that they would receive some land of their own—promising them that "if you clean two acres you get two acres; if you clean ten acres you get ten acres" of farmland. It was this promise which kept some freedmen on the Marshall land until it was sold to the Land Commission. They cut and cleared part of the tract of the native pines and readied it for planting in anticipation of ownership. But the promise proved empty, and Marshall's death and the subsequent sale of his lands to the state deprived many of those who labored day and night on the land of the free farms they hoped would be theirs. "After they had cleaned it up they still had to pay for it." Other freedmen in the county "moved off after

[12]Interview with Cora Frazier Hall, 15 February 1978, Promised Land, S.C., and Isaac Moragne, 14 September 1979, New York, N. Y.

slavery ended but couldn't get no place" of their own to farm.[13] Unable to negotiate labor or lease arrangements, they faced a time of homelessness with few resources and limited options until the farms became available to them. A few entered into labor contracts supervised by the Freedman's Bureau or settled on rented farms in the county for a time.

The details of the various postemancipation economic arrangements made by the freedmen who settled on the small tracts at Dr. Marshall's farm, whatever the form they assumed, were dominated by three conscious choices all had in common. The first was their decision to stay in Abbeville County following emancipation. For most of the people who eventually settled in Promised Land, Abbeville was their home as well as the site of their enslavement. There they were surrounded by friends, family and a familiar environment. The second choice this group of freedmen shared was occupational. They had been Piedmont farmers throughout their enslavement, and they chose to remain farmers in their freedom.

Local Negroes made a third conscious decision that for many had long-range importance in their lives and those of their descendents. Through the influence of the Union League, the Freedman's Bureau, the African Methodist Church, and each other, many of the Negroes in Abbeville aligned politically with the Republicans between 1865 and 1870. In Abbeville as elsewhere in the state, this alliance was established enthusiastically. The Republicans promised land as well as suffrage to those who supported them. If their political activities became public knowledge, the freedmen "were safe nowhere"; and men like Wilson Nash, Willis Smith, Washington Green, and Allen Goode who were highly visible Negro politicians took great risks in this exercise of freedom. Those risks were not without justification. It was probably not a coincidence that loyalty to the Republican cause was followed by a chance to own land.

[13]Interview with Cleora Wilson Turner, 5 June 1978, Greenwood, S.C. On the matter of immediate postemancipation Negro mobility Samuel A. Stouffer and Lyonel C. Florant, with Eleanor C. Isabell and Rowena Wyant, "Negro Population Movements, 1860–1940," Preliminary Draft of a Memorandum Prepared for the Carnegie-Myrdal Manuscripts, n.d., Schomburg Collection, New York Public Library, note that migration from the South prior to 1910 was minimal, although there was a moderate degree of intraregional movement among the newly emancipated Negroes, typically a rural to urban drift. David H. Donald, *Liberty and Union* (Boston, 1978), is more emphatic in his summary of the immediate post-1865 population shifts, stating that "thousands of former slaves flocked to Southern cities where the Freedman's Bureau was issuing rations." Social services provided by the bureau combined with personal concerns as former bondsmen "set about to find husbands, wives, or children from whom they had been forcibly separated during slavery" (p. 186). Migration, in any case, was purposeful rather than random wandering. The role of kinship in Negro migration is an issue with broad implications, which extend over the whole of Afro-American history. See especially Carol B. Stack, *All Our Kin* (New York, 1974); and Herbert G. Gutman, *The Black Family in Slavery and in Freedom* (New York, 1976), esp. pp. 185–229; for discussions of the interplay between kinship bonds and motives for migration. The behavior of future settlers at Promised Land was wholly consistent with those patterns noted, for they were tied to the region through a complex network of kinship bonds and their own heritage as slaves.

LAND FOR SALE TO THE COLORED PEOPLE

*I have 700 acres of land to sell in lots of from 50 to 100 acres or more
situated six miles from Abbeville.* Terms: *A liberal cash payment;
balance to be made in three annual payments from date of purchase.*
J. Hollinshead, Agent
(Advertisement placed by the Land Commission
in Abbeville *Press*, 2 July 1873)

The Land Commission first advertised the farms on the Marshall Tract in
January and February 1870. Eleven freedmen and their families established
conditional ownership of their farms before spring planting that year. They
were among a vanguard of some 14,000 Negro families who acquired small
farms in South Carolina through the Land Commission program between
1868 and 1879. With a ten-dollar down payment they acquired the right
to settle on and till the thin soil. They were also obliged to place at least
half of their land under cultivation within three years and to pay all taxes
due annually in order to retain their ownership rights.[14]

Among the earliest settlers to the newly created farms was Allen Goode,
the precinct manager at White Hall, who bought land in January 1870,
almost immediately after it was put on the market. Two brothers-in-law,
J. H. Turner and Primus Letman, also bought farms in the early spring
that year. Turner was married to LeAnna Moragne and Letman to LeAnna's
sister Francis. Elias Harris, a widower with six young children to raise,
also came to his lands that spring, as did George Hearst, his son Robert,
and their families. Another father-son partnership, Carson and Will Don-
nelly, settled on adjacent tracts. Willis Smith's father Daniel also bought a
farm in 1870.

Allen Goode was the wealthiest of these early settlers. He owned a
horse, two oxen, four milk cows, and six hogs. For the other families, both
material resources and farm production were modest. Few of the homesteaders produced more than a single bale of cotton on their new farms
that first year; but all, like Wilson Nash two years earlier, had respectable
corn harvests, a crop essential to "both us and the animals."[15] Most house-

---

[14]Statutes at Large for the State of South Carolina, 1869, Act No. 186, 27 March 1869 set forth
the legal stipulations for buyers of Land Commission farms.

[15]Interview with John Hall, 1 December 1978, Promised Land, S.C. The names of the original
purchasers are listed in: Secretary of State, Duplicate Titles A., pp. 249–277, SCDAH. Agricultural data are derived from: U.S. Bureau of the Census, 1870 Agricultural Census Manuscripts, Smithville and White Hall Enumeration Districts, Abbeville County, S.C. Family
relationships were provided by George L. Wilson, Lettie Richie Moragne, Cora Frazier Hall,
Elese Morton Smith, Benetta Morton Williams, Lilly Wimms Evans, Cleora Wilson Turner,
and Balus Glover, all of Promised Land, S. C.

Farm production for these earliest settlers on the Marshall Tract farms during the
1870 census year revealed a distinct disinterest in cotton cultivation. Crops were equally
divided between cotton, corn, and oats. The average ($\overline{X}$) corn yield was 47.8 bushels per
household, and the cotton crop averaged ($\overline{X}$) 1.1 bales. Average ($\overline{X}$) value of farms was
listed at $404, farm machinery at $6.20, and personal/household property at $282.11.
Agricultural resources were minimal and counted as much in terms of human labor as in
material assets. Half of these households owned draft animals, 78 percent owned at least

holds also had sizable pea, bean, and sweet potato crops and produced their own butter. All but the cotton crops were destined for household consumption, as these earliest settlers established a pattern of subsistence farming that would prevail as a community economic strategy in the coming decades.

This decision by the Promised Land farmers to intensify food production and minimize cotton cultivation, whether intentional or the result of other conditions, was an important initial step toward their attainment of economic self-sufficiency. Small scale cotton farmers in the Black Belt were rarely free agents. Most were quickly trapped in a web of chronic indebtedness and marketing restrictions. Diversification of cash crops was inhibited during the 1870's and 1880's not only by custom and these economic entanglements but also by an absence of local markets, adequate roads, and methods of transportation to move crops other than cotton to larger markets. The Promised Land farmers, generally unwilling to incur debts with the local lien men if they could avoid it, turned to a modified form of subsistence farming as their only realistic land-use option. Through this strategy many of them avoided the "economic nightmare" which fixed the status of other small-scale cotton growers at a level of permanent peonage well into the twentieth century.[16]

The following year, 1871, twenty-five more families scratched up their ten-dollar down payment; and upon presenting it to Hollinshead obtained conditional titles to farms on the Marshall Tract. The Williams family, Amanda and her four adult sons—William, Henry, James, and Moses— purchased farms together that year, probably withdrawing their money from their accounts at the Freedman's Savings and Trust Company Augusta Branch for their separate down payments. Three of the Moragne brothers—Eli, Calvin, and Moses—joined the Turners and the Letmans, their sisters and brothers-in-law, making five households in that corner of the tract soon designated "Moragne Town." John Valentine, whose family was involved in A.M.E. organizational work in Abbeville County, also obtained a conditional title to a farm, although he did not settle there permanently. Henry Redd, like the Williamses, withdrew his savings from the Freedman's Bank and moved to his farm from Newberry, a small town about thirty miles to the east. Moses Wideman, Wells Gray, Frank Hutchison, Samuel Bulow, and Samuel Burt also settled on their farms before spring planting.[17]

---

one milk cow and/or hog. A pattern of subsistence farming, clearly evident in these data, was to be a persistent and dominant pattern of economic behavior for the entire community in the coming years.

[16]C. Vann Woodward, *Origins of the New South*, rev. ed. (Baton Rouge, La., 1971), pp. 182 ff., provides an excellent overview of the difficulties small farmers faced during the 1870's and 1880's, particularly with regard to crop diversification.

[17]Register of Signatures of Depositors in Branches of the Freedman's Savings and Trust Company, 1865–1874, Augusta, Georgia Branch, 23 November 1870–19 June 1874, showed savings accounts for Amanda Williams, her adult son Henry Williams, Charles Jackson, and the Redd family, all future purchasers of farms at Promised Land. Although the immediate postemancipation experiences of the first Promised Land settlers are largely a matter of speculation, these data suggest gainful employment away from agriculture for some. Others,

As the cluster of Negro-owned farms grew more densely populated, it gradually assumed a unique identity; and this identity, in turn, gave rise to a name, Promised Land. Some remember their grandparents telling them that "the Governor in Columbia [South Carolina] named this place when he sold it to the Negroes." Others contend that the governor had no part in the naming. They argue that these earliest settlers derived the name Promised Land from the conditions of their purchase. "They only promised to pay for it, but they never did!" Indeed, there is some truth in that statement. For although the initial buyers agreed to pay between nine and ten dollars per acre for their land in the original promissory notes, few fulfilled the conditions of those contracts. Final purchase prices were greatly reduced from ten dollars to $3.25 per acre, a price more in line with prevailing land prices in the Piedmont.[18]

By the end of 1873 forty-four of the fifty farms on the Marshall Tract had been sold. The remaining land, less than seven hundred acres, was the poorest in the tract, badly eroded and at the perimeter of the community. Some of those farms remained unsold until the early 1880's, but even so the land did not go unused. Families too poor to consider buying the farms lived on the state-owned property throughout the 1870's. They were squatters, living there illegally and rent-free, perhaps working a small cotton patch, always a garden. Their condition contrasted sharply with that of the landowners who, like other Negroes who purchased farmland during the 1870's, were considered the most prosperous of the rural freedmen. The freeholders in the community were among the pioneers in a movement to acquire land, a movement that stretched across geographical and temporal limits. Even in the absence of state or federal assistance in other regions, and despite the difficulties Negroes faced in negotiating land purchases directly from white landowners during Reconstruction, by 1875 Negroes across the South owned five million acres of farmland. The promises of emancipation were fulfilled for a few, among them the families at Promised Land.

Settlement of the community coincided with the establishment of a public school, another of the revolutionary social reforms mandated by the 1868 constitution. It was the first of several public facilities to serve community residents and was built on land still described officially as "Dr. Marshall's farm." J. H. Turner, Larkin Reynolds, Iverson Reynolds, and

---

like Wilson Nash, were probably surviving for the period between their emancipation and their move to Promised Land on rented farms or by even more direct labor-subsistence exchanges with white employers; a few of the original settlers obtained work for cash wages sufficient to begin minimal savings programs. Of equal importance is the indication from these savings patterns that there was among the first community residents an ideology of futurism and an ability to direct their behavior in such a way as to empirically realize personal goals and plans. These fundamental personality traits came to characterize much of the community's collective behavior as well as individual actions and in part account for the longevity of the Promised Land community.

[18]Interviews with Cora Frazier Hall, 15 February 1978, Promised Land, S.C.; John Cole, 19 August 1978, Mt. Vernon, N.Y.; Ada Letman Wilson, 27 September 1979, Chicago, Ill.

Hutson Lomax, all Negroes, were the first school trustees.[19] The families established on their new farms sent more than ninety children to the one-room school. Everyone who could be spared from the fields was in the classroom for the short 1870 school term. Although few of the children in the landless families attended school regularly, the landowning families early established a tradition of school attendance for their children consonant with their new status. With limited resources the school began the task of educating local children.

The violence and terror experienced by some of the men of Promised Land during 1868 recurred three years later when Eli and Wade Moragne were attacked and viciously beaten with a wagon whip by a band of Klansmen.[20] Wade was twenty-three that year, Eli two years older. Both were married and had small children. It was rumored that the Moragne brothers were among the most prominent and influential of the Negro Republicans in Abbeville County. Their political activity, compounded by an unusual degree of self-assurance, pride, and dignity, infuriated local whites. Like Wilson Nash, Willis Smith, Washington Green, and Allen Goode, the Moragne brothers were victims of insidious political reprisals. Involvement in Reconstruction politics for Negroes was a dangerous enterprise and one which addressed the past as well as the future. It was an activity suited to young men and those who faced the future bravely. It was not for the timid.

The Republican influence on the freedmen at Promised Land was unmistakable, and there was no evidence that the "outrages" and terrorizations against them slowed their participation in local partisan activities. In addition to the risks, there were benefits to be accrued from their alliance with the Republicans. They enjoyed appointments as precinct managers and school trustees. As candidates for various public offices, they experienced a degree of prestige and public recognition which offset the element of danger they faced. These men, born slaves, rose to positions of prominence as landowners, as political figures, and as makers of a community. Few probably had dared to dream of such possibilities a decade earlier.

During the violent years of Reconstruction there was at least one official attempt to end the anarchy in Abbeville County. The representative to the state legislature, J. Hollinshead—the former regional agent for the Land Commission—stated publicly what many local Negroes already knew pri-

[19]Teachers' Monthly Reports, 1870, State Superintendent of Education, SCDAH; W. O. B. Hoitt to Governor R. K. Scott, 12 May 1869, Governor Scott's Papers, SCDAH: and *AP*, 13 and 14 May and 3 June 1870. White attitudes toward public education were varied and shifted from year to year. In general, there was opposition to racial mixing within the educational system; and the possibility of integrated schools was the focus of most of the white opposition to the education of Negro children. See especially, Mary Catherine Davis, "Ten O'Clock Scholars, Black Education in Abbeville County, 1865–1870" (Paper, Department of History, University of South Carolina, 1978), for a cogent survey from the First Freedman's Bureau schools to the implementation of a common school system.

[20]Reports and Resolutions of the State of South Carolina, 1869–1870, pp. 1061–1064.

vately, that "numerous outrages occur in the county and the laws cannot be enforced by civil authorities." From the floor of the General Assembly of South Carolina Hollinshead called for martial law in Abbeville, a request which did not pass unnoticed locally. The Editor of the *Press* commented on Hollinshead's request for martial law by declaring that such outrages against the freedmen "exist only in the imagination of the legislator."[21] His response was probably typical of the cavalier attitude of southern whites toward the problems of their former bondsmen. Indeed, there were no further reports of violence and attacks against freedmen carried by the *Press*, which failed to note the murder of County Commissioner Henry Nash in February 1871. Like other victims of white terrorists, Nash was a Negro.[22]

While settlement of Dr. Marshall's Farm by the freedmen proceeded, three community residents were arrested for the theft of "some oxen from Dr. H. Drennan who lives near the 'Promiseland.' "[23] Authorities found the heads, tails, and feet of the slaughtered animals near the homes of Ezekiel and Moses Williams and Colbert Jordan. The circumstantial evidence against them seemed convincing; and the three were arrested and then released without bond, pending trial. Colonel Cothran, a former Confederate officer and respected barrister in Abbeville, represented the trio at their trial. Although freedmen in Abbeville courts were generally convicted of whatever crime they were charged with, the Williamses and Jordan were acquitted. Justice for Negroes was always a tenuous affair; but it was especially so before black, as well as white, qualified electors were included in the jury pool. The trial of the Williams brothers and Jordan signaled a temporary truce in the racial war, a truce which at least applied to those Negroes settling the farms at Promised Land.

In 1872, the third year of settlement, Promised Land gained nine more households as families moved to land that they "bought for a dollar an acre." There they "plow old oxen, build log cabin houses" as they settled the land they bought "from the Governor in Columbia." Colbert Jordan and Ezekiel Williams, cleared of the oxen stealing charges, both purchased farms that year. Family and kinship ties drew some of the new migrants to the community. Joshuway Wilson, married to Moses Wideman's sister Delphia, bought a farm near his brother-in-law. Two more Moragne brothers, William and Wade, settled near the other family members in "Moragne

[21]*AP*, 20 January 1871. Hollinshead, a carpetbagger from Ohio, came to South Carolina as an Internal Revenue Service agent during Reconstruction. He also served for a time as the local agent for the Land Commission and was probably well known among the county's freedmen. He was elected to the state senate from Abbeville in 1870 and served one term.

[22]Drumm, "The Union League," p. 186. Whether or not Henry Nash and Wilson Nash of Promised Land were related is not clear. Both were involved with the Republicans in county politics, both were Negroes, and both lived in the county. There is also a question as to whether either of these men were related to Beverly Nash, a prominent Negro legislator from Columbia during Reconstruction. There was some probability of a link between the three Nash men and Promised Land, however; for the property James Fields owned in Columbia was less than two blocks away from a lumber yard owned and successfully operated by Beverly Nash during Reconstruction.

[23]*AP*, 23 February 1871.

Town." Whitfield Hutchison, a jack-leg preacher, bought the farm adjacent to his brother Frank. "Old Whit Hutchison could sing about let's go down to the water and be baptized. He didn't have no education, and he didn't know exactly how to put his words, but when he got to singing he could make your hair rise up. He was a number one preacher."[24] Hutchison was not the only preacher among those first settlers. Isaac Y. Moragne, who moved to Promised Land the following year, and several men in the Turner family all combined preaching and farming.

Not all of the settlers came to their new farms as members of such extensive kinship networks as the Moragnes, who counted nine brothers, four sisters, and an assortment of spouses and children among the first Promised Land residents. Even those who joined the community in relative isolation, however, were seldom long in establishing kinship alliances with their neighbors. One such couple was James and Hannah Fields who lived in Columbia before emancipation. While still a slave, James Fields owned property in the state capitol, which was held in trust for him by his master. After emancipation Fields worked for a time as a porter on the Columbia and Greenville Railroad and heard about the up-country land for sale to Negroes as he carried carpet bags and listened to political gossip on the train. Fields went to Abbeville County to inspect the land before he purchased a farm there. While he was visiting, he "run up on Mr. Nathan Redd," old Henry Redd's son. The Fieldses' granddaughter Emily and Nathan were about the same age, and Fields proposed a match to young Redd. "You marry my granddaughter, and I'll will all this land to you and her." The marriage was arranged before the farm was purchased, and eventually the land was transferred to the young couple.[25]

By the conclusion of 1872 forty-eight families were settled on farms in Promised Land. Most of the land was under cultivation, as required by law; but the farmers were also busy with other activities. In addition to the houses and barns which had to be raised as each new family arrived with their few possessions, the men continued their political activities. Iverson Reynolds, J. H. Turner, John and Elias Tolbert, Judson Reynolds, Oscar Pressley, and Washington Green, all community residents, were delegates to the county Republican convention in August 1872. Three of the

[24]Interviews with Rufus Nash, 27 May 1978; Promised Land, S.C.; Cleora Wilson Turner, 30 May 1978, Greenwood, S.C.; Cora Frazier Hall, 15 February 1978, Promised Land, S.C. There are few surviving details of the first community settlers among contemporary residents. Rarely does family or community oral history at Promised Land extend beyond three generations, and for the most part aspects of the third generation back are recalled only in hazy terms and with few details. Generally community residents emphasize the future rather than the past. This is in part a function of local childrearing practices which drew sharp distinctions between generations and limited communication between parents and children to instructional rather than narrative forms. None of the contemporary residents reported interactions with their parents at the informal level. Intergenerational exchanges focused on order and commands issued by the parents and obeyed by the children.

[25]Interview with Cora Frazier Hall, 15 February 1978, Promised Land, S.C. This information was relayed as gossip to the interviewer. Land management strategies and financial matters are held as private family concerns at Promised Land and are generally not open to scrutiny by others in the community.

group were landowners. Their political activities were still not received with much enthusiasm by local whites, but reaction to Negro involvement in politics was lessening in hostility. The *Press* mildly observed that the fall cotton crop was being gathered with good speed and "the farmers have generally been making good use of their time." Cotton picking and politics were both seasonal, and the newspaper chided local Negroes for their priorities. "The blacks have been indulging a little too much in politics but are getting right again." Iverson Reynolds and Washington Green, always among the community's Republican leadership during the 1870's, served as local election managers again for the 1872 fall elections.[26] The men from Promised Land voted without incident that year.

Civic participation among the Promised Land residents extended beyond partisan politics when the county implemented the new jury law in 1872. There had been no Negro jurors for the trial of the Williams brothers and Colbert Jordan the previous year. Although the inclusion of Negroes in the jury pools was a reform mandated in 1868, four years passed before Abbeville authorities drew up new jury lists from the revised voter registration rolls. The jury law was as repugnant to the whites as Negro suffrage, termed "a wretched attempt at legislation, which surpasses anything which has yet been achieved by the Salons in Columbia." When the new lists were finally completed in 1872 the *Press*, ever the reflection of local white public opinion, predicted that "many of [the freedmen] probably have moved away; and the chances are that not many of them will be forthcoming" in the call to jury duty. Neither the initial condemnation of the law nor the optimistic undertones of the *Press* prediction stopped Pope Moragne and Iverson Reynolds from responding to their notices from the Abbeville Courthouse. Both landowners rode their mules up Five Notch Road from Promised Land to Abbeville and served on the county's first integrated jury in the fall of 1872. Moragne and Reynolds were soon followed by others from the community—Allen Goode, Robert Wideman, William Moragne, James Richie, and Luther (Shack) Moragne. By 1874, less than five years after settlement of Dr. Marshall's farm by the new Negro landowners began, the residents of Promised Land remained actively involved in Abbeville County politics. They were undaunted by the *Press* warning that "just so soon as the colored people lose the confidence and support of the North their doom is fixed. The fate of the red man will be theirs."[27] They were voters, jurors, taxpayers, and trustees of the school their children attended. Their collective identity as an exclusive Negro community was well established.

ONLY COLORED DOWN IN THIS OLD PROMISED LAND

Abbeville County, South Carolina
Mr. John Lomax passed through the Promised Land yesterday, and
he thinks the crops there almost a failure. The corn will not average

---

[26]*AP*, 7 August 1872.
[27]*AP*, 25 September 1872, 8 October 1873, and 8 April and 13 May 1874.

*two bushels to the acre, and the cotton about 300 pounds [less than
one bale] to the acre. A large quantity of sorghum cane was planted.
It was almost worthless. The land appeared as if it had been very well
cultivated.*
Abbeville *Press*
30 September 1874

The forty-eight men and women who established conditional ownership
of the farms at Promised Land between 1870 and 1872 were required by
law to place at least half of their land under cultivation within three years
of their purchase. There was, however, no requirement about the crops to
be planted. The men who established that cultivation standard probably
assumed that cotton would be the major cash crop, as it was throughout
the Piedmont. At Promised Land cotton was indeed planted on every one
of the farms, but not in overwhelming amounts. The relatively small cotton
fields were overshadowed by fields of corn, peas, and sorghum cane; and
the sense of permanence among the settlers was clearly evident when "they
planted peach trees and pear trees and had grape vines all over" the land,
which only a few years before was either uncleared of native pine forests
or part of the up-country plantation system. Cotton, the antebellum crop
of the slaves, became the cash crop of freedom. It would never dominate
the lives of the farmers at Promised Land.[28]

The 1870's were economically critical years for the new landowners.
They had mortgage payments to meet and taxes to pay, but they also had
families to feed. In 1870, when the price of cotton reached twenty-two
cents a pound, all this was possible. In the following years, however, cotton
prices declined dramatically. This, combined with generally low cotton
yields, resulted in economic hardship for many of the farmers. Poverty
was their constant neighbor, and their struggle for survival drew them into
a cycle of indebtedness to white "lien men."

In those depression years there was little credit in the Piedmont. "The
poor people wasn't able to buy their fertilize. That's what makes your
cotton."[29] Storekeepers and merchants reserved their resources for the
local white planters, and the Negro farmers were forced to find credit
from other sources. They turned to their white landowning neighbors and
in some cases their former masters, the Devlin family in Verdery; the Tuck
family, nearby farmers; and the Hendersons, Verdery merchants. To them
the Promised Land farmers paid usurious interest rates for the fertilizer
they needed "to make a bale of cotton" and the other supplies and food-
stuffs they required to survive the growing season.

[28]Interview with John Turner and Cleora Wilson Turner, 30 May 1978, Greenwood, S.C. The
trend toward subsistence farming was a common one during the 1870's, explained by
DuBois, *Black Reconstruction*, p. 75, in more global terms: "emancipation had enlarged the
Negro's purchasing power, but instead of producing solely for export, he was producing to
consume. His standard of living was rising." Although agricultural statistics for Reconstruction indicate an overall decline in production in the South, these data neglect the increase
in subsistence production among freedmen like the Promised Land farmers. It was this
subsistence production, as DuBois suggested, that offset the decline in cash crop production.
[29]Interview with Cora Frazier Hall, 1 December 1978, Promised Land, S.C.

It was during this decade that the community farmers learned to maintain a skillful balance between a small cotton cash crop and their subsistence fields. Careful in the management of debt, most landowners probably used their cotton crop to meet their mortgage payment to the Land Commission and their tax bill to the county. There was never any surplus on the small farms, and a crop failure had immediate and personal consequences. At best a family would go hungry. At worst they would lose their farm.

Times were hard; and, despite generally shrewd land and debt management, twenty of the original settlers lost title to their land during the early 1870's. All migrated from Promised Land before the 1875 growing season. An advertisement in the *Press* attracted some new purchasers to the vacated farms, but most buyers learned of the land through friends and relatives. New families once again moved on to the land.[30] Wilson Nash bought the farm originally purchased by John Valentine; both men were church leaders and probably discussed the transaction in some detail before the agreement was finalized.

Allen Goode, Wells Gray, and James Fields added to their holdings, buying additional farms from discouraged families who were leaving. Moses Wideman's younger brothers, William and Richmond, together bought an eighty-five-acre farm and then divided it, creating two more homesteads in the community. J. H. Turner, who secured a teaching position in an Edgefield County public school, sold his farm to his brother-in-law Isaac Y. Moragne. Each of the landowners had a brother, a cousin, or a friend who was eager to assume the financial burden of landownership; and none of the twenty vacated farms remained unoccupied for long. Promised Land quickly regained its population. The new arrivals strengthened and expanded the kinship bonds, which already crisscrossed and united individual households in the community.

Marriage provided the most common alliance between kinship groups. The Wilson and Wideman families and the Fields and Redds were both so related. The use of land as dowry, first employed by James Fields to arrange his granddaughter's marriage to Nathan Redd, provided a convenient and viable bargaining tool. When Iverson Reynolds bought his thirty-acre farm he also purchased a second, twenty-acre tract in his daughter's name, looking forward to the time of her marriage. "When Oscar Pressley married Iverson Reynolds' daughter, Janie, Iverson Reynolds give him that land or sold it to him. But he got that farm from old Iverson Reynolds when he got married." The Moragnes, Turners, Pinckneys, and Letmans were also united through land-based dowry arrangements. "The Moragne women is the ones that had the land. All them, the Turners, the Pinckneys, and the Letmans—all them got into the Moragnes when the women married these men."

[30]Secretary of State, Duplicate Titles B, n.p., SCDAH. The average $(\overline{X})$ size of the farms on the Marshall Tract was 48.14 acres. Final purchase prices averaged $(\overline{X})$ $3.24 per acre, a significant decline in price from the original $9.20 per acre contract costs. The Land Commission paid $10.00 per acre for the land and thus absorbed a loss in excess of $18,000 on this single transaction. It was this pattern of fiscal mismanagement which led ultimately to the bankruptcy of the commission.

Marriage did not always accompany kinship bonds, for at Promised Land, like every place else, "some folks have childrens when they not married. Things get all mixed up sometimes." Still, the community was a small and intimate place, woven together as early as the 1880's by a complex and interlocking series of kin ties, which were supplemented by many other kinds of personal relationships. The separation of public and private spheres blurred; and, married or not, "when the gals get a baby" everyone was aware of the heritage and family ties of new babies. "Andrew Moragne supposed to been his daddy, but his momma was a Bradley so he took the name Bradley." Even so, promiscuity and illegitimacy were not casually accepted facts of life. Both were sinful and disgraceful not just to the couple but to their families as well. For women a pregnancy without marriage was particularly painful. "Some might be mean to you then," and many refused to even speak publicly to an unmarried woman who became pregnant. "All that stop when the baby is born. Don't want to punish an innocent baby."[31] Legitimate or not, babies were welcomed into families and the community, and the sins of the parents were set aside. Ultimately, the bonds of kinship proved more powerful than collective morality, and these bonds left few residents of the community excluded from an encompassing network of cousins, aunts, uncles, and half-brothers and sisters.

As the landowning population of Promised Land stabilized, local resources emerged to meet day-to-day needs. A molasses mill, where the farmers had their sorghum cane ground into molasses by Joshuway Wilson's oldest son Fortune, opened in the community. Two corn and wheat grist mills opened on Curltail Creek. One, the old Marshall Mill, was operated by Harrison Cole, a Negro who subsequently purchased a vacant farm in the community. The other, the former Donalds Mill, was owned and operated by James Evans, an Irish immigrant whose thirst for land equaled that of his Negro neighbors.[32] North Carter, the youngest son of landowner Marion Carter, opened a small general store at the east-west crossroads, where he sold candy, kerosene, salt, and other staples to his neighbors, extending credit when necessary, knowing that they would pay when they could. Long before the final land purchase was completed, the freedmen at Promised Land had established a framework for economic and social self-sufficiency.

The farms, through hard work, decent weather, and an eight-month growing season, soon yielded food for the households. A pattern of subsistence agriculture provided each Promised Land family a degree of independence and self-reliance unknown to most other Negro families in the area. Cows produced milk and butter for the tables, and chickens eggs and fresh poultry. Draft animals and cash money were both scarce commodities, but "in them days nobody ever went hungry." Hogs provided the major source of meat in the community's subsistence economy. "My mother and them used to kill hogs and put them down in salt in wood boxes and

---

[31]Interviews with Cora Frazier Hall, 1 December 1978, Promised Land, S.C.; John Turner and Cleora Wilson Turner, 30 May 1978, Greenwood, S.C.

[32]AP, 17 June 1870. Both mills were renovations, not new structures. Cole's establishment was upstream of the Evans Mill, and the latter was more central to most Promised Land farmers.

cover them so flies couldn't get to them for about five or six weeks. Take it out and wash it, put on red pepper and such, hang it up to dry, and that meat be *good*."[33] The absence of an abundant cotton crop was not a sign of lack of industry. Prosperity, as well as productivity, was measured against hunger; and, in the never-ending farm cycle, fields were planted according to the number of people in each household, the number of mouths to be fed.

Community and household autonomy were firmly grounded in the economic independence of the land. Both were strengthened with the establishment of a church in Promised Land. In 1875, fully a decade before the final farms were settled, James Fields sold one acre of his land to the Trustees of Mt. Zion A.M.E. Church.[34] It was a sign of the times. At Promised Land, as elsewhere in the South, freedmen withdrew from white churches as quickly as possible. Membership in the Baptist and Methodist denominations increased tenfold between 1860–1870 as the new Negro churches in the South took form. Mt. Zion was relatively late in emerging as a part of that movement for independence from white domination, but the residents of Promised Land were preoccupied for a time with more basic concerns. The fields had to be established as productive before community residents turned their energies to other aspects of community development.

The Field's land, located squarely in the geographical center of Promised Land, was within a two-mile walk of all the houses in the community. On this thinly wooded tract the men carved out a brush arbor, a remnant of slavery days; and Isaac Y. Moragne led everybody in the young settlement in prayers and songs. From the beginning of their emancipation schools and churches were central components of Negro social life; and at Promised Land religion, like education, was established as a permanent part of community life while the land was still being cleared.

NEWCOMERS AND COMMUNITY GROWTH

Most families survived those first settlement years, the droughts and crop failures, Ku Klux Klan attacks, and the violent years of Reconstruction. They met their mortgage payments and their taxes, and the years after 1875 were relatively prosperous ones. Promised Land was well established before the Compromise of 1877, the withdrawal of federal troops from the state, and the election of Wade Hampton as governor. The political squabbles among the white Democrats during the years after Hampton's redemption of South Carolina touched the folks at Promised Land only indirectly. The community was, for the most part, preoccupied with internal events.

By 1880 the community had expanded from forty-nine to eighty-nine households, an average growth of four new families each year for the

---

[33]Interview with George L. Wilson, 7 November 1977, Promised Land, S.C.

[34]Direct Index to Deeds, Abbeville County Courthouse, Abbeville, S.C. This information had been lost to contemporary community residents, who commonly date the beginning of Mt. Zion from the erection of the first church building during the 1880's. The donor of the land, James Fields, was not known until the land records were examined.

previous decade. Fifty of those families were landless, attracted to Promised Land for a combination of reasons. Probably at least some of them hoped to acquire land there. Promised Land was the only place in the area where Negroes had even minimal hope of buying land after 1877. Local farmers and planters, never eager to sell land to Negroes, now grew even more recalcitrant as Democratic white rule was re-established. Sharecropping dominated farming arrangements between whites and Negroes throughout the Cotton Belt. The landowners at Promised Land, "well, they was wheels. They *owned* their farms."[35] And the respect and prestige they commanded within the county's landless Negro population were another kind of attraction for landless families.

The violence of Reconstruction was moderated only slightly, and a concern for personal safety was surely another reason Negroes moved to Promised Land. Few of the early settlers, those who came before the mid-1880's, could have escaped that violence, even if their contact was indirect. Wilson Nash, Willis Smith, Allen Goode, Washington Green, Wade and Eli Moragne all headed landowning households. For any who might forget, those men were constant reminders of the dangers which lay just beyond the community's perimeter.

The men at Promised Land still exercised their franchise, fully aware of both the dangers and the benefits which they knew accompanied political activity. Together they walked the three miles to Verdery and collectively cast their ballots at the post office "where Locket Frazier held the box for the niggers and Red Tolbert for the whites." Perhaps they walked together as a symbolic expression of their solidarity, but much more likely it was because of a practical concern for their own safety. They were less vulnerable to attack in a group. As it had in the past, however, this simple exercise of citizenship enraged the local whites; and, once again, in the early 1880's the men at Promised Land faced the threat of violence for their partisan political activities.

> Them old Phoenix rats, the Ku Klux, come up here to beat up the niggers 'cause they went to Verdery and voted. Them old dogs from Phoenix put on red shirts and come up here to beat the poor niggers up. Old George Foster, the white man, he told them "Don't go down in that Promiseland. Josh Wilson and Colbert Jordan and them got some boys up there, and they got shotguns and Winchesters and old guns. Any white man come in to Promiseland to beat the niggers up, some body going to die. They'll fight 'til hell freezes over. You Phoenix rats go back to Phoenix." So they went on down to Verdery, and they told them the same thing.[36]

---

[35]Comments by Amos Wells, Sr., at Jacob's Chapel Baptist Church Meeting, 16 July 1978.

[36]Interview with Cora Frazier Hall, 1 December 1978, Promised Land, S.C. The Red Shirts were active white Wade Hampton supporters. The Phoenix community was fraught with racial tensions, which erupted in a riot there on 8 November 1898. See Bruce Lee Kleinschmidt, "The Phoenix Riot," *Furman Review* 5 (Spring 1971): 27–31, for a discussion of the local conditions in the Phoenix community and details of the riot. The aborted invasion of Promised Land by this same group during the same period indicates the extent to which racial tension pervaded and dominated black-white interchanges in Abbeville County during the 1880's and 1890's. That the Promised Land community was able to insulate itself to some extent from these tensions is one indicator of community solidarity. Isolated Negroes in the county were considerably more vulnerable to attack.

Their reputation, their readiness, and their willingness to defend their land were clearly well-known facts about the people at Promised Land. The "Red Shirts" heeded the warning, and white terrorists never again attempted to violate Promised Land. This, too, must have been a part of the community's attraction to landless families who moved there.

Promised Land in 1880 was a community which teemed with activity. Most of the newcomers joined in the brush arbor worship services and sent their children to the community schools. Liberty Hill School and the white schoolmaster were replaced by "schools scattered all around the woods" taught by Negro men and women who lived at Promised Land. Abbeville County maintained a public school. Crossroads School for Colored was taught by H. L. Latimer. The Mill School, maintained by the extensive Moragne family for their children, was held in James Evans' mill on Curltail Creek and was taught by J. H. Turner, Moragne brother-in-law. The Hester School, located near the southern edge of the community, was so named because it met in the Hester family's home. All three private schools supplemented the meager public support of education for Negro children; and all were filled to capacity, because "folks had big families then—ten and twelve childrens—and them schools was crowded."[37]

The representatives to the 1868 South Carolina Constitutional Convention who formulated the state's land redistribution hoped to establish an economically independent Negro yeomanry in South Carolina. The Land Commission intended the purchase and resale of Dr. Marshall's farm to solidify the interests of radical Republicanism in Abbeville County, at least for a time. Both of these designs were realized. A third and unintended consequence also resulted. The land fostered a socially autonomous, identifiable community. Drawing on resources and social structures well established within an extant Negro culture, the men and women who settled

[37]Interviews with George L. Wilson, 30 March 1978; Balus Glover, 1 April 1978, both at Promised Land, S.C. The pattern of private education at Promised Land was consistent with other educational efforts among the freedmen. See especially: Bureau Letters, Farrow to Headquarters, 6 March and 15 May 1867, for two early cases in the district in which groups of freedmen generated cash and labor for independent educational facilities; ibid., Freedpeople to Headquarters, 8 August 1867, in which a group of freedmen from Due West, S.C. requested funds from the Bureau to supplement the small wages of a teacher they had employed for their children; ibid., Allen to Headquarters, 4 December 1867, containing a request for $200 to support another independent school in the county. Martin Abbott, *The Freedman's Bureau in South Carolina, 1865–1872* (Chapel Hill, N.C., 1967), p. 91, noted that these early educational efforts, whether supported in part by the Bureau or instigated and maintained independently by freedmen, were "concerned with substance and content, with moral maxims, and with promoting mental and social discipline . . . and often alien to the needs of children so recently come from bondage." Abbott's criticism that the schools lacked practical application and an orientation toward vocationalism seems to ignore the fact that this was largely learned by most Negro children through apprenticeship and the fact that the few months children spent in the schoolhouse until as late as the 1940's were a precious time for them. That was the only opportunity most would have for intellectual pursuits. By the age of twelve Negro children assumed adult labor responsibilities in the fields alongside their parents. Negro parents understood this fact in a way neglected by scholars, and their initiative in establishing and supporting schools for their children bears witness to the value placed on education by nineteenth-century Negroes.

Promised Land established churches and schools and a viable economic system based on landownership. They maintained that economic autonomy by subsistence farming and supported many of their routine needs by patronizing the locally owned and operated grist mills and general store. The men were actively involved in Reconstruction politics as well as other aspects of civil life, serving regularly on county juries and paying their taxes. Attracted by the security and prestige Promised Land afforded and the possible hope of eventual landownership, fifty additional landless households moved into the community during the 1870's, expanding the 1880 population to almost twice its original size. Together the eighty-nine households laid claim to slightly more than four square miles of land, and within that small territory they "carved out their own little piece of the world."[38]

[38]U. S. Bureau of Census, 1880 Household and Agricultural Manuscripts, Smithville and White Hall Enumeration Districts, Abbeville County, S.C. All subsequent demographic, agricultural, and household data are derived from these sources unless otherwise noted. Interview with Isaac H. Moragne, 14 September 1979, New York, N.Y.

Typewriting had become women's work by 1915

The New Technology and Women's Work

SHEILA M. ROTHMAN

Rarely in history has the female role been as clearly defined as in Victorian America, when women were expected to dedicate their lives to "the cult of true womanhood" or "the cult of domesticity."

Before the nineteenth century, most women worked alongside their husbands in agricultural pursuits or domestic manufacture. With the growth of cities, however, and the rise of the middle class, women lost their traditional economic function and were admonished to withdraw behind the domestic curtain. There they were to practice the virtues of piety, purity, submissiveness, and domesticity, as described in Barbara Welter's seminal essay, "The Cult of True Womanhood." Their station in life was determined by the achievements and social status of their husbands, and women were expected to maintain the home as a refuge to which their husbands could retreat from the hurly-burly of nineteenth-century business dealings. Increasingly, women became the primary child rearers.

The conventions that fixed this burden upon women did not imply that women were inferior. On the contrary, they were considered superior and were expected to serve as the guardians of faith and morals. But this strict separation of sex roles was a much more effective tool for male dominance than any theory of superiority or inferiority could have been. The principal assumption of this dichotomy was that men and women were intended to occupy different spheres in society. The male sphere was public life; the female, private life—positions derived from religious teachings, traditions, and biological differences.

The developing technology of the late nineteenth century had a significant impact on the lives of middle-class women. This was particularly true in urban areas, where electricity made possible a variety of labor-saving devices and the development of apartment houses and department stores helped reduce the amount of time and effort spent. The lightening of household drudgery and the changing patterns of responsibility enabled women to become the primary consumers within the family. Nevertheless, the distinctive spheres of male and female remained intact.

Working women were also affected by the new technology. Employed women were not a new phenomenon in American life, but up until the late nineteenth century job opportunities for female workers were quite limited. Many young women from the countryside and small towns found employment in the developing factories of the United States in the middle of the nineteenth century. They typically worked for a few years and then retired to marriage and motherhood. In the late nineteenth century, however, new inventions such as the telephone and typewriter opened up new areas of employment for urban women. These new jobs quickly became sex-typed and largely restricted to females. The positions did not offer much possibility of job mobility, and supervisory positions tended to be held by men. So while more women were able to find employment, they remained in gender ghettoes, prevented from advancing into positions of responsibility. The traditional pattern of authority was retained.

Sheila M. Rothman has written about the changing place of women in American life. In the selections from her book printed below, the reasons why expanding opportunity did not change the structure of gender relationships are explored. Women sought and gained an expanded arena in which to operate, but for the most part their new fields were merely incorporated into the already clearly defined spheres. The careers favored by educated women were those which reflected what was assumed to be woman's natural character—nurturing, compassionate, and submissive. It would remain for the mid-twentieth century to see women seeking with moderate success to break through the barrier of the spheres in the realm of employment.

T he closing decades of the nineteenth century present two contradictory and yet authentic images. In the first instance, the period appears to be remarkably open and fluid, filled with marvelous innovations and technological advances. Over these thirty years, America did become modern. Industrial production transformed the economic life of the nation: large-scale corporations distributed mass-produced goods to national markets over an elaborate network of railroads. Americans in unprecedented numbers began to move to the cities. A restless energy drove them from the countryside and the small towns to the new urban centers. At the same time, great numbers of Europeans, particularly Eastern Europeans, migrated to take their chances in a New World. A sense of ambition and adventure seemed to pervade every place and enterprise. But these same decades were no less marked by constraints and restrictions. The gap between the rich and the poor widened, the distance between mansion and tenement becoming so great that only a very lucky few could ever bridge it. The discipline of work took on a new relentlessness: the factory machine and the office routine imposed their own kind of tyranny. Thus one vacillates, properly, between a sense of opportunity and creativity and a sense of fixity and rigidity.[1]

Although many of these images come from the world of men, the same tension predominated in the world of women. In a variety of ways, technological innovations transformed women's lives and particularly the lives of middle-class, urban women. Technology liberated them from much of the drudgery of household tasks. The appliances that electricity powered freed women from traditional and incredibly onerous household chores. Further, new types of institutions for women, particularly the women's colleges, came into existence during these years, providing an altogether novel kind of experience. Still further, new occupations opened up to women, especially in offices and department stores, while the number of teaching positions in the public schools increased. Finally, this era witnessed the vigorous and energetic activities of women's clubs; benevolent-minded women set out to reform the almshouses and eliminate the saloon. As the Woman's Christian Temperance Union (WCTU) motto proclaimed: "Woman will bless and brighten every place she enters, and will enter every place."

Yet again, in each of these instances, liberation seems to be only part of the story. A very special ideology defined women's proper social roles in narrow and restricted ways. Ideas that we may lable "virtuous womanhood" dominated their lives, closing off opportunities, fostering a sexstereotyping of jobs, and ruling out options. Both in the private and public arena—in the home, in the club, and in the workplace—women's actions had to be consistent with moral sensibility, purity, and maternal affection, and no other code of behavior was acceptable. Hence, to understand the experience of women in the post-Civil War decades, particularly as it helped to shape social policy by women and on behalf of women, requires a full appreciation of the interaction between opportunity and obligation, between social reality and ideology.

TECHNOLOGY AND THE WHITE WOMAN'S BURDEN

Almost every technological innovation in the period 1870–1900 significantly altered the daily routine of middle-class women. During these years, city after city, responding to the demands of engineers and real estate promoters, constructed and extended water and sewerage lines. It was not unusual for as much as one-third of a municipal budget to go to improving sanitation.[2] By 1890, even moderate-priced homes in many cities were equipped with hot and cold water, water closets, and bathrooms. These

[1]David Potter, *People of Plenty* (Chicago, 1954); Robert Wiebe, *The Search for Order 1877–1920* (New York, 1967); and Stephen Thernstrom, *Poverty and Progress* (Cambridge, Mass., 1964).
[2]Daniel Boorstin, *The Americans: the Democratic Experience* (New York, 1973), p. 352.

conveniences are so much a part of our lives that we may easily forget their significance to the first generation of women who enjoyed them: they reduced—almost eliminated—an extraordinary amount of menial tasks. Hot and cold running water within a private dwelling simplified the most demanding domestic task that a woman faced, the weekly wash. Laundering probably took as much as one-third of her working hours. To Marion Harland, one of the most prolific writers of household advice books, laundry was "the white woman's burden . . . the bane of American housemother's professional life."[3] The new water supply eliminated not only the endless parade of bucket-carrying from the outdoor well to the kitchen, but also the enervating task of pumping water from a hand pump, then lifting and lowering heavy washtubs of hot water from the stove. More, the piping of water prepared the way for the arrival of the great household appliance, the washing machine.[4] The hand pump, the copper washtub, and the wooden scrubbing board were on their way to becoming antiques, relics of a primitive past.

So, too, the municipal power companies began to harness electricity to light city streets and stores, and before very long they were providing electric light for private dwellings.[5] Electricity expanded the hours of the day in a literal sense, and it was soon reducing the drudgery of housework. Electricity, reported one architect by 1903, "is used in operating telephones, call bells . . . for driving laundry, kitchen ventilating and pumping apparatus, and in some cases for refrigerating machinery."[6] And each of these appliances saved women time and energy.

The technological improvements in water supply, sewerage, and electricity all contributed directly to the creation of a novel form of residential living, and one that would prove exceptionally convenient for women— the apartment house. Part of the stimulus for the erection of apartment houses came from real estate developers. As the cost of land climbed in every major urban area and as real estate values doubled and tripled in short periods of time, the use of commercial residential space was fundamentally altered. When land values soared, so did buildings—and hence the new office skyscrapers. At the same time, the possibility of owning a private home within the city became more and more the prerogative of the very rich, the mansion dwellers along New York's Fifth Avenue. For the middle classes there was the suburb, and they did flock to the perimeters of the city along the new urban transportation networks.[7] But many middle-class families were eager to remain close to the urban core, and for them the apartment dwelling was eminently attractive.[8]

[3]Marion Harland, *The Housekeeper's Week* (Indianapolis, Ind., 1908), p. 13.

[4]Boorstin, *The Americans*, p. 254.

[5]Ibid., pp. 530–535.

[6]P. R. Moses, "Some Data on Electricity in Apartment Houses," *Architectural Review* 10 (1903), p. 11.

[7]Sam B. Warner, Jr., *Streetcar Suburbs* (Cambridge, Mass., 1962).

[8]A. C. David, "A Cooperative Studio Building," *Architectural Record* 14 (October 1903), p. 243. David notes that while in 1870 the island of Manhattan was dominated by single-family homes and tenements, by 1900 this had changed. That year only ten single-family homes were built and apartment buildings were dotting the skyline.

Developers quickly understood the need to build not only offices but also apartment houses as high as possible. But before they could carry out the plan, they had to be able to deliver critical kinds of services. In the case of the office building, electricity made the essential service of an elevator easily available. But home residences required more complex facilities, particularly in the kitchen. Some apartment houses had been constructed before the advent of electricity, but invariably they served a very limited clientele, generally the rich, precisely because they could not provide kitchens. The first apartment buildings were appropriately known as "apartment hotels," buildings that substituted a communal dining room for a private kitchen. The family took its meals on the hotel's main floor with other residents. The lack of privacy under this arrangement did prompt some buildings to offer an additional service—the private servants of the family could prepare meals in the downstairs kitchen and then use dumbwaiters to lift the food upstairs. In either case, apartment hotels were suitable only for a very wealthy minority.[9]

By the later 1880s, technological developments transformed apartment hotels into apartment houses. Builders installed a central refrigeration plant that cooled each apartment refrigerator. They piped gas into kitchen stoves and, of course, provided elevators to move the tenant and her groceries upstairs.[10] Thus, in 1901 the apartment, to quote one architect, became "a substitute for the home," able to supply "what the house gives."[11]

The innovation was quick to spread. Developers found that economies of scale paid well, and so they built apartment houses taller and wider. The first structures occupied one city lot; the newer ones covered two or three. The high initial cost of wiring and providing elevators could be offset by increasing the number of units in each building.[12] Thus, middle-class families who did not wish to move to the suburbs could live comfortably and even cheaply within the city. Apartments were less costly to maintain than homes and were more efficient besides. The new kitchens were especially attractive: the floors were typically covered with rubber tile, and the lower half of the walls had white tile that was easy to clean. A gas stove, a hot water heater, a sink with hot and cold running water, and a refrigerator with "glass or tile linings and compartments for every conceivable use" were all in place, simplifying almost every household task. Further, the entire arrangement obviated the need for servants just at a time when domestic help was becoming less available. In 1870, one of every eight families had a servant; by 1900 the number had dropped to one in fifteen.[13] Clearly, an apartment kitchen made full-time help much less necessary.

Technological innovations and apartment units became more available to still larger numbers of American families in the opening decades

[9]Ibid., p. 242; T. Richardson, "New Homes of New York," *Scribner's Monthly* 8 (1874), p. 68.

[10]O. F. Semsch, "The Heating, Plumbing, and Refrigerating in Apartment Houses," *Architectural Review* 10 (1903), p. 106.

[11]Ernest Flagg, "Planning of Apartment Houses and Tenements," *Architectural Review* 10 (1903), p. 89.

[12]Moses, "Some Data," p. 11.

[13]D. N. B. Sturgis, "The Planning and Furnishing of the Kitchen in the Modern Residence," *Architectural Record*, 16 (1904), p. 391.

of the twentieth century. More electrical power was harnessed to light homes, to drive washing machines, and to heat ovens. More apartment dwellings were built as land costs rose in small as well as large municipalities. Indeed, to a local chamber of commerce, apartment houses represented municipal prosperity, a sign that land in the town was too valuable for constructing private homes. To the tenants, the units symbolized the quintessence of modern living. "Apartment dwelling is both simplified and intensive living," one observer reported. "The smoothly run private house, with one or two good servants doing practically all the work, is for those of moderate means largely a recollection of the happy past. . . . We may contrast with this the life of the well-managed apartment house. At once is the heating problem disposed of, with its laborious care of the furnace and its coal and dirt. . . . Packages, mail, and messages are received, receipted for, and delivered by attendants. Rubbish and garbage are taken away daily, and papers, milk, bread, and ice are brought to the apartment doors. . . . If plumbing or electrical trouble develops, the engineer is at hand; if a trunk or piece of furniture needs shifting, there is the elevator man." So, too, the "servantless electric kitchen" became popular. Builders substituted refrigerators, electric ranges, and even dishwashers for roomy kitchens, pantries, and maids' rooms. One favorite cartoon of the 1920s portrayed the servantless housewife asleep while her electric machines did all the chores.[14]

In the newly expanded city, women found a host of labor-saving services. In 1870, for example, most urban women were still canning and preserving fruits and vegetables; over the course of the next two decades, the technology of commercial canning advanced so that women could vary the family diet in little time and at little expense. The Campbell soup jingle now boasted that "it only takes a ten-cent can to make enough for six," and the Heinz Company had developed not only their famous ketchup but also fifty-seven varieties of pickles and relishes. (To advertise their products, Heinz in 1897 erected a fifty-foot electric sign in mid-Manhattan, whose green bulbs made up an enormous pickle.) At the same time, the combination of national railway lines and refrigerated railway cars brought fresh meat from Midwestern slaughterhouses to butchers and to housewives in well-wrapped and precisely cut packages. The presence of commercial local bakeries in the cities and the distribution of national food company products like Uneeda Biscuits meant that women no longer had to reserve one day of the week to bake the family bread and cakes. (Uneeda Biscuits promised that its inner wrap seal would deliver a product "as fresh as mother's.") By 1900, 90 percent of urban homes used bakers' bread only, and two-thirds of urban families sent some laundry out of the home to be finished. All these developments represented a fundamental change in the consumption patterns. More middle-class families were spending a larger proportion of their funds on durable goods and services and less on purchasing homes and the services of domestic servants.[15]

[14]Edward Stratton Holloway, "Apartments and How to Furnish Them," *House Beautiful*, 56 (1924), p. 130; I. M. Rubinow, "Discussion," Third Annual Meeting of The American Sociological Society *Papers and Proceedings* (1908), p. 38.

[15]Frank Presbrey, *The History and Development of Advertising* (New York, 1929), pp. 379, 417, 421–422; Boorstin, *The Americans*, pp. 318–321.

Only a few nostalgic critics lamented these changes. " 'The Homemade Loaf,' " Marion Harland declared, "stands with so many of us as a symbol of the wholesome good cheer beloved in our childhood's days that we are disposed to class the phrase with the traditional open fireplaces, doughnuts 'such as mother used to make,' and other reminiscences of 'the days that are no more.' "[16] But others, like Thomas Edison, spread a very different message. Praising the wonders of electricity, he predicted that woman "will give less attention to the home, because the home will need less; she will be rather a domestic engineer than a domestic laborer, with the greatest of all handmaidens, electricity, at her service. This and other mechanical forces will so revolutionize the woman's world that a large portion of the aggregate of woman's energy will be conserved for use in broader, more constructive fields."[17] Technology had the potential to make women's lives much less isolated and home-bound.

No change better exemplified the way in which technology increased women's efficiency and encouraged their movement outside the home than the department store. Just as Americans quickly incorporated the variety of new, mass-produced products in their homes, so, too, women with equal ease moved to take advantage of the bargains and delights of shopping in the new department stores. These stores, another innovation of the post-Civil War decades, revolutionized the patterns of retail trade and the shopping habits of middle-class women. Wanamaker's in Philadelphia, Marshall Field's in Chicago, and Macy's in New York wanted to make it more economical for women to shop at their stores. They defended a cash-only system of business by claiming that it allowed them to offer lower prices than the local shops. "For every cent expended in our store," Macy's told their customers, "we return full value, because we give no credit and, therefore, incur no losses. . . . Every article in our store is a BARGAIN."[18] The stores' size also enabled them to eliminate many middleman costs; they could buy directly from the manufacturer or even produce the goods themselves. By 1885, Macy's manufactured "ladies' and children's underwear, men's shirts, linen collars and cuffs for both men and women, women's dresses, bustles . . . velvet wraps and linen handkerchiefs," selling the goods under their private label.[19] They were further able to reduce prices by placing orders in bulk. John Wanamaker proudly noted that a purchase of pins for his store took an entire freight car to transport and that he could then sell pins to his customers at a lower cost.

The department store also offered women a dazzling variety of products. Macy's boasted that it had the "most extensive assortment of china [and] glassware . . . ever displayed in America."[20] And the opening of a new Wanamaker's store gave President William Howard Taft the occasion to declare that Americans could now purchase "under one roof . . . at the lowest reasonable, constant, and fixed price, everything that is usually

[16]Harland, *Housekeeper's Week*, p. 74.

[17]Edward Marshall, "The Woman of the Future," *Good Housekeeping*, 55 (October 1912), p. 436.

[18]Ralph M. Hower, *History of Macy's of New York, 1858–1919* (Cambridge, Mass., 1943), pp. 271–272.

[19]Ibid., p. 163.

[20]Ibid., p. 104.

needed upon the person or in the household for the sustaining of life, for recreation, and for intellectual enjoyment."[21]

The department store added other efficiencies to attract women. It delivered packages to apartments in the city, to the suburbs, or to nearby summer communities. It repaired jewelry and watches and framed pictures. It even stored furs during the hot summer months, a particular convenience to customers living in small apartments.[22]

The department store's popularity also testified to its ability to capture the imagination and interest of the middle-class woman. It resorted to so many promotional devices that a trip to the department store had the quality of an adventure. *The New York World* was right to call Macy's "a bazaar, a museum, a hotel and a great fancy store all combined."[23]

The architecture of the new stores was monumental in design. The "cast-iron palaces" were almost cathedral-like in character. Wanamaker, for example, instructed his architect: "What you must do for me is to strive to say in stone what this business has said to the world in deed. You must make a building that is solid and true. It shall be granite and steel throughout . . . simple, unpretentious, noble, classic—a work of art, and, humanly speaking, a monument for all time." The result was a building that contained a huge auditorium with almost 2,000 seats, a pipe organ of nearly 3,000 pipes, a Grand Court with towering marble columns, and a Greek Hall with 600 more seats.[24] Shoppers entering New York's Siegel & Cooper Company faced an enormous fountain of a Greek goddess over twenty feet high. Plush and ornate trimmings ran through every corner of the stores. The ladies' waiting room at Macy's was described as "the most luxurious and beautiful department devoted to the comforts of ladies to be found in a mercantile establishment in the city. The style of decoration is Louis XV, and no expense has been spared in the adornment and furnishing of this room"[25] Adjoining the waiting room was an art gallery with an extensive exhibit of oil paintings.

The department store provided customers with still more comforts and conveniences. As early as 1878, Macy's set aside space where women could sit and write letters or read its collection of the latest editions of the daily newspapers. The newspapers, of course, always contained the store's advertisement, usually placed directly across the page from an article of special interest to women. The Wanamaker advertisement was seemingly so popular a feature of the Philadelphia press that the store claimed: "Women of the city and suburbs refused to take a daily paper that did not contain the Wanamaker advertisement."[26] In 1890, when a biking craze swept New York City, women could not only purchase their bicycles at Macy's but also learn to ride them there. In all, these stores had an irresistible appeal. As Macy's told its customers: "Ride our bicycles, read our books, cook in our

---

[21]William H. Taft, "The Dedication of Wanamaker's 1911," *Golden Book of the Wanamaker Store Jubilee Year*, 1861–1911 (Philadelphia, 1911), Vol. 2, p. 3.

[22]Hower, *Macy's*, pp. 280, 235.

[23]Ibid., p. 164.

[24]*Golden Book*, pp. 150–151.

[25]Hower, *Macy's*, p. 284.

[26]Ibid., p. 166; *Golden Book*, p. 285.

saucepans, dine off our china, wear our silks, get under our blankets, smoke our cigars, drink our wines—Shop at Macy's—and life will Cost You Less and Yield You More Than You Dreamed Possible."[27]

Department store customers were among the first to experience technological innovations. New York City streets were not lit by electricity until 1882, but in 1879 Macy's display windows were "brilliantly illuminated with electric lights until 10 o'clock." In 1878 the first telephone was installed in the White House, and within two years Macy's had the device. One of the earliest steam-powered elevators in the country ran in Strawbridge and Clothier of Philadelphia. The Otis hydraulic model in the Eiffel Tower took tourists to the top in seven minutes in 1889. The electric elevators installed by Macy's and Wanamaker's in 1888 went faster.[28]

Urban living meant that many middle-class women did not have to be at home to prepare a noonday meal. Men's workplaces were typically too distant from their residences to allow the family to lunch together. So daytime visiting between women, once confined to the parlor, more frequently took place in centrally located public restaurants. The department stores, as well as the commercial tea parlors, offered a Ladies' Luncheon. The first ladies' lunchroom opened at Macy's in 1878, the same year the Sixth Avenue Elevated brought rapid transit to Fourteenth Street. The lunchroom was so successful that, when opening its new Herald Square store in 1902, Macy's installed a public restaurant for 2,500 people.[29] The Womans Exchange, a charitable and social organization commonly found in cities, also ran dining rooms. The Boston Exchange, with its several thousand women members, was reputedly "the one place we can surely find good food at moderate prices."[30] By 1910, as Marion Talbot, Dean of Women at the University of Chicago, aptly concluded, "the sewing circle, the husking bee, the afternoon visit are things of the past."[31] Now women would meet in the grand reception hall of the department store, see the newest sights, shop with friends, and then lunch together. A stop before returning home allowed them to purchase a "home-baked" bread or cake to place on the table.

• • •

DEFINING WOMAN'S WORK:
TYPEWRITERS, SALESGIRLS, AND TEACHERS

The contrast between opportunity and rigidity, innovation and fixity that marked the world of urban women and college girls also characterized the world of working women. To many observers, women were enjoying an

[27]Hower, *Macy's*, p. 273.
[28]Boorstin, *The Americans*, pp. 536 and 103; Hower, *Macy's*, p. 166.
[29]Hower, *Macy's*, pp. 160, 325.
[30]Agnes S. Donham, "History of Woman's Educational & Industrial Union" (Boston, 1955), typewritten manuscript. Papers of the Boston Woman's Educational and Industrial Union. Schlesinger Library, Radcliffe College.
[31]Marion Talbot, *The Education of Women* (Chicago, 1910), p. 46.

unparalleled freedom to enter traditional professions and to hold newly created positions in an expanding economy. And yet, their actual distribution in the labor force and their chances for promotion do not bear out such optimistic pronouncements. In fact, the late nineteenth century began a sex-stereotyping of occupations that would persist through most of the twentieth century. This was the moment when typists, stenographers, department store clerks, and school teachers all became prototypically female.

The definition of what constituted a woman's occupation owed much to purely market forces. Employers hired women when men, because of their social class or education, were either unwilling or unable to fill the positions—or, put another way, when women made up the cheapest available and suitable labor pool. Yet the prevailing concepts of virtuous womanhood that we have been exploring had an impact, too; they helped to buttress and support this process of selection and labeling. Notions of when women could properly work and what they could properly do contributed in critical ways to legitimating distinctions that were frankly discriminatory.

It was those women most active in public life—heading up newly established clubs or agitating for suffrage—who were most convinced of novel opportunities in the work force. Taking as their point of comparison Harriet Martineau's observation in the 1830s that only seven occupations were open to women in the United States, these women insisted that nothing less than a revolution had occurred: in 1900, women could be found in 295 of the 303 occupations listed in the United States Census. "When I was a girl," recalled suffrage leader Lucy Stone, "I seemed to be shut out of everything I wanted to do. I might teach school . . . I might go out dressmaking or tailoring, or trim bonnets, or I might work in a factory or go out to domestic service; there the mights ended and the might nots began."

For her children, however, conditions seemed altogether different. "A few years ago when my daughter left Boston University with her degree of B.A., she might do what she chose; all the professions were open to her; she could enter any line of business." Frances Willard, another suffragist, agreed. "Nowadays, a girl may be anything, from a college president down to a seamstress or a cash girl. It depends only upon the girl what rank she shall take in her chosen calling." Opportunities appeared to be limitless, bounded only by individual choice. "Set the goal of your ambitions," Willard advised young women, "and then climb to it by steady, earnest steps." So too, Marion Harland told her many readers: "Choose Something to Do *and do it!* Thirty years back this injunction would have meant to a young woman, reputably-born and in moderate circumstances, 'Prepare yourself to become a governess or the principal of a school.' Now—what may it not signify and include? If we would know how times have changed, and we with them . . . survey . . . the fallen and disintegrating boundary-walls."[32]

This insistence that unmarried women could and should "do something" reflected a belief that the chance to work would relieve the tedium

[32]Frances E. Willard, *Occupations for Women* (New York, 1897), p. 23, 142; Harland, *Eve's Daughters*, p. 258.

that often afflicted their lives. Specifically, new job opportunities seemed not only to explain but to justify the fact that so many country girls were flocking to the city. "Young girls," declared Arnold Wolfe, a remarkably perceptive student of urban lodging and boardinghouses, "come from rocky farms and hill towns to escape the irksome drudgery and monotony of petty household duties; girls who have grown tired . . . of helping their mothers wash the dishes and pare the potatoes . . . have set their eyes to the city as a sort of Mecca for all in search of opportunity."[33] Nor were they likely to be disappointed: "If a girl has the right sort of business ability behind her ambition," noted one advice-book writer, "the city holds wonderful possibilities for her. There is always room for the girl with an idea; for the girl who does one thing well; for the girl who is willing, nay anxious to learn to work." To be sure, in this Mecca a woman would have to be careful to preserve her virtue: "No mother should permit her daughter to go to a strange city unless she can provide the girl with funds to pay for board and room for a month. . . . The mother who recklessly allows her unskilled daughter to enter a strange city armed with only a week's board and high hopes is guilty of criminal neglect as the guardian of her child's future." But as long as the girl had good moral training or skill and something of a financial stake, she would realize the promise of the city.[34]

Even more important, employment possibilities would rescue not only country girls from the farm, but all girls from the perils of a hasty and unwise marriage. To this end, the concepts of virtuous womanhood actually encouraged work for single and middle-class girls. To a suffragist like Mary Livermore, women's entrance into the labor force was another way to bring feminine, as opposed to masculine, qualities into the society. Pleased that "the doors of colleges, professional schools, and universities, closed against them [women] for ages, are opening to them," and that "trades, business, remunerative vocations and learned professions seek them," Livermore contended that such changes demonstrated that "the leadership of the world is being taken from the hands of the brutal and low, and the race is groping its way to a higher ideal than once it knew. It is the evolution of this tendency that is lifting women out of their subject condition, that is emancipating them from the seclusion of the past." But Livermore herself, and others as well, placed these general observations into a more specific context: the woman who could earn her own living would not be a captive of the male beast. "This fact," declared Laura Clay, the daughter of Henry Clay and a noted feminist, "would avail more to prevent unworthy and loveless marriages, entered into for the sake of support, than all the exhortations of moralists."[35]

Marion Harland, a far more traditional-minded writer, was no less certain that a young girl should abandon altogether the precept, "Do noth-

---

[33] Arnold B. Wolfe, *The Lodging House Problem* (Boston, 1906), pp. 81–82. See also John Modell and Tamara K. Hareven, "An Examination of Boarding and Lodging in American Families," *Journal of Marriage and the Family* 35 (August 1973), p. 471.

[34] Anna S. Richardson, *The Girl Who Earns Her Own Living* (New York, 1909), p. 282.

[35] Mary A. Livermore, *What Shall We Do with Our Daughters?* (Boston, 1883), pp. 13, 14; Laura Clay, "Responsibility of Women to Society," Association for the Advancement of Women, Fifteenth Congress, *Proceedings*, 1887, p. 12.

ing, but be as happy as the day is long," precisely because "in the endeavor to follow the prescription, she falls in love." And that kind of fall could be disastrous; "Many a woman, after wasting years of time and wealth of devotion upon an undeserving object, has died of a broken heart, who would never have loved a worthless man and suffered unto death if she had had regular employment for her thoughts and hands. Occupation, congenial and continuous, is the best panacea for ill-directed fancies."[36]

Livermore elaborated this message in her 1883 volume, *What Shall We Do With Our Daughters?* "The substance of this book," she explained, "has been before the public for more than a decade, in the form of lyceum lectures, delivered hundreds of times to audiences in all sections of the country from Maine to California." The core of the advice that she spread so energetically was that parents should train daughters to support themselves, to enable them "to maintain themselves by their own labor." Livermore insisted that "it is not safe, neither is it wise or kind, to rear our daughters as if marriage were their only legitimate business." First, some of them would not find husbands, because men were killing themselves off through addiction to corruption and vice: "If it were possible to obtain statistics on drunkenness," noted Livermore, "we should see that its draughts on the male population exceed that made by war." Remember, too, "the inevitable fatalities attending the pursuits of men in pleasure and business, by overwork and excessive haste to be rich." More, the men who did survive were not always "good or competent husbands. Some become permanent invalids; others are dissolute and unambitious [Livermore damned men either way], and not a few desert entirely both wives and children." Thus, women had to choose their mates wisely and even then be prepared for all sorts of contingencies. Only a "practical knowledge of a trade, a paying business, or a profession" would allow for that.

Such training, Livermore argued, had another advantage: "Girls would then escape one of the most serious dangers to which inefficient women are liable—the danger of regarding marriage as a means of a livelihood." The self-sufficient woman who married would not view the future with "the vague terror with which aimless untrained women regard it." Clearly, a moral imperative informed all these dicta, drawn directly from the precepts of virtuous womanhood. "No woman," Livermore declared, "has the moral right to become the mother of children whose father is drunken and immoral. For this perpetuates the brutishness of the race and extends evils that should be eliminated from humanity." In sum, concluded Livermore, when women "are trained and self-poised, they will not be in bondage to ignorance; nor will they be as liable to become dupes or the prey of others. A wife and mother should be mistress of herself and of her department and never a slave of another—not even when that other is her husband, and the slavery is founded on her undying love."[37]

In fact, mothers learned that working was less dangerous to their daughter's health than attending college, provided, that is, that the work was not too intellectual. Physicians believed that even physically demand-

---

[36]Harland, *Eve's Daughters*, pp. 278–279.

[37]Livermore, *Our Daughters*, pp. 3, 132, 149; Mary A. Livermore, "Superfluous Women," an undated article found in the WCTU papers of the Sophia Smith Collection, p. 216–17.

ing occupations were not as harmful as concentrated study. "There are two reasons," maintained Dr. Edward Clark, "why female operatives of all sorts are likely to suffer less, and actually do suffer less, from such persistent work than female students; why Jane in the factory can work more steadily with the loom than Jane in college with the dictionary." The average female worker, Clarke argued, had already passed puberty, the time when reproductive organs placed their heaviest demands on the body; the female student, on the other hand, has "these tasks before her." (Clarke's chronology, incidentally, was inaccurate—the majority of women in the work force were actually between 14 and 18, just the ages that doctors found so worrisome.) Clarke also insisted, in the tradition of Jacksonian medical superintendents, that factory girls were healthier because they "work their brains less." Finally, he and his colleagues were acutely concerned about the ill effects of idleness, convinced that moral degeneration and corrupt habits had their source in a life of leisure. Hence, just as medical superintendents instituted a routine of steady work to cure the mentally ill, so these doctors advocated it to protect the young woman.[38]

College presidents used a variant of Livermore's arguments as another justification for female higher education. A college experience, like training for a job, would enable graduates to marry better than others. A liberal education, contended Vassar President John Raymond, made a young woman into "a fit companion for a wiser and nobler man, than she otherwise would have been. If he be a professional man, she will feel an enlightened sympathy in his intellectual pursuits, and may often find it in her power to render him valuable counsel and effective aid." And many others agreed. "Educated women," reported one journalist, "subject their impulses to the test of their reason in study; this gives them an advantage in choice of husbands." Insisted still another: "The college woman is not only more exacting in her standards of marriage, but under less pressure to accept what falls below her standard than the average woman. . . . Unhappy marriages are almost unknown among college women."[39]

These comments, to be sure, were intended to offset the popular assumption that college unfitted girls to marry—a notion that did have a base in reality. The 1885 survey of the Association of Collegiate Alumnae (which reported so favorably upon the health of college women) noted that only 28 percent of women graduates were married. Vassar, surveying its first twenty-four graduating classes in 1894, discovered that of the 815 living graduates, only 315 (39 percent) had married, and most of them did so many years after graduation. But proponents of women's education had a ready answer. Maria Mitchell coined the slogan that would be heard well into the twentieth century: "Vassar girls marry late, but they marry well."[40]

All of these claims exaggerated and distorted both the number of opportunities that women enjoyed in the labor force and, no less impor-

---

[38]Edward H. Clarke, *Sex in Education* (Boston, 1874), pp. 131, 133.

[39]Raymond, "The Demand of the Age," p. 43; Gilman, *Thoughts*, p. 84; Millicent Washburn Shinn, "The Marriage Rate for College Women," *Century Magazine*, 50 (October 1895), p. 948.

[40]Howe, *Health Statistics*, p. 29; Elizabeth C. Boyd, "Vassar College," *Godey's Magazine* (February 1895), p. 197.

tant, the amount of freedom of choice that the role of virtuous womanhood allowed them outside the home. The occupational distribution of women was nowhere near as balanced as the rhetoric of Lucy Stone implied. The principles that were to guide women in selecting a job and remaining at work were far more confining than the language of Mary Livermore suggested.

Frances Willard once described the reality of the situation accurately when noting, "The American woman . . . has taken a *dip* into every occupation." Although one could find a woman here or there in many job categories, most women were grouped into a select few. College graduates ended up as school teachers (of those 815 Vassar graduates, 805 worked at some time as teachers). Women with less education entered offices; those with still less, retail stores. (In 1870 the number of women in offices and stores was 10,798 or under 1.0 percent of the women employed in non-agricultural jobs; by 1900 the number had risen to 394,747 or 9.1 percent of the total.[41] And no matter what the job, women remained at the lower end of the ladder. In the public schools they were the classroom teachers, not the principals or superintendents; in offices, they made up the ranks of typists and stenographers, not the executives; in the retail stores, they were the clerks and cashiers, not the floorwalkers or managers. In other words, the job that a woman first assumed was generally the one that she kept as long as she worked. Men had careers, rising from clerks to become managers, from teachers to become principals; women remained locked in the same position. Once a typist, always a typist; once a clerk, always a clerk. Indeed, the job discrimination that they suffered was so obvious, the situation that they confronted so bleak, that the point that needs explaining is why some jobs opened up for women at all.

By the same token, even the staunchest proponents of women's work wanted them—and everyone else—to think of labor essentially as a temporary state (something to do until the right man came along), as a form of insurance (something to do if an emergency arose), or, in a still more restricted way, as a last resort (something to do if the sex ratio remained grossly imbalanced). A woman's job skills were to improve her marital choices, to allow her and her husband to sleep more securely, and to demonstrate her moral worth through self-support under the most trying circumstances. But a woman was not to work in order to advance a career. In fact, these postulates assumed a self-fulfilling quality. Encouraged to think of themselves in some sense or other as part-time workers, women did not generally expect or press for promotion and equal pay. So, too, employers defined women as temporary workers and were accordingly reluctant to advance them or to raise their salaries. The graduate and professional schools also took refuge in this argument (more or less honestly). Why invest in so expensive a training program for a woman if she would only practice law or medicine temporarily? Again, what now seems most puzzling is that *any* job actually became a woman's job.

The dynamic that operated in the post-Civil War decades to create new and exclusive positions for women emerges with special clarity in white-collar occupations. An expanding and modernizing economy did increase

---

[41]Willard, *Occupations*, p. 172 (italics added); Boyd, "Vassar College," p. 197; Joseph A. Hill, *Women in Gainful Occupations, 1870 to 1920* (Washington, D.C., 1929), p. 45.

the number of clerical and office jobs, particularly for typists and stenographers—and it was women who filled them. In the 1870s, men typically worked as stenographers and scriveners; women composed less than 5 percent of this group. By 1900, the women held fully three-quarters of these jobs.[42]

The change began with the typewriter. It altered both the style of office work and the composition of the office staff. Although the Remington Company developed the first writing machines in 1874, typewriters were not sold in significant numbers until the 1880s. They remained a novelty, mostly because few people had the necessary skills to use them. Remington soon understood that to market its product it would have to train operators; only when typists, like spare parts, were available on demand would businesses invest in the machines. The company therefore opened typewriting schools in the large cities and established an employment bureau as an adjunct to each of them. The strategy worked well. By 1890, Remington could barely keep up with orders for machines and demands for operators. Between 1897 and 1902 it supplied New York City alone with 25,262 typists, and Chicago with 23,368.[43]

Nearly all of Remington's students were women. One of the designers of the machine even boasted that its most important achievement "was to allow women an easier way to earn a living." But why did Remington's schools recruit—and recruit successfully—among women? Because the company recognized that a typist had to "be a good speller, a good grammarian and have the correct knowledge of the use of capitals and the rules of punctuation."[44] Where might it find a ready source of labor with such educational qualifications? Lower-class men did not have the literacy skills necessary for the job; skilled male workers were well paid in other positions. Middle-class men with high school educations had still more opportunities for responsible and upwardly mobile employment elsewhere. Recognizing that men were either ineligible or uninterested, the company then turned to women, to the large pool of female high school graduates.

The high school system had only recently come to hold a significant place in urban educational systems, and its new popularity was linked in part to its filling up a young girl's time. "Boys drop out of high school," as one superintendent explained, "some [to] go to college; others because they get tired of school; others to engage in business; and still others because they had formed bad associations; but the girls remain and graduate if not obliged to quit."[45] Put another way, boys had options (to go to college or into business); girls did not, so they stayed on to graduate. But what

[42]May Allison, *The Public Schools and Women in Office Service* (Boston, 1914), p. 6.

[43]For the early history of the typewriter see Richard N. Current, *The Typewriter and the Men Who Made It* (Urbana, Ill., 1954); Bruce Bliven, *That Wonderful Writing Machine* (New York, 1954). For the role of the Remington Company as an employment agency, see *The Typewriter and Phonographic World*, 20 (1902), p. 125.

[44]Arthur T. Foulke, *Mr. Typewriter* (Boston, 1961), p. 79; G. Shankland Walworth, "How to Get a Situation," in *The Typewriter and Phonographic World*, 18 (Oct. 1901), p. 191; Anna Wade Westabrook, "Young Ladies as Stenographers and Typewriters," *The Typewriter and Phonographic World*, 6 (Feb. 1891).

[45]In 1891, for example, there were 239,556 high school graduates in the United States, 60 percent of whom were women; U.S. Commissioner of Education, *Report*, 1891–92, p. 686; Board of Education, Kansas City, Missouri, *Sixteenth Annual Report*, 1887, p. 24.

were they to do when commencement finally came? For many of them, as we shall see, a teaching position was the answer. But over the 1870s and 1880s, competition so increased that a sizable number of girls could no longer find open posts. There was always the factory, but that was a last resort. Clearly, work at the typewriter in an office was a far more attractive option. The girls could remain in a middle-class, respectable setting, one that was clean, well lit, quiet, and safe. The typewriter was an easy machine to run, and the wages paid were no lower than those of skilled female machine operators. How much better, then, to be a typewriter (as these girls were called) than a factory worker. This fact of life gave Remington and other companies like Royal their labor supply.

Given the desirability of this sort of office work, the manufacturers, the commercial schools, and soon the high schools themselves, rushed to train girls at typewriting. In the early 1880s, one commercial school prospectus still had to concede that "it was an uncommon thing to find a girl living in a respectable home and moving in good society who would not consider herself somewhat degraded by going into a business office and earning a living. And more than that, her father and brother—if she had them—would feel it would be greatly to their discredit to permit such a thing."[46] But by the 1890s, views had changed. The mayor of New York could now tell the graduating class at the Packard Commercial School, "You will lift the tone of those offices . . . and win the lasting respect of your associates. The men around you will grow nobler and better." He assured them that the women working in his office had not only made it a finer place, but "they have made me better, and there is not a person about the office who has not been improved by the presence of the ladies."[47]

From the employers' perspective, women were perfectly suited to be "typewriters." The temporary nature of their work commitment posed no problem; if one operator left to be married, a call to the Remington Company quickly produced another. And since each typing assignment was discrete, the continuity of service of any particular operator was unimportant. Another typist could just as well copy the next letter or bill. Further, wages could be kept low—office managers recognized that their working conditions were superior to those in the factory. Finally, the women's presence did not threaten the ambitions of the men in the office. They could be added to the staff with a minimum of trouble.

In much the same way, women took over stenographic positions, mastering the skills of shorthand and learning to take dictation and then to type the letters. These were well-paying jobs, and women eagerly filled them; a typist earned $6 to $10 a week, a stenographer between $12 and $16. An income of $700 a year put a stenographer well up on the scale of earnings at a time when unskilled labor received about $200 annually, and semi-skilled workers about $400 to $500.

Why did these remunerative positions go to women? Why did a job that in the pre-1860 period was held almost exclusively by men now become

[46]Packard's Business College *Prospectus* 1897–1898, pp. 17–18.
[47]Packard Commercial School *Graduation Exercises* (1895), p. 15. See also Jessica Kemm, *Women as Stenographer/Typist: 1880–1900*, unpublished paper (1976), pp. 6, 12.

defined as female work? Obviously, lower-class men lacked the educational qualifications (or in the case of immigrants, the necessary language skills) to compete for these positions; nor were they about to enroll in a 6- to 9-month course in stenography. As for middle-class men, they did remain the first choice for some employers. (In 1902, when women filled over three-quarters of the positions, the Remington Bureau noted that 40 percent of prospective employers still first requested male stenographers.[48]) But in most cases, office work had become so much more specialized that neither employers nor middle-class men continued to define stenography as a desirable position, that is, one with a potential for promotion. As offices grew larger and the routine within them more specialized, stenography became one of several bureaucratic chores; the time when the male clerk worked alongside the proprietor and might well anticipate advancement had passed. And then it became appropriate to make stenography, and so many other office positions, women's work. Women had the requisite skills, and again, the tasks were so discrete that turnover did not matter.

From one perspective, it is clear that specialization in office work did create new job opportunities for women. The number of all types of female clerks climbed dramatically over the period. In 1880, women composed only 6 percent of the half million clerical workers. By 1910, they were 35 percent of a group that numbered over one and a half million.[49] Yet, at the same time, office work offered few occasions for promotion. It really could not have been different—had the positions allowed for upward mobility, men would have held them. Only because they were dead-end jobs did these positions go to women. One poll taken in the 1920s reported that two-thirds of typists and stenographers never expected advancement. And the companies themselves frankly admitted the correctness of these negative expectations. "It is a commonly accepted fact," noted Grace Coyle, a student of office work, "that such promotion as does exist is much more common for men than for women." Part of the explanation that employers offered was frankly sexist: "It is not assumed that they [women] have the calibre for executive positions." They suggested, too, that the temporary character of women's work ruled out promotion. "The fact that they are likely to marry and leave the business also tends to keep them out of positions which are regarded as training for the higher levels." Whatever the reason, Coyle concluded—accurately—that such assumptions were likely to persist, so that the number of women working in offices would increase but the number who would be promoted would not. "The nature of the work seems to be well adapted to women; they afford a less expensive labor supply than men and their more or less temporary relation to the job enables them to adjust themselves to the lack of opportunity for advancement which is characteristic of many office positions. There seems

[48]Jean Cunningham, "Character of Office Service," in Allison, The Public Schools, pp. 29, 74–75; Hazel Manning, "Home Life Responsibilities" in Allison, The Public Schools, p. 166; John F. Soby, "Male Stenographers Required," The Typewriter and Phonographic World, 20 (July 1902), pp. 38–39.
[49]Grace C. Coyle, Present Trends in Clerical Occupations (New York, 1928), p. 13.

to be every reason to expect that succeeding census figures will show a growing proportion of women in the major clerical fields."[50]

In the exceptional instance when stenography retained its traditional place as a starting point for a career, it was men, and not women, who filled the posts. Thus one trade journal reported that some employers "are actually seeking the boy who understands shorthand." Why? For "no other purpose than to train him with a view of placing him ultimately in some responsible position." When the goal was promotion, the right employee was a male. So, too, the Chicago and Northwestern Railroad announced in 1898 that it was no longer hiring women stenographers. "The move is not because women proved inefficient," they reported, "but it is simply carrying out the company's policy in the matter of promotion of employees. The Northwestern will advance its employees from low positions to officers of trust. Can you imagine a woman as general superintendent or general manager of the affairs of its great railroad system? I think not. But just as long as we have women in clerical positions, the source from which to draw valuable officials in the future is narrowed to small limits."[51] A policy to promote up through the ranks was therefore a policy that prohibited bringing women into the ranks at any level.

The department stores, which revolutionized the buying habits of one class of women, also provided novel employment opportunities for another. As they proliferated, so did the number of women employed as cash girls, saleswomen, and cashiers. Because middle-class men (and in this case, middle-class women, too) did not want these low-paying and tedious jobs, and because store owners considered lower-class men unsuitable, it was lower-class women who filled them.

In the pre-Civil War decades, men had typically worked as clerks in small retail stores, doing the bargaining and selling, and even purchasing the merchandise. To be a clerk in a dry goods shop was a position of some responsibility. The post-Civil War department store, however, with its "one price" formula and specialized buying staff, made the sales clerk's job into a menial position. Department stores actually prided themselves on the passive and routine quality of the help. One general manager boasted that his "salespersons do not urge the customer to buy, and dilate upon the beauties of his wares. They simply ask the customer what he or she wants, and make a record of the sale."[52] The stores generally did not pay their clerks a commission on sales, reducing in still another way the possible returns from the position. Under these circumstances, middle-class men preferred to look elsewhere for jobs that valued their initiative or allowed more responsibility and better prospects for advancement.

[50]Ibid., pp. 14, 37. There was also an assumption that the stenographer could and should be better educated than her employer; clearly educational attainments were unrelated to advancement, Potential workers were told: "Your employer may not use correct grammar, but he will want his stenographer to be able to correct his mistakes. He may not understand the proper use of capitals, or be a good speller, but he pays his stenographer for this, and she must not be found deficient" (Westabrook, "Young Ladies," p. 191).

[51]Soby, "Male Stenographers," p. 40; *Illustrated Phonographic World*, 14 (January 1899), p. 223.

[52]John S. Steck, "Storekeeping in New York City," *Arena*, 22 (August 1899), p. 179.

But young women whose only other choice was factory work or domestic service found the department store a very attractive option. Since it was designed to attract middle-class women as customers, the store was far cleaner and more pleasant than a factory. The work was also less tiring. However demanding the customer might be, the machine was much more ruthless. A department store clerk was much less isolated than a domestic. (Indeed, more than one reformer worried that salesgirls met *too many* people.) And even the most dictatorial company rules and autocratic managers were mild in comparison to the regimen that middle-class housewives imposed on their maids.

Department store employment created its own hierarchy. The youngest workers, those around fourteen years old, took their first jobs as cash girls and moved up to become wrappers and stock girls. Each promotion carried a slight increase in pay—a stock girl earned between $2 and $3 a week, less than an unskilled factory worker. The cash girls raced between salesclerks and cashiers, delivering payments and bringing back change. (In the twentieth century the pneumatic tube and then the computerized cash register would take over this job.) The wrapper "artfully" packaged the merchandise, and the stock girl "neatly" replenished the shelves. At age 16, usually after two years of service, a girl might become a salesclerk (receiving $6 to $7 weekly, better than an unskilled factory worker and about the same as a typist). Clerks who proved both "intelligent and responsible" went on to become cashiers (earning $8 to $10 a week).[53]

Owners preferred to hire women for all these positions, so that three-quarters of department store employees were female. They believed that women were more honest than men. In an establishment with two or three thousand workers, owners and managers—unlike their counterparts in a retail shop—could not expect to oversee every detail. "Honesty on the part of employees," one observer reported, "must of necessity be taken for granted." Therefore, as one manager told Helen Campbell, an investigator of conditions of women's work, "We don't want men; we wouldn't have them even if they came at the same price. No, give me a woman every time. I've been a manager thirteen years, and we never had but four dishonest girls, and we've had to discharge over forty boys in the same time."[54]

Women also seemed easier to discipline and manage. "Boys smoke and lose at cards," Helen Campbell learned, "and do a hundred things that women don't and they get worse instead of better." The girls, drilled in obedience and politeness in an almost military manner, proved tractable. "We want it said of our employees that they are a credit to the house," the Siegel and Cooper Company told its workers. "Be civil and polite to your superiors. Should those in authority not be civil to you, OBEY." The store's manual went on to establish the following rules:

[53]Samuel Hopkins Adams, "The Department Store," *Scribner's Magazine*, 21 (June 1897); Anonymous, "A Salesgirl's Story," *Independent*, 54 (July 31, 1902), pp. 1815–1821; Hower, *Macy's*, pp. 194–199; Helen Campbell, *Darkness and Daylight* (Hartford, Conn., 1892), pp. 256–259.

[54]Adams, "Department Store," p. 19; Helen Campbell, *Prisoner of Poverty* (Boston, 1887), p. 173.

THINGS NOT TO DO

Do not stand in groups.
Do not chew gum, read books, or sew.
Do not giggle, flirt, or idle away your time.
Do not walk together through the store.
Do not be out of your place.
Do not take over fifteen minutes on a pass.
Do not be late at any time.
Do not make a noise when going up in elevators.
Do not push when going into elevators, but always stand in line.
Do not talk across aisles, or in a loud voice.
Do not gossip; mind your own affairs and you will have enough to do.
Do not sit in front of the counter.

TRY TO BE

Polite, neat; dress in black.
Serious in your work.
Punctual, obliging, painstaking.
Keep your stock in good order, and follow the rules of the house.[55]

To enforce these regulations, the stores hired floorwalkers, a post that always went to men. Better paid than the female help (receiving up to $40 a week), the floorwalker was the sergeant in charge of the army of clerks. It was his duty "to keep his salespeople up to the standard in dress, deportment and activities." He was to be the "arbiter on conduct and store etiquette." In addition, the companies relied not only on the threat of dismissal but also on a system of fines to implement their codes. They docked the girls' pay for lateness, for gum chewing, and for standing in front of (instead of behind) the sales counter. Some stores were even prepared to police the moral habits of their employees after work hours. As Siegel and Cooper informed the girls: "You would be very much surprised if you knew the trouble and expense we go to find out character and habits. Detectives you don't know often are detailed to report on all your doings for a week. Don't flirt. . . . Don't lie. . . . Don't live beyond your income, or go into debt. . . . DON'T BORROW OR LEND. . . . Entertaining, even while selling goods in a long, drawn-out way, will not be allowed. Floor managers are particularly instructed to enforce this rule and are to remember that they are to guard the young ladies from annoying visitors."[56]

Most important of all, the department stores hired women for their

---

[55]Campbell, *Prisoner*, p. 174: Siegel and Cooper Company of New York, *Rules and Regulations for the Government of the Employees* (New York, c. 1900), pp. 4–7.

[56]Adams, "Department Store," pp. 14–15. Adams also notes that the position of floorwalker invariably went to a man. Generally the floorwalker had been a clerk himself, but in a wholesale house or other business. "Managers of departments are not generally promoted from the ranks or educated to these positions, but are drawn by offers of larger salaries or better opportunities from other establishments where they have attracted attention through their success" (p. 9). See also Siegel and Cooper Company, *Rules and Regulations*, pp. 36–37.

manners, or, more precisely, for their suitability in dealing with middle-class women customers. The owners did not hire lower-class males to do the job, on the assumption that the ladies simply would not buy household goods and clothing from rough-and-ready immigrant men. Indeed, the owners did not want to hire just any type of female worker. "A girl who obtains employment at even the lowest work in any department store I know of," one salesgirl reported, "must be neat, bright, smart, in good health and have some education." Or, as another journalist noted: "For every woman who means to enter the retail trade, manners should be considered by her and her employer as necessary as neat dress or stools to sit on, or ability to add and subtract, or English speech. They should be learned and cultivated, like typewriting and stenography, as among the qualifications for a particular kind of business."[57]

Given the attractions the job had for women, the managers could be particular about whom they hired. And given the styles of their customers, they kept the social habits of their employees very much in mind. Just as middle-class women preferred to employ servants of English stock or second- and third-generation Irish, so did the department stores. During these decades, almost every Macy's employee was English or second- or third-generation immigrant. Not until 1900 did German or Eastern European girls begin to appear in the sales ranks. As late as 1909, native-born girls made up the majority of employees in Baltimore's retail stores. "Two stores employ only American girls," one researcher noted. "This preponderance is due to the fact that many customers prefer to be served by Americans, and in part to the fact that native-born girls of Anglo-Saxon stock prefer, when possible, to choose an occupation socially superior to factory work."[58] The department stores also preferred to hire only young women who lived at home, reducing the possibility of a scandal, and—in terms of the girls' appearance—getting more for their money. "Two-thirds of the girls here are public school girls and live at home," one manager boasted to Helen Campbell. "You see that makes things pretty easy, for the family pool their earnings and they dress well and live well."[59]

In the department store, as in the office, the women's jobs were the dead-end jobs. Girls did not rise from clerical positions to become floor-walkers; they did not earn promotions to become buyers or assistants to the managers. They could move from cash girl to cashier, but never beyond that. Had the position held out more promise, it might well have become the preserve of middle-class men. So once again, opportunity for women in the post-Civil War decades came in a very particular way: through novel job openings that were preferable to factory work but that led nowhere.

For all the availability of novel types of employment, teaching remained women's primary role in the work force. Large numbers of women had entered the profession in the pre-Civil War decades, and the dynamic that first made teaching a woman's job continued to operate through the post-

[57]Anonymous, "A Salesgirl's Story," p. 1818; Anonymous, "Some Manners," *Nation*, 63 (1896), p. 470.
[58]Hower, *Macy's*, pp. 199, 383; Elizabeth Beardsley Butler, *Saleswomen in the Mercantile Stores of Baltimore* (New York, 1913), pp. 143–144.
[59]Campbell, *Prisoners*, p. 174.

Civil War period. In schools, as in offices and factories, women did what men would not or could not do.

No sooner were public schools founded in the 1820s than a seemingly endless number of complaints began to circulate about the unsatisfactory nature of the teaching staffs. School reformers had assumed that educated, sober, and even refined middle-class men would make a career of teaching the young. Instead, the male teachers either were poorly educated or were using the post as a steppingstone to another career; many would-be lawyers, for example, supported themselves by classroom teaching. In 1837, George Emerson, one of Massachusetts' most distinguished educators, drew a discouraging portrait of the average teacher for the state legislature. Public school teachers, he contended, were either "young men in the course of their studies, teaching from necessity, and often with a strong dislike for the pursuit," or they were "mechanics and others wanting present employment," or "persons who, having failed in other callings, take to teaching as a last resort with no qualifications for it, and no desire of continuing in it longer than they are obliged by absolute necessity." Emerson believed that local boards were "baffled by the want of good teachers; that they have been sought for in vain; the highest salaries have been offered, to no purpose; that they *are not to be found* in sufficient numbers to supply the demand." As a remedy, he proposed a system of state normal schools. Emerson's ideal teacher was "to know *how* to teach," to "have a thorough knowledge of whatever he undertakes to teach," and to have such an "understanding of *the ordering and discipline* of a school, as to be able at once to introduce system, and to keep it constantly in force."[60] He insisted that the state normal school would inculcate just such traits in its students. Graduates would be able to fulfill the seemingly masculine task of ordering and disciplining a classroom.

But it was women, and not men, who flocked to the normal schools. The men found better opportunities elsewhere. "When we consider the claims of the learned professions," explained Catharine Beecher, "the excitement and profits of commerce, manufactures, agriculture, and the arts; when we consider the aversion of most men to the sedentary, confining, and toilsome duties of teaching and governing young children; when we consider the scanty pittance that is allowed to the majority of teachers; and that few men will enter a business that will not support a family, when there are multitudes of other employments that will afford competence, and lead to wealth; it is chimerical to hope that the supply of such immense deficiencies in our national education is to come from that sex." Yet, the very reasons that made teaching so unattractive to men made it more suitable and appealing for women. "It is woman," Beecher continued, "fitted by disposition, and habits, and circumstances for such duties, who, to a very wide extent, must aid in educating the childhood and youth of this nation; and therefore it is, that females must be trained and educated for this employment." In following a teaching career, a woman helped herself as well as improved society. "Most happily," concluded Beecher,

[60]"Memorial of the American Institute of Instruction to the Legislature of Massachusetts in Normal School," January 1837, in Henry Barnard, *Normal Schools and Other Institutions* (Hartford, Conn., 1851), pp. 85–87.

"the education necessary to fit a woman to be a teacher, is exactly the one that best fits her for that domestic relation she is primarily designed to fill."[61]

The fit between women and teaching seemed no less ideal to local school boards. Women not only were willing to work for low salaries but, in the absence of competing opportunities, composed a very pliable staff. Thus, one Ohio school superintendent confidently told his fellow educators: "As the business of teaching is made more respectable, more females engage in it, and the wages are reduced. Females do not . . . expect to accumulate much property by this occupation; if it affords them a respectable support and a situation where they can be useful, it is as much as they demand. I, therefore, most earnestly commend this subject to the attention of those counties which are in the habit of paying men for instructing little children, when females would do it for less than half the sum, and generally much better than men can."[62]

These judgments on the suitability and convenience of employing women teachers persisted through the post-Civil War decades. As school systems expanded, so did the percentage of women on their staffs. In 1870, women constituted 60 percent of the nation's teachers; by 1900 they made up 70 percent, and by 1910, 80 percent.[63] That boards continued to find them so satisfactory is not surprising—middle-class men still looked for opportunities elsewhere and the newly arrived immigrant men were obviously unsuitable for the positions. But why did women continue to seek out teaching? Indeed, why did college graduates as well as normal school graduates persist in moving into the classroom?

In the first instance, college girls learned that teaching was a significant task and one that they could perform exceptionally well, From the moment that Vassar opened, its president lectured on the graduates' duty to improve the quality of public schools. "I do not hesitate to avow the belief," John Raymond declared, "that the education of the nation is today emasculate and weak, compared with what it might easily be made by simply raising the qualifications of its female instructors. . . . Elevating the character of women instructors alone might raise the standard of the national intelligence a hundred percent in a generation,"[64] and Vassar was going to help do just that. In fact, as the colleges grew confident of their ability to train vigorous young women, they became even more certain that their students belonged in teaching. "The college woman is also proving herself the most efficient of all women," contended M. Carey Thomas in 1901. "She makes so successful a teacher that she is swiftly driving untrained women teachers out of the private and public secondary schools and will soon begin to drive them from the elementary schools; she is also driving men from the schools."

[61]Catharine E. Beecher, *An Essay on the Education of Female Teachers* (New York, 1835), p. 18.

[62]Thomas Woody, *History of Women's Education in the United States*, I (New York, 1929), p. 491.

[63]Willard S. Elsbree, *The American Teacher* (New York, 1939), p. 554.

[64]Raymond, "Demands of the Age," pp. 47–48.

Women heeded the message. Perhaps they did so in a spirit of resignation, recognizing that business and the professions were closed to them.
Or perhaps, in keeping with the precepts of virtuous womanhood, they
were most comfortable in the role of moral counselor and teacher to the
young. "There are more reasons," insisted Marion Harland, "for the press
of women who are obliged to earn a livelihood, into the profession of
teaching than the one usually assigned and accepted, namely, that it is an
eminently respectable occupation and involves little physical drudgery. It
is the nature of being of the mother-sex to gather together into her care
and brood over and instruct creatures younger and feebler than herself."[65]
Or perhaps women calculated that teaching wages were the best available
for the least onerous work. The salaries were higher than factory girls
earned and identical with those of stenographers. In all events, women
crowded into teaching jobs.

Despite their numerical dominance in the teaching ranks and seemingly natural suitability for the jobs, female teachers suffered the same
kind of discrimination in school systems that their counterparts did in
offices and department stores. School boards paid men more than women
for carrying out the same assignments ($35 a week compared to $14). As
the Massachusetts Board of Education reported in 1893, women's wages,
when contrasted with men's, "are so low as to make it humiliating to report
the two in connection. Moreover, the advance in the wages of male teachers
in ten years has been at the rate of 36.2 percent, while that for female
teachers has been at the rate of 14.8 percent."[66] Even more important, the
men held practically all the influential and well-paying administrative
positions. (Probably the boards hired men as school teachers so as to be
able to promote them up the ranks to run the system.) If men composed
only a small minority of classroom teachers, they made up a heavy majority
of the principals and superintendents. "There is some slight relief from
. . . the steady falling off of male teachers," declared the Massachusetts
Board of Education, "in the fact that it is more than compensated for in
the number of male teachers transferred to the ranks of school superintendents." Put another way, women with similar credentials remained
elementary and secondary school teachers. "While 67 percent of all the
teachers in the country are women," on investigator reported to the Association for the Advancement of Women in 1888, "less than 4 percent of
those who direct what shall be taught and teaching what shall be done are
women." Women were permitted to teach children in every state of the
union, but in only 13 states were they even eligible to hold all school offices.
In 1900, only two women held the position of state superintendent of
schools and only twelve were superintendents of city school systems.[67]

School boards explained the situation in terms of rapid turnover and
immaturity, as though female teachers were typically young girls of sixteen

[65]M. Carey Thomas, "The College Woman of the Present and Future," *McClure's Syndicate*
(1901), p. 3; Harland, *Eve's Daughters*, p. 271.

[66]Massachusetts Board of Education, *57th Annual Report*, 1893, p. 70.

[67]Ibid., p. 70; May Sewall, "Women as Educators," in Association for the Advancement of
Women, *Proceedings* (1888), pp. 126–127; U.S. Commissioner of Education, *Report*, 1900–
1901, II, pp. 2406–2407.

or seventeen with two years of high school education. But such a claim was inaccurate. The average city school teacher was in her early twenties when first appointed and had completed at least a normal school course. She also tended to hold her teaching position for almost a decade. The tenure of the teaching staff in Columbus, Ohio was one case in point. As the Columbus school system grew, so did the length of service of its female teachers. In 1875, Columbus employed 97 teachers, 91 of whom were women who remained on the job for an average of 5.3 years. In 1891, the city employed 256 teachers, 251 of whom were women who typically served 9 years. In 1875, only 5 percent of the women had been employed for over 19 years; by 1888, the figure climbed to 34 percent. So, too, in neighboring Indianapolis the average length of tenure for women teachers in 1888 was 8 years; 29 percent of the female staff had taught more than a decade. Indeed, the keen competition for the positions made such an outcome logical and predictable.

Cities or states that had created normal schools in the 1850s and 1860s to ensure a ready supply of teachers found themselves in the 1880s and 1890s with a surplus of highly qualified applicants. Waiting lists for jobs were commonplace, and the larger the city, the longer the list. In 1898, Columbus, Ohio could no longer place the graduates of its normal school into the system. "If the order of the present reserve list is followed," declared the principal of the normal school, "it will be some time before many of the class are assigned to duty in our schools."[68] Thus, despite their degrees, women could not translate their qualifications into better positions. A diploma became an entry card into a profession already overcrowded with women—and one that would not allow for mobility.

In the world of work as elsewhere, new opportunities were counterbalanced, if not quite canceled out, by restrictions and qualifications. The post-Civil War decades created many types of novel settings for women, and yet within each of them women had to know their very special place.

---

[68]See, for example, Massachusetts Board of Education, *Fortieth Annual Report* 1875–1876, p. 160; Chicago, Ill. Board of Education *Report for 1873*, pp. 26–27; Sewall, "Women as Educators," pp. 124–125; Columbus Ohio Board of Education, *Annual Reports* 1875, 1886–1887, and 1891.

Tea time on the porch of a New England home, c. 1900

The Social Defenses of the Rich

E. DIGBY BALTZELL

The myth of equality has had a powerful influence in shaping American attitudes. Beginning in the colonial period and continuing until today, foreign visitors
as well as native writers have commented on what they have perceived as the
high degree of social mobility available to Americans as a result of the basic
equality of opportunity that is their birthright. Of course, many of these same
writers have also pointed out that certain elements of the population were left
out of the equality scheme by definition, for example, women and nonwhites. But
the myth persisted, even among those denied access to its rewards.

At least one group of Americans, however, knew better—the wealthy traditional elite (which did assimilate newcomers, but slowly). From the colonial
period to the Civil War, many wealthy citizens of WASP (white Anglo-Saxon
Protestant) ancestry believed they had a special place in society. Their wealth
and traditions insulated them from the entrepreneurial clamor of the Jacksonian
period, and they maintained a castelike existence in the cities of the eastern
seaboard.

After the Civil War, however, traditions and family connections were no
longer sufficient to maintain the exclusivity of the caste structure. The route to
riches had shifted, and holders of the new wealth aspired to the life-style previously available primarily to the WASP elite. The homogeneous quality of upper-
class existence began to break down under the onslaught of rapid economic
growth and the extraordinary financial success of an increasing number of non-
WASP families.

Initially, the traditional elite had supported open immigration from eastern
and southern European countries in order to insure an overabundance of common laborers that would tend to keep wages down, but as participants in this
new immigration began to rise in economic status, and in some cases to become
actually wealthy, the elite began to reconsider their position. Although they were

unable to restrict immigration until well into the twentieth century, they were able to take steps soon after the Civil War to insulate themselves from the society of wealthy non-WASPs.

E. Digby Baltzell, a sociologist at the University of Pennsylvania, has taken as his field of study the traditional elite of the Eastern seaboard. After publishing a book on the upper-class families of Philadelphia, he enlarged his focus to consider the exclusionary tactics of the WASP elite through the last hundred years. In the chapter reprinted below, he focuses on the anti-Semitic practices of the traditional families and enumerates the various devices by which the traditional upper class insulated itself socially from non-WASP wealth. Several features of the social life of the upper class taken so much for granted today have their origin in this period. Exclusive prep schools, college societies, restricted suburbs, summer resorts, and city clubs were founded in order to enable the traditional elite to protect what they saw as their caste privileges. Consequently, the excluded wealthy families formed their own parallel network of social organizations that were designed to reflect the class, if not the caste, prerogatives of upper-class existence.

We are still in power, after a fashion. Our sway over what we call society is undisputed. We keep the Jew far away, and the anti-Jew feeling is quite rabid.

HENRY ADAMS

The Civil War was fought, by a nation rapidly becoming centralized economically, in order to preserve the political Union. Although the Union was preserved and slavery abolished, the postwar Republic was faced with the enormously complex and morally cancerous problem of caste, as far as the formally free Negroes were concerned. The solution to this problem has now become the central one of our own age. But the more immediate effect of the Civil War was that, in the North at least, the nation realized the fabulous potential of industrial power. The Pennsylvania Railroad, for instance, began to cut back operations at the beginning of the war, only to realize a tremendous boom during the remainder of the conflict (total revenue in 1860: $5,933 million; in 1865: $19,533 million). But the profits of the war were nothing compared to those of the fabulous postwar years. Between 1870 and 1900, the national wealth quadrupled (rising from $30,400 million to $126,700 million and doubled again by 1914—reaching $254,200 million).[1]

During this same period, wealth became increasingly centralized in the hands of a few. In 1891, *Forum* magazine published an article, "The

[1]Here I have followed Richard Hofstadter, *The Age of Reform*. New York: Vintage Books, 1960, Chap. IV.

Coming Billionaire," which estimated that there were 120 men in the nation worth over $10 million. The next year, the *New York Times* published a list of 4,047 millionaires, and the Census Bureau estimated that 9 per cent of the nation's families owned 71 per cent of the wealth. By 1910 there were more millionaires in the United States Senate alone than there were in the whole nation before the Civil War. This new inequality was dramatized by the fact that, in 1900, according to Frederick Lewis Allen, the former immigrant lad Andrew Carnegie had an *income* of between $15 and $30 million (the income tax had been declared unconstitutional in a test case in 1895), while the average unskilled worker in the North received less than $460 a year in wages—in the South the figure was less than $300. It is no wonder that the production of pig iron rather than poetry, and the quest for status rather than salvation, now took hold of the minds of even the most patrician descendants of Puritan divines.

This inequality of wealth was accompanied by an increasing centralization of business power, as the nation changed, in the half century after Appomattox, from a rural-communal to an urban-corporate society. President Eliot of Harvard, in a speech before the fraternity of Phi Beta Kappa in 1888, noted this new corporate dominance when he pointed out that, while the Pennsylvania Railroad had gross receipts of $115 million and employed over 100,000 men in that year, the Commonwealth of Massachusetts had gross receipts of only $7 million and employed no more than 6,000 persons.[2] And this corporate economy was further centralized financially in Wall Street. The capital required to launch the United States Steel Corporation, for example, would at that time have covered the costs of all the functions of the federal government for almost two years. J. P. Morgan and his associates, who put this great corporate empire together in 1901, held some three hundred directorships in over one hundred corporations with resources estimated at over $22 billion. This industrial age, in which the railroads spanned the continent and Wall Street interests controlled mines in the Rockies, timber in the Northwest, and coal in Pennsylvania and West Virginia, brought about a national economy and the emergence of a national mind.

And the prosperity of this new urban-corporate world was largely built upon the blood and sweat of the men, and the tears of their women, who came to this country in such large numbers from the peasant villages of Southern and Eastern Europe. Whereas most of the older immigrants from Northern and Western Europe had come to a rural America where they were able to assimilate more easily, the majority of these newer arrivals huddled together in the urban slums and ghettos which were characteristic of the lower levels of the commercial economy which America had now become.

Except for the captains of industry, whose money-centered minds continued to welcome and encourage immigration because they believed it kept wages down and retarded unionization, most old-stock Americans were frankly appalled at the growing evils of industrialization, immigration

[2]Charles William Eliot, *American Contributions to Civilization*. New York: The Century Company, 1897, pp. 85–86.

and urbanization. As we have seen, the closing decades of the nineteenth century were marked by labor unrest and violence; many men, like Henry Adams, developed a violent nativism and anti-Semitism; others, following the lead of Jane Addams, discovered the slums and went to work to alleviate the evils of prostitution, disease, crime, political bossism and grinding poverty; both Midwestern Populism and the Eastern, patrician led Progressive movement were part of the general protest and were, in turn, infused with varying degrees of nativism; and even organized labor, many of whose members were of recent immigrant origin, was by no means devoid of nativist sentiment.

In so many ways, nativism was part of a more generalized anti-urban and anti-capitalist mood. Unfortunately, anti-Semitism is often allied with an antipathy toward the city and the money-power. Thus the first mass manifestations of anti-Semitism in America came out of the Midwest among the Populist leaders and their followers. In the campaign of 1896, for example, William Jennings Bryan was accused of anti-Semitism and had to explain to the Jewish Democrats of Chicago that in denouncing the policies of Wall Street and the Rothschilds, he and his silver friends were "not attacking a race but greed and avarice which know no race or religion."[3] And the danger that the Populist, isolationist and anti-Wall Street sentiment in the Middle West might at any time revert to anti-Semitism continued. As we shall see in a later chapter, Henry Ford, a multimillionaire with the traditional Populist mistrust of the money-power, was notoriously anti-Semitic for a time in the early 1920's.

Nativism was also a part of a status revolution at the elite level of leadership on the Eastern Seaboard. "The newly rich, the grandiosely or corruptly rich, the masters of the great corporations," wrote Richard Hofstadter, "were bypassing the men of the Mugwump type—the old gentry, the merchants of long standing, the small manufacturers, the established professional men, the civic leaders of an earlier era. In scores of cities and hundreds of towns, particularly in the East but also in the nation at large, the old-family, college-educated class that had deep ancestral roots in local communities and often owned family businesses, that had traditions of political leadership, belonged to the patriotic societies and the best clubs, staffed the government boards of philanthropic and cultural institutions, and led the movements for civic betterment, were being overshadowed and edged aside in making basic political and economic decisions. . . . They were less important and they knew it."[4]

Many members of this class, of old-stock prestige and waning power, eventually allied themselves with the Progressive movement. Many also, like Henry Adams, withdrew almost entirely from the world of power. The "decent people," as Edith Wharton once put it, increasingly "fell back on sport and culture." And this sport and culture was now to be reinforced by a series of fashionable and patrician protective associations which, in turn, systematically and subtly institutionalized the exclusion of Jews.

The turning point came in the 1880's, when a number of symbolic events forecast the nature of the American upper class in the twentieth

[3]Richard Hofstadter, *op. cit.*, p. 80.
[4]*Ibid.*, p. 137.

century. Thus, when President Eliot of Harvard built his summer cottage at Northeast Harbor, Maine, in 1881, the exclusive summer resort trend was well under way; the founding of *The* Country Club at Brookline, Massachusetts, in 1882, marked the beginning of the country-club trend; the founding of the Sons of the Revolution, in 1883, symbolized the birth of the genealogical fad and the patrician scramble for old-stock roots; Endicott Peabody's founding of Groton School, in 1884, in order to rear young gentlemen in the tradition of British public schools (and incidentally to protect them from the increasing heterogeneity of the public school system) was an important symbol of both upper-class exclusiveness and patrician Anglophilia; and finally, the Social Register, a convenient index of this new associational aristocracy, was first issued toward the end of this transitional decade in 1887 (the publisher also handled much of the literature of the American Protective Association, which was active in the nativist movement at that time).

The Right Reverend Phillips Brooks—the favorite clergyman among Philadelphia's Victorian gentry, who was called to Boston's Trinity Church in 1869, the year Grant entered the White House and Eliot accepted the presidency at Harvard—was one of the most sensitive barometers of the brahmin mind. Thus, although he himself had graduated from the Boston Latin School along with other patricians and plebeian gentlemen of his generation, he first suggested the idea of Groton to young Peabody in the eighties and joined the Sons of the Revolution in 1891, because, as he said at the time, "it is well to go in for the assertion that our dear land at least used to be American."[5]

ANCESTRAL ASSOCIATIONS AND THE QUEST FOR OLD-STOCK ROOTS

The idea of caste dies hard, even in a democratic land such as ours. Our first and most exclusive ancestral association, the Society of the Cincinnati, was formed in 1783, just before the Continental Army disbanded. Its membership was limited to Washington's officers and, in accord with the rural traditions of primogeniture, was to be passed on to the oldest sons in succeeding generations. The society's name reflects the ancient tradition of gentlemen-farmers, from Cincinnatus to Cromwell, Washington and Franklin Roosevelt, who have served their country in times of need. Just as the founding of the Society of Cincinnati reflected the rural values of the gentleman and his mistrust of grasping city ways, it was quite natural that the new wave of ancestral associations which came into being at the end of the nineteenth century was a reaction to the rise of the city with its accompanying heterogeneity and conflict. As Wallace Evan Davies, in *Patriotism on Parade*, put it:

> "The great Upheaval," the Haymarket Riot, the campaigns of Henry George, and the writings of Edward Bellamy crowded the last half of the eighties. The nineties produced such proofs of unrest as the Populist

[5]Barbara Miller Solomon, *Ancestors and Immigrants: A Changing New England*. Cambridge, Mass.: Harvard University Press, 1956, p. 87.

Revolt, the Homestead Strike with the attempted assassination of Henry Clay Frick, the Panic of 1893, the Pullman Strike, Coxey's Army, and finally, the Bryan campaign of 1896. Throughout all this the conservative and propertied classes watched apprehensively the black cloud of anarchism, a menace as productive of alarm and hysteria as bolshevism and communism in later generations.[6]

These old-stock patriots, desperately seeking hereditary and historical roots in a rapidly changing world, flocked to the standards of such newly founded societies as the Sons of the Revolution (1883), the Colonial Dames (1890), the Daughters of the American Revolution (1890), Daughters of the Cincinnati (1894), the Society of Mayflower Descendants (1894), the Aryan Order of St. George or the Holy Roman Empire in the Colonies of America (1892), and the Baronial Order of Runnymede (1897). It is no wonder that genealogist, both amateur and professional, rapidly came into vogue. Several urban newspapers established genealogical departments; the Lenox Library in New York purchased one of its largest genealogical collections, in 1896, setting aside a room "for the convenience of the large number of researchers after family history"; the *Library Journal* carried articles on how to help the public in ancestor hunting; and, as of 1900, the *Patriotic Review* listed seventy patriotic, hereditary and historical associations, exactly *half* of which had been founded during the preceding decade alone.

This whole movement was, of course, intimately bound up with anti-immigrant and anti-Semitic sentiments. Thus a leader of the D.A.R. saw a real danger in "our being absorbed by the different nationalities among us," and a president-general of the Sons of the American Revolution reported that: "Not until the state of civilization reached the point where we had a great many foreigners in our land . . . were our patriotic societies successful."[7] The Daughters of the American Revolution was indeed extremely successful. Founded in 1890, it had 397 chapters in 38 states by 1897. That the anti-immigrant reaction was most prevalent in the urban East, however, was attested to by the fact that the Daughters made slow headway in the West and South and had a vast majority of its chapters in New York and Massachusetts.

But, as Franklin Roosevelt once said, "we are all descendants of immigrants." While old-stock Americans were forming rather exclusive associations based on their descent from Colonial immigrants, newer Americans were also attempting to establish their own historical roots. Such organizations at the Scotch-Irish Society (1889), the Pennsylvania-German Society (1891), the American Jewish Historical Society (1894), and the American Irish Historical Society (1898) were concerned to establish ethnic recognition through ancestral achievement. "The Americanism of all Irishmen and Jews," writes Edward N. Saveth, "was enhanced because of the handful of Irishmen and Jews who may have stood by Washington in a moment of crisis."[8]

---

[6]Wallace E. Davies, *Patriotism on Parade: The Story of Veteran's and Hereditary Organizations in America, 1783–1900.* Cambridge, Mass.: Harvard University Press, 1956.
[7]*Ibid.*, p. 48.
[8]Edward N. Saveth, *American Historians and European Immigrants, 1875–1925.* New York: Columbia University Press, 1948, p. 194.

The genealogically minded patrician has remained a part of the American scene down through the years. The front page of any contemporary copy of the Social Register, for instance, lists a series of clubs, universities and ancestral associations, with proper abbreviations attached, in order that each family may be identified by its members' affiliations. A recent Philadelphia Social Register listed an even dozen such societies, and a venerable old gentleman of great prestige (if little power) was listed in a later page as follows:

> Rittenhouse, Wm. Penn—Ul.Ph.Myf.Cc.Wt.Rv.Ll.Fw.P'83 . . . Union
> League

It was indeed plain to see (after a bit of research on page 1) that this old gentleman was nicely placed as far as his ancestral, college and club affiliations were concerned. He belonged to the Union League (Ul) and Philadelphia clubs (Ph), had graduated in 1883 from Princeton University (P'83), and was apparently devoting himself to some sort of patriotic ancestor worship in his declining years, as suggested by his ancestral association memberships: Mayflower Descendants (Myf); Society of Cincinnati (Cc); Society of the War of 1812 (Wt); Sons of the Revolution (Rv); Military Order of the Loyal Legion (Ll); and the Military Order of Foreign Wars (Fw). And, as the final entry shows, he was living at the Union League.

THE SUMMER RESORT AND THE QUEST FOR HOMOGENEITY

Americans have always longed for grass roots. In a society of cement, the resort movement in America paralleled the genealogical escape to the past. The physiological and physical ugliness of the city streets gradually drove those who could afford it back to nature and the wide-open spaces. Men like Owen Wister, Theodore Roosevelt and Madison Grant went out to the West, and the more timid, or socially minded, souls sought refuge at some exclusive summer resort. In spite of the efforts of men like Frederick Law Olmstead and Madison Grant to bring rural beauty into the heart of the city (Olmstead built some fifteen city parks from coast to coast, Central Park in New York City being the most well known), first the artists and writers, then the gentry, and finally the millionaires were seeking the beauty of nature and the simple life among the "natives" of coastal or mountain communities along the Eastern Seaboard. President Eliot and his sons spent the summers during the seventies camping in tents before building the first summer cottage in Northeast Harbor, Maine, in 1881.[9] Charles Francis Adams, Jr., saw his native Quincy succumb to industrialism and the Irish (the Knights of Labor gained control of the Adams "race-place" in 1887), gave up his job with the Union Pacific in 1890, and finally escaped to the simple life at Lincoln, Massachusetts, in 1893.

The summer resort increased in popularity after the Civil War and went through its period of most rapid growth between 1880 and the First War. Long Branch, New Jersey, summer capital of presidents from Grant

---

[9]Henry James, *Charles W. Eliot*. Vol. I. Boston: Houghton Mifflin Company, 1940, p. 344.

to Arthur, was filled with proper Philadelphians and New Yorkers. Further south, Cape May—where Jay Cooke, financier of the Civil War, spent every summer—was the most fashionable Philadelphia summer resort until well into the twentieth century. Boston's best retreated to the simple life at Nahant. Others went to the Berkshires, where large "cottages," large families and large incomes supported the simple life for many years (Lenox boasted thirty-five of these cottages as of 1880, and seventy-five by 1900).[10] Between 1890 and the First War, Bar Harbor became one of America's most stylish resorts. By 1894, the year Joseph Pulitzer built the resort's first hundred-thousand-dollar "cottage," Morgan and Standard Oil partners were the leaders of the community (when a Vanderbilt bought a cottage in 1922, it was the first to change hands in fifteen years; within the next three years, forty-seven such cottages changed hands). Less fashionable, but no less genteel, Northeast Harbor grew at the same time. Anticipating modern sociology, President Eliot made a study of the community in 1890. Among other things, he found that, as of 1881, nonresident summer people owned less than one-fifth of the local real property; only eight years later, in 1889, they owned over half (and total property values had almost doubled).[11]

Just as the white man, symbolized by the British gentleman, was roaming round the world in search of raw materials for his factories at Manchester, Liverpool or Leeds, so America's urban gentry and capitalists, at the turn of the century, were imperialists seeking solace for their souls among the "natives" of Lenox, Bar Harbor or Kennebunkport. Here they were able to forget the ugliness of the urban melting pot as they dwelt among solid Yankees (Ethan Frome), many of whom possessed more homogeneous, Colonial-stock roots than themselves. And these rustic "types" kept up their boats, taught their children the ways of the sea, caught their lobsters, served them in the stores along the village streets, and became temporary servants and gardeners on their rustic estates. But although most old-time resorters were patronizingly proficient with the "Down East" accent, and appreciated the fact that the "natives" were their "own kind" racially, sometimes the idyllic harmony was somewhat superficial, at least as far as the more sensitive "natives" were concerned. Hence the following anecdote circulating among the "natives" at Bar Harbor: "They emptied the pool the other day," reported one typical "type" to another. "Why?" asked his friend. "Oh, one of the natives fell in."

But the simple life was, nevertheless, often touching and always relaxing. All one's kind were there together and the older virtues of communal life were abroad; Easter-Christmas-Wedding Christians usually went to church every Sunday; millionaires' wives did their own shopping in the village, and walking, boating and picnicking brought a renewed appreciation of nature. And perhaps most important of all, one knew who one's daughter was seeing, at least during the summer months when convenient alliances for life were often consummated.

When J. P. Morgan observed that "you can do business with anyone, but only sail with a gentleman," he was reflecting the fact that a secure

[10]Cleveland Amory, *Last Resorts*. New York: Harper & Brothers, 1952, p. 21.
[11]Henry James, *op. cit.*, p. 111.

sense of homogeneity is the essence of resort life. It is no wonder that anti-Semitism, of the gentlemanly, exclusionary sort, probably reached its most panicky heights there. Thus one of the first examples of upper-class anti-Semitism in America occurred, in the 1870's, when a prominent New York banker, Joseph Seligman, was rudely excluded from the Grand Union Hotel in Saratoga Springs. This came as a shock to the American people and was given wide publicity because it was something new at that time. Henry Ward Beecher, a personal friend of the Seligmans, reacted with a sermon from his famous pulpit at Plymouth Church: "What have the Jews," he said, "of which they need be ashamed, in a Christian Republic where all men are declared to be free and equal? . . . Is it that they are excessively industrious? Let the Yankee cast the first stone. Is it that they are inordinately keen on bargaining? Have they ever stolen ten millions of dollars at a pinch from a city? Are our courts bailing out Jews, or compromising with Jews? Are there Jews lying in our jails, and waiting for mercy. . . . You cannot find one criminal Jew in the whole catalogue. . . ."[12]

The Seligman incident was followed by a battle at Saratoga Springs. Immediately afterwards, several new hotels were built there by Jews, and by the end of the century half the population was Jewish; as a result, it is said that one non-Jewish establishment boldly advertised its policies with a sign: "No Jews and Dogs Admitted Here." At the same time, other prominent German Jews were running into embarrassing situations elsewhere. In the 1890's Nathan Straus, brother of a member of Theodore Roosevelt's Cabinet and a leading merchant and civic leader himself, was turned down at a leading hotel in Lakewood, New Jersey, a most fashionable winter resort at that time. He promptly built a hotel next door, twice as big and for Jews only. And the resort rapidly became Jewish, as kosher establishments multiplied on all sides.

Even the well-integrated and cultivated members of Philadelphia's German-Jewish community eventually had to bow to the trend. As late as the eighties and nineties, for instance, leading Jewish families were listed in the Philadelphia Blue Book as summering at fashionable Cape May, along with the city's best gentile families. But this did not continue, and many prominent Philadelphia Jews became founding families at Long Branch, Asbury Park, Spring Lake or Atlantic City, where the first resort synagogues were established during the nineties: Long Branch (1890), Atlantic City (1893), and Asbury Park (1896).[13]

As the East European Jews rapidly rose to middle-class status, resort-hotel exclusiveness produced a running battle along the Jersey coast and up in the Catskills. One resort after another changed from an all-gentile to an all-Jewish community. Atlantic City, for example, first became a fashionable gentile resort in the nineties. By the end of the First War, however, it had become a predominantly Jewish resort, at least in the summer months (the first modern, fireproof hotel was built there in 1902; there were a thousand such hotels by 1930). According to Edmund Wilson, it was while visiting Atlantic City in the winter of 1919 that John Jay Chap-

[12]Quoted in Carey McWilliams, *A Mask for Privilege.* Boston: Little, Brown & Company, 1948, p. 6.
[13]E. Digby Baltzell, *Philadelphia Gentlemen.* Glencoe, Ill.: The Free Press, 1958, p. 285.

man first became anti-Semitic. "They are uncritical," he wrote to a friend after watching the boardwalk crowd of vacationing Jews. "Life is a simple matter for them: a bank account and a larder. . . . They strike me as an inferior race. . . . These people don't know anything. They have no religion, no customs except eating and drinking."[14]

Just before the First World War, resort establishments began to advertise their discriminatory policies in the newspapers. The situation became so embarrassing that New York State passed a law, in 1913, forbidding places of public accommodation to advertise their unwillingness to admit persons because of race, creed or color.

Although the high tide of formal resort society has declined in recent years, the rigid exclusion of Jews has largely continued. As Cleveland Amory has put it:

> Certain aspects of the narrowness of the old-line resort society have continued, not the least of which is the question of anti-Semitism. Although certain Jewish families, notably the Pulitzers, the Belmonts and the Goulds have played their part in resort Society—and Otto Kahn, Henry Seligman, Jules Bache and Frederick Lewison have cut sizeable figures—the general record of resort intolerance is an extraordinary one; it reached perhaps its lowest point when Palm Beach's Bath and Tennis Club sent out a letter asking members not to bring into the club guests of Jewish extraction. Among those who received this letter was Bernard Baruch, then a member of the club and a man whose father, Dr. Simon Baruch, pioneered the Saratoga Spa. Several of Baruch's friends advised him to make an issue of the affair; instead, he quietly resigned. "No one," he says today, "has had this thing practiced against him more than I have. But I don't let it bother me. I always remember what Bob Fitzsimmons said to me—he wanted to make me a champion, you know—'You've got to learn to take it before you can give it out.' "[15]

THE SUBURBAN TREND, THE COUNTRY CLUB AND THE COUNTRY DAY SCHOOL

The resort and the suburb are both a product of the same desire for homogeneity and a nostalgic yearning for the simplicities of small-town life. Just as, today, white families of diverse, ethnic origins and newly won middle-class status are busily escaping from the increasingly Negro composition of our cities, so the Protestant upper class first began to flee the ugliness of the urban melting pot at the turn of the century. In Philadelphia, for instance, the majority of the Victorian gentry lived in the city, around fashionable Rittenhouse Square, as of 1890; by 1914, the majority had moved out to the suburbs along the Main Line or in Chestnut Hill. And this same pattern was followed in other cities.

[14]Edmund Wilson, *A Piece of My Mind.* New York: Doubleday Anchor Books, 1958, p. 97.
[15]Cleveland Amory, *op. cit., p. 48.*

In many ways Pierre Lorillard was the Victorian aristocrat's William Levitt. Just as Levittown is now the most famous example of a planned community symbolizing the post World War II suburban trend among the middle classes, so Tuxedo Park, New York, established on a site of some 600,000 acres inherited by Pierre Lorillard in 1886, was once the acme of upper-class suburban exclusiveness. According to Cleveland Amory, the Lorillards possessed a foolproof formula for business success which, in turn, was exactly reversed when they came to promoting upper-class exclusiveness. He lists their contrasting formulas as follows:

For Business Success:
1) Find out what the public wants, then produce the best of its kind.
2) Advertise the product so that everybody will know it is available.
3) Distribute it everywhere so that everybody can get it.
4) Keep making the product better so that more people will like it.

For Snob Success:
1) Find out who the leaders of Society are and produce the best place for them to live in.
2) Tell nobody else about it so that nobody else will know it's available.
3) Keep it a private club so that other people, even if they do hear about it, can't get in.
4) Keep the place exactly as it was in the beginning so that other people, even if they do hear about it and somehow do manage to get in, won't ever like it anyway.[16]

At Tuxedo Park, Lorillard produced almost a caricature of the Victorian millionaire's mania for exclusiveness. In less than a year, he surrounded seven thousand acres with an eight-foot fence, graded some thirty miles of road, built a complete sewage and water system, a gate house which looked like "a frontispiece of an English novel," a clubhouse staffed with imported English servants, and "twenty-two casement dormered English turreted cottages." On Memorial Day, 1886, special trains brought seven hundred highly selected guests from New York to witness the Park's opening.

Tuxedo was a complete triumph. The physical surroundings, the architecture and the social organization were perfectly in tune with the patrician mind of that day. In addition to the English cottages and the clubhouse, there were "two blocks of stores, a score of stables, four lawn tennis courts, a bowling alley, a swimming tank, a boathouse, an icehouse, a dam, a trout pond and a hatchery. . . . The members sported the club badge which, designed to be worn as a pin, was an oakleaf of solid gold; club governors had acorns attached to their oakleafs and later all Tuxedoites were to wear ties, hatbands, socks, etc., in the club colors of green and gold. . . . No one who was not a member of the club was allowed to buy property."

[16]*Ibid.*, p. 83.

Tuxedo Park was perhaps a somewhat exaggerated example of an ideal. It certainly would have suggested the conformity of a Chinese commune to many aristocrats seeking real privacy (in the eighties at Nahant, for example, Henry Cabot Lodge built a high fence between his place and his brother-in-law's next door). The upper-class suburban trend as a whole, nevertheless, was motivated by similar, if less rigid, desires for homogeneity. Unlike Tuxedo, however, the country club and the country day school, rather than the neighborhood *per se*, were the main fortresses of exclusiveness. Thus the beginning of a real suburban trend can conveniently be dated from the founding of *The* Country Club, at Brookline, Massachusetts, in 1882. In the next few decades similar clubs sprang up like mushrooms and became a vital part of the American upper-class way of life. Henry James, an expert on Society both here and abroad, found them "a deeply significant American symbol" at the turn of the century, and an English commentator on our mores wrote:

> There are also all over England clubs especially devoted to particular objects, golf clubs, yacht clubs, and so forth. In these the members are drawn together by their interest in a common pursuit, and are forced into some kind of acquaintanceship. But these are very different in spirit and intention from the American country club. It exists as a kind of center of the social life of the neighborhood. Sport is encouraged by these clubs for the sake of general sociability. In England sociability is a by-product of an interest in sport.[17]

This English commentator was, of course, implying that the real function of the American country club was not sport but social exclusion. And throughout the twentieth century the country club has remained, by and large and with a minority of exceptions, rigidly exclusive of Jews. In response to this discrimination, wealthy Jews have formed clubs of their own.[18] When many wealthy German Jews in Philadelphia first moved to the suburbs, as we have seen, the famous merchant Ellis Gimbel and a group of his friends founded one of the first Jewish country clubs in the nation, in 1906.[19] After the Second War, when many Jewish families began to move out on the city's Main Line, another elite club, largely composed of East European Jews, was opened.

If the country club is the root of family exclusiveness, the suburban day school provides an isolated environment for the younger generation. Thus a necessary part of the suburban trend was the founding of such well-known schools as the Chestnut Hill Academy (1895) and Haverford School (1884) in two of Philadelphia's most exclusive suburbs; the Gilman School (1897) in a Baltimore suburb; the Browne and Nichols School (1883) in Cambridge, Massachusetts; the Morristown School (1898), the Tuxedo Park School (1900), and the Hackley School (1899) in Tarrytown, to take care of New York suburbia.[20] While not as rigidly exclusive as the country

---

[17]George Birmingham, "The American at Home and in His Club," in *America in Perspective*, edited by Henry Steele Commager. New York: New American Library, 1947, p. 175.

[18]John Higham, *Social Discrimination Against Jews in America, 1830–1930.* Publication of the American Jewish Historical Society, Vol. XLVII, No. 1, September 1957, 13.

[19]Mr. Gimbel had only recently been "blackballed" by the Union League Club in the city.

[20]Porter Sargent, *Private Schools.* Boston: Porter Sargent, 1950.

club as far as Jews are concerned, these schools have been, of course, overwhelmingly proper and Protestant down through the years. Few Jews sought admission before the Second War, and since then some form of quota system has often been applied (this is especially true of the suburban schools run by the Quakers in Philadelphia, largely because of their extremely liberal policies of ethnic, racial and religious tolerance).

The greatest monuments are often erected after an era's period of greatest achievement. Versailles was completed after the great age of Louis XIV, the finest Gothic cathedrals after the height of the Catholic synthesis, and the neoclassic plantation mansions after the South had begun to decline. As we shall see below, upper-class suburban homogeneity and exclusiveness are rapidly vanishing characteristics of our postwar era. And when the upper class reigned supreme in its suburban glory (1890–1940), discriminatory practices were genteel and subtle when compared, for example, with the methods of modern automobile magnates in Detroit. The grosser, Grosse Pointe methods, however, will serve to illustrate (in the manner of our discussion of Tuxedo Park) the anti-Semitic and anti-ethnic values of suburban upper class, especially at the height of its attempted escape from the motley urban melting pot. As a somewhat tragic, and slightly ludicrous, monument to the mind of a fading era, the following paragraphs from *Time* magazine must be reproduced in full:

> Detroit's oldest and richest suburban area is the five-community section east of the city collectively called Grosse Pointe (pop. 50,000). Set back from the winding, tree-shaded streets are fine, solid colonial or brick mansions, occupied by some of Detroit's oldest (pre-automobile age) upper class, and by others who made the grade in business and professional life. Grosse Pointe is representative of dozens of wealthy residential areas in the U. S. where privacy, unhurried tranquility, and unsullied property values are respected. But last week, Grosse Pointe was in the throes of a rude, untranquil exposé of its methods of maintaining tranquility.
>
> The trouble burst with the public revelation, during a court squabble between one property owner and his neighbor, that the Grosse Point Property Owners Association (973 families) and local real estate brokers had set up a rigid system for screening families who want to buy or build homes in Grosse Pointe. Unlike similar communities, where neighborly solidarity is based on an unwritten gentleman's agreement, Grosse Pointe's screening system is based on a written questionnaire, filled out by a private investigator on behalf of Grosse Point's "owner vigilantes."
>
> The three-page questionnaire, scaled on the basis of "points" (highest score: 100), grades would-be home owners on such qualities as descent, way of life (American?), occupation (Typical of his own race?), swarthiness (Very? Medium? Slightly? Not at all?), accent (Pronounced? Medium? Slight? None?), name (Typically American?), repute, education, dress (Neat or Slovenly? Conservative or Flashy?), status of occupation (sufficient eminence may offset poor grades in other respects). Religion is not scored, but weighted in the balance by a three-man Grosse Pointe screening committee. All prospects are handicapped on an ethnic and racial basis: Jews, for example, must score a

minimum of 85 points, Italians 75, Greeks 65, Poles 55; Negroes and Orientals do not count.[21]

On reading this questionnaire, one could not fail to see that these Detroit tycoons were, after all, only reflecting their training in the methodology of modern social science. One might prefer the less-amoral world of William James, who once said: "In God's eyes the difference of social position, of intellect, of culture, of cleanliness, of dress, which different men exhibit . . . must be so small as to practically vanish." But in our age, when the social scientist is deified, several generations of young Americans have now been scientifically shown that men no longer seek status "in God's eyes." Instead they are asked to read all sorts of status-ranking studies, often backed by authoritative "tests of significance," which show how one is placed in society by one's cleanliness, dress, and drinking mores. How, one may ask, can one expect these suburbanites, most of whom have been educated in this modern tradition, not to use these methods for their own convenience.

THE NEW ENGLAND BOARDING SCHOOL

The growth in importance of the New England boarding school as an upper-class institution coincided with the American plutocracy's search for ancestral, suburban and resort-rural roots. At the time of Groton's founding in 1884, for example, these schools were rapidly becoming a vital factor in the creation of a national upper class, with more or less homogeneous values and behavior patterns. In an ever more centralized, complex and mobile age, the sons of the new and old rich, from Boston and New York to Chicago and San Francisco, were educated together in the secluded halls of Groton and St. Paul's, Exeter and Andover, and some seventy other, approximately similar, schools. While Exeter and Andover were ancient institutions, having been founded in the eighteenth century, and while St. Paul's had been in existence since before the Civil War, the boarding school movement went through its period of most rapid growth in the course of the half century after 1880. Exeter's enrollment increased from some 200 boys in 1880, to over 400 by 1905. The enrollment reached 600 for the first time in 1920, rose to 700 in the 1930's, and has remained below 800 ever since. St. Paul's went through its period of most rapid growth in the two decades before 1900 (the school graduated about 45 boys per year in the 1870's and rose to 100 per year by 1900, where it has remained ever since).

It is interesting in connection with the growth of a national upper class that the founding of many prominent schools coincided with the "trust-founding" and "trust-busting" era. Thus the following schools were founded within a decade of the formation of the United States Steel Corporation, in 1901:

---

[21]*Time*, April 25, 1960. Copyright 1960 Time Inc. All rights reserved. [Reprinted by permission from *Time*.]

The Taft School in Watertown, Connecticut, was founded by Horace Dutton Taft, a brother of President Taft, in 1890; the Hotchkiss School, Lakeville, Connecticut, was founded and endowed by Maria Hotchkiss, widow of the inventor of the famous machine-gun, in 1892; St. George's School, Newport, Rhode Island, which has a million-dollar Gothic chapel built by John Nicholas Brown, was founded in 1896; in the same year, Choate School, whose benefactors and friends include such prominent businessmen as Andrew Mellon and Owen D. Young, was founded by Judge William G. Choate, at Wallingford, Connecticut; while the elder Morgan was forming his steel company in New York and Pittsburgh in 1901, seven Proper Bostonians, including Francis Lowell, W. Cameron Forbes; and Henry Lee Higginson, were founding Middlesex School, near Concord, Massachusetts; Deerfield, which had been a local academy since 1797, was reorganized as a modern boarding school by its great headmaster, Frank L. Boydon, in 1902; and finally, Father Sill of the Order of the Holy Cross, founded Kent School in 1906.[22]

While the vast majority of the students at these schools were old-stock Protestants throughout the first part of the twentieth century at least, it would be inaccurate to suppose that the schools' admission policies rigidly excluded Catholics or even Jews. Few Catholics and fewer Jews applied (Henry Morgenthau attended Exeter. As he never referred to the fact, even in his *Who's Who* biography, he probably had a pretty lonely time there). As a matter of historical fact, these schools were largely preoccupied, during the first three decades of this century, with assimilating the sons of America's newly rich Protestant tycoons, many of whom were somewhat spoiled in the style of the late William Randolph Hearst, who had been asked to leave St. Paul's.

On the whole . . . , these schools have continued to assimilate the sons of the newly rich down through the years. John F. Kennedy, for example, was graduated from Choate School in the thirties, after spending a year at Canterbury. In this connection, it was a measure of the increasingly affluent status of American Catholics that the nation's two leading Catholic boarding schools, Portsmouth Priory and Canterbury, were founded in 1926 and 1915 respectively.

THE COLLEGE CAMPUS IN THE GILDED AGE: GOLD COAST AND SLUM

The excluding mania of the Gilded Age was of course reflected on the campuses of the nation, especially in the older colleges in the East. In his book, *Academic Procession*, Ernest Earnest begins his chapter entitled "The Golden Age and the Gilded Cage" as follows:

It is ironic that the most fruitful period in American higher education sowed the seeds of three of the greatest evils: commercialized athletics, domination by the business community, and a caste system

[22]E. Digby Baltzell, *op. cit., p. 302.*

symbolized by the Gold Coast. . . . A smaller percentage of students came to prepare for the ministry, law, and teaching; they came to prepare for entrance into the business community, especially that part of it concerned with big business and finance. And it was the sons of big business, finance, and corporation law who dominated the life of the campus in the older Eastern colleges. To an amazing degree the pattern set by Harvard, Yale and Princeton after 1880 became that of colleges all over the country. The clubs, the social organization, the athletics—even the clothes and the slang—of "the big three" were copied by college youth throughout the nation. In its totality the system which flowered between 1880 and World War I reflected the ideals of the social class which dominated the period.[23]

It is indeed appropriate that Yale's William Graham Sumner added the term "mores" to the sociological jargon, for the snobbish mass mores of the campuses of the Gilded Age were nowhere more binding than at New Haven. In the nineties, Yale became the first football factory and led the national trend toward anti-intellectualism and social snobbishness. Between 1883 and 1901, Yale plowed through nine undefeated seasons, piled up seven hundred points to its opponents' zero in the famous season of 1888, and produced Walter Camp, who picked the first All-American eleven and who produced Amos Alonzo Stagg, who, in turn, taught Knute Rockne everything he knew about football. By the turn of the century, "We toil not, neither do we agitate, but we play football" became the campus slogan. And cheating and the use of purchased papers almost became the rule among the golden boys of Yale, most of whom lived in "The Hutch," an expensive privately owned dormitory where the swells patronized private tailors, ruined expensive suits in pranks, sprees and rioting, ordered fine cigars by the hundred-lot, and looked down on those poorer boys who had gone to public high schools. The Yale Class Book of 1900, appropriately enough, published the answer to the following question: Have you ever used a trot? Yes: 264, No: 15. At the same time, in a survey covering three floors of a dormitory, it was found that not a single student wrote his own themes. They bought them, of course. After all, this sort of menial labor was only for the "drips," "grinds," "fruits," "meatballs," and "black men" of minority ethnic origins and a public school education. But at least one gilded son was somewhat horrified at the mores of Old Eli in those good old days before mass democracy had polluted gentlemenly education. A member of the class of 1879, this young gentleman asked an instructor in history to recommend some outside reading. The reply was "Young man, if you think you came to Yale with the idea of reading you will find out your mistake very soon."[24]

This anti-intellectual crowd of leading Yale men was composed primarily of boarding school graduates who began to dominate campus life at this time. Owen Johnson, graduate of Lawrenceville and Yale (1900), wrote about this generation in his best seller, *Stover at Yale.*[25] Stover soon

[23]Ernest Earnest, *Academic Procession.* New York: Bobbs-Merrill Company, Inc., 1953.
[24]*Ibid.*, p. 232.
[25]*Ibid.*, p. 208.

learned that the way to success at Yale meant following the mores established by the cliques from Andover, Exeter, Hotchkiss, Groton and St. Paul's:
"We've got a corking lot in the house—Best of the Andover crowd." Even
in the famous senior societies, caste replaced the traditional aristocracy
of merit. Thus a committee headed by Professor Irving Fisher found that,
whereas twenty-six of the thirty-four class valedictorians had been tapped
by the senior societies between 1861 and 1894, after 1893 not a single one
had been considered.[26]

By the turn of the century, the College of New Jersey which had only
recently changed its name to Princeton was far more homogeneously upper
class than Yale. "The Christian tradition, the exclusiveness of the upper-
class clubs, and the prejudices of the students," wrote Edwin E. Slosson in
Great American Universities in 1910, "kept away many Jews, although not
all—there are eleven in the Freshman class. Anti-Semitic feeling seemed
to me to be more dominant at Princeton than at any of the other universities I visited. "If the Jews once get in,' I was told, 'they would ruin
Princeton as they have Columbia and Pennsylvania.' "[27]

Football mania and the snobberies fostered by the eating-club system
gradually dominated campus life at Princeton. Thus in 1906, Woodrow
Wilson, convinced that the side shows were swallowing up the circus, made
his famous report to the trustees on the need for abolishing the clubs.
Although many misunderstood his purpose at the time, Wilson actually
desired to make Princeton an even more homogeneous body of gentlemen-
scholars. His preceptorial and quadrangle plans envisioned a series of small
and intimate groups of students and faculty members pursuing knowledge
without the disruptive class divisions fostered by the existing club system.
Wilson was defeated in his drive for reform (partly because of his tact-
lessness) and was eventually banished to the White House, where he would
be less of a threat to the system so dear to the hearts of many powerful
trustees.

One should not dismiss Princeton's idea of homogeneity without mentioning one of its real and extremely important advantages. Princeton is
one of the few American universities where an honor system is still in
force, and presumably works. In this connection, Edwin E. Slosson's observations on the system as it worked in 1910 should be quoted in full:

> At Harvard I saw a crowd of students going into a large hall, and
> following them in, I found I could not get out, that no one was allowed
> to leave the examination room for twenty minutes. The students were
> insulated, the carefully protected papers distributed, and guards walked
> up and down the aisles with their eyes rolling like the search lights of
> a steamer in a fog. Nothing like this at Princeton; the students are on
> their honor not to cheat, and they do not, or but rarely. Each entering
> class is instructed by the Seniors into the Princeton code of honor,
> which requires any student seeing another receiving or giving assis-
> tance on examination to report him for a trial by his peers of the

[26]*Ibid.*, p. 230.
[27]Edwin E. Slosson, *Great American Universities.* New York: The Macmillan Company, 1910,
  p. 105.

student body. . . . I do not think the plan would be practicable in the long run with a very large and heterogeneous collection of students. It is probable that Princeton will lose this with some other fine features of its student life as the university grows and becomes more cosmopolitan. The semimonastic seculsion of the country village cannot be long maintained.[28]

In contrast to Princeton, and even Yale, Harvard has always been guided by the ideal of diversity. A large and heterogeneous student body, however, is always in danger of developing class divisions. Like his friend Woodrow Wilson, A. Lawrence Lowell was disturbed by this trend at Harvard at the turn of the century. In a letter to President Eliot, written in 1902, he mentioned the "tendency of wealthy students to live in private dormitories outside the yard" and the "great danger of a snobbish separation of the students on lines of wealth."[29] In a committee report of the same year, he noted how one of the finest dormitories was becoming known as "Little Jerusalem" because of the fact that some Jews lived there.

Samuel Eliot Morison, in his history of Harvard, shows how the college gradually became two worlds—the "Yard" and the "Gold Coast"—as Boston society, the private schools, the club system and the private dormitories took over social life at the turn of the century.[30] "In the eighties," he writes, "when the supply of eligible young men in Boston was decreased by the westward movement, the Boston mammas suddenly became aware that Harvard contained many appetizing young gentlemen from New York, Philadelphia, and elsewhere. One met them in the summer at Newport, Beverly, or Bar Harbor; naturally one invited them to Mr. Papanti's or Mr. Foster's 'Friday Evenings' when they entered College, to the 'Saturday Evening Sociables' sophomore year, and to coming-out balls thereafter."[31] These favored men were, at the same time, living along Mount Auburn Street in privately run and often expensive halls, and eating at the few final clubs which only took in some 10 to 15 per cent of each class. Closely integrated with the clubs and Boston Society were the private preparatory schools. Until about 1870, according to Morison, Boston Latin School graduates still had a privileged position at Harvard, but "during the period 1870–90 the proportion of freshmen entering from public high schools fell from 38 to 23 per cent." About 1890 the Episcopal Church schools and a few others took over. "Since 1890 it has been almost necessary for a Harvard student with social ambition to enter from the 'right' sort of school and be popular there, to room on the 'Gold Coast' and be accepted by Boston society his freshman year, in order to be on the right side of the social chasm . . . conversely, a lad of Mayflower or Porcellian ancestry who entered from a high school was as much 'out of it' as a ghetto Jew."[32]

During most of Harvard's history, according to Morison, a solid core

---

[28]*Ibid.*, p. 106.
[29]Ernest Earnest, *op. cit.*, p. 216.
[30]Samuel Eliot Morison, *Three Centuries of Harvard, 1636–1936.* Cambridge, Mass.: Harvard University Press, 1937.
[31]*Ibid.*, p. 416.
[32]*Ibid.*, p. 422.

of middle-class New Englanders had been able to absorb most of the students into a cohesive college life which was dominated by a basic curriculum taken by all students. The increasing size of the classes (100 in the 1860's to over 600 by the time Franklin Roosevelt graduated in 1904), the elective system which sent men off to specialize in all directions, and the increasing ethnic heterogeneity of the student body, paved the way for exclusiveness and stratification. By 1893, for example, there were enough Irish Catholics in the Yard to support the St. Paul's Catholic Club, which acquired Newman House in 1912. The situation was similar with the Jews. "The first German Jews who came were easily absorbed into the social pattern; but at the turn of the century the bright Russian and Polish lads from the Boston public schools began to arrive. There were enough of them in 1906 to form the Menorah Society, and in another fifteen years Harvard had her 'Jewish problem.' "[33]

The "Jewish problem" at Harvard will be discussed below. Here it is enough to emphasize the fact that it grew out of the general development of caste in America at the turn of the century. And this new type of caste system was supported by all kinds of associations, from the suburban country club to the fraternities and clubs on the campuses of the nation. Not only were two worlds now firmly established at Harvard and Yale and to a lesser extent at Princeton; at other less influential state universities and small colleges, fraternities dominated campus life.

Although fraternities grew up on the American campus before the Civil War, they expanded tremendously in the postwar period. By the late 1880's, for instance, the five hundred undergraduates at the University of Wisconsin were stratified by a fraternity system which included no less than thirteen houses.[34] As class consciousness increased, campus mores of course became more rigidly anti-Semitic and often anti-Catholic. Bernard Baruch, who entered the College of the City of New York in 1884 (as he was only fourteen at the time, his mother would not let him go away to Yale, which was his preference), felt the full weight of campus anti-Semitism. Although he was extremely popular among the small group of less than four hundred undergraduates, and although he was elected president of the class in his senior year, young Baruch was never taken into a fraternity at C.C.N.Y. "The Greek-letter societies or fraternities," he wrote years later in his autobiography, "played an important part at the college. Although many Jews made their mark at the college, the line was drawn against them by these societies. Each year my name would be proposed and a row would ensue over my nomination, but I never was elected. It may be worth noting, particularly for those who regard the South as less tolerant than the North, that my brother Herman was readily admitted to a fraternity while he attended the University of Virginia."[35] In response to the "Anglo-Saxon-Only" mores which accompanied the fraternity boom in the eighties and nineties, the first Jewish fraternity in America was founded at Columbia, in 1898.

[33]*Ibid.*, p. 417.
[34]Ernest Earnest, *op. cit.*, p. 207.
[35]Bernard M. Baruch, *Baruch: My Own Story.* New York: Pocket Books, Inc., 1958, p. 54.

The campus mores were, of course, modeled after the adult world which the students in the Gilded Age were preparing to face. For the large corporations, banks and powerful law firms—in the big-city centers of national power—increasingly began to select their future leaders, not on the basis of ability alone, but largely on the basis of their fashionable university and club or fraternity affiliations. "The graduate of a small college or a Western university," writes Ernest Earnest, "might aspire to a judgeship or bank presidency in the smaller cities and towns; he might get to Congress, become a physician or college professor. Particularly west of the Alleghenies he might become a governor or senator. But he was unlikely to be taken into the inner social and financial circles of Boston, New York or Philadelphia."[36] In the first half of the twentieth century, five of our eight Presidents were graduates of Harvard, Yale, Princeton and Amherst. A sixth came from Stanford, "the Western Harvard," where the social system most resembled that in the East.

THE METROPOLITAN MEN'S CLUB: STRONGHOLD OF PATRICIAN POWER

When the gilded youths at Harvard, Yale and Princeton finally left the protected world of the "Gold Coast" to seek their fortunes in the Wall streets and executive suites of the nation, they usually joined one or another exclusive men's club. Here they dined with others of their kind, helped each other to secure jobs and promotions, and made friends with influential older members who might some day be of help to them in their paths to the top. Proper club affiliation was, after all, the final and most important stage in an exclusive socializing process. As a character in a novel about Harvard, published in 1901, put it: "Bertie knew who his classmates in college were going to be at the age of five. They're the same chaps he's been going to school with and to kid dancing classes . . . it's part of the routine. After they get out of college they'll all go abroad for a few months in groups of three or four, and when they get back they'll be taken into the same club (their names will have been on the waiting list some twenty-odd years) . . . and see one another every day for the rest of their lives."[37] But, by the century's turn, the metropolitan club was gradually becoming more than a congenial gathering-place for similarly bred gentlemen.

British and American gentlemen, especially after the urban bourgeoisie replaced the provincial aristocracy, soon realized that the club was an ideal instrument for the gentlemanly control of social, political and economic power. For generations in England, top decisions in the City and at Whitehall have often been made along Pall Mall, where conservatives gathered at the Carlton and liberals at the Reform. But perhaps the best illustration of the role of the club in the making of gentlemen, and its use as an instrument of power, was a "gentlemanly agreement" which was made in the late nineteenth century at the frontiers of empire. And it is indeed

[36]Ernest Earnest, *op. cit.*, p. 218.
[37]*Ibid.*, p. 217.

symbolic and prophetic that it should have been made in racialist South Africa by the great Cecil Rhodes, that most rabid of racialists who dreamed of forming a Nordic secret society, organized like Loyola's, and devoted to world domination. The club served Rhodes well on his way to wealth.[38]

The exploitation of Africa became a full-fledged imperialist enterprise only after Cecil Rhodes dispossessed the Jews. Rhodes' most important competitor in the fight for control of the Kimberley diamond mines was Barney Barnato, son of a Whitechapel shopkeeper, who was possessed by a passionate desire to make his pile and, above all, to become a gentleman. Both Rhodes and Barnato were eighteen years of age when they arrived in Kimberley in the early seventies. By 1885 Rhodes was worth fifty thousand pounds a year, but Barnato was richer. At that time Rhodes began his "subtle" and persistent dealings with Barnato in order to gain control of de Beers. Nearly every day he had him to lunch or dinner at the "unattainable," at least for Barnato, Kimberley Club (he even persuaded the club to alter its rules which limited the entertainment of nonmembers to once-a-month). At last, Barnato agreed to sell out to Rhodes for a fabulous fortune, membership in the Kimberley Club, and a secure place among the gentlemanly imperialists. While Rhodes had perhaps used his club and his race with an ungentlemanly lack of subtlety, "no American trust, no trust in the world, had such power over any commodity as Rhodes now had over diamonds." But in the end, his dream that "between two and three thousand Nordic gentlemen in the prime of life and mathematically selected" should run the world became the very respectable Rhodes Scholarship Association, which supported selected members of all "Nordic Races," such as Germans, Scandinavians and Americans, during a brief stay in the civilizing atmosphere of Oxford University (the "Nordic" criterion for selection has since been abandoned). In the meantime, his friend Barney Barnato, soon after realizing his dream of becoming both a millionaire and a gentleman, drowned himself in the depths of the sea.

Many such dreams of corporate and financial empire-building have been consummated within the halls of America's more exclusive clubs. The greatest financial imperialist of them all, J. Pierpont Morgan, belonged to no less than nineteen clubs in this country and along Pall Mall. One of his dreams was realized on the night of December 12, 1900, in the course of a private dinner at the University Club in New York. Carnegie's man, Charles M. Schwab, was the guest of honor and the steel trust was planned that night.

In the 1900's the metropolitan club became far more important than the country club, the private school and college, or the exclusive neighborhood as the crucial variable in the recruitment of America's new corporate aristocracy. Family position and prestige, built up as a result of several generations of leadership and service in some provincial city or town, were gradually replaced by an aristocracy by ballot, in the hierarchy of metropolitan clubdom. In New York, for example, this process can be illustrated by the club affiliations of successive generations of Rockefellers:

---

[38]See Hannah Arendt, *The Origins of Totalitarianism*. New York: Harcourt, Brace and Company, 1951, p. 203. And S. Gertude Millin, *Cecil Rhodes*. London: Harper & Brothers, 1933, pp. 99–100.

John D. Rockefeller belonged to the Union League; John D., Jr., to the University Club; and John D. III to the Knickerbocker. Thus is a business aristocracy recruited.

And this associational, rather than familistic, process was certainly democratic, except for one thing. That is the fact that, almost without exception, every club in America now developed a castelike policy toward the Jews. They were excluded, as a people or race, regardless of their personal qualities such as education, taste or manners. It is important, moreover, to stress the fact that this caste line was only drawn at the end of the nineteenth century, when, as we have seen, the members of the upper class were setting themselves apart in other ways. Joseph Seligman's experience at Saratoga Springs was part of a general trend which came to a head again when Jesse Seligman, one of the founders of New York's Union League, resigned from the club in 1893, when his son was blackballed because he was a Jew. Apparently this sort of anti-Semitism was not yet a norm when the club was founded during the Civil War.

Nor was it the norm among the more exclusive clubs in other cities. The Philadelphia Club, the oldest and one of the most patrician in America, was founded in 1834, but did not adhere to any anti-Semitic policy until late in the century. During the Civil War, for instance, Joseph Gratz, of an old German-Jewish family and a leader in his synagogue, was president of the club. The membership also included representatives of several other prominent families of Jewish origin. Yet no other member of the Gratz family has been taken into the Philadelphia Club since the nineties, a period when countless embarrassing incidents all over America paralleled the Seligman incident at the Union League.[39] The University Club of Cincinnati finally broke up, in 1896, over the admission of a prominent member of the Jewish community. Elsewhere, prominent, cultivated and powerful Jews were asked to resign, or were forced to do so by their sense of pride, because of incidents involving their families or friends who were refused membership solely because of their Jewish origins. Gentlemanly anti-Semitism even invaded the aristocratic South. As late as the 1870's one of the more fashionable men's clubs in Richmond, the Westmoreland, had members as well as an elected president of Jewish origins. But today all the top clubs in the city follow a policy of rigid exclusiveness as far as Jews are concerned. This is the case even though the elite Jewish community in Richmond, as in Philadelphia, has always been a stable one with a solid core of old families whose members exhibit none of the aggressive, *parvenu* traits given as a reason for the anti-Semitic policies of clubs in New York, Chicago or Los Angeles.

Yet the inclusion of cultivated Jews within the halls of the Philadelphia or Westmoreland clubs in an earlier day was characteristic of a provincial and familistic age when the men's club was really social, and membership was based on congeniality rather than, as it has increasingly become, on an organized effort to retain social power within a castelike social stratum. George Apley, whose values were the product of a rapidly departing era,

---

[39]As a matter of "subtle" fact, there were no "Jewish" members of the Gratz family left in the city by this time.

threatened to resign from his beloved Boston Club when he thought it was being used, somewhat in the style of Cecil Rhodes, as an agency for the consolidation of business power. At a time when his clubmates Moore and Field were apparently violating his gentlemanly code in seeking the admission of their business associate Ransome, Apley wrote the admissions committee as follows:

> I wish to make it clear that it is not because of Ransome personally that I move to oppose him.
> Rather, I move to oppose the motive which actuates Messrs. Moore and Field in putting this man up for membership. They are not doing so because of family connections, nor because of disinterested friendship, but rather because of business reasons. It is, perhaps, too well known for me to mention it that Mr. Ransome has been instrumental in bringing a very large amount of New York business to the banking house of Moore and Fields. This I do not think is reason enough to admit Mr. Ransome to the Province Club, a club which exists for social and not for business purposes.[40]

Today many other clubs like Apley's Province, but unlike Pittsburgh's Duquesne, are fighting the intrusion of business affairs into a club life supposedly devoted to the purely social life among gentlemen. "A year or two ago," wrote Osborn Elliott in 1959, "members of San Francisco's sedate Pacific Union Club (known affectionately as the P.U.) received notices advising them that briefcases should not be opened, nor business papers displayed, within the confines of the old club building atop Nob Hill."[41] At about the same time, patrician New Yorkers were shocked at a *Fortune* article which reported that "at the Metropolitan or the Union League or the University . . . you might do a $10,000 deal, but you'd use the Knickerbocker or the Union or the Racquet for $100,000, and then for $1 million you'd have to move on to the Brook or the Links."[42]

In this chapter I have shown how a series of newly created upperclass institutions produced an associationally insulated national upper class in metropolitan America. I have stressed their rise in a particular time in our history and attempted to show how they were part of a more general status, economic and urban revolution which, in turn, was reflected in the Populist and Progressive movements. All this is important as a background for understanding the present situation, primarily because it shows that upper-class nativism in general and anti-Semitism in particular were a product of a particular cultural epoch and, more important, had not always been characteristic of polite society to anywhere near the same extent. This being the case, it may well be true, on the other hand, that new social and cultural situations may teach new duties and produce new upper-class mores and values. As a measure of the success of these caste-creating associations, the following remarks made by the late H. G. Wells after a visit to this country soon after the turn of the century are interesting.

---

[40]John P. Marquand, *The Late George Apley*. New York: The Modern Library, 1940, p. 189.
[41]Osborn Elliott, *Men at the Top*. New York: Harper & Brothers, 1959, p. 163.
[42]*Ibid.*, p. 164.

In the lower levels of the American community there pours per-
petually a vast torrent of strangers, speaking alien tongues, inspired
by alien traditions, for the most part illiterate peasants and working-
people. They come in at the bottom: that must be insisted upon. . . .
The older American population is being floated up on the top of this
influx, a sterile aristocracy above a racially different and astonishingly
fecund proletariat. . . .

Yet there are moments in which I could have imagined there were
no immigrants at all. All the time, except for one distinctive evening,
I seem to have been talking to English-speaking men, now and then,
but less frequently, to an Americanized German. In the clubs there are
no immigrants. There are not even Jews, as there are in London clubs.
One goes about the wide streets of Boston, one meets all sorts of Boston
people, one visits the State-House; it's all the authentic English-speaking America. Fifth Avenue, too, is America without a touch of foreign-
born; and Washington. You go a hundred yards south of the pretty
Boston Common, and behold! you are in a polyglot slum! You go a
block or so east of Fifth Avenue and you are in a vaster, more Yiddish
Whitechapel.[43]

At this point, it should be emphasized that it was (and still is) primarily the patrician without power, the clubmen and resorters and the
functionless genteel who, as Edith Wharton wrote, "fall back on sport and
culture." It was these gentlemen with time on their hands who took the
lead in creating the "anti-everything" world which Henry Adams called
"Society." So often, for example, it was the men of inherited means, many
of them bachelors like Madison Grant, who served on club admission
committees, led the dancing assemblies and had their summers free to
run the yacht, tennis and bathing clubs at Newport or Bar Harbor. And
these leisurely patricians were, in turn, supported by the new men, and
especially their socially ambitious wives, who had just made their fortunes
and were seeking social security for their children. In all status revolutions,
indeed, resentment festers with the greatest intensity among the new rich,
the new poor, and the functionless genteel. And these gentlemen of resentment responded to the status revolution at the turn of the century by
successfully creating, as H. G. Wells so clearly saw, two worlds: the patrician and Protestant rich, and the rest.

[43]H. G. Wells, *The Future in America*. New York: Harper & Brothers, 1906, p. 134.

Suggestions for Further Reading

Few general works try to cover this period from the perspective of everyday life. One popular and entertaining work that attempts this view is J. C. Furnas, *The Americans: A Social History of the United States, 1587–1914** (New York, 1969), available in a two-volume paperback edition. Other works that present some coverage of everyday life during the Gilded Age are Ray Ginger, *Age of Excess: The United States from 1877–1914** (New York, 1965); Henry F. May, *Protestant Churches and Industrial America** (New York, 1949); and Thomas Cochran and William Miller, *The Age of Enterprise: A Social History of Industrial America** (New York, 1961). For a view of the closing decade, see Larzer Ziff, *The American 1890's: Life and Times of a Lost Generation** (New York, 1966). Tamara Hareven has edited a useful collection of essays in *Anonymous Americans: Explorations in Nineteenth Century Social History** (Englewood Cliffs, N.J., 1971). Fictional treatments of the period that are revealing are Mark Twain and Charles Warner, *The Gilded Age** (New York, 1874), and two works by William Dean Howells, *The Rise of Silas Lapham** (Boston, 1884) and *The Hazard of New Fortunes** (New York, 1889).

For material on everyday life on the Middle Border and Great Plains, see Robert Dykstra, *The Cattle Towns** (New York, 1968); Merle Curti, *The Making of an American Community: A Case Study of Democracy in a Frontier County** (Stanford, 1959); and Everett Dick, *The Sod-House Frontier, 1854–1890: A Social History of the Northern Plains from the Creation of Kansas and Nebraska to the Admission of the Dakotas** (New York, 1937), and Lewis Atherton, *Main Street on the Middle Border** (Bloomington, 1954). Developments in agriculture are covered in Fred A. Shannon, *The Farmer's Last Frontier, Agriculture, 1860–1897** (New York, 1945). Fiction provides an excellent source of information about life in the Midwest. Classic works of American literature on this subject are Mark Twain, *Life on the Mississippi** (Boston, 1883), *Huckleberry Finn** (New York, 1885), *Tom Sawyer** (Hartford, Conn., 1892); Sherwood Anderson, *Winesburg, Ohio** (New York, 1919); Sinclair Lewis, *Main Street** (New York, 1920); and, most sympathetically,

*Available in paperback edition.

111

Willa Cather, *My Antonia** (Boston, 1926); and Hamlin Garland's auto-biographical *A Son of the Middle Border* (New York, 1918).

The standard short revisionist history of Reconstruction is Kenneth M. Stampp, *The Era of Reconstruction, 1865–1877** (New York, 1965). For South Carolina specifically, see Joel Williamson, *After Slavery: The Negro in South Carolina During Reconstruction, 1861–1877** (Chapel Hill, 1974). Leon Litwack presents a richly detailed description of the beginning of Reconstruction in *Been in the Storm So Long: The Aftermath of Slavery** (New York, 1979). In *Exodusters: Black Migration to Kansas after Reconstruction** (New York, 1977), Nell Irwin Painter tells of one attempt of the freedpeople to escape white domination. Norman Crockett describes some of the separatist settlements in *The Black Towns* (Lawrence, Kansas, 1979). The role of the federal government in land reform is explored in Claude F. Oubre, *Forty Acres and a Mule: The Freedmen's Bureau and Black Land Ownership* (Baton Rouge, 1978).

Recent surveys of America's working women include Alice Kessler-Harris, *Out to Work: A History of Wage-Earning Women in the United States* (New York, 1982); Barbara Mayer Wertheimer, *We Were There: The Story of Working Women in America** (New York, 1977); and Rosalyn Baxandall, Linda Gordon, and Susan Reverby (eds), *America's Working Women: A Documentary History—1600 to the Present** (New York, 1976). Of interest is Susan Estabrook Kennedy's *If All We Did Was to Weep at Home: A History of White Working-Class Women in America** (Bloomington, 1979). Two studies of expanding opportunities for women in this period are Karen Blair, *The Clubwoman as Feminist: True Womanhood Redefined, 1868–1914* (New York, 1980) and Barbara J. Harris, *Beyond Her Sphere: Women and the Professions in American History* (Westport, 1981).

For a study of the Philadelphia elite, see E. Digby Baltzell, *Philadelphia Gentleman: The Making of a National Upper Class** (Glencoe, Ill., 1958). Glimpses of the life-style of the wealthy are found in Stewart Holbrook, *The Age of the Moguls* (Garden City, N. Y., 1953), and Stephen Birmingham, *The Right People: A Portrait of America's Social Establishment* (Boston, 1968). A contemporary critical analysis is Thorstein Veblen, *The Theory of the Leisure Class** (New York, 1899), and a recent critique is C. Wright Mills, *The Power Elite** (New York, 1956). William G. Domhoff has probed the upper class of today in *The Higher Circles: The Governing Class in America** (New York, 1971) and *The Bohemian Grove and Other Retreats: A Study in Ruling Class Cohesiveness** (New York, 1975). Popular treatments of non-Anglo-Saxon wealth are found in Stephen Birmingham, *Our Crowd: The Great Jewish Families of New York** (New York, 1967), *The Grandees: America's Sephardic Elite** (New York, 1971), and *Real Lace: America's Irish Rich** (New York, 1973). Higher education is scrutinized in Richard Hofstadter and Walter P. Metzger, *The Development of Academic Freedom in the United States** (New York, 1955), available in a two-volume paperback edition.

The Early
Twentieth Century

1900–1930

"He's not heavy; he's my brother."
Photo taken by Jacob A. Riis, c. 1900

Growing Up in the Ghetto

IRVING HOWE

In the early twentieth century, an American Jewish playwright coined a phrase that entered the common language as a description of American society's absorption of various immigrant streams. The United States was the "melting pot" of nations. Although some authorities, like the Dillingham Commission, questioned the validity of the melting-pot theory, for half a century this metaphor influenced the popular mind as a fulfillment of the promise of the founding fathers: *e pluribus unum* (out of many, one).

Up until the Civil War period, most voluntary immigrants had been rather easily assimilated into the dominant culture. The major exception among European immigrants had been the large numbers of Irish peasants who migrated during the 1840s and 1850s. Even the German Jews who had come to this country before the late nineteenth century had been largely absorbed. With the coming of the new immigrants from Southern and Eastern Europe in the late nineteenth and early twentieth centuries, however, the assimilation process shifted its intent. The new immigrants, Roman Catholic or Jewish for the most part, were not wanted in the dominant culture. Theories of racial superiority and social evolution were drawn on by the defenders of the "traditional American way of life" in order to demonstrate the danger these newcomers posed to the older values. As a result of their efforts, restrictive legislation was passed in the 1920s, virtually precluding further migration from the countries of the new immigration. Although the exclusion acts led to a surge of ethnic consciousness on the part of those excluded, the conventional wisdom about the immigration process came to be found in the melting-pot metaphor.

After the Second World War, however, it seemed to many that only the surface had been melted, producing an overlay of general cultural traits developed in the United States, while underneath remained a strong, distinctly traditional ethnic way of life that derived largely from old-world traditions. Beginning with the publication of **Beyond the Melting Pot** by Daniel P. Moynihan and Nathan Glazer in 1963, scholars began to reconsider the nature of ethnic survivals in American society. In the late 1960s, partly in response to the perceived gains of the civil rights and black militant movements of that decade, ethnic consciousness began to grow, and the children and grandchildren of the new immigration started to reevaluate their traditional cultures and to seek a more aggressive stance against an overall culture that they found chauvinistically denying the validity of ethnic pluralism.

The Eastern European Jews provide a special case in this ethnic history. The centuries-long religious and cultural oppression experienced by the Jewish people created in them an exceedingly strong sense of identity that survived intact the transfer to the United States. In addition, because discriminatory laws deprived Jews of access to certain kinds of work and career lines in Eastern Europe, they had learned to fill the interstices in the economic structure as peddlers, small shopkeepers, and artisans. These skills proved useful in America, since there were areas of great need in the rapidly expanding economy of the late nineteenth and early twentieth centuries. Like most of the new immigrants, Jews tended to form distinct communities and were, therefore, in a position to develop special markets for culture-specific items.

Jews provide a special case in another respect. Their relatively high level of literacy, or at least respect for literacy, found outlet and market in the growth of a literary culture, particularly on New York's Lower East Side. It also provided access to upward mobility through the educational process in the public schools. While most of the Jews of the immigrant generation found work in light industry, particularly in the garment business, many in the second generation moved into other areas of employment that proved to be upwardly mobile. In other immigrant groups, there was a greater tendency for children to follow in the line of work of their parents.

In a prize-winning memoir and history of the Jews of the Lower East Side, Irving Howe, of the City University of New York, has provided a richly textured and highly personalized account of an important American ethnic culture. His recounting of the problems and prospects of growing up in the ghetto, reprinted here, helps put in perspective certain cultural myths (for example, the bookishness of Jewish youth) and describes the awesome struggle of young immigrant women to free themselves to participate in the promise of American life.

The socio-economic rise of many of the descendants of this ghetto is one of America's great success stories. Many Jews have so successfully adopted the "American Dream" that some of their community leaders fear their distinctiveness may be lost through intermarriage and assimilation. In relation to Jewish immigration, then, perhaps the melting-pot metaphor was right, only expressed fifty years ahead of its time.

The streets were ours. Everyplace else—home, school, shop—belonged to the grownups. But the streets belonged to us. We would roam through the city tasting the delights of freedom, discovering possibilities far beyond the reach of our parents. The streets taught us the deceits of commerce, introduced us to the excitement of sex, schooled us in strategies of survival, and gave us our first clear idea of what life in America was really going to be like.

We might continue to love our parents and grind away at school and college, but it was the streets that prepared the future. In the streets we were roughened by actuality, and even those of us who later became intellectuals or professionals kept something of our bruising gutter-worldliness, our hard and abrasive skepticism. You could see it in cab drivers and garment manufacturers, but also in writers and professors who had grown up as children of immigrant Jews.

T he streets opened a fresh prospect of sociability. It was a prospect not always amiable or even free from terror, but it drew Jewish boys and girls like a magnet, offering them qualities in short supply at home: the charms of the spontaneous and unpredictable. In the streets a boy could encircle himself with the breath of immigrant life, declare his companionship with peddlers, storekeepers, soapboxers. No child raised in the immigrant quarter would lack for moral realism: just to walk through Hester Street was an education in the hardness of life. To go beyond Cherry Street on the south, where the Irish lived, or west of the Bowery, where the Italians were settling, was to explore the world of the gentiles—dangerous, since one risked a punch in the face, but tempting, since for an East Side boy the idea of *the others*, so steadily drilled into his mind by every agency of his culture, was bound to incite curiosity. Venturing into gentile streets became a strategy for testing the reality of the external world and for discovering that it was attractive in ways no Jewish voice had told him. An East Side boy needed to slip into those gentile streets on his own. He needed to make a foray and then pull back, so that his perception of the outer world would be his own, and not merely that of the old folks, not merely the received bias and visions of the Jews.

When he kept to the Jewish streets, the East Side boy felt at home, free and easy on his own turf. Even if not especially friendly or well mannered, people talked to one another. No one had much reason to suppose that the noisiest quarrel between peddler and purchaser, or parents and children, was anything but a peaceful ritual. Within the tight circle of the East Side, children found multiple routes for wandering, along one or another way:

• Toward Canal Street, "suit-hunting avenue," as they called it, the stores bright with ties, *mezuzas*, hats, Hebrew books, *taleysim*, where you could jest with the hawkers, stare at the bowls shaped like hourglasses and filled with colored liquids which were kept in the drugstores, feast on windows, savor the territory.

• Toward Hester or, a bit later, Orchard Street, pushcart territory: shawls, bananas, oilcloth, garlic, trousers, ill-favored fish, ready-to-wear spectacles. You could relax in the noise of familiars, enjoy a tournament of bargains, with every ritual of haggling, maneuver of voice, expertly known and shrewdly appraised. "After a light diet of kippered herring I would wander among the pushcarts for my dessert. I developed a knack for slipping bananas up my sleeve and dropping apples into my blouse while the peddler was busy filling some housewife's market bag. I used to pack a peach into my mouth with one snap of the jaws and look deeply offended when the peddler turned suspiciously upon me."

• Toward Rutgers Square, with a stop in the summer to cool off at the Schiff Fountain, and then a prowl into the crammed adjacent streets: boys playing stickball or stoopball, and "on one corner the water hydrant turned on to clear the muck of the gutter. Half-naked children danced and shouted under the shower. . . . They pushed out the walls of their homes to the street." At night Rutgers Square changed colors, and it was fun to sidle along, watching the intellectuals as they strolled on East Broadway, and street speakers variously entertaining, some with little more than lung power, others artists in low-keyed enticement.

• Toward the East River, in warm months, with a dive off the docks, where a blue film of oil from passing tugs coated the water "and a boy who didn't come out looking brown hadn't bathed." Once, after "washing away our sins in the water, we had to pass by gentile lumber yards, and the men there used to throw bricks at us. Then some of us got together and beat them up with sticks, and they never bothered us again."

• Toward Allen Street, center of darkness and sin, "with its elevated structure whose trains avalanched between rows of houses and the sunlight never penetrated. I see the small shops, which somehow never achieved the dignity of selling anything new . . . a street which dealt in castoff merchandise. Even the pale children seemed old, secondhand."

These "ways," while hardly as elegant as more celebrated ones in modern literature, tracked discoveries into the familiar and the forbidden, into that which stamped one as a true son of the immigrants and that which made one a future apostate. Learning the lessons of cement, one lost whatever fragments of innocence remained. The apartments were crowded, the streets were crowded, yet for boys and girls growing up in the ghetto, the apartments signified a life too well worn, while the streets, despite their squalor, spoke of freedom. Freedom to break loose from those burdens that Jewish parents had come to cherish; freedom, if only for an hour or two, to be the "street bum" against whom fathers warned; freedom to live by the senses, a gift that had to be learned and fought for; freedom to sin. Cramped or denied, shushed or repressed, sexual yearnings broke out on the streets and were expressed through their grubby poetry, in hidden corners, black basements, glowering roofs: wherever the family was not.

To be poor is something that happens to one; to experience poverty is to gain an idea of what is happening. All the evidence we have suggests that the children of the East Side rarely felt deprived. They certainly knew that life was hard, but they assumed that, until they grew up and got a grip on things, it had to be hard. Only later, long after the proper occasion had passed, did self-pity enter their psyche. In the actual years of childhood, the streets spoke of risk, pleasure, novelty: the future—that great Jewish mania, the future.

Legends of retrospect, woven from a wish to make the past seem less rough and abrasive than it actually was, have transformed every Jewish boy into a miniature scholar haunting the Seward Park library and, before he was even out of knee pants, reading Marx and Tolstoy. The reality was different. Scholarly boys there certainly were; but more numerous by far were the street boys, tough and shrewd if not quite "bums," ready to muscle their way past competitors to earn half a dollar, quick to grasp the crude wisdom of the streets. Sammy Aaronson, who would rise to distinction as a fight manager, spent his boyhood as a street waif, sometimes sleeping in the Christopher Street public baths, sometimes at Label Katz's poolroom in Brownsville, sometimes riding the subways all night for a nickel. His family was the poorest of the poor, his mother worked as a junk peddler, their furniture often landed on the street after an eviction, but "there was nothing particularly tragic about that. . . . We didn't feel sorry for ourselves and nobody felt sorry for us." Harry Golden, whose youth was softer, assures us that he too was no Goody Two-shoes. "I played hooky and went to the movies. . . . I was unconscionably capable of forging a note the next day to explain my absence. 'My son Herschele was sick yesterday. (Mrs.) Anna Goldhurst.' Instinctively I knew 'Herschele' and the parentheses would lend absolute verisimilitude to my forgery." Eddie Cantor, before he began to appear in vaudeville skits in Chinatown, did come close to being a "bum." By the age of thirteen, he had "socked a teacher," lost a job through talking too much, perfected his game of pool, learned to hustle a few pennies by jigging and singing on a street corner, and taken up with an immigrant Russian girl, not Jewish, but with melancholy black eyes.

The streets were the home of play. Jewish boys became fanatics of baseball, their badge as Americans. In the narrow streets baseball was narrowed to stickball: a broomstick used as a bat, a rubber ball pitched on a bounce or sped into the catcher's glove, the ball hit high to fielders pinched into the other end of the street, with quarrels as to whether passers-by or wagons (later, cars) had hindered ("hindoo'd") the play. Or stoopball, with a rubber ball thrown smartly against the outer steps of a tenement—a game mostly for eleven-to-fourteen-year-olds.

> We'd go to play ball in Tompkins Park. If we couldn't afford a bat we'd bat a can around. The girls played jacks. We'd make a big circle and play marbles. The highly colored ones we called "immies," I couldn't tell my father I played ball, so my mother would sneak out my baseball gear and put it in the candy store downstairs. . . . Later, when I played semipro baseball I'd bring home five dollars and give it to my mother.

Jewish boys were said to be terribly competitive at games, as if already playing by adult norms: "You see it in the street where they delight in 'spiking' tops, playing marbles 'for keeps,' and 'pussy cat,' in all of which the sole idea is to win as an individual boy." The East Side allowed no lingering in childhood; it thrust the ways of the world onto its young. In their middle teens the boys turned clannish, forming "social and athletic clubs," partly to imitate American models.

Girls had their own games, since "the separation of boys and girls so rigidly carried out in the public schools also held for the street; boys played with boys, girls with girls." Sophie Ruskay, who lived on Henry Street, continues:

> Occasionally we girls might stand on the sidelines and watch the boys play their games, but usually our presence was ignored. . . . We knew it to be a boy's world, but we didn't seem to mind it too much. . . . Tagging after us sometimes were our little brothers and sisters whom we were supposed to mind, but that was no great hardship. We would toss them our bean-bags [to play with], little cloth containers filled with cherry pits. . . . Then we could proceed to our game of potsy. Mama didn't like me to play potsy. She thought it "disgraceful" to mark up our sidewalk with chalk for our lines and boxes; besides, hopping on one foot and pushing the thick piece of tin, I managed to wear out a pair of shoes in a few weeks.
>
> Neither my friends nor I played much with dolls. Since families generally had at least one baby on hand, we girls had plenty of opportunity to shower upon the baby brothers or sisters the tenderness that would otherwise have been diverted to dolls. Besides, dolls were expensive.
>
> Regardless of season, the favorite game of both boys and girls was "prisoner's base." We lined up on opposite sides of the curb, our numbers evenly divided, representing two enemy camps. One side turned its back to invite a surprise attack. Stealthily a contestant advanced and either safely reached the "enemy" and captured a "prisoner," or, if caught, "became a prisoner." When a sufficient number of prisoners had been taken, a tug of war followed to rescue them. Trucks and brewery wagons lumbered by. We looked upon them merely as an unnecessary interference.

The streets meant work. Children, like nine-year-old Marie Ganz, went out to pick up bundles of sewing for her mother and was told they could bring in "maybe five dollars a week if she's a good sewer." But the full-time employment of children in shops and factories was rare on the East Side, partly because there was not much for them in the "Jewish industries," partly because the Jewish sense of family prompted fathers to resist with every ounce of their being the idea of children as full-time workers.

By about 1905 most immigrant Jewish families were trying to keep their children in school until at least the age of fourteen; but almost all of them worked in the afternoons, evenings, weekends. Henry Klein, whose story is quite ordinary, peddled matches at the age of six and a bit later, with his ten-year-old brother Isadore, shined shoes at the Houston Street ferry. When he became experienced, he peddled with a professional named

"Sammy" Cohen, working after school and earning twenty-five cents an hour extra when he taught English to his boss. He sold vegetables, fruit, fish; he hauled coal and wood from the Rheinfrank coalyard at the foot of East Third Street and ice from the Fifth Street dock. While attending high school and, later, City College, he spent weekends selling lozenges in Central Park, fearful of the police because he had no license and making his sister Estelle sit on the benches with boxes of lozenges hidden under her skirt. He would average about two dollars a day, on good days as much as three.

PARENTS AND CHILDREN

Between Jewish immigrant parents and the world of the streets there was a state of battle, not quite a declared war but far from a settled peace. To the older generations the streets enclosed dangers and lusts, shapeless enemies threatening all their plans for the young. The parents could not, nor did they really wish to, distinguish between their received sense of the gentile world and the streets to which their children fled. The older immigrants were too suspicious, too thoroughly under the sway of past humiliations, to believe there might really be some neutral ground, neither moral nor immoral, neither wholly purposive nor merely corrupting, for the years of adolescence. Immigrant parents feared the streets would lure their children from the Jewish path, would soften their will to succeed, would yield attractions of pleasure, idleness, and sexuality against which, they suspected, they were finally helpless.

"We push our children too much," wrote a Dr. Michael Cohen, who lived on the East Side. "After school they study music, go to Talmud Torah. Why sacrifice them on the altar of our ambition? Must we get *all* the medals and scholarships? Doctors will tell you about students with shattered nerves, brain fever. Most of them wear glasses. Three to five hours of studying a day, six months a year, are better than five to twelve hours a day for ten months a year." The *Forward* labored to explain to its readers:

> There is no question but that a piano in the front room is preferable to a boarder. It gives spiritual pleasure to exhausted workers. But in most cases the piano is not for pleasure but to make martyrs of little children, and make them mentally ill. A little girl comes home, does her homework, and then is forced to practice under the supervision of her well-meaning father. He is never pleased with her progress, and feels he is paying fifty cents a lesson for nothing. The session ends with his yelling and her crying. These children have not a single free minute for themselves. They have no time to play.

The testimony we have on these matters comes from the sons and daughters, hardly a word from the older people. What might *they* have said? That they brought with them a bone knowledge of the centuries and that being born a Jew meant to accept a life frugal in pleasures? Or that, seeing opportunities for their children such as Jews had never dreamed of, they felt it was necessary to drive them to the utmost?

The costs were high. "Alter, Alter," cried a mother, "what will become of you? You'll end up a street bum!" What had this poor Alter done? He had been playing ball on the street. Later, when he broke a leg, his mother came weeping to the hospital: "Alter, Alter, do you want to kill me?" Trying to joke, he answered, "Wait, Mama, whose leg is broken?" But as he realized later, "to the folks from the old country sports always remained something utterly pagan." A good many Jewish children would always suffer from a life excessively cerebral and insufficiently physical; they would always be somewhat unnerved by the challenge of the body and fearful before the demands of sports.

By their mid-teens, if not earlier, the children of the immigrants began to shift the focus of their private lives from home to street. The family remained a powerful presence, and the young could hardly have envisaged its displacement had they not kept an unspoken sense of its strength. But in their most intimate feelings they had completed a break which in outer relations it would take several years to carry through. This was, in part, no more than the usual rupture that marks the storms of adolescence, but among the immigrant Jews it took a peculiarly sharp form, a signal for a Kulturkampf between the generations.

The immediate occasions for battle were often matters of private experience. That sex could be coped with only through stealth and secrecy, and in accordance with norms appropriated from the outer world—most East Side boys and girls simply took this for granted. Sex was not merely a pleasure to be snatched from the meagerness of days, it was the imaginative frontier of their lives, a sign of their intention to leave behind the ways of their parents. Sex might begin as an embarrassed fumbling toward the life of the senses, but it soon acquired a cultural, even an ideological aspect, becoming an essential part of the struggle to Americanize themselves. Day by day, the wish to be with one's girlfriend or boyfriend, modest enough as a human desire, brought the most exasperating problems. "On the East Side there was no privacy. Couples seized their chance to be together when they found it; they embraced in hallways, lay together on roofs. I passed them all with eyes averted."

In this tangle of relationships, the young could rarely avoid feelings of embarrassment. One's mother spoke English, if she spoke it at all, with a grating accent; one's father shuffled about in slippers and suspenders when company came, hardly as gallant in manner or as nicely groomed as he ought to be; and both mother and father knew little about those wonders of the classroom—Shakespeare, the Monroe Doctrine, quadratic equations—toward which, God knows, they were nevertheless sufficiently respectful. The sense of embarrassment derived from a half-acknowledged shame before the perceived failings of one's parents, and both embarrassment and shame mounted insofar as one began to acquire the tastes of the world. And then, still more painful, there followed a still greater shame at having felt ashamed about people whom one knew to be good.

> There never seemed any place to go. The thought of bringing my friends home was inconceivable, for I would have been as ashamed to show them to my parents as to show my parents to them. Besides, where would people sit in those cramped apartments? The worldly manner

affected by some of my friends would have stirred flames of suspicion in the eyes of my father; the sullen immigrant kindliness of my parents would have struck my friends as all too familiar; and my own self-consciousness, which in regard to my parents led me into a maze of superfluous lies and trivial deceptions, made it difficult for me to believe in a life grounded in simple good faith. . . .

So we walked the streets, never needing to tell one another why we chose this neutral setting for our escape at evening.

DELINQUENTS AND GANGS

When Alter's mother grew fearful that her son would end as a "street bum," she was not merely indulging a fantasy. All through the decades of immigration, the East Side and its replicas elsewhere in the country were harassed by outbreaks of juvenile crime and hooliganism, ranging in character from organized bands of pickpockets to young gangs half-social and half-delinquent. Crime had flourished in the Jewish immigrant quarters since the early 1880's . . . but the rise of a distinctive youth delinquency seems to have become especially troubling shortly after the turn of the century. The mounting congestion of the East Side drove more and more children into the streets, while the gradual improvement in economic conditions enabled them to acknowledge the extent of their desires.

By 1902, reported Louis Marshall, there were "upwards of 300 boys and girls of Jewish parentage" in the House of Refuge on Randall's Island, the New York Juvenile Asylum, and other municipal and non-Jewish institutions. By 1904 the children's courts, "which handle children under fifteen, are packed. Police courts are filled with boys over fifteen, second and third offenders who started at age thirteen-fourteen." The *Forward* printed discussions as to whether erring children should be driven out, as they sometimes were by enraged Orthodox fathers, or kept at home; its editors favored the latter course, "since if you let them out they will go to the dogs completely. They have aggressive natures; if they can't get to their sister's pocketbook for a few cents, they'll try to get the money by stealing. It is preferable that parents should suffer from a bad child."

In 1906 the head of the New York YMHA, Falk Younker, reported that "between 28 and 30 percent of all children brought to the children's court in New York, are Jewish. There are three and a half times as many children among this number who are the children of recently arrived immigrants as there are of native born parents. Fifteen years ago Jewish prisoners were an unknown quantity." The main reason cited by Younker was blunt enough: "home life is unbearable."

So acute had the problem become by 1902–1903 that communal figures like Louis Marshall and Jacob Schiff—once relations with government were involved, German Jews still took the lead—started to apply pressure on municipal authorities. They proposed that Jewish children under sixteen committed for misdemeanors be sent, with a subvention from the city, to a reformatory organized by the Jewish community itself. A similar arrangement was already in effect within the Protestant and Catholic communities. Mayor Seth Low vetoed the necessary bill in 1902, but Marshall was a very stubborn man and he kept badgering city officials until the bill was passed a few years later. With a $110 annual contribution per child from the city, and a building fund of several hundred thousand dollars from wealthy donors, the Jewish Protectory Movement built the Hawthorne School, a reformatory in Hawthorne, New York, and supervised probationary work in the city. It tells us something about the magnitude of this problem that the Protectory Movement had to continue its work through and beyond the First World War.

In the gap between Jewish family and gentile world, the children of the immigrants improvised a variety of social forms on the streets. At one extreme were the good and earnest boys, future reformers and professionals, who organized the Social, Educational and Improvement Club of the late 1890's, built up a treasury averaging $11.50 in any given month, and listened to talks by "Mr. Ordway on his experience in the Arctic" (it seems, the secretary archly noted, that "he received a warm reception in a cold climate") and by Mr. Mosenthal on "the theory of our government." At the other extreme were the "tough" gangs, made up of boys from six to twenty years of age, popularly known as "grifters," or pickpockets. These gangs, devoted more to thievery than violence, were sometimes so successful that they could hire furnished rooms to shelter those bolder members living away from home. Their customary hangouts were street corners, alleyways, poolrooms. Crowded streetcars and parks were favorite arenas for "grifting." A frequent strategy would be to start a fake street fight between two of the older members and then, as a crowd collected, the younger ones would go through to pick pockets.

Members of these gangs would later graduate into the ranks of Jewish criminality, such figures as Arnold Rothstein and Legs Diamond becoming masters of their craft; but in any sober light, these formed only a small, marginal group. Far more characteristic were the gangs combining an urge toward social ritual and a staking of turf with occasional forays into petty lawbreaking. Rough schools of experience, these gangs were seldom as violent as those that would later spring up in American urban life. On the East Side they gave a certain structure to the interval between childhood and independence—half-illicit, half-fraternal agencies for a passage into adult life.

GIRLS IN THE GHETTO

For girls in the immigrant Jewish neighborhoods there were special problems, additional burdens. Both American and Jewish expectations pointed in a single direction—marriage and motherhood. But the position of the Jewish woman was rendered anomalous by the fact that, somehow, the Jewish tradition enforced a combination of social inferiority and business activity. Trasported to America, this could not long survive.

In the earlier years of the migration, few Jewish women rebelled against the traditional patterns—life was too hard for such luxuries. Early union organizers repeatedly found, Lillian Wald reported, that a great obstacle to organization was "a fear of young women that it would be considered 'unladylike' and might even militate against their marriage." In the 1890's, after the Council of Jewish Women was started, with a membership drawing only slightly on immigrant women from eastern Europe, Rebecca Kohut "was sent on a series of speaking tours, and I frequently had to face hostile crowds" in Jewish neighborhoods. For "Jewish women were expected to stay at home. . . . To have opinions and to voice them was not regarded as good form even in the home."

A glimpse into the conditions under which immigrant shopgirls had to work is provided by Rose Schneiderman's sober account of her teenage years:

> So I got a place in the factory of Hein & Fox. The hours were from 8 AM to 6 PM, and we made all sorts of linings—or, rather, we stitched in the linings—golf caps, yachting caps, etc. It was piece work, and we received from 3½ cents to 10 cents a dozen, according to the different grades. By working hard we could make an average of about $5 a week. We would have made more but we had to provide our own machines, which cost us $45. . . . We paid $5 down [for them] and $1 a month after that.
>
> I learned the business in about two months, and then made as much as the others, and was consequently doing quite well when the factory burned down, destroying all our machines—150 of them. This was very hard on the girls who had paid for their machines. It was not so bad for me, as I had only paid a little of what I owed.
>
> The bosses got $500,000 insurance, so I heard, but they never gave the girls a cent to help them bear their losses. I think they might have given them $10, anyway. . . .
>
> After I had been working as a cap maker for three years it began to dawn on me that we girls needed an organization.

It made all the difference, growing up in the ghetto, whether a girl had come with her parents from Europe or had been born here. The *Forward*, with its roving sociological eye, noted that

> When a grown girl emigrates to America, she becomes either a finisher or an operator. Girls who have grown up here do not work at these "greenhorn" trades. They become salesladies or typists. A typist represents a compromise between a teacher and a finisher.
>
> Salaries for typists are very low—some work for as little as three dollars a week. . . . But typists have more *yikhes* [status] than shopgirls; it helps them get a husband; they come in contact with a more refined class of people.
>
> Typists therefore live in two different worlds: they work in a sunny, spacious office, they speak and hear only English, their superiors call them "Miss." And then they come home to dirty rooms and to parents who aren't always so courteous.

Other kinds of "refined" work were even less lucrative, department stores paying salesgirls in 1903–1904 only ten dollars a month to start with, and rarely more than five dollars a week when experienced. Librarians in those years started at three dollars a week, even though special training was required. The most desirable job for a Jewish girl, then as later, was felt to be in teaching, but this meant that she had to be supported in her schooling until she was at least eighteen or nineteen. Many families could not do that. Or, if they had to choose between keeping a son in college and sending a girl to high school, they would usually prefer the former, both for traditional and economic reasons.

Even Jewish girls who had come from Europe as children and were therefore likely to remain fixed in the progression from shopgirl to housewife found themselves inspired—or made restless—by American ideas. They came to value pleasure in the immediate moment; some were even drawn to the revolutionary thought that they had a right to an autonomous selfhood. Carving out a niche of privacy with the cluttered family apartment, they responded to the allure of style, the delicacies of manners, the promise of culture.

Hannah Chotzinoff, going out one evening to a ball at Pythagoras Hall,

> looked radiant in a pink silk shirtwaist and a long black satin skirt.
> . . . [How had] Hannah obtained her beautiful outfit? There never
> seemed to be an extra quarter around the house. . . . If the pink silk
> shirtwaist was an extravagance, Hannah took measures to preserve its
> freshness. She had tied a large white handkerchief around her waist,
> so arranged that it would protect the back of her shirtwaist from the
> perspiring right palms of her dance partners. . . . To [those who placed
> their hands above the handerchief] Hannah said politely: "Lower, please."

Girls like Hannah were close to the small group of young immigrants who tried to model themselves on the styles of the late-nineteenth-century Russian intelligentsia. Tame enough by later standards but inspired by a genuine spiritual loftiness, the style of these young immigrants might be described as a subdued romanticism, a high-minded bohemianism. One of the topics in the air during these years was

> the double standard of morality. The Russian author Chernyshevsky
> had written a novel on the subject, and the book, though not new, was
> enjoying a vogue on the East Side. . . . It posed for its heroine and, by
> extension, to all women, the question of the acceptance or rejection of
> the hitherto unchallenged promiscuity of males. . . . It was earnestly
> debated in my own house, on the sidewalks, and on the benches by
> the Rutgers Square fountains. . . . The male arguments against a single
> standard appeared to lack force, and almost always capitulated to the
> sterner moral and spiritual convictions of the opposition.

Though snatches and echoes of such debates occasionally reached them, the double standard could hardly have been a major preoccupation of most immigrant shopgirls. Their lives were too hard for anything but the immediacy of need—especially those who, because they had come to America by themselves or had lost their parents through death, were now forced to live alone in hall bedrooms and support themselves over sewing machines. Lonely, vulnerable, exhausted, these girls were the lost souls of the immigrant Jewish world, rescued, if they were "lucky," by marriage or solaced by political involvement. In the years slightly before and after 1900, the

Yiddish press carried reports of such girls taking their lives—"*genumen di gez*" ("took the gas") ran the headlines.

For the Jewish girl who had been born in America, or had come here at an age young enough so that she could learn to speak English reasonably well, there were other difficulties. Jewish boys faced the problem of how to define their lives with relation to Jewish origins and American environment, but Jewish girls faced the problem of whether they were to be allowed to define their lives at all. Feminism as a movement or ideology seems to have touched no more than a small number of Jewish girls, mostly those who had already been moved to rebellion by socialism. (The fiery socialist Rose Pastor became famous only after, or because, she married the millionaire Graham Stokes; the idea of a red Yiddish Cinderella made its claims on the popular imagination as the idea of a brilliant rebel girl could not.)

What stirred a number of young Jewish women to independence and self-assertion was not so much an explicit social ideology as their fervent relation to European culture, their eager reading of nineteenth-century Russian and English novels. One such young woman, Elizabeth Stern, recalls how her father

> had come to look with growing distrust on my longing to know things; upon my books especially. . . . He discovered me with *Oliver Twist* bulging from the covers of my prayer book where, with trembling hands, I was trying to hide it. He flung the novel on top of the book case. He told me in his intense restrained angry voice that my English books, my desire for higher education, were making me an alien to my family, and that I must give up all dreams of continuing beyond the grammar school.

An intelligent woman who wished to be just toward her own memories, Elizabeth Stern remembered that her father later spoke in "a voice of rare tenderness" when he told her that "he wished me to grow up a pride to our people, quiet, modest. . . . I was to marry; I too could be another Rachel, another Rebecca." Her father "would joyfully sacrifice himself for any of his children, that they might follow the path he believes the ideal one. He could not see that I might have ideals different from those held by him."

When the moment came to decide whether Elizabeth would continue with her studies, her father kept repeating "impossible"—though all the poor girl wanted was to be allowed to enter high school! Finally her mother intervened with a memorable remark: "Let her go for a year. We don't want her to grow up and remember that we denied her life's happiness."

So it was with many other Jewish girls. Golda Meir, growing up in an immigrant home in Milwaukee, had to run away in order to assert her independence. Anzia Yezierska (1885–1970), for a time a well-known novelist, was locked in a struggle with her father that lasted for years. Her story, quite typical in its beginnings, turned at its end into an American legend:

She arrived in New York in 1901, sixteen years old. Her first job was as a servant in an Americanized Jewish family "so successful they were ashamed to remember their mother tongue." She scrubbed floors, scoured pots, washed clothes. At the end of a month she asked for her wages, and was turned out of doors: "Not a dollar for all my work." Her second job was in a Delancey Street sweatshop kept by "an old wrinkled woman that looked like a black witch." Anzia sewed buttons from sunup to sundown. One night she rebelled against working late and was thrown out: "I want no clock-watchers in my shop," said the old witch.

Her third job was in a factory where she learned a skill and, luxury of luxuries, "the whole evening was mine." She started to study English. "I could almost think with English words in my head. I burned to do something, be something. The dead work with my hands was killing me."

She began to write stories with heroines—Hannahs and Sophies—who were clearly projections of her own yearnings. They were not really good stories, but some streak of sincerity and desperation caught the fancy of a few editors and they were published in magazines. By now, she was no longer young—a woman in her mid-thirties, trying to make up for years of wasted youth.

A first novel, *Hungry Hearts*, won some critical praise. Like all her books, it was overwrought, ungainly, yet touching in its defenselessness. No woman from the immigrant Jewish world had ever before spoken with such helpless candor about her fantasies and desires. In one of her novels, *Salome of the Tenements*, a young immigrant girl named Sonia says of herself: "I am a Russian Jewess, a flame, a longing. A soul consumed with hunger for heights beyond reach. I am the ache of unvoiced dreams, the clamor of suppressed desires." Sonia meets and marries a Yankee millionaire, the elegant Manning, and for a moment she thinks that she has won the world; but it all turns to dust, as in such novels it has to, and in the end what remains is the yearning of a Jewish girl, far more real than anything else in the book.

All the while, in the forefront of her imagination, loomed the figure of her father, a stern pietist who regarded her literary efforts with contempt. "While I was struggling, trying to write, I feared to go near him. I couldn't stand his condemnation of my lawless, godless, selfish existence." There were bitter quarrels. "He had gone on living his old life, demanding that his children follow his archaic rituals. And so I had rebelled . . . I was young. They were old."

Her first book published, Anzia confronted her father. "What is it I hear? You wrote a book about me? How could you write about someone you don't know?" Words of wrath flew back and forth, but Anzia, staring at her father in his prayer shawl and phylacteries, "was struck by the radiance that the evils of the world could not mar." He again threw up the fact that she had not married: "A woman alone, not a wife and not a mother, has no existence." They had no meeting ground but anger.

One morning a telegram was delivered to her room: ten thousand dollars for the movie rights to *Hungry Hearts!* She went to Hollywood, Yiddish accent and all; she wore expensive clothes, enjoyed the services of a secretary, met the "greats" of the movie world. But alas, not a word came out of her. The English she had worked so painfully to master ran dry.

Back home, defeated, she drifted through years of loneliness and poverty again. A few books published but little noticed: all with her fervent signature, pitiful in their transparency. At sixty-five, quite forgotten, she wrote an autobiography, *Red Ribbon on a White Horse*, summoning memories of the time when she had been a young immigrant woman locked in struggle with her father. By now she shared his view that the fame and money of her middle years had been mere delusion, and for the title of her book she chose a phrase from an old Jewish proverb: "Poverty becomes a wise man like a red ribbon on a white horse." In some groping, half-acknowledged way she had returned to the world of her fathers—a final reconciliation, of sorts.

The case of Anzia Yezierska was an extreme one, in that she had to confront, at their stiffest, the imperatives of both Jewish and American culture. Most Jewish girls of her day were neither wholly submissive nor wholly rebellious; within the bounds of the feminine role they found stratagems for cultivating their private interests and developing their private sensibilities. By 1914 a growing number of girls from East Side homes were going to high school and a small number to college; by the mid-twenties, about a generation later than the daughters of the German Jews, a good many girls from east European Jewish families had beguan attending Hunter College and, in smaller numbers, Barnard.

A check of the graduating classes at Hunter—admittedly imprecise, since it is difficult to know whether certain names are Jewish, let alone German-Jewish or east European-Jewish—confirms this trend.

Year of Graduation	Number of Graduates	Estimated Jewish Graduates	Estimated East European Jewish Graduates
1906	156	43	13
1910	186	40	25
1912	155	36	25
1913	295	85	56
1914	273	102	66
1916	245	71	58

If these figures are at all indicative, it would seem that by the years immediately before the First World War, the girls from east European Jewish families had become the majority within the graduating Jewish population at Hunter. Since there is no reason to suppose that the number of German-Jewish girls going to college declined, it would follow that at about the same time numbers of German-Jewish girls started going to private colleges like Barnard.

With eager if shy determination, the Jewish girls were redefining their lives. Elizabeth Stern, having won the battle for high school, found that she "wanted a room in which one simply sat. I had no clear idea of what I would do in it. But I had no room of my own yet. . . . Neighbors and relatives laughed in amusement at my wish." Like thousands of others, this young immigrant woman struck intuitively upon the demand that Virginia Woolf would voice in another setting: a room of one's own, a room with a view. . . .

JEWISH CHILDREN, AMERICAN SCHOOLS

For the New York school system, the pouring in of these immigrant Jews—as well as Italians, Germans, Poles, Slavs—seemed like an endless migraine. Language, curriculum, habits, manners, every department of the child's life and study had to be reconsidered. While the educational system was mostly in the hands of the Irish, there were a good number of German Jews among both administrators and teachers, and it was they, "progressive" in educational thought and eager to speed the assimilation of their east European cousins, who developed new educational strategies for the immigrants. Given the poor conditions—overcrowding in the schools, fear and suspicion among the immigrants, impatience and hostility among some teachers, and an invariably skimped budget (often worse during reform administrations than when Tammany dealt out the spoils)—a summary conclusion would be that the New York school system did rather well in helping immigrant children who wanted help, fairly well in helping those who needed help, and quite badly in helping those who resisted help.

In 1905, a peak year of immigration, the Jewish pupils on the East Side were concentrated in thirty-eight elementary schools. These contained 65,000 students, of whom some 61,000, or almost 95 percent, were Jewish. Certain schools, like P.S. 75 on Norfolk Street, were totally Jewish. That condition which a half-century later would be called *de facto* segregation did not deeply trouble the Jewish immigrants—on the contrary, they found a certain comfort in sending their children to public schools overwhelmingly Jewish. Children who knew a little English served as translators for those who a week or two earlier had stepped off the boats. In the years between, say, 1900 and 1914 there were sporadic efforts by Jewish groups to pressure the Board of Education with regard to overcrowding of schools, released time for religious training, and the teaching of foreign languages; but we have no record of major objection to the racial homogeneity of a given school or district.

"The school personnel," writes a historian of New York education,

> considered it easier to teach English to a class in which all the youngsters spoke the same foreign language. . . . Only the social workers raised questions about the ethnic homogeneity of the schools. The assimilation of the immigrant would be retarded, they feared, and the learning of English impeded when the children used their native tongue everywhere but in the classroom. . . . But even the settlement house workers concentrated their fire on the methods of Americanization they saw [in the schools]. . . . They commented angrily on the gulf the teachers were creating between the foreign born parents and their native born children. Grace Abbott, Jane Addams, and Sophinisbe Breckenridge exhorted the schools to recognize the importance of foreign cultures.

From the immigrant spokesmen there were similar complaints, often furious in the Yiddish press and stiff even in the writings of so reasonable a man as David Blaustein. "Respect for age," he noted, "is certainly not an American characterisitic, and this is an upsetting of all the immigrant's preconceived idea of society. . . . The children are imbued with the idea that all that is not American is something to be ashamed of. It is an unfortunate but indisputable fact that cheap and superficial qualities are the more likely to be assimilated."

But segregation of Jewish pupils failed to arouse any concerted protest among immigrant parents. It was a condition to which they had long been accustomed; it helped make the first years of settlement somewhat less frightening; and it also seemed, in its distinctive American form, a social springboard for plunging into the new world. The immigrants were prepared, indeed, eager, to have their children Americanized, even if with some psychic bullying, but they did not want to see themselves discarded in the process. As time went by, however, they came close to accepting even this fate as a price that had to be met.

Not without some dragging of feet—a mode of locomotion endemic to educational bodies—the Board of Education began to restructure the New York schools in order to "connect" with immigrant children. Good and even imaginative work was undertaken. Bilingualism in the schools was rejected out of hand: the authorities never saw it as a serious option, the immigrants would have been deeply suspicious of it. But an effort was made by such East Side superintendents as Gustave Straubenmuller, a specialist in teaching English to foreigners, and Julia Richman, an enthusiast for "progressive" education, to make their teachers sensitive to the special problems of Jewish pupils. One study of these problems, after listing the familiar virtues of Jewish students ("idealistic, thirst for knowledge," etc.), is candid enough to mention "other characteristics" that teachers might find disturbing: "occasional overdevelopment of mind at expense of body; keen intellectualism often leads toward impatience at slow progress; extremely radical; many years of isolation and segregation give rise to irritability and supersensitivity; little interest in physical sports; frank and openminded approach in intellectual matters, especially debatable questions."

Public school curriculums were revised to place a smaller stress on the memorizing of fixed materials (e.g., dates and names in American history) and a greater stress on what Julia Richman called "practical civics," study of the actual workings of American government and society. Schools and playgrounds were opened for afternoons, evenings, and weekends, to provide social centers for children and to lure them away from the streets. (Nothing could finally do that . . .) Emphasis was placed on manners, grooming, little courtesies, often annoying to immigrant pupils but which in later years they would be wryly grateful for. Miss Richman, ruling her school district with a stern hand, instituted a range of practical reforms, from regular eye examinations for children to the organization of parent groups.

The main problem, of course, was to teach children to read, write, and speak a new, a *second*, language. Good sense, even imaginative sympathy, is shown in a 1907 syllabus designed for special English classes for immigrant children:

> Spoken language is an imitative art—first teaching should be oral, have children speak.
> Teach children words by having them work with and describe objects.

Words should be illustrated by means of pictures, toys, etc.

Presentation of material should keep pace with the pupil's growth in power.

A bright pupil should be seated next to one less bright, one should teach the other.

In copying, the purpose is language, not penmanship.

Until 1903 immigrant children had been placed in classes together with much younger American-born children, and as the English of the immigrant pupils improved they were promoted into classes with children nearer their own age. But by 1903-1904 the Board decided, in accord with a plan developed by Straubenmuller, that this method no longer worked, since it tended to humiliate the immigrant children and slow down the American ones. Special classes were therefore set up to teach pupils of foreign parentage whose intellectual condition was in advance of their ability to express themselves in English. Pupils would remain in these special classes for a period of four or five months and then, having gained the rudiments of English, be assigned to regular classes.

Of the 250 special classes organized in 1905, 100 were held on the East Side. Most were smaller in size than normal classes, containing 30 to 35 pupils rather than the usual 45 to 50. The peak year for these special classes was 1912, when 31,000 pupils attended them: after that, the number steadily declined.*

Once immigration came to a stop with the outbreak of the First World War, these problems, though still unsolved, seemed less acute. Yet as late as 1914 a law was enacted in New York stipulating that children under sixteen who left school would have to complete at least the sixth grade—indicating, it would seem, that a good number were still failing to get through grammar school. It is chastening to note that in 1910 only some 6,000 out of 191,000 Jewish pupils in New York were attending high school. One of three pupils in New York was Jewish, but only one out of four high-school pupils was Jewish. Allowing for the probability that the proportion

---

*To deal with varying abilities of the immigrant children, a complex system of special classes was elaborated in 1905–1906. "C" classes were held for immigrant pupils between eight and fourteen years old who could speak no English. After a few months of intensive work they were either sent to regular classes or shifted to a special "E" class. The "E"classes were for pupils over the normal age who were enabled to advance rapidly through a modified course of instruction that relaxed the usual demands with regard to English. Most children in "E" classes were between eleven and fifteen. Finally, "D" classes were organized for children approaching fourteen who had no prospects of finishing the eighth grade; they were given the bare elements of literacy so they could get working papers. Over the years, the "E" classes became the most numerous and important, while "D" classes were gradually eliminated.

This system worked with a certain rough effectiveness—best, as usual, for the best students. In a little while, however, it began to decline into an informal track system, especially in schools with the least sympathetic principals: slow pupils and those for whom English formed a hopeless barrier were allowed to linger, or waste, in the "E" classes. One East Side principal, Edwin Goldwasser of P.S. 20, complained about this trend in 1912 and proposed that "E" classes be abolished; he wanted immigrant children to be either transferred quickly from special to regular classes or directed toward entering the labor force in their mid-teens.

of Jewish children under high-school age was greater than among the rest of the population, these figures still suggest that the dropout rate among Jewish children at or before the end of grammar school was not significantly better than for the remaining two thirds of the school population taken as a whole. It was better, however, than for other immigrant segments such as the Irish and Italians. A 1908 study of laggard students in the New York schools showed that no simple correlations could be established between command of English and classroom performance: children of German-born parents did better than children of American-born parents, the latter better than children of Russian-born parents, and the latter better than the children of Irish-born and Italian-born parents. The bulk of Jewish immigrant children, studies indicate, were not very different in their capacities or performances from the bulk of pupils from most other ethnic groups.

During the years between 1900 and 1914 the Board of Education published quantities of material on these matters, some of it notable for flashes of insight and sympathy in regard to immigrant children, but still more for honesty in grappling with problems of handicapped, ungifted, and recalcitrant children. Conscientious efforts were made to provide the rudiments of learning to immigrant children, within the financial constraints imposed by the city and the intellectual limits of a culture persuaded that a rigorous, even sandpapery Americanization was "good" for the newcomers. To read the reports of the school superintendents is to grow impatient with later sentimentalists who would have us suppose that all or most Jewish children burned with zeal for the life of the mind. Some did, seemingly more so than among other immigrant communities, and these comprised a layer of brilliant students who would be crucial for the future of the American Jews. What made the immigrant Jewish culture distinctive was the fierce attention and hopes it lavished upon this talented minority.

NOTES

"streets were ours": Irving Howe, unpublished memoir. "diet of kippered herring": Eddie Cantor, *My Life Is in Your Hands*, 1928, p. 21. "on one corner": Anzia Yezierska, *Red Ribbon on a White Horse*, 1950, p. 101. "boy . . . looking brown": Cantor, p. 31. "washing away our sins": Dr. Herman Welkowitz, interview, Hebrew Home for the Aged, New York, July 1970. Allen Street: Louis Waldman, *Labor Lawyer*, 1944, p. 27. Sammy Aaronson: Sammy Aaronson, *As High as My Heart*, 1957, p. 18. "I played hooky": Harry Golden, *The Right Time*, 1969, p. 49. close to being a bum: Cantor, pp. 47–62. "We'd go to play ball": Louis Green, interview, Hebrew Home for the Aged, New York, July 1970. Jewish boys competitive: Charles H. Warner, "Tendencies in East Side Boy's Clubs," *USS [University Settlement Society] Reports, 1901*, p. 43. "separation of boys and girls": Sophie Ruskay, *Horsecars and Cobblestones*, 1948, pp. 41–42. "maybe five dollars": Marie Ganz, *Rebels: Into Anarchy—and Out Again*, 1920, p. 56. Henry Klein's story: Henry Klein, *My Last Fifty Years*, 1935, p. 10.

Parents and Children

"We push our children": *For.* [*Jewish Daily Forward*], 20 January 1911. "piano in front room": *For.*, 6 July 1903. "Alter, Alter": Arthur Goldhaft, *The Golden Egg*, 1957, p. 122. East Side, no privacy: Yezierska, p. 110. "There never seemed": Irving Howe, "A Memoir of the Thirties," in *Steady Work*, 1966, p. 355.

Delinquents and Gangs

"upwards of 300 boys and girls": Louis Marshall to Nathaniel Elsberg, 25 February 1902, in American Jewish Archives, Cincinnati. children's courts: *For.*, 18 April 1904. drive children out?: *For.*, 18 April 1904. Younker quote: "Jewish Delinquent Children," *Charities*, 26 May 1906. "Mr. Ordway": minutes, Social, Educational and Improvement Club. pickpockets: Frederick King, "Influences in Street Life," *USS Reports*, 1900, p. 31. Rough schools of experience: *ibid.*

Girls in the Ghetto

"fear of young women": Lillian Wald, *The House on Henry Street*, 1915, p. 203. Council of Jewish Women: Rebecca Kohut, *His Father's House*, New Haven, 1938, p. 254. "So I got a place": Rose Scheiderman, "A Cap Maker's Story," *Independent*, 27 April 1905, p. 936. "When a grown girl": *For.*, 8 September 1905. Hannah's blouse: Samuel Chotzinoff, *A Lost Paradise*, 1955, p. 173. Chernyshevsky: *ibid.*, p. 83. One such young woman: Elizabeth Stern, *My Mother and I*, 1917, pp. 84–87. Yezierska's jobs: Anzia Yezierska, "America and I," *Scribner's*, February 1922. "I am a Russian Jewess": Anzia Yezierska, *Salome of the Tenements*, 1923, p. 65. "While I was struggling," "What is it I hear," "struck by the radiance": Anzia Yezierska, *Red Ribbon on a White Horse*, 1950, pp. 31, 93, 216. "wanted a room": Stern, pp. 99–100.

Jewish Children, American Schools

school figures, 1905: Charles Bernheimer, ed., *The Russian Jew in the United States*, Philadelphia, 1905, p. 185. Jewish groups vis-à-vis Board of Ed.: [Selma] Berrol, ["Immigrants at School, 1898–1914," dissertation, City University of New York, 1967] p. 52; *Tageblatt*, 25 September 1908. historian of New York education: Berrol, pp. 53–54. "Respect for age": David Blaustein, *Memoirs*, ed. Miriam Blaustein, 1913, p. 61. "other characteristics," Jewish students: David Snedden, *Civic Education*, Yonkers, N. Y., 1922, pp. 291–92. 1907 syllabus: Board of Superintendents, New York, *Syllabus for C Classes*, 1907. C, D, E classes: Board of Superintendents, New York, *Report*, 1912. study of laggard students, 1908: L. P. Ayers, *Laggards in Our Schools*, 1909, pp. 106–107.

Confrontation between strikers and National Guard,
Lawrence, Massachusetts, 1912

"Not Enough Pay": Lawrence, 1912

HENRY F. BEDFORD

When the textile mills of the eastern Massachusetts river towns were built in the first half of the nineteenth century, they were looked upon as models of industrial development. Totally planned economic systems, paternalistically managed, staffed with young American women, they augured a period of relatively peaceful economic expansion.

By the end of the nineteenth century, however, the mill towns were not as idyllic as they had appeared to be, at least to the proprietors. Of the variety of social changes that had affected industrial America, the coming of the new immigrants was perhaps the most widely noted. This new wave of largely unskilled settlers of diverse cultural backgrounds, combined with an increasing trend toward radicalism among labor, brought crisis after crisis to America's industrial towns and cities around the turn of the century.

Because of their high visibility and strange ways, the new immigrants seemed to present a real threat to traditional American institutions. The theory of race suicide that was propounded at this time was a manifestation of the fear that the new immigration created in the existing population. Both the basis of the fear and the reality of the threat can be appraised through an investigation of the immigration statistics covering this period.

There was a veritable tidal wave of immigrants between 1900 and 1915; nine and one-half million persons emigrated to the United States from southern and eastern Europe. That is almost equal to the total number of emigrants from the United Kingdom for the previous one hundred years. Most of the new immigrants poured into the country through the seaports of the Northeast, and most of them never left the cities of the eastern seaboard. Those who did leave tended to settle in the new and old industrial cities of the East and the Great

Lakes area. The massive concentration of immigrants in these cities gave them a greater visibility than would have occurred had they been more evenly dispersed among the general population. In spite of the vast number of immigrants during this period, however, a study carried out in the 1920s showed that 51 percent of the American people were descended from families who had lived here during colonial times. Also, further studies have demonstrated that in 1880 about 12 percent of the population was foreign-born and that, while the figure for the foreign-born rose to 15 percent at the height of the new immigration, by 1930 the percentage had receded to 12. It seems, then, that the fears of being overwhelmed by an alien horde were based more on xenophobia (fear of strangers) than on reality. As for race suicide, studies have indicated that between 1890 and 1930 the total number of children born to native whites more than doubled, while the number of children born of foreign or mixed parentage did no quite double. So "the race" did not die out but, rather, continued to dominate the country's life and institutions.

There were occasions, however, when new immigrants and labor radicals successfully combined to challenge the industrial hierarchy. Such a case occurred in Lawrence, Massachusetts, in 1912, and is the subject of the next selection, one of a series of essays on local history written by Henry F. Bedford, of Amherst College. According to Bedford's account of the 1912 textile workers' strike, the new immigrants were not so much interested in labor organizations as they were in relieving their economic distress. The International Workers of the World (IWW), perhaps America's most radical labor organization, assisted the Lawrence strikers in their campaign. But once the strike was settled the workers showed little inclination to join the union. The Wobblies (as the union members were called) were destroyed by the United States government during the First World War. Today the textile industry continues to be the most under-organized industry of the advanced industrial sector of the economy. The essay that follows gives some indication of the living conditions of the workers and the means by which the forces of society attempted to subdue the protests of textile workers.

T he looms stopped. An eerie stillness settled over the weaving room of the Everett Mill. News of the interruption reached the offices, where the staff was busy with the payroll for about 2000 employees. On an ordinary day, one man might have investigated. Thursday, January 11, 1912, was no ordinary day, and several officials, joined by an interpreter, made their way toward the weaving room. Through the interpreter, someone asked one of the weavers why she had shut down her machine. Using English instead of her usual Polish, the woman replied, "Not enough pay." She was right on two counts: her envelope contained less money than

" 'Not Enough Pay': Lawrence, 1912." From *Trouble Downtown: The Local Context of Twentieth-Century America* by Henry F. Bedford (New York: Harcourt Brace Jovanovich, 1978), pp. 9–45. © 1978 by Harcourt Brace Jovanovich, Inc. and reprinted with their permission.

she usually received, and, by most measures, even her usual wage was too low. One of the men explained that a new state law permitted women and children under eighteen to work no more than fifty-four weekly hours, two fewer than before. Surely, he went on, the weavers expected wages to fall in proportion. The woman heard him out, and repeated "Not enough pay."

The looms remained still. The managers concluded that a strike had begun and asked the idle weavers to leave the mill quietly. As they left, the weavers persuaded other workers to join them. When the mills closed on Thursday evening, a third of the looms lacked operators. On Friday morning, one in eight was in service. At noon on Saturday, the Everett Mill closed. That was only the beginning.

"AMERICA IN MICROCOSM"

"Lawrence, Massachusetts," one historian has written, "was America in microcosm" in the winter of 1912.[1] The mills that now seem dingy and brooding were new and throbbing then, symbols of the country's vigorous industrialization. The mixed accents and tongues that bubbled through tenements and factories illustrated the collision of "new" immigrants from southern and eastern Europe with northern Europeans who had arrived a generation or two earlier. In the city's suburbs and middle-class neighborhoods, concerned professional and business people worried about the potential political power of naturalized but unassimilated immigrants, about the exploitation of factory workers by corporate employers, about the social consequences of industrial and urban growth.

The strike held the nation's attention because other Americans had the same fears. The solidarity of Lawrence's ethnically diverse workers suggested the existence of social classes and the possibility of class warfare, developments that belied much national folklore. The glimpse of social and economic upheaval both enraged and terrified those with most to lose. Reformers understood, and to some extent shared, that reaction. But the strike also emphasized for them the necessity of enlightened change, the need for more tolerable working conditions and fairer wages. The apparent success of a radical labor union, which thrilled those opposed to capitalism, revealed to other Americans the weakness of ordinary labor organizations and the inadequacy of factory legislation already enacted. For a few months, Lawrence became a social laboratory, testing for a fascinated nation beliefs that had evolved in a simpler society.

Those beliefs were best expressed by people called progressives in the years before the First World War. The term "progressive" lacked precision and the "progressive movement" certainly was neither coherent nor unified. Indeed, most Americans subscribed to much of the progressive creed, which held that the American system, although fundamentally sound, could be improved through the careful effort of decent, disinterested people. Progressives tended to see most other Americans in their own image—

[1]Melvyn Dubofsky, *We Shall Be All* (New York: Quadrangle, 1974), p. 235.

as calm and reasonable citizens, more sympathetic to individualism and property rights than recent immigrants and laborers, less greedy and cynical than industrial oligarchs. It was a confident vision, sometimes condescending, but rarely arrogant or mean.

Nor was it entirely accurate. Industrialization seemed merely to alter the scale of things: factories replaced shops, cities grew from towns, proprietors became corporations, employees joined unions. But a qualitative change accompanied this change of scope. The tasks of city governments were not only greater than those of towns but were often entirely different tasks. Factories not only produced more shoes than had artisans, but converted shoemakers from craftsmen to unskilled "hands." Immigrants, who arrived in mounting numbers, differed in language, religion, tradition, and property from those who had come earlier.

Most progressives recognized the existence of social injustice, but they did not always correctly identify its causes. Often they explained social dislocation as the result of inefficiency or some local or individual "abuse," such as political corruption or monopolistic power. The most obvious evils were those closest to home—dishonest aldermen, noisome slums, high fares on streetcars. And the first line of defense was also local: better candidates, judicious pressure on landlords and employers, municipal regulation or even ownership of public services. The variety of the so-called progressive movement, and much of its vitality as well, reflected its origin in local circumstance. The smorgasbord of solutions reflected the diverse provisions of dozens of state constitutions and hundreds of municipal charters, as well as the interests of reformers themselves.

Two groups of Bay State reformers seemed rivals as often as allies. One was Yankee, patrician or middle-class, professional, Republican, Protestant, and personally tied to industry only through dividends. Cities and immigrants, as these progressives saw them, were part of the problem. The other progressive strain consisted of just the sort of people that made the first group apprehensive. City-dwellers, of Irish or more recent immigrant stock, Catholic, and often connected with labor unions and Democratic political machines, these urban liberals were developing a program that foreshadowed a half century of American reform.

Massachusetts reformers had enacted during the nineteenth century much of the legislation that engaged their counterparts elsewhere in the years before the First World War. The state's legislature established commissions to regulate railroads and public utilities, a bureau of labor statistics to permit informed industrial regulation, and incorporation laws that discouraged "trusts." Several Massachusetts communities experimented with municipal ownership of generating plants to supply power for street lights, and a few with municipal distribution of fuel and other consumer goods. The state had tried to restrict child labor as early as 1836, and subsequently provided for the inspection of factories to insure decent conditions and appropriate safety procedures. In 1874, ten hours became the legal working day for women and children; the maximum work week was reduced to fifty-eight hours, to fifty-six in 1910, and then to fifty-four, effective January 1, 1912.[2]

[2]Richard M. Abrams, *Conservatism in a Progressive Era* (Cambridge: Harvard University Press, 1964), *passim*, especially chapter 1.

Ironically, that final reduction triggered the strike in Lawrence. Before 1912, most industrial managers had adjusted wages so that fewer hours had not caused thinner pay envelopes. The action was voluntary, because most judges agreed that states could not enact a minimum wage. In 1912, Lawrence's managers refused to discuss a compensatory raise, and anxious employees concluded that there would be none. On the first payday in January, then, the Polish weaver and her companions found "not enough pay." However pleasant the two weekly hours of additional leisure, she needed the money more.

After the strike began, in response to a resolution of the United States Senate, the Commissioner of Labor sent statisticians to Lawrence to find out where the money went. The strikers claimed their weekly wage averaged between $5 and $6, but Commissioner Charles P. Neill's careful figure was $8.76–about 15¢ or 16¢ an hour. The "full-time earnings of a large number of adult employees," Neill found, "are entirely inadequate to maintain a family." People apparently subsisted on bread (about 3¢ per loaf), beets and onions (a nickel per pound), potatoes (40¢ per peck), and cheap cuts of meat ("pork neck . . . 12¢"). Stew beef, eggs, and butter were luxuries.

The commissioner's investigators found that six families in ten took in lodgers to share the average $3 weekly rent; seven occupants in a four- or five-room flat seemed the usual census. Almost all of these dwellings had running water and toilets, but Lawrence's building code did not regulate lighting, ventilation, or the structural adequacy of a building. In the wooden tenements of central Lawrence, Commissioner Neill observed, "the fire risk both to life and property is very great." Even without a fatal fire, long hours, congested living, and inadequate diet shortened lives. Textile cities, like Lawrence, had a notoriously high incidence of pneumonia and tuberculosis, and a notoriously high rate of infant mortality. The mean age at death in Lawrence was fifteen.[3]

At fifteen, many of Lawrence's residents had been at work for a year, and some for more than that. The state required attendance at school to age fourteen, a well-meant provision that both parents and employers too often had an interest in evading. Family income was so low that the few dollars a child earned could make the difference between eating and hunger. An inquiring congressman asked a boy in 1912 whether he regretted his departure from school at the fourth grade and whether he wished the state had required him to attend until he was sixteen. Sure, the lad replied, and he continued with a question of his own: "but what would we eat?" At fifteen, his wages exceeded his father's; he was the oldest child and there were six others at home.[4]

Like most of Lawrence's inhabitants, the boy was the child of immigrants. Indeed most of the people in Massachusetts were either immigrants

[3]The report of the Commissioner of Labor was published as U. S., Congress, Senate, *Report on Strike of Textile Workers in Lawrence, Mass. in 1912*, 62nd Cong., 2d sess., 1912, Senate Document 870. The references in these paragraphs may be found at pages 20, 486, and 27. See also Donald B. Cole, *Immigrant City* (Chapel Hill: University of North Carolina Press, 1963), p.212.

[4]U. S., Congress, House, Committee on Rules, *The strike at Lawrence, Mass., Hearings Before the Committee on Rules . . . 1912*, 62nd Cong., 2d sess., 1912, House Document 671, p. 153.

or the children of immigrants, though the foreign element in Lawrence was unusually large and diverse. Only 14 percent of the city's 85,000 inhabitants were native-born of native parents; almost half had been born abroad: nearly 8000 in Canada, most of whom spoke French as their native tongue; about 6500 in Italy; 6000 in Ireland; more than 4000 in parts of the Russian Empire, including Poland; and about 2000, called Syrians in Lawrence, who had been born in the Turkish Empire.[5]

THE FIRST DAYS

Formal delegations of employees ordinarily met a frosty reception in the offices of the Lawrence mills. Lest courtesy be mistaken for recognition of a labor organization, management routinely refused to answer questions from groups with any resemblance to a union. Late in 1911, when workers tried to discover how the fifty-four-hour law would be implemented, local managers turned them aside or referred them to corporate headquarters in Boston, whence no answer was forthcoming either. Lawrence officials reassured an executive from Boston, who asked whether a proportional reduction in wages would cause trouble. "At worst," they reported, a strike would "probably be confined . . . in a single mill."

Management, Commissioner Neill observed later, had lost touch with the people on the payroll. Posting the new law in the mills, as the law itself required, hardly constituted informing the employees and might be deliberately evasive, since Polish- and Italian-speaking workers could not reasonably be expected to understand legal English. Answering the questions of representative employees could not, Neill thought, imply official recognition of a union; corporate refusal to talk with employees was a lame excuse for arrogance.[6]

William Madison Wood—behind his back people called him "Billy"—certainly thought he knew his employees. To be sure, he was the president of the American Woolen Company, the largest corporation in the business; as much as anyone, he was responsible for the mergers that built the hundred-million-dollar trust that owned the most important mills in Lawrence and employed several thousand people there. The orphaned son of a Portuguese sea cook, Wood himself had started in a New Bedford textile mill when he was eleven. He worked hard, attracted the paternal interest of his employer, and moved up, and eventually on, to Lawrence where he married the boss's daughter. Wood always maintained that the interests of capital and labor coincided, and not even radicals doubted his sincerity. He believed he deserved the confidence of his employees, that he knew what was best for them. The workers would soon realize, he remarked at the outset of the strike in 1912, that "justice [was] not on their side," and that their action was "hasty and ill-advised." He was, Wood said, as much a corporate employee as they were.

---

[5]Cole, *Immigrant City*, p. 209.
[6]Senate Document 870, pp. 10–11.

... I am bound ... to take proper care of the interests of 13,000 stockholders [and] ... of some 25,000 employees. It is my duty to see that each side has a square deal. ... I have consulted long and anxiously with the directors. ... Reluctantly and regretfully we have come to the conclusion that it is impossible ... to grant any increase in wages. ... I ask you to have confidence in this statement and to return to your work. ... [F]our times this company has increased your wages without your asking. ... This proves that I have looked after your interests pretty well in the past. Why should I not have your confidence for the future?[7]

There was, Joe Ettor thought, an answer to that question in the first sentence of the basic document of the Industrial Workers of the World (IWW): "The working class and the employing class have nothing in common." Like William Wood, Joe Ettor was the son of a working man; like Wood, Ettor had started early to make his own way. He drifted from Brooklyn to Chicago to San Francisco, where he learned a skilled trade, survived the 1906 earthquake, and watched the great fire with his friend the proletarian novelist Jack London. At seventeen Ettor sent his nickel to Socialist party headquarters to purchase a red button; in 1907, at twenty-two, he was in the logging camps of Oregon enrolling lumberjacks in the IWW. Soon he had a hand in the IWW's efforts to organize workers in steel mills, shoe shops, and mining camps.

Joe Ettor could deliver the union's simple message in English, Italian, Polish, Yiddish, and broken Hungarian. He told his audiences that one industrial union of skilled and unskilled, male and female, immigrant and native, was the only effective force against the united bosses. He called industrial sabotage a legitimate weapon in that no-holds-barred struggle. He damned private property as legal theft and the government as the agent of the exploiting class. Not for Joe Ettor the moderate's search for harmonious compromise; he had chosen the workers' side. The workers in Lawrence never thought of him as the outsider Wood tried to paint him when Ettor arrived in January 1912.

Organizing industrial workers was difficult because they had little bargaining power. The nation's major labor union, the American Federation of Labor (AFL), concentrated on craftsmen whose skills gave them an economic leverage that textile workers, for instance, lacked because unskilled labor abounded. Still, the AFL chartered a textile affiliate, the United Textile Workers (UTWU), and spent money, energy, and prestige in a futile drive in Lawrence, where in 1912 fewer than one in ten textile workers belonged to any labor organization. John Golden, president of the UTWU, attributed his union's failure to the presence of "these new people, unacquainted with our ways, unable to speak our language," who were willing to work for wages that would have outraged "English-speaking people. ..." He told the congressional committee investigating the strike that "the Federal Government should seriously consider the restricting of immigration," an ironic stance for one who had himself immigrated about twenty

---

[7]*Ibid.*, p. 40, see also John B. McPherson, *The Lawrence Strike of 1912* (Boston: The Rockwell and Churchill Press, 1912), p. 15.

years earlier. The workers in Lawrence displayed their own sense of irony in a booklet entitled *What John Golden Has Done for the Textile Workers;* bound inside the impressive cover were several eloquent blank pages.[8]

Even without a union, the strike quickly spread beyond the Everett Mill. Payday elsewhere in the city was Friday, January 12, and most employees expected less money than usual and more trouble. The worried paymaster at the Washington Mill delayed his rounds when he heard that knots of workers were collecting, talking instead of working. When disorder began, he suggested that Frank Sherman at the Wood Mill ought to secure the doors. Sherman moved too slowly. "Within three minutes," he said later, "I heard the most ungodly yelling and howling and blowing of horns I ever heard. . . ." The paymaster, "scared white," reported that the mob had come through the doors and overpowered the watchman. Sherman told the paymaster to lock up the cash and let the crowd run its course until the police came. As they had done in the Washington Mill, strikers shut down machinery, by throwing the switch, by slashing the belt, or simply by pulling the operator into the throng that rushed on. Untended machines ruined some unfinished fabric, and the unruly crowds knocked over stacks of finished goods. Sherman waited until the wave subsided; it lasted about thirty minutes.[9]

Sherman's tactics foreshadowed management's approach to the strike: lock up the money, let the first spontaneous energy dissipate, send for the police, and distribute thin pay envelopes. While employers sat tight, disgruntled employees sought a method of converting the demonstration to a strike. A few members of the IWW—in more or less good standing—sent for Joe Ettor, who arrived on Saturday and used the weekend to devise an organizational structure that raised money, sustained morale, and kept the strikers united and the community on edge for almost two months. Ettor used the threat of violence, and the city's fear of it, to counter management's strategy of delay. He could not prevent every thrown rock and fist, but even an unfriendly observer noted that Ettor controlled the strikers "as completely as any general ever controlled his disciplined troops."[10]

Ettor's device was a strike committee organized by ethnic group, rather than by craft as the AFL would have done, or by mill or employer, a pattern the owners preferred. Each group elected three representatives, who typically assembled in the morning to receive reports ("The Syrians are standing firm"; "there are a few scabs among the Jews.") and to discuss plans. The representatives returned to their neighborhoods later in the day to carry instructions and to encourage the faint-hearted. Ettor presided, but the committee was not an arm of the IWW. It was the strike, not the union, that was important.

On Sunday, the newly formed committee agreed on a set of demands. Fifty-six-hours' pay for fifty-four-hours' work was no longer enough. The strikers asked an immediate 15 percent increase in wages and double pay

---

[8]House Document 671, p. 81; see also Henry F. Bedford, *The Socialists and the Workers in Massachusetts, 1886–1912* (Amherst: University of Massachusetts Press, 1966), p. 248.

[9]House Document 671, pp. 439–40.

[10]McPherson, *Lawrence Strike,* p. 9.

for overtime. In addition, they demanded abolition of the "premium system," a schedule of monthly bonuses employers used to speed up production. To protect their jobs, strikers wanted management's promise not to discharge anyone because of activity during the strike. Significantly, they did not insist on recognition of their union. The committee encouraged workers to gather at the gates of the mills on Monday morning to persuade (or intimidate) those who might want to return to work.

That was the sort of activity Mayor John Scanlon intended to prevent. He called the city's commissioners into session at 5:45 on Saturday morning to provide more policemen for the emergency. He warned strikers against violence, asked that they not congregate in the streets, and suggested that they start negotiations with management promptly. He probably could not have done more. Mayor Scanlon had taken office only two weeks before under a new city charter that replaced politicians with commissioners. The new officials were supposed to be experts, capable of providing services more efficiently and less expensively than corruptible politicians. Progressives around the country advocated the city commission form of government partly to avoid the ethnic politics to which Lawrence was especially susceptible. But ethnic representatives, as Joe Ettor recognized, at least had standing in their neighborhoods, which "experts" sometimes lacked. And the experts in Lawrence, like the politicians they succeeded, all seemed to be Irish anyhow.

Mayor Scanlon took another step on Sunday with an order that sent one company of militia to the armory. He asked for two more on Monday morning, when police met pickets on the bridges leading to the mills. The crowd surged up the bridges, and harried officials turned on the fire hoses. Strikers parried with hunks of ice, coal, and other handy trash. Panic mounted inside the mills as windows smashed. About thirty strikers braved the barricades and the water and attempted to shut down the mill. Soldiers and police reinforcements arrived, scattered the crowd, and arrested thirty-six strikers. The city's courts acted promptly: within hours of their arrest, twenty-four rioters had been sentenced to a year in jail, and those carrying weapons received two years.

The mayor's attempt to promote negotiations foundered when management refused to meet with mediators. The strike committee did assemble and outlined the demands strikers had approved the day before. But, William Wood said, employers had no counterproposals for workers who destroyed property and were "in no frame of mind to discuss conditions." The city's responsibility, Wood continued, was not to find a compromise, but to end "mob rule." Mayor Scanlon had already sent for more soldiers.[11]

Scanlon's request went to Governor Eugene Foss, whose preelection record had contained little to cheer advocates of industrial reform. Foss himself owned textile mills; his success as a businessman plus his ability to contribute heavily to Democratic campaigns combined to bring him a slightly tainted nomination for governor in 1910. He won the election, reelection twice, and promised to run the state "along well established business lines."

[11]*New York Call*, January 16, 1912; Senate Document 870, pp. 37–38, 60.

Yet once in office Foss was not the stereotypical probusiness executive. Instead he compiled a progressive record of the urban liberal stripe. Although he vetoed bills that permitted picketing, he signed other labor legislation, including the fifty-four-hour law, which he did not like, and a first attempt to establish workman's compensation. He approved statutes that regulated railroad rates, monopolistic prices, and tenement housing. It was sober legislation, offering more to organized labor than unions had had before, and annoying "the interests" without undermining them. The Foss administration, in short, encouraged a somewhat more democratic and humane society, but did not fundamentally challenge the existing social order.[12]

The governor sent troops to Lawrence, and his secretary, Dudley Holman, as well. Foss wanted a first-hand report and, if possible, a resolution of the strike before events slipped out of control. Holman met late Monday night with Mayor Scanlon, police officials, and Colonel Leroy Sweetser, the officer in charge of the militia. Early the next morning, Holman prowled the mill district looking for Ettor, whose office seemed to be in the streets. Accompanied at first by Ettor's self-appointed bodyguards, who feared he might be arrested, the two men walked and talked in the subzero dawn. Holman reported the governor's hope that the state board of arbitration might be helpful. Ettor did not like the idea, but presented it to the strike committee, where a majority overruled him. Holman telephoned Foss to convey the strikers' willingness to take their case to the state agency.

The meeting never took place. The strikers sent the delegation they had promised. The state board of arbitration appeared. But several employers, including American Woolen, refused to send representatives. Consequently, Holman said, "the thing fell through." A committee of the Massachusetts legislature subsequently held an equally barren session in Lawrence. Two weeks later, Foss himself sought a way out of the impasse. He asked the workers to return to the mills for thirty days, and he asked the employers to keep weekly wages at the fifty-six-hour level. A month, Foss thought, should suffice for him to find a solution. He pledged his "best efforts" and expected "a settlement satisfactory to all parties." Nobody answered his letter.[13]

VICTORY!

The strike in Lawrence began about six weeks after James McNamara had ended a sensational trial by pleading guilty to blowing up the headquarters of the *Los Angeles Times* in the course of labor warfare in southern California. For some time after that explosion, any American labor dispute inspired rumors of dynamite. Stories flashed through Lawrence and surfaced in the press—prematurely in one instance when a Boston newspaper described a cache police located about the time the headline appeared.

[12]Abrams, *Conservatism in a Progressive Era*, pp. 251–61.
[13]House Document 671, 347–48, 350; Senate Document 870, p. 44.

Checking reports of three other bombs, Lawrence police raided a tenement in the Syrian district, where they found some explosives and arrested seven residents. More dynamite turned up in the cobbler shop in the Italian district Joe Ettor used as an address; the cobbler was arrested. But the police had trouble with the third batch they had heard about, which was supposed to be somewhere near the cemetery.

Who knew more about Lawrence's cemeteries than John Breen, the genial undertaker who had first told the police about the dynamite? Breen drew a map for the officers, who returned to the cemetery and found what they were looking for. It seemed a little strange that the explosives were wrapped in an undertaker's trade journal; it seemed even more strange when the police discovered that only Breen, of all the city's undertakers, did not have that issue. The judge at the local police court, who without hesitation had sentenced "rioters" to a year, threw out the cases against the Syrians and the cobbler. Persons "interested in maintaining a reign of terror in this city," said Judge J. J. Mahoney, not the immigrant defendants in his courtroom, had planted the dynamite.

As a matter of fact—and of increasingly common knowledge—John Breen had. A local contractor, showing the effect of too much drink and perhaps of a troubled conscience as well, blurted to the prosecuting attorney that William Wood had had his hands on the dynamite. Or at least that was the story the prosecutor told to a grand jury. But the contractor sobered up and killed himself, and the indictment of Wood did not stick. Breen was convicted, fined, and recalled from the school committee, which was supposed to have been the first step toward succeeding his father as the city's Irish political boss.

The bungled dynamite plot was only one indication of rising tension as the days became weeks and neither side flinched. The strike committee improved its organization by adding alternates and designating substitutes to take over if leaders were arrested. A major effort to raise funds among radicals and labor groups brought in nearly $1000 each day to provide soup kitchens and living allowances for strikers and their families. Ettor designed new tactics to make picketing more effective and to harass the inexperienced militiamen. Parading pickets carried the American flag, taunted the soldiers to salute it, and then pushed through the formation that was supposed to be a barrier, shouting, "The American flag can go anywhere." Women—pregnant women if possible—marched in the first ranks of the strikers' demonstrations in order to make security forces think twice about nightsticks and bayonets. Other women, when arrested, refused to post bond or otherwise to expedite trial, and then nursed and cared for their children while in jail. When authorities forbade pickets to stop and talk with employees willing to return to work, Ettor marshaled 10,000 strikers who moved continuously through the mill district, thereby complying with the order and defeating its purpose. Pickets linked arms and swept singing through the streets four- or five-abreast. When police or militia disrupted the columns, large groups, still singing and still with linked arms, moved from the streets to the stores. Nervous customers departed and nervous merchants protested. A congressman subsequently asked the acting chief of police why he had not arrested the leaders of these demonstrations. "There are no leaders in the streets," the bewildered chief replied.[14]

Monday, January 29, started badly when strikers stopped streetcars in order to keep passengers from reaching the mills. By seven in the morning, derailed cars, broken windows, and bruised patrons persuaded managers of the street railway company to shut the line down. The crowd, its anger momentarily dampened, flowed off singing radical songs. Several thousand jeering strikers paused in front of the residence of a priest who had urged his flock to return to work. People loudly discussed demolition of church and rectory, and then the throng moved along. When the bayonets of militiamen blocked further progress, Ettor tactfully diverted the demonstrators up a side street to avoid confrontation, for the mood of the city became increasingly ugly as the day wore on.

That afternoon strikers and police clashed in one of the residential neighborhoods. The jostling ended in shots, and a young striker named Annie LoPezzi died on the sidewalk. Strikers claimed a police officer fired the fatal shot; the police alleged that someone shooting at an officer had accidentally killed a bystander instead. Joe Ettor and Arturo Giovannitti, the radical editor and poet who had accompanied Ettor to Lawrence, were arrested the following day, charged with having incited an unknown killer. Both men had been in other parts of the city when the shooting took place, but they were denied bail and remained in prison for the next ten months.[15] The strike committee added a new demand to the list: Ettor and Giovannitti must be released.

Murder inspired a formal resolution from the city council asking the militia to restore order. Governor Foss raised the available force to 1300 men by sending twelve additional companies of infantry and two troops of cavalry to Lawrence. Colonel Sweetser forbade meetings, parades, picketing, and intimidation, and stationed his troops all over the city. The next day, a detachment responded to a report that a parade was forming in the Syrian section. Troops moved to disperse the band. John Ramy, a young musician, did not move quickly enough and died of a bayonet wound in the back. There was a perfunctory investigation that disclosed no names. A congressman later remarked sarcastically that he had missed in the account of Lawrence's chief of police "what sort of deadly weapon the boy had in his hand at the time he was killed." "I did not say he had a deadly weapon," the chief replied; "I said he had a musical instrument."[16]

Colonel Sweetser had made his point. The strikers stayed at home. So did many of those whom the strikers had been intimidating. Unions representing skilled workers decided they were on strike too. In the second month of the strike the number of employees actually present in the mills dipped to its lowest point. A reporter visited the Washington Mill, where the machinery hummed. But, he noted, "not a single operative was at

[14]House Document 671, pp. 261ff, 292, 302; Philip S. Foner, *The Industrial Workers of the World* (New York: International Publishing Co., 1965), pp. 321–22.

[15]House Document 671, pp. 290–94; McPherson, *Lawrence Strike*, pp. 26–27; *New York Call*, January 29, 30, 1912.

[16]House Document 671, p. 296; Foner, *IWW*, p. 331; Senate Document 870, pp. 44–45.

work and not a single machine carried a spool of yarn."[17] His visit verified Big Bill Haywood's remark that "You can't weave cloth with bayonets."

Members of the IWW were often called "wobblies" and one-eyed William D. (Big Bill) Haywood had a national reputation as the wildest "wobbly" of them all. His foes, and some of his radical comrades, exaggerated Haywood's penchant for violence, but he was indeed a charismatic man with a genuine outrage about the exploitation of industrial workers and a demonstrated ability to inspire them. After Ettor's arrest, Haywood replaced him on the strike committee and assumed much of the responsibility for directing the strike. Together with Elizabeth Gurley Flynn, the twenty-two-year-old "red flame," and others of the union's hierarchy, he whipped up the spirit of workers on the scene and raised money outside the city for their support.

An Italian immigrant at a meeting in New York City did not have much money. But his family, he said, would welcome a child or two from a striker's family. Although one or two more mouths at his table would not make much difference, the absence of hungry babies might stiffen the resistance of wavering workers in Lawrence. That was how workers in the old country helped one another. Haywood and the strike committee liked the idea. *The Call*, a socialist daily in New York, made an appeal on behalf of "the little children of Lawrence," and volunteers appeared from all over the city.[18]

Other radicals in other places wanted their share of the heroic "little children." Emotional departures from the train station in Lawrence triggered one set of news releases, greetings at host cities another. Physicians examined the children and gave out statements about rickets and malnutrition. Observers remarked the shabby clothing children wore and the paradoxical fact that those who wove woolen cloth could not afford to wear it. Margaret Sanger, an idealistic young nurse whose experience in public health would make her the nation's foremost proponent of birth control, testified that only 4 of the 119 children she examined wore underwear.[19]

As the children moved out, the money rolled in, and the strike dragged on. The Lawrence city fathers, proud of their city, thought it deserved better than the publicity the "little children" generated, and decided to keep them at home. Colonel Sweetser informed the strike committee that he would not "permit the shipping off of little children . . . unless I am satisfied that this is done with the consent of their parents."[20]

Within a few days, the strike committee announced that 150 children would, with the consent of their parents, accept invitations to visit Philadelphia for the duration of the strike. On the day of departure, almost two months after the walkout began, early arrivals at the depot noticed a company of militia parading in the street outside. Inside, an inordinate number of policemen fanned out through the station, clearing out loiterers

[17]*New York Times*, February 1, 1912.
[18]*New York Call*, February 8–11, 1912.
[19]*Ibid.*, February 12, 1912; House Document 671, pp. 232–33.
[20]Senate Document 870, p. 51.

and then assembling in two parallel ranks leading toward a door. Outside the door, the chief had parked an open truck he had borrowed from the militia. He approached the children, who had clustered in the waiting room, and told them of the city's readiness to supply charitable relief: "[I]f any of you make a . . . request for aid or assistance you will receive it." Only about 40 children, and fewer adults, had withstood the intimidating show of force, and they were not deterred by the chief's kind words. They declined to argue, waited for the train, and moved to board it when it was announced. The police diverted them to the truck, and thence to jail.

But not without an uproar. The radical press described beatings, blood, miscarriages, and weeping, bruised children in cells. The rhetoric was borrowed from Russian uprisings—Cossacks, tyranny, pogroms. Even Samuel Gompers, the president of the AFL and no supporter of the tactics of the IWW, grumbled that nobody would have detained the sons and daughters of millionaires. Judge Ben Lindsay, a reformer from Denver known as "the children's judge," noted that "those children will probably not miss the Constitution—they have missed so much else." The Attorney General of the United States said the authorities had made "a stupid blunder." Months later, the police chief was still bewildered. He had not seen any violence, he said; he was just enforcing the statue that prohibited parental neglect of children.[21]

One of the congressmen investigating the strike was delighted at last to have a statute to discuss. He tried to pin down the chief's superior, Lawrence's Commissioner of Public Safety: "Under what law of the State of Massachusetts were you acting in the matter?" The commissioner did not know "offhand." The congressman kept at it: "Did you know what the law was at the time?" The commissioner said somebody had looked it up. The congressman tried once more: Was there any applicable statute, he asked. "I think there is," was the best the commissioner could do. "Did you read that law?" the congressman inquired. "I did not read it; no sir," the commissioner replied. "I think not," the exasperated congressman remarked, and turned to another topic.[22]

Mill officials knew immediately that the scene at the station disgraced the one-sided law enforcement upon which they relied. They authorized a defensive statement denying responsibility for the city's effort to detain the children. "The manufacturers did not ask for this [action]; they were not consulted about it; they were not informed of the contemplated action of the local authorities."[23] The owners knew they were in trouble; the struggle could no longer be kept in Lawrence where they had a chance to control it. The Senate would soon send Commissioner Neill's investigators to Lawrence; the Committee on Rules of the House of Representatives convened hearings on the strike. Congressional criticism of the industry's labor practices might undermine support for the textile schedules of the protective tariff.

And by the end of February, Governor Foss had had enough too. His disclaimer about events at the station echoed that of the mill owners: local

[21]*New York Call*, February 25, 29, 1912; House Document 671, pp. 303–09.
[22]House Document 671, p. 281.
[23]McPherson, *Lawrence Strike*, pp. 37–38; *New York Call*, February 29, 1912.

authorities controlled the police; he had not been consulted; the militia was not involved. Indeed, Foss wrote the owners, it was time to send the militia home; he did not propose to have the military forces of Massachusetts used to break the strike. Both the governor and the owners knew that the militia's departure would leave discredited police officials responsible for law and order. Foss asked the state's attorney general to look into the incident at the depot to see whether any citizen's constitutional rights had been abridged. Foss then let the pressure build with the word that he was "disappointed" that management had not tried more diligently to settle the strike.[24]

In fact management had begun to seek a settlement, less because of political pressure than because of a flood of orders. On March 1, Wood met a delegation from the strike committee. American Woolen would raise wages 5 percent, he said, and similar notices appeared in the other mills. The strikers thought Wood's offer too little, too late, and too vague. Within a week, the delegation had another invitation. It would take time, Wood said, to spell out the new rates for each employee. The strikers replied that they could wait until the lists were prepared, even though some of the skilled employees had already accepted Wood's terms. On March 9, Wood clarified his offer another time, with a schedule that showed a raise up to 11 percent. The strikers waited again. Three days later, Wood gave in: the raise for the most poorly paid workers was more than 20 percent, and no one received less than 5; an additional 25 percent would be paid for overtime. Premiums would be calculated every two weeks instead of once a month. No worker would be penalized for participation in the strike. The strikers met on the Lawrence Common, cheered, sang, and accepted.[25]

One troubling loose end remained: Ettor and Giovannitti were still in jail. The employers promised to use their influence to achieve the prisoners' release, but Essex County's legal staff stubbornly did its duty. Spring became summer, and summer turned to fall. Haywood and Flynn went on to other struggles in other cities, where they occasionally took up a collection to help pay their comrades' legal expenses. Roland Sawyer, a socially conscious minister from Ware and the Socialist's party's candidate for governor against Eugene Foss, subordinated his political campaign to an effort to reach the jurors who might judge Ettor and Giovannitti. Sawyer made a batch of slides from his photographs of the strike, prepared a set of resolutions, and wrote an all-purpose speech, which he gave wherever he could find an audience.

Joe Ettor knew who his friends were. He sent Sawyer a warm note, thanking him for his public effort and private encouragement. Tell everybody for me, Ettor wrote, that "I am putting my time to good use reading and studying," that I "am enjoying my usual good health," that I "am not discouraged. [but] buoyant as ever." He was, Ettor claimed, guilty only of his "loyalty to the working class." If he were convicted, "and if the reward be death," he wrote, "I will part with life with a song on my lips."[26]

[24]*New York Call*, February 9. 1912; Foner, *IWW*, p. 341.
[25]Senate Document 870, pp. 54–59.
[26]Joe Ettor to Roland D. Sawyer, June 1912, ms in possession of author.

There was no need for that. The jury acquitted Ettor and Giovannitti and ended their months of imprisonment. The verdict came at Thanksgiving time, and there was indeed much to be thankful for. Textile workers elsewhere in New England received wage increases comparable to those in Lawrence, often without more than mentioning a strike. New windows and new belts made the mills as good as new, and the confidence of employers returned when membership in the IWW shrank as quickly as once it had grown. Civic boosters mounted a parade for "God and Country" to dramatize the transcience of radicalism and the permanence of conventional values, and to restore the city's morale and public reputation.

Anxiety about Lawrence's reputation stemmed from intense national interest in the strike. Social workers, labor leaders, journalists, politicians, and miscellaneous tourists swarmed to the city to see events at first-hand. Senator Miles Poindexter of Washington, barred by police from interviewing those arrested at the railway station, told reporters the city was a "concentration camp." William Allen White, whose Emporia, Kansas, newspaper had a national circulation, remarked that the immigrant strikers possessed a "clearer vision of what America stands for than did many of those who sneered at them."[27] When Congressman Victor Berger, a Socialist from Milwaukee, introduced a resolution authorizing a congressional investigation, he submitted a sheaf of supportive petitions. They came from labor organizations in Mattoon, Illinois, and Moundsville, West Virginia; from Bellingham, Washington, and Bellefontaine, Ohio; from the city council of Thief River Falls, Minnesota, and the Socialists of Jersey City; from reformers in Spokane, Washington, and Washington, D. C.[28]

The strike caught the nation's attention because it offered a glimpse of what might be the future—a sobering preview for progressive, middle-class Americans, a shocking one for conservatives, and an exhilarating one for radicals and factory workers. To be sure, Lawrence was a unique community, and conditions there did not obtain in every other industrial center. But conditions might rapidly change: if immigration were not restricted, if wealth were not more equitably distributed, if unions and bosses were not restrained—if somebody, in short, did not do something—any place might become a Lawrence in the none-too-distant future.

That was no pleasant prospect—for progressives, in many ways, least pleasant of all. Through reform, they had intended to enable Americans to avoid precisely the sort of class confrontation that had manifestly occurred in Lawrence. Progressives hoped to convince employers that justice and self-interest alike demanded decent wages and working conditions. And progressives believed that those concessions, whether coerced by legislation or freely offered by enlightened businessmen, ought to persuade employees that the American system worked. Progressives advocated reform because they believed the nation's institutions were fundamentally fair. The strike in Lawrence suggested that reformers might have to choose between their acceptance of social stability and their sympathy for the victims of social injustice.

---

[27]*New York Call*, February 27, March 1, 1912.
[28]House Document 671, pp. 11–23.

Walter Weyl, a journalist and student of labor disputes, continued to postpone the choice. As he surveyed the strike for *The Outlook*, a progressive weekly that carried Theodore Roosevelt's name on the masthead, Weyl favored both the strikers and the militia—well-behaved lads, Weyl thought, who ought to have been playing ball. He condemned radical labor leaders, particularly Ettor and Haywood, and also "ruthless, immoral, ill-advised" employers for creating an explosive situation: "If out of this caldron of disillusion there should come a quick, hot flame of violence, it must be promptly extinguished. *Neither may we allow men, however wealthy or respectable, to scatter explosives on the ground.*"[29]

In condemning impartially all parties to an industrial dispute, progressives often unconsciously paraded their own purity of motive. The "best citizens" of Lawrence—"judges, ministers, . . . bankers, shopkeepers, and workingmen of character and reputation," *The Outlook* reported—had begun a disinterested search for compromise. These people, "who are viewed with confidence by all classes," the editorial continued, should urge "operators to return to work at once."[30] And that, presumably, would be that. In the public interest, workers and owners alike ought to defer to middle-class citizens. The proposition was not necessarily wrong, but it had no connection with the behavior of real people in Lawrence, Massachusetts, or much of anywhere else.

Yet the people who faced Eugene Foss were real enough, as were those during other industrial disputes who visited other progressive mayors, governors, and Presidents. In difficult circumstances, Foss struck a progressive balance with more skill than contemporaries saw: he sent troops to restore order and prepared to withdraw them when their presence enhanced unduly the bargaining power of the mill owners. In other circumstances, other progressive politicians had to find a similar balance between order and justice, between the rights of employees and those of employers, between the need for governmental regulation and the tradition of individual liberty, between the protection of existing interests and the preservation of opportunity in the future.

That balance became increasingly elusive in the years before the First World War, and the optimistic faith of progressives increasingly difficult to sustain. In Lawrence, employers showed no shame about their unawakened social consciences, and employees spurned progressive remedies in favor of unions and radicalism and solutions they designed themselves. Even progressive legislation, administered by progressive executives, had unpredictable, and sometimes unprogressive, results. Had the fifty-four-hour law improved life in Lawrence? If the commissioners enacted a new building code, would mill workers be able to secure better housing? If William Wood were converted to welfare capitalism, would the stockholders of American Woolen indulge him? Did it all come down to restricting immigration, as labor leaders and patricians alike suggested, or to Prohibition, which became the crusade of Governor Foss? Was that the best the nation could do in the face of manifest injustice in Lawrence?

---

[29]The italics are Weyl's; the reference is not literally to dynamite, but to social explosives.
   Walter Weyl, "The Strikers at Lawrence," in *Outlook*, February 10, 1912, pp. 309, 312.
[30]*The Outlook*, February 17, 1912, pp. 352, 353, 358.

Walter Weyle kept coming back to a meeting in Mayor Scanlon's office. The visiting state legislators were seeking a middle ground and trying to impress the strikers with their good intentions and good will. Finally one of the strikers asked the legislators just how far they would go:

> If you find one party wrong, can your state force it to do right? . . .
> Would you arbitrate a question of life and death, and are the worst
> wages paid in these mills anything short of death? Do you investigate
> because conditions are bad, or because the workers broke loose and
> struck? Why did you not come before the strike? What can your state
> of Massachusetts do to make wrong right for the workingmen who are
> the bulk of your citizens?

That last one was the central question, Weyl thought. "What can the state do? What can we do to make wrong right for the people of our mills and factories?"[31] That was the question the strike had posed. And the nation had, as yet, no certain answer.

[31]Weyl, pp. 311–312

John Scopes being sentenced in Dayton, Tennessee, 1925

Religion, Politics, and the Scopes Trial

RAY GINGER

The history of religion in America has often been viewed as the intellectual and institutional history of the mainstream Protestant churches. The changing patterns of theology, from Calvinistic Puritanism with its harsh doctrines of original sin and unconditional election, through the more "democratic" Arminianism, which offered freedom of choice, to the liberal theology of twentieth-century Protestantism, with its emphasis on social action and forgiveness, the stress has been on viewing institutional religion from the top down. The actual beliefs and practices of religious Americans have usually been left to sociologists and anthropologists.

Although the Puritan tradition looms large in the literature of American religion, evangelical Protestantism has been the dominant style of religious life in the United States since the early nineteenth century. From its spiritual beginnings in the Great Awakening of the eighteenth century, with its emphasis on individual consciousness of sin and salvation, the institutional basis for evangelicalism developed in the Great Revival of the early 1800s. The Camp Meeting movement and the growth of Methodist and Baptist churches with their anti-hierarchical bias led to the domination of American religious life by evangelicalism.

Among the many differences between this new movement and the traditional churches is the former's stress on the individual conversion experience. With certain exceptions, this stress on individualism has caused evangelicalism to resist the emphasis of some religious people on social reform and has led the movement, particularly in recent times, to become a bulwark of socio-economic conservatism. Its slogan has become: "First save the individual souls, then the society will be transformed."

Even though evangelicals agree on the importance of individual conversion, they have differed on a variety of issues. One influential wing of evangelicalism in the twentieth century is fundamentalism. Taking its name from a series of publications (1910–13), fundamentalism insisted that true Christianity required

157

acceptance of the following tenets: the Bible is verbally inspired by God and therefore without error; the virgin birth of Jesus; the satisfaction theory of the atonement; the bodily resurrection of Jesus; and the miracles of Jesus.

It was the doctrine of the Bible's literal inerrancy that led to the struggle between fundamentalism and the growing emphasis on scientific education in the early twentieth century. As the Darwinian theory of evolution came to dominate biological thinking, a conflict with Biblical history was unavoidable. After all, if the Bible were literally true, the world was created in six days. Darwin's theories applied to natural history required one to believe that the world evolved over a period of millions of years. Scientific theory generally, and biology and geology specifically, came to be seen as anti-God and, therefore, of the Devil.

In an attempt to stem this apparent evil, in the 1920s laws were passed in certain southern states where fundamentalism was particularly influential which forbade the teaching of evolutionary theory in the public schools. The most well known of these laws was enacted in Tennessee, leading to the notorious trial of Tennessee V. John Thomas Scopes. In the first chapter of his book on the Scopes trial, reprinted below, the late Ray Ginger describes how the Tennessee antievolution law came to be passed and the decision of certain citizens of the state to challenge that law in the courts. The outcome of the case was obvious; after the verbal pyrotechnics of the opposing attorneys, William Jennings Bryan for the prosecution and Clarence Darrow for the defense, Scopes was found guilty of violating the law. The decision was reversed on a technicality, and the law remained on the books, though it was never again enforced.

With the resurgence of fundamentalism in the 1980s, antievolution laws are again being brought into play. A widely publicized trial in Arkansas in 1981–82 led to the conclusion that fundamentalist creation theory had no place in the public school curriculum in that state. The growing political power of the movement, however, leads one to conclude that the creation/evolution controversy is by no means over. Fundamentalism's power encourages it to seek to impress its theories on the American people through the legislative process if it cannot do so through its spiritual influence.

And the seed of Israel separated themselves from all strangers, and stood and confessed their sins, and the iniquities of their fathers.

NEHEMIAH ix:2

I

The human eye and mind do not readily grasp the unfamiliar. Were two icebergs to collide so that one of them emerged from the water for half or more of its bulk, hung thus momentarily, and sank back to its customary immersion, the event would leave us uncertain. What was it we saw? That part of the iceberg that emerged from the water—was it just more of the same? Or was it wondrously different?

Similarly when massive social forces collide, as they did in the trial of John Thomas Scopes for teaching Darwinism, we can hardly credit the facts. We focus on the easy, because the familiar: the evidences of vanity and foolishness, the brilliant quip and the preposterious statement, a three-time candidate for President hoist on his own canard. Three decades have passed since the trial took place, and perhaps now we can understand the deeper realities that it thrust momentarily into view: the tortured issues of social policy, how the trial expressed the age-old craving of this man and that one, of you and me, to escape by spiritual rebirth from a past soiled with compromise. "And I will sprinkle clean water upon you, and ye shall be clean: from all your filthiness, and from all your idols, will I cleanse you. A new heart also will I give you, and a new spirit put within you: and I will take away the stony heart out of your flesh, and I will give you an heart of flesh" (Ezekiel xxxvi:25–6).

Like so much evil, the Scopes trial began with a sincere effort to do good. John Washington Butler, the Tennessee legislator who sponsored the law that Scopes violated, won the affection, even the respect, of all who met him. He was a broad-shouldered six-footer, with kindly Indian-brown face, ready smile. A straightforward man who, in 1925, had lived all his 49 years on the family farm in Macon County that had been worked successively by his greatgrandfather, grandfather, father. Located in north central Tennessee, Macon County did not have a single mile of railroad track. The same year in which he first saw a train, his twenty-first year, John Washington Butler took over the family farm. He also taught school for five years, teaching in the fall, planting his crop in the spring. After that he settled down to raising a variety of plants and animals on his 120 acres. Once a week or so he would go the three miles to LaFayette, the county seat of 800 residents. Every Sunday he went to church.

About 1921 an itinerant preacher who came once each month to Butler's church mentioned a young woman from the community who had gone away to a university. She had returned believing in the theory of evolution and not believing in the existence of God. This set Butler to thinking of his own children: two daughters, three sons. What might happen to them? No need even to go to the universities to be corrupted; Darwin's theory of evolution was taught in the public high schools of Macon County.

The next year Butler was urged to run for the state legislature. He agreed, and his campaign circulars stated the need for a law to prohibit teaching the theory of evolution in the public schools. The Bible said that God had created man in his own image, so man could not have evolved from lower animals as the scientists said. Those were the alternatives, and Butler found the choice easy. "Put not your trust in princes, nor in the son of man, in whom there is no help" (Psalms cxlvi:3). Butler was sure that in the three counties of his district—Trousdale and Sumner were farming country like Macon—99 people out of 100 agreed with him about this.

"Religion, Politics, and the Scopes Trial," From *Six Days or Forever: Tennessee v. John Thomas Scopes*, by Ray Ginger (Boston: The Beacon Press, 1958), pp. 1–21.

Maybe so. At least, they elected him. As a freshman legislator he was not aggressive enough to introduce his anti-evolution bill, but during the 1924 campaign he resolved that if re-elected he would do his utmost to get the bill passed. It came to that.

On the morning of his 49th birthday Butler was thinking, "What'll I do on my birthday?" And he said to himself, "Well, the first thing I'll get that law off my mind." He sat down in the homely comfortable living room of his farm home before a fireplace with stone jambs (it had been built before the days of fire brick), and composed a bill.

> An Act prohibiting the teaching of the Evolution Theory in all the Universities, Normals, and all other public schools of Tennessee, which are supported in whole or in part by the public school funds of the State, and to provide penalties for the violations thereof.
>
> Section 1. Be it enacted by the General Assembly of the State of Tennessee, That it shall be unlawful for any teacher in any of the Universities, Normals and all other public schools of the State which are supported in whole or in part by the public school funds of the State, to teach any theory that denies the story of the Divine Creation of man as taught in the Bible, and to teach instead that man has descended from a lower order of animals.
>
> Section 2. Be it further enacted, That any teacher found guilty of the violation of this Act shall be guilty of a misdemeanor and upon conviction, shall be fined not less than One Hundred ($100.00) Dollars nor more than Five Hundred ($500.00) Dollars for each offense.
>
> Section 3. Be it further enacted, That this Act take effect from and after its passage, the public welfare requiring it.

Butler wrote three or four other versions. In the end he returned to his first effort.

Why had he done it? He explained later: "In the first place, the Bible is the foundation upon which our American Government is built. . . . The evolutionist who denies the Biblical story of creation, as well as other Biblical accounts, cannot be a Christian. . . . It goes hand in hand with Modernism, makes Jesus Christ a fakir, robs the Christian of his hope and undermines the foundation of our Government . . ."

Butler was no vindictive, pleasure-hating, puritanical fanatic. In maturity he looked back with pride to his youthful skill at baseball. He loved music, and his three sons had a band. His religion looked toward love rather than toward retribution. Clerk of his own congregation and clerk of the district session of the Primitive Baptists, he had chosen this sect over the more popular Missionary Baptists because of a doctrinal issue: "Now *I* don't believe, and *no* Primitive Baptist believes, that God would condemn a man just because he never heard of the gospel."

Butler carried his bill to Nashville, got a stenographer in the Capitol to type a clean draft, and threw it in the legislative mill. Mainly the other members were indifferent. Some thought the bill would make the state of Andrew Jackson seem ridiculous. An effort was made to pigeonhole it in committee. But Butler called it out, as he could do under the House rules.

And the pressures for it in Nashville began to build up. A representative from one of the leading evangelical schools gave a series of five lectures on the Virgin Birth. Dr. W. F. Powell, pastor of the First Baptist Church, declared strongly for the bill. His weight counted: the Baptists were the largest denomination in the state, and Powell lectured every Sunday morning at the Knickerbocker Theater to the largest Bible class in Tennessee.

Baptists could easily view the situation as a variant on the main chance. Nashville was the national capital of the Methodist Church, and Methodists, following Wesley's lead in setting less stock in words than in deeds, in grace than in works, had been generally inactive in the fundamentalist campaigns against evolution and higher criticism of the Bible. Some Baptist ministers now saw in the Butler Bill a weapon that could be used to embarrass their chief rivals in the competition for members. Churches, like other institutions, can be influenced by imperialist ambitions.

Meanwhile there was almost no vocal opposition to the bill. The officials and faculty of the University of Tennessee turned their backs; the legislature was considering a handsome new appropriation for the university, whose president privately disapproved the bill but would say nothing publicly. Officials of the state Department of Education likewise kept silent; the legislature had under consideration a bill to establish a compulsory school term of eight months in the public schools instead of the five or six months' schooling then common in rural counties of the state. Leaders of the Tennessee Academy of Science were not heard from. The main newspapers of the state either approved the measure or ignored it.

And so on January 28, 1925, the lower house passed Butler's bill by a vote of 71 to 5. The next evening William Jennings Bryan, three times the Democratic nominee for President, Secretary of State under Woodrow Wilson, the lifelong apostle of rural America and the acknowledged leader of the crusade against Darwinism, swept through Nashville with his masty physique and his silver voice. His subject: "Is the Bible True?" His reply: It is. Every word of it. Every comma. Jesus Christ was born of the Holy Spirit and the Virgin Mother. He died to redeem man's sins. He was born again. Every miracle recorded in the Bible actually happened. The Bible is the word of God, who dictated it verbatim to the Apostles: "holy men of God spake as they were moved by the Holy Ghost" (II Peter i:21).

As the Butler Bill went to the senate, a Nashville attorney named W. B. Marr, who had heard Bryan's lecture, went into action. He and some friends printed and distributed widely several thousand copies of "Is the Bible True?" About 500 of the pamphlets went to members of the legislature. The anti-evolution lobby, if small, was making itself heard. On the other side, silence. Most voters in the state didn't care a hang either way. Neither did most legislators. But they were politicians who had to stand for re-election. Few of them were willing to give their opponents a chance to say: "Well, there's Bill. He's a good fellow, but he's an atheist. He believes that you are descended from a monkey. I don't. I believe in the Bible." When the measure came to a vote in the senate, only two members spoke against it. Then the speaker of the upper house, Lew Hill, Democrat and ardent Campbellite, took the floor. "Save our children for God!" The vote was 24 to 6.

Even William Jennings Bryan could not affect the steamroller. On February 9 he wrote to a senator, John A. Shelton, suggesting that the bill should not contain any penalty for violations. He pointed out that the joint resolution against the teaching of evolution that he had written and that had been passed the previous year by the Florida legislature did not carry any penalty. This course, Bryan said, was wise for two reasons: A penalty could be used as a diversion by enemies of the bill, as had been done in defeating an anti-evolution bill in Kentucky. Also the law was to apply to an educated class who presumably would obey the law. If they did not, a later legislature could add a penalty for violations. Bryan's letter went for naught. The legislature of Tennessee passed the measure exactly as Butler had written it.

Most legislators did not take the matter very seriously. "The gentleman from Macon wanted a bill passed; he had not had much during the session and this did not amount to a row of pins; let him have it." One senator later claimed that the bill would not have passed at all if students from the local Vanderbilt University had not crowded the galleries during debate and heckled proponents of the bill, but this argument sounds like justification after the fact. Others claimed that most senators felt the governor would veto the bill. That makes more sense.

Austin Peay was a popular governor. And not a bad one. Elected governor in 1922 and re-elected in 1924, he had a progressive program for Tennessee. In his first term he had cleared away the state's financial deficit and given it a balance of $2 million. Then he started spending money. Highways. Schools. Hospitals and prisons. He wanted the compulsory eight-months school term and the largest appropriation in history for the University. To achieve these reforms, he needed the votes of a strategic bloc of rural legislators, men like John Washington Butler. The governor was in a true dilemma. He hesitated. When one of the senators who had spoken against the bill visited him, Governor Peay protested that the measure was absurd and that the legislature should have saved him from this predicament by failing to pass the bill. As the senator left Peay's office, a large delegation of Dr. Powell's Baptists entered. Governor Peay was a Baptist too. On March 21, eight days after the Butler Bill cleared the legislature, Peay signed it. It took effect at once.

The governor explained his action in a special message to the legislature. He noted first that the state consitution mentioned the people's belief in God and immortality. Obviously if man was to be judged after death, he must be judged by some laws, and the only source of those laws was the Bible. The Butler Act did not require the public schools to teach any one interpretation of the Biblical account of Creation. Peay added:

> After a careful examination I can find nothing of consequence in the books now being taught in our schools with which this bill will interfere in the slightest manner. Therefore it will not put our teachers in any jeopardy. Probably the law will never be applied. It may not be sufficiently definite to admit of any specific application or enforcement. Nobody believes that it is going to be an active statute.

If the Butler Act was not intended to be enforced, it can hardly have been a law. And it was not. It was a gesture, a symbolic act. Governor Peay said so: "But this bill is a distinct protest against an irreligious tendency to exalt so-called science, and deny the Bible in some schools and quarters—a tendency fundamentally wrong and fatally mischievous in its effects on our children, our institutions and our country."

The Butler Act was a stump speech; it was each legislator telling his constituents that he very much wanted to be re-elected. It was an expression of the belief of many Americans that law is magic, the sort of belief that led the lower house of the Indiana legislature in 1899 to pass a law fixing the value of pi as 4, that led the Tennessee legislature in 1908, at the behest of the Methodists, to outlaw cigarettes, that led John Washington Butler, that man of sound instincts and kindly heart, to announce that he would introduce a bill to ban gossip in the state. And the Butler Act was prayer, prayer emerging from an overwhelming but vague anxiety.

II

Governor's Peay's message on the Butler Act noted the "deep and widespread belief that something is shaking the fundamentals of the country." The anxiety was nationwide, because some of its major causes were nationwide. In the nineteenth century most Americans had lived on farms or in small towns. While dependent on the impersonalities of the market, they were not directly under the power of any other man who could be pointed out and called by name. A man could, in satisfying ways, still call his soul his own. The emphasis was on character rather than on personality, and the traditional Protestant code of morality was almost universal in a nation that still derived overwhelmingly from British and West European ancestry.

After 1890 this changed with incredible speed. The breathtaking growth of industry resulted in a vast expansion of cities, and the industrial cities overflowed with immigrant laborers from Eastern and Southern Europe. Most of the new arrivals were Catholics and peasants with a moral code that, if neither less strict nor more humane, was yet noticeably different. Overcrowding and poverty meant slums; slums meant political bosses and organized crime. The new immigrant groups came to be voting blocs of more significance than were native-born Americans in one city after another, and acquired influence even in Washington. The erstwhile independent men joined up in the new industrial armies, the new bureaucracies in which each man was subject to the personal dictation of his superior. The farm boy came to the city, and he was often revolted and outraged by what he saw there. And above all, he was frightened and tormented by his loneliness. How can you make them happy up in Detroit, after they've lived on the farm?

All this was summarized in 1926 by the Imperial Wizard and Emperor of the Ku Klux Klan:

> . . . Nordic Americans for the last generation have found themselves increasingly uncomfortable and finally deeply distressed. There appeared first confusion in thought and opinion, a groping hesitancy about national affairs and private life alike, in sharp contrast to the clear, straightforward purposes of our earlier years. There was futility in

religion, too, which was in many ways even more distressing. . . . Finally
there came the moral breakdown that has been going on for two decades. . . . The sacredness of our Sabbath, of our homes, of chastity,
and finally even of our right to teach our children in our own schools
fundamental facts and truths were torn away from us.

The sense of losing one's birthright, of alienation, of betrayal, was
heightened by World War I. Before the war Christianity had turned increasingly toward the Social Gospel, which sought to face the social problems
of industrialism and urbanism and to deal with them in a spirit of practical
idealism. The prevailing mood was hope. The representative men were
happy men: Theodore Roosevelt, in spite of his splenetic forebodings; Eugene
Debs, sure of socialism in the United States in his own lifetime; even Clarence Darrow, certainly one of the most disillusioned men of that generation.
     Then came the war. Many persons never stopped thinking that we
should stay out of it; not improbably a plebescite in 1917 on the question
of American entry would have resulted in negative majorities in the whole
region from the Appalachians to the Rockies. Many of those who supported
American entry did so, not with sober realism, but with impossible objectives. This would be the last war, and then the world would be safe for
democracy. But war itself meant bloodshed and terror, publication of the
secret Allied treaties, rejection by the Senate of the Covenant of the League
of Nations. The reins of power passed to the flaccid hands of Warren
Gamaliel Harding. Everybody—those who had supported American participation as well as those who had opposed it—felt betrayed. Gone now
was more than the illusions of the war. Gone was the previous hopefulness,
the cheery conviction that progress is inevitable. In its place was a massive
distrust, the sort of distrust you would feel if a man stole your silverplate
and your wife after you had invited him into your house and fed him at
your table. And the distrust was directed toward Europe, things European,
anything that could be called European.
     Present too, with many, was a vague sense of guilt. For persons steeped
from birth in Christian doctrine, the idea of original sin may lead to pervasive anxiety. How much worse for such persons, taught to regard every
temporal defeat as divine retribution, to confront the staggering defeat of
American purposes in the war. The feeling of having sinned, of being at
the verge of eternal damnation, was intolerable, and men had to assure
themselves of their basic goodness. This effort required a simple definition
of morality: A good man is a man who does not drink, or smoke, or gamble,
or commit adultery, or contravene the Word of the Bible, and who punishes
the sins of others. A desperate flight backward to old certainties replaced
the pre-war belief in gradual adaptation to new conditions. In a convulsion
of filiopiety, men tried to deny the present by asserting a fugitive and
monastic virtue. Not progress, but stability and certainty. "How blessed
that some things, after all, are static—the love of God, the way of life, and
the revealing Book, that have not changed through all the centuries." Thus
a fundamentalist.
     From such roots sprang a multifoliate plant. The Red Hunt, with its
insistence that radicalism was a foreign doctrine and that no native-born

American could adhere to it, culminated logically in the wave of brutal deportations. The Knights of Columbus, the American Legion, and the Daughters of the American Revolution made a furor about the "pro-British" bias of textbooks on American history; official clamors on the subject occurred in New York City, in Chicago, in other cities from Portland, Oregon, to Boston. New York, Wisconsin, and Oregon were among the states that, as Walter Lippmann wrote, "passed laws designed to do for patriotic fundamentalism what the Tennessee statute had been designed to do for religious fundamentalism." The xenophobia also erupted in the massive, and almost unopposed, demand for restriction of immigration, which resulted in the 1921 and 1924 laws setting quotas based on national origins.

Even before the war, many Protestant advocates of the Social Gospel had believed in prohibition; after passage of the Volstead Act, its strict enforcement became for them a means of solving all social problems. Alcoholic beverages were, simultaneously, European, Catholic, and sinful. A moralizing, if immoral, impulse was likewise basic in the Ku Klux Klan, which in many areas punished adultery as well as Jewish birth, drunkenness as well as Catholic faith, failure to attend church as well as failure to look white: inflicted punishments even on white Protestant Americans. The Klan, in one of its several aspects, was the Ten Commandments swinging a whip. Or rather, some of the Ten Commandments; the moralizing was selective.

Leaders of the anti-evolution crusade, including Bryan, George M. Price, and William Bell Riley, tried too to exploit the current fear of Bolshevism by linking Darwinism to it. Thus T. T. Martin, author of *Hell in the High Schools* and other tracts against evolution, flung down a challenge to the Mississippi legislature when it was considering an anti-evolution bill: "Go back to the fathers and mothers of Mississippi and tell them because you could not face the scorn and abuse of Bolsheviks and Anarchists and Atheists and agnostics and their co-workers, you turned over their children to a teaching that God's Word is a tissue of lies."

All of these movements—the fundamentalist crusade against evolution, anti-radicalism, immigration restriction, prohibition, the Ku Klux Klan—originated in the same state of mind, and each helped to create an atmosphere congenial to the others. But in the actual struggle for members they were largely competitive with each other. While a few prominent Klansmen were prompted by their greed for money to switch to fundamentalist organizations, such fundamentalist stalwarts as the Moody Bible Institute and John Roach Straton attacked the Klan. And a statistical study of Klan membership showed it to be strongest in states where fundamentalism was unimportant, but weak in Tennessee and Mississippi which adopted anti-evolution statutes.

It was charged at the time, by the Harvard theologian Kirsopp Lake and others, that "large financial interests" might take up fundamentalism as part of their general opposition to revolutionary ideas. Such instances did occur, but direct support by big business of the anti-evolution movement accounts at most for a minor part of its strength. Doubtless other businessmen had the perception to see what a machinery manufacturer of Fort Wayne, Indiana, expressed: "American business must raise its voice against thought that is against the best interests of business and denies the theory of evolution. For evolution is no longer a theory. Science could not be studied without it. Business is dependent on science."

The social creed expounded in the 1920's by the two influential business groups, the National Association of Manufacturers and the United States Chamber of Commerce, clashed head-on at crucial points with the views of William Jennings Bryan. Bryan stood squarely for the direct rule of the majority in all matters; the business groups stood equally squarely for rule by an elite because they believed the great mass of the people were ignorant and could not recognize their own best interests. The business groups acclaimed the American system of checks and balances and placed particular faith in the judiciary, especially the Supreme Court; Bryan believed in an unrestrained legislature because that branch of government was most responsive to the popular will. The business groups thought it was the nature of man to concentrate on material rewards; Bryan spoke for the primacy of spiritual values.

But in other respects these big business groups helped to create good growing weather for the anti-evolution movement. They too preached the overwhelming need for social order, for stony-faced resistance to change. When the Butler Act was violated by John Thomas Scopes, the president of the N.A.M. pointed to "America's greatest menace today—the popular contempt in which many of the laws and much of its constitutional authority are held." The *Manufacturers' Record* was explicitly religious, denouncing theories of evolution as "silly twaddle" and asserting that "one must believe in the Bible in its entirety or not believe in it at all."

The big business groups and the fundamentalists likewise agreed that education should consist in the inculcation of received truths, not in the development among students of certain modes of analysis, not in the discovery of new truths. Truth is known. Teach it. Who knows it? We do. How did you learn it? The fundamentalists replied: God revealed it to us. The business groups replied: We are the elite. We know everything.

And yet, ironically, fundamentalism was in part an effort by Protestant clergymen to regain some of the power and prestige that they were losing to the burgeoning business classes. This condition for fundamentalism, like many others, existed with peculiar intensity in the South.

III

The South is perhaps unique in world history in that the growth of industry, cities, and education stimulated church membership, which rose nearly 50 per cent between 1906 and 1926. This phenomenon was especially marked in the cities; in Memphis, for example, population grew 23 per cent in this period, church membership 62 per cent. Slightly more than a third of the adults in the Southeast were not affiliated with any church; most of these were Negroes or isolated, uneducated whites. Newly arrived in the growing cities, men found themselves faced with an aching solitude and alienation, and they sought an emotional haven in religion.

They also sought emotional excitement that was not given them elsewhere in life, and religion in the South, as earlier on the Western frontier, was often corybantic. The two creeds that claimed three fourths of all church members in the region, the Baptists and the Methodists, were strongly revivalistic. The more ritualistic Protestants were losing ground, and in Tennessee there was only one Roman Catholic in every hundred persons. The arcanum was the Word—or words, which had a special fascination for many Southerners. Mere announcement of a speech would draw an enormous crowd; it would, that is, if the speech met a few simple requirements. It had to be delivered with florid gestures and rotund eloquence. It had to deal in the received words and phrases, so that efforts to follow it would not exacerbate the mind.

But it might torment the spirit. Most Southerners were reared on endless iterations of the same sermon about hellfire and brimstone, about fiery pits and demons with pitchforks. They were conditioned to believe that we are all sinners. Since, like the prisoner in Kafka's *The Trial*, they were not told what specific crime they were charged with, they were not clear just how they could modify their practical actions in order to get right with God; they were left with what the psychologists term "free-floating" anxiety and guilt. Because their humanity was their sin, their sin seemed irremediable. This state of mind, especially if the feeling was not too intense, made them vulnerable to such ritualized acts of expiation as the Butler Bill. "And Aaron shall lay both his hands upon the head of the live goat, and confess over him all the iniquities of the children of Israel, and all their transgressions in all their sins, putting them upon the head of the goat, and shall send him away by the hand of a fit man into the wilderness: And the goat shall bear upon him all their iniquities unto a land not inhabited: and he shall let go the goat in the wilderness" (Leviticus xvi:21–2).

Other Southern institutions did little to offset the theological dominance. Higher education was largely controlled by the churches; each of the major denominations felt constrained to provide at least one college for men and one for women in every Southern state. Although clergymen were being steadily displaced as trustees of these colleges by more opulent businessmen who, if themselves usually conservative in their religious views, were yet more liberal than the clergy, the typical college curriculum consisted of religion and the classics. This limitation was partly due to policy, partly to lack of money; in 1903 the total funds available for higher education in nine Southern states combined were less than the income that year of Harvard. Twenty years later, the entire South held not a single university of the first rank, and its training facilities in engineering and science were particularly poor. The South had no public forums on scientific or social topics. Libraries were rare, poorly stocked, and infrequently visited. Walter Hines Page claimed that the chief element distinguishing Southerners from, say, citizens of Massachusetts was their utter lack of intellectual curiosity. And many Southerners took a perverse pride in their plight. Huey Long knew it was good politics when he declaimed in the Senate: "It is true. I am an ignorant man. . . . I know the hearts of my people because I have not colored my own. I know when I am right in my own conscience."

Although a few fundamentalists sought to show that Darwin's findings were unscholarly, the movement typically catered to the smugly ignorant. A writer in *Christian Fundamentals* declared that almost the only believers in evolution were "the university crowd and the social Reds." A Georgia legislator, Hal Kimberly, who had doubtless never heard of Aquinas' *Summa Theologica*, nonetheless used its distinction between natural and revealed knowledge to reach a conclusion that would have stunned Aquinas: "Read the Bible. It teaches you how to act. Read the hymn book. It contains the finest poetry ever written. Read the almanac. It shows you how to figure out what the weather will be. There isn't another book that is necessary for anyone to read, and therefore I am opposed to all libraries."

The Bible is the medium of revelation. Anybody who wants to be saved should stake his chips on revealed truth—and the Southern churches never doubted that their mission was individual salvation rather than social reform. The mind and body last but a day, but the soul is immortal. "Love not the world, neither the things that are in the world. If any man love the world, the love of the Father is not in him" (I John ii:15). Not surprising, therefore, that during the entire dispute about evolution no Southern theological school took a stand against the efforts to ban Darwinism by law. Of the theology professors who grumbled privately about it, few dared open their mouths. In Tennessee an estimated fifty ministers held modernist opinions, but only ten would declare themselves publicly.

It was not that the South had no liberals, or that they were without influence. Some of the major Southern newspapers had recently acquired liberal editors; Southern liberals had begun to achieve the highest political offices. But they were fighting an uphill fight, and many hesitated to dissipate in quasi-religious disputes the influence they might need on issues of economic policy or of policy toward Negroes.

Beginning about 1896, the Southern states had launched a rigorous and systematic segregation of Negroes—something that had not existed even under slavery. So massive a reshaping of society required more than laws and illegal violence, it required too a reshaping of men's minds. There took place a concentrated effort to persuade everybody that segregation was natural and inevitable, that it had always existed, that it was how matters were arranged by our noble ancestors. The campaign for Jim Crow laws, superbly analyzed by C. Vann Woodward in *The Strange Career of Jim Crow*, was strikingly similar in some ways to the later campaign for anti-evolution laws: both were greatly facilitated by the lack of opposition, and both were dependent on a favorable national climate of opinion.

The authentic traditionalism of the South, which grew out of a relatively simple, homogeneous, and unchanging way of life, was reinforced by a spurious and manufactured traditionalism enshrined in the myth of the Confederacy. The drive for segregation bred intolerance, and the intolerance spread to other topics. A new idea on any subject would further the habit of discussion, of rational consideration, and these habits would impede the effort to impose segregation. This consideration—in addition to a desire to protect religion for its own sake, or for the sake of social order, or a desire to give harmless diversion to the common folks—may explain why prominent businessmen and lawyers endorsed the antievolution movement and why the journal that was virtually the official publication of the Southern textile industry applauded the passage of the Butler Act.

The traditionalism in religion was shored up by the region's ubiquitous ancestor worship. Men voted the way their fathers had, thought the way their fathers had. Cordell Hull testified that in his native Pickett County, Tennessee, a candidate for county office could predict within two or three votes the vote he would get. J. Frank Norris, a fundamentalist leader, told with undoubted effect how a Tennessean had walked up to Clarence Darrow, the chief attorney for John Thomas Scopes, clenched his fist under Darrow's nose and shouted: "Damn you, don't you reflect on my mother's Bible. If you do I will tear you to pieces." John Washington Butler summed the point well; when asked if he knew that many good Baptists believed in evolution, he said yes, and added: "I reckon it's a good deal like politics—the way you've been raised."

But if the South was susceptible to the anti-evolution movement, so were other regions, and the rest of the country was more active in pursuing the moral equivalents of fundamentalism. Two Southerners could write with justice: "In a way it may be said that the Fundamentalist craze was the Southern counterpart of the Northern red-hunt. . . . If Southern reactionaries were more successful in passing 'monkey laws,' Northerners were more active in discharging professors because of their opinions." And Tennessee was by no means the most daddy-ridden of the Southern states; unlike nine of them, it had ratified the Nineteenth Amendment giving women the right to vote.

IV

That the Butler Act was intended as gesture rather than as "active statute," in Governor Peay's words, is confirmed by the failure of the law-enforcing agencies to make any effort to execute it in the classrooms. Teachers taught as they had taught, out of the same books. The Chattanooga *Times* broke its silence to editorialize against the law. And some citizens of the state began to think about seeking a legal test of the Butler Act's constitutionality.

The normal, ordinary way to do this in Tennessee was for a plaintiff to file a bill in chancery court challenging the questionable law. The judge then ruled the law constitutional or not, with his reasons. Appeals could be carried to the court of appeals and to the supreme court of the state. It was rumored that plans were laid to challenge the Butler Act in this way, but that the men who should have been the plaintiffs balked finally for fear of fundamentalist wrath if the law were actually voided by the courts. Such a procedure would have avoided the sensationalism of a criminal trial. But a woman in New York City made the move that started events down a different path.

Lucile Milner was the secretary of the American Civil Liberties Union, which had been organized during World War I to defend pacifists and had continued after the war with the more general purpose of upholding the Bill of Rights. In the course of her regular chore of clipping civil-liberties news from the press, she came upon a three-inch item in a Tennessee paper about the passage of the Butler Act. Seeing the importance of the story, she showed it to Roger Baldwin, director of the organization. As a result, the Board of the ACLU agreed to raise a special fund to finance a test case and to hire distinguished lawyers to handle it. They got off to a slow start. Their first choice as attorney, John W. Davis, who had been the Democratic Presidential nominee in 1924, turned them down. And how could an organization with offices in New York City find a plaintiff in Tennessee? Finally they sent a story to the Tennessee papers announcing that the ACLU would finance a test case if some teacher were willing to cooperate.

George W. Rappelyea, on May 4, was sitting in his office in a coal yard at Dayton, Tennessee. He was an unimpressive figure: 31 years old, slight, swarthy, untidy, with horn-rimmed glasses and bushy black hair. He had grown up in New York City, and he was a mining engineer. Trained men were scarce in the South. He was in charge of six coal and iron mines for the Cumberland Coal Company, with 400 men under his direction.

Rappelyea saw in a newspaper that Chattanooga had give up its plans to start a case to test the Butler Act. He got an idea, and he telephoned F. E. Robinson, local druggist and head of the county board of education, and Walter White, county superintendent of schools. He argued earnestly with them. The next day he was at them again. They gave in. Then Rappelyea sent for John Thomas Scopes and asked him to come down to Robinson's drugstore. When Scopes arrived, Rappelyea was deep in an argument about evolution with two young local lawyers, Sue K. Hicks (a man whose parents had played him a grim joke) and Wallace C. Haggard. Rappelyea was arguing that the Bible was "mere history"; the two lawyers insisted that it must be taken literally. What, they asked, did Scopes think?

John Scopes was a guileless young man, with blue, contemplative eyes. Only 24 years old, he had graduated from the University of Kentucky the preceding year and had come to the high school at Dayton as science teacher and football coach. His local popularity was very great. Here was the man Rappelyea wanted. Scopes was drawn into the discussion, and found himself observing that nobody could teach biology without using the theory of evolution. Being the person he was, he was trapped. Rappelyea said, "You have been violating the law."

"So has every other teacher," said Scopes. "This is the official textbook," and he went to the shelf in the drugstore, which was also the town's bookstore, and took down a copy of George Hunter's *Civic Biology.* This book was officially prescribed for the public schools by the state textbook commission appointed by the governor.

Rappelyea produced the news item about the ACLU offer, and made a proposal to Scopes. "It's a bad law. Let's get rid of it. I will swear out a warrant and have you arrested. . . . That will make a big sensation. Why not bring a lot of doctors and preachers here? Let's get H. G. Wells and a lot of big fellows." Scopes demurred. He did not like the idea of having an arrest on his record. He was a modest man, distressed by the mere thought of being in the limelight. Besides, he believed that "evolution is easily reconciled with the Bible."

But Rappelyea persisted, and finally Scopes agreed. Describing the episode later, Scopes said: "It was just a drugstore discussion that got past control."

Rappelyea wired the ACLU in New York. They replied promptly: "We will cooperate Scopes case with financial help, legal advice and publicity."

On May 7 John Scopes was arrested. Three days later he had a preliminary hearing before three squires. It was charged that on April 24 he had taught the theory of evolution to his class. It was shown that Hunter's *Civic Biology* contained such sentences as: "We have now learned that animal forms may be arranged so as to begin with the simple one-celled forms and culminate with a group which contains man himself." The justices decided there was ample evidence, and Scopes was bound over to the grand jury that would meet the first Monday in August. Bond was fixed at $1,000.

Roger Baldwin announced in New York for the American Civil Liberties Union: "We shall take the Scopes case to the United States supreme court if necessary to establish that a teacher may tell the truth without being thrown in jail."

If Governor Peay and other saw the Scopes trial partly as political speech and partly as pious gesture, such men as George Rappelyea, Sue Hicks, and Dayton merchants viewed it as a civic promotion. This could really put Dayton in the headlines, on the map. It could bring a lot of business to local stores. But it needed celebrities. Who better than William Jennings Bryan, the one man of world reputation in the fundamentalist movement?

So Hicks sent Bryan several telegrams asking him to affiliate with the prosecution in the case. But before Hicks succeeded in reaching him, Bryan announced in Pittsburgh on May 13 that, if the Tennessee officials agreed, he would accept the appointment by the World's Christian Fundamentals Association to represent them in the prosecution of the case. His tone was determined: "We cannot afford to have a system of education that destroys the religious faith of our children. . . . There are about 5,000 scientists, and probably half of them are atheists, in the United States. Are we going to allow them to run our schools? We are not." He was less happy when he actually read the law whose "integrity" he had sworn to protect; he thought it muddled and written in faulty English.

Thus Bryan joined the prosecution, an occurrence that largely determined future events. And a remarkable fact, although few commentators have found it so. State governments sometimes retain prominent specialists and tril lawyers to handle complicated cases before appellate courts, but a simple criminal prosecution in a trial court? Never. And Bryan at that—a man whose brief lackluster career at the bar had ended thirty years earlier.

On the eve of the Scopes trial a Tennessean, an able lawyer and prominent Baptist layman, said to a reporter: "What business do you think William Jennings Bryan, who has not tried a law-suit in twenty-five years, has coming here to assist the bench and bar of Tennessee in the trial of a little misdemeanor case that any judge ought to be able to dispose of in a couple of hours?" The answer was to emerge only gradually. Before the Scopes trial began, few foresaw what kind of ritual it would contain, or what role in it a high priest might play.

Studying Latin in a high school classroom in the 1920s

Training the Young

ROBERT S. LYND AND HELEN M. LYND

Americans take the existence of compulsory public schooling for granted. Probably no other institution in American life receives as much support from the general population. Even those who choose not to send their children to the public schools rarely criticize or challenge the system. Many in fact, particularly the parochial school parents, want to become part of the system, at least financially, by having public monies allocated for the support of their children's schools. Today most of the attacks on the public schools are not aimed at the notion of publicly supported education but at the monopoly of public education by local school boards. These critics support the free market in education in which families with school-age children are given public funds which they might spend in any available school. The policy of providing ten to thirteen years of free education for all remains one of the mainstays of American institutional life.

It was not always this way, of course. Except for the colonial New England experience, and that more in theory than in practice, the public schools that existed before the Civil War were voluntary, and their very existence was controversial. Education was viewed as the responsibility of the family, and the middle and upper classes sent their children to private schools or taught them at home. The strongest impulse for the creation of a universal system of public education in the United States came in the middle and late nineteenth century as a response to the increasing immigration of non-Protestant, non-Anglo-Saxon peoples who did not fit neatly into the official culture of the nation.

Recent scholarship has demonstrated that public schools functioned, not so much as a route to upward mobility for immigrant populations, but as a form of social control. The immigrants found the public schools to be, in effect, Protestant parochial schools in which the dominant values of the society were the substance of the curriculum. This curriculum, with its inclusion not only of Protestant values but also of the myths of American history, had the intention of training a devout and loyal citizenry, that would acquiesce in the dominant values and follow the leadership of the traditional elite. In struggling against this cultural chauvinism, Roman Catholics and others established competing school systems in an attempt to create and sustain their own particular loyalties.

What public education did exist in the nineteenth century consisted mainly of grammar schools that rarely were compulsory in attendance. After the Civil War, compulsory schooling became a controversial issue in many communities as parents saw in the compulsion an intrusion of the state into the management of children, which generally had been recognized by law as an almost exclusively parental function. By the turn of the century, however, even such establishment stalwarts as Theodore Roosevelt recognized that the state could serve as an "overparent" capable of providing services, including education, that an urban population found it increasingly difficult to manage for itself.

During the twentieth century, acceptance of education as a function of government has led to an increased desire for secondary schooling until, today, a high-school diploma has become the minimum educational goal sought by most American parents for their children. Colleges and junior colleges, particularly public institutions with open enrollment policies, are today in a comparable position in terms of function to the secondary schools early in this century.

The selection reprinted below from Robert and Helen Merrill Lynd's classic study of Muncie, Indiana, describes and evaluates the educational system found there in the 1920s. After the passing of a compulsory schooling law in Indiana in 1897, the school population of Muncie increased dramatically. An even more dramatic increase occurred in the number of high-school students. Between 1890 and 1924, high-school enrollment increased from 8 percent to 25 percent to total school enrollment. As the selection indicates, much of the high-school growth was in the area of vocational training. But more importantly, neither the students nor the townspeople saw the school as performing a basically educational function. Social and athletic activities as well as general socialization functions seemed more significant to all concerned.

Many of the Lynds'criticisms of the Muncie public schools are being echoed by critics of the schools today. Small but increasing numbers of parents and children are seeking alternate forms of schooling, including community control of schools in racial ghettos, in order to circumvent the political and social indoctrination encountered in the public schools. There is no doubt, however, that for the foreseeable future the traditional public school will be the dominant institution, more dominant even than the family, in the life of America's young.

WHO GO TO SCHOOL?

In an institutional world as seemingly elaborate and complex as that of Middletown, the orientation of the child presents an acute problem. Living goes on all about him at a brisk pace, speeded up at every point by the utilization of complex shorthand devices—ranging all the way from the alphabet to daily market quotations and automatic machinery—through which vast quantities of intricate social capital are made to serve the needs of the commonest member of the group. As already noted, the home operates as an important transfer point of civilization, mediating this surrounding institutional world to the uninitiated newcomer. Religious agencies take a limited part in the child's training at the option of his parents. *True Story* on the news-stand, *Flaming Youth* on the screen, books from the public library, the daily friction of life with playmates—all these make their casual though not insignificant contributions. But it is by yet another agency, the school, that the most formal and systematic training is imparted.

When the child is six the community for the first time concerns itself with his training, and his systematic, high-pressure orientation to life begins. He continues to live at home under the nominal supervision of his parents, but for four to six hours a day,[1] five days a week, nine months of the year, his life becomes almost as definitely routinized as his father's in shop or office, and even more so than his mother's at home; he "goes to school".

Prior to 1897 when the first state "compulsory education" law was passed, the child's orientation to life might continue throughout as casually as in the first six years. Even after the coming of compulsory schooling only twelve consecutive weeks' attendance each year between the ages of eight and fourteen was at first required. During the last thirty years, however, the tendency has been not only to require more constant attendance during each year,[2] but to extend the years that must be devoted to this formal, group-directed training both upward and downward. Today, no person may stop attending school until he is fourteen,[3] while by taking over and expanding in 1924 the kindergartens, hitherto private semi-charitable organizations, the community is now allowing children of five and even of four, if room permits, to receive training at public expense.

This solicitude on the part of Middletown that its young have "an education" is reflected in the fact that no less than 45 per cent of all money expended by the city in 1925 was devoted to its school. The fourteen school plants are valued at $1,600,000—nearly nine times the value of the school

[1]Ranging from three hours and fifty minutes, exlusive of recess periods, in the first and second years, to five hours and fifty minutes in every year above the seventh. In 1890 it was five hours daily for all years.

[2]The average daily attendance in the two school years 1889–91 was 66 per cent. of the school enrollment as against 83 per cent. for the two school years 1922–24.

[3]Children of fourteen who have completed the eighth grade in school may be given a certificate allowing them to start getting a living, provided they can prove that money is needed for the support of their families and that they attend school in special part-time classes at least five hours a week; children who have not finished the eighth grade may start getting a living at sixteen; the community supervises the conditions under which they shall work until they are eighteen. Until 1924 the upper age limit for required school attendance was fourteen. The state law allows a city to require the minimum school attendance (five hours a week) for all children up to eighteen, but Middletown does not do this.

"Training the Young." From *Middletown* by Robert S. and Helen M. Lynd, pp. 181–205, 211–22, copyright, 1929, by Harcourt Brace Jovanovich, Inc.; renewed, 1957, by Robert S. Lynd and Helen M. Lynd. Reprinted by permission of the publishers.

equipment in 1890.[4] During 1923–24 nearly seven out of ten of all those in the city between the ages of six and twenty-one were going regularly to day school, while many others of all ages were attending night classes.

No records are kept in the Middletown schools of the ages and grades at which children withdraw from school. The lengthening average number of years during which each child remains in school today can only be inferred from the heavier attendance in high school and college. While the city's population has increased but three-and-one-half-fold since 1890, enrollment in the four grades of the high school has mounted nearly elevenfold, and the number of those graduating has increased nineteenfold. In 1889–90 there were 170 pupils in the high school, one for every sixty-seven persons in the city, and the high school enrollment was only 8 per cent. of the total school enrollment, whereas in 1923–24 there were 1,849 pupils in high school, one for every twenty-one persons in the city, and the high school enrollment was 25 per cent. of the total school enrollment. In other words, most of Middletown's children now extend their education past the elementary school into grades nine to twelve. In 1882, five graduated from high school, one for each 1,110 persons in the community;[5] in 1890 fourteen graduated, one for each 810 persons; in 1899 thirty-four graduated, "one of the largest graduating classes the city ever had," making one for each 588 persons;[6] in 1920, 114 graduated, or one for each 320 persons; and in 1924, 236 graduated, or one for each 161.[7]

Equally striking is the pressure for training even beyond high school. Of those who continue their training for twelve years, long enough to graduate from high school, over a third prolong it still further in college or normal work. Two of the fourteen members of the high school graduating class of 1890 and nine of the thirty-two graduates of 1894 eventually entered a college or normal school, while by the middle of the October following graduation, a check of 153 of the 236 members of the class of 1924 revealed eighty as already in college, thirty-six of them in colleges other than the local college and forty-four taking either the four-year college course or normal training at the local college.[8] Between 1890 and

---

[4]The annual expenditures of the state for elementary and secondary education, meanwhile, increased from $5,245,218 in 1890 to $63,358,807 in 1922.

[5]Population estimated at 5,550.

[6]Population estimated at 20,000.

[7]The 1920 Federal Census showed 76 per cent. of the city's population aged fourteen and fifteen and 30 per cent. of the group aged sixteen and seventeen as in attendance at school; the doubling of the high school graduating class between 1920 and 1924 suggests a substantial increase today over these 1920 percentages. According to the State Department of Public Instruction, high school attendance throughout the state increased 56 per cent. during the five years 1920 to 1924.

The high school in Middletown is used by the township, but the number of pupils from outside the city is small and the population of Middletown has therefore been used above as the basis in figuring.

[8]The 1924 data are from published lists in the high school paper and are not a sample, but probably include the majority of those who went to college. In addition to the eighty accounted for above, seven more were in business college, one in art school at the state capitol, and three were taking post-graduate courses in high school.

1924, while the population of the state increased only approximately 25 per cent., the number of students enrolled in the State University increased nearly 700 per cent., and the number of those graduating nearly 800 per cent. During the same period the numer of students enrolled in the state engineering and agricultural college increased 600 per cent., and the number of those graduating over 1,000 per cent.

Even among those who do not go on to college or do not finish high school the same leaven is working; there were, in the spring of 1925, 1,890 enrollments in evening courses in the local schools—719 of them in trade and industry courses,[9] 175 in commercial courses, and 996 in home-making courses.[10]

In addition to other forms of training, fifty to one hundred people of both sexes take correspondence courses annually in the city. The Middletown Business College has an annual enrollment of about 300 students, roughly half of them coming from Middletown.

So general is the drive towards education in Middletown today that, instead of explaining why those who continue in high school or even go on to college do so, as would have been appropriate a generation ago, it is simpler today to ask why those who do not continue their education fail to do so. Answers to this question were obtained from forty-two mothers who had a total of sixty-seven children, thirty-seven girls and thirty boys, who had left high school. Fourteen girls and six boys had left because their financial help was needed at home; three girls and twelve boys because they "wanted to work"; six girls because of "poor health," and one boy because of bad eyes; seven girls and six boys because they "didn't like high school"; three of each left to go to business college and one girl to study music; one girl and two boys "had to take so many things of no use"; one girl was married; and one stayed home to help during her mother's illness.

Obviously such answers are superficial explanations, masking in most cases a cluster of underlying factors. The matter of mental endowment is, naturally, not mentioned, although, according to Terman, "The pupils who drop out [of high school] are in the main pupils of inferior mental ability."[11] And yet, important though this consideration undoubtedly is, it must not too easily be regarded as the prepotent factor in the case of many of those who drop out of high school and in that of perhaps most of those

---

[9]Machine shop practice, carpentry, blue printing, drafting, pattern making, lathe and cabinet work, shop mathematics, chemistry.

[10]Sewing, dressmaking, millinery, applied design, basketry, planning and serving meals.

In general, attendance at evening courses of all kinds tends to be larger in "bad times." The director of this work attributes this to two factors: (1) people out of work have more time on their hands; (2) when competition for jobs is severe, workers realize the desirability of having education in addition to mere trade skill. A third factor, touching women only, is the increase in home sewing and the making of one's own hats when times are bad and the family pocket-book empty; these women may join a course to make one hat or dress and then drop out.

In 1923–24 the modal group among the men students were in their early twenties, while the modal group of women were in their thirties.

[11][Lewis M.] Terman, *The Intelligence of School Children* (Boston: Houghton Mifflin, 1919), pp. 87–90.

who complete high school but do not go on to college;[12] standards are relatively low both in the high school and in a number of near-by colleges. The formal, remote nature of much school work probably plays a larger role in discouraging children from continuing in school than the reference above to having "to take so many things of no use" indicates; save in the case of certain vocational courses, a Middletown boy or girl must take the immediate relevancy and value of the high school curriculum largely on faith.

Potent among the determining factors in this matter of continuance in school is the economic status of a child's family; here again, as in the case of the size of the house a given family occupies and in other significant accompaniments of living, we observe this extraneous pecuniary consideration dictating the course of the individual's life. The emphasis upon this financial consideration in the answers of the Middletown mothers cited above probably underestimates the importance of money. A number of mothers who said that a child had left school because he "didn't like it" finally explained with great reluctance, "We couldn't dress him like we'd ought and he felt out of it," or, "The two boys and the oldest girl all quit because they hated Central High School. They all loved the Junior High School[13] down here, but up there they're so snobbish. If you don't dress right you haven't any friends." "My two girls and oldest boy have all stopped school," said another mother. "My oldest girl stopped because we couldn't give her no money for the right kind of clothes. The boy begged and begged to go on through high school, but his father wouldn't give him no help. Now the youngest girl has left 10B this year. She was doing just fine, but she was too proud to to go to school unless she could have clothes like the other girls." The marked hesitation of mothers in mentioning these distasteful social distinctions only emphasizes the likelihood that the reasons for their children's leaving school summarized above understate the real situation in this respect.

This influential position of the family's financial status emerges again in the answers of the women interviewed regarding their plans for their children's future, although these answers cannot be satisfactorily tabulated as they tended to be vague in families where children were still below high school age. Every business class mother among the group of forty interviewed was planning to send her children through high school, and all but three of the forty were definitely planning to send their children to

[12]In Middletown as in the rest of the state there seems to be little direct relation between the ability of high school seniors and the selection of those who go to college. Book says of the state, "Almost as many students possessing E and F grades of intelligence are going to college as merit a ranking of A-plus or A.

"Many of the brightest students graduating from our high schools are not planning to go to college at all. Of those rated A-plus, 22 per cent. stated that they never expected to attend a college or university. Of those rated A, 24 per cent. did not intend to continue their education beyond the high school. . . . Of those ranking D and E, 64 and 62 per cent. respectively stated they would attend college next year." (*Op. cit.*, pp. 39–40.)

[13]Working class children go to the Junior High School on the South Side until they have finished the ninth grade. For the last three years of the high school—tenth, eleventh, and twelfth grades—all children of the city go to the Central High School on the North Side.

college; of these three, two were planning a musical education for their children after high school, and the third had children under eight. Eight of those planning to send their children to college added, "If we can afford it." Three were planning graduate work in addition to college. Two others said that musical study might be an alternative to college.

The answers of the working class wives were in terms of "hope to" or "want to"; in almost every case plans were contingent upon "if we can afford it." Forty of these 124 working class families had no plans for their children's education, eighteen of the forty having children in high school; the attitude of some of these mothers is expressed by the mother of nine children who said wearily, "I don't know; we want them all to go as far as they can." Of those who had plans for their children's future, three were planning definitely to have their children stop school at sixteen, the legal age limit of compulsory attendance. Thirty-eight were planning if possible to have their children continue through high school. Five planned on the local Business College in addition to one or more years at high school; four on the local Normal School; twenty-eight on college following high school; one on musical training in addition to high school; five on music without high school; and one on Business College with high school.[14] The answer of one mother conveys the mood of many other families: "Our oldest boy is doing fine in high school and his father says he'd like to send him to some nice college. The others will go through high school anyhow. If children don't have a good education they'll never know anything except hard work. Their father wants them to have just as much schooling as he can afford." Over and over again one sees both parents working to keep their children in college. "I don't know how we're going to get the children through college, but we're *going* to. A boy without an education today just ain't *anywhere!*" was the emphatic assertion of one father.

If education is oftentimes taken for granted by the business class, it is no exaggeration to say that it evokes the fervor of a religion, a means of salvation, among a large section of the working class. Add to this the further fact, pointed out below, that the high school has become the hub of the social life of the young of Middletown, and it is not surprising that high school attendance is almost as common today as it was rare a generation ago.

THE THINGS CHILDREN LEARN

The school, like the factory, is a thoroughly regimented world. Immovable seats in orderly rows fix the sphere of activity of each child. For all, from the timid six-year-old entering for the first time to the most assured high school senior, the general routine is much the same. Bells divide the day into periods. For the six-year-olds the periods are short (fifteen to twenty-five minutes) and varied; in some they leave their seats, play games, and act out make-believe stores, although in "recitation periods" all movement

---

[14]These figures are given in terms of families, not children. In some cases the plans given apply to only one or two children in a family when the parents have no plans for the others.

is prohibited. As they grow older the taboo upon physical activity becomes stricter, until by the third or fourth year practically all movement is forbidden except the marching from one set of seats to another between periods, a brief interval of prescribed exercise daily, and periods of manual training or home economics once or twice a week. There are "study-periods" in which children learn "lessons" from "textbooks" prescribed by the state and "recitation-periods" in which they tell an adult teacher what the book has said; one hears children reciting the battles of the Civil War in one recitation period, the rivers of Africa in another, the "parts of speech" in a third; the method is much the same. With high school come some differences; more "vocational" and "laboratory" work varies the periods. But here again the lesson-textbook-recitation method is the chief characteristic of education. For nearly an hour a teacher asks questions and pupils answer, then a bell rings, on the instant books bang, powder and mirrors come out, there is a buzz of talk and laughter as all the urgent business of living resumes momentarily for the children, notes and "dates" are exchanged, five minutes pass, another bell, gradual sliding into seats, a final giggle, a last vanity case snapped shut. "In our last lesson we had just finished"— and another class is begun.

All this ordered industry of imparting and learning facts and skills represents an effort on the part of this matter-of-fact community immersed in its daily activities to endow its young and certain essential supplements to the training received in the home. A quick epitome of the things adult Middletown has come to think it important for its children to learn in school, as well as some indication of regions of pressure and change, is afforded by the following summary of the work in Grades I and VII in 1890 and in 1924:

1890	1924
GRADE I	
Reading	Reading
Writing	Writing
Arithmetic	Arithmetic
Language	Language
Spelling	Spelling
Drawing	Drawing
Object Lessons (Science)	Geography
Music	Music
	Civic Training
	History and Civics
	Hygiene and Health
	Physical Education
GRADE VII	
Reading	Reading
Writing	Writing
Arithmetic	Arithmetic
Language	Language
Spelling	Spelling

1890	1924
Drawing	Drawing
Music	Music
Geography	Geography
Object Lessons (Science)	Civic Training
Compositions and Declamation	History and Civics
	Manual Arts (Boys)
	Home Economics (Girls)
	Physical Education

In the culture of thirty-five years ago it was deemed sufficient to teach during the first seven years of this extra-home training the following skills and facts, in rough order of importance:[15]

   a. The various uses of language. (Overwhelmingly first in importance.)
   b. The accurate manipulation of numerical symbols.
   c. Familiarity with the physical surroundings of peoples.
   d. A miscellaneous group of facts about familiar physical objects about the child—trees, sun, ice, food, and so on.
   e. The leisure-time skills of singing and drawing.

Today the things for which all children are sent to school fall into the following rough order:

   a. The same uses of language.
   b. The same uses of numerical figures.
   c. Training in patriotic citizenship.
   d. The same familiarity with the physical surroundings of peoples.
   e. Facts about how to keep well and some physical exercise.
   f. The same leisure-time skills of singing and drawing.
   g. Knowledge and skills useful in sewing, cooking and using tools about the home for the girls, and, for the boys, an introductory acquaintance with some of the manual skills by which the working class members get their living.

   Both in its optional, non-compulsory character and also in its more limited scope the school training of a generation ago appears to have been a more casual adjunct of the main business of "bringing up" that went on day by day in the home. Today, however, the school is relied upon to carry a more direct, if at most points still vaguely defined, responsibility. This has in turn reacted upon the content of the teaching and encouraged a

[15]The state law of 1865 upon which the public school system rests provided for instruction in "orthography, reading, writing, arithmetic, English, grammar, and good behavior," and the minutes of the Middletown School Board for 1882 (the only minutes for a decade on either side of 1890 which describe the course of study in detail) affirm that "reading, writing, and arithmetic are the three principal studies of the public schools, and if nothing more is possible, pupils should be taught to read the newspapers, write a letter, and perform the ordinary operations of arithmetic."

more utilitarian approach at certain points. A slow trend toward utilizing material more directly instrumental to the day-by-day urgencies of living appears clearly in such a course as that in hygiene and health, epitomized in the text-books used a generation ago and today, Jenkins' *Advanced Lessons in Human Physiology* in the one case and Emerson and Betts' *Physiology and Hygiene* in the other. The earlier book devoted twenty-one chapters, 287 of its 296 pages, to the structure and function of the body—"The Skeleton," "The Skin and the Kidneys," "The Anatomy of the Nervous System," and so on, and a final chapter, eight and one-quarter pages, to "the laws of health"; a three-page appendix on "Poisons and Antidotes" gave the various remedies to be used to induce vomiting after poisoning by aconite, arsenic, and so on, as well as rules for treating asphyxia. The current book, on the other hand, is primarily concerned throughout with the care of the body, and its structure is treated incidentally. Examination questions in the two periods show the same shift. Characteristic questions of 1890 such as "Describe each of the two kinds of matter of the nervous system" and "Tell weight and shape of brain. Tell names of membranes around it" are being replaced by "Write a paragraph describing exactly the kind of shoe you should wear, stating all the good points and the reasons for them," and "What is the law of muscles and bones (regarding posture)? How should it guide you in your daily life?"

Geography, likewise, according to the printed courses of study for the two periods, is less concerned today with memorizing "at least one important fact about each city located" and more with the "presence of storm and sunshine and song of bird," "interests of the child"; but classes visited are preoccupied with learning of facts, and 1890 and 1924 examination questions are interchangeable. Reading, spelling, and arithmetic, also, exhibit at certain points less emphasis upon elaboration of symbols and formal drill and more on the "practical application" of these skills; thus in reading, somewhat less attention is being paid to "clear and distinct enunciation" and "proper emphasis and expression" and more to "silent reading," which stresses content. But, in general, these subjects which are "the backbone of the curriculum" show less flexibility than do the subjects on the periphery or the newcomers. Most of these changes are indeed relatively slight; the social values represented by an "elementary education" are changing slowly in Middletown.

When we approach the high school, however, the matter-of-fact tendency of the city to commandeer education as an aid in dealing with its own concerns becomes more apparent. Caught less firmly than the elementary school in the wake of tradition and now forced to train children from a group not heretofore reached by it, the high school has been more adaptable than the lower school. Here group training no longer means the same set of facts learned on the same days by all children of a given grade. The freshman entering high school may plan to spend his four years following any one of twelve different "courses of study",[16] he may choose the

[16] 1. General Course
2. College Preparatory Course
3. Music Course
4. Art Course

7. Applied Electricity Course
8. Mechanical Drafting Course
9. Printing Course
10. Machine Shop Course

sixteen different yearly courses which will make up his four years of training from a total of 102.[17] All this is something new, for the 170 students who were going to high school in the "bursting days of boom" of 1889–90 had to choose, as Middletown high school students had done for thirty years, between two four-year courses, the Latin and the English courses, the sole difference between them being whether one did or did not take "the language." The number of separate year courses open to them totaled but twenty.

The facts and skills constituting the present-day high school curriculum present a combination of the traditional learning reputed to be essential to an "educated" man or woman and newer applied information or skills constantly being inserted into the curriculum to meet current immanent concerns. Here, too, English, the successor in its varied forms of the language work in the grades, far outdistances all competitors for student time, consuming 22 per cent. of all student hours. It is no longer compulsory throughout the entire four years as it was a generation ago; instead, it is required of all students for the first two years, and thereafter the earlier literary emphasis disappears in seven of the twelve courses, being replaced in the third year by commercial English, while in the fourth year it disappears entirely in five courses save as an optional subject. Both teaching and learning appear at times to be ordeals from which teachers and pupils alike would apparently gladly escape: "Thank goodness, we've finished Chaucer's *Prologue!*" exclaimed one high school English teacher. "I am thankful and the children are, too. They think of it almost as if it were in a foreign language, and they *hate* it."

| 5. Shorthand Course | 11. Manual Arts Course |
| 6. Bookkeeping Course | 12. Home Economics Course |

Courses Three to Twelve inclusive have a uniform first-year group of required and elective subjects. Four subjects are taken each half of each year, of which two or three are required and the rest selected from among a list offering from two to nine electives, according to the course and the year. The indispensables of secondary education required of every high school student are:

Four years of English for those taking Courses One through Six.
Three years of English for those taking Courses Seven through Twelve.
One year of algebra.
One year of general history
One year of American history.
One-half year of civics.
One-half year of sociology.
One year of science.
One-half year of music.
One-half year of gymnasium.

This constitutes a total of ten required and six elective one-year courses or their equivalents during the four years for the academic department (Courses One through Six) and nine required and seven elective courses for those in the vocational department (Courses Seven through Twelve).

[17]The year unit rather than the term or semester unit is taken here as the measure of the number of course, since it furnishes the only basis of comparison with 1890. When different subjects make up one year's course they are almost invariably related, e.g., civics and sociology, zoölogy and botany.

Latin, likewise, though still regarded by some parents of the business class as a vaguely significant earmark of the educated man or woman, is being rapidly attenuated in the training given the young. It is not required of any student for even one year, though in one of the twelve courses it or French is required for two years. Gone is the required course of the nineties taken by over half of the high school students for the entire four years and enticingly set forth in the course of study of the period as "Latin, Grammar, Harkness: Begun-Completed. Latin, Reader, Harkness: Begun-Completed. Latin, Caesar, Harkness: Begun-Completed. Latin, Virgil, Harkness: Begun-Completed." The "Virgil Club's" annual banquet and the "Latin Wedding" are, however, prominent high school social events today, and more than one pupil confessed that the lure of these in the senior year helped to keep him through four years of Latin. Although Latin is deader than last summer's straw hat to the men joshing each other about Middletown's Rotary luncheon table, tradition, the pressure of college entrace requirements, and such incidental social considerations as those just mentioned still manage to hold Latin to a place of prominence in the curriculum: 10 per cent. of all student hours are devoted to Latin, as against but 2 per cent. each to French and Spanish;[18] only English, the combined vocational courses, mathematics, and history consume more student hours.

The most pronounced region of movement appears in the rush of courses that depart from the traditional dignified conception of what constitutes education and seek to train for specific tool and skill activities in factory, office, and home. A generation ago a solitary optional senior course in bookkeeping was the thin entering wedge of the trend that today controls eight of the twelve courses of the high school and claimed 17 per cent. of the total student hours during the first semester of 1923–24 and 21 per cent. during the second.[19] At no point has the training prescribed for the preparation of children for effective adulthood approached more nearly actual preparation for the dominant concerns in the daily lives of the people of Middletown. This pragmatic commandeering of education is frankly stated by the president of the School Board: "For a long time all boys were trained to be President. Then for a while we trained them all to be professional men. Now we are training boys to get jobs."

Unlike Latin, English, and mathematics in that they have no independent, honorific traditions of their own, these vocational courses have frankly adopted the canons of office and machine shop: they must change in step with the coming of new physical equipment in machine shops and offices,

---

[18]Since the World War German has not been taught in Middletown.

[19] . . . In the case of English, the only subject or group of subjects to exceed the time spent on these non-academic courses, it should be borne in mind that in seven of the twelve courses of study offered by the high school one-third of the total English work required is a new vocational kind of English called commercial English, reflecting the workaday emphasis rather than the older academic emphasis in the curriculum.

It should also be recalled that, in addition to this high school work, manual arts is compulsory for all boys in Grades VI to VIII of the elementary school, and home economics is also compulsory for girls in Grades VII and VIII.

or become ineffective.[20] A recently organized radio class shows the possibility of quick adaptability to new developments. More than any other part of the school training, these vocational courses consist in learning *how* rather than learning *about*. Actual conditions of work in the city's factories are imported into the school shops; boys bring repair work from their homes; they study auto mechanics by working on an old Ford car; they design, draft, and make patterns for lathes and drill presses, the actual casting being done by a Middletown foundry; they have designed and constructed a house, doing all the architectural, carpentry, wiring, metal work, and painting. A plan for providing work in a local machine shop, alternating two weeks of this with two weeks of study throughout the year, is under discussion.

Under the circumstances, it is not surprising that this vocational work for boys is the darling of Middletown's eye—if we except a group of teachers and of parents of the business class who protest that the city's preoccupation with vocational work tends to drag down standards in academic studies and to divert the future college student's attention from his preparatory courses.[21] Like the enthusiastically supported high school basketball team, these vocational courses have caught the imagination of the mass of male tax-payers; ask your neighbor at Rotary what kind of schools Middletown has and he will begin to tell you about these "live" courses. It is not without significance that vocational supervisors are more highly paid than any other teachers in the school system.

Much of what has been said of the strictly vocational courses applies also to work in bookkeeping and stenography and in home economics. The

[20]This conformity to existing conditions is accentuated by the necessity of bidding for union support and falling in with current trade union practices. The attitude of the unions toward this school training varies all the way from that of the carpenters whose president attends the evening classes and who start a high school trained boy with a journeyman's card and corresponding wages to that of the bricklayers and plasterers who start a high school vocational graduate at exactly the same wage as an untrained boy.

[21]Many Middletown people maintain that the coming of vocational work to the high school has tended greatly to lower its standing as a college preparatory school. More than one mother shook her head over the fact that her daughter never does any studying at home and is out every evening but gets A's in all her work. It is generally recognized that a boy or girl graduating from the high school can scarcely enter an Eastern college without a year of additional preparatory work elsewhere.

Leading nationally known universities in neighboring states gave the following reports of the work of graduates of the Middletown high school: In one, of eleven Middletown students over a period of fifteen years, one graduated, none of the others made good records, four were asked to withdraw because of poor scholarship; of the four in residence in 1924, two were on probation, one was on the warned list, and one was doing fair work. In another, of five Middletown students in the last five years, one did excellent work, one fair, two did very poor work and dropped out after the first term, one had a record below requirement at the time of withdrawal. In a third, of eight Middletown students in the last five years, one was an excellent student, four were fair, and three were on probation. The single Middletown student in a fourth university attended for only a year and was on probation the entire time.

last-named, entirely new since 1890, is devised to meet the functional needs of the major group of the girls, who will be home-makers. Beginning in the seventh and eighth years with the study of food, clothing, and house-planning, it continues as an optional course through the high school with work in dressmaking, millinery, hygiene and home nursing, household management, and selection of food and clothing. As in the boys' vocational work, these courses center in the more obvious, accepted group practices; much more of the work in home economics, for example, centers in the traditional household productive skills such as canning, baking, and sewing, than in the rapidly growing battery of skills involved in effective buying of ready-made articles. The optional half-year course for the future business girl in selection of food and clothing, equipping a girl "to be an intelligent consumer," marks, however, an emergent recognition of a need for training in effective consumption, as does also the class visiting of local stores to inspect and discuss various kinds of household articles. In 1925 a new course in child care and nutrition was offered in one of the grade schools; while it consists almost entirely in the study of child feeding rather than of the wider aspects of child care, it is highly significant as being the first and sole effort on the part of the community to train women for this fundamental child-rearing function. Standard women's magazines are resorted to in these courses for girls as freely as technical journals are employed in the courses for boys.

Second only in importance to the rise of these courses addressed to practical vocational activities is the new emphasis upon courses in history and civics. These represent yet another point at which Middletown is bending its schools to the immediate service of its institutions—in this case, bolstering community solidarity against sundry divisive tendencies. A generation ago a course in American history was given to those who survived until the eighth grade, a course in general history, "covering everything from the Creation to the present in one little book of a hundred or so pages," followed in the second year of the high school, and one in civil government in the third year. Today, separate courses in civic training and in history and civics begin with the first grade for all children and continue throughout the elementary school, while in high school the third-year course in American history and the fourth-year course in civics and sociology are, with the exception of the second-year English course, the only courses required of all students after the completion of the first year. Sixteen per cent. of the total student hours in the high school are devoted to these social studies—history, sociology, and civics—a total surpassed only by those of English and the combined cluster of vocational, domestic science, manual arts, and commercial courses.

Evidently Middletown has become concerned that no child shall be without this pattern of the group.[22] Precisely what this stamp is appears clearly in instructions to teachers:[23]

[22]"Good citizenship as an aim in life is nothing new. . . . But good citizenship as a dominant aim of the American public school is something new. . . . For the first time in history, as I see it, a social democracy is attempting to shape the opinions and bias the judgment of oncoming generations." From the *Annual Report* of Dean James E. Russell of Teachers College for the year ending June, 1925.

"The most fundamental impression a study of history should leave on the youth of the land when they have reached the period of citizenship," begins the section on history and civics of the Middletown Course of Study of the Elementary Schools, "is that they are their government's keepers as well as their brother's keepers in a very true sense. This study should lead us to feel and will that sacrifice and service for our neighbor are the best fruits of life; that reverence for law, which means, also, reverence for God, is fundamental to citizenship; that private property, in the strictest sense, is a trust imposed upon us to be administered for the public good; that no man can safely live unto himself. . . ."

"History furnishes no parallel of national growth, national prosperity and national achievement like ours," asserts the State Manual for Secondary Schools for 1923. "Practically all of this has been accomplished since we adopted our present form of government, and we are justified in believing that our political philosophy is right, and that those who are today assailing it are wrong. To properly grasp the philosophy of this government of ours, requires a correct knowledge of its history."

The State Manual for Elementary Schools for 1921 instructs that "a sense of the greatness of their state and a pride in its history should be developed in the minds of children," and quotes as part of its directions to teachers of history: "The right of revolution does not exist in America. We had a revolution 140 years ago which made it unnecessary to have any other revolution in this country. . . . One of the many meanings of democracy is that it is a form of government in which the right of revolution has been lost. . . . No man can be a sound and sterling American who believes that force is necessary to effectuate

---

In view of the manifest concern in Middletown to dictate the social attitudes of its young citizens, the concentration of college attendance of local high school graduates in local or near-by institutions is significant. As noted in the preceding chapter, forty-four of the eighty members of the high school class of 1924 who were attending college were enrolled in the small local college; twelve more were in the two state universities, ten more in other small colleges within the state, nine were in small colleges in adjoining states, two in nationally known state universities in adjoining states, two in prominent eastern colleges, and one in an eastern school giving specialized training—a total of sixty-six within the city or state, eleven in immediately adjoining states, and three in distant states. This when coupled with the tendency already pointed out for from one-third to one-half of each high school graduating class, including almost certainly many of the most enterprising and original members, to migrate to other communities, and the further tendency of Middletown to favor teachers trained within the state, presents some interesting implications for the process of social change in Middletown.

[23]Descriptions of courses and instructions to teachers as set forth by the School Board or State Department of Education sometimes bear little relation to what children are actually being taught in the classroom. But they do show what those directing the training of the young think *ought* to be taught and what they believe the public thinks ought to be taught. As indicating major characteristics of this culture, therefore, they are, in one sense, even more significant than the things that actually go on in the class-room. And by and large they do, of course, indicate trends in teaching.

the popular will. . . . Americanism . . . emphatically means . . . that we have repudiated old European methods of settling domestic questions, and have evolved for ourselves machinery by which revolution as a method of changing our life is outgrown, abandoned, outlawed."

The president of the Board of Education, addressing a meeting of Middletown parents in 1923, said that "many educators have failed to face the big problem of teaching patriotism. . . . We need to teach American children about American heroes and American ideals."

The other social studies resemble history in their announced aims: civic training, with its emphasis upon respect for private property, respect for public property, respect for law, respect for the home, appreciation of services of good men and women, and so on; economics, with its stressing of "common and fundamental principles," "the fundamental institutions of society: property, guaranteed privileges, contracts, personal liberty, right to establish private enterprises"; and sociology.

Nearly thirty-five years ago the first high school annual summarized the fruits of four years of high school training as follows: "Many facts have been presented to us and thus more knowledge has been attained." Such a summary would be nearly as applicable today, and nowhere more so than in these social studies. Teaching varies from teacher to teacher, but with a few outstanding exceptions the social studies are taught with close reliance upon textbooks prescribed by the state and in large measure embodying its avowed aims. A leading teacher of history and civics in the high school explained:

"In class discussion I try to bring out minor points, two ways of looking at a thing and all that, but in examinations I try to emphasize important principles and group the main facts that they have to remember around them. I always ask simple fact questions in examinations. They get all mixed up and confused if we ask questions where they have to think, and write all over the place."

In the case of history, facts presented in the textbooks are, as in 1890, predominantly military and political, although military affairs occupy relatively less space than in the nineties. Facts concerning economic and industrial development receive more emphasis than in the earlier texts, although political development is still the core. Recent events as compared with the colonial period in colonial history are somewhat more prominent today.[24] Examination questions of the two periods indicate so little change in method and emphasis in teaching that it is almost impossible simply

[24]See W. C. Bagley and H. O. Rugg, *The Content of American History as Taught in the Seventh and Eighth Grades* (University of Illinois School of Education Bulletin No. 16, Vol. XIII, 1916), comparing textbooks from 1865 to 1911, with a supplementary study by Earle Rugg of *Eight Current Histories*, and Snyder's *An Analysis of the Content of Elementary High School History Texts* (University of Chicago Doctor's Dissertation, 1919). Montgomery's *The Leading Facts of American History*, used in the Middletown schools in the nineties, and Woodburn and Moran's *American History and Government*, used in 1924, were included in the Rugg-Bagley study. Fite's *History of the United States*, used in the Middletown schools in 1924, was included in Snyder's study.

by reading a history examination to tell whether it is of 1890 or 1924 vintage.

It may be a commentary upon the vitality of this early and persistent teaching of American history that when pictures like the Yale Press historical series are brought to Middletown the children say they get enough history in school, the adults say they are too grown up for such things, and the attendance is so poor that the exhibitor says, "Never again!"

Further insight into the stamp of the group with which Middletown children complete their social studies courses is gained through the following summary of answers of 241 boys and 315 girls, comprising the social science classes of the last two years of the high school, to a questionnaire:[25]

Statement	Percentage answering "True"		Percentage answering "False"		Percentage answering "Uncertain"		Percentage not answering	
	Boys	Girls	Boys	Girls	Boys	Girls	Boys	Girls
The white race is the best race on earth	66	75	19	17	14	6	1	2
The United States is unquestionably the best country in the world	77	88	10	6	11	5	2	1
Every good citizen should act according to the following statement: "My country—right or wrong!"	47	56	40	29	9	10	4	5
A citizen of the United States should be allowed to say anything he pleases, even to advocate violent revolution, if he does no violent act himself	20	16	70	75	7	7	3	2
The recent labor government in England was a misfortune for England	16	15	38	20	38	57	8	8
The United States was entirely right and England was entirely wrong in the American Revolution	30	33	55	40	13	25	2	2

(Continued on next page)

[25]Students were requested to write "true," "false," or "uncertain" after each statement. No answers of Negroes are included in this summary. The greater conservatism of the girls in their answers to some of the questions is noteworthy.

Statement	Percentage answering "True"		Percentage answering "False"		Percentage answering "Uncertain"		Percentage not answering	
	Boys	Girls	Boys	Girls	Boys	Girls	Boys	Girls
The Allied Governments in the World War were fighting for a wholly righteous cause	65	75	22	8	11	14	2	3
Germany and Austria were the only nations responsible for causing the World War	22	25	62	42	15	31	1	2
The Russian Bolshevist government should be recognized by the United States Government	8	5	73	67	17	24	2	4
A pacifist in war time is a "slacker" and should be prosecuted by the government	40	36	34	28	22	28	4	8
The fact that some men have so much more money than others shows that there is an unjust condition in this country which ought to be changed	25	31	70	62	4	5	1	2

Other new emphases in the training given the young may be noted briefly. Natural sciences, taught in 1890 virtually without a laboratory[26] by a teacher trained in English and mathematics and by the high school principal who also taught all other junior and senior subjects, is today taught in well-equipped student laboratories by specially trained teachers. In the first and second semesters of 1923–24, 7 per cent. and 8 per cent. respectively of the student hours were devoted to the natural sciences.

Although art and music appear to occupy a lesser place in the spontaneous leisure-time life of Middletown than they did a generation ago, both are more prominent in the training given the young. In 1890 both

[26]Says the high school annual in 1804: "The laboratory is situated in what is known as the south office—a room six by four feet. On the east side of the room are a few shelves containing a half dozen bottles of chemicals. This is the extent of the chemical 'laboratory.' The physical laboratory will be found (with the aid of a microscope) in the closet adjoining the south office. Here will be found the remants of an old electric outfit, and a few worn-out pieces of apparatus to illustrate the principles of natural philosophy."

were unknown in the high school except for the informal high school choir; a lone music teacher taught three hours a day in the grades; and "drawing" was taught "as an aid to muscular coördination" on alternate days with writing. Today art is taught in all eight years of the grades, while in high school a student may center his fours years' work in either art or music, two of the twelve courses being built around these subjects. The high school art courses consist in creative work, art history, and art appreciation, while art exhibits and art contests reach far beyond formal class-room work.[27] Over and above the work in ear training and sight reading throughout the grades, there are today sixteen high school music courses in addition to classes in instrumental work. They include not only instruction in harmony, history of music, and music appreciation, but a chorus, four Glee Clubs, three orchestras, and two bands. Victrolas, now a necessary part of the equipment of all schools, and an annual music memory contest in the schools, further help to bring music within the reach of all children.[28]

Another innovation today is the more explicit recognition that education concerns bodies as well as minds. Gymnasium work, required of all students during the last year of the elementary school and the first year of the high school, replaces the earlier brief periods of "setting-up exercises" and seems likely to spread much more widely.

Abundant evidence has appeared throughout this chapter of the emphasis upon values and "right" attitudes in this business of passing along the lore of the elders to the young of Middletown. Since the religious attitudes and values are nominally held in this culture to overshadow all others, no account of the things taught in the schools would be adequate without a discussion of the relation of the schools to the religious beliefs and practices of the city. Getting a living, as we have observed, goes forward without any accompanying religious ceremonies or without any formal relation to the religious life of the city save that it "keeps the Sabbath day." Religion permeates the home at many points: marriage, birth, and death are usually accompanied or followed by religious rites, the eating of food is frequently preceded by its brief verbal blessing, most children are taught to say their prayers before retiring at night, a Bible is found in nearly every home, and the entire family traditionally prays together daily, though this last, as noted elsewhere, is becoming rare; the family itself is regarded as a sacred institution, though being secularized at many points. Leisure-time practices are less often today opened by prayer or hymns;

[27]The class work itself reaches all groups of students. A barber commented proudly on the interest of his daughter, a high school junior, in her art work: "We have some friends that made fun of her for taking art—they thought it meant painting big pictures. My wife heard her talking art to some people the other day and says she could hold up her end with the best of 'em. I'm all for it. Now it has practical application. When it comes to fixing up a house she'll know what things go good together."

[28]Neither this music work nor the art work in the schools appears to be as rooted in the present-day local life as the emphasis upon vocational education and the social studies. In fact, they represent a tradition less strong in the everyday life of the city today than a generation ago. Whether they will tend to increase spontaneous and active participation in music and art, as opposed to the passive enjoyment of them that predominates in this culture today, is problematical.

though they have traditionally "observed the Sabbath," abundant testimony appears throughout this study of the attenuation of such observance of the "Lord's Day" by young and old. The common group affairs of the city, likewise, are increasingly carried on, like getting a living, without direct recourse to religious ceremonies and beliefs. In the midst of the medley of secularized and non-secularized ways of living in the city, education steers a devious course. One religious group, the Catholics, trains its children in a special school building under teachers who are professional religious devotees and wear a religious garb; this school adjoins the church and the children attend a church service as part of their day's schooling. For the great mass of children, however, separate Sunday Schools, in no way controlled by the secular schools, teach the accepted religious beliefs to those who choose to attend. The Y.M.C.A. and Y.W.C.A. serve as a liaison between church and school, teaching Bible classes in all elementary schools, for the most part on school time, and giving work in the high school for which credit is granted towards graduation. But while the public schools themselves do not teach the group's religious beliefs directly, these beliefs tacitly underlie much that goes on in the class-room, more particularly those classes concerned not with the manipulation of material tools but with the teaching of ideas, concepts, attitudes. The first paragraph in the "Course of Study of the Elementary Schools" enjoins upon the teachers that "all your children should join in opening the day with some exercise which will prepare them with thankful hearts and open minds for the work of the day. . . . The Bible should be heard and some sacred song sung." The School Board further instructs its teachers that geography should teach "the spirit of reverence and appreciation for the works of God—that these things have been created for [man's] joy and elevation . . . that the earth in its shape and movements, its mountains and valleys, its drought and flood, and in all things that grow upon it, is well planned for man in working out his destiny"; that history should teach "the earth as the field of man's spiritual existence"; that hygiene create interest in the care of the body "as a fit temple for the spirit"; finally that "the schools should lead the children, through their insight into the things of nature that they study, to appreciate the power, wisdom, and goodness of the Author of these things. They should see in the good things that come out of man's struggle for a better life a guiding hand stronger than his own. . . . The pupils should learn to appreciate the Bible as a fountain of truth and beauty through the lessons to be gotten from it. . ."

This emphasis was if anything even stronger in 1890. At the Teachers' Institute in 1890 botany was discussed as a subject in which "by the study of nature we are enabled to see the perfection of creation," and a resolution was passed that "the moral qualifications of the teachers should be of such a nature as to make them fit representatives to instruct for both time and eternity." "In morals, show the importance of building upon principles. Encourage the pupil to do right because it is right," said the School Board instructions for 1882. One gains a distinct impression that the religious basis of all education was more taken for granted if less talked about thirty-five years ago, when high school "chapel" was a religio-inspirational service with a "choir" instead of the "pep session" which it tends to become today.

Some inkling of the degree of dominance of religious ways of thinking at the end of ten or twelve years of education is afforded by the answers of the 241 boys and 315 girls in the social science classes of the last two years of the high school appraising the statement: "The theory of evolution offers a more accurate account of the origin and history of mankind than that offered by a literal interpretation of the first chapters of the Bible": 19 per cent. of them marked it "true," 48 per cent. "false," 26 per cent. were "uncertain," and 7 per cent. did not answer.

SCHOOL "LIFE"

Accompanying the formal training afforded by courses of study is another and informal kind of training, particularly during the high school years. The high school, with its athletics, clubs, sororities and fraternities, dances and parties, and other "extracurricular activities," is a fairly complete social cosmos in itself, and about this city within a city the social life of the intermediate generation centers. Here the social sifting devices of their elders—money, clothes, personal attractiveness, male physical prowess, exclusive clubs, election to positions of leadership—are all for the first time set going with a population as yet largely undifferentiated save as regards their business class and working class parents. This informal training is not a preparation for a vague future that must be taken on trust, as in the case with so much of the academic work; to many of the boys and girls in high school this is "the life," the thing they personally like best about going to school.

The school is taking over more and more of the child's waking life. Both high school and grades have departed from the attitude of fifty years ago, when the Board directed:

> "Pupils shall not be permitted to remain on the school grounds after dismissal. The teachers shall often remind the pupils that the first duty when dismissed is to proceed quietly and directly home to render all needed assistance to their parents."

Today the school is becoming not a place to which children go from their homes for a few hours daily but a place from which they go home to eat and sleep.[29]

An index to this widening of the school's function appears in a comparison of the 1924 high school annual with the first annual, published thirty years before, though even this comparison does not reflect the full extent of the shift since 1890, for innovations had been so numerous in the years just preceding 1894 as to dwarf the extent of the 1890–1924 contrast. Next in importance to the pictures of the senior class and other class data

---

[29]This condition is deplored by some as indicative of the "break-up of the American home." Others welcome it as freeing the child earlier from the domination of parents and accustoming him to face adjustments upon the success of which adult behavior depends. In any event, the trend appears to be in the direction of an extension of the present tendency increasingly into the grades.

in the earlier book, as measured by the percentage of space occupied, were the pages devoted to the faculty and the courses taught by them, while in the current book athletics shares the position of honor with the class data, and a faculty twelve times as large occupies relatively only half as much space. Interest in small selective group "activities" has increased at the expense of the earlier total class activities.[30] But such a numerical comparison can only faintly suggest the difference in tone of the two books. The description of academic work in the early annual beginning, "Among the various changes that have been effected in grade work are . . ." and ending, "regular monthly teachers' meetings have been inaugurated," seems as foreign to the present high school as does the early class motto "Deo Duce"; equally far from 1890 is the present dedication, "To the Bearcats."

This whole spontaneous life of the intermediate generation that clusters about the formal nucleus of school studies becomes focused, articulate, and even rendered important in the eyes of adults through the medium of the school athletic teams—the "Bearcats."[31] The business man may "lay down the law" to his adolescent son or daughter at home and patronize their friends, but in the basket-ball grandstand he is if anything a little less important than these youngsters of his who actually mingle daily with those five boys who wear the colors of "Magic Middletown." There were no high school teams in 1890. Today, during the height of the basket-ball season when all the cities and towns of the state are fighting for the state championship amidst the delirious backing of the rival citizens, the dominance of this sport is as all-pervasive as football in a college like Dartmouth or Princeton the week of the "big game." At other times dances, dramatics, and other interests may bulk larger, but it is the "Bearcats," particularly the basket-ball team, that dominate the life of the school. Says the prologue to the high school annual:

> "The Bearcat spirit has permeated our high school in the last few years and pushed it into the prominence that it now holds. The '24 *Magician* has endeavored to catch, reflect and record this spirit because it has been so evident this year. We hope that after you have glanced at this book for the first time, this spirit will be evident to you.
>
> "However, most of all, we hope that in perhaps twenty years, if you become tired of this old world, you will pick up this book and it will restore to you the spirit, pep, and enthusiasm of the old 'Bearcat Days' and will inspire in you better things."

[30]The following shows the percentage of the pages of the annual occupied by the chief items in 1894 and 1924, the earlier year being in each case given first: Class data—39 per cent., 19 per cent.; faculty–16 per cent., 8 per cent. (brief biographies and pictures in 1894, list of names only and picture of principal in 1924), athletics–5 per cent., 19 per cent.; courses of study–6 per cent., 0.0 per cent.; class poems–13 per cent., 0.0 per cent.; activities other than athletics–5 per cent. (one literary society), 13 per cent. (thirteen *kinds* of clubs); jokes—5 per cent., 17 per cent.; advertisements and miscellaneous—11 per cent., 24 per cent.

[31]In the elementary grades athletics are still a minor interest, though a school baseball and basket-ball league have been formed of recent years and the pressure of inter-school leagues and games is being felt increasingly.

Every issue of the high school weekly bears proudly the following "Platform":

    "1. To support live school organizations.

    "2. To recognize worth-while individual student achievements.

    "3. Above all to foster the real 'Bearcat' spirit in all of Central High School."

Curricular and social interests tend to conform. Friday nights throughout the season are preëmpted for games; the Mothers' Council, recognizing that every Saturday night had its own social event, urged that other dances be held on Friday nights instead of school nights, but every request was met with the rejoinder that "Friday is basket-ball night."

This activity, so enthusiastically supported, is largely vicarious. The press complains that only about forty boys are prominent enough in athletics to win varsity sweaters. In the case of the girls it is almost 100 per cent. vicarious. Girls play some informal basket-ball and there is a Girls' Athletic Club which has a monogram and social meetings. But the interest of the girls in athletics is an interest in the activities of the young males. "My daughter plans to go to the University of—" said one mother, "because she says, 'Mother, I just *couldn't* go to a college whose athletics I couldn't be proud of!' " The highest honor a senior boy can have is captaincy of the football or basket-ball team, although, as one senior girl explained, "Every member is almost as much admired."

Less spectacular than athletics but bulking even larger in time demands is the network of organizations that serve to break the nearly two thousand individuals composing the high school microcosm into the more intimate groups human beings demand. These groups are mainly of three kinds: the purely social clubs, in the main a stepping down of the social system of adults; a long distance behind in point of prestige, clubs formed around curriculum activities; and, even farther behind, a few groups sponsored by the religious systems of the adults.

In 1894 the high school boasted one club, the "Turemethian Literary Society." According to the early school yearbook:

> "The Turemethian Society makes every individual feel that practically he is free to choose between good and evil; that he is not a mere straw thrown upon the water to mark the direction of the current, but that he has within himself the power of a strong swimmer and is capable of striking out for himself, of buffeting the waves, and directing, to a certain extent, his own independent course. Socrates said, 'Let him who would move the world move first himself.' . . . A paper called the Zetetic is prepared and read at each meeting. . . . Debates have created . . . a friendly rivalry. . . . Another very interesting feature of the Turemethian Society is the lectures delivered to us. . . . All of these lectures help to make our High School one of the first of its kind in the land. The Turemethian Society has slowly progressed in the last year. What the future has in store for it we can not tell, but must say as Mary Riley Smith said, 'God's plans, like lilies pure and white, unfold; we must not tear the close-shut leaves apart; time will reveal the calyxes of gold.' "

Six years later, at the turn of the century, clubs had increased to the point of arousing protest in a press editorial entitled "Barriers to Intellectual Progress." Today clubs and other extracurricular activities are more numerous than ever. Not only is the camel's head inside the tent but his hump as well; the first period of the school day, often running over into the next hour, has recently, at the request of the Mothers' Council, been set aside as a "convocation hour" dedicated to club and committee meetings.

The backbone of the purely social clubs is the series of unofficial branches of former high school fraternities and sororities; Middletown boasts four Alpha chapters. For a number of years a state law has banned these high school organizations, but the interest of active graduate chapters keeps them alive. The high school clubs have harmless names such as the Glendale Club; a boy is given a long, impressive initiation into his club but is not nominally a member of the fraternity of which his club is the undergraduate section until after he graduates, when it is said that by the uttering of a few hitherto unspoken words he comes into his heritage. Under this ambiguous status dances have been given with the club name on the front of the program and the fraternity name on the back. Two girls' clubs and two boys' clubs which every one wants to make are the leaders. Trailing down from them are a long list of lesser clubs. Informal meetings are usually in homes of members but the formal fall, spring, and Christmas functions are always elaborate hotel affairs.

Extracurricular clubs have canons not dictated by academic standards of the world of teachers and textbooks. Since the adult world upon which the world of this intermediate generation is modeled tends to be dominated primarily by getting a living and "getting on" socially rather than by learning and "the things of the mind," the bifurcation of high school life is not surprising.

"When do you study?" some one asked a clever high school Senior who had just finished recounting her week of club meetings, committee meetings, and dances, ending with three parties the night before. "Oh, in civics I know more or less about politics, so it's easy to talk and I don't have to study that. In English we're reading plays and I can just look at the end of the play and know about that. Typewriting and chemistry I don't have to study outside anyway. Virgil is worst, but I've stuck out Latin four years for the Virgil banquet; I just sit next to —and get it from her. Mother jumps on me for never studying, but I get A's all the time, so she can't say anything."

The relative status of academic excellence and other qualities is fairly revealed in the candid rejoinder of one of the keenest and most popular girls in the school to the question, "What makes a girl eligible for a leading high school club?"

"The chief thing is if the boys like you and you can get them for the dances," she replied. "Then, if your mother belongs to a graduate chapter that's pretty sure to get you in. Good looks and clothes don't necessarily get you in, and being good in your studies doesn't necessarily keep you out unless you're a 'grind.' Same way with the boys— the big thing there is being on the basket-ball or football team. A fellow who's just a good student rates pretty low. Being good-looking, a good dancer, and your family owning a car will help."

The clubs allied to curricular activities today include the Dramatic Club–plays by sophomore, junior, and senior classes in a single spring have replaced the "programs of recitations, selections, declamations, and essays" of the old days; the Daubers, meeting weekly in school hours to sketch and in evening meetings with graduate members for special talks on art; the Science Club with its weekly talks by members and occasional lectures by well-known scientists; the Pickwick Club, open to members of English classes, meeting weekly for book reviews and one-act plays, with occasional social meetings; the Penmanship Club; and the Virgil Club, carrying with it some social prestige. Interest in the work of these clubs is keen among some students. All have their "pledges," making their rituals conform roughly to those of the more popular fraternities and sororities.

On the periphery of this high school activity are the church and Y.M.C.A. and Y.W.C.A. clubs. All these organizations frankly admit that the fifteen to twenty-one-year [old] person is their hardest problem. The Hi-Y club appears to be most successful. The Y.M.C.A. controls the extracurricular activities of the grade school boys more than any other single agency, but it maintains itself with only moderate success in the form of this Hi-Y club among the older boys. A Hi-Y medal is awarded each commencement to the boy in the graduating class who shows the best all-round record, both in point of scholarship and of character. The Y.W.C.A. likewise maintains clubs in the grades but has rough sledding when it comes to the busy, popular, influential group in high school. According to one representative senior girl:

> "High School girls pay little attention to the Y.W. and the Girl Reserves. The boys go to the Y.M. and Hi-Y club because it has a supper meeting once a month, and that is one excuse for getting away from home evenings. There aren't any supper meetings for the girls at the Y.W. It's not much good to belong to a Y.W. club; *any one* can belong to them."

All manner of other clubs, such as the Hiking Club and the Boys' and Girls' Booster Club and the Boys' and Girls' Pep Club hover at the fringes or even occasionally take the center of the stage. Says the school paper:

> "Pep Clubs are being organized in Central High School with a motive that wins recognition. Before, there has been a Pep Club in school, but this year we are more than fortunate in having two. Their business-like start this year predicts a good future. Let's support them!"

Pep week during the basket-ball season, engineered by these Pep Clubs, included:

> *"Monday:* Speakers in each of the four assemblies. . . .
> *"Tuesday:* Poster Day.
> *"Wednesday:* Reverend Mr. —in chapel. Booster pins and pep tags.
> *"Thursday:* Practice on yells and songs.
> *"Friday:* Final Chapel. Mr. —speaks. Yells and songs.

"Pep chapel[32] for all students will be held in the auditorium the ninth period. Professor —and his noisy cohorts will furnish the music for the occasion. Immediately following the chapel the students will parade through the business district."

With the growth of smaller competitive groups, class organization has also increased, reaching a crescendo of importance in the junior and senior years. In a community with such a strong political tradition it is not surprising that there should be an elaborate ritual in connection with the election of senior and other class officers. The senior officers are nominated early in the school year, after much wire-pulling by all parties. "The diplomatic agents of the candidates have been working for weeks on this election," commented the school paper. The election comes a week later so as to allow plenty of electioneering; the evening before election an "enthusiasm dinner" is held in the school cafeteria at which nominees and their "campaign managers" vie with each other in distributing attractive favors (menus, printed paper napkins, and so on), and each candidate states his platform.

Amid the round of athletics, clubs, committees, and class meetings there is always some contest or other to compete for the time of the pupils. Principals complain that hardly a week passes that they do not have to take time from class work in preparation for a contest, the special concern of some organization. In 1923–24 these included art and music memory contests, better speech and commercial department contests, a Latin contest, a contest on the Constitution, essays on meat eating, tobacco, poster making, home lighting, and highways.

In this bustle of activity young Middletown swims along in a world as real and perhaps even more zestful than that in which its parents move. Small wonder that a local paper comments editorially, "It is a revelation to old-timers to learn that a genuine boy of the most boyish type nowadays likes to go to school." "Oh, yes, they have a much better time," rejoined the energetic father of a high school boy to a question asked informally of a tableful of men at a Kiwanis luncheon as to whether boys really have a better time in school than they did thirty-five years ago or whether they simply have more things. "No doubt about it!" added another. "When I graduated early in the nineties there weren't many boys—only two in our class, and a dozen girls. All our studies seemed very far away from real life, but today—they've got shop work and athletics, and it's all nearer what a boy's interested in."

The relative disregard of most people in Middletown for teachers and for the content of books, on the one hand, and the exalted position of the social and athletic activities of the schools, on the other, offer an interesting commentary on Middletown's attitude toward education. And yet Middletown places large faith in going to school. The heated opposition to compulsory education in the nineties[33] has virtually disappeared; only three

[32]The evolution of the chapel to anything from a "Pep chapel" to a class rally is an interesting example of the change of custom while the label persists.

[33]The following, from editorials in the leading daily in 1891, reflect the virulence with which compulsory education was fought by many, and incidentally exhibit a pattern of opposition to social change that bobs up from time to time today as innovations appear:

of the 124 working class families interviewed voiced even the mildest impatience at it. Parents insist upon more and more education as part of their children's birthright; editors and lecturers point to education as a solution for every kind of social ill; the local press proclaims, "Public Schools of [Middletown] Are the City's Pride"; woman's club papers speak of the home, the church, and the school as the "foundations" of Middletown's culture. Education is a faith, a religion, to Middletown. And yet when one looks more closely at this dominant belief in the magic of formal schooling, it appears that it is not what actually goes on in the schoolroom that these many voices laud. Literacy, yes, they want their children to be able to "read the newspapers, write a letter, and perform the ordinary operations of arithmetic," but, beyond that, many of them are little interested in what the schools teach. This thing, education, appears to be desired frequently not for its specific content but as a symbol—by the working class as an open sesame that will mysteriously admit their children to a world closed to them, and by the business class as a heavily sanctioned aid in getting on further economically or socially in the world.

Rarely does one hear a talk addressed to school children by a Middletown citizen that does not contain in some form the idea, "Of course, you won't remember much of the history or other things they teach you here. Why, I haven't thought of Latin or algebra in thirty years! But . . ." And here the speaker goes on to enumerate what *are* to his mind the enduring values of education which every child should seize as his great opportunity: "habits of industry," "friendships formed," "the great ideals of our nation." Almost never is the essential of education defined in terms of the subjects taught in the class-room. One member of Rotary spoke with pitying sympathy of his son who "even brought along a history book to read on the

---

"Taxpayers of this country are upset by the state and county teachers' resolutions favoring compulsory education. . . . The teachers in our schools are not well versed in political economy. The most of them are young, and have had little time to study anything other than textbooks and their reports and programs. The idea of compulsion is detestable to the average American citizen. Men do not become good under compulsion. Two classes of men are clamoring for compulsory education: those who are depending upon school work for a living and for place and power, and those who are afraid of the Catholic Church. . . . The school system has not done what was expected of it. Immorality and crime are actually on the increase. . . . The states that have the greatest percentage of illiteracy have the smallest percentage of crime. . . . Compulsory education has failed wherever tried on American soil."

"The danger to the country today is through too many educated scoundrels. Boys and girls learn to cheat and defraud in copying papers for graduation essays. . . . A law compelling a child seven years of age to sit in a poorly ventilated school room and inhale the nauseous exhalations from the bodies of his mates for six hours a day for three or four months at a time, is a wicked and inhuman law. . . . Children forced into schools are morally tainted—and neutralize the virtues of well-bred children. It is a great mistake for the state to undertake to carry forward the evolution of the race from such bad material when there is so much good material at hand. Every movement that tends to relieve the father or mother of the moral responsibility of developing, training and directing the moral and intellectual forces of their own children, tends to reduce marriage and the home to a mere institution for the propagation of our species."

The press of 1900 noted that "the problem of securing boy labor is still worrying [state] manufacturers. The truancy law, they say, is detrimental to their business."

train when he came home for his Christmas vacation—the poor over-worked kid!"

Furthermore, in Middletown's traditional philosophy it is not primar-ily learning, or even intelligence, as much as character and good will which are exalted. Says Edgar Guest, whose daily message in Middletown's lead-ing paper is widely read and much quoted:

> "God won't ask you if you were clever,
> For I think he'll little care,
> When your toil is done forever
> He may question: 'Were you square?' "

"You know the smarter the man the more dissatisfied he is," says Will Rogers in a Middletown paper, "so cheer up, let us be happy in our igno-rance." "I wanted my son to go to a different school in the East," said a business class mother, "because it's more cultured. But then I think you can have too much culture. It's all right if you're living in the East—or even in California—but it unfits you for living in the Middle West." Every one lauds education in general, but relatively few people in Middletown seem to be sure just how they have ever used their own education beyond such commonplaces as the three R's and an occasional odd fact, or to value greatly its specific outcome in others.

Some clew to these anomalies of the universal lauding of education but the disparagement of many of the particular things taught, and of the universal praise of the schools but the almost equally general apathy towards the people entrusted with the teaching, may be found in the disparity that exists at many points between the daily activites of Middletown adults and the things taught in the schools. Square root, algebra, French, the battles of the Civil War, the presidents of the United States before Grover Cleve-land, the boundaries of the state of Arizona, whether Rangoon is on the Yangtze or Ganges or neither, the nature or location of the Japan Current, the ability to write compositions or to use semicolons, sonnets, free verse, and the Victorian novel—all these and many other things that constitute the core of education simply do not operate in life as Middletown adults live it. And yet, the world says education is important; and certainly edu-cated men seem to have something that brings them to the top—just look at the way the college boys walked off with the commissions during the war. The upshot is, with Middletown reasoning thus, that a phenomenon common in human culture has appeared: a value divorced from current, tangible existence in the world all about men and largely without com-merce with these concrete existential realities has become an ideal to which independent existence is attributed. Hence the anomaly of Middletown's regard for the symbol of education and its disregard for the concrete pro-cedure of the school-room.

But the pressure and accidents of local life are prompting Middletown to lay hands upon its schools at certain points, as we have observed, and to use them instrumentally to foster patriotism, teach hand skills, and serve its needs in other ways. This change, again characteristically, is tak-ing place not so much through the direct challenging of the old as through the setting up of new alternate procedures, e.g., the adding to the traditional high school, offering only a Latin and an English course in 1890, of ten complete alternate courses ranging all the way from shorthand to home economics and mechanical drafting. The indications seem to be that the optional newcomers may in time displace more and more of the traditional education and thus the training given the young will approach more nearly the methodically practical concerns of the group.

Lest this trend of education overtaking the life of Middletown appear too simple, however, it should be borne in mind that even while Middletown prides itself on its "up-to-date" schools with their vocational training, the local institutional life is creating fresh strains and maladjustments heretofore unknown: the city boasts of the fact that only 2.5 per cent. of its population ten years of age or older cannot read and write, and meanwhile the massed weight of advertising and professional publicity are creating, as pointed out above, new forms of social illiteracy, and the invention of the motion picture is introducing the city's population, young and old, week after week, into types of vivid experience which they come to take for granted as parts of their lives, yet have no training to handle. Another type of social illiteracy is being bred by the stifling of self-appraisal and self-criticism under the heavily diffused habit of local solidarity in which the schools coöperate. An organized, professional type of city-boosting, even more forceful than the largely spontaneous, amateur enthusiasm of the gas boom days, has grown up in the shelter of national propaganda during the war. Fostered particularly by the civic clubs, backed by the Chamber of Commerce and business interests, as noted elsewhere, it insists that the city must be kept to the fore and its shortcomings blanketed under the din of local boosting—or new business will not come to town. The result of this is the muzzling of self-criticism by hurling the term "knocker" at the head of a critic and the drowning of incipient social problems under a public mood of everything being "fine and dandy." Thus, while education slowly pushes its tents closer to the practical concerns of the local life, the latter are forever striking camp and removing deeper into the forest.

Suggestions for Further Reading

The classic description of American life in this period is Mark Sullivan, *Our Times, 1900–1925*, 6 vols. (New York, 1926–35). Other general treatments that consider various periods of the early twentieth century are Henry May, *The End of American Innocence: A Study of the First Years of Our Time, 1912–1917** (New York, 1959); Walter Lord, *The Good Years** (New York, 1960); and Gilman Ostrander, *American Civilization in the First Machine Age, 1890–1940** (New York, 1970). J. C. Furnas has extended his popular history of American life with *Great Times: An Informal History of the United States, 1914–1929* (New York, 1974). The standard popular treatment of the 1920s is Frederick Lewis Allen, *Only Yesterday** (New York, 1931). Two recent works that challenge Allen's interpretations are Paul Carter, *The Twenties in America** (New York, 1968), and John Braeman, Robert H. Bremner, and David Brody, eds., *Change and Continuity in Twentieth-Century America: The 1920's* (Columbus, Ohio, 1968). The novelist John Dos Passos' classic trilogy, *U. S. A.** (Boston, 1937), contains much valuable material on this period.

On immigration, see Oscar Handlin, *The Uprooted*, rev. ed.* (Boston, 1973). The basic theoretical work on assimilation is Milton Gordon, *Assimilation in American Life** (New York, 1964). Other works dealing with the Jewish community are Moses Rischin, *The Promised City: New York's Jews, 1870–1914** (Cambridge, Mass., 1962); Arthur A. Cohen, *New York Jews and the Quest for Community: The Kehillah Experiment, 1908–1922* (New York, 1970); and a novel by Abraham Cahan, *The Rise of David Levinsky** (New York, 1917).

On the conditions of labor in the early twentieth century, see Harry Braverman, *Labor and Monopoly Capital: The Degradation of Work in the Twentieth Century** (New York, 1974); Milton Meltzer, *Bread—and Roses: The Struggle of American Labor, 1865–1915** (New York, 1977); and John Bodnar, *Immigration and Industrialization: Ethnicity in an American Mill Town, 1870–1940* (Pittsburgh, 1978). For the struggles of labor, see Bruno Ramirez, *When Workers Fight: The Politics of Industrial Relations in the Progressive Era, 1898–1916* (Westport, Conn., 1978). The standard work on the IWW is Melvyn Dubofsky, *We Shall*

*Available in paperback edition.

Be All: A History of the Industrial Workers of the World* (New York, 1969). See also Gerard Rosenblum, *Immigrant Workers: Their Impact on American Labor Radicalism* (New York, 1973). Herbert G. Gutman's excellent labor essays have been collected in *Work, Culture and Society in Industrializing America** (New York, 1977).

The standard history of American religion is Sydney E. Ahlstrom, *A Religious History of the American People** (New Haven, 1972). For a short introduction to protestantism, see Martin E. Marty, *Righteous Empire: The Protestant Experience in America** (New York, 1970). The idea that there were distinctive regional religious cultures is expounded in Samuel Hill, Jr., *The South and the North in American Religion* (Athens, Georgia, 1980). Recent studies of the fundamentalist/modernist debate are George M. Marsden, *Fundamentalism and American Culture: The Shaping of Twentieth-Century Evangelicalism, 1870–1925** (New York, 1980) and William R. Hutchison, *The Modernist Impulse in American Protestantism** (New York, 1982). For background on the antievolution crusade, see James R. Moore, *The Post-Darwinian Controversies: A Study of the Protestant Struggle to Come to Terms with Darwin in Great Britain and America, 1870–1900* (New York, 1979).

Very little outstanding work has been produced on the history of education in the twentieth century. Most of what has been done concerns intellectual history rather than institutional history. See, for example, the excellent work by Lawrence Cremin, *The Transformation of the School: Progressivism in American Education, 1876–1957** (New York, 1961). Richard Hofstadter deals with many of the same ideas in the last section of *Anti-Intellectualism in American Life** *(New York, 1963)*. To appreciate the difficulties of writing education history, see Ellwood P. Cubberley, *Public Education in the United States* (New York, 1934), which must be read in conjunction with Lawrence Cremin, *The Wonderful World of Ellwood Patterson Cubberley: An Essay on the Historiography of American Education** (New York, 1965). Cremin has also contributed an essay on secondary education during this period, "The Revolution in American Secondary Education, 1893–1918," *Teachers College Record* 56 (1955): 295–308. For public education in the nineteenth century, see Rush Welter, *Popular Education and Democratic Thought in America** (New York, 1962), and Michael B. Katz, *The Irony of Early School Reforms: Educational Innovation in Mid-Nineteenth Century Massachusetts** (Cambridge, Mass., 1968). For recent criticisms of the public schools in the United States, see the writings of Charles Silberman, Jonathan Kozol, Herbert Kohl, and John Holt. Perhaps no better description of the modern high school exists than Frederick Wiseman's documentary film, *High School*. An unusual collection of extremely provocative source material is found in Robert H. Bremner et al., eds., *Children and Youth in America: A Documentary History*, 3 vols. (Cambridge, Mass., 1970–74).

Depression, War, and After

1930–1960

A "black blizzard" over Manter, Kansas, on April 14, 1935

The Dust Bowl

DONALD WORSTER

Coming at the same time as the Great Depression, the Dust Bowl of the 1930s on the Great Plains seemed to be adding insult to injury. Was it not enough that the American economy was at its worst point in modern times? Was nature itself, by denying rain and by increasing wind, seeking to wreak vengeance on those who were trying to make a living on the Great American Desert?

In order to understand the causes of the Dust Bowl it is necessary to consider both the nature of American agriculture and the ideology of capitalism. Donald Worster of the University of Hawaii has done both in his outstanding study of the Dust Bowl. The selection reprinted below describes the impact of the ecological disaster on people living in the area, but he indicates elsewhere in his book where the responsibility for the situation must rest.

The basic fault lies, according to Worster, with the ecological values which are expressed in the capitalist ethos. He cites three maxims: "Nature must be seen as capital. . . . Man has a right, even an obligation, to use this capital for constant self-advancement. . . . The social order should permit and encourage this continual increase of personal wealth. . . ." (p.6). The implications of these maxims are evident throughout the history of American agriculture. Farming in the United States has always been looked upon as a profit-making enterprise. Although there have been subsistence farmers in our history, they have occupied a marginal place in the business of agriculture. From the tobacco farmers of seventeenth-century Virginia to corporate agribusiness in California today, profit and not subsistence has been the goal of the nation's farmers.

Nature is not to stand in the way of profit; it is to be the capital on which the increase is to be based. Until recently nature was seen as an enemy to be feared, placated, and accommodated. The forces of nature were beyond our control, and we had to temper our desires to their demands. The expanding spirit of capitalism, however, challenged those age-old attitudes. People are now in control of nature, bending it to our will. This attitude, along with the growing mechanization of agriculture, combined to produce the conditions which made the Dust Bowl so devastating.

Cycles of drought and fertility have probably always been a part of the ecological structure of the Great Plains. Archaeologists have identified dust storms in the area as long ago as approximately 500 A. D., but the tough sod grasses which covered the plains tended to minimize their impact. In the last hundred years, however, the grasses have been destroyed in the interest of profitable agriculture. The availability of the land to settlers through the homestead acts caused thousands of people to move into the area and start carving up the sod. The First World War and the demands for American wheat from our European allies led farmers to invest in more productive and more expensive farm machinery, and to plow under millions more acres of grassland. In the 1920s when lessening demand caused the price of wheat to fall precipitously, many farmers went bankrupt and their lands were left without crops or grass. When the drought and wind hit, these farms just literally blew away.

Even though the Dust Bowl of the 1930s went the way of previous drought with the return of normal rainfall and increased irrigation, the Great Plains is still a precarious place to farm. The irrigation is seriously lowering the water table in the area, and periodic droughts threaten a return to the conditions of the 1930s. Only with reduced expectations for productivity on the plains and a careful marshaling of the available resources will it be possible to restore a relatively stable ecology to the region.

I. The Black Blizzards Roll In

The thirties began in economic depression and in droughts. The first of those disasters usually gets all the attention, although for the many Americans living on farms drought was the more serious problem. In the spring of 1930 over 3 million men and women were out of work. They had lost their jobs or had been laid off without pay in the aftermath of the stock market crash of the preceding fall. Another 12 million would suffer the same fate in the following two years. Many of the unemployed had no place to live, nor even the means to buy food. They slept in public toilets, under bridges, in shantytowns along the railroad tracks, or on doorsteps, and in the most wretched cases they scavenged from garbage cans—a Calcutta existence in the richest nation ever. The farmer, in contrast, was slower to feel the impact of the crash. He usually had his own independent food supply and stood a bit aloof from the ups and downs of the urban-industrial system. In the twenties that aloofness had meant that most farm families had not fully shared in the giddy burst of affluence—in new washing machines, silk stockings, and shiny roadsters. They had, in fact spent much of the decade in economic doldrums. Now, as banks began to fail and soup lines formed, rural Americans went on as before, glad to be spared the latest reversal and just a little pleased to see their proud city cousins humbled. Then the droughts began, and they brought the farmers to their knees, too.[1]

During the spring and summer of 1930, little rain fell over a large part of the eastern United States. A horizontal band on the map, from Maryland and Virginia to Missouri and Arkansas, marked the hardest hit area of wilting crops, shrinking ground-water supplies, and uncertain income. Over the summer months in this drought band the rainfall shortage was 60,000 tons for each 100–acre farm, or 700 tons a day. Seventeen million people were affected. In twelve states the drought set record lows in precipitation, and among all the Eastern states only Florida was above normal. Three years earlier the Mississippi River had overflowed in banks and levees in one of the most destructive floods in American history. Now captains there wondered how long their barges would remain afloat as the river shrank to a fraction of its average height.[2]

During the thirties serious drought threatened a great part of the nation. The persistent center, however, shifted from the East to the Great Plains, beginning in 1931, when much of Montana and the Dakotas became almost as arid as the Sonoran Desert. Farmers there and almost everywhere else watched the scorched earth crack open, heard the gray grass crunch underfoot, and worried about how long they would be able to pay their bills. Around their dried-up ponds the willows and wild cherries were nearly leafless, and even the poison ivy drooped. Drought, of course, is a relative term: it depends upon one's concept of "normal." But following the lead of the climatologists of the time, we can use a precipitation deficiency of at least 15 per cent of the historical mean to qualify as drought. By that standard, of all the American states only Maine and Vermont escaped a drought year from 1930 to 1936. Twenty states set or equaled record lows for their entire span of official weather data. Over the nation as a whole, the 1930s drought was, in the words of a Weather Bureau scientist, "the worst in the climatological history of the country."[3]

Intense heat accompanied the drought, along with economic losses the nation could ill afford. In the summer of 1934, Nebraska reached 118 degrees, Iowa, 115. In Illinois thermometers stuck at over 100 degrees for so long that 370 people died—and one man, who had been living in a refrigerator to keep cool, was treated for frostbite. Two years later, when the country was described by *Newsweek* as "a vast simmering caldron," more than 4500 died from excessive heat, water was shipped into the West

[1] *Fifteenth Census of the United States:* 1930. Unemployment (Washington, D.C., 1931), 1:8– 9. William Leuchtenburg, *Franklin D. Roosevelt and the New Deal, 1933–1940* (New York: Harper & Row, Torchbooks, 1963), p. 19. Dixon Wecter, *The Age of the Great Depression, 1929– 1941* (New York: Macmillan, 1948), p. 123.

[2] John Hoyt, *Drought of 1930–34,* U. S. Geological Survey, Water Supply Paper 680 (Washington, D. C., 1936), p. 6. Ivan Tannehill, *Drought: Its Causes and Effects* (Princeton: Princeton University Press, 1947), p. 83. Harley Van Cleve, "Some of the Biological Effects of Drought," *Scientific Monthly, 33* (Oct. 1931), 301–6.

[3] John Hoyt, *Drought of 1930–34,* pp. 8–9, 66: Hoyt, *Drought of 1936,* U. S. Geological Survey, Water Supply Paper 820 (Washington, D. C., 1938), pp. 1, 7, 27. *Newsweek,* 15 Aug. 1936, pp. 17–18. "The Effect of Drought on Prairie Trees," *Science,* 8 Mar. 1935, Supp. p. 7. Joseph Kincer, "The Drought of 1934," *Scientific Monthly, 39* (July 1934), 95–96.

by diverted tank-cars and oil pipelines, and clouds of grasshoppers ate what little remained of many farmers' wheat and corn—along with their fenceposts and the washing on their clotheslines. The financial cost of the 1934 drought alone amounted to one-half the money the United States had put into World War I. By 1936, farm losses had reached $25 million a day, and more than 2 million farmers were drawing relief checks. Rexford Tugwell, head of the Resettlement Administration, who toured the burning plains that year, saw "a picture of complete destruction"—"one of the most serious peacetime problems in the nation's history."[4]

As the decade reached its midpoint, it was the southern plains that experienced the most severe conditions. During some growing seasons there was no soil moisture down to three feet over large parts of the region. By 1939, near Hays, Kansas, the accumulated rainfall deficiency was more than 34 inches—almost a two-year supply in arrears. Continued long enough in such a marginal, semiarid land, a drought of that magnitude would produce a desert. Weathermen pointed out that there had been worse single years, as in 1910 and 1917, or back in the 1890s, and they repeatedly assured the people of the region that their records did not show any modern drought lasting more than five years, nor did they suggest any long-range adverse climatic shift.[5] But farmers and ranchers did not find much comfort in statistical charts; their cattle were bawling for feed, and their bank credit was drying up along with the soil. Not until after 1941 did the rains return in abundance and the burden of anxiety lift.

Droughts are an inevitable fact of life on the plains, an extreme one occurring roughly every twenty years, and milder ones every three or four. They have always brought with them blowing dust where the ground was bare of crops or native grass. Dust was so familiar an event that no one was surprised to see it appear when the dry weather began in 1931. But no one was prepared for what came later: dust storms of such violence that they made the drought only a secondary problem—storms of such destructive force that they left the region reeling in confusion and fear.

"Earth" is the word we use when it is there in place, growing the food we eat, giving us a place to stand and build on. "Dust" is what we say when it is loose and blowing on the wind. Nature encompasses both—the good and the bad from our perspective, and from that of all living things. We need the earth to stay alive, but dust is a nuisance, or, worse, a killer. On a planet such as ours, where there is much wind, where there are frequent dry spells, and where we encounter vast expanses of bare soil, dust is a constant presence. It rises from the hooves of animals, from a

[4]*Newsweek*, 19 May, pp. 5–6; 4 Aug., pp. 6–7; 18 Aug. 1934, pp. 5–6, 4 July, p. 10, 11 July, p. 13, 18 July, pp. 7–11, 25 July 1936, p. 72. M.L.G., "The Drought and Its Effect on Agricultural Crops," *Scientific Monthly*, 39 (Sept. 1934), 288. Martha Bruère, "Lifting the Drought," *Survey Graphic*, 23 (Nov. 1934) 544–47.

[5]P. H. Stephens, "Why the Dust Bowl?" *Journal of Farm Economics*, 19 (Aug. 1937), 750–55. F. W. Albertson and J. E. Weaver, "History of the Native Vegetation of Western Kansas during Seven Years of Continuous Drought," *Ecological Monographs*, 12 (Jan. 1942), 26, 31. S. D. Flora, "Is the Climate of Kansas Changing?" Kansas State Board of Agriculture, *31st Annual Report* (Topeka, 1938), pp. 30–33. Willis Ray Gregg, "Meteorological Aspects of the 1936 Drought," *Scientific Monthly*, 43 (Aug. 1936), 190.

wagon's wheels, from a dry riverbed, from the deserts. If all the continents were an English greensward, there would be no dust. But nature has not made things so. Nor has man, in many times and places.

Dust in the air is one phenomenon. However, dust storms are quite another. The story of the southern plains in the 1930s is essentially about dust storms, when the earth ran amok. And not once or twice, but over and over for the better part of a decade: day after day, year after year, of sand rattling against the window, of fine powder caking one's lips, of springtime turned to despair, of poverty eating into self-confidence.

Explaining why those storms occurred requires an excursion into the history of the plains and an understanding of the agriculture that evolved there. For the "dirty thirties," as they were called, were primarily the work of man, not nature. Admittedly, nature had something to do with this disaster too. Without winds the soil would have stayed put, no matter how bare it was. Without drought, farmers would have had strong, healthy crops capable of checking the wind. But natural factors did not make the storms—they merely made them possible. The storms were mainly the result of stripping the landscape of its natural vegetation to such an extent that there was no defense against the dry winds, no sod to hold the sandy or powdery dirt. The sod had been destroyed to make farms to grow wheat to get cash. But more of that later on. It is the storms themselves we must first comprehend: their magnitude, their effect, even their taste and smell. What was it like to be caught in one of them? How much did the people suffer, and how did they cope?

Weather bureau stations on the plains reported a few small dust storms throughout 1932, as many as 179 in April 1933, and in November of that year a large one that carried all the way to Georgia and New York. But it was the May 1934 blow that swept in a new dark age. On 9 May, brown earth from Montana and Wyoming swirled up from the ground, was captured by extremely high-level winds, and was blown eastward toward the Dakotas. More dirt was sucked into the airstream, until 350 million tons were riding toward urban America. By late afternoon the storm had reached Dubuque and Madison, and by evening 12 million tons of dust were falling like snow over Chicago—4 pounds for each person in the city. Midday at Buffalo on 10 May was darkened by dust, and the advancing gloom stretched south from there over several states, moving as fast as 100 miles an hour. The dawn of 11 May found the dust settling over Boston, New York, Washington, and Atlanta, and then the storm moved out to sea. Savannah's skies were hazy all day 12 May; it was the last city to report dust conditions. But there were still ships in the Atlantic, some of them 300 miles off the coast, that found dust on their decks during the next day or two.[6]

"Kansas dirt," the New York press called it, though it actually came from farther north. More would come that year and after, and some of it was indeed from Kansas—or Nebraska or New Mexico. In a later spring, New Hampshire farmers, out to tap their maples, discovered a fresh brown

[6]Eric Miller, "The Dust Fall of November 12–13, 1933," *Monthly Weather Review* 62 (Jan. 1934), 14–15. W. A. Mattice, "Dust Storms, November 1933 to May 1934," *ibid.* 63 (Feb. 1935), 53–55. Charles Kellogg, "Soil Blowing and Dust Storms," USDA Miscellaneous Publication 221 (Washington, D. C., 1935).

snow on the ground, discoloration from transported Western soil.[7] Along
the Gulf Coast, at Houston and Corpus Christi, dirt from the Llano Esta-
cado collected now and then on windowsills and sidewalks. But after May
1934 most of the worst dust storms were confined to southern plains
region; less frequently were they carried by those high-altitude currents
moving east or southeast. Two types of dusters became common then: the
dramatic "black blizzards" and the more frequent "sand blows." The first
came with a rolling turbulence, rising like a long wall of muddy water as
high as 7000 or 8000 feet. Like the winter blizzards to which they were
compared, these dusters were caused by the arrival of a polar continental
air mass, and the atmospheric electricity it generated helped lift the dirt
higher and higher in a cold boil, sometimes accompanied by thunder and
lightning, other times by an eerie silence. Such storms were not only terrifying to observers, but immensely destructive to the region's fine, dark
soils, rich in nutrients. The second kind of duster was a more constant
event, created by the low sirocco-like winds that blew out of the southwest
and left the sandier soils drifted into dunes along fence rows and ditches.[8]
Long after New York and Philadelphia had forgotten their taste of the
plains, the people out there ate their own dirt again and again.

   In the 1930s the Soil Conservation Service compiled a frequency chart
of all dust storms of regional extent, when visibility was cut to less than
a mile. In 1932 there were 14; in 1933, 38; 1934, 22; 1935, 40; 1936, 68;
1937, 72; 1938, 61—dropping as the drought relented a bit—1939, 30;
1940, 17; 1941, 17. Another measure of severity was made by calculating
the total number of hours the dust storms lasted during a year. By that
criterion 1937 was again the worst: at Guymon, in the panhandle of Oklahoma, the total number of hours that year climbed to 550, mostly concentrated in the first six months of the year. In Amarillo the worst year was
1935, with a total of 908 hours. Seven times, from January to March, the
visibility there reached zero—all complete blackouts, one of them lasting
eleven hours. A single storm might rage for one hour or three and a half
days. Most of the winds came from the southwest, but they also came from
the west, north, and northeast, and they could slam against windows and
walls with 60 miles-per-hour force.[9] The dirt left behind on the front lawn
might be brown, black, yellow, ashy gray, or, more rarely, red, depending
upon its source. And each color had its own peculiar aroma, from a sharp
peppery smell that burned the nostrils to a heavy greasiness that nauseated.

   In the memory of older plains residents, the blackest year was 1935,
particularly the early spring weeks from 1 March to mid-April, when the
Dust Bowl made its full-blown debut. Springtime in western Kansas can
be a Willa Cather world of meadowlarks on the wing, clean white curtains
dancing in the breeze, anemones and wild verbena in bloom, lilacs by the
porch, a windmill spinning briskly, and cold fresh water in the bucket—
but not in 1935. After a February heat wave (it reached 75 degrees in

[7]W. O. Robinson, "The 'Brown' Snowfall in New Hampshire and Vermont," *Science*, 19 June
  1936, pp. 596–97.
[8]B. Ashton Keith, "A Suggested Classification of Great Plains Dust Storms," *Kansas Academy
  of Science Transactions*, 47 (Sept. 1944), 96–109.
[9]Soil Conservation Service, "Some Information about Dust Storms and Wind Erosion in the
  Great Plains" (Washington, D. C., 1953), p. 9. H. F. Choun, "Duststorms in the Southwestern
  Plains Area," *Monthly Weather Review*, 64 (June 1936), 195–99.

Topeka that month), the dust began moving across Kansas, Oklahoma, and Texas, and for the next six weeks it was unusual to see a clear sky from dawn until sundown. On 15 March, Denver reported that a serious dust storm was speeding eastward. Kansans ignored the radio warnings, went about their business as usual, and later wondered what had hit them. Small-town printer Nate White was at the picture show when the dust reached Smith Center: as he walked out the exit, it was as if someone had put a blindfold over his eyes; he bumped into telephone poles, skinned his shins on boxes and cans in an alleyway, fell to his hands and knees, and crawled along the curbing to a dim houselight. A seven-year-old boy wandered away and was lost in the gloom; the search party found him later, suffocated in a drift. A more fortunate child was found alive, tangled in a barbed wire fence. Near Colby, a train was derailed by dirt on the tracks, and the passengers spent twelve dreary hours in the coaches. The Lora-Locke Hotel in Dodge City overflowed with more than two hundred stranded travelers; many of them bedded down on cots in the lobby and ballroom. In the following days, as the dust kept falling, electric lights burned continuously, cars left tracks in the dirt-covered streets, and schools and offices stayed closed. A reporter at Great Bend remarked on the bizarre scene: "Uncorked jug placed on sidewalk two hours, found to be half filled with dust. Picture wires giving way due to excessive weight of dust on frames. Irreparable loss in portraits anticipated. Lady Godiva could ride thru streets without even the horse seeing her.[10]

The novelty of this duster, so like a coffee-colored winter snow, made it hard for most people to take it seriously. But William Allen White, the Emporia editor, called it "the greatest show" since Pompeii was buried in ashes. And a Garden City woman described her experience for the *Kansas City Times*:

> All we could do about it was just sit in our dusty chairs, gaze at each other through the fog that filled the room and watch that fog settle slowly and silently, covering everything—including ourselves—in a thick, brownish gray blanket. When we opened the door swirling whirlwinds of soil beat against us unmercifully. . . . The door and windows were all shut tightly, yet those tiny particles seemed to seep through the very walls. It got into cupboards and clothes closets; our faces were as dirty as if we had rolled in the dirt; our hair was gray and stiff and we ground dirt between our teeth.

By the end of the month conditions had become so unrelenting that many Kansans had begun to chew their nails. "Watch for the Second Coming of Christ," warned one of Topeka's unhinged, "God is wrathful." Street-corner sects in Hill City and other towns warned pedestrians to heed the signs of the times. A slightly less frenetic Concordian jotted in her log: "This is ultimate darkness. So must come the end of the world."[11] The mood of the

[10]*Kansas City Times*, 22 Feb. 1935; *Dodge City Globe*, 16 Mar. 1935; *Topeka Capital*, 17, 19 Mar. 1935; *Amarillo Sunday News-Globe*, 17, 26 Mar. 1935; *Kansas City Star*, 20–24 Mar. 1935. Smith Center Centennial Committee, *History of Smith Centre, Kansas, 1871–1971* (n.p., 1971), pp. 14–15.

[11]*Kansas City Star*, 21 Mar. 1935; *Kansas City Times*, 20 Mar. 1935; *Topeka Journal*, 10, 23 Mar. 1935.

people had begun to change, if not to apocalyptic dread in every case, at least to a fear that this was a nightmare that might never end.

By 24 March southeastern Colorado and western Kansas had seen twelve consecutive days of dust storms, but there was worse to come. Near the end of March a new duster swept across the southern plains, destroying one-half the wheat crop in Kansas, one-quarter of it in Oklahoma, and all of it in Nebraska—5 million acres blown out. The storm carried away from the plains twice as much earth as men and machines had scooped out to make the Panama Canal, depositing it once again over the East Coast states and the Atlantic Ocean.[12] Then the wind slackened off a bit, gathering strength, as it were, for the spectacular finale of that unusual spring season—Black Sunday, 14 April.

Dawn came clear and rosy all across the plains that day. By noon the skies were so fresh and blue that people could not remain indoors; they remembered how many jobs they had been postponing, and with a revived spirit they rushed outside to get them done. They went on picnics, planted gardens, repaired henhouses, attended funerals, drove to the neighbors for a visit. In midafternoon the summery air rapidly turned colder, falling as many as 50 degrees in a few hours, and the people noticed then that the yards were full of birds nervously fluttering and chattering—and more were arriving every moment, as though fleeing from some unseen enemy. Suddenly there appeared on the northern horizon a black blizzard, moving toward them; there was no sound, no wind, nothing but an immense "boogery" cloud. The storm struck Dodge City at 2:40 p.m. Not far from there John Garretson, a farmer in Haskell County, Kansas, who was on the road with this wife, Louise, saw it coming, but he was sure that he could beat it home. They had almost made it when they were engulfed; abandoning the car, they groped for the fencewire and, hand over hand, followed it to their door. Down in the panhandle Ed and Ada Phillips of Boise City, with their six-year-old daughter, were on their way home too, after an outing to Texline in their Model A Ford. It was about five o'clock when the black wall appeared, and they still had fifteen miles to go. Seeing an old adobe house ahead, Ed realized that they had to take shelter, and quickly. By the time they were out of the car the dust was upon them, making it so dark that they nearly missed the door. Inside they found ten other people, stranded, like themselves, in a two-room hut, all fearing that they might be smothered, all unable to see their companions' faces. For four hours they sat there, until the storm let up enough for them to follow the roadside ditch back to town. By then the ugly pall was moving south across the high plains of Texas and New Mexico.[13]

Older residents still remember Black Sunday in all its details—where they were when the storm hit, what they did then. Helen Wells was the wife of the Reverend Rolley Wells, the Methodist minister in Guymon. Early

[12]*Newsweek*, 30 Mar. 1935, pp. 5–6. For early April storms, see *Garden City Telegram*, 10 Apr. 1935; *Amarillo Globe*, 11 Apr. 1935; *Kansas City Star*, Apr. 11, 1935. According to J. S. Ploughe, there were 19 days of dust between March 15 and April 15. ("Out of the Dust," *Christian Century*, 22 May 1935, pp. 691–92.)

[13]John and Louise Garretson to author, taped interview, 9 Sept. 1977. Ed and Ada Phillips to author, taped interview, 21 Sept. For other dust-storm experiences see Stanley Vestal, *Short Grass Country* (New York: Duell, Sloan & Pearce, 1941), pp. 196ff.; and Vestal papers, Western History Collection, University of Oklahoma, Norman.

that morning she had helped clean the accumulated dust from the church pews, working until she was choking and exhausted. Back in the parsonage she switched on the radio for some inspiring music and what she heard was the hymn "We'll Work Till Jesus Comes." "I just had to sit down and laugh," she recalls; she had worn out her sweeper but still had a broom if that was needed. Later that day her husband, partly to please two visiting *Saturday Evening Post* reporters, held a special "rain service," which concluded in time for the congregation to get home before the dust arrived.[14]

A Kansas cattle dealer, Raymond Ellsaesser, almost lost his wife that day. She had gone into Sublette with her young daugher for a Rebekah lodge meeting. On the way home she stopped along the highway, unable to see even the winged hood ornament on her car. The static electricity in the storm then shorted out her ignition, and foolishly, she determined to walk the three-quarters of a mile home. Her daughter plunged ahead to get Raymond's help, and he quickly piled into a truck and drove back down the road, hallooing out the window. Back and forth he passed, but his wife had disappeared into the fog-like dust, wandering straight away from the car into the field, where she stumbled about with absolutely no sense of direction. Each time she saw the truck's headlights she moved that way, not realizing her husband was in motion too. It was only by sheer luck that she found herself at last standing in the truck's beams, gasping for air and near collapse.[15]

The last of the major dust storms that year was on 14 April, and it was months before the damages could be fully calculated. Those who had been caught outside in one of the spring dusters were, understandably, most worried about their lungs. An epidemic of respiratory infections and something called "dust pneumonia" broke out across the plains. The four small hospitals in Meade County, Kansas, found that 52 per cent of their April admissions were acute respiratory cases—thirty-three patients died.[16] Many dust victims would arrive at a hospital almost dead, after driving long distances in a storm. They spat up clods of dirt, washed the mud out of their mouths, swabbed their nostrils with Vaseline, and rinsed their bloodshot eyes with boric acid water. Old people and babies were the most vulnerable to the dusters, as were those who had chronic asthma, bronchitis, or tuberculosis, some of whom had moved to the plains so they might breathe the high, dry air.

Doctors could not agree on whether the dust caused a new kind of pneumonia, and some even denied that there were any unusual health problems in their communities. But the Red Cross thought the situation was so serious that it set up six emergency hospitals in Kansas, Colorado, and Texas, and it staffed them with its own nurses. In Topeka and Wichita volunteers worked in high school sewing rooms to make dust masks of cheesecloth; over 17,000 of those masks were sent to the plains, especially to towns where goggles had been sold out.[17] Chewing tobacco was a better remedy, snorted some farmers, who thought it was too much of a bother

---

[14]Helen Wells to author, taped interview, 10 Sept. 1977.

[15]Raymond Ellsaesser to author, taped interview, 8 Sept. 1977.

[16]Lawrence Svobida, *An Empire of Dust* (Caldwell, Id.: Caxton, 1940), p. 97.

[17]*Kansas City Star*, 27, 30 Apr.; 1, 2 May 1935. "Effect of Dust Storms: Replies of County Health Officers," Mar. 1935, National Archieves Record Group (RG) 114.

to wear such gadgets when driving their tractors. But enough wore the Red Cross masks or some other protection to make the plains look like a World War I battlefield, with dust instead of mustard gas coming out of the trenches.

On 29 April the Red Cross sponsored a conference of health officers from several states. Afterward the representatives of the Kansas Board of Health went to work on the medical problem in more detail, and eventually they produced a definitive study on the physiological impact of the dust storms. From 21 February to 30 April they counted 28 days of "dense" dust at Dodge City and only 13 days that were "dust free." Dirt deposited in bakepans during the five biggest storms gave an estimated 4.7 tons of total fallout per acre. Agar plate cultures showed "no pathogenic organisms" in the accumulation, only harmless soil bacteria, plant hair, and micro-fungus spores. But the inorganic content of the dust was mainly fine silicon particles, along with bits of feldspar, volcanic ash, and calcite; and silica," they warned, "is as much a body poison as is lead"—"probably the most widespread and insidious of all hazards in the environment of mankind," producing, after sufficient contact, silicosis of the lungs. These scientists also found that a measles outbreak had come with the black blizzards, though why that happened was not clear; in only five months there were twice as many cases as in any previous twelve-month period. The death rate from acute respiratory infections in the 45 western counties of Kansas, where the dust was most intense, was 99 per 100,000, compared with the statewide average of 70; and the infant mortality was 80.5, compared with the state's 62.3.[18]

The medical remedies for the dust were at best primitive and make-shift. In addition to wearing light gauze masks, health officials recommended attaching translucent glasscloth to the inside frames of windows, although people also used cardboard, canvas, or blankets. Hospitals covered some of their patients with wet sheets, and housewives flapped the air with wet dish towels to collect dust. One of the most common tactics was to stick masking tape, felt strips, or paraffin-soaked rags around the windows and door cracks. The typical plains house was loosely constructed and without insulation, but sometimes those methods proved so effective that there was not enough air circulation inside to replenish the oxygen supply. Warren Moore of southwestern Kansas remembers watching, during a storm, the gas flame on the range steadily turn orange and the coal-oil lamp dim until the people simply had to open the window, dust or no dust.[19] But most often there was no way to seal out the fine, blowing dirt: it blackened the pillow around one's head, the dinner plates on the table, the bread dough on the back of the stove. It became a steady part of one's diet and breathing. "We thrived on it," claim some residents today; it was their "vitamin K." But all the same they prayed that they would not ingest so much it would maim them for life, or finish them off, as it had a neighbor or two.

[18]Earle Brown, Selma Gottlieb, and Ross Laybourn, "Dust Storms and Their Possible Effects on Health," U. S. Public Health Reports, 50 (4 Oct. 1938), 1369–83. See also Dallas Morning News, 14 Apr. 1935, for another study of dust composition.
[19]Warren Moore to author, taped interview, 9 Sept. 1977.

Livestock and wildlife did not have even those crude defenses. "In a rising sand storm," wrote Margaret Bourke-White, "cattle quickly become blinded. They run around in circles until they fall and breathe so much dust that they die. Autopsies show their lungs caked with dust and mud." Newborn calves could suffocate in a matter of hours, and the older cattle ground their teeth down to the gums trying to eat the dirt-covered grass. As the dust buried the fences, horses and cattle climbed over and wandered away. Where there was still water in rivers, the dust coated the surface and the fish died too. The carcasses of jackrabbits, small birds, and field mice lay along roadsides by the hundreds after a severe duster; and those that survived were in such shock that they could be picked up and their nostrils and eyes wiped clean.[20] In a lighter vein, it was said that prairie dogs were now able to tunnel upward several feet from the ground.

Cleaning up houses, farm lots, and city stores after the 1935 blow season was an expensive matter. People literally shoveled the dirt from their front yards and swept up bushel-basketfuls inside. One man's ceiling collapsed from the silt that had collected in the attic. Carpets, draperies, and tapestries were so dust-laden that their patterns were indiscernible. Painted surfaces had been sandblasted bare. Automobile and tractor engines operated in dust storms without oil-bath air cleaners were ruined by grit, and the repair shops had plenty of business. During March alone, Tucumcari, New Mexico, reported over $288,000 in property damage, although most towns' estimates were more conservative than that: Liberal, Kansas, $150,000; Randall County, Texas, $10,000; Lamar, Colorado, $3800. The merchants of Amarillo calculated from 3 to 15 per cent damage to their merchandise, not to mention the loss of shoppers during the storms. In Dodge City a men's clothing store advertised a "dust sale," knocking shirts down to 75 cents. But the heaviest burdens lay on city work crews, who had to sweep dirt from the gutters and municipal swimming pools, and on housewives, who struggled after each blow to get their houses clean.[21]

The emotional expense was the hardest to accept, however. All day you could sit with your hands folded on the oilcloth-covered table, the wind moaning around the eaves, the fine, soft, talc sifting in the keyholes, the sky a coppery gloom; and when you went to bed the acrid dust crept into your dreams. Avis Carlson told what it was like at night:

> A trip for water to rinse the grit from our lips. And then back to bed
> with washcloths over our noses. We try to lie still, because every turn
> stirs the dust on the blankets. After a while, if we are good sleepers,
> we forget.

After 1935 the storms lost much of their drama; for most people they were simply a burden to be endured, and sometimes that burden was too heavy. Druggists sold out their supplies of sedatives quickly. An Oklahoman took

---

[20]Margaret Bourke-White, "Dust Changes America," *The Nation*, 22 May 1935, pp. 597–98. *Kansas City Star*, 30 Apr. 1935. Caroline Henderson, "Spring in the Dust Bowl," *Atlantic Monthly*, 159 (June 1937), 715. Marilyn Coffey, "Dust Storms of the 1930s," *Natural History*, 87 (Feb. 1978), 80–81.

[21]*Kansas City Star*, 22 Apr. 1935. "Effects of Dust Storms: Chambers of Commerce Reports," Mar. 1935, National Archives RG 114.

down his shotgun, ready to kill his entire family and himself—"we're all better off dead," he despaired.[22] That, to be sure, was an extreme instance, but there were indeed men and women who turned distraught, wept, and then, listless, gave up caring.

The plains people, however, then as now, were a tough-minded, leatherskinned folk, not easily discouraged. Even in 1935 they managed to laugh a bit at their misfortunes. They told about the farmer who fainted when a drop of water struck him in the face and had to be revived by having three buckets of sand thrown over him. They also passed around the one about the motorist who came upon a ten-gallon hat resting on a dust drift. Under it he found a head looking at him. "Can I help you some way?" the motorist asked, "Give you a ride into town maybe?" "Thanks, but I'll make it on my own," was the reply, "I'm on a horse." They laughed with Will Rogers when he pointed out that only highly advanced civilizations—like ancient Mesopotamia—were ever covered over by dirt, and that California would never qualify. Newspaper editors could still find something to joke about, too: "When better dust storms are made," the *Dodge City Globe* boasted, "the Southwest will make them." Children were especially hard to keep down; for them the storms always meant adventure, happy chaos, a breakdown of their teachers' authority, and perhaps a holiday.[23] When darkness descends, as it did that April, humor, bravado, or a childlike irresponsibility may have as much value as a storm cellar.

Whether they brought laughter or tears, the dust storms that swept across the southern plains in the 1930s created the most severe environmental catastrophe in the entire history of the white man on this continent. In no other instance was there greater or more sustained damage to the American land, and there have been few times when so much tragedy was visited on its inhabitants. Not even the Depression was more devastating, economically. And in ecological terms we have nothing in the nation's past, nothing even in the polluted present, that compares. Suffice it to conclude here that in the decade of the 1930s the dust storms of the plains were an unqualified disaster.

At such dark times the mettle of a people is thoroughly and severely tested, revealing whether they have the will to go on. By this test the men and women of the plains were impressive, enduring, as most of them did, discouragements the like of which more recent generations have never had to face. But equally important, disasters of this kind challenge a society's capacity to think—require it to analyze and explain and learn from misfortune. Societies that fail this test are sitting ducks for more of the same. Those that pass, on the other hand, have attained through suffering and hardship a more mature, self-appraising character, so that they are more aware than before of their vulnerabilities and weaknesses. They are stronger because they have been made sensitive to their deficiencies. Whether the dust storms had this enlarging, critical effect on the minds of southern plainsmen remains to be seen.

[22]Avis Carlson, "Dust," *New Republic*, 1 May 1935, p. 333. Ira Wolfert, *An Epidemic of Genius* (New York: Simon & Schuster, 1960), pp. 61–62.

[23]*Dodge City Globe*, 18 Mar. 1935. Charles Peterson, "Drama in the Dustbowl," *Kansas Magazine* (1952), 94–97. For samples of Dust Bowl humor, see Vance Johnson, *Heaven's Tableland: The Dust Bowl Story* (New York: Farrar, Straus, 1947), p. 194.

II. IF IT RAINS

The American plains are a "next year" country. This season the crops may wither and die, the winds may pile up dirt against the barn, but next time we will do better—we will strike a bonanza. If we are poor today, we will be rich tomorrow. If there is drought, it will rain soon. In the dirty thirties that quality of hope was strained to the breaking point. But for every discouraged resident who wanted to leave, or did so, there were two more who were determined to stick it out, hang on, stay with it. Some remained out of sheer inertia or bewilderment over what else to do, or because they had the economic means to stay where others did not. Whatever the reasons people had for not moving away, hope was commonly a part of them. The people were optimists, unwilling to believe that the dust storms would last or that their damage would be very severe. That attitude was not so much a matter of cold reason as it was of faith that the future must be better. Optimism may be an essential response for survival in this sometimes treacherous world; it certainly brought many Western farmers through to greener days. But it also can be a form of lunancy. There is about the perennial optimist a dangerous naïveté, a refusal to face the grim truths about oneself or others or nature. Optimism can also divert our attention from critical self-appraisal and substantive reforms, which is exactly what happened on the plains.

Optimism may rest either on a confidence in one's ability to affect the course of events or, paradoxically, on a happy, fatalistic belief that the world is preordained to promote one's welfare. Plainsmen in the 1930s went both ways. They were sure that they could manage the land and bring it under control, especially if Franklin Roosevelt's New Deal would give them a bit of help. Hard work and determination would pay off in the end. They were even surer that the laws of nature were on their side. A perceptual geographer, Thomas Saarinen, has concluded that Great Plains farmers consistently and habitually underrate the possibility of drought— that they minimize the risks involved in their way of life. When drought occurs, they insist that it cannot last long. Consequently, although they may become unhappy or upset by crop failures, they feel no need to seek out logical solutions or change their practices. They are prouder of their ability to tough it out than to analyze their situation rationally, because they expect nature to be good to them and make them prosper.[1] It is an optimism at heart fatalistic—and potentially fatal in a landscape as volatile as that of the plains.

The source of that optimism is cultural: it is the ethos of an upwardly mobile society. When a people emphasize, as much as Americans do, the need to get ahead in the world, they must have a corresponding faith in the benignity of nature and the future. If they are farmers on the Western plains, they must believe that rain is on its way, that dust storms are a temporary aberration, and that one had better plant wheat again even if there is absolutely no moisture in the soil. The black blizzards said, however, that there was something seriously amiss in the plainsmen's think-

---

[1]Thomas Saarinen, *Perception of Drought Hazard on the Great Plains*, Department of Geography Research Paper 106 (Chicago: University of Chicago Press, 1966), p. 132.

ing—that nature would not yield so easily, so reliably, all the riches expected, and that the future would not necessarily bring higher and higher levels of prosperity. Blowing dirt challenged the most cherished assumptions of middle-class farmers and merchants about the inevitability of progress; therefore the dirt had to be minimized, discounted, evaded, even ignored. The bedrock plainsmen's response was to shout down nature's message with a defense of the old assumptions. Changes in attitudes did occur, to be sure, but the most incredible fact of the dirty thirties was the tenacity of bourgeois optimism and its imperviousness to all warnings.

The pattern of reaction among plainsmen went something like this: fail to anticipate drought, underestimate its duration when it comes, expect rain momentarily, deny that they are as hard hit as outsiders believe, defend the region against critics, admit that *some* help would be useful, demand that the government act and act quickly, insist that federal aid be given without strings and when and where local residents want it, vote for those politicians who confirm the people's optimism and pooh-pooh the need for major reform, resent interference by the bureaucrats, eagerly await the return of "normalcy" when the plains will once more proceed along the road of steady progress. Accepting the coming of the New Deal fit into that pattern more or less easily. The region received more federal dollars than any other, along with reassurance, solicitation, and encouragement. But whenever the New Deal really tried to become new and innovative, plainsmen turned hostile. The fate of the plains lay in the hands of Providence, and Providence, not Washington, would see them come out all right.

The day after Black Sunday the Dust Bowl got its name. Robert Geiger, an Associated Press reporter from Denver, traveled through the worst-hit part of the plains, and he sent a dispatch to the *Washington Evening Star*, which carried it on 15 April 1935: "Three little words," it began, "achingly familiar on a Western farmer's tongue, rule life in the dust bowl of the continent—if it rains." That Geiger meant nothing special by the label was apparent two days later, when in another dispatch he called the blow area the "dust belt." But, inexplicably, it was "bowl" that stuck, passing quickly into the vernacular, its author soon forgotten and never really sure himself where it all began. Some liked the name as a satire on college football— first the Rose Bowl and the Orange Bowl, now the Dust Bowl—or they thought it described nicely what happened to the sugar bowl on the table. Geiger more likely had recalled the geographical image of the plains pushed forward by another Denver man, William Gilpin. In the 1850s, the continent, Gilpin had thought, was a great fertile bowl rimmed by mountains, its concave interior destined one day to become the seat of empire. If that was the unconscious precedent, then Geiger's "dust bowl" was more ironic than anyone realized.[2]

[2]Robert Geiger, *Washington Evening Star*, 15–17 Apr. 1935. Geiger's priority was established by Fred Floyd, A History of the Dust Bowl, (Ph.D. thesis, University of Oklahoma, 1950), Chap. 1. An earlier effort to locate the origin of the phrase "Dust Bowl" is discussed in David Nail, *One Short Sleep Past: A Profile of Amarillo in the Thirties* (Canyon, Tex.: Staked Plains Press, 1973), p. 124. William Gilpin's major work was *The Central Gold Region* (Philadelphia: Sower, Barnes & Co.; St. Louis: E. K. Woodward, 1860).

Within weeks the southern plains had a new identity, one that they would never be able to shake off. The label came spontaneously into the speeches of the region's governors, into the pressrooms of city newspapers, and into the private letters of local residents to their distant friends—for all of them it was a handle to put on this peculiar problem. When the Soil Conservation Service capitalized it and began using it on their maps, even setting up a special office in the area, "Dust Bowl" became official. The SCS followed Geiger's own delineation rather closely: "the western third of Kansas, Southeastern Colorado, the Oklahoma Panhandle, the northern two-thirds of the Texas Panhandle, and Northeastern New Mexico." But the SCS's Region VI also covered an extensive fringe that made a total of almost 100 million acres, stretching 500 miles from north to south, 300 from east to west—about one-third of the entire Great Plains. A serious blowing hazard existed on a shifting 50 million of those acres from 1935 to 1938. In 1935 the Dust Bowl reached well down into the cotton belt of west Texas, but three years later it had moved northeastward, making Kansas the most extensively affected state. By 1939 the serious blow area within the Bowl had shrunk to about one-fifth its original size; it increased again to 22 million acres in 1940, then in the forties it disappeared.[3]

The difficulty in making the Dust Bowl more fixed and precise was that it roamed around a good deal—it was an event as well as a locality. A puzzled tourist stopped George Taton, a Kansas wheat farmer, in Garden City one day: "Can you tell me where this Dust Bowl is?" "Stay where you are," Taton told him, "and it'll come to you." Even locals could not always discover the exact boundaries, wondering exasperatedly, "Are we in it or ain't we?"[4] In a sense, wherever there were recurring dust storms and soil erosion there was a dust bowl, and by that test most of the Great Plains was "in it" during a part of the 1930s, some of the most severe conditions occurring as far north as Nebraska and the Dakotas. But SCS officials, surveying the entire plains, placed their Dust Bowl perimeters around the most persistent problem area, and there was no doubt which counties were at the heart of this Bowl: Morton in Kansas, Baca in Colorado, Texas and Cimarron in Oklahoma, Dallam in Texas, and Union in New Mexico.

By 1935 the landscape in those and surrounding counties had become, in Geiger's words, "a vast desert, with miniature shifting dunes of sand." The fences, piled high with tumbleweeds and drifted over with dirt, looked like giant backbones of ancient reptiles. Elsewhere the underlying hardpan was laid bare, as sterile and unyielding as a city pavement. The winds exposed long-buried Indian campgrounds, as well as arrowheads, pioneer wagon wheels, Spanish stirrups, branding irons, tractor wrenches, the chain someone had dropped in the furrow the previous year. By 1938, the peak year for wind erosion, 10 million acres had lost at least the upper five inches of topsoil; another 13.5 million acres had lost at least two and a half inches. Over all the cultivated land in the region, there were 408

[3]Tom Gill to Robert Geiger, 14 Apr. 1941, along with "Blow Area Map," National Archives RG 114. An earlier map is in H. H. Finnell Correspondence, *ibid.* Roy Kimmel, "A United Front To Reclaim the Dust Bowl," *New York Times Magazine*, 14 Apr. 1938, pp. 10–11, 20.

[4]George Taton to author, taped interview, 11 Sept. 1977. *Dalhart Texan*, 5 July 1937. Hugh H. Bennett, "The Vague, Roaming 'Dust Bowl,'" *New York Times Magazine*, 26 July 1936, pp. 1–2, 17.

tons of dirt blown away from the average acre, in some cases only to the next farm, in others to the next state or beyond. According to Roy Kimmel, the special federal coordinator assigned to the Dust Bowl, in 1938 they were still losing 850 million tons of earth a year to erosion, far more than was washed down the Mississippi. The dirt that blew away, one Iowa-deposited sample revealed, contained ten times as much organic matter and nitrogen—the basics of fertility—as did the sand dunes left behind in Dallam County, Texas.[5]

After Geiger, other journalists came to the Dust Bowl, and they described the scene to urban Americans. They usually carried with them a license for hyperbole and a capacity for shock. George Greenfield of the *New York Times*, passing through Kansas on the Union Pacific, was the most funereal: "Today I have seen the cold hand of death on what was one of the great breadbaskets of the nation . . . a lost people living in a lost land." But more cutting was the 1937 *Collier's* article by Walter Davenport, "Land Where Our Children Die," which found in the Dust Bowl only "famine, violent death, private and public futility, insanity, and lost generations." For Davenport the source of the devastation lay in its Dogpatch residents—its Willie Mae Somethings, Jere Hullomons, Twell Murficks, all too stupid or greedy to be trusted with the land. Then there were the newsreel photographers from the *March of Time*, who had heard about Texas crows being forced to build their nests out of barbed wire and, of course, hurriedly came to exploit the rumor rather than examine it.[6] In theaters, newspapers, and magazines, Americans began to see more of the southern plains, a place remote from their experience and heretofore ignored, but invariably what they saw was the same extreme slice of reality, the most sensationally barren parts of that land.

These outside reports, however, were not total fabrications, as many local residents admitted in their own descriptions of what they saw. Albert Law of the *Dalhart Texan* published this frank account in 1933, well before the peak years:

> Not a blade of wheat in Cimarron County, Oklahoma; cattle dying there on the range; a few bushels of wheat in the Perryton area against an average yield of from four to six million bushels; with all the stored surplus not more than fifty per cent of the seeding needs will be met—ninety per cent of the poultry dead because of the sand storms; sixty cattle dying Friday afternoon between Guymon and Liberal from some disease induced by dust—humans suffering from dust fever—milk cows going dry, turned into pasture to starve, hogs in such pitiable shape that buyers will not have them; cattle being moved from Dallam and other counties to grass; no wheat in Hartley County; new crops a remote possibility, cattle facing starvation; Potter, Seward and other Panhandle counties with one-third of their population on charity or

[5]Soil Conservation Service, "Some Information about Dust Storms and Wind Erosion in the Great Plains" (Washington, D. C., 1953), p. 10. H. H. Finnell, "Southern Great Plains Region," Oct. 1940, National Archives RG 114. Kimmel, "A United Front," p. 11.

[6]George Greenfield, *New York Times*, 8 Mar. 1937. Walter Davenport, "Land Where Our Children Die," *Collier's*, 18 Sept. 1937, pp. 11–13, 73–77. *Dalhart Texan*, 24 Mar. 1936.

relief work; ninety per cent of the farmers in most counties have had to have crop loans, and continued drought forcing many of them to use the money for food, clothes, medicine, shelter.

Confirmation of those details came from all over. In Moore County, Texas, for example, the welfare director, on behalf of the Dumas Chamber of Commerce, reported to federal officials in March 1935 that it was "an impossible task to describe the utter destruction": roads obliterated, the crops all gone, "no hope or ambition left," and many farmers "near starvation."[7] Today, more than forty years later, oldtimers often point out that outsiders never knew what the dirty past of the thirties was really like, never appreciated how severe the problem was.

But at the same time there were many on the plains, especially businessmen in the towns, who bitterly resented their "Dust Bowl" reputation, so much so that they formed truth squads to get the straight facts to the rest of the nation. Usually "straight" meant "most flattering," and those who did not conform, who saw things differently, could be in for trouble. Albert Law's paper lost more than $1000 in advertising after his frank article appeared, and in later years he learned to speak more carefully, even to join the truth-squad vigilantes. In 1936 he referred to that "harebrained individual" who "in an abortive fit" misnamed the plains "Dust Bowl." Leadership for the defensive campaign came from several west Texas chambers of commerce, particularly Dalhart's, and from editor John L. McCarty of Dalhart and, later, of Amarillo, McCarty's style was at its shoot-em-up best in this refutation of the *Collier's* article by Walter Davenport: "a vicious libel," "compounded of lies and half-truths," "bunk," "more bunk," "sissy." The outrage lay not only in that outside critics were condemning "a group of courageous Americans for a six-year drought cycle and national conditions beyond their control"; they were also destroying the property values, bank credit, and business prospects of the region.[8]

A minor but extreme episode in this effort to clear away the dust from the plains' reputation centered on painter Alexandre Hogue. The son of a Missouri minister, Hogue had spent much of this youth on his brother-in-law's ranch near Hartley, Texas, not far from Dalhart, where he had learned to love the country and the cowhand's life. In his mid-thirties when the dusters appeared, he began painting the ravaged panhandle landscape. Dust drifts, starved cattle, broken-down windmills, and rattlesnakes were the principal features of his works, scenes as hopeless and grim as Hogue could manage. The paintings were obviously fictions, exaggerated for dramatic effect—"superrealism" or "psycho-reality" he called his style—but brilliantly conveying the painter's ambivalent mood about the disaster. There was the utter destruction of a rural way of life, which he deeply regretted, but there was also a fascination with the forms of disorder. "They were *not* social comment," Hogue insists; "I did them because to me, aside from the tragedy of the situation, the effects were beautiful,

---

[7]Albert Law, *Dalhart Texan*, 17 June 1933. Mrs. M. A. Turner, Moore County, Tex., "Effects of Dust Storms: Chambers of Commerce Reports," Mar. 1935, National Archives RG 114.

[8]Albert Law, *Dalhart Texan*, 24 Mar. 1936. John McCarty, *Amarillo Globe-Times*, 13 Sept. 1937.

beautiful in a terrifying way." But the Dalhart Chamber of Commerce was not ready for Hogue's aestheticism, and when *Life* magazine published some of his works in 1937 and called him "artist of the dust bowl" (he hated that phrase), the vigilantes went into action. Hogue, they insisted, was "some upstart sent down from New York who knows nothing about the region and so painted isolated cases that are not typical if they even exist." An emissary was sent to Dallas to purchase the painting "Drought Survivors" from the Pan-American Exposition there; the truth squad planned to burn it on the streets of Dalhart. But when the emissary discovered that he had been given only $50 to buy a $2000 work, he trudged back home— and art triumphed over local pride, or at least cost more.[9]

To admit that the plains had in fact become a disaster area was to give up faith in the future and the productive potential of the land. Many simply could not bring themselves to do it. They were quick to deny, and to repress, the Dust Bowl label. But they were even quicker to announce that the Bowl was shrinking. One month after Black Sunday rain was falling everywhere; Baca County got one inch and a half—it's a "mud bowl" now, they exulted. Floods were rampaging in Hutchinson and Augusta, Kansas, just east of the blow area. It was a short-lived phenomenon, as were other moments of respite in the later part of the decade. But it was enough to renew faith in the future and to vindicate the vigilantes. One year later, in March 1936, Robert Geiger came back to Oklahoma and wrote that, with more rains, "the 'Dust Bowl' is losing its handle." Ida Watkins, a large-scale wheat farmer in southwestern Kansas, was so encouraged that she began planting, explaining to a visitor:

> I guess the good Lord is going to lead us out into the promised Land again. . . . For five years we have been living here in the desert of the dust bowl and now the abundant rains have taken us up into a high mountain and shown us close ahead the bounteous land of Canaan, blossoming with wheat and a new prosperity.[10]

Like President Herbert Hoover, who kept reassuring the public that the Depression was almost over, these hopeful souls were false prophets. There were at least five more difficult years ahead, five years when the dust masks came out repeatedly, trains continued to be derailed by dust, and wheat fields often stood empty and dry. Most of those later storms were only "gray zephyrs" compared with those of 1935, but some could be awesomely devastating. One of the biggest ever came three years after Watkins's glimpse of the promised land—on 11 March 1939, when a Stillwater, Oklahoma, agronomist estimated there was enough dirt in the air to cover 5 million acres one foot deep. That storm raged over a 100,000-square-mile spread.[11] A too-ready optimism was no more an effective defense against the winds of ruin than was censorship.

[9]Hogue to author, 2 Mar. 1978. Ironically, Hogue's "Drouth Survivors" was burned after all— in an accidental fire in Paris at the Jeu de Paume Museum, which had purchased it. See also *Life*, 21 June 1937, pp. 60–61. Drought, incidentally, is always spelled "drouth" on the plains.

[10]*Kansas City Star*, 12, 13 May 1935. Ida Watkins, *ibid.* 7 June 1936. *Dodge City Glove*, 12 May 1935. Robert Geiger, *Amarillo Sunday News-Globe*, 15 Mar. 1936. Ward West, "Hope Springs Green in the Dust Bowl," *New York Times Magazine*, 16 July 1939, pp. 7, 21.

[11]Robert Martin, "Duststorms of 1938 in the United States," *Monthly Weather Review*, 67 (Jan.

Even as the John McCartys were defending the region's credit rating and the Ida Watkinses were straining their eyes toward Canaan, plains residents were collecting federal aid. The benign arm of Providence could use a little government muscle, apparently. Things were not going to change for the better with time, it was feared—or a least few people were patient enough to wait around for that to happen. The plains were in serious trouble and getting worse, and no amount of faith in the inevitability of progress would save them unless prompt action were taken. What the plains wanted was a speedy restoration of "normal" expectations and the means to satisfy them. The New Deal promised that restoration, just as it offered factory workers the chance to go back to work in the same factory under the old ownership. In the mid-1930s out on the plains, federal money began raining down with the sweet smell of a spring shower, nourishing the seeds of hope that had so persistently been planted. In the absence of the real thing, such outpourings were the best available substitute. And for a while Washington became the new Providence.

It was a long way from the federal government to the Dust Bowl. The region was then, and still is, one of the most remote and rural parts of America. The largest city in the region was Amarillo, with a population of 43,000 in 1930. Denver, with almost 300,000 inhabitants, lay at the extreme northwest corner of the Bowl, out on the fringe, as were all the other state capitals—Topeka, Oklahoma City, Austin, and Albuquerque. Scattered over the SCS's Region VI were 2 million people, most of them living not in cities, but in very small towns or on farms. And they were spiralling downward into desperate poverty as their crops failed year after year. In Hall and Childress counties in Texas, average cotton ginnings fell from 99,000 bales in the late 1920s to 12,500 in 1934. The next year Kansans cut wheat on only half their planted acreage; Stanton County reaped nothing.[12] Those two years were especially bad, to be sure, but with the exception of 1938, a wetter year, not one in the decade saw a significantly improved harvest. As the agricultural base of the region's economy was buried under dust, extreme hardship loomed over the southern plains, and rescue by a distant government was the only hope.

In 1936, to determine which areas were in the most desperate straits, the federal government's Works Progress Administration (WPA) sent out two investigators, Francis Cronin and Howard Beers, to survey the entire Great Plains. Cronin and Beers compiled data in five categories—precipitation, crop production, status of pasturelands, changes in number of cattle, and federal aid per capita—all the way back to 1930. Taken together, the categories gave an index of "intense drought distress." Out of 800 counties they surveyed, from Minnesota and Montana to Texas, two centers of rural poverty emerged: first, an area that covered almost all of North and South Dakota, along with contiguous counties in neighboring states;

1939), 12–15; Martin, "Duststorms of 1939," *ibid.* (Dec.), 446–51. *Daily Oklahoman* (Oklahoma City), 19 Mar. 1939.

[12]Dorothea Lange and Paul Taylor, *An American Exodus* (New Haven: Yale University Press, 1969), p. 70. Vance Johnson, *Heaven's Tableland: The Dust Bowl Story* (New York: Farrar, Straus, 1947), pp. 173–76. "Effect of Dust Storms: County Agents' Reports," Mar.–Apr. 1935, National Archives RG 114.

and second, the Dust Bowl on the southern plains. Altogether, 125 counties from both foci qualified as "very severe" and another 127 as "severe." South Dakota led, with 41 counties in the bottom-most category; North Dakota had 23, as did Texas; Kansas, 20; Oklahoma, 5; Colorado, 2. By 1936, in each of the counties, federal aid for agricultural failure had already totaled at least $175 per person. Other studies revealed that government payments for the fourteen southwestern counties of Kansas came to $100 a year per capita, and Morton received twice that much. One-third to one-half of the farm families in that corner of the state depended upon some kind of government relief in 1935; it was still much less than the 80 per cent found in one North Dakota county, but it was well above the national average. "The prairie," observed a reader of the *Dallas Farm News* in 1939, "once the home of the deer, buffalo and antelope, is now the home of the Dust Bowl and the WPA."[13]

Rural Americans had been more reluctant to ask for outside help than the city poor, even after they too had begun to feel the pinch of hard times. Nowhere was this aversion to "charity" more fierce than on the southern plains. To ask for aid implied personal and providential failure—the very "insult" that the McCarthy brigade had resented. In any case, there was little charity to be had, at least locally: no effective organization to give it out, public or private, in most counties; and nothing to give. State capitals were slow to learn about conditions, and slower to act, excusing themselves by reason of tight budgets. Thus there was only Washington, far away and highly suspect, but the last resort. At the onset of the drought President Hoover turned to the Red Cross, which had performed wonderfully in the Mississippi flood of 1927, to devise another rescue. But the Red Cross leaders, many of them appointed by Hoover, seriously underestimated the Western relief needs, appropriating only a third of what they had spend on the flood. At last, when it became apparent that these private efforts were pathetically inadequate, Congress set up a $45 million seed-and-feed loan fund. Hoover denounced it as "a raid on the public treasury" and a slide toward the degenerate "dole"—but he signed it into law.[14] That was the beginning of federal initiatives to save the Great Plains from utter ruin.

The loan fund was not by any token adequate to the relief task, nor by 1932 was Hoover's gloomy mien or budget-consciousness acceptable to most Dust Bowl voters. In the national elections that year, the plains joined with the rest of the nation to elect Franklin Roosevelt, a gentleman farmer from New York, to the presidency. Traditionally Democratic Texas, Oklahoma, and New Mexico gave Roosevelt 88, 73, and 63 per cent of their votes, respectively; while in Kansas and Colorado the victory margin, although below the national level (almost 58 per cent), was a major departure from

[13]Francis Cronin and Howard Beers, *Areas of Intense Drought Distress*, 1930–1936, WPA Research Bulletin, Series V, no. 1 (Washington, D. C., 1937). Charles Loomis, "The Human Ecology of the Great Plains," *Oklahoma Academy of Science Proceedings*, 17 (1937), 21. Johnson, *Heaven's Tableland*, pp. 190–91. Lange and Taylor, *American Exodus*, p. 82. Howard Ottoson et al., *Land and People in the Northern Transition Area* (Lincoln: University of Nebraska Press, 1966), p. 73.

[14]Paul Kellogg, "Drought and the Red Cross," *Survey*, 15 Feb. 1931, pp. 535–38, 72–76. See also Pete Daniel, *Deep'n As It Come: The 1927 Mississippi River Flood* (New York: Oxford University Press, 1977), pp. 10–11, 84–95.

their loyal Republican past.[15] It was time, the plainsmen agreed, for something beyond rugged individualism, even if they were unsure what and and how much the federal government ought to do for them. Perhaps Roosevelt's style, however, was more important to them than any specific program. His easy and buoyant manner appealed to a people who felt their traditional optimism slipping and wanted it shored up.

During his first year in office Roosevelt ignored the Great Plains, as his predecessor had done. It was perhaps understandable: there was a drought going on, but the dust storms had not yet reached continental proportions and he had his hands full with greater emergencies—thousands of bank failures and industrial shutdowns, national income cut in half, one out of every four workers unemployed. He did establish important new programs that would come to play a critical role in the region's recovery, such as the Agricultural Adjustment Administration, the Federal Emergency Relief Administration, and the Farm Credit Administration, all of which were set in motion during the famous first hundred days of the Roosevelt presidency in 1933.[16] But it took the May 1934 dust storm to make the plains visible to Washington. As dust sifted down on the Mall and the White House, Roosevelt was in a press conference promising that the Cabinet was at work on a new Great Plains relief program. Desperate appeals were being heard from farmers, ranchers, politicians, and businessmen out West, some of them demanding money, others, more humble, wanting advice and comfort. "Please do something," one lady wrote, "to help us save our country, where one time we were all so happy."[17] Alf Landon, the governor of Kansas, got letters too, as did other area governors, but in effect they forwarded them to Washington by requesting federal relief money that they could disperse to their voters—the 1930s version of states' rights.

While Roosevelt and his Cabinet worked out a drought relief package, the American public put its own ingenuity to work and sent the results to the President and other public officials. Ideas began coming in during the spring of 1934 and kept coming over the next few years, from citizens in every part of the country and even from observers in China, England, and Czechoslovakia. They came from barnyard inventors and company engineers, from immigrants eager to do something for their adopted Uncle Sam, from former plains farmers retired in Los Angeles, and from the city unemployed who hoped their notions would produce a job or a fat check. The obvious remedy, according to many of these letter writers, was simply to cover the Dust Bowl over. The Sisalkraft Company of Chicago had a tough waterproof paper that could do the job, while the Barber Asphalt Company in New Jersey recommended an "asphalt emulsion" at $5.00 an acre, and a Pittsburgh steel corporation had wire netting for sale. One man urged that the ground be covered with concrete, leaving holes for planting seeds, and another that rocks be hauled in from the mountains. Mrs. M. L. Yearby of Durham, North Carolina, saw a chance to beautify

[15]Bureau of the Census, *Vote Cast in Presidential and Congressional Elections, 1928–1944* (Washington, D. C., 1946).

[16]The record of F. D. R.'s first 100 days is summed up in Arthus Schlesinger, Jr., *The Coming of the New Deal* (Boston: Houghton Mifflin, Sentry ed., 1965), pp. 1–23.

[17]Mary Gallagher of Amarillo to F.D.R., 15 Mar. 1934, National Archives RG 114.

her own state by shipping its junked automobiles out to the plains to anchor the blowing fields, and several others proposed spreading ashes and garbage from Eastern cities or leaves from forests to create a mulch over the plains and restore a binding humus to the soil. Building wind deflectors also appealed to many—cement slabs or board fences, as much as 250 feet high, or shelterbelts of pine trees, alfalfa, greasewood, and even Jerusalem artichokes. An Albuquerque writer blamed the dust storms on "German agents"; a Russian-born chemist in New York City suggested radio waves instead; the Lions Club in Perryton, Texas, pointed to pollution from local gas and oil refineries; and there were some who worried about the carbon-black plant near Amarillo.[18]

But for plains residents the most widely favored panacea was, understandably, water. "You gave us beer," they told Roosevelt, "now give us water." That was all they really needed, they were sure, and the federal government was wasting its time with anything else. "Every draw, arryo [sic], and canyon that could be turned into a lake or lagoon," wrote a clothing store manager, "should be made into one by dams and directed ditches & draws until there are *millions* of them thru these mid western states." A Texas stockman wanted to use natural gas to pump flood waters from the Mississippi River to the plains. Deep-water irrigation wells was another scheme; 5000 of them, it was said, would cost only $17.5 million. And then there were the perennially hopeful rainmakers, long familiar on the southern plains, always popping up with a "scientific" method, new or old, to extract rain out of a cloudless sky. An old soldier from Denver penciled his ideas on ruled tablet paper: stage sham battles with 40,000 Civilian Conservation Corps boys and $20 million worth of ammunition— the noise would be sure to stir up some rain, as it always did in wartime. "Try it," he finished, "if it works send me a check for $5000 for services rendered."[19]

Each of those letters and dozens more like them, got a patient answer from a federal administrator, but no check. The Roosevelt advisers settled on a more prosaic, if more expensive program for the Great Plains. On 9 June 1934 the President asked Congress for $525 million in drought relief, and it was promptly given. The biggest chunks, totaling $275 million, were for cattlemen—to provide emergency feed loans, to purchase some of their starving stock, and to slaughter the animals and can their meat for the poor. Destitute farmers would get more public jobs, often building ponds and reservoirs, as well as cash income supplements, costing $125 million. Other features of the program included acquiring submarginal lands, relocating rural people in better environments, creating work camps for young men, and making seed loans for new crops. A few days later Roosevelt squeezed in a shelterbelt program, too.[20] For the remainder of the thirties

[18]All these suggestions are from letters in the National Archives RG 114. See also Dr. Preston Pratt, *Kansas City Star*, 11 May 1935; and Harlan Miller, "Dust Rides the Winds Out of the West," *New York Times Magazine*, 11 Mar. 1935, pp. 11, 14.

[19]H. H. Finnell Correspondence, National Archives RG 114. For an actual rainmaking experiment, see R. Douglas Hurt, "The Dust Bowl," *American West*, 14 (July–Aug. 1977), 26.

[20]Samuel Rosenman (ed.), *The Public Papers and Addresses of Franklin D. Roosevelt*, (13 vols., New York: Random House, 1938), Vol. III, pp. 293–97. See also Michael Schuyler, "Federal Drought Relief Activities in Kansas, 1934," *Kansas Historical Quarterly*, 42 (Winter 1976), 403–24.

most of these strategies became familiar fixtures in the federal budget, evolving, along with other farm and relief legislation, into a more specifically directed Dust Bowl rehabilitation effort.

As for the most immediate need to stop the blowing dust, the federal government heeded regional advice and in 1935 adopted a program of emergency "listing."[21] The lister, a standard farm implement on the plains, was a double mold-board that dug deep, broad furrows and threw the dirt upto high ridges. Once used for planting corn, it now served the function of creating a corduroy-like ground surface that would slow erosion, or at least it would if the listing were done crosswise to the prevailing winds. In a stiff blow the ridges would still drift back into the furrows, forcing the farmer to list his fields repeatedly to keep them stabilized. Sometimes a chisel would be employed too, breaking the hard subsurface and bringing up heavy clods to hold down the dust. But when you were broke, with no money for gasoline or tractor repairs, constant lister-plowing or chiseling was impossible. Or if you lived a hundred miles away from your farm, visiting it only twice a year, once at planting and again harvesting time, the work would not get done. The government, therefore, proposed to pay plains farmers for working their own land or having it worked by someone on the scene. And the Texas and Kansas legislatures allowed counties to list the land of irresponsible neighbors, charging the expense to the owner, where all other inducements had failed. As an effort to legalize community control over recalcitrant individuals, these state laws were too hedged about with delays, and too seldom used, to be especially effective.[22] But self-interest, along with government money, was generally adequate to put the bare fields under some control.

Emergency listing continued to get federal funds virtually every year thereafter in the decade. In the 1936 Soil Conservation and Domestic Allotment Act, $2 million was the sum allowed for this work. Kansas and Texas received about half of the money, the other three southern plains states what was left over. In each state the money first passed through the hands of the land-grant colleges and their county extension agents, then through local committees that supervised contracts and made sure the listing was actually done, and done properly. Dust Bowl farmers listed more than 8 million acres in the 12 months prior to July 1937, for which the government paid them 20 cents an acre where they worked their own land, 40 cents where they had to hire others to do it.[23] It was not much money; many thought they should get more. Nor did emergency listing address the deeper issues of man and the land on the southern plains or stop a full-fledged black blizzard. But it gave farmers something to do, and it kept some of the dirt from going too far.

[21]Memorandum, C. W. Warburton to Henry Wallace, 22 Dec. 1937, National Archives RG 16.

[22]George Wehrwein, "Wind Erosion Legislation in Texas and Kansas," *Journal of Land and Public Utility Economics.* 12 (Aug. 1936), 312–13.

[23]This program was called the "Kansas Plan," after Governor Landon, on the advice of state agriculturists, presented the idea to F.D.R. (*Kansas City Star*, 29 Mar. 1935). Kansas received the first federal grant for listing—$250,000 paid out at 10 cents an acre. See also Edgar Nixon (ed.), *Franklin D. Roosevelt and Conservation, 1911–1945* (2 vols., New York: Arno Press, 1972), 1:367–68; and Donald McCoy, *Landon of Kansas* (Lincoln: University of Nebraska Press, 1966), p. 325.

The people of the plains made it clear in the 1936 elections how well they liked this rain of federal money. Despite the fact that the Republican party chose Alf Landon of Kansas for their presidential nominee, Roosevelt was again triumphant in the region, winning 54 per cent of the votes in Kansas, 60 in Colorado, 63 in New Mexico, 67 in Oklahoma, and 87 in Texas. Landon, who conducted a fumbling and waffling campaign, had nothing fresh or appealing to offer the Dust Bowl states and had been regionally upstaged and outmaneuvered by Roosevelt's "fact-finding" swing through the northern Great Plains in September.[24] Two years later Roosevelt and the New Deal were still immensely popular in the Southwest. When the President went to Amarillo on 11 July 1938, in his only venture into the Dust Bowl itself, the city assembled the largest massed marching band in the history of the nation to greet him, thousands lined the streets, and, *mirabile dictu*, rain began to fall shortly before he arrived. As he stood hatless in the downpour, uttering genial platitudes in his clear ringing style, a woman in the audience exclaimed: "I am ready to make him king, anybody who can smile like that."[25] So warm a reception was bound to cool, of course, and by 1940 portions of the dust belt began to defect, reverting to their traditional political views. But throughout the dirty thirties it was all New Deal country.

Some of the most insistent proponents of government intervention were Dust Bowl businessmen. While farmers tended to resist too much interference with their freedom to do as they liked with the land, there were business groups that demanded more authoritarian control by Washington, including a declaration of martial law. The Liberal, Kansas, Chamber of Commerce, for instance, insisted on "a force program, under government supervision," which would see that every field was listed properly. The federal soil erosion agent there noted in 1937 that businessmen, who had been arguing that "the conditions were being over emphasized and this area was getting more than its share of adverse publicity," now were agreed that "the control of wind erosion in the dust bowl is well out of hand and are willing to allow any action that the federal government may take to put into operation." Down in Dalhart the truth squad had to send out a new emissary, this one to a Washington congressional committee, to admit there was some truth in Alexandre Hogue's paintings and to plead for passage of a $10-million water-facilities bill.[26]

But there was one government proposal that never failed to arouse hostility—resettlement or relocation. Leaving the plains meant giving up, admitting defeat, and possibly losing the future altogether; Providence never rewards the quitters. Resettlement was never really a serious idea in Washington either, not at least to the extent of removing all of the people

---

[24]The itineraries and correspondence for this trip are in Official File 200, F.D.R. Library, Hyde Park, N. Y. See also Nixon (ed.), *Roosevelt and Conservation*, 1: 559–67, for the follow-up conferences in Des Moines, Iowa; and Michael Schuyler, "Drought and Politics, 1936: Kansas as a Test Case," *Great Plains Journal*, 14 (Fall 1975), 3–27.

[25]Nixon (ed.), *Roosevelt and Conservation*. 2:247–49. *Amarillo Daily News*, 12 July 1935.

[26]Telegram, Emergency Dust Bowl Committee, Liberal, Kansas, to Governor Walter Huxman, 23 Apr. 1937, Huxman Papers, Kansas State Historical Society, Topeka. Letter, H. A. Kinnery to Huxman, 29 April 1937, *ibid*. Telegram, Liberal committee to F.D.R., 22 April 1937, National Archives RG 114. Letter, Fred Sykes to H. H. Finnell, 23 Apr. *ibid*.

from the Dust Bowl, but plains residents were forever on their guard after the Harold Ickes incident. Secretary of the Interior Ickes, when presented in November 1933 with a proposal to build expensive dams in the Oklahoma panhandle, turned thumbs down; he felt that it would be a waste of money. "We'll have to move them [the people] out of there," he said, "and turn the land back to the public domain." The howls of protest from 40,000 Oklahomans could be heard all the way to Capitol Hill. Ickes is "entirely ignorant of the possibilities this country affords," retorted the *Boise City News*.[27] But the subsequent setting up of a Resettlement Administration in 1935 under Rexford Tugwell, a Columbia University professor, kept the plains wall-eyed. Following Black Sunday, as more rumors of forced evacuation came from the East Coast, John McCarty and his Dalhart boosters organized a Last Man's Club, each member pledging on his sacred honor never to abandon the plains. And farther west, in New Mexico, where the prospects of removal were just as unwelcome, a farmer spoke for many when he warned: "They'll have to take a shotgun to move us out of here. We're going to stay here just as long as we damn please."[28]

That fierce resolve to stay, even as the tawny dust was making their land of opportunity a dreary wasteland, followed in large part from an assumption that the plains people made. It was drought, they were confident, and drought alone, that had made the Dust Bowl: "That drought put the fixins to us." But with a gambler's trust in better luck, they knew the rains would return. "This land will come back," most were sure: "it'll make good agin—it always has." Franklin Roosevelt, although he hardly knew what real drought was, or poverty, for that matter, shared the plainsmen's optimism, and, to a large extent, their analysis of the problem. "Drought relief" was what they most needed, he believed, and when the rains returned the people would be back on their feet, restoring the land to the rich agricultural empire it had been. That confidence was not absolutely misplaced, as later history showed. But it was all too simple and easy, and the farmers too quick to blame nature for the dust storms, too ready to lay all their misfortunes on the lack of rain. Although drought assistance was obviously needed, as flood or earthquake aid was needed elsewhere, a few of Roosevelt's administrators soon began to see that something more was required: a more far-reaching conservation program that would include social and economic changes.

Without the abrupt drop in precipitation the southern plains would never have become so ravaged a country, nor would they perhaps have needed, even during the Depression, much government aid: this much is true. But the drought, though a necessary factor, is not sufficient in itself to explain the black blizzards. Dry spells are an inevitable fact of life on the plains, predictable enough to allow successful settlement, but only if the settlers know how to tread lightly, look ahead, and shape their expectations to fit the qualities of the land. As the federal administrators studied the problem more fully, they came to see that the settlers of the West had never shown those qualities. They had displayed instead a naïve hopeful-

[27]*Boise City* (Ok.) *News* (hereafter cited as *BCN*), 2 Nov. 1933.
[28]*Dalhart Texan*, 29 Apr. 1935. *Amarillo Daily News*, 27 May 1936. Evon Vogt, *Modern Homesteaders* (Cambridge: Harvard University Press, 1955), p. 66.

ness that the good times would never run out, that the land would never go back on them. Some officials, therefore, began to call for major revisions in the faulty land system; others emphasized new agronomic techniques, rural rehabilitation, more diversified farming, or extensive grassland restoration. But their common theme was that staying meant changing. The Dust Bowl, in this evolving government view, must be explained as a failure in ecological adaptation—as an absence of environmental realism.

Farmers and ranchers on the plains were not so recalcitrant as to reject that analysis totally, although, understandably, it was hard for them to admit that what they had learned and had always been told was right could now be responsible for their predicament. It was natural for them to be defensive. They felt unfairly singled out for blame and criticism by many outsiders, when it was they who had to face the dust and struggle hard to save the farms that produced much of the nation's food. And they were right to this extent: it was indeed unjust and misdirected to blame everything on the Dust Bowl residents themselves, for they were largely unwitting agents—men and women caught in a larger economic culture, dependent on its demands and rewards, representing its values and patterns of thought. The ultimate meaning of the dust storms in the 1930s was that America as a whole, not just the plains, was badly out of balance with its natural environment. Unbounded optimism about the future, careless disregard of nature's limits and uncertainties, uncritical faith in Providence, devotion to self-aggrandizement—all these were national as well as regional characteristics.

The activism of the federal government was appropriate and essential; a national problem demanded national answers. But the situation also demanded a more than superficial grasp of what was responsible for the disaster and of how it could be prevented from occurring again. What the plainsmen needed was hope, of course—but the mature hope that does not smooth over failure, deny responsibility, or prevent basic change. They needed a disciplined optimism, tempered with restraint and realism toward the land. But all that required a substantial reform of commercial farming, which neither Roosevelt nor most of his New Deal advisers were prepared or able to bring about. Even as it evolved toward a more comprehensive program, the New Deal did not aim to alter fundamentally the American economic culture. Washington became and remained throughout the decade a substitute for a benign Providence, trying to give the plainsmen their "next year."

Racial segregation was rigidly observed in the South

Race Relations in
a Southern Town

HORTENSE POWDERMAKER

In the southern United States prior to the end of the Civil War, the relationship between blacks, most of whom were slaves, and whites was carefully regulated by a complex of laws and customs based on the institution of slavery. After abolition, for a few years, race relations were in a relatively ambiguous state. C. Vann Woodward's *The Strange Career of Jim Crow,* revised for the third time in 1974, and the controversy this work has engendered have charted for us the formulation of a new pattern of southern race relations that was substantially complete by the opening years of the twentieth century. The resulting system of segregation, or "Jim Crow," called for legally enforced separation of the races into a two-level caste system that permeated both public and private life in the South.

The public aspects of segregation, because of their basis in law and local ordinance, finally came under attack by the federal judiciary after years of litigation forced primarily by the National Association for the Advancement of Colored People. The decision of the United States Supreme Court in 1954 declaring school segregation unconstitutional rang the death knell for official racial discrimination in the public sphere. But it has been a long time dying. In the years after 1954, continued litigation brought many areas of segregation under public scrutiny, and as federal legislation was gradually enforced in the South and border regions, the long-standard structure of race relations began to crumble.

Less well known, but in many ways more dehumanizing, were the private patterns of racial discrimination throughout the South. Historians have been more interested in the larger, public institutions and their change over time. Sociologists, however, and particularly social and cultural anthropologists, have through the years been concerned with the more intimate relationships within communities and groups of all sorts. During the 1930s and 1940s, several excellent studies of black communities and race relations in the South were published. Perhaps the best of these is an anthropological study of Indianola, Mississippi, published in 1939 by Hortense Powdermaker, formerly of Queens College of the City University of New York. While the primary purpose of Powdermaker's work was to provide a social portrait of the black people in Indianola (called Cottonville in the study), she necessarily included a great deal of material on the relationship between the races. Few people who have not lived in the segregated South can understand the extent to which race relations formed a major topic of interest and concern for all involved, the dominant as well as the dominated. This same level of concern, however, is now being approached in urban centers, which have taken the place of the South as the major area of racial conflict.

It has often been said that the major difference between northern and southern white attitudes toward blacks in past times has been that in the North black people were loved as a race and despised as individuals, while in the South they were loved as individuals and despised as a race. The practical application of this southern attitude, however, was set within narrow limits. In the selection from Powdermaker's book reprinted below, she explores these limitations and delineates the ways in which the racial attitudes of whites work themselves out in action. Her concern here is not with the segregation of public institutions but with the refusal of whites to grant to blacks the common respect of humanity. The constant interpersonal humiliation, and its ultimate form, lynching, rather than the better known institutional discrimination is her subject in this section.

As the pattern of public segregation began to break down in recent years, a concomitant change often occurred in interpersonal relations. The "affection" based on hard and fast caste lines often was lost as the caste lines became more permeable. But, at the same time, a grudging acknowledgment of respect based on a common humanity began to develop. A major factor in the elimination of the kind of discriminatory behavior described below has been the increasing refusal of black Americans to accept such treatment. And, as far as racial attitudes and patterns of racial relationships are concerned, the nation now more nearly resembles the condition described by Malcolm X: "The South begins at the Canadian border." For the first time in American history, race relations now are being looked at from a national, rather than a regional, perspective.

What the white inhabitants of the Cottonville community think and feel about the Negro finds expression whenever there is contact between the two races. The more subtle manifestations of prevailing attitudes appear only after examination, but the cruder expressions are apparent to any visitor who is not so familiar with them as to take them for granted. That the local Whites do take them for granted so thoroughly as hardly to be aware of them until they are commented upon or violated is an essential feature of the social scene.

Any American visitor is prepared to find the well-known Jim Crow arrangements of the railroad station with its separate waiting-rooms and toilets. He will know that there are separate and inferior day coaches reserved for the Negroes at the standard fares, and that they are not permitted to ride in Pullmans at any price. He will note that here, as in many places up north, Negroes are not allowed to eat in white restaurants, but may patronize two or three small eating places run by and for colored people. The balcony of the one moving picture theater is reserved for them. Seats here are cheaper than those downstairs, and they may not buy the more expensive seats. There are separate schools and churches for Negroes, in buildings removed from the white neighborhood—either Across the Tracks or in the country. These divisions are absolute. No white person would attend a Negro insitution or sit in the places reserved for Negroes, though presumably he could if he would. No Negro would be admitted to the institutions or places reserved for Whites.

Hardly less rigid are the social mechansims which express the conviction that the two races are distinct and that one of them is distinctly inferior, and which confirm the well-known fact that in this section of our democracy the accepted order is analogous to, though not identical with, a caste system. These social mechanisms are familiar enough to American readers so that brief mention of a few will suffice to indicate their nature and their relation to factors already discussed. They take the form of prohibitions, injunctions, usages; they may be chiefly "social," or may carry economic and even legal consequences. They vary also in the significance attached to them, which is not always in proportion to their apparent magnitude.

A social prohibition to which great weight is attached is that which forbids addressing a Negro as "Mr.," "Mrs.," or "Miss." Just what the white person withholds in avoiding the use of these titles is suggested by those he is willing to employ. Ordinarily, a Negro is simply called by his first name, regardless of his age, attainments, or wealth, and often by Whites who may be less endowed in any of these respects. "Doctor" and "Professor" are readily granted to professional people, however. A teacher who has charge of a small one-room country school, and who himself has never been to high school, is regularly called Professor. A medical man will be addressed as "Doctor" by Whites who could not conceivably bring themselves to call him "Mister." It may not seem entirely inappropriate that members of a race considered inferior should more easily be accorded an indication of status achieved by effort than one which stands for respect and social parity acquired by birth. It is to be remembered, however, that special titles are used more easily and with less significance in the South than in the North, and that the general American attitude toward members of the learned professions is somewhat ambiguous.

It is quite in order for Whites to address Negroes by terms which imply relationship or affection. Women are called "Aunty" and men "Uncle" even when they are younger than the person speaking to them. On the other hand, Whites often say "Boy" or "Girl" to Negroes who are much older than themselves.

A moderately prosperous man in his late fifties is a highly respected member of the Negro group. As presiding elder in his church on Sunday, wearing gloves and a neatly pressed suit, he presents a most dignified appearance. On Monday, going to work, he is stopped by a young white woman who is having tire trouble. Both have lived in the same town all their lives and she knows his name very well. She addresses him only as "Boy," repeating the word sharply as she orders his moves in rendering her this unpaid service.

The prohibition against courtesy titles extends to the telephone. If a Negro puts in a long-distance call for "Mr. Smith" in a town fifty miles away, the operator, who can tell where the call comes from, will ask: "Is he colored?" On being told that he is, she replies: "Don't you say 'Mister' to me. He ain't 'Mister' to me."

To violate this strong taboo is to arouse the resentment, suspicion, fear, which attends the breaking of taboos or customs in any culture. If a Melanesian is asked what difference it would make if he failed to provide a feast for his dead maternal uncle, or if he broke the rule of exogamy, his attitude is one of complete bewilderment and strong fear at the mere suggestion. If a member of his community should actually commit such a breach, he would resent it as an invitation to general disaster. The exogamy rule is felt, inarticulately, to be an inherent and indispensable part of the Melanesian *status quo*, one of the balances which keep the culture revolving in orderly fashion. The title taboo is sensed as equally essential to the *status quo* in Mississippi. To question either is to question the whole system; to violate either is to violate, weaken, endanger, the entire *status quo*. In either case this is merely the background to the immediate reaction, which is seldom reasoned, and may be intensified by the secondary meanings which become attached to any social pattern.

The rule for forms of address is concerned also with what the Negro calls the White. The white person's name is never to be mentioned without some title of respect. It may be the first or the last name, depending on the degree of acquaintance. Military titles, traditionally accorded to Whites, are less frequently heard today, and the old-time "Massa" has given way to "Boss." If no other title is used, the Negro says "Ma'am" or "Sir." Among Whites and among Negroes, this is a matter of courtesy; but when a Negro is speaking to a white person it is compulsory. If he mails a package at the post office he must be very careful to observe this usage toward the clerk who is serving him. He must be equally careful in addressing the telephone operator.

A man who had lived in a large city for several years forgot the injunction when he was putting in a long-distance call. The operator repeated his number several times, each time asking if it was correct, and each time receiving the answer: "Yes." Finally in an ominous stone she said: "You'll say 'Yes, Ma'am' to me." The Negro canceled his call. Since then a kind of secret warfare has gone on. Whenever he uses the phone the operator asks a question that would ordinarily be answered with a "Ma'am," and he extricates himself by saying: "That's it," "That is correct," or some phrase that evades the difficulty. The operator continues her campaign, undaunted.

There often appears to be a relation between the insistence of the White upon observance of such a usage, and his own adjustment within his group.

A woman who was disliked and resented by both races tried to get the Negroes to call her Miss Sylvia instead of Mrs. T. The Negro who spoke of this said: "Miss Sylvia is more like slavery times," and added scornfully that she guessed Mrs. T. didn't know other people have been born since slavery.

Closely connected with the title taboo is the term used when Whites talk among themselves about Negroes. "Nigger" is the term used almost universally. Its emotional tone varies according to the context of the situation and the individual using it. It ranges from contempt to affection, and its use is so prevalent and so much a part of the *mores*, that it may not necessarily be deeply charged. "Darky" is sometimes substituted for "nigger," and then the tone is practically always one of affection. When a white is talking to a Negro, and wishes to use the third person, "nigger" is the common term. There are occasional exceptions. A sensitive and "good White" may substitute "your people." State and county officials in addressing Negro groups use this term, or "colored people," or "Negroes." The latter is the one to which the Whites show the most resistance, and several linguistic variations have occurred as a result, such as "niggra."

Although all these terms occur in intra-Negro conversation, they always resent intensely "nigger" and "darky" when used by the Whites. "Negro" and "colored people" are the preferred terms. Among themselves, "darky" is heard rarely, but "nigger" is used frequently, and again its emotional tone varies. A colored person may call another "nigger" in either affection or anger, and the emotion connected with the term may be small or great. The term does not usually call forth resentment when used by a Negro, as it always does when used by a White.

The taboo against eating with a Negro is another which suggests analogies from different cultures. Eating with a person has strong symbolic value in many societies, and usually signifies social acceptance. White children may on special occasions eat with Negroes, but for colored and white adults to eat together under ordinary conditions is practically unheard of. If a white person in the country would for some reason ask for food at a Negro home, he would eat apart. Special circumstances may, however, constitute an exception to the rule: if a white man and a colored man went fishing, they might grill their fish over an open fire and eat together, in the open. Exceptions are extremely rare, and the taboo is extended to colored people who are not Negroes.

A Chinese doctor who was participating in a public health study lived at one of the town's boarding houses. Several of the boarders objected to sitting at the same table with him. The woman who told about it added: "You know, we are so narrow down here."

The rule that a Negro should not enter the front door of a house is so taken for granted that many white people, when they go out for a short time, will lock the back door against thieves, and leave the front door open. They assume that no colored person would go in the front way and, apparently, that no white person would steal. The visibility of the front entrance in the daytime lends a practical support to the assumption.

The front-door prohibition is far less important to some Whites than to others.

"A poor-raised white person can work alongside of you," one Negro said, "and then if he gets a fortune, you can't come to the front door but have to go round to the back. But a rich-raised White don't care if you walk out of the front door."

Two women, each of whom considers herself a typical Southerner, illustrate divergent attitudes. Both are members of the middle class, but they represent as much contrast as can be found within the limits of that comparatively homogeneous group. One belongs to the "best people" of the town; the other has recently acquired a small competence, after years of insecurity and strain. The son of the second woman happened to see the first woman's cook leave the house by the front door. "Do you allow your cook to go out that way?" he asked in surprise. His hostess replied that it didn't make any difference to her which door her cook used. The boy exclaimed that his mother would never allow anything like that; one day when their cook did try to go out the front way, his mother picked up a piece of wood from the fireplace and threw it at her.

Few cooks would attempt to leave by the front door, and still fewer mistresses would be indifferent to it. The amount of individual variation with regard to this prohibition, however, suggests that it is not one of those which carry the strongest symbolic force for the Whites.

In connection with shaking hands, it again appears that affection may be permissible where respect is denied. A colored mammy may kiss her charges, perhaps even on rare occasions after they have grown up. But colored people and white people do not as a rule shake hands in public. If a white educator addresses a group of Negro teachers, he might shake hands with them after his speech. On such occasions refreshments might also be served, but it would be lap service, with no question of sitting at the same table.

It is of course taken for granted that ordinary courtesies have no place between the two races. A white man thinks nothing of sitting while a colored woman stands, regardless of who she is. A highly educated woman who always stood in talking to the white man under whose direction she worked was frightened when on one occasion he invited her to sit.

Courtesies of the road are among those withheld. Negroes in Cotton-ville are very cautious drivers, and they have need to be, since white drivers

customarily ignore the amenities toward a car driven by a colored person.
A white Northerner driving through the town with Negro passengers in
the rumble seat of her car was startled to find other machines passing her
without sounding their horns. It is simply assumed that the Negro will
proceed with caution, keep to the side of the road, and not count on the
right of way. The assumption is sound, since if there is an accident the
Negro as a rule shoulders the penalty.

A white lawyer driving at about fifty miles an hour came to a cross
road. He saw another car coming but did not stop, figuring that the
other would do so. He figured wrong, and there was a collision in
which he was slightly bruised and his car was battered. A white bystander
urged him to "just kill the nigger," since he couldn't collect any money
for damages. "That's the only thing to do—just kill him." The lawyer
said he would not kill him, but would take the case to court. When it
came up, the Negro pleaded guilty and was fined $25, which he had
to work out at the county work house, as he did not have the money.
The white woman who told the story said it was good he pleaded
guilty or "he'd have got worse." It might be unjust, she admitted, but
"you have to treat the niggers that way; otherwise nobody knows what
would happen." The lawyer received insurance for his car and nothing
but satisfaction from the Negro's sentence.
Exceptions happen to this rule also. One occurred when the mayor
of the town happened to witness an accident in which the white man
was unmistakably at fault. The white driver, not knowing this, had
the Negro arraigned and brought before the mayor, who promptly
dismissed the case. The Negroes' comment was that the mayor "is
mighty fair for a southern man."

It is of course assumed that Negroes always wait until white people
are served. In the case of an appointment, the Negro waits until all Whites
have been taken care of, even if they come in after him. If someone comes
in during an interview, he is expected to step aside and wait. He may also
expect to be kept waiting even if nobody else is there. There are always
and everywhere people ready to employ this popular device for putting
others in their places and feeling that one is in his own place. Certain local
Whites derive obvious satisfaction from being able to keep Negroes waiting
as long as possible, and for no reason—especially the educated, prosperous, or "uppity" Negroes.
In the white stores, where Negroes do the bulk of their buying, they
have to wait until the white clientele has been served. A Negro who has
money for purchases is permitted to enter almost any store and buy, although
certain ones cater to the colored trade and others do not. Even in the latter,
however, the more distinguished individuals among the Negroes may expect
to receive courteous treatment. The depression has wrought a definite
change in the policy of most white shops toward the other race. Under
stress of hard times, the shopkeepers made an effort to attract Negro trade
as they had never done before. Negro customers were no longer kept waiting indefinitely for attention. In many cases they were permitted to try on

garments rather than, as before, being required to buy shoes, gloves, hats, without first finding out whether they were the right size or shape. Once such concessions have been granted, they cannot easily be withdrawn.

The granting of the privilege of trying on garments before they are bought has an economic value for the Whites not directly involved in such a usage as, for example, the front-door prohibition. Economic implications are strong in several others among the mechanisms expressing white attitudes toward the Negro—notably the Jim Crow arrangements, which are also more official in their manner of enforcement. In the subtle gradation from social through economic to legal aspects, one comes finally to issues which seem of a different order, although they rest upon the same basis. The attitudes that prompt minor social taboos, prohibitions, injunctions, also underlie the disenfranchisement of the Negro, his exclusion from jury service, and his liability to lynching. These have been investigated throughout the deep South, and the reports and discussions published cover Mississippi. They will be touched upon here only in connection with the attitudes that surround them.

The device for withholding the franchise from Negroes in the community is very simple. In order to qualify as a voter, one must have paid one's taxes, including the two-dollar poll tax, and must be able to read and interpret a paragraph of the Constitution. This test is admittedly designed to prevent Negroes from voting; no white person in charge of it would admit that a Negro's interpretation was correct. Knowing this, the Negroes make no attempt to qualify. The Whites justify the prohibition on the ground that, since the Negroes are in the majority, the franchise would give them polictical control, which would spell disaster: a Negro might even be elected to office. It is assumed that the Negroes would all vote Republican, because that party freed the slaves. The Whites feel that any measure is justifiable that would prevent control by the Negroes or the Republicans, and that either eventuality might lead to the other. One reason for fearing the entrance of the Republican Party is the suspicion that it would give the Negro the vote in order to strengthen its following. The danger is not imminent, since the community is so strongly Democratic that no Republican primaries are held there.[1]

That no Negro should serve on a jury is as universally taken for granted by the Whites as that no Negro should vote. The two prohibitions are closely linked, and the fact that Negroes pay so small a percentage of the taxes is offered as partial justification for both.

Denial of legal rights guaranteed by the Constitution is more severe and more tangible in its effects than denial of social amenities. Most severe of all are the denials involved in lynching. Nevertheless, it too is a mode of behavior customary in certain situations, and is a direct product of the creed and attitudes which have been described. It differs from the other mechanisms in its spectacular nature, in the fact that it is a sporadic manifestation, and in the more limited and covert social sanction which supports it.

[1]The author's impression is that, if they had had the chance, most Negroes during the period of this survey would have voted the Democratic ticket because of their faith in the New Deal.

Very few white men except the Poor Whites would declare in favor of lynchings. Very few white men would actively try to halt one. There is a report from another community that a member of the aristocracy did once come out definitely against a lynching and succeeded in stopping it. A middle-class storekeeper, under rather special circumstances, did much the same thing in a case given earlier. The rarity of such an act is due chiefly to the danger of opposing a mob. In addition, many a White who deplores lynching yet feels it may serve a beneficent purpose. There are good and kind Christians who will explain that lynchings are terrible, but must happen once in a while in order to keep the Negro in his place.

It is generally assumed that lynching as a rule occurs because of an alleged sexual crime. This is not strictly true, but it is usually associated with the cry of rape. The alarm is calculated to set off a maximum of excitement. It awakens latent fears in connection with the Negro man and the white woman, against a background of guilt and fear related to the white man and the Negro woman. It brings out into the open the forbidden subject of sex. And in addition, it affords the Poor Whites their one opportunity to avenge themselves for the degradation and misery of their own position. A lynching is the one occasion when they can vent all their stored-up resentment without fear of the other Whites, but rather with their tacit consent.

Under proper stimulation, the consent becomes more than tacit. The following reports and editorials in a local paper concern an incident which took place in a near-by community during the course of this study.

> Crimes like the one that shocked this county last week call for the most severe and swift penalty that can be invoked. Our officers are doing their utmost to capture the guilty fiends, and when caught "may the Lord have mercy on their souls." The swiftest penalty that will be given them will be entirely too slow for the temper of the people at present.

> One of the most horrible crimes ever attempted in the county occurred about two miles west of M. Tuesday evening, when two negroes attempted to kill a young man . . . and after cutting his throat, stabbing him several times in the chest, and throwing him in the rear of the car, drove off toward a secluded place with the young lady. . . .

> After going some distance the young lady, with rare presence of mind, when they came near a house, told one of them to open the car door as she wanted to spit. When he opened the door she jerked the key out of the car and threw it away, and jumped out screaming. People who lived in the house came running and the negroes fled. When assistance came the wounded young man was taken . . . to the hospital . . . where his wounds were pronounced fatal, as his jugular vein was almost severed, besides the chest wounds.

> The alarm was quickly sounded and posses rapidly assembled organized for the man hunt. . . . [The sheriff] was quickly on the scene with his deputies and hunted all Tuesday night but failed to capture them. The sheriff found out where they lived and arrested a brother of one of the fiends, who told all he knew of them. That they had come to his house with bloody clothes and changed the clothes and

told him they had gotten into some trouble and had to run for it. They left and up to this time they have not been captured, although Sheriff L. is still on the trail. The bloody clothes were secured by the sheriff. It is a miracle that the young lady was unharmed and had the presence of mind to distract their attention while she threw the car key away.

We hope they will be speedily caught near the scene of their crime. We do not think the county jail has any room at present for such criminals, but we feel certain that the splendid citizens of C. and vicinity will properly place them should they get hold of them.

These newspaper accounts and comments were hardly calculated to act as a deterrent to the mob, made up mainly of Poor Whites. On the day after the attack, a group of these shabby men, their eyes burning, tramped up and down the road and through the woods, mingling their oaths with the barking of their dogs. The middle-class white men sitting in their offices or homes remarked that of course they did not approve of lynching, but that undoubtedly these Negroes would be lynched, and "what can you do when you have to deal with the primitive African type, the killer?" The Negroes in the neighborhood sat at home all day, afraid to go out. Those in a town thirty miles distant said that things must be getting better because a few years ago, if the mob had not found the men they wanted by this time, they would have lynched someone else.

The town in which the murder had been committed was quiet. The Negroes had escaped into another state. Nobody knew where they were. At last the mob broke up; the dogs were quiet. A few of the middle-class Whites murmured that perhaps the Negroes were after the man and not the girl; that maybe there was some real ground for their grudge against him. These were a few almost inaudible whispers. Most of the people said nothing. The eyes of the shabby men no longer gleamed with excitement. They had gone back to the dull routine of the sharecropper. The middle class sat back and reaffirmed that they did not believe in lynching.

Not all of them say so, however. A few openly condone it. Interestingly enough, of the group who answered the questionnaire, more young people than old said that lynching for rape is justifiable, and slightly more women than men. If any weight can be attached to this type of sampling, it must be assumed that, despite the more liberal and less emotional attitude of the younger generation in general, a "nigger'hunt" appeals to them more than to their parents. The vigor of youth may have something to do with this, and the type of imagery that would be evoked by the suggestion of a Negro raping a white woman. Perhaps also there is less interference by social and religious inhibitions. It is hardly to be supposed that when these Junior College students are middle-aged they will be more in favor of lynching than their parents are today. The differential between men and women could not be accepted as reliable in itself, but corresponds to the difference in attitudes generally expressed, and is not at odds with impressionistic evidence. It is to be remembered of course that none of the Whites who answered the questionnaire was of the class that takes an active part in this practice.

Of the social mechanisms described, lynching is the one that has the least consistent, the least whole-hearted, and certainly the least open sanction from the white group. It is also the one that has roused the most active protest from the North. If a Federal law is passed prohibiting it, change will be enforced from the outside. In any case, the pressure of outside opinion is a potent factor in its gradual decline. Furthermore, the attention drawn to the South by lynching tends to overflow onto mechanisms of racial discrimination that might otherwise be less noticed from the outside.

From the sketch of white attitudes and the social mechanisms that express them, it can readily be seen that the Negro carries a large load of the white man's prejudices and fears. All peoples in all cultures have both prejudice and fear; the forms they take are determined by the historical accidents that have shaped the culture and the way the culture impinges upon the individuals who participate in it. In a community such as this, where there are socially sanctioned channels for group fear and prejudice and a socially determined object for them, their effects become somewhat specialized. We shall be concerned chiefly with the effects on the Negroes, although it may be assumed that they are equally profound for the Whites, and would well repay investigation.

New Yorkers celebrate the surrender of Japan on August 14, 1945

The Veterans Return

JOSEPH C. GOULDEN

To the victor belong the spoils. The spoils of war had been shared among the victorious military forces of the world since the dawn of history. Fighting men have expected to garner loot of some kind at the successful completion of any military enterprise—until the present time. In our enlightened age these benefits are no longer expected to be supplied by the defeated enemy but by a grateful government in whose service the fighting was done.

In the early years of American history, soldiers were rewarded upon the completion of their service with grants of land. After all, both the British colonies and later the young United States had more land than money to distribute to veterans of the armed forces. The idea of pensions for retired or disabled veterans began to grow around the turn of the nineteenth century, and in the Age of Jackson pensions were awarded to the few remaining survivors of the War for Independence.

The end of the Civil War saw the pattern of benefits change, partly because of the unusually large percentage of the population who served and partly because of the development of the first massive veterans' organization—the Grand Army of the Republic. The political power of this veterans' lobby was such that by the end of the century over forty percent of federal expenditures went to pay the pensions of veterans and their dependents.

When the United States entered the First World War, the government, anxious to avoid the bonus issue, arranged for allotments to be paid to servicemen's dependents while they were at war, and for an insurance plan which would provide for disability and death benefits. After the war, however, the American Legion organization of veterans pushed hard for an additional bonus. In 1924, Congress passed a measure which provided for pension payments for veterans to begin in 1945. As the Great Depression deepened in the early 1930s, it was the veterans' demand for immediate payment of the pension which led to the infamous expulsion from the nation's capital of the "Bonus Marchers" in 1932.

Several factors altered the situation for veterans during and after the Second World War. For one thing, the war was the most widely supported military enterprise in which this nation had yet been engaged. For another, the number of service people was extraordinary. At least fifteen million Americans served in the armed forces during the war. So the question was not whether there would be veterans' benefits; the question was how much and how paid. These issues are discussed in the selection reprinted below from Joseph C. Goulden's book on the postwar years. The conflicting efforts of competing veterans' organizations led to a variety of programs that affected different sectors of the economy in varying ways. Perhaps the most important of these is described below in the section on the educational benefits offered under the G.I. Bill of Rights. This program drastically altered the face of American higher education by increasing the number of students attending colleges and universities and the role of the federal government in providing funds for these institutions. Both of these developments turned out to be permanent, and the era of mass higher education was upon us.

Veterans' benefits continued to be paid as the American military developed for the first time in our history a large standing army. The G.I. Bill remained in force, though with decreasing benefits through the Korean and Vietnamese Wars. Veterans of the latter enterprise have had a particularly difficult time reentering civilian society. The growing unpopularity of the war in its later stages led both the general population and the government to take out their frustrations on those who had performed military service in Viet Nam. It remains to be seen whether an *un*grateful nation will attempt to salvage the lives and careers of American service people who fought in the losing struggle in Indochina.

VETERANS—OR CITIZENS?

The 52–20 Club flourished because Americans accept as a matter of faith that men who go to war should be rewarded when they return home. Land grants, cash bonuses, free medical and hospital care, pensions, gratis fishing and hunting licenses, preferential hiring for governmental jobs, streetcar passes, even lifetime movie passes—such is the largess a grateful country has bestowed upon its fighting men after battle. "There aren't going to be any apple sellers on the street corners after this war if we can prevent it," vowed Lieutenant General Brehon Somervell, chief of the army service forces.[1] President Roosevelt, in a 1944 letter to Congress, said, "It is impossible to take millions of our young men out of their normal pursuits for the purpose of fighting to preserve the nation, and then expect them to resume their normal activities without having any special consid-

---

[1]Washington *Post*, April 22, 1944.

eration shown them." FDR instructed federal agencies to give preference to veterans in their hiring. (The Washington *Post* disagreed: "Why not give veterans' preference benefits to former servicemen who might want to run for election in the national legislature? The status of these men can only be debased by treating them as inferiors incapable of securing jobs through free competition with their fellow citizens."[2]) That a program would be created for World War Two servicemen was never doubted; the only questions were how much and in what type of package.

Fiscal conservatives expressed wariness of locking the country into an open-ended program of cash benefits, fearing that euphoric generosity at war's end would burden future generations. Veterans' programs do have a marked tendency toward longevity: not until March 1946 did the government finish paying off claims from the War of 1812, upon the death of an eighty-eight-year-old Oregon woman, daughter of a soldier who fought in the Battle of New Orleans.[3] The operative criteria, based upon congressional decisions beginning in 1944, were to give the veterans enough to "catch up" with civilians who had not gone off to war, but to avoid turning the national treasury into a cornucopia that would make former servicemen an overprivileged class. Overhanging the debate was the political realization that if history could be considered a guide, veterans would come home howling for hard cash, payable immediately, and that the initial mass public reaction would be, "Give our boys anything they want." Even before the war ended, the Veterans of Foreign Wars lobbied for $5,000 in paid-up cash or in bonds maturing over five years. The Philadelphia *Bulletin*, in a poll in November 1945, found citizens favoring some form of bonus by a margin of 14–1—greater even then the 10–1 sentiment of veterans. Precedent existed for a cash bonus: after the First World War veterans received $1 for each day of service in the United States and $1.25 for each day overseas. But the House Committee on World War Veterans Legislation, in a report in May 1944, opposed a cash bonus, pointing out that, at the First World War rates, the cost would be $20 billion cash immediately. Nonetheless Congress found itself uneasy. As a body Congress' instinctive nature is to take the least hazardous available path: if the public cried for a free Cadillac and $50 a week for each returning GI, many politicians would oblige and worry about the consequences later. Many congressional elders had been around Washington during the traumatic Bonus March of 1932, when thousands of veterans descended on the capital to demand a bonus for their war service. Army troops dispersed the marchers, brutally but efficiently, an experience no one in government wished to relive.

In all the clamor for benefits, the loudest voice of the organized veteran belonged to the American Legion. Boasting 2,000,000 members when the war ended, and a chapter system that made it visible in every American hamlet, the Legion towered over rival groups like some elephantine colossus. When the Legion's Washington office growled, politicians paid attention. One index of the Legion's political eminence is that officeholders of all parties found it expedient to join. When Congress convened in 1946, 44

[2]*Ibid.*, July 11, 1944.
[3]Gray, *The Inside Story of the Legion.*

of 96 senators carried Legion cards, and 195 of 435 representatives. President Truman was a Legionnaire; so were five of his cabinet members, three Supreme Court justices, and twenty-six state governors. At the end of 1945 the Legion was signing 70,000 new members weekly, more than the combined membership of AMVETS and the American Veterans Committee, and comfortably ahead of the archrival Veterans of Foreign Wars. Although the Legion charter prohibited enrolling men still on active duty, Legion recruiters literally camped outside the gates to await dischargees. A field office in Honolulu, manned by four publicists, distributed pony editions of the *American Legion Monthly,* disbursing both news and appeals to stay away from VFW recruiters (who could sign active servicemen). Many vets came home to find that their Legionnaire fathers had already signed them into the local post. In small-town America the Legion built phenomenal strength: in Luray, Kansas, the Legion had 234 members of a total population of 380 persons; the entire town turned out for meetings. Although Luray was an extreme example of hyper-Legionism, other tank towns approached its enthusiasm. In Bagley, Minnesota, the Legion post had 448 members in a population of 1,248; in Loris, South Carolina, 604 of 1,298.

Incentives to join the Legion were many. Often the local Veterans Administration official was a Legionnaire and gave fellow members preferential treatment. The Legion had tight liaison with the VA at all levels, and its Washington office could expedite claims. In small towns such local powers as the banker, insurance agent, leading merchants, even the police chief and sheriff, were often Legionnaires. For a young veteran, membership was the chance to hobnob with people who could give him a job or approve his loan. In middle America the Legion exuded a respectability rivaling that of organized religion. As a Legion national commander once said, "The time should come soon, and I think it will be here soon, when any man eligible to become a member of the Legion who does not belong will be looked upon with suspicion, and justly so, by the community where he lives." And, finally, there was the social factor. In the bone-dry towns of the Bible and corn belts, the Legion hall was the only place in town where a man could buy a bottle of beer and idle away a Saturday afternoon shooting pool. In larger cities, the Legion bar was popular because as a private, nonprofit club it undersold competitors and followed loose closing hours. The Legion sponsored dances and picnics and showed movies; veterans (and their families) gravitated to the Legion hall often because the town offered no other social attractions.

Politically, the Legion's consistent demand was that the country "not forget" the veteran once the immediate postwar euphoria subsided. The Legion's stated goals—to help veterans get better education, housing, and medical care—had undeniable surface attraction. But the fine print in the specific programs the Legion was willing to accept on the veteran's behalf is yet another story, and one that can be explained only in the context of the group's origins, its internal politics, and the causes it espoused over the years.

A group of army officers who served in France in the First World War is credited with planning the Legion. Headquarters had asked the officers how to improve morale. Lieutenant Colonel Theodore Roosevelt, Jr., son of the former President, suggested a veterans organization, and the Legion resulted. According to an official history published by former Legion publicist Richard Sellye Jones in 1946, "There was a general concern about the postwar attitude of the average soldier toward extreme political radicalism." Officers worried about "rumors and reports from America on radical, Communistic movements," and the formation of "soldiers' and sailors' councils among men who had been discharged quickly after the armistice. . . . Even the restless lack of discipline in the [army] itself was vaguely attributed by some to Soviet ideas. A safe and sound organization of veterans might be the best insurance against their spread." Thus did "antiradicalism" become a leitmotiv of the American Legion. On the positive side the Legion helped the individual veteran in his dealings with the mare's-nest bureaucracy of the Veterans Administration, and the Legion's employment service in the 1920's surpassed anything offered by official agencies.

Concurrently, however, the Legion spent almost as much time helping authorities suppress the politically suspect. Labor organizers especially were harassed. In agricultural areas of California Legionnaires wearing overseas caps and Sam Browne belts and acting as "special deputies" helped bully migrant farm workers into staying on jobs that paid near-starvation wages. The Legion maintained close ties with such groups as the National Association of Manufacturers (which underwrote the Legion's annual national high-school oratorical contest), the American Medical Association, and the real estate industry. Coincidentally or not, the views of these friends were consistently reflected in the Legion's positions when it began working in Congress for post-World War Two veterans' benefits.

The Legion's first concern was the inability of the Veterans Administration to care for thousands of servicemen discharged because of disability. The law provided that they be hospitalized and given compensation. But the VA, a horror house of red tape and inefficiency, could not do its job, and thousands of veterans received neither money nor care for months on end. The VA, as did other wartime federal agencies, suffered manpower problems. More crippling, however, was its hypercautious director, Brigadier General Frank T. Hines, a fussy bureaucrat who had run the VA since the 1920's. (Hines' title was real: he had enlisted as a private in the Spanish-American War, and earned his brigadiership in 1918.) So far as anyone could deduce, Hines ran the VA on the theory that the less he did, the better his chances of avoiding trouble. A conservative, anti-New Deal Republican, and a favorite of economy-minded congressmen, Hines ran the VA as penuriously as possible. Not even the start of the war and the prospect of caring for millions of veterans in one manner or another stirred Hines into preparing the VA for its expanded responsibilities. Although hospital care for veterans was a major VA function, Hines' attitude toward medicine was not only ignorant but hostile. Brushing aside criticisms of his refusal to permit VA hospitals to associate themselves with medical schools, Hines once said, "I don't want any interns experimenting on my veterans." So when the wounded began returning home the VA sat immobile, unable to care for them or to pay their benefits promptly. Many cases dragged for months. One particularly pitiable and publicized incident involved a GI, blinded in combat, who was discharged June 20, 1943, and who still awaited his first VA pension check on November 29. The American Legion, which itself had close relations with General Hines (the Legion, after all, itself reflexively opposed most federal spending), finally cried "enough." If anything was to be done for veterans, initiative must come from other than the Veterans Administration. So the Legion began a vigorous lobbying campaign with separate but overlapping purposes: the immediate reform of the VA, so that it could process the increasing flow of disabled dischargees; and a package of long-range benefits.

Harry W. Colmery, an attorney from Topeka, Kansas, who had been both Republican national chairman and national commander of the Legion (both in the 1930's), took responsibility for writing specific legislation. Working in the Legion offices overlooking K Street Northwest in downtown Washington, often through the night, Colmery saw two broad purposes in the GI legislation. When veterans returned to civilian life "they should be given the opportunity to reach that place, position or status which they normally expected to achieve, and probably would have achieved, had their war service not interrupted their careers." Secondly, Colmery thought it "sound national policy" to adopt a benefits program "to see us through the troublous times which [are] ahead of us, by giving stability and hope and faith to the men and women who would return." Veterans should be assured of their benefits before leaving the military. "When the time comes to get out," Colmery said, "most men will sign almost anything, without any thought of the fact or the future." So the bill contained a section to the effect that no predischarge declaration should be held against a veteran if he asked for benefits later. In one public talk asking support for veterans legislation Colmery declared:

> There are those who worry about making the veteran shiftless, and unwilling to work, and desirous of loafing and leaning on the government for sustenance. Would you take that position toward the boy in need of a job, without whose fighting you wouldn't have any government on which to lean or depend to protect your freedom?

As a lobbying ally, the Legion relied upon the not inconsiderable publicity resources of the Hearst newspaper organization. David Comelon of Hearst's Washington bureau had helped the Legion in a 1943 campaign to boost the mustering-out bonus from the $300 sought by the Roosevelt Administration to $500. Although Camelon favored the benefits as "a matter of principle," a personal feud gave added fire to his enthusiasm. He and the Legion had thought the bonus was in hand until Representative Andrew Jackson May, chairman of the House Military Affairs Committee, went home to Tennessee in late December before adjournment, permitting the legislation to die. Camelon wrote that May had "slipped out of Washington." A few days later, after returning to town, the angry congressman bearded him in a Capitol corridor. "If you say any more about me sneaking out of Washington, you make arrangements with the undertaker before you do—because, brother, you'll need him." According to Camelon, May's threat "made it my personal fight." Concurrently, the Hearst organization concluded that fighting for veterans would be good promotion for the newspapers as well as good citizenship, so an extraordinary thing happened in early 1944. On the orders of William Randolph Hearst, Ted Sloan, political editor of the Chicago *Herald-American*, sought out Legion national commander Warren Atherton, a fellow Illinoisan, and offered him "all the facilities of the [Hearst] organization to help the Legion insure passage " of the bills. Hearst said he wanted no credit, just the legislation. According to Camelon, "three Hearst men—Frank Reilly [of the Boston *American*], Roy Topper, crack promotion manager of the [Chicago] *Herald-American*, and I—were assigned to the Legion's Washington headquarters for the duration of the campaign. We functioned as aides in the Legion's public relations department. The Legionnaires accepted us completely; they made us a part of the team. We sat in on all conferences—we were in the fight every minute, and we shared all the heartaches and the joys of the long campaign. We did whatever we could to help under their leadership." The Hearst team wrote "news stories" about veterans legislation while acting as Legion lobbyists. During a brainstorming session at Legion headquarters one afternoon Jack Cejnar, a Legion publicist, came up with a catchall slogan describing the benefit package—a phrase that became an integral part of the veteran's vocabulary, one so much a part of the American language that it is a subject heading in encyclopedias: "The GI Bill of Rights." Camelon felt the slogan "was something close to genius. It was short, punchy, easily grasped. It told the whole story—and it became a fighting slogan from coast to coast."*

Yet did the American Legion strike the best deal possible for the veterans it purported to represent? Returning veterans read in the papers of the splendid benefits being readied for them—only to find that in reality not all that much had been changed. And the American Legion, in the legislative infighting on the GI Bill, consistently took conservative positions that worked to the disadvantage of the veteran.

A prime example was housing. One section of the GI Bill provided financing for veterans who wanted to buy or build homes. The real estate lobby (specifically, the National Association of Real Estate Boards and the National Association of Home Builders) liked the concept of the bill, for it was certain to touch off a postwar housing boom. But the real estate people wanted a bill of their own design. A key issue was whether the home-finance section of the bill should be administered by the existing Federal Housing Administration or the VA. The FHA was the logical agency, for it had the staff and experience. The VA would have to create a duplicate bureaucratic apparatus. The real estate interests, however, distrusted the FHA because of its involvement in public housing (an unpleasant association in their industry) and did not want to give it a toehold in the veterans' program. So the Legion fought alongside the real estate lobby for VA control. Another issue was a proposal in the original version of the GI Bill that the government make housing loans outright for three percent. Again, there was strong business opposition: the real estate industry and its allies (including the Legion) argued for conventional financing through banks

*The bill's formal title was "The Serviceman's Readjustment Act of 1944." Another version of the source of the name "GI Bill" came from Chester Bowles, director of the Office of Price Administration, who proposed that President Roosevelt spell out a "Second Bill of Rights" in his 1944 State of the Union message. Roosevelt used the title, but extended coverage of the "rights" to all Americans, not just veterans. Chester Bowles, *Promises to Keep*, Harper & Row, 1971.

and savings and loan associations. As a result, the GI paid higher interest than necessary when he went into the home market. One close critic of the Legion's role in the GI Bill, Justin Gray, commented that, contrary to popular expectation, the legislation did *not* provide new housing for veterans; it ended up "merely helping the vet finance a house if he could find one." Another critic, Charles G. Bolte, a founder of the progressive American Veterans Committee, found any number of flaws in the Legion's handiwork. Under its provisions, Bolte wrote,

> . . . the veteran could resume his education, *if* he could live on $50 a month; could get the government to guarantee up to $2,000 of a loan at four percent interest to buy a house or a farm or to go into business, *if* the lending agency thought he was a good risk; could get up to $20 a week unemployment compensation for up to 52 weeks, *if* he was unemployed through no fault of his own within two years after his discharge or after the end of the war, whichever was later.

Bolte charged that the bill was sold "like a new breakfast food," to the grave disappointment of GIs, who discovered they simply couldn't walk into a bank and ask, "Where's my $2,000?"

The Legion groused about "outrages" of another sort—the realization that it would not be permitted to dominate the Veterans Administration after the war. Soon after peace, President Truman dismissed General Hines and installed General Omar N. Bradley as head of the VA. One of the most popular field commanders of the war, a brass hat who convinced the GI he was a true friend, Bradley agreed to try to straighten out two decades of administrative chaos. He made headway. For instance, he persuaded the nation's seventy-seven leading medical colleges to let doctors work as resident physicians for the VA while completing three years of specialist training. In a year's time Bradley reduced the average hospital stay from forty-two to twenty days. But in remaking the VA, Bradley also alienated old-line allies of the Legion, and brought all sorts of troubles on himself. For one thing, Bradley told his physicians to buck up and not admit patients just because a Legion "case officer" had promised them a hospital bed, needed or not. Bradley also had the audacity to refuse to build a hospital in Decatur, Illinois—a project dear to an Illinois politican named John Stelle, the Legion's postwar commander. When Bradley supported legislation limiting on-the-job training payments to $200 per month, Stelle jumped him for "breaking faith with the veterans" and all but dared the general to defend himself at the Legion's convention.

Bradley did. He took out after the "high-salaried professional veterans . . . who forget that the veteran has paid, and is paying, for all that he gets. . . . More dangerous than the German army is the demagoguery that deceives the veteran today by promising him something for nothing." As the Legion hierarchy listened in pained silence, Bradley said, "Anyone, whether he be the spokesman of veterans or any other group of American citizens, is morally guilty of betrayal when he puts special interests before the welfare of this nation. . . . The American veteran is first a citizen of these United States. He is thereafter a veteran." (Bill Mauldin, at the convention as an amused observer, said, "From the stony silence that greeted his speech . . . one would have thought the general had recommended the use of veterans for vivisection.") Stelle replied at the convention, "The main difference between General Bradley and myself, apparently, is that the general thinks that the citizen should be considered first and then the veteran." After a year Bradley fled back to the army, exhausted (according to Mauldin) from "wading through political slop and dodging floating pork barrels."

Despite its defects, the GI Bill did avoid the obvious pitfall of simply paying off servicemen with a lump sum bonus and leaving them on their own. And, in the long run, the approach of the GI Bill was economical to the nation as well as beneficial to the veteran. The total cost of the World War Two GI Bill, for education and training, was $14.5 billion when it ended July 25, 1956.* During its twelve-year existence, 7,800,000 veterans (50 percent of the 15,600,000 eligible) received training: 2,200,000 in institutions of higher learning; nearly 3,500,000 below college level; 1,400,000 on-the-job; and almost 700,00 in institutional on-farm courses.[4]

The GI Bill notwithstanding, enough veterans preferred immediate cash payments to make the "war bonus" a major political issue in state after state. And the bonus seekers wanted more than token payments. At a rally in Boston in March 1946, veterans hooted and howled at speakers opposed to increasing the Massachusetts state bonus from $100 to $1,000. The clamor over bonuses irritated *Time:* "The country had promised to cushion the shock of their return and the country, for the most part, had made good. No soldier could deny that. If anything, the cushion was too soft." *Time* said the GI Bill and other benefits made previous veterans' programs "look like nickel jitney rides." But such criticisms did not deter the bonus seekers, who had mixed luck at the state level. In West Virginia voters rejected a new state sales tax to raise the $90,000,000 needed for bonuses; similarly, New Jersey rejected a $105,000,000 state lottery. The Pennsylvania legislature, however, approved a $500,000,000 bond issue without a dissenting vote. By mid-1949, according to a survey by the American Legion, eleven states and two territories had approved bonus payments, ranging from South Dakota's 50 cents a day for U. S. Service and 75 cents daily for overseas to $10 and $15 monthly in Pennsylvania.

But was material gain all that should concern the veterans? Should not veterans' organizations deal with matters more important than a pension check, cut-rate license tags, and cheap after-hours beer? One person who looked beyond the bonus and benefit checks was Gilbert A. Harrison, who had gone from UCLA to the air force. In 1943 Harrison wrote about twenty-five college friends in the service suggesting that they keep in touch through a regular channel so they could share their thoughts about postwar Amer-

---

*By one estimate, the government made a net profit on the GI Bill. According to the Department of Labor, a male college graduate will earn (and pay income tax on) in excess of a quarter-of-a-million dollars more in his lifetime than the high-school graduate. The VA asserts, "The federal tax on this added income alone will be several times the total cost of his GI Bill education and "training assistance from VA."

[4] A good summary of benefits paid under the GI Bill is a fact sheet, "Thirty Years of Service to Those Who Served," Veterans Administration information service, June 1974.

ica. Most of the men had backgrounds in UCLA's University Religious Conference, an ecumenical umbrella under which campus liberals did good works rather than simply talk about them. Harrison's friends liked the idea, and the URC supplied the logistics for a periodic bulletin through which servicemen could vent their thoughts. Many were frightened at the prospects of postwar America. A serviceman from overseas wrote: "We'll have all the ingredients for a first-class fascistic government—all that's needed now is a catalytic agent, such as a breakdown of our internal structure. A military group returning to find their services no longer needed, a working class without jobs, a middle class a thing of the past, governmental irresolution, are fatal ingredients. We will have all of them if we don't begin now to decide what we are going to do with them."* Another man wrote: "See how everyone is preparing for the postwar grab. . . . People who organize seem to do so for the purpose of going out to grab, and the ones who pay are the poor dev'ls who have not learned the ropes, or do not care to play in a game where life is valued in decimals."

So what should be done? Harrison and his friends realized the practical futility of "reforming" the far-flung American Legion from within. Better to create their own organization of like-minded persons rather than squander energy with internal fights. Eventually Harrison got to Charles G. Bolte, a Dartmouth graduate who had joined the British army before Pearl Harbor, lost a leg in the battle of El Alamein, and come home to write news copy as a civilian for the Office of War Information. Bolte heard of Harrison's loosely organized correspondence group, they talked and found their ideas markedly parallel, and so in January 1944 Bolte became chairman of the American Veterans Committee. Bolte tells what happened thereafter:

"At the end of the war the magazines were full of stuff about what the veteran would or wouldn't do, and how he was a new force that could dominate the country politically. That was a lot of crap. Most of us just wanted to get home and rescue our lives again. Most veterans expressed their individuality by not joining any organization at all—a majority of them, in fact. They said to hell with the Legion, the VFW, the AVC—"Thanks very much, but I'll be my own spokesman."

"Our guiding philosophy at the AVC was that we were 'citizens first, veterans second.' We didn't want special privileges—we wanted a better society. At our peak we didn't have more than 100,000 members, but we made about as much noise, and attracted as much attention, as the American Legion. The columnist Thomas Stokes once asked why the AVC got so much publicity, and answered his own question: 'Because every single son-of-a-bitching one of them owns a typewriter.' That was true; we had a heavy concentration of members in publishing and the media, and we took advantage of it.

---

*Demagogues certainly expected sunshiny times. The Reverend Gerald L. K. Smith said in 1944: "My time will come in the postwar period—the election of '48. The candidate will not be me—it will be a young veteran of this war, but I'll be behind him." Smith forecast inflation, widespread unemployment, and farm foreclosures because "professional politicians are too cautious" to face up to readjustment. "Then the flame will spread, and the extreme nationalist will come to power."

"*The lack of numbers didn't bother us. We were not deliberately elitist— in fact, we made a deliberate appeal to political moderates and conservatives—but we did not aim at signing up everyone we could. When we were still talking about the kind of organization we wanted, Gil Harrison and I visited Walter Lippmann. He listened with care and said, 'Go ahead, but keep it small. Try to get men who are going to govern the country in twenty-five years, and don't let the big numbers join.'*

"*Well, we beat Lippmann's goal by ten years. Five members of JFK's first cabinet were AVCers* and there were many, many more at the under secretary level.*

"*Thoughtful congressmen were grateful for AVC because it gave them a chance to say that 'not all veterans are for this particular grab.' Our emphasis was on benefits for all, without veterans' preference. For instance, we wanted a national medical care program for all Americans, not just the ex-GIs. We wanted the Wagner-Ellender-Taft housing bill to give good low-cost housing to everyone in the country, not just our people—as hard up as vets were for housing. Our attitude was that what is good for the nation is good for the veteran; that what vets needed was help in picking up the threads of civilian life, not continuing handouts.*

"*The Communists wouldn't join AVC at first because they thought we'd be a small elitist group. They went to the Legion and found they could get nowhere there; it was too tightly controlled. So they came back to the AVC.*

"*For most people the transition period was very short. The veteran lost his novelty in a hurry. After the first few hundred men came home the fact that you were a veteran didn't make that much difference. By late '45 they were nothing special—less than a dime a dozen. This was good. One of our chief objectives was to reassimilate veterans into the general community as fast as possible, so they would not stand apart and feel oppressed.*

"*My fears of fascism, which were very real near the end of the war, wound down very fast—that is, until the end of the decade, when McCarthyism was upon us. The day I stopped worrying was when the FBI came around checking on an AVC member who was accused of involvement in radical activities of one sort or another. The agent asked, 'Was he with you or with the Communists?' I realized the FBI was getting sophisticated, when it could look at an organization as complex as AVC, which did have a Communist problem, and realize that not everyone in it should be so tainted.*"

Measured against the bread-and-potatoes goals of the Legion and the VFW, the AVC's aims had a refreshing visionary appeal for veterans not content with the same old prewar world. The Legion's banana-republic zest for pomp, ceremony, and fancy uniforms amused even its own members. A letter writer to the *American Legion Magazine* suggested that old-timers stop cluttering their uniforms and caps with medals showing past offices and honors. "The caps together with the hardware are worn pulled down over the ears in order to carry the weight of scrap," he said. If an *American Legion Magazine* editorial rumbled with suspicion about "entanglement" with the United Nations, a letter to the *AVC Bulletin* suggested that AVC members volunteer for a (nonexistent) UN military reserve. While

---

*Dean Rusk, Orville Freeman, Stewart Udall, Arthur J. Goldberg, and Abraham Ribicoff.

the VFW fretted over obscure details of pension bills, the AVC discussed the idea of having GI Bill benefits made available to children of vets who did not wish to attend college. While Legion lobbyists sat jowl-to-jowl with the real estate people before congressional committees, the AVC was the sole veterans' group to testify for continued federal rent controls. The AVC staged public forums and demonstrations across the nation in favor of low-cost-housing programs; 2,500 members and families slept overnight in MacArthur Park in Los Angeles to dramatize the need for the Wagner-Ellender-Taft (W-E-T) Housing Bill, which the Legion denounced as "radical," despite the conservative pedigree of Senator Robert A. Taft, one of the authors. The AVC spoke the truths other veterans' groups ignored: in the words of Clinton E. Jencks, of Denver, vice-chairman of its mountain states region, all that veterans received from the housing programs were a "a few army barracks reconverted down by the stockyards and railroad shops," while contractors busied themselves with "bars, garages, beauty parlors, ski shops, supermarkets."

The AVC did not hesitate to call names. Franklin D. Roosevelt, Jr., a national AVC officer, termed the Legion's opposition to W-E-T a surrender to the real estate interests. "One wonders what the privates in the Legion think of it." He called the Legion's then national commander, Paul Griffith, "the principal errand boy on Capitol Hill for the powerful real estate lobby." Editorially, the *AVC Bulletin* charged that the Legion "is well on the road to making suckers of the veterans of World War II. It has enrolled several millions of veterans of the last war with rosy promises. But the kingmakers of the Legion are paying no heed to the promises they made."*

Inevitably, of course, the AVC's nervy activism got it dangerously crosswise with the Legion, the VFW, and other powerful adversaries. The AVC insisted on its chapters and meetings being integrated, even in the South, and it supported the fair employment practices commission and antilynching and antipoll tax legislation (the latter three the civil rights causes célèbres of the late 1940's). So Representative Rankin, the avowed white supremacist from Mississippi who chaired the House Veterans Affairs Committee, banned AVC from appearing before his committee to testify on legislation—some of which, ironically, AVC had written. Rankin did so by restricting testimony to organizations whose members were "exclusively active, participating veterans of American wars." AVC had on its rolls 400 merchant seamen and men, such as Bolte, who had served in foreign armies. (The VFW had demanded just such a legislative rule for months.) Rankin's order survived only briefly before the full committee

*Whether Legion opposition to W-E-T and other housing measures represented rank-and-file sentiment is undeterminable. World War Two vets comprised 70 percent of the Legion's membership in 1947—but only 5 percent of the delegates to the national convention. Commander Griffith would not permit W-E-T advocates to speak; when a resolution supporting W-E-T came to a vote, he ruled that any delegate absent from the floor would be considered in opposition, and so recorded. The VFW hierarchy used another form of parliamentary legerdemain on housing issues. A few days after a national convention approved W-E-T, national commander Louis Starr said the resolution was not biding; acoustics in the auditorium were so poor, Starr said, that members didn't understand what they were voting on. Starr's ploy did not work: a young VFW housing enthusiast named John F. Kennedy, a first-term Democrat congressman from Massachusetts, made the commander back down.

overturned it, but it did set an irksome precedent. Later in 1947 the California and North Carolina legislatures, at Legion urging, used the same excuse to bar AVC from public facilities. In 1948, when AVC pressured Army Secretary Kenneth C. Royall to end segregation in the army, he retaliated by withdrawing its accreditation as a bona fide veterans' organization (meaning AVC could no longer use military bases for meetings and other activities).

Threatening though the external foes were, the issue that ultimately stifled AVC was an internal one: a traumatic fight against Communists who attempted to seize the organization and turn it into a propaganda arm of the far left. The AVC's leadership's first tactic was to admit Communists to membership, and then to work hard to outvote them when they ran for national office. The very presence of the Communists prompted the right-wing press to denounce AVC as a fellow traveler of Moscow or worse, and AVC civil libertarians spent considerable time in pained and often murky explanations of their containment of the infiltrators. For example, in early 1947 the Washington *Times-Herald* published a vitriolic series of articles citing Communists active in various AVC chapters, and depicting AVC as a sort of veterans' wing of the Communist Party, USA (CPUSA). The attack touched a sore spot, for one non-Communist AVC faction was arguing that taking a hard line against the internal Communists was nothing more than "red-baiting." Rebutting, Franklin D. Roosevelt, Jr., wrote in the *AVC Bulletin* that while communism was not an issue in many chapters, "there are no civil liberties or anti-Russian issues involved in the necessity of non-Communist members of AVC being organized to combat Communist influence and infiltration . . . to maintain AVC as a genuine independent organization." Merle Miller, the writer, who was a member of AVC's national planning committee, disagreed with "those wonderfully honest progressives who think that a liberal movement in America must accept the help of the Communist Party." He wanted continued election of AVC leaders "whose understanding of independent liberalism as against Party-line thought is clear and unmistakable."

The climactic confrontation with the Communists came in 1948, when the AVC decided that the advantages of taking Communists as members were far outweighed by the dangers. In midsummer a federal grand jury indicted John Gates, editor of *The Daily Worker*, and a member both of the CPUSA and the AVC, under the Smith Act. The AVC national governing board promptly expelled him on grounds it was "inconsistent" for him to "sign the preamble to the [AVC] constitution in good faith while a member of the Communist Party." Because the CPUSA was a "tight conspiracy" demanding "rigid adherence . . . a member of the CPUSA is neither a free agent in his own party nor in AVC. As a party member he can join AVC only for the purpose of furthering the objectives of the CPUSA." Gates called the statement "too childish to answer," but his supporters took the issue to the floor of the AVC convention in November. They lost, and Gilbert Harrison, running for AVC president, easily beat down a Communist-supported candidate. The convention declared Communists ineligible for AVC membership, and instructed the national officers to purge them.

The Communists fought no longer. Communist-dominated AVC chapters in Los Angeles and elsewhere simply vanished, with members moving into leftist organizations such as the "Progressive Veterans of America." But for non-Communist members victory proved Pyrrhic. As Roosevelt admitted, "From a flowering, inspiring group of young Americans, interested in the nation's welfare, we have become a tattered and torn group."

The American Veterans Committee survives today, but only tenuously. Although its national advisory council boasts eight congressmen, two senators, and two United States district judges, AVC is virtually anonymous in Washington; the windy "position papers" that flow from its second-floor walk-up offices in a ramshackle old building south of Dupont Circle are apparently read (and heeded) by few save its 50,000-odd members. Nonetheless Bolte* thinks AVC did what needed to be done in the postwar years. "We were an alternative to the American Legion, and a loud one," he said. "For one hundred thousand of us, at least, the AVC was a way of saying that winning the war didn't mean a damned thing unless the end result was a better country, a better world. Am I satisfied? Oh, one looks at any situation, any outcome, and thinks about 'what could have been.' At least we provided a forum for the thinking veteran."

BOOKS AND BONUSES

Chesterfield Smith, *a curly-haired, booming-voiced kid from rural Florida, never seemed able to settle down before the war. When he entered the University of Florida for prelaw studies in 1935, "I'd go to school a semester and then drop out a semester to earn enough money to return. I chose the easy life in college: I'd rather drop out and work than skimp in school." He worked as a clerk in the Florida legislature, jerked sodas at a tourist fishing resort in Boca Raton, ranged over central Florida as a debt collector, and sold tobacco and candy from a route truck. Smith's childhood sweetheart, Vivian Parker, whom he married in 1944, said of him: "He was just a poker-playing, crap-shooting boy who wouldn't settle down." Between 1935 and 1940 Smith managed to complete only 3½ years of school. "I'd had the highest average in my high-school class, but I had few targets, and I never worked very hard." In 1940 he went on active duty with the National Guard, attended officer candidate school, and served with a field artillery battery in France, beginning "about D-Day plus 45," through the Battle of the Bulge to peace. Smith saved $5,000 from his army pay, won another $3,000 shooting craps on the homeward troop ship, and reentered the University of Florida in 1946.*

"Something happened to Chesterfield's attitude in the war," Mrs. Smith said of her husband years later. "I don't know just what, but he was a serious man when he returned." Carefully budgeting his money ("What with the GI Bill, the money from the war, and a teaching job, beginning my second year in law school, we had more than most") and his hours (he found time to golf five times weekly), Smith led his class academically and politically, and took about every BMOC honor available. "I didn't go drink

---

*Bolte ended his career as an official of the Carnegie Endowment for International Peace, from which he retired in 1973.

*coffee or sit out on the bench and bull it all the time. I never missed a day
of class. I kept a work schedule just like I had a job. If I had a paper due
in three weeks, I started it right away and finished a week early. Hell, here
I was, almost thirty years old—I wanted to get that law license and get into
practice and make myself some money. The idea of playing around a university for unnecessary months or years had no appeal to me whatsoever."*

*Twenty-five years later Smith was the lead partner in a prestigious
Tampa-Orlando firm, with a six-figure annual income, and held the presidency of the American Bar Association. "The way I was going before the
war," Smith said, "I don't think I would ever have made it through law
school. But after the war I felt I had something invested in my country—
five years of my life. I said to myself, 'Boy, you've got to settle down and
make something of yourself, otherwise you ain't agonna 'mount o nothin'.'
My classmates in the forties, after the war, we wanted to get on with our
lives. We were men, not kids, and we had the maturity to recognize we had
to go get what we wanted, and not just wait for things to happen to us."*

In terms of sheer revolutionary impact upon American society, the
most important feature of the GI Bill was higher education. Through its
financial assistance, the GI Bill brought a college degree to within reach
of millions of persons who otherwise would have gone directly into trades
or blue-collar jobs. Between 1945 and 1950, according to VA figures, 2,300,000
veterans studied in colleges and universities under the GI Bill. The GI Bill
provided a special incentive to older veterans and to those whose families
were ill-educated and low-income. Educational Testing Service, in a study
of postwar vets, found that 35 percent of the older GIs (twenty-two years
or more) would not have attended college had not the GI Bill existed.[5] For
all the vets, 10 percent "definitely" would have forgone college; another
10 percent "probably" would not have gone. Even so, the GI Bill had a
more profound implication: It marked the popularization of higher education in America. After the 1940's, a college degree came to be considered
an essential passport for entrance into much of the business and professional world. And mass America, once the GI Bill afforded it a glimpse at
higher education, demanded no less an opportunity for successive generations. Pushed beyond their prewar capacity by the glut of veteran students, colleges and universities vastly expanded their physical plants. Once
the space existed, academia fillied it, and the educational boom was on.
Some decade-apart statistics show the intensity with which postwar Americans pursued higher education. In 1939–40, U.S. colleges and universities
conferred 216,521 degrees. In 1949–50 the number more than doubled,
to 496,661.

America's postwar affluence and emphasis on technology undoubtedly
would have boosted college enrollment even if the GI Bill had not existed.
But the GI Bill was important because it was tantamount to a forced
feeding of the universities: the veterans demanded schooling, and in a
hurry, and their very presence jolted academia into a double-time expansion inconceivable to an earlier educational generation. Further, the GI Bill

[5]Norman Frederiksen and W. B. Schrader, *Adjustment to College. A Study of 10,000 Veterans
and Non-veteran Students in Sixteen American Colleges* (Education Testing Service, 1951).

marked the first federal contributions to higher education since establishment of the land-grant colleges in the late 1800's, a political precedent of no little significance. That the spending was "for our boys" enabled legislators to brush aside engrained prejudices against federal aid to education. The money went not only to the veterans, but to the colleges as well, $9.65 for every credit hour taken by a student enrolled under the GI Bill.

Colleges realized even before the war ended that they faced unprecedented enrollments once the servicemen returned home. A War Department survey taken in 1944, before the benefits of the GI Bill were firmly set, showed that at least 8 percent of the 16,000,000 people in uniform intended to enter college. So the universities began to think seriously about what veterans would expect of them. Beginning in 1943, Columbia University sent its former students in the military a periodic "Memorandum from Morningside" to tell them what was happening on their old campus.[6] Near the war's end, 1,200 servicemen were asked what they wanted from Columbia, both as students and as humans. Virtually every man who responded urged that he and fellow veterans be treated exactly like other students. They asked only that recognition be given their age, their varied experience, and their desire to make up for lost time. An officer aboard the USS *Chief*, in the Pacific, reported, "Much as I'd like to, I don't expect to take very much more liberal arts work. By the time I get back to school, I'll be getting on in years, and with several more years of professional study contemplated, the problem of when I'll start earning a living will begin to be a serious one." The officer nonetheless had mixed feelings about suggestions that Columbia accelerate its courses. "Education is too important to me now to be raced through. I want to have the feeling of leisure to do an honest job with the most valuable time of my life." Going to a year-round three-semester plan "would turn college into a factory." But a P-51 pilot was not worried about twelve unbroken months of classes: "I remember how we used to think that a full year would be a tough grind, but it was probably laziness that prompted that feeling."

A condescending tone frequently crept into college bureaucrats' house organs as they discussed what to do with the veteran. As was much else of America, the educators were prepared to treat the veteran as somewhat of a special animal, and they didn't know quite what to expect of him, or vice versa. "Because the veteran fought our fight," President Paul Klapper of Queens College wrote in *School and Society*, "because the victory he brings is purchased all too frequently at the expense of his health and his integrated personality, ours is the obligation to make him at home in the society he has served." But Klapper warned that universities "must guard against mawkish generosity toward the veteran-student. If he receives a substandard education because of our mistaken kindness, he will become a substandard member of his vocational and cultural group." Klapper didn't like the notion of accelerating classes, regardless of what the eager veterans demanded; to permit a veteran to finish college in less than three years "is a delusion and a snare. One must live with ideas to understand them. Unless they are applied and reapplied in successive challenges, they degenerate into mere words, mere mouthings."

[6]Servicemen's responses to the Columbia questionnaires are quoted in McKnight, "They Know What They Want." *School & Society*, December 21, 1946.

Klapper was not alone in his worries about the demands the vet would make upon universities. Frederic W. Ness, assistant to the vice-chancellor of New York University, said many veterans came to college with unrealistic expectations, foxhole and barracks dreams they had scant chance of realizing. A navy storekeeper, twenty-five years old, married with three children, his only formal education a single year at a commercial high school, wanted to be a doctor. Another veteran "whose campaign ribbons outnumbered Hermann Goering's medals" wanted three business courses but lacked the required preparatory schooling that would enable him to understand the material. Both men had to be rejected. Ness did not disguise his frustration with vets who acted as if earning a college degree involved nothing more than showing up for classes: "If we think that the primary objective of a college course in French is to give only a speaking acquaintance with the language, then we limit the function of a college," he wrote. "Why bother to pass a GI Bill of Rights to send the veteran to college? Let us buy him a set of Victrola records!"

The fretting of the academics, however, was beyond the earshot of the veteran student, who saw considerable visible evidence that the colleges were preparing for him. College after college created special programs tailored for the veteran. The University of Nebraska, for example, waived its entrance requirement of a high-school diploma for anyone who could prove his "capability" of doing college-level work; it created one-, two-, and three-year curricula for veterans wanting to rush through specialized courses. North Dakota Agricultural College added a "school of veteran education" to "provide for the returning veteran such training as will prepare him for a pleasant and profitable place in the postwar world." Chancellor Rober M. Hutchins of the University of Chicago worried about "educational hoboes" who would drift into school for lack of anything better to do. Western Reserve University in Cleveland set up a course in small business management for the veteran. At North Carolina State College, the Navy closed its diesel engineering school, which had trained hundreds of technicians for sea duty, and the head of the ceramics department returned from service with the War Production Board. The universities were ready for peace.

"Being somewhat of a sentimentalist," former paratrooper Jack Fisler wrote in *The Technician* at North Carolina State College in 1946, "I just couldn't keep that lump in my throat from bobbing right up and knocking a few very dry tears out of my eyes as I gazed on our beautiful Memorial Tower last March after three long, long years of drilling, KPing, griping, jumping from airplanes, and in general, making a monkey out of myself and the Japs." A columnist in *The Texas Ranger*, student magazine at the University of Texas, wrote in the September 1946 issue: "This is a different campus now, even if the buildings look the same. You see fellows in prewar saddleshoes, but when you get close you hear them trading baby formulas." Goodfriends, a campus area women's shop, advertising in the same issue, advised coeds, "That guy, who was someone nice to send your letters to last year, is back in your college life. Vaulted corridors will resound once more to the tread of size twelve brogans. And what a welcome change the boys make in your college life, in your college wardrobe. . . . Even campus and classroom fashions are softer, prettier, packed with man-appeal. G. I. (Guy Interest) is the theme song of Goodfriends campus college. . . ."

And North Carolina State's *Technician* directed an editorial at newcomers that was both a welcome and a warning:

> Your new freshmen comprise a class unique in the history of State College because of the wide variance in age range, amount of experience, and maturity of the different individuals. . . . Only one of three new entrants graduate, even in peacetime. . . . So it appears that if you are starting in college just to have a good time, it would be best to stop now before you have wasted too much money and too much of your own and other people's time.

For veterans who had been in college before the war, homecoming had its disappointments. The demands of war had stripped campuses of many of their old traditions and activities, and now the Veterans Association elbowed aside prewar political blocs and established itself as the most powerful student group on many campuses. For example, at North Carolina State it ran the United War Fund Drive (campus form of the community chest), lobbied through reduced ticket rates for vets at the little theater, formed a cooperative store, and won four of six sophomore offices. The Interfraternity Council, nervous about the depletion of Greek letter societies, pledged to eliminate the "old collegiate snobbery" by broadening fraternity membership so that returning veterans "will find on the campuses a true manifestation of the democracy for which the war was waged." Unimpressed, vets on some campuses formed their own highly informal fraternity: Chi Gamma Iota, whose Greek letters are X-G-I. Old customs also withered at Duke University in nearby Durham. Campus editor Clay Felker* wrote that shouts of "Button, freshmen," were replaced by "Square that hat, sailor," during the war, when naval officers trained at Duke, and somehow never revived. First-semester freshmen sat on the broad steps of Duke Chapel, off limits to them before the war. Upperclassmen dutifully handed out "blue dinks"—beanies bearing class numbers which traditionally had been worn until the Duke-North Carolina football game (and to Christmas if Carolina won). The veterans threw them away. And when nonveteran upperclassmen attempted to revive "Rat Court" hazing of freshmen, student columnist Jack Fisler cautioned, "Being an enlisted veteran of the parachute infantry, we understand that no strongarm tactics would be advisable to apply on indifferent freshmen of the veteran group."

An air of solemnity pervaded. There was a determined preoccupation with books and study, a frenetic hurrying to *finish*, to earn the degree and enter the job market, to "make up for lost time," the five words that summarized the overriding goal of the postwar campus veteran. A *Time* reporter, asking graduating vets about their "problems" in June 1947, got this answer from a student at Indiana University: "Pardon me, but you'll have to hurry, because I've got to get along. Problem? The main problem of everybody is to catch up. We're all trying to get where we would have been if there hadn't been a war."

Late in the war University of Texas sociologists Drs. Harry Moore and Bernice Moore speculated on what the returning veteran would think of the coed: "He will not be staggered if when he returns she has changed

*Now editor of *New York Magazine*.

not at all; if she has refused to grow up; if she has not kept up with the times; if she has not learned what the war really meant. He expects and needs a *woman* [the sociologists' emphasis] when he returns." But did the coeds fit the veterans' definition of "woman"? And were coeds fresh from home prepared for men three, four, five years older, and experienced in subjects other than warfare? In retrospect, no other aspect of postwar campus life had such long-range insignificance as the debate over boy-girl relationships, an argument waged with windy fury in dormitory bull sessions, the letters columns of campus newspapers, college political campaigns, even in quasi-learned sociological tracts; so intense, in fact, that when the *New York Times* published an article by a veteran comparing American girls unfavorably with Europeans ("being nice is almost a lost art among American women"), the storm of protesting mail was so immense that the *Times* self-defensively devoted two full pages to the females' rebuttal.

For the veterans, a major irritant was a frequently outrageously one-sided male-female ratio. At the University of Texas, an archetypical large state university, the ratio was three males for each woman, a figure that provoked an ominous opinion from a professor of anthropology: "Not even warfare has ever put such a strain on any civilized or primitive society. There have been isolated cases of such a ratio, but it is definitely an artificial phenomenon." John Bryson, writing in a special issue of *The Texas Ranger* devoted to women, commented, "The contrast between ego-inflated young girls, blessed with such a ratio, and the women that veteran met in a realistic outside world has provided a comparison that only invites unpleasantness and hard feelings. The female excuse, 'Look how unhappy we were during the manpower shortage; we have to make up for lost time,' is hardly logical to men who spent their formative years enduring the loneliness of jungles, trenches, and barracks in similar lost time, intensified by the ultimate in suffering."

Another Texas veteran, Downs Matthews, wrote that ex-GIs knew what was "wrong" with the average coed but were at a loss on how to go about improving her. "The biggest factor involved is one of contrast," Matthews wrote. "Through a quick, sobering maturity and the sweeping education of war travels, they know what they want in a woman. They have been awakened to possibilities in the female by association with women all over America and the rest of the world. Not loose, wild women without morals. Just women, not girls." In the next lines, however, Matthews made some criticisms that tended to confirm the direst suspicions of coeds: that the phrase "lack of maturity" was a euphemism for girls who refused to be bedded in a motel or the back seat of a car. Matthews complained that the college girl "expects too much of her boyfriend, and gives too little in return. She makes no attempt at being a good date, or trying to show the boy, who is willing to spend his time, money and efforts in obtaining her company, that she is appreciative." Matthews frowned at coeds who "pretend . . . to be shocked at the mention of a drink or talk of going off to another city for a party and football game. . . . The college girl has absolutely no concept of what pleases a man." By contrast, Matthews wrote, "working girls . . . have learned the hard way that such attitudes do not pay. They are forced to face the unadorned facts that if they want to have a good time they will have to have something to offer the man. Being thrown into the terrific competition of the working world, where there are few opportunities to meet eligible men, girls get terribly lonely and bored with nobody asking for a date every day or so. When a date comes along, they really appreciate him and they do their utmost to show their appreciation of his attention." Veterans writing to *The Daily Texan* drummed home much the same theme. One student defiantly called upon all male students to make three dates for the night of February 8, then gather for a stag party, standing up the entire female population of the university. A few weeks of such treatment, the veteran suggested, would result in "the most cowed, trustworthy group of women to be found anywhere in the world outside Moslem India." Said another writer: "There's really nothing wrong with those Texas coeds that a change of diapers wouldn't cure." Responding, females generally equated criticisms as reflections upon their virtue. A letter signed by three coeds stated: "We regret that we cannot measure down to the standard you lived by in the streets of Paris, London, Frisco, and a few other hot spots of the universe. Perhaps [the veterans are] confusing immaturity with chastity. The average girl on the campus does not want to be a mature woman in the sense that she forfeit her gaiety, her laughter, and even her coquettishness. We are proud to be young and full of life. We are proud to be innocent." Some coeds found a self-assurance among the vets that set them apart from the younger undergraduates. Mary Matossian, as a freshman at Stanford in the 1940's,* dated many older vets and found them more pleasant, mature company than the run-of-the-mill sophomore. "They treated you like a lady, they knew you were young and inexperienced, they didn't spend all their time trying to lay you," Dr. Matossian related. One of Dr. Matossian's colleagues at Maryland (she begged anonymity) said, "I had offers and propositions made to me at UCLA and Michigan, by these horny vets, that were so direct I won't repeat them even today, and I consider myself a broad-minded person." And Ivamae Brandt, in a letter to the University of Iowa's *Daily Iowan* in 1946, warned, "Your [the veterans'] prewar manners need a little brushing up. You're no longer the fair-haired boys the war has made you. Girls like to have doors opened for them, to be called respectable names, and to be treated with what chivalry there is left in the world. You fellows are going to be hard up unless something is done about your repulsive selves in a hurry." Joan Walker, giving the women's viewpoint in *The Texas Ranger* symposium, scoffed at the vets as crybabies, and suggested some self-examination:

> The women think you're the ones that have changed, and I agree with them. You've ruined the curve on quizzes. You're too self-sufficient. You talk about radar and the cap'n and the B.O.Q. You spend too much of your time living over your buzz-boy days. You're still in that period that's called "postwar readjustment." And I could go on. But you don't hear women griping much. We're glad to have you back—the pickin's were pretty slim for a long time. But we're beginning to get a little tired waiting for your "Here-I-am-welcome-me-with-open-arms" attitude to be over, and we're beginning to be a little tired of your complaints. We're not so bad.

*Now a professor of history at the University of Maryland.

> So shut up, remember where you are, look around, and there she
> is. I know some guys that have already done this, and they're just that
> far ahead of you.

But where to live, and where to study? Increased enrollments staggered the capacity of colleges to absorb the gush of students. A *School and Society* survey of 450 institutions found increases of up to 580 percent in teachers' colleges; 125 percent in agricultural and engineering colleges; 280 percent in arts and sciences. The surge surprised even the educational bureaucrats: In early 1946 the U. S. Office of Education had estimated that college enrollments would reach 2,000,000 in 1949 and 3,000,000 some five years later. But by November 1946 enrollments were 2,062,000, of whom 1,073,000 were veterans (and 667,000 were women). Further, the demands came after more than a decade of financial starvation for the colleges, whose income dropped precipitously during the Depression and war years because of lower investment income and decreased enrollment and gifts.

So the colleges scrambled. "Education proceeds with a student, a teacher, a book and a laboratory," President Henry Wriston of Brown University said in 1946. "Students there are in plenty but everything else is scarce." Temple University in Philadelphia bought an old aircraft-parts plant and converted it into classrooms. The state of New York set up a college at a naval training station near Geneva, and enrolled 12,000 students. "Let's get them in this year even though you will have to sacrifice some of your standards," Governor Thomas E. Dewey told state college presidents. The University of Connecticut took part of a coast guard facility at Fort Sampson; the University of Oklahoma got a naval air station at Norman. Colleges and universities in New York City combined to convert barracks at Camp Shanks into housing for 2,400 families, and buses hauled the students to and from classes. The Federal Public Housing Authority dismantled more than 100,000 housing units built for war workers and transported them, complete with surplus furniture, to campuses. The University of Wisconsin established branches in thirty-four cities to give the first two years of college work; the University of Illinois managed to obtain an old amusement pier in Chicago, used for navy classes during the war, and squeeze in 4,000 students. Texas Christian University in Fort Worth put its geology labs in a gymnasium. Wisconsin bedded 1,866 vets in an old munitions plant thirty-five miles from campus, another 1,600 at an airbase.

Student ingenuities were no less active. At the University of Iowa, three students found living space in the basement of a funeral parlor. Les Cramer, a navy vet at Ohio Wesleyan University, rented a house trailer in a preacher's back yard and got water through a garden hose. At the University of Southern California, two men lived in an auto for seven months, studying at night under a street light. At Auburn University in Alabama, two students persuaded a sympathetic Episcopal minister to let them live in the belfry of his church. At North Carolina State, engineering student Charles C. Elder, Jr., who spent eighteen war months in remote weather stations in Canada and Greenland, balked at leaving his wife in his home town when he couldn't find conventional housing. So Elder made himself a trailer of wood and sheet metal and friends helped him haul it to Raleigh— twenty-four feet long, eight feet wide, seven feet tall, but a temporary home nonetheless. Princeton, breaking a 200-year tradition, let student wives live on campus. At Rhode Island State, housing officials crammed eleven students into each Quonset hut.

Gripe though they did, most student vets philosophically accepted the housing mess as an unpleasant extension of wartime hardship, a discomfort that could be endured because school, unlike war, had a definite completion date. The vets and their families lived in tight camaraderie: in "villages" of house trailers, Quonset huts, plywood houses, and old army barracks that had been hauled to campuses and converted into housing. Many of the dwellings were little more than sparsely furnished housekeeping rooms. At North Carolina State, for instance, the majority of couples lived in quarters without cooking facilities. But the vets built a markedly cohesive community.

Consider Monroe Park, an enclave of ninety-five house trailers for vet families at the University of Wisconsin, dubbed the "state's most fertile five acres" because of the high birth rate the year after former servicemen and their wives reunited and settled down to study. (In one week in the spring of 1947 babies were born to five Monroe Park families.) Monroe Park was as tightly organized as an army battalion, albeit on a more convivial basis. It elected a mayor (term: one semester) to serve as liaison with university and town officials. Six "constables" had arrest power but, aside from quieting roisterous Saturday night parties, spent most of their time handling such emergencies as defective oil heaters. The park's cooperative grocery store grossed $5,000 weekly and gave eight vets part-time work; its prices were about 10 percent lower than private stores'. The park sponsored a bowling league, a softball team, semimonthly dances at a community recreation center (with music by radio or jukebox), and classes on sewing, cooking, and child care. The Monroe Park vets skimped. Trailer rent ranged from $25 to $32.50 monthly, including electricity for light and cooking, and oil for heating (but no running water). Estimated expenses for a family with one child were $150 monthly, $60 more than the GI Bill stipend. But a park resident, Pauline Durkee, wife of an engineering student and mother of girls eight and nine, was philosophical when she talked with a writer for the *American Legion Magazine*. Although she clerked in a grocery store to help balance the family budget, Mrs. Durkee found time to be the Monroe Park social chairman, and she said it was "good discipline" for the families to haul their own water and live communally. "It keeps us from becoming softies, and makes us remember that our forefathers had to go without conveniences we consider indispensable, and thought nothing of it."

Michigan State College boasted its own fertile valley in a vet village of apartments, trailers, and prefabricated huts. A count in April 1947 turned up 800 children of less than five years among the 2,000 veteran couples; 288 wives were pregnant. Here, too, the families banded closely together. A young wife named Marian McGregor, shocked by general loneliness when she moved into the village in 1946, began bringing women together for picnics and discussions on homemaking. The response was so warm that Mrs. McGregor arranged a mass meeting in a college ballroom to organize a formal association, Spartan Wives. College officials detailed a woman professor and the director of the adult extension division to help develop a program. Soon the Spartan Wives had classes on subjects ranging from swimming to motherhood and how to make kids' clothes from cast-off GI garb. The wives sponsored a weekly program on the campus radio station on such subjects as "How to Live on $90 a Month." Their cooperative store undercut local grocers by 10 percent. But more important than the formal programs, Mrs. McGregor mused in 1947, was the cohesiveness the Spartan Wives brought to the village, and the excitement of a shared adventure. "Our men didn't sit around and gripe when they were overseas fighting; they went ahead and did the job. The least we wives can do is to make the home life as easy as possible while they finish the other job, that of getting their degrees."

Dick Mullan* was a freshman at Pennsylvania State College when drafted into the infantry for "three kind of grim years." At age twenty-one, he and his new wife, Peggy, returned to State College, Pa., in 1947 to pursue a degree in biochemistry. They lived briefly in a small upstairs apartment with no stove or refrigerator. "We kept things outside the window to keep them cool, milk and cream for breakfast. We tried to cook on a hot plate, cleaning the dishes in the bathroom sink." Mullan car-pooled with neighbors to the campus, three miles distant, often waiting hours in the library for a ride home at night. Peggy had problems getting to and from her job in the graduate school. Hence they felt themselves lucky when a vacancy suddenly developed for an apartment on Beaver Street, State College's main thoroughfare near the campus.

"Our new apartment was really a front porch, right on the main street, with venetian blinds separating us from the outside world. The 'living room' consisted of a desk and a chair. The stove had three gas burners. We had some sort of tin contraption, a Dutch oven, which we put on top of the stove for an oven. But we did all sort of wild things with it. We'd bake cakes and roasts. One time my brother came for dinner and said, 'Peggy, sometimes I think you are going to open that thing and take out a suckling pig!'

"But the bathroom was the real riot. There was no shower, no bathtub. We were never really sure how the landlady expected us to keep clean; I guess she really didn't. Everything in the bathroom was miniature—little tiny john, little tiny sink. The problem was to figure out how to take a bath. I could always go up the street and take showers at the fraternity house. But this really wasn't going to do for Peggy.

"I was down at Sears one day and saw a collapsible bathtub—a camping type of thing, which you opened up like a cot and filled with water, using a pan or a bucket. You had to be careful about scraping or tearing the thing—which we did at the end, anyway—but it worked, sort of. Since we lived right on the main street, if you wanted to take a bath you had to pull the blinds and lock the front door. If anyone came to the door, you quickly said, 'Sorry, I'm taking a bath.'" ("When I got pregnant, it was a real drag," recollected Peggy Mullan. "It was hard enough getting in and out, but there was no way I could fill or empty it, no way.")

"The landlady didn't even know we had the thing until we moved; I don't think she was particularly interested in how we kept clean, if we did.

---

*Now an executive with a national food chain, living in a Philadelphia suburb.

I really felt we were not too welcome by the town, that the people wanted to exploit us. When we finally left, though, after one and one-half years, we sold it to her at the price we had paid for it, leak and all.

"The bedroom was approximately seven by eight feet, with a double bed six and three-quarters by seven and three-quarters feet. It took up the whole room. You walked in and fell right into bed—the bedroom was really that, a bedroom." ("You crawled in from the end," Peggy Mullan said. "That got funny when I was pregnant—I needed Dick to pull me in from the foot of the bed.")

"The front porch had no insulation. We'd start a bridge game, and it would get colder and colder and colder; there was no answer but for everyone to go home. Sometimes we'd come in from a weekend outing when the temperature was ten below zero, and there was a big rush to get hot chocolate and crawl into bed and attempt to get warm."

Peggy Mullan was 8½ months pregnant the snowy February day in 1950 when Dick received his degree. ("There was a real baby explosion the last year at State College, when everyone was finishing; most all of our friends were pregnant.") They returned to the apartment and crammed their belongings into a 1938 Plymouth. "The last thing we put in was the broom we used to sweep the snow off the top of the car. We had a drink with a fraternity brother and drove away in ten inches of snow, ready for the world.

"It was one of the best times of our life. We were young. What we had to contend with was more in the pioneer tradition of the country. We survived, and we learned, which was good for all of us."

As inflation pushed the cost of living steadily upward, Congress heard an increasing crescendo of cries by veteran students that they could not survive on GI Bill payments. A conference of veterans, labor, and education officials in January 1947 produced considerable data to support the complaints. Stipends at the time were $65 monthly for a single vet, and $90 for a man with dependents. The VA also paid up to $500 annually for tuition, books and supplies. But for most vets the GI Bill was a supplement, not a supporting income. A survey of 132 campuses by veterans' groups found single vets paying as much as $120 monthly for living expenses (the low was $32 monthly, the average $53.33). The range for married ex-GIs was from $47 to $165 monthly, with an average of $79. Regardless of the disparities in living costs, however, vets received the same amount, no matter where they lived and the amount they spent for subsistence. So in early 1947 the veterans lobby put forth a bill increasing stipends to $75 for single students and $100 for married vets, plus $15 for the first child and $10 per child thereafter.[7] The vets had the statistics on their side, a fact everyone conceded; nonetheless surprisingly diverse protestants opposed any increase. Dr. Francis J. Brown, speaking for the 829 colleges and universities in the American Council on Education, endorsed higher pay for couples with children, but for no one else. Brown acknowledged the vets' financial plight. Yet the purpose of the GI Bill, he noted, was to "assist" and encourage vets to go to college, "not to give them a free education." A

[7]"Increasing Subsistence Allowances for Education," hearings, House Committee on Veterans Affairs, February 1947.

token $5 monthly increase would cost the Treasury $150 million a year, he noted. Charles A. Shields, a student at Haverford College outside Philadelphia, supported Brown: "It would be just expense money, spending money," Shields testified before the House Committee on Veterans Affairs. "We never had it so good." A committee member, Representative W. Howes Meade of Kentucky, chimed that the majority of committee members were Second World War veterans, and all had a college education. "So far as I know," he said, "all had difficult times. Yet, without any assistance from the government, they got their college education." Representative Olin Teague of Texas, a wounded combat hero, was also cool. He put into the record a letter from a college student saying single vets griped chiefly because they were too lazy to earn money to supplement the GI Bill. "Not only do the majority of them refuse to work, but they all drive nice automobiles, take weekend trips practically every weekend, and . . . spend considerable money on whiskey and beer." Other congressmen were hostile because two-thirds of the vets were not in programs of any sort; hence why give more money to those in college?

Student supporters of an increase talked about both immediate needs and the long-range benefits of the GI Bill. Gary Reynolds, student editor of *Mail Call*, the veterans magazine at George Washington University, Washington, D.C., said about 10 percent of the 6,000 vets at the school couldn't find part-time jobs; that his personal monthly expenses were $100, including $69 for a boarding-house room. Without an increase, Reynolds said, veteran enrollment would drop by half. James T. Roberts, a student at the University of Baltimore, said he wouldn't wave the flag for more money, but that he would talk about practical reasons: "I am sick and tired of hearing this 'I faced death' stuff," Roberts said. "I don't want anything for that, but I do want an education, and I feel I can serve my country better as an educated man than I can as 'John Doe, ditch digger,' or a man who runs a machine."

The veterans' demands were irresistible: in 1948 Congress kicked up the benefits to $75 monthly for a single vet; $105 for a couple, $120 for a family with a child. Budgets nonetheless remained tight, but the veterans tugged their belts and kept at their studies.

Regardless of their desires to blend into the general student population, veterans did retain a separate identity. Because of their intensity of purpose, the conventional wisdom among college bureaucrats was that they accomplished far more academically than did nonveterans. But the difference was more imagined than real. The Educational Testing Service studied 10,000 veteran and nonveteran students at sixteen colleges during the late 1940's and arrived at the carefully hedged conclusion that among freshmen "there is a tendency for veterans to achieve higher grades in relation to ability than do nonveteran students." But ETS said the "actual magnitude of the difference is small, however. In the most extreme case, the advantage of the veterans would on the average amount to no more than the difference between a C and a C-plus." But for "interrupted veterans" (that is, those who had attended college before military service, and then returned) there was "marked superiority" at four of five large universities studied. ETS also turned up an apparent anomaly: despite their seriousness, the veterans "on the whole . . . attached less importance to college grades and to college graduation than the nonveterans." They attended college to obtain higher-paying jobs, not to prepare for a profession.

The veterans' emphasis on the practical offended many professorial sensitivities. Were the universities destined to be nothing more than academic factories, producing graduates in assembly-line fashion, with the emphasis upon speed rather than quality? Must the popularization of higher education mean also its vulgarization?

But according to S. N. Vinocour, a veteran who taught speech at the University of Nevada, "If pedagogic desks were reversed and the veteran now in college were given the opportunity to grade his professor, he would give him a big red 'F' and rate him as insipid, antiquated and ineffectual." Reporting on a 5,000-mile research tour of campuses in *School and Society* in 1947, Vinocour wrote that many vets feared an economic depression was imminent. Hence they wanted career training rather than theoretical courses. The veteran, Vinocour maintained, did not want to "fritter away his time cramming inconsequential facts, such as learning the names of all the signers of the Declaration of Independence, conjugation of the vulgar Latin verbs, memorizing the date that Shakespeare first said 'Hello' to Ann Hathaway, or how many hours Benjamin Franklin had to stand in the rain with his kite." The veteran felt he entered college as a full-fledged and mature citizen, "not as an adolescent high school graduate eager to participate in the old rah-rah days of Siwash." He considered the collegiate atmosphere "not only very stupid, but a definite hindrance to his acquiring an education." Vinocour argued that the veteran wanted more practical courses (such as radio technique) and "more realistic English courses," rather than the "minor poems of Milton" and "history of oratory." Concluding, Vinocour charged that veterans are "living and studying in a vacuum covered with the moss of the professor's yellow lecture notes."

Such a broadside, of course, could not go unchallenged. *School and Society* bristled with angry rebuttals from professors claiming that the indolent veteran was the major educational problem of the nation. Most of the vets, asserted the correspondents, would be better off in trade schools, not universities; they decried their lack of intellectual curiosity and abhorrence of serious scholarship. So frothful was the debate (or, more accurately, the attack upon Vinocour) that it eventually burst from the pages of *School and Society* into other academic trade journals. One must speculate at the magnitude of the classroom slight that prompted the retaliatory outburst of the venerable Professor Bayard Quincy Morgan, of Stanford University, in the *Pacific Spectator*, a West Coast intellectual quarterly. Morgan scoffed at the complaint about "professors mumbling from notes yellow with age" (a paraphrase of one of Vinocour's laments). He asked: "Does that mean to you that the ideas embodied there are *necessarily* flyblown and fit only for the ash can? Must I write a fresh set of lecture notes every year, ignoring everything I said the year before?" Morgan continued: "They want a degree, oh yes, but about as a man buys a railway ticket or secures a passport. . . . [A]nything that doesn't contribute directly and demonstrably to the quickest acquisition of a degree is not only not wanted, it is resented." Veterans wanted "training" rather than "education." Morgan summarized their attitude: " 'Never mind the theory; that takes too long, and we won't understand it anyway. What we want is the know-how.' So they demand just enough English to talk to a day laborer; just enough of a foreign language to order a meal or engage a hotel room; just enough mathematics to check the bills and the bank statement."[8]

Beneath Morgan's wrath was a serious criticism of an ominous drift in American higher education. The new generation of students, he said, was resentful of courses that did not provide "results." Confronted with a course outside their narrow professional field, they asked, "What good will it do me?" The veterans, he maintained, were scornful of free discussion of political, economic, and social ideas. Morgan felt he knew why: "The armed forces were always intent on 'getting the job done,' and always in a hurry. They rushed the recruits thorugh 'just enough' of everything, trusting . . . to the exigencies of actual fighting to augment the scanty education of the trainee. It is not surprising if the veteran thinks all education is like that, and expects the college to give him the same kind of training he got in the army or navy." (Critical as Morgan was of the veteran, he said academicians should listen to the complaints, and, "perhaps, with the veteran's help and counsel, improve on our present system.")

Guy Owen is a writer who has earned more satisfaction, and quiet reputation, than money. His The Flim Flam Man and The Apprentice Grifter, *published in 1972, the truly uproarious account of the adventures of a con man in rural North Carolina, is at once a handbook on how to fleece larcenous rednecks and a comic narrative of the genre of Mark Twain's* Huckleberry Finn. *The book sold 3,000 copies, the movie was not the box office success it had promised to be, and Pocket Books remaindered the paperback edition. But these matters are inconsequential to Owen himself. He has staked for his personal literary province the changing character of the coastal regions of North Carolina, the subject of three other novels; he writes poetry; he teaches English at North Carolina State University; and he has been active in the civil rights and peace movements. After graduation from high school in 1942, the seventeen-year-old Owen lied about his age to get a job as a welder in a shipyard, and made so much money that he was reluctant to leave to enter the University of North Carolina. He managed one year before being drafted, and eventually landed with the 13th Armored Division under Major General George S. Patton. Owen won't—or can't— talk about his specific war experiences, other than to say that he heard "considerable gunfire."*

"There is a reason my story is not 'typical.' I came out of the war mentally . . . [Owen paused many seconds] mentally wounded. I guess you would say. I spent a month in a hospital in California. I don't think I was batty or anything like that, but I had nervous tics in my face. The psychiatrists gave me a fifty percent disability. So a good part of the postwar years, so far as I was concerned, was spent trying to find myself, to prove to myself that I was not sick.

"Looking toward peace, for me the main thing was to get back to a sane world where the ground would not buckle under your feet, to a world

[8]"Let's Give the Veterans an Education," by Bayard Quincy Morgan, *the Pacific Spectator,* Winter 1948.

that was not a slaughterhouse. I was young and sensitive, maybe hypersensitive; after all, I'm a youngster who published poetry in high school, mind you. But during the war me and other soldiers, we just turned ourselves into monomaniacs, in a way. The main thing was to stop the Germans, stop the Japs. There was no arguing about it, it damned simply had to be done. There was no romance about it.

"I guess what happened to me, when I returned to Chapel Hill [site of the University of North Carolina], was a gradual withdrawing into a safe world, a little island, a retreat into an aesthetic world, away from the brutality of the shipyards and the army. I had two goals: to prove that I could make it in the world even though I had been labeled fifty percent disabled; and to get a college education. I did this by going to my private inner island. I cut off relations with the church and became an agnostic; I had no interest in politics, no belief in economic salvation, no thoughts about science. I didn't even care enough about politics to argue them.

"Financially, I was better off than before the war; I didn't have to wait tables. I didn't have a lot of money to throw around, to buy records and books I wanted. But I didn't miss it, because I never had it. It was a pretty austere life, living in those little old boxed-up Quonset huts and 'victory villages.' I couldn't get any work done in a crowded dorm, so I'd take off to the library: after all, how do you study in a double-bunk bed?

"But I don't think I bitched very much. There were people who couldn't even get into the university because they didn't have a place to stay. I remember a few tents thrown up around the campus. Plus the fact that when you are in the army, and a private, you are used to sleeping on the ground. I felt grateful running my hands over the smoothness of a clean sheet.

"For the vets, college was a sort of no-nonsense thing. They worked hard, they concentrated on the main thing, the degree, married or not. Oh, there were blowups on the weekends, when people would sit around and drink beer. But the main thing was 'Man, I've got three, four, five years down the drain; we've got to work.' Myself, I graduated in three years by going to summer school.

"Sure, we felt an apartness from nonveterans. I resented it very much when I went home on my furlough from overseas, and going up and shaking hands with a man on the street who said, 'Hello, there, where have you been?'"

"It was like we were in a cancer ward looking out the window at people who were very healthy, and who couldn't communicate with us.

"I don't think it was a fun time for us. I worked too hard. Those days, I didn't even drink, so I kept out of the weekend parties. A part of it was that I came from a very small high school, and was not ready for Chapel Hill; I was always sort of running scared.

"Also, there was this 'fifty percent disabled' label put on me, and having this psychiatrist tell me, 'You are going to make it okay, but don't try to do anything that will tax you too hard, don't get too involved, don't set your goals too high.' I still resent that. I got rid of the percentages in a few years, and I was no longer getting a $10 check each month to remind me that I shouldn't try too hard.

"The GI Bill, I can't emphasize enough, really saved me. I don't think I would have been able to go on for the doctorate. Sure, I would have gotten an AB, but that would have meant teaching in a high school, where I wouldn't

*have the spare time to write the novels. The GI Bill took me well into my
doctorate, and enabled me to get outside the state, to places such as the
University of Chicago, where I had different experiences from what I would
have ever seen in Carolina.*

*"The war is something I've tried to dismiss, and I've done a pretty good
job of blanking it out. Anybody who can't tell you the name of his first
sergeant—and I can't—has it out of mind. Still, when I hear machine-gun
fire, I begin to tremble. I wouldn't go see* Patton *[a film with George C. Scott
in the title role]. I had the shaking experience just last week watching
Charlie Chaplin's* Modern Times *again. It doesn't hurt me, but my body
still takes over.*

*"I thought, when I was floundering around at Chapel Hill, that if I had
any story to tell, it was about the war. A lot of GIs who wanted to be writers
felt the same way, mostly as a means of working off grudges against officers
and sergeants, and the waste of war—the horror, the boredom, the regi-
mentation, the dehumanizing things. I remember once drawing up a list of
things I'd like to write about, and one of them was the war. But I haven't
written anything about it. For a long time I was so close to it, so haunted
by it, that I couldn't be objective.*

*"Going back to my immediate postwar feelings: sure, I was apolitical.
(I'm not now: I helped organize peace vigils in Raleigh, and marches against
the [Vietnam] war, and I made trips to Washington, and I helped integrate
Raleigh by demonstrating in the streets.) But I make no apologies for the
postwar period. We did stop the Japs, we did stop the Germans. I'm a little
bit impatient with youngsters who want to picture us as American Legionnaires and hard hats and whatnot. This is all that anyone has the right to
demand of my generation: that we stopped the Japs, we stopped the Germans.*

*"Now if we want to turn on the TV, drink beer, even to vote for George
Wallace, it may be that we should be forgiven in a sense. We cut away
everything to make up for those lost years. Maybe that's why my generation
was called the 'silent generation.'"*

Summing up the first full campus year of peacetime, *The Texas Ranger*
at the University of Texas noted, "All in all, it was a year of everyone trying
to return to normal. Khaki leftovers from the army gradually disappeared
from the campus as clothes became available to the new civilians. There
was less and less talk about old outfits and more and more discussion of
what lies ahead. All in all, it looked like American college life was on the
way back."

So, too, was the American economy, but with a mass of problems that
far surpassed any troubles faced by the academicians. The question, in
essence, was whether business and labor could survive peace.

NOTES

Two persons who were especially helpful in interviews, beyond
credit given in the text, were Harry W. Colmery, of Topeka, Kansas, an
attorney and a past national commander of the American Legion who
did much of the legal draftsmanship of the GI Bill, and Charles G.

Bolte, the first chairman of the American Veterans Committee. Although in his eighties Colmery granted me a "dinner" interview that lasted until four o'clock the next morning; he also supplied a 23-page memorandum about the origins of the GI Bill. Bolte's book, *The New Veteran* (Reynal & Hitchcock, 1945), is a moving exposition on the origins and philosophy of the AVC. The Hearst papers' role in passage of the GI Bill, and the political infighting, are detailed in a series of articles, "I Saw the GI Bill Written," by David Camelon in *The American Legion Magazine* (September, October and November 1949).

Two extraordinarily critical—and readable—studies of the American Legion are in *The Inside Story of the Legion*, by Justin Gray (Boni and Gaer, 1948); and *Back Home* by Bill Mauldin.

School & Society, a magazine for educational administrators, was invaluable for insight into how colleges planned for the postwar years, and especially "The Place of the College in Educating the Veteran for Civilian Life" by Paul Klapper (March 24, 1945); "Education and the Older Veteran" by Henry G. Kobs (February 23, 1946); "To What Extent Will Colleges Adjust to the Needs of Veterans?" by Loren S. Hadley (February 23, 1946); "They Know What They Want" by Nicholas M. McKnight (December 21, 1946); "The College Versus the Veteran" by Frederic W. Ness (December 21, 1946); "A New Angle in Higher Education" by Doris P. Merrill (February 1, 1947); and "The Veteran Flunks the Professor: A GI Indictment of Our Institutions of Higher Learning" by S. N. Vinocour (April 7, 1947).

*Undocumented Mexican workers arrested on a train
in Los Angeles in the 1950s*

The Bracero Program and Undocumented Workers

JUAN RAMON GARCÍA

Americans of Mexican ancestry occupy a special place in our ethnic history. Unlike blacks and American Indians, the first Mexican-Americans were neither brought here in chains nor conquered in battle; they became Americans by treaty. After the Mexican War (1846–48), the Treaty of Guadalupe Hidalgo transferred thousands of Mexicans and Indians from the jurisdiction of Mexico to that of the United States. The terms of the treaty provided for protection of their rights and claims, but, as is so often the case in matters of this sort, they found themselves deprived of promised lands and resources by the Anglo population.

As the southwestern territories of the United States began to organize themselves for statehood, people of Mexican ancestry stood at a distinct disadvantage. They had three characteristics that automatically made them subject to discriminatory action by the dominant society: many were of mixed "racial" ancestry (Spanish and Indian), the majority spoke little or no English, and they were overwhelmingly Roman Catholic. These features of the population delayed the acceptance of New Mexico as a state for fifty years.

As the settlement of the Southwest by people from the eastern states increased, so did the need for unskilled labor, both in agriculture and in construction. The primary source of that labor which was not supplied domestically was the northern states of Mexico. Immigrants have been pouring across the border from Mexico to fulfill the demand for labor for over a hundred years, and any history of Mexican-Americans has to deal with both the long-settled population and the constant stream of migrants north.

Immigrants worked in the expanding agricultural lands in Texas and California, toiled in the mines of the West, provided the majority of laborers in railroad construction around the turn of the century, migrated farther northward into the sugar-beet fields of Colorado and Idaho, and supplied industrial workers in the expanding factory cities of the upper Midwest. Their traditional life-style and apparent acceptance of oppressive working conditions made the Mexican immigrants seem like an ideal source of labor for the rapidly growing economy of the West in the early twentieth century.

After the upheavals of revolution in Mexico in the early part of this century, migration to the United States increased significantly, and more of the newcomers sought permanent residence here. Most of the work they found was temporary and low-paying. Many joined the stream of migratory farm workers, which deprived them of any opportunity to become economically stable or politically influential. Many others found themselves among the ranks of the urban poor, segregated on the edges of the cities of the Southwest and the West Coast, where they met with widespread social, economic, and political discrimination, particularly in Texas and southern California.

As is the case with other minority groups in recent years, the Mexican-Americans have formed protest organizations and political movements. In some areas of high concentrations, Chicanos (as Mexican-Americans like to call themselves) have wrested political control from the Anglos. The successes of Cesar Chavez and the United Farm Workers union movement among agricultural workers have inspired migrant workers and their allies throughout the United States to attempt to organize in order to combat some of the worst aspects of agricultural labor.

In attempts both to control the flow of immigration and to protect the Mexican workers in the United States, the government of Mexico has from time to time entered into contract labor agreements with the United States. In these agreements, Mexico promised to supply a certain numbers of workers, primarily for southwestern agriculture, for periods of up to six months; the United States government promised, among other things, to see to it that proper wages were paid and that living and working conditions were tolerable. They also agreed to try to lessen discrimination.

An agreement of this sort was set up in the early days of the Second World War. *Braceros* (as the contract workers were called) would be used to replace American workers engaged in the war effort. Along with the braceros, many thousands of "undocumented" Mexicans entered the United States illegally to benefit from the higher wages being offered here. In his study of the mass deportation of these "illegals" in 1954, Juan Ramon García of the University of Michigan at Flint describes the plight of both the braceros and the undocumented workers during and just after the war years. It is clear from his study that the United States government was doomed to fail in its attempt to regulate the conditions of farm labor—as it has continued to fail in this area up to the present time.

CONTRACT LABOR PROGRAM AND ILLEGAL IMMIGRATION

T he unregulated exodus of Mexican workers was not a new problem for Mexico. Mexican nationals had been entering the United States for decades, and the flow was increased with the completion of railroad lines to the northern frontier during the regime of Porfirio Diaz. The flow continued unabated during the 1920s, when the southwestern United States experienced an agricultural and railroad building boom that required large amounts of cheap labor. Because of immigration restrictions against Asians and East Europeans, employers increasingly turned to the readily available supply of Mexican laborers.[67]

In the late 1920s and early 1930s, Manuel Gamio, a noted Mexican sociologist who was deeply involved in the study of Mexican emigration, charged that the wholesale emigration of Mexicans to the United States was detrimental to Mexico, primarily because it drained the nation of its best working population. As an alternative he proposed the creation of a contract labor arrangement whereby Mexicans would go into selected agricultural regions of the United States for seasonal work. As part of the arrangement such workers would be covered by written guarantees and supervised by both governments.[68] Although not adopted at the time, his ideas would have a strong influence on the Mexican government when it developed its contract labor program during World War II.

Mexico's plan to use the bracero agreement as a means of controlling the "wetback" influx was to prove unsuccessful. Numerous reports and scholarly studies have established the fact that the bracero program played a major role in causing increased "illegal" immigration to the United States.[69] With the onset of World War II and the signing of the bracero agreement, "the bracero program was as important a catalyst as the Revolution of 1910 in the first exodus"[70] in increasing the influx of "illegal aliens" into the United States.

The bracero program catalyzed the second exodus of Mexican emigrants in several ways. The program acted like a magnet, drawing thousands upon thousands of hopeful applicants to the recruiting centers. Usually contract workers returned with exciting tales of the money that could be earned in the United States. With each new harvest season, those who had participated in the program wanted to return to earn more money. Naturally their friends also wished to participate and applied as braceros. The end result was that the number of those applying for admission into the United States far exceeded the labor needs certified by the Secretary

[67] Juan R. García, *A History of the Mexican American People of Chicago Heights, Illinois* (Chicago Heights: Prairie State College, 1976), chapter 1.

[68] Manuel Gamio, *Mexican Immigration to the United States* (New York: Dover, Inc., 1971), pp. 177–82.

[69] For example, *see:* Leo Grebler, *Mexican Immigration to the United States: The Record and Its Implications*, Mexican American Study Project, Advance Report 2 (Los Angeles: University of California, 1966); Eleanor Hadley, "A Critical Analysis of the Wetback Problem," *Law and Contemporary Problems* 21 (1956): 334–57; Julian Samora, *Los Mojados: The Wetback Story* (South Bend, Ind.: University of Notre Dame Press, 1971); Lyle Saunders and Olen E. Leonard, "The Wetback in the Lower Rio Grande Valley of Texas," in *Inter-American Education, Occasional Papers*, vol. 7 (Austin: University of Texas, July 1951).

[70] Corwin, "Causes of Mexican Emigration," p. 567.

"The Bracero Program and Undocumented Workers." From *Operation Wetback: The Mass Deportation of Mexican Undocumented Workers in 1954*, by Juan Ramon García, pp. 35–61. Used with the permission of the publisher, Greenwood Press, a division of Congressional Information Service, Inc., Westport, Connecticut.

of Labor. It was estimated by Miguel Calderon, who held the office of Director General of Migratory Workers Affairs in the Department of Foreign Relations from 1947 to 1960, that only one out of every ten applicants ever received a contract.[71]

Needless to say, those who had made the often long, arduous, and expensive trip to the recruiting centers were generally reluctant to return home empty-handed if they were refused a contract, and many of them entered illegally.[72] In this way the bracero program acted as a pump primer for a second wave of Mexican emigration, both legal and illegal.

Another cause for increased entry of undocumented workers was the widespread practice of bribery in the bracero program. Because so many people in Mexico were destitute, a bracero contract very often meant the difference between starvation and survival. That this made the contract a very valuable document, Mexican officials were not slow to recognize. Further, the very mechanisms set up to operate the program in Mexico provided a great deal of opportunity for graft. For one thing one had to go through a prolonged process even to be considered for application. Potential braceros had to receive clearance from their local authorities that no labor shortage existed in that particular area and that men were free to make application for a contract. Without some sort of bribe to local officials, the chances of receiving clearance were slim. Once clearance was obtained, an individual had to make his way to one of the recruiting stations, which often required a great deal of time and expense, as most of the recruiting stations were located along the United States-Mexican border. This worked a particular hardship on bracero applicants from the densely populated central plateau region of Mexico, which would provide the majority of braceros throughout the life of the program. For example, during the period from 1942 to 1954, the states of Durango, Zacatecas, Guanajuato, Jalisco, Michoacan, and Aguascalientes provided 74 percent of the braceros contracted by employers in the United States.[73]

By the time most Mexicans had reached a recruiting station they had paid a bribe of about fifty pesos to the Municipal President to be allowed to leave that particular municipality. Once at the contracting center the potential bracero had to pay some three hundred pesos to an official to gain admittance. Inside, Mexicans had to pass rigorous health inspections and run a gauntlet of quotas and security checks. Even before they had entered the United States, many Mexicans had already invested fifty dollars or more,[74] no mean sum when one stops to consider the extreme poverty of these people. For many, fifty dollars amounted to almost half a year's income.

Graft was widespread and, for those officials on the take, extremely lucrative. Various factors contributed to its prevalence, including the low salaries of officials, the refusal of many Mexicans to complain or file

---

[71] Personal interview with Manuel G. Calderon in November, 1969, Mexico City, cited in Campbell, "Bracero Migration," p. 93.

[72] Hadley, "A Critical Analysis," p. 344.

[73] Hancock, *The Role of the Bracero*, p. 21.

[74] Tomasek, "The Political and Economic Implications," pp. 180–81 and 190–91; Otey M. Scruggs, "The United States, Mexico, and the Wetbacks, 1942–1947," *The Pacific Historical Review* 30, no. 2 (May, 1961): 163.

complaints, and the fact that more money in the economy made the opportunities greater than ever. Oftentimes, those who could afford to pay the bribes were braceros who had already been to the United States and had set aside money to acquire another contract. Graft was so widespread that in 1952 President Adolfo Ruiz Cortines started a cleanup campaign that led to the temporary dismissal of some one hundred Mexican immigration inspectors, largely because of complaints by foreigners concerning bribery attempts.[75] Of course the mordida trade (another name for bribery) was so lucrative that many inspectors and officials continued to risk the consequences. By 1957 it was estimated to involve more than 72. million dollars annually.[76]

Many Mexicans who would have preferred to enter the United States legally were discouraged by the way the bracero system operated. Moreover, not even paying the bribes guaranteed that a contract would be awarded. After all, almost everyone else at the contracting centers had also paid a bribe to get there.

Following admission to a center, an indeterminate period was spent waiting to be examined and checked. After that more waiting, this time to be contracted. For every job opening there were ten to fifteen applicants or more. These people were forced to mill around in large waiting areas, sleeping outside and eating whatever food they could afford.[77] This situation created headaches for local and federal officials in the Mexican government. It also aroused the ire of certain segments of the Mexican press, who criticized the government for its conflicting bracero politics and its inability to provide for the economic well-being of its citizens.[78]

In spite of the lack of shelter, food, and proper sanitation facilities, and temperatures that often exceeded 100° during the day, the great majority of Mexicans waiting to be contracted comported themselves so well that officials in border towns like Mexicali and Chihuahua sang their praises. For example, even though some 17,000 men were waiting for a contract in Chihuahua, Salvador Razura, manager of the Chamber of Commerce of Retailers of Chihuahua, commented that although many of the hapless braceros were hungry and lacked the money to buy food, they nonetheless behaved themselves, "so that I cannot do other than praise them."[79]

Officials recognized that when cities having recruiting stations became crowded with men hopeful for contracts a potentially explosive situation was created. Yet they also realized that these men were only seeking to

[75] New York Times (2 April 1954), p. 2.

[76] Hispanic American Report, no. 10 (November 1957), p. 520.

[77] Record Group 166, Foreign Agricultural Service, Box 299, Folder on Mexican Labor, 1950–1948, National Archives, Washington, D.C. (hereafter cited as R.G. 166, Box 299, Mexican Labor Folder, 1950–1948, N.A.); the author was also provided with a special box of materials and documents dealing with Mexican labor from 1946 to 1949, no Record Group Number, National Archives (hereafter cited as Box on Mexican Labor, 1946–1949, N.A.).

[78] Gustavo Duran de la Huerta, "17,000 Campesinos Sin Abrigo Ni Comida Luchan Por Emigrar," Excelsior (1 June 1951); Robert L. Ghisi, "Inhumana Explotacion Han Hecho Con Los Braceros Contratados," article in the Mexicali Daily ABC (6 September 1951); Robert L. Ghisi, "Transportation Como Bestias Desde Guadalajara, A 25,000 Braceros," ABC (7 September 1951).

[79] de la Huerta, "17,000 Campesinos," Excelsior (1 June 1951).

better their lot and that if local officials could not house and feed them then the least they could do was to treat them with as much courtesy, kindness, and respect as possible.

Not only were aspirants for contracts subject to harsh climatic conditions or physical hardships, but they also often became the victims of unscrupulous "coyotes" who preyed upon their meager personal or financial holdings with the promise of a contract. Local officials did what they could to control this form of exploitation, but individuals were either afraid to testify or refused to identify culprits for fear of jeopardizing their chances for a contract—a contract that more often than not never materialized.

At times even the system served to discourage individuals, for even though the government tried to establish an orderly method of assigning contracts by issuing numbers to men as they arrived, the numerical ordering was usually not adhered to, through bureaucratic bungling or bribery or both. And so it continued until the contracting period ended, when the governor of the state would take the necessary measures to dislodge from the city those who had not been contracted.[80]

Because of such conditions, entering illegally proved to many an easier and far less expensive way to come to the United States. Through illegal entry many Mexicans avoided the numerous bribes, the waiting, anxiety, and bureaucratic red tape. Others entered illegally because they learned that if one had been in the United States before then the chances of getting a bracero contract were much better, a situation which will be discussed in more detail later.[81]

From the outset the Mexican government had been opposed to opening recruiting stations along the border. In 1942 it had opened a recruiting station in Mexico City, D.F., but found it was not prepared to deal with the mass of humanity that poured into the city in search of contracts. Within a very short period Mexico City's population had increased by about 50,000. Lacking the public facilities to house or feed the applicants, officials decided to move the centers away from Mexico City.[82] In 1944 centers were opened in Guadalajara and Irapuato, while in 1947 centers operated in the cities of Zacatecas, Chihuahua, Tampico, and Aguascalientes.[83]

Between 1942 and 1950 the majority of recruiting stations operated away from the border regions, which presented a point of controversy between Mexico and the United States because the latter, moved by grower pressure, consistently argued for centers located along the border. Both countries based their stance on well-defined economic interests. On the one hand, Mexico realized that border recruiting would hurt the large commercial growers along its own northern frontier by drawing potential laborers to the United States. Such a shortage of labor would force Mexican growers to pay higher wages if they were to be competitive with wages in the United States.[84] Mexico also wanted to limit the number of braceros

[80] Department of State, Washington, Foreign Service Dispatch (7 September 1951), Subject: "Arrival and Processing of Mexican Agricultural Workers at Calexico, California, under the Migrant Labor Agreement of 1951," located in R. G. 166, Box 299, Mexican Labor Folder, 1950–1948, N.A.

[81] Scruggs, "The United States," p. 163.

[82] Galarza, Merchants, p. 52.

[83] Ibid.

[84] Ibid., pp. 56–57 and 77.

who emigrated in an effort to operate the program more efficiently and to keep the demand high for braceros in the United States. Finally, from Mexico's perspective, if recruiting centers were located along the border then the probability of illegal entry by uncontracted applicants would be dramatically increased.

The United States, on the other hand, wanted recruiting centers along the border because contracting braceros would prove cheaper and more convenient for Americans. Under the agreement, first the government and later the employer was responsible for paying the cost of a bracero's transportation and meals from the recruiting center and back. The further the center was from the border the greater the expense. Congressional supporters of the program were quite sensitive to expenses as it cost hundreds of thousands of dollars to operate the program every year. The government and growers wanted to shift this expense to the applicants by making them pay their way to contracting stations along the border,[85] and supporters of the program hoped thus to alleviate some of the criticism about the high operating cost of the program from some individuals in Congress.

In August of 1950 Mexico reversed its position against border contracting stations when it opened centers at Hermosillo, Chihuahua, and Monterrey, which provided United States employers with all the braceros they needed. Mexico also acquiesced to the continued legalization of Mexicans who had emigrated illegally and dropped all demands for an entry cutoff date for those who were to be legalized. In essence this marked a triumph for proponents of the open border, reflecting the fact that for the moment Mexico's bargaining strength was at low ebb. Aware of the implications and ramifications that news of this might have in Mexico, the Mexican government requested that publicity concerning this concession "be restricted."[86]

Though one of the purposes of the bracero program had been to curb illegal entry, this purpose was never achieved.[87] In 1952, a spokesman for the National Agricultural Workers Union, which represented the small farmer, made the following statement:

> Agreements with the Republic of Mexico for the legal entry of 45,000 to 200,000 contract workers each year since 1942 . . . acted as a magnet drawing hundreds of thousands to the border from deep in the interior of Mexico. When the worker arrives at the border and finds that he cannot be accepted as a legal contract worker . . . it is a relatively easy matter to cross the 1,600 miles of practically unguarded boundary. Once in the United States there are always employers who will hire them at wages so low that few native Americans will accept. Thus legal importation of Mexicans has created the vicious situation now prevailing.[88]

[85] Ibid., p. 57; and Craig, *The Bracero Program*, p. 82.

[86] Kirstein, "Anglo over Bracero," pp. 170–71.

[87] Hancock, *The Role of the Bracero*, p. 66.

[88] U.S. Congress, House, Committee on the Judiciary, *Hearings before the President's Commission on Immigration and Naturalization*, 82d Cong., 2d sess., September and October, 1952, pp. 41–42. This union, a strong opponent of the illegal influx, consistently pointed to the bracero program as the chief cause of the great increase in the number of illegal entrants. National Agricultural Workers Union *Proceedings: Seventh National Convention of the National Farm Labor Union* (Memphis, 1951), Resolution 2.

Subsequent figures have borne out such allegations. There were nearly 856,000 recorded expulsion cases in the last half of the 1940s as against a little over 57,000 in the first half of that decade. Deportation cases rose to 70,505 in the latter half of the 1940s as compared to 17,078 in the earlier period.[89]

In examining the statistics on the number of braceros, one can find further proof of the bracero program's impact in bringing about illegal immigration. As the number of braceros increased there occurred a concomitant rise in the number of illegal entries (see figure 1). Chihuahua, the largest state in Mexico, was the greatest supplier of braceros to the United States.[90] During the period from 1951 to 1964, however, the state of Guanajuato supplied the most braceros. During this period Guanajuato provided 12.91 percent of 567,514 braceros, Jalisco 10.59 percent, Michoacan 10.55 percent, Chihuahua 9.89 percent, Zacatecas 8.87 percent, and Durango 8.87 percent. (Table 5) For this eleven-year period these six states provided about 65 percent of all braceros.[91]

Figure 1
Number of Mexican undocumented persons and
contract laborers in the United States,
1941–1956

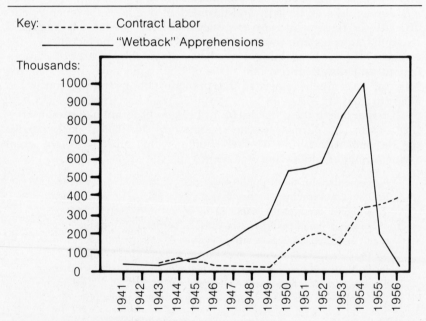

Key: ----------- Contract Labor
        _____ "Wetback" Apprehensions

Source: Records of U.S. Immigration and Naturalization Service

[89] Grebler, *Mexican Immigration*, p. 32.
[90] Hancock, *The Role of the Bracero*, p. 3.
[91] Gloria R. Vargas y Campos, *El Problema del Bracero Mexicano* (Mexico: Universidad Autonoma de Mexico, 1964), Table 7; and Mexico, Direccion General de Estadistica, *Anuarios estadisticos*, 1962/1963 and 1964/65 (distributed by Somerset House, Teaneck, New Jersey). The reader should note that percentages will vary among different authors.

Table 5
Numbers of Braceros, by State of Origin,
1951–1964

State	Total Number	Percentage of the Total
Mexico	4,395,622	—
Aguascalientes	80,970	1.84
Baja California	21,078	.48
Campeche	1,256	.03
Coahuila	191,074	4.34
Colima	12,190	.28
Chiapas	1,473	.03
Chihuahua	434,938	9.89
Distrito Federal	44,431	1.01
Durango	386,260	8.78
Guanajuato	567,514	12.91
Guerrero	133,821	3.04
Hidalgo	33,712	.77
Jalisco	465,396	10.59
Mexico	79,288	1.80
Michoacan	463,811	10.55
Morelos	38,376	.87
Nayarit	46,660	1.06
Nuevo Leon	185,311	4.22
Oaxaca	126,453	2.88
Puebla	63,381	1.44
Queretaro	50,853	1.16
Quintana Roo	75	—
San Luis Potosi	211,703	4.82
Sinaloa	42,546	.97
Sonora	44,527	1.01
Tabasco	16,032	.37
Tamaulipas	56,652	1.29
Tlaxcala	29,430	.67
Veracruz	10,802	.25
Yucatan	47,285	1.08
Zacatecas	390,061	8.87

Sources: 1951–1960 Oficina Central de Trabajadores Emigrantes cited in: Gloria R. Vargas y Campos, "El problema del bracero mexicano" (Ph.D. diss., Universidad Nacional Autonoma de Mexico, 1964), table 7. 1961–1964 *Anuarios Estadisticos*, 1962/63–1964/65.

Approximately 94 percent of all braceros employed went to the states of Texas, California, Arizona, New Mexico, and Arkansas. Of these, California and Texas employed the greatest number of braceros. The remaining 6 percent were divided among twenty-four other states.[92]

The majority of undocumented workers came from the very Mexican states that provided the majority of the bracero population. It is also significant that the American states that contracted most of the braceros were the same states that contained the largest proportions of undocumented workers.

[92] Craig, *The Bracero Program*, pp. 130–31; and Hancock, *The Role of the Bracero*, p. 3.

The state of Texas had a bad reputation among Mexican officials and Mexican citizens in general because of its preference for hiring "illegals," its early and blatant violation of bracero contracts, and its discriminatory practices against people of Mexican descent. These activities had led Mexico to blacklist Texas from 1943 to 1947, but even after Texas was removed from the list and was permitted again to contract Braceros, word had gotten out about conditions there. Even as late as 1951, while thousands of braceros awaited contracts in towns along the border, their tendency was not to accept a contract in Texas. As some braceros put it, they preferred to work in the United States because most of them knew they would be paid fairly well. With regard to treatment, the truth was "that with the exception of Texas," most of the places they went to treated them fairly well and only those who "misbehaved" were "punished."[93]

It appears that for the most part Texas employers were little fazed by the blacklisting and regarded the imposition of contracts for hiring Mexicans as burdensome, bureaucratic, and unjust. Many of them preferred to hire undocumented Mexican workers, the majority of whom came from the states of Guanajuato, Jalisco, Michoacan, Zacatecas, and San Luis Potosi.[94] Generally speaking, when Texas employers did hire legally contracted braceros, they often violated contract guarantees. When this happened, dissatisfied braceros either complained to officials or they "skipped" their contracts. If a bracero "skipped" his contract then he was classified as an "illegal alien" by immigration authorities.

"Skipping" one's contract meant that, once in the United States, a bracero left his assigned employer and struck out on his own to seek employment elsewhere.[95] The majority of those who "skipped" were forced into doing so by a variety of reasons and circumstances, although the most frequent causes cited were abuse, exploitation, violation of contract guarantees, or a combination of these. Another factor involved in "skipping" was the character and background of the "typical" bracero.

Generally speaking most braceros were single and between the ages of 17 and 22 years of age, with the median age between 21.78 years.[96] Most of them came from communities with populations of 2,500 or less,[97] and largely belonged to the landless *jornalero* population. While not among the poorest of the poor, these people nonetheless felt compelled by economic circumstances to seek greater opportunity elsewhere.[98] Initially many of these rural *campesinos* migrated to urban areas in search of employment, thereby creating a surplus labor supply. Unfortunately many of them

[93] de la Huerta, "17,000 Campesinos," *Excelsior* (1 June 1951).

[94] Saunders and Leonard, "The Wetbacks," p. 30.

[95] Samora, *Los Mojados*, p. 39.

[96] Robert C. Jones, *Los Braceros Mexicanos en los estados unidos durante el periodo belico* (Washington, D.C.: Union Panamericana, 1946), pp. 29–42. According to the figures presented, 83 percent of the braceros contracted were under 24 years of age and 76 percent of those who were contracted were unmarried.

[97] According to Nathan Whetten nearly 65 percent of the Mexican people in 1940 lived in rural communities of 2,500 or less. By 1960 the percentage had dropped to 49 percent. Nathan Whetten, "Population Growth in Mexico," *Report of the Select Commission on Western Hemisphere Immigration* (Washington, D.C.: G.P.O., 1968), p. 175.

[98] Campbell, "Bracero Migration," p. 180.

lacked the necessary skills to work in industrial occupations and thus became braceros employed primarily in the agricultural sector.

Those who sought contracts as braceros were generally the more aggressive and more determined to improve their economic condition. With their decision to emigrate they had developed certain economic expectations with regard to the wages to be earned while braceros. As they struggled to obtain a contract and as the cost of obtaining a contract increased, so did their expectation that the returns would make the effort and the expense worthwhile. To bolster their expectations there were the ever-present "success" stories of those who had already been there.

The initiative, determination, and assertiveness displayed by many would-be braceros in search of a contract did not bear out the incorrect stereotypes of their docility and laziness. For the most part these men were not prepared to accept anything less than what had been promised or perceived as promised. The awarding of a contract renewed their hopes for a better life for themselves and their families. It also reinforced in many the obligation to repay those who had provided the money to travel to recruiting centers. Most, if not all, of these factors were generally at work when a bracero accepted a contract, and although a large number of them swallowed the bitter pill of disappointment in terms of earnings, there were those who refused to accept their fate at the hands of unscrupulous employers. It was from this latter group that the majority of "skips" came.

According to the 1942 Agreement, which was to serve as the prototype for all subsequent bracero agreements, contractors had to fulfill certain obligations to the braceros once they were employed.

> The contract, legally supported by the United States government, afforded the bracero the following guarantees: (1) payment of at least the prevailing area wages received by natives for performing a given task, (2) employment for three-fourths of the contract period, (3) adequate and sanitary free housing, (4) decent meals at reasonable prices, (5) occupational insurance at the employer's expense, and (6) free transportation back to Mexico once the contract period was completed.[99]

Other provisions stated that deductions were to be made from paychecks only for those items that appeared in the contract, that adequate employment records be kept, and that each individual's earnings be itemized each pay period.

Unfortunately, the bracero program was to be plagued by widespread evasion of regulations, which victimized those the program was designed to protect, in part because some of the requirements were vague or contained loopholes that created a wide margin for interpretation and evasion of responsibilities on the part of employers. Perhaps the greatest weakness lay in the area of compliance, where enforcement was at best patchy and at times almost nonexistent.

A common problem that caused dissatisfaction among braceros and consternation among Mexican officials was the lack of clarity over the so-called prevailing wage rate. As stated in the agreements, all legally con-

---

[99] Craig, *The Bracero Program*, p. 60.

tracted braceros were to be paid the "prevailing wage" of the area in which they were hired or a minimum of fifty cents, whichever was higher. On paper this sounded fair enough, but in reality there were at least two significant drawbacks. The first was that the "prevailing wage" was determined before the season began by the growers themselves.[100] This was advantageous to the growers as it kept wage levels as low as possible. Although these wage levels were either equal to or slightly higher than those paid to domestic migrants, the fact remained that the pay was not significant. An amendment to Public Law 78 in 1955 changed this practice. According to this amendment both employees and employers would negotiate with respect to the wages to be paid.[101] Nonetheless, wages never reached the level expected by the braceros or the Mexican government.

A second drawback was that the prevailing wage rate was extremely difficult to enforce, as it fluctuated from area to area. For the most part the size of the labor pool determined wage rates. In areas saturated with undocumented workers, wage rates were extremely low. For example, in 1950 the average wage for farm work in California was eighty-eight cents per hour. In Texas it was fifty-four cents per hour. In the lower Rio Grande Valley, an area highly saturated with "illegals," the wage was fifteen to twenty-five cents an hour.[102] Braceros assigned to low-paying areas were often dissatisfied, and many "skipped" in order to find better wage rates elsewhere.

In essence the minimum wage guarantee was a myth. According to Walter J. Mason, a member of the Legislative Committee for the American Federation of Labor, there appeared little hope that the issue would ever be resolved in favor of the worker. To support his views he cited the findings of Jerry Holleman who, as executive secretary of the Texas State Federation of Labor, had investigated conditions under which braceros worked. Holleman reported that:

> Most of the Mexican consular offices in the areas involved are reporting literally thousands of complaints in this minimum wage violation. There are more cases filed than the (Mexican) consuls can investigate. It may be years before they can process the cases already filed with them. The same complaints cover housing, bedding, cooking utensils, and so forth.[103]

Critics of program abuses charged that things had become worse when the United States had ceased being the major contractor in 1947. From that year until 1951 individual growers or their representatives were allowed to directly negotiate with and contract braceros. Thus the individual con-

---

[100] Hadley, "A Critical Analysis," p. 354.

[101] Ibid.

[102] Sheldon L. Greene, "Immigration Law and Rural Poverty: The Problems of the Illegal Entrant," *Duke Law Journal* 1969, no. 3 (June 1969): p. 479. This practice was not new to Mexico or Mexicans since minimum wages were set biannually by wage boards made up of government representatives, workers, and employers in the municipios of Mexico. Because of this, Mexico also had wage rates that differed from state to state. Campbell, "Bracero Migration," p. 146.

[103] Walter J. Mason to George Meany (18 October 1954), cited in U.S. Congress, House, Mexican Farm Labor Program, *Hearings Before the Subcommittee on Agriculture on H.R. 3822*, 84th Cong., 1st sess., March 1955, p. 160 (hereafter cited as *Hearings on H.R. 3822*).

tractor rather than the federal government was legally responsible for fulfilling the agreements in the contract. With the elimination of direct government supervision over working and living conditions, a plethora of abuses and violations arose.

While some braceros attempted to deal with employer-employee problems themselves, others turned to Mexican consuls for help and succour. Generally speaking, when consuls visited sites of alleged violations, they usually found evidence to substantiate bracero complaints.

For example, an inspection tour of camps in August of 1947 by the consul at Kansas City, Missouri, uncovered a series of contract violations. At one camp the consul found twenty-four nationals crowded into two wooden shacks measuring five meters by four meters. These shacks lacked proper ventilation and were in a state of complete neglect. The kitchen and dining area were "filthy," and the utensils used for cooking were "repellent for lack of cleanliness." To add to the distress of the men the camp lacked bathing and washing facilities.[104]

Inspection of other camps by this consul uncovered conditions worse than those he had encountered in the first camp. Workers in one camp complained of insults, abusive language, and brutal treatment on the part of the foreman, employees of the company, "and even at times by the representatives of the Department of Agriculture," some of whom were of Hispanic descent.[105] Workers complained to him that certain individuals had informed them that their contracts and guarantees meant nothing. Some stated that some of them had been threatened with expulsion from the camp or deportation if they got sick, were too exhausted to do the work, or protested against poor treatment, bad food, lack of work, or errors in their salaries.[106]

The consul heard similar complaints from workers at Montgomery, Minnesota, where some two hundred braceros were employed. Workers claimed that at times they had been forced to work from 15 to 19 hours a day and that the foreman frequently abused them. It was at this camp that the Regional Representatives of the Department of Agriculture had cancelled the contracts of five workers and had refused to pay for their return transportation after they had acted as co-spokesmen for the discontented workers. According to the consul, the Regional Representative had taken this action because he considered these men to be "agitators."[107]

Russek, who wrote a report based on his visits to some of the camps and on information provided by other consuls, placed much of the blame for the abuses on the Regional Representative, who, he said, had shown little sympathy for Mexican workers in the past. In fact his attitude was one of "a great deal of callousness" with regard to the plight of the braceros.[108]

---

[104] Note #6770, from Mexican Embassy to Department of State, 10 September 1947, in Record Group 244, Office of Labor, General Correspondence, 1947, Health Services 6, Box 114, Folder 3, Laborers, National Archives, Washington, D.C. (hereafter cited as Note #6770, R.G. 244, Box 114, Folder 3, 1947, N.A.).

[105] Ibid.

[106] Ibid.

[107] Ibid., p. 2.

[108] Ibid.

Another common complaint voiced by braceros was that they had not received full payment of wages by the contracting companies. Numerous letters written either by the braceros themselves or by their legal representatives to consuls or directly to the companies asked that back wages be forwarded. In many instances such pay failed to materialize.[109]

In 1947 Karl L. Zander, a public health engineer, complained to his director about budget cuts that would make it difficult for him to do an effective job in the Southwest. He stated that upon hearing of the legislative directive to liquidate the federally operated farm labor supply centers he immediately contacted the State Health Department and the California Division of Housing in order to ascertain whether or not they could handle the responsibility of administering this program. Both state agencies indicated to him that they were unprepared to do so.[110]

Zander believed it was a mistake to lease federally owned camps to local growers, because past experience had proven that they did little to keep up the facilities. He stated that even when the camps had been federally funded, supervised, and inspected they still suffered from substandard facilities and limited equipment.[111] He described many of the camps as battered by heavy use and in need of extensive repair. Furthermore, most of the housing available to California migrants was in the form of one-room cabins, shelters, or tents that contained an oil stove for cooking. Most of them lacked adequate food storage facilities, heating facilities, or running water. He was very critical of the federal migratory program, which, he said, "wreaked [sic] with reports (and) citations of sordid conditions," largely because of the dominant legislative influence of farm groups, who were primarily concerned "with the economics of crops and a cheap and ready labor market."[112]

Although Zander was complaining about problems encountered by migrants in Arizona and California and was opposed to the control of housing by growers, his statements are relevant, as most of these facilities would be leased by growers in order to house braceros.

Complaints concerning contract violations also emanated from the Mexican government itself. In 1949 Mexican officials objected to the actions of an individual who had repeatedly violated portions of the bracero agreement. According to the complaint, the Foreign Office in Mexico had had problems with this person in the past and because of these "held him in low esteem." Officials were loath to permit him to contract braceros as he was "regarded as a slave driver who on every occasion would not fail to take advantage of Mexican workers."[113] Because of this the Mexican government informed U.S. officials that they would no longer furnish

[109]Letters in Folder 3, Ibid.

[110]Karl L. Zander to W. T. Harrison, Medical Director, District No. 5, 1947, p. 3, in Record Group 224, Office of Labor, General Correspondence, 1947, Box 114, Health Services, Sanitation, Folder 7, National Archives, Washington, D.C. (hereafter cited as Zander Memorandum, R.G. 244, Box 114, 1947, Folder 7, N.A.).

[111]Ibid., p. 4.

[112]Ibid., p. 5.

[113]Airgram from Walter Thurston, American Embassy, Mexico, D.F., to Secretary of State, 26 August 1949, in Special Box, no Record Group, Folder, Mexico, 1949–1946, N.A.

braceros to an organization that allowed the individual in question to contract braceros.

Another common complaint voiced by Mexican officials concerned the tendency of growers to violate regulations governing the employment and placement of braceros. This was the subject of a complaint filed by Manuel Aguilar, a member of the Ministry of Foreign Affairs. Aguilar informed the American Consul Harwood Blocker that a private contractor had transferred the braceros encharged to him to another employer in Mississippi without authorization to do so. To make matters worse the employer who had accepted the braceros was a person blacklisted by the Mexican government for repeated contract violations.[114] According to Aguilar about twenty of the fifty-one men who had been sent to work for this person had "skipped" their contracts as a result of inadequate housing and cooking facilities and being overcharged for food.[115] Others had "skipped" after some of their colleagues had been incarcerated by this person after they had verbally protested the poor conditions in which they were forced to live. Because the U.S. government had failed to take necessary measures to protect these braceros, wrote Aguilar, his government had ordered the Mexican consul in Memphis, Tennessee, to cancel the contracts of the remaining braceros and see to it that they were turned over to an employer who would abide by the terms of the agreement.[116]

In several incidents U.S. officials charged with enforcing the contract agreements were accused by Mexican officials of not fulfilling these responsibilities and failing to cooperate with them. One such incident involved a representative of the U.S. at the El Paso contracting station. This official had not demonstrated any desire to cooperate with Mexican officials and had repeatedly exhibited negative feelings toward them whenever any problems concerning braceros arose.[117] He had refused to intervene on behalf of 2,500 braceros who had filed complaints and claims for back wages against the Trans Pecos Cotton Association. The fact that he had not even bothered to investigate their claims had resulted, according to Liciencado Miguel C. Calderon, Chief of the Department of Bracero Affairs, in considerable financial losses to those involved.[118]

The tone of Calderon's report about the lack of cooperation by this person reflected his anger and frustration. What particularly irked him was the poor attitude toward Mexicans this person had displayed. The actions of Mr. B., wrote Calderon, mirrored his belief that the Mexicans had no rights in the operation of the program. In fact he had voiced this

---

[114]Dispatch, to Department of State, from Mexico, D.F., 9 November 1950. Subject: "Braceros: Cancellation of Contracts," Record Group 166, Foreign Agricultural Service, Narrative Reports 1950–1954, Box 299, Mexican Labor Folder 1950–1948, National Archives, Washington, D.C. (hereafter cited as R.G. 166, Box 299, Mexican Labor Folder, 1950–1948, N.A.).

[115]Ibid.

[116]Ibid.

[117]Foreign Service Dispatch from American Embassy, Mexico, D.F., to Department of State, Reference to Embassy's Dispatch No. 1806 of 25 January 1952, Subject: Braceros: Incident, 1 February 1952, in Record Group 166, Foreign Agricultural Service, Narrative Reports 1950–1954, Box 299, Mexican Labor Folder, 1952–1951, National Archives, Washington, D.C. (hereafter cited as R.G. 166, Box 299, Mexican Labor Folder, 1952–1951, N.A.).

[118]Ibid., pp. 1–2.

opinion to several Mexican officials when he had decided to furnish braceros to some California growers in spite of their protestations. According to one representative Mr. B. had told them that he would furnish braceros to whomever he pleased, "with or without the authorization of the Mexican representative."[119] When one of the Mexican representatives asked that he at least check with Washington, Mr. B. replied: "What for? What can they do to me?" Exasperated by these remarks Mexican representatives asked how U.S. officials could expect them to work with anyone who had expressed himself in this way.[120]

Both Blocker and the State Department were sympathetic to Calderon's complaints, and the transfer of Mr. B. was arranged. The United States apologized for his actions, although no personal apology came from the individual involved. American officials asked that Lic. Calderon do them the favor of not making incidents of this nature the subject of future official correspondence. Instead the Embassy requested that matters such as these be taken up with them "unofficially," so that their handling could be accomplished more expeditiously. It is somewhat ironic that the U.S. Embassy asked the injured party to show his good faith by withdrawing his note of 2 February 1952, which asked for an official investigation and some satisfaction on the matter. Apparently Calderon was satisfied enough to acquiesce to the request.[121]

Much of the correspondence already alluded to points to the fact that lack of effective enforcement plagued the program. More often than not certain groups or companies were guilty of repeated violations, and the fact that sanctions were not imposed on them only encouraged continued violations on their part. Although Mexican officials repeatedly called for cancellation of contracts against groups, companies, or individuals, few if any were cancelled, even when such cancellation was clearly merited.[122]

Because of these widespread violations Mexico sought to regain closer control over the program by having both governments assume direct responsibility for the contracting of braceros again. To bolster its argument Mexico pointed to the increasing number of braceros who were "skipping" their contracts because of poor working and living conditions, violation of wage guarantees, and discriminatory practices in states such as Arkansas, Mississippi, and Texas.[123] Mexican officials, such as Manuel Tello from the Ministry of Foreign Relations, claimed that their offices were receiving more and more complaints from workers concerning contract violations. The lack of compliance made it imperative, in the eyes of Mexican officials, to revise the bracero agreement so that a new, more stringent contracting system could be implemented.[124]

---

[119] Ibid., p. 2.

[120] Ibid.

[121] Foreign Service Dispatch from American Embassy, Mexico, D.F., to Department of State, 26 February 1952, in R.G. 166, Box 299, Mexican Labor Folder, 1950–1948, N.A.

[122] Foreign Service Dispatch to State Department from American Embassy, Mexico, D.F., Dispatch No. 1187, 8 November 1951, R.G. 166, Box 299, Mexican Labor Folder, 1952–1951, N.A.

[123] Foreign Service Dispatch to State Department from W.K. Alshie, American Consul General, Mexico, D.F., Dispatch No. 1135, 31 October 1951, ibid.

[124] Foreign Service Dispatch from Manuel Tello, Mexico, D.F., to Department of State, Dispatch No. 1, 2 July 1951, ibid.

Although it appears that both governments attempted to play down incidents, violations, and abuses because of political and diplomatic reasons, they could not keep information concerning these problems from leaking out. In Mexico the opposition seized upon this information and used it to attack the program and the government for its failure to provide adequate protection for braceros. The opposition also criticized the weak economic structure that forced people to leave their homeland in search of work.

The program and its accompanying abuses, particularly in Texas, also drew fire from critics in the United States. Pauline Kibbe, a member of the Texas Good Neighbor Commission, an organization established in the aftermath of Mexico's blacklisting of that state in the early 1940s, called the program "bankrupt" and a "shocking disgrace to the entire country." She charged the agencies responsible for enforcement with "open connivance with private interests" and said that the violations and the insults against Mexico on the part of these agencies could not be "overlooked or condoned."[125] According to Kibbe, Texas had been negligent in rectifying the unsavory conditions under which Mexicans had labored and had too long hidden behind the battle cry of states rights, which to her was merely a "smoke screen for bigotry, avarice, (and) failure."[126]

In 1952 the Most Reverend Leo F. Dworschak wrote that farmers in his area appeared to have no sense of responsibility towards braceros or any other workers they brought in. He remarked sadly that "in some instances they provide better care for their cattle than they do for 'their workers.'"[127]

Archbishop Robert E. Lucey of San Antonio was not surprised to receive such information as that found in Reverend Dworschak's letter. A strong advocate of rights for migrant workers, Lucey was a consistent critic of the bracero program. Although on several occasions he criticized the program because it provided contract guarantees to aliens instead of domestic migrants, he nonetheless realized that braceros were not that much better off. In a letter to Reverend Matthew Kelly, the Archbishop wrote that Reverend Kelly had been too "kind" in his remarks concerning the bracero agreement before a senate committee. Kelly had credited the agreement with providing braceros with proper housing, adequate pay, and humane treatment. The truth of the matter was, wrote Lucey, that "the housing is sometimes pretty atrocious and a wage of fifty cents an hour is pretty far below a decent income."[128]

Lucey complimented Kelly for his testimony concerning the abuses of migrant workers and told him that his appearance was an honor to the Church. "We cannot deny," concluded Lucey, "that in times past too many of our priests and practically all of our laymen were silent about the obvious

[125] Pauline R. Kibbe, "The Economic Plight of Mexicans," *Ethnic Relations in the United States*, ed. Edward C. McDonagh and Eugene S. Richardo (New York: Appleton-Century Crofts, Inc., 1953), p. 106.

[126] Ibid., p. 197.

[127] Most Reverend Leo F. Dworschak (Auxiliary Bishop of Fargo, North Dakota) to Most Reverend Robert E. Lucey, 27 October 1952, letter in Archbishop Robert E. Lucey Papers, Notre Dame Archives, University of Notre Dame, South Bend, Ind. (hereafter cited as Lucey Papers, N.D. Archives).

[128] Archbishop Robert E. Lucey to Reverend Matthew Kelly, July 1954, p. 1, Lucey Papers, N.D. Archives.

crimes committed in our country in industry and agriculture."[129] Not all Catholic priests felt as Lucey did. Earlier Lucey had received a preliminary report from Reverend James A. Hickey, a member of the Diocese of Saginaw, Michigan, who said that seminarians were cautioned "to avoid entanglements with the farmers and (sugar) companies. . . . We feel it best to stress the religious character of the work rather than get into arguments over housing, etc."[130]

Yet members of the Catholic hierarchy in the United States believed that they should get more involved in the temporal problems and needs of their Mexican parishioners, for they were well aware of the fact that the Protestants had begun to make inroads into the Mexican community. That is one of the reasons that the Bishops Committee on the Spanish Speaking was formed in 1945.

Various Protestant denominations had been actively involved in proselytizing among Mexican migrants for years, although the number of converts had not increased dramatically. Nonetheless some ministers took a keen interest in the plight of the Mexicans, especially when growers or contractors abused them. One such complaint was voiced by Father John F. Godfrey, pastor of the Ascension Church in Chesterfield, Missouri, who wrote to Secretary of Agriculture Mitchell about the abuse of Mexican nationals by a local employer. In his letter Godfrey charged that "very few of the agreements in the work contract" were being observed by the contractor. He wrote that his church had made repeated efforts to get the braceros, whom he described as humble and hard-working, to attend church services on Saturday and Sunday. After some coaxing several of the braceros had come to the church dressed in ragged clothes. Most of them arrived barefooted, while others simply had tied old pieces of auto tires to their feet. Godfrey, who was moved by their poverty, complained that the company did everything that it could to keep the braceros from church. Even though their contract did not require them to work on weekends, Godfrey explained, many of them were afraid to refuse work in order to attend services. Those who chose to attend often found themselves locked out when they returned to the compound. On other occasions the church vehicle was not allowed to pick up braceros so that they might participate in church activities. To Godfrey this situation was the "worst form of slave labor and denial to our Mexican neighbors of the fundamental rights of our country especially the right of religious freedom."[131] Informed of these conditions, Mexican authorities investigated the situation and shortly thereafter refused to contract any more braceros to this particular employer.

Another strong critic of the program and its abuses was Ernesto Galarza, a labor activist, who at this time was serving as Director of Research and Education for the National Agricultural Workers Union. Galarza had long been an advocate of social legislation for domestic migrants and,

[129] Ibid., pp. 1–2.

[130] "A preliminary report on the work of Mexican 'Chaplains' for Migrants in the Michigan Area," p. 3, from Reverend James A. Hickey, Diocese of Saginaw, to Archbishop Robert E. Lucey, 8 July 1953, in Lucey Papers, N.D. Archives.

[131] Father John F. Godfrey to James P. Mitchell, 23 November 1953, R. G. 174, Department of Labor, Box 54, Mexican Labor Program, Miscellaneous Folder, National Archives, Washington, D.C.

although he was sympathetic to the plight of braceros, he believed that the program served to undermine labor-organizing efforts among migrants and delay the passage of laws designed to help migratory workers. Galarza, a meticulous scholar, published a pamphlet in 1956 entitled *Strangers in Our Fields*, in which he exposed the widespread abuse suffered by braceros. In his pamphlet Galarza attacked those who exploited braceros, criticized government agencies for their lack of enforcement, and attempted to discredit the arguments of those who defended the program on a variety of levels. The contents of the pamphlet, based on interviews with braceros and examination of reports, statistics, and other relevant documents pertaining to the bracero program, elicited much attention. Most of it was critical in nature and emanated from the targets of Galarza's pen. Critics charged him with exaggeration, poor research, and character assassination. Several angry letters were fired off to different senators and congressmen and a few to the Secretaries of Agriculture and Labor demanding that they refute the charges or force Galarza to retract his statements.[132] Of course the latter proved an unrealistic and unworkable request, and Galarza's pamphlet was widely circulated.

Strangers in Our Fields addressed itself to issues that plagued the program and contributed to the "wetback" influx. Galarza charged that the wages paid braceros were insufficient to meet their normal living needs.[133] According to him, braceros were required to pay $12.50 per week for room and board. This amount was deducted from their wages whether they worked or not. Although $12.50 represented the maximum that could be deducted under contract guidelines, Galarza stated that in most cases the maximum became the minimum charged in the camps.

Other charges and costs further served to reduce bracero earnings. Braceros were required to pay between 69 cents and one dollar per week for premiums on nonoccupational insurance negotiated for them by the Mexican government. Yet in spite of insurance premiums, braceros complained that medical attention was costly and at times difficult to get. When injuries or disabilities did occur, braceros often found it difficult to collect on their health insurance.[134]

Depending upon the arrangements, braceros sometimes had to pay for their room and board separately. If this was the case, the most that could be charged for meals was $1.75 per day. As in the case of the maximum for room and board, $1.75 became the minimum charged.[135]

Again, braceros found the food not to their liking. In many cases the food was carelessly prepared, sometimes rancid, and not enough to satisfy their appetites.[136]

Another abuse concerned the wages paid. As growers often did not bother to post wages, braceros seldom knew exactly how much they were

[132] Correspondence in Record Group 174, Box 140, Department of Labor, Mexican Labor Program Folder, July-December 1956, National Archives, Washington, D.C.

[133] Ernesto Galarza, *Strangers in Our Fields* (Washington, D.C.: Joint United States-Mexico Trade Union Committee, 1956), p. 35.

[134] Rocco C. Siciliano, Assistant Secretary of Labor, to Estes Kefauver 6 July 1956, in R.G. 174, Box 140, Mexican Labor Program File, July-December 1956, N.A.

[135] Galarza, *Strangers*, p. 30.

[136] *Los Braceros*, pp. 97–99.

earning, and it was not surprising that many found themselves short-changed when they were paid. This and other violations of contract guarantees were reported by the Reverend Joseph H. Crosthwait during a trip through the western states on behalf of the Bishop's Committee for the Spanish Speaking. According to Crosthwait, records of working hours were not properly kept in many instances. "I have seen certificates of men I knew were all working twelve hours a day and who were being credited and paid for six or seven hours of work."[137] Braceros he questioned were aware of this. When asked why they did not complain to the employer, they responded that they did not want to be sent back until they had made a little money.[138] Crosthwait argued that the basic rights of freedom of speech had been denied to these braceros and that he had encountered these violations not only in California but also in other contracting states he had visited. In his opinion, these men were being treated worse than animals. "The very setup of the Program tends to herd them into a mass of nonentities."[139]

All of this worked to the detriment of the bracero and ate away at his earnings, which were meager to begin with. If, according to Galarza, a bracero had a contract for a period of 45 days,

> with a wage rate of 70 cents per hour and assuming steady work of 48 hours a week, a National will have $79.05 deducted from his total earnings, leaving an average of little over $20.00 a week. If he is paid 90 cents an hour he may expect to average, on a full work week, $29.70.[140]

From this amount a bracero set aside $10.00 per week to send to his family in Mexico. Subtracted from this was about $2.50 per week required for such needs as clothing and cigarettes. The tight budget on which braceros lived left no room for other deductions for work equipment such as gloves, blankets, or other needs. Many braceros also had to earmark about $5.00 from their weekly earnings to repay money they had borrowed to finance their trip.[141] Given this situation it is little wonder that many braceros decided to break their contracts and strike out on their own. Those who endured the contract period often did not return as braceros the following year. Instead they decided that the expense, the trouble, and the potential earnings were not really worth the effort and the investment and instead opted for entering illegally.[142]

In spite of the numerous complaints, growers and contractors generally believed that there was little to fear from government reprisals. The

---

[137]Excerpts from Report of Field Trip to the Western States by Reverend Joseph H. Crosthwait, Field Representative, Bishop's Committee for the Spanish-speaking, October 1957, BCSS File, Annual Report, Lucey Papers, N.D. Archives.

[138]Ibid.

[139]Ibid.

[140]Galarza, *Strangers*, pp. 35–6.

[141]Ibid.

[142]There were braceros who felt that the contract was worth it. As the program continued, growers began recontracting many of the same braceros who had worked for them in previous seasons. There soon emerged a group of "professional" braceros who were repeatedly contracted, which served to reduce the number of new contracts available. Those unable to receive contracts because they were superseded by these "professionals" also entered illegally. Campbell, "Bracero Migration," pp. 103–4.

size of the program alone and the vast area involved tended to preclude strict enforcement. For example, in California the Division of Housing had some 4,818 camps of all types under its jurisdiction in 1953, some 1,200 camps short of the estimated number of camps in operation. That year the Division of Housing was able to inspect 2,375 camps, leaving 2,443 camps not inspected. If the actual number of camps operating in California is taken into account, the number of camps uninspected rises to 3,625.[143] Given the lack of inspections, there is little wonder that growers often failed to meet contract standards in working and living conditions.

The agency charged with enforcing the contract agreements was the Labor Department. Its compliance officers were charged with the responsibility of enforcing contract agreements and were empowered to deny contract labor to any employer who violated any of the guarantees or who abused or exploited braceros. They were also required to remove braceros from growers who used "wetback" labor, or during domestic migrant strikes. Unfortunately the job required a greater amount of manpower than the Department of Labor had or was prepared to furnish.

In the postwar period the Department of Labor had only ten to twenty compliance agents to enforce contract agreements and to investigate violations. Hampered by a lack of personnel, the department was not effective in fulfilling its role as a compliance agency, nor did it on occasion carry out its responsibilities with much zeal. For example, in several instances the Border Patrol offered some assistance by furnishing compliance agents with lists of employers who had been caught using "wetbacks," but the Department of Labor continued to allow these employers to use contract workers.[144] Critics of the program were not slow to point this out, charging the department with a conflict of interest as the Secretary of Labor had the responsibility of assuring that the use of Mexican workers would not adversely affect the wages and working conditions of domestic migrants while also certifying that a bona fide shortage of domestic workers existed before braceros could be contracted.

The problem was that grower associations set the prevailing wage, which was usually low. Most domestic migrants found that they could not earn a decent living on such wages and thus refused to work. In this way the growers themselves had created a labor shortage by offering low wages and the Department of Labor was, in a sense, forced to declare that a labor shortage existed and permit the importation of braceros.[145] Representatives of the Labor Department at times admitted that this was the case

---

[143] Galarza, *Strangers*, p. 26.

[144] Tomasek, "The Political and Economic Implications," p. 132.

[145] U.S., Congress, House, *Congressional Record*, 83d Cong., 2d sess., 1954, 100, pt. 2: 2432; President's Commission on Migratory Labor, *Migratory Labor in American Agriculture* (Washington, D.C.: G.P.O., 1951), p. 62; Ellis W. Hawley, "The Politics of the Mexican Labor Issue, 1950–1965," *Agricultural History* 40, no. 2 (July 1966): 169. Hawley states that contrary to outward appearances, the Department of Labor was not really a hostile agency with regard to the growers. Although the United States Employment Agency was charged with certifying labor shortages, it was only a coordinating agency for the state services and their farm placement divisions. The crucial day-to-day decisions were made on the local and state levels where employer influence was strong. It was usually certain that labor shortages would be certified so that growers and their associations would be eligible for braceros.

but added that the problem was not a simple one. According to Robert C. Goodwin, determining whether Mexican workers adversely affected the wages of domestic migrants was extremely difficult, because adverse effects occurred slowly and were not often discernable until the passage of more than one crop season. Even then, Goodwin concluded, it was difficult to prove that the foreign workers were the sole cause, as other intangible and unexpected factors such as climate, crop yields, earnings, competitive employment, and technological changes also influenced wage rates.[146] Goodwin nonetheless admitted that there had been a relative decline in domestic wage rates, particularly in those areas where braceros were employed.[147]

By 1951 the Department of Labor was responsible for covering thirty thousand growers and other employers who had contracted braceros, while the number of compliance men had grown only to fifty.[148] This apparent laxity in ensuring that contract guarantees were carried out and enforced frustrated groups and individuals concerned with the plight of braceros and their effect on domestic migrants.

In 1954 Jerry Holleman wrote that the Texas Federation of Labor had been unable to find any genuine sincerity of purpose in the administration of the bracero program. According to him, "The absence of a United States employment service compliance program and compliance staff has caused a complete breakdown in the International Migratory Labor Agreement. Practically all articles for the protection of the bracero are being flagrantly and openly violated."[149] To illustrate his point Holleman listed examples of failure to enforce the agreement. He noted the absence since April of 1953 of published blacklists providing the names of all contractors and growers who had been caught using "wetbacks." Failure to publish these lists, he said, was in clear violation of the terms of the agreement.[150]

Complaints of abuses were also forthcoming from the braceros themselves. They were among the first to point out that violation of contract guarantees was a major reason for the large number of "skips." An interview with Carlos Morales that appeared in the Washington *Daily News* in 1956 gave a clear indication of the plight of many Mexicans. Morales was a man who had seen both sides of the issue, as a bracero and as an "illegal," and the *Daily News* reporter referred to him as a "legal slave" who had worked on a Texas ranch. In the interview Morales indicated he would rather be a "wetback" than do it all over again the legal way. He was not alone in his feelings, he stated, for they were shared by thousands like him who believed they had been cheated by greedy American farmers and grafting Mexican officials and abused by tyrannical foremen.[151]

[146]Robert C. Goodwin to Secretary of Labor James P. Mitchell, December 12, 1956, R.G. 174, Box 140, Mexican Labor Program File, 1956, N.A.

[147]Ibid.

[148]Tomasek, "The Political and Economic Implications," pp. 226–27.

[149]*Hearings on H.R. 3822*, p. 159.

[150]Ibid.

[151]Don McLean and Walter Wings, "U.S. Farms Breed Wetbacks?" clipping from *Washington Daily News* (19 November 1956), p. 30, found in R. G. 174, Box 140, Mexican Labor Program File, 1956.

Morales spoke of his hopes of earning sixty dollars for three month's work, and of the forty-eight dollars he paid for a work contract, a contract that was supposedly free. He described his long wait in the courtyard with about fifteen thousand other hopeful workers.

> If your name is called, you may have a job. Sometimes it costs still more money to get your name called. If it is called you take a physical. After that someone pats your back, someone shakes your hand . . . it is all so friendly, you think the first time. Actually, they are finding out if your back is strong and your hands rough, as if they were buying a horse.[152]

Those interviewed by Galarza were simply expressing what men such as Morales and others had experienced as braceros. Although happy to have a contract, they found that its promises were far greater than its actual benefits. Experience proved to them that the contract had little value when it came right down to guaranteeing their rights. As one bracero told Galarza, the boss was not interested in what it said. In the words of one contractor, the contract was "a filth of a paper. If you want to see how useless (it is) try to tell somebody about it."[153] The same bracero told Galarza that he was the first person they had spoken to who was willing to listen. To him the sheep in the adjoining field were better off, for they had a shepherd to watch over them and a dog to protect them. "Here" the bracero concluded, "it is one bite after another. They bite your wages and they bite your self love."[154]

Different authors have questioned Galarza's study, claiming that the abuses were not as widespread as he asserted[155] or that although grievance procedures were inadequate, most of the guarantees were fairly well kept.[156] Others have pointed to the fact that most braceros who were interviewed held positive views about their experiences in the United States and made little or no reference to abuses and violations.[157] Yet their findings are subject to question for several reasons. One reason is the official records and statements of officials on both sides of the border and of braceros themselves that speak of the myriad violations that were never investigated because of indifference, political reasons, or lack of sufficient staff. There was the blacklisting of Texas by the Mexican government after World War II because of widespread violations and acts of open discrimination. So flagrant were the latter that popular weeklies and newspapers in Mexico carried numerous articles and editorials on the subject of American racism. One such weekly was the Mexican *Mañana*, which referred to the Texans as Nazis who, though "not political partners of the Fuhrer of Ger-

---

[152] Ibid.
[153] Galarza, *Strangers*, p. 79.
[154] Ibid., p. 18.
[155] Hancock, *The Role of the Bracero*, p. 126.
[156] Tomasek, "The Political and Economic Implications," p. 75.
[157] Norman D. Humphrey, "The Mexican Image of Americans," *Annals of the American Academy of Political and Social Science* 295 (September 1954): 116; William H. Form and Julius Rivera, "Work Contracts and International Evaluations," *Social Forces* 37 (May, 1959): 334–35; Campbell, "Bracero Migration," p. 276.

many," were nevertheless "slaves to the same prejudices. . . ."[158] Even Hart Stillwell, a popular novelist, was moved to comment on the widespread discrimination extant in his home state when he wrote:

> We can bring ten thousand Tipica Orchestras to Texas and send five thousand Rotary Clubs and Kiwanis Clubs . . . into Mexico, yet so long as the Mexican knows that he may be killed with impunity by an American who chooses to kill him, then all our talk about being good neighbors is merely paying lip service to a friendship we both know is a joke.[159]

There is also the fact that for the most part the interviews were held with braceros who had served the full length of their contract terms. Braceros who had been returned or who had "skipped" appear not to have been interviewed.

Further supporting Galarza's work are the findings of the so-called *Secret Study* written during the administration of Harry S. Truman. This report, based on State Department files and correspondence, identified five critical problem areas affecting the bracero program up until that time, including numerous violations committed by Texas employers with regard to recruiting, wages, general living conditions, and the utilization of undocumented workers; the failure of the United States Employment Service to enforce certain wage requirements and its tendency to favor agribusiness; numerous violations of Article 9 of the 1949 Agreement, which guaranteed braceros work for three-fourths of their contract; employers returning braceros to Mexico without first notifying the appropriate authorities; and the unjust encarceration of Mexican braceros following an incident in the town of Tivoli, Texas.[160] Finally, adding further credence to Galarza's studies, there was the increasing number of braceros who "skipped" yearly because of widespread dissatisfaction with their treatment at the hands of unscrupulous growers. These "skips" often felt frustrated, for it was difficult to even begin to demand their rights. Those who were willing to complain often found their efforts thwarted by insensitive bureaucrats, by a complex grievance system, or by the very brevity of their contract term. Of the three obstacles, the latter two proved the most discouraging.

For example, if one filed a complaint and action was taken, the bracero was in danger of losing a lot of valuable time in processing the complaint and seeing it to its conclusion, which reduced his time in the fields and curtailed his earning capacity. Other braceros believed it did little good to complain. One described how fifty of them had stopped work in the fields one day in order to protest. The bracero said that one among them who could speak English spoke on behalf of the others. He told the foreman that they did not wish to strike, but that they wanted either eight hours of work or free board if conditions allowed them to work only one or two

---

[158]Carey McWilliams, *Factories in the Fields* (Boston: Little, Brown, 1939), pp. 270–71, citing *Mañana*, p. 21.

[159]*The Texas Spectator* (11 October 1946), p. 21.

[160]*Secret Study*, n.d., report housed in the David H. Stowe Papers, Truman Library, Independence, Mo. (hereafter cited as *Secret Study*).

hours. The foreman assured them that he would look into the matter, and they returned to work. The following day the braceros noticed that the man who had spoken for them was not around. They were told that if they would not do the work for what they received, then there were plenty more to take their place.[161] The bracero stated that he had read his contract, but that it was not worth the trouble to insist that the terms be observed. "Here the contract has no value," said the bracero.[162] Another bracero who spoke with Galarza put the issue more succinctly. "Eight times I have been in the United States, four times as a wetback and four times as a bracero. . . . The new ones without any experience have the illusion of the contract, but not me. When you come as a bracero it passes the same as when you come as a wetback."[163]

Increasingly this became the attitude of many braceros, who either "skipped" or returned as "illegals." Rather than complain and protest, many braceros voted with their feet. Contract skipping became a frequent occurrence in many camps, and the growing numbers of "skips" attested to the poor conditions in the camps and to the belief by braceros that the grievance procedure of the Bracero Agreement was of little value. In skipping out many braceros expressed their basic agreement with the Department of Labor official who stated that "the National cannot change jobs freely, thus seeking better conditions or higher pay."[164] In the eyes of many braceros the undocumented worker had more freedom to do just that. Unfortunately the plight of the undocumented worker was little better, and more often much worse.

There exist no accurate figures as to the number of braceros who "skipped" their contracts, yet their numbers were sufficient enough to concern officials in the United States. A report to the Secretary of Labor written in 1953 stated that in addition to "wetbacks" there were "hundreds of abscondees from contracts."[165] According to Rocco C. Siciliano, Assistant Secretary of Labor, the percentage of "skips" during the period from July 1951 to July 1953 was about 4.4 percent, or about 8,000 out of some 180,000 braceros sampled.[166] In later testimony Siciliano stated that the number of "skips" was fairly substantial, ranging anywhere from 15 to 20 percent.[167] Nonetheless Siciliano inferred at this time that the fault lay not with the growers but rather with the Mexican braceros who set out on their own in an effort to make better wages. He made no mention of what may have been the root causes of the problem, which were employer abuse, exploitation, and contract violations.

Opponents of the program were not as hesitant to discuss the problem of bracero "skips" as were government officials. In testimony before a

[161] Galarza, *Strangers*, p. 18.

[162] Ibid.

[163] Ibid.

[164] Ibid.

[165] Bureau of Labor Standards, "The Migratory Labor Story, 1953," report prepared for Secretary of Labor (July 1953), Folder 10, Box 78, A72–8, Dwight D. Eisenhower Library, Abilene, Kansas.

[166] Ibid.

[167] Ibid.

Senate Committee in 1952, reference was made to a study conducted in 1951 concerning the number of braceros who had not completed their contract terms. Of the 30,200 Mexicans involved in the study, 5,466 had left their employers because of dissatisfaction. Another 6,122 had returned of their own volition to Mexico before the end of their contract period. All told, 39 percent of the 30,200 braceros had broken their contracts.[168]

In 1954 Walter Reuther complained to Secretary of Labor Mitchell that as a result of gross abuses and violations "thousands" had "skipped" their contracts and had entered the "industrial areas, swelling the ranks of the several million illegal entrants estimated to come here each year."[169] In that same year the Executive Council of the American Federation of Labor stated that "wetbacks" and braceros were both part of the same problem, as evident from the fact that "thousands of contracted aliens have either 'skipped' their contract or have continued to live in the United States after the expiration of their contracts. In either case they have automatically become 'wetbacks' who work and live at the mercy of easy-money employers or unscrupulous labor contractors."[170]

While accurate figures do not exist as to the number of braceros who actually "skipped," the fact remains that those who did "skip" often did so because of real or perceived unfair treatment at the hands of their employers. Inadequate and cumbersome grievance procedures also tended to encourage "skipping," for in pursuing the grievance procedure the bracero was bound to lose, either through lost time and wages or by the loss of his job.

It was also not unusual to find employers who encouraged braceros to "skip" their contracts and return illegally to them. Growers were loathe to release braceros whom they had trained to perform skill-related work, as those braceros might not be available for the next contracting period. Through this arrangement braceros could avoid an uncertain fate at contracting centers, and growers were assured of the renewed services of individuals who were of value to them.[171] This arrangement also saved growers the cost of bracero contracts, which after 1949 ran as high as fifty dollars per contract.[172]

---

[168]U.S., Congress, Senate, *Migratory Labor Hearings* before the subcommittee on Labor-Management Relations of the Committee on Labor and Public Welfare, 82d Cong., 2d sess., 1952, pt. 1:888.

[169]Walter P. Reuther to James P. Mitchell (11 January 1954), Record Group 174, Box 54, Mexican Labor Program-Miscellaneous (January-June), National Archives, Washington, D.C.

[170]Harvey A. Levenstein, *Labor Organizations in the United States and Mexico: A History of Their Relations* (Westport, Ct.: Greenwood Press, 1971), p. 209.

[171]Corwin, "Causes of Mexican Emigration," p. 568.

[172]It appears that on occasion employers were given to extreme practices in protecting their investments. Fully aware that "skipping" was on the increase, some growers took the precaution of placing armed guards in the camps and fields to prevent runaways. Ted Le Berthon, "At the Prevailing Rate," *Commonweal* 67 (1 November 1957): 123. Similar precautions had been taken during the 1920s by labor contractors when they chained braceros together and delivered them under armed guard to the depots for transporting to their assigned areas. Victor S. Clark, "Mexican Labor in the United States," *Bulletin of the Bureau of Labor*, 17, no. 78 (Washington, D.C.: Bureau of Labor, 1908): 471–75.

Conclusion

In discussing the ways in which the bracero program contributed to the illegal influx, this chapter raises a number of questions about the operation of the program. For example, if widespread abuse did exist, why did so many braceros crowd into contracting stations seeking a contract? Why did so many others return year after year as contracted braceros? Of the many questions raised about the program perhaps these are the most difficult to answer, and one must rely largely on speculation in attempting to answer them.

Existing records seem to leave little doubt that abuse, exploitation, and violations did occur. The sheer size of the program and the numbers involved precluded strict enforcement of the contract agreements. Those braceros who complained often found their grievances unanswered or thwarted. Others elected to "skip" and strike out on their own in hopes of finding better jobs and wages and greater opportunity, yet they soon found that they were subject to even greater exploitation as "illegals." Thus the majority of Mexicans, whether happy with their lot as braceros or not, decided to fulfill their contract obligations. While the wages and the living and working conditions were not what they had been led to expect, they were for the most part tolerable.

Those who stayed did so out of a sense of obligation to those they had left behind and to those they owed money to. Most had been unemployed or underemployed in Mexico, and as braceros they were at least working and eating. They also knew that acquiring a contract greatly improved their chances for renewal when the next contract period came about. Others stayed because they had little choice. They understood neither the language nor the alien culture in which they found themselves. While conditions might not have been that good where they were, the uncertainty of what lay ahead should they leave was great enough to dissuade them from striking out on their own. Still others decided to take advantage of their contract to learn some English and to pick up whatever knowledge they could so that one day they might return and seek employment on their own. Some felt that they had put too much money and effort into getting contracts and therefore were loathe not to complete their terms as braceros. They therefore completed their obligation and chalked it up to experience. Also, there was the concept of "honor," wherein braceros viewed their acceptance of a contract as a bargain they were obligated to fulfill even if the other party could violate it with impunity. Of course, there were those whose employers abided by the contract rules and treated braceros with kindness and respect, which made the contract period worthwhile both economically and personally. Braceros fulfilled their contracts for various and sundry reasons. Certainly the same question can be asked as to why undocumented workers risked so much and endured such hardships for the meager sums they were paid.

The question also arises as to why Mexico repeatedly acquiesced to renewals of the contract labor program, given the plethora of problems that plagued it. Here the answer appears somewhat more clear.

The bracero program proved of tremendous economic benefit to Mexico, although official Mexican sources tended to play down the program's economic impact. Nonetheless figures indicate that Mexico's economy experienced growth during the 1950s and 1960s, much of which was due to tourism, broader transactions, and bracero remittances, all of which helped reduce Mexico's trade deficit with the United States.[173]

Conflicting figures exist as to the actual amount that Mexico received as a result of bracero remittances. It has been estimated that from 1942 to 1947 Mexico received $318 million from braceros. Of this, $118 million came as a result of the forced and voluntary savings sent to Mexico.[174] Another $31 million was brought back by returning braceros, while $106 million came from individuals who had entered without a contract.[175]

In 1952 it was estimated that bracero remittances totalled some $70 million.[176] Other sources stated that during the decade of the 1950s remittances ranged from $22 million to $120 million annually.[177] Mexico's statistics are at variance with these figures. Mexican sources listed remittances at slightly more than $200 million for the period 1954–1959.[178] In 1954 a nationwide survey of bracero earnings by the Mexican Bankers Association revealed that $67 million had been sent to Mexico through postal and bank money orders during the five-month peak of contracting. A report released by the Mexican Treasury Department in 1954 estimated that $67 million had been brought back by braceros, thus bringing the estimated total of bracero remittances for that year, which by the way represented the peak load for bracero contracting, to $134 million.[179]

Hancock estimated that between 1956 and 1957 braceros either sent back or took no less than $120 million dollars annually.[180] The U.S. Department of Labor estimated that braceros earned approximately $200 million in 1957, half of which went back to Mexico.[181]

Whatever the precise amount of the remittances, they were of crucial importance to Mexico's balance of payments.[182] Bracero remittances contributed between 1 and 2 percent annually to Mexico's national income

[173] Campbell, "Bracero Migration," p. 209.

[174] Prior to 1951 all braceros were required to deposit ten percent of their earnings into banks specifically designated by the Mexican government. The monies were held there until the braceros returned at the end of their contract period, to insure that the braceros saved some of their earnings and to discourage them from remaining in the United States after their contracts expired. This practice was discontinued after 1951.

[175] These figures are based on 52 percent savings figures. Pedro Merla, "El Bracero Mexicano en la Economia Nacional," *Revista del Trabajo* 3, no. 143 (December 1949): 9–10.

[176] "Wetback Flood," *Newsweek* 41, no. 21 (25 May 1953): 56.

[177] Craig, *The Bracero Program*, p. 17.

[178] Secretaria de Industria y Commercio, *Direccion General de Estadistica*, M. 19:422, 421; 12:112; 22:108; 23:168.

[179] A. C. McLellan, "Down in the Valley: A Supplementary Report on Developments in the Wetback and Bracero Situation of the Lower Rio Grande Valley of Texas Since Publication of 'What Price Wetbacks?'" (Austin: Texas State Federation of Labor, 1953), p. 3.

[180] Hancock, *The Role of the Bracero*, p. 37.

[181] U.S., Department of Labor, *Farm Labor Fact Book* (Washington, D.C.: G.P.O., 1958), p. 176.

[182] U.S., Congress, Senate, Committee on Appropriations, *Department of Agriculture and Related Agencies' Appropriations. Hearings before Subcommittee on H.R. 10509*, 90th Cong.; 1st sess., Fiscal Year 1968, pp. 55–57. A study completed three years after the bracero program ended showed that there was a substantial increase in the balance of payments in favor of the U.S. in those years following the end of the program.

(see table 6). The importance here is not so much the percentage but rather its "multiplier effect" on the national economy.[183] According to Henry P. Anderson, a strident critic of the bracero program, each bracero supported an average of six people, which placed the number of people dependent upon bracero earnings at two-and-one-half million people.[184] Thus, unlike other sources of foreign exchange, these remittances went directly to the most economically depressed groups (see table 7).

Because of the economic importance of the program, Mexico allowed it to continue through 1964. Mexican officials well realized that their country's economy could not keep pace with the demand for jobs and land produced by the tremendous population growth that Mexico was experiencing. They also knew that the impoverished state of many *campesinos* made them a politically and socially explosive force. The bracero program, along with increasing illegal emigration, served as a safety valve that relieved Mexico of some of its hungry and discontented populace. This exodus probably spared Mexico a great deal of social unrest and upheaval.[185]

Even if Mexico had discontinued the program at the end of World War II, it is quite doubtful that large-scale emigration to the United States could have been prevented. Mexico well realized that it could do little to stop the exodus. Faced with this reality, Mexico opted for a contract program. At least an international agreement, reasoned Mexican officials, would allow for some protection of their citizens while in the United States. If

Table 6
Bracero Remittances as a Percentage of
the Mexican National Income,
1954–1964

Year	National Income[a] (Billions of Pesos)	Bracero Remittances[b] (Billions of Pesos)	Percent
1954	64,432	938	1.46
1955	69,290	1,313	1.89
1956	75,470	1,613	2.14
1957	83,120	1,500	1.80
1958	88,560	1,463	1.65
1959	93,750	1,625	1.73
1960	101,150	1,400	1.38
1961	106,480	1,338	1.26
1962	113,570	900	0.79
1963	122,300	638	0.52
1964	137,200	588	0.43

[a]Real Terms, 1954 prices
[b]All figures rounded off.

Sources: Column 2, *Review of the Economic Situation of Mexico* 43,498 (May 1967): 11. Column 3, U.S., Department of Commerce.

[183]Campbell, "Bracero Migration," pp. 212–13.
[184]Henry P. Anderson, *The Bracero Program in California with Particular Reference to Health Status, Attitudes, and Practices* (Berkeley: School of Public Health, University of California, 1961), p. 17.
[185]Craig, *The Bracero Program,* p. 60.

Table 7
Average Remittance by Mexican Braceros, 1954–1964

Year	Dollar Amount	Peso Equivalent	Mexican Estimate
1964	264	3300	2026
1963	273	3413	2038
1962	369	4613	2038
1961	367	4588	1463
1960	355	4438	1425
1959	297	3713	1075
1958	270	3375	1025
1957	275	3438	957
1956	290	3625	1063
1955	263	3288	775
1954	243	3038	1125

Sources: Column 3, $1:12.50 pesos (all figures rounded off). Column 4, González Navarro, "Historia Demográfica," p. 411.

mass emigration seemed inevitable, then let it occur under government auspices.

What Mexican officials failed to realize was that they were not dealing solely with the government of the United States. They were also dealing with strong interest groups who considered the bracero program as their own domain and had long resisted government interference or control in agriculture. These officials also failed to recognize that their goals differed from those of the United States.

Generally speaking, Mexico can be credited with doing a good job in getting so many guarantees for its workers. Unfortunately they had little or no direct control over those who would contract workers. A contract could not change ingrained attitudes or historical relationships. For example, a pattern of caste relationships had developed in California between racial minorities such as Mexicans, Filipinos, and other Asian groups and the white population. To the white Californians who generally employed them, all field workers were social inferiors.[186]

Similar attitudes were perhaps even more evident in Texas, where Mexicans and white Texans had been in cultural conflict since the early part of the nineteenth century. The independence of Texas in 1836 and the end of the Mexican War in 1848 only served to intensify hatred between the two groups. Negative feelings and stereotypes hardened on the part of the "conquerors" and the "conquered." The Mexicans were viewed and depicted as either dirty, cowardly, bloodthirsty bandits or as ignorant, lazy, docile, childlike peasants who needed to be prodded along or cared for. These stereotypes tended to evoke feelings of hostility toward people of Mexican descent on the part of Anglo-Texans. Attitudes, stereotypes, and perceptions were slow to die; and the miserable conditions characterizing the lives of many Mexicans and Mexican Americans in the Southwest served only to reinforce negative views about them and their culture. Some perceived this situation as the natural order of things and resented anyone who attempted to change it. As one Texan expressed it: "As soon as you

[186]Stein, *California*, p. 60.

begin to Americanize a Mexican he's no longer any good. He just won't work anymore."[187]

In essence, a contract did not alter the fact that the braceros were Mexicans, a fact that determined in large part how the braceros were treated. Once braceros were contracted, employers generally reverted to the same practices of exploitation and abuse that have characterized much of the history of agribusiness in the Southwest. A contract without teeth and without enforcement mechanisms became just another piece of paper to most growers. It was, in most cases, a means to an end, with the end being a large supply of cheap labor.

While braceros theoretically had certain rights, in many ways they were no better off than the domestic migrants who suffered from many of the same abuses. Working and living conditions for both braceros and domestic migrants left much to be desired, although braceros did find themselves the objects of great concern on the part of their government while in the United States. The same was true of domestic migrants, whose cause was espoused by a vocal, although poorly organized and ineffective group of social-reform, labor, and religious advocates.

At the very bottom was the worker who had entered illegally. Living outside the law, he had no one to champion his cause. He had only those who sought to exploit him and those who sought to expel him. Of the three groups, bracero, domestic migrant, and undocumented worker, the last was the least understood and the most exploited.

[187]Hawley, "The Politics," p. 169.

Suggestions for Further Reading

William Manchester has provided an exhaustively detailed history of the years since 1932 in *The Glory and the Dream: A Narrative History of America, 1932–1972** (Boston, 1974). Frederick Lewis Allen followed his work on the 1920s, *Only Yesterday*, with a work on the 1930s, *Since Yesterday** (New York, 1940). Two popular histories of the depression that consist partly of recollections are Carolyn Bird, *The Invisible Scar** (New York, 1966), and Robert Bendiner, *Just Around the Corner: A Highly Selective History of the Thirties** (New York, 1967). David A. Shannon has edited a collection of documents detailing the social impact of the depression in *The Great Depression** (Englewood Cliffs, N.J., 1960). See also Milton Meltzer, *Brother, Can You Spare a Dime? The Great Depression, 1929–1933** (New York, 1969). A view of the American workingman during this period is given in Irving Bernstein, *The Lean Years: A History of the American Worker, 1920–1933** (Boston, 1961) and *The Turbulent Years: A History of American Labor, 1933–1941** (Boston, 1970).

The impact of the depression is measured in the essays collected by Bernard Sternsher in *Hitting Home: The Depression in Town and Country** (Chicago, 1970) and *The Negro in Depression and War: Prelude to Revolution** (Chicago, 1970). The long-term impact on children raised during the 1930s is analyzed in a unique longitudinal study by Glen H. Elder, Jr., *The Children of the Great Depression: Social Change in Life Experience** (Chicago, 1974). Robert and Helen Merrill Lynd returned to Muncie, Indiana, to measure the changes wrought by the depression, which they describe in *Middletown in Transition** (New York, 1937). An important demographic shift is outlined by Walter J. Stein in *California and the Dust Bowl Migration** (Westport, Conn., 1973). The classic statement on this westward migration is found, of course, in John Steinbeck, *The Grapes of Wrath** (New York, 1939). For the effects of the depression on Appalachia, see Harry M. Caudill, *Night Comes to the Cumberlands: A Biography of a Depressed Area** (Boston, 1963). Recollections of the depression have been compiled by Studs Terkel in *Hard Times: An Oral History of the Great Depression** (New York, 1970), also available in a two-disc, long-playing record album. Woody Guthrie's autobiography, *Bound for Glory** (New York, 1943), contains a great deal of material on growing up in the dust bowl and bumming around the country in the 1930s.

The classic study of the Dust Bowl region is *The Great Plains** (Boston, 1931) by Walter Prescott Webb. Paul Bonnifield has studied

*Available in paperback edition.

the Depression Dust Bowl in *The Dust Bowl: Men, Dirt, and Depression* (Albuquerque, 1979). The University of Kansas has explored various aspects of Great Plains life in Brian W. Blouet and Frederick C. Leubke (eds.), *The Great Plains: Environment and Culture* (Lincoln, 1979) and Merlin P. Lawson and Maurice E. Baker (eds.), *The Great Plains: Perspectives and Prospects** (Lincoln, 1980).

W. J. Cash, *The Mind of the South** (New York, 1941), is an impressionistic and insightful study of Southern life and culture. Among the studies of race relations in the South, the following were produced in the period of the 1930s and 1940s: John Dollard, *Caste and Class in a Southern Town** (New Haven, Conn., 1937); Allison Davis, B. G. Gardner, and Mary R. Gardner, *Deep South: A Social Anthropological Study of Caste and Class** (Chicago, 1942); Allison Davis and John Dollard, *Children of Bondage** (Washington, 1940); Arthur F. Raper, *Preface to Peasantry** (Chapel Hill, N.C., 1934); and three works by Charles S. Johnson, *Shadow of the Plantation** (Chicago, 1934), *Growing Up in the Black Belt** (Washington, 1941), and *Patterns of Negro Segregation** (New York, 1943). A later community study is Hylan Lewis, *Blackways of Kent** (Chapel Hill, N.C., 1955). Sharecroppers are the subject of a recent study by Pete Daniel, *The Shadow of Slavery: Peonage in the South, 1901–1969** (Champaign-Urbana, Ill., 1972). Ernest J. Gaines' fictional *The Autobiography of Miss Jane Pittman** (New York, 1971), a narration of one woman's experiences, gives a sympathetic and brilliant portrait of black life from the end of the Civil War to the present. Autobiographical episodes about growing up in the depression South are found in Richard Wright, *Black Boy** (New York, 1945). Ralph Ellison, *Invisible Man** (New York, 1952), one of the best American novels of the century thus far, provides useful information about various facets of black life.

The home front during the Second World War is described in *Don't You Know There's a War On? American Home Front, 1941–1945** (New York, 1970) by Richard R. Lingeman and *Days of Sadness, Years of Triumph: The American People, 1939–1945** (New York, 1973) by Geoffrey Perrett. For background on the veterans' bonus issue see Roger Daniels, *The Bonus March* (Westport, 1971). On education benefits for veterans, see Keith W. Olson, *The G.I. Bill, the Veterans, and the Colleges* (Lexington, Kentucky, 1974).

The issue of Mexican immigration to the United States in an earlier period has been explored in Mark Reisler, *By the Sweat of Their Brow: Mexican Immigrant Labor in the United States, 1900–1940** (Westport, 1976) and Lawrence A. Cardoso, *Mexican Emigration to the United States, 1897–1931: Socio-Economic Patterns** (Tucson, 1980). Different aspects of the bracero program are described in Ernesto Galarza, *Merchants of Labor: The Mexican Bracero Story** (San Jose, 1964) and Richard B. Craig, *The Bracero Program: Interest Groups and Foreign Policy* (Austin, 1971). A comparative study of migrant labor is found in Michael J. Piore, *Birds of Passage: Migrant Labor and Industrial Societies** (Cambridge, England, 1979). A recent series of essays on the question of Mexican immigrants edited by Arthur F. Corwin is *Immigrants—and Immigrants: Perspectives on Mexican Labor Migration to the United States* (Westport, 1978).

Contemporary Society

1960–Present

The suburban ideal: Willingboro (formerly Levittown), New Jersey

The Quality of
Suburban Life

HERBERT J. GANS

Although scholars have been writing for some time about the United States as an urban nation, as early as the 1920s, an important new demographic trend was noticed—the increasing growth of suburbs.

Before the advent of mass transportation facilities, the wealthy tended to live in the central city and the outlying areas were populated by the less wealthy and the poor. As the cities continued to grow, however, the older housing began to deteriorate, and the wealthy moved to newer, more fashionable urban neighborhoods, leaving the rundown areas to the working people and the poor. With the arrival of the first breakthrough in urban mass transit—the horse-drawn streetcar—some of the more well-to-do citizens decided to abandon the older portions of the city altogether for new, culturally homogeneous settlements on the periphery called suburbs.

In the 1880s a socialist critic had pointed out that "this modern fashionable suburbanism and exclusiveness is a real grievance to the working class. Had the rich continued to live among the masses, they would with their wealth and influence make our large towns pleasant places to live. . . ." What could not be seen at the time, of course, was the increased prosperity of the working classes that, along with the automobile, would make suburban living available to all except the poorest and most discriminated against among our citizens by the middle of the twentieth century.

By the 1920s, the rate of growth of the suburbs began to exceed that of the cities. The goal of almost every American family seemed to be the purchase of a single-family detached house in a suburban development. While many people moved to the suburbs to escape real or imagined perils in the city, most simply moved there because they found it a more congenial way of life.

Aided by federal legislation, suburban growth rocketed after the Second World War. Veterans Administration loans, Federal Housing Administration mortgage policy, and federally funded highway and road building all contributed to this development. In 1970, the census indicated that more people were living in the suburbs—defined as the metropolitan area outside the central city—than in the cities themselves. By 1972, the number of jobs was about equal in both areas. Thus we are rapidly becoming, not an urban nation, but a suburban one.

In the late 1950s, social critics began to find in suburbia the source of many of the ills they saw plaguing American society. And what one sociologist called the myth of suburbia emerged. The fault, the myth ran, lay in the homogeneity of both the population and lifestyle in the typical suburb. This sameness led to a mass culture and the apparent ethic of conformity that so concerned the critics.

As serious scholarly studies of suburban communities began to appear, however, it became evident that, no matter how much the critics deplored the quality of life in the suburbs, the people who lived there liked it. Herbert J. Gans, of Columbia University, a sociologist who had previously studied an urban working-class community, decided to analyze suburban life firsthand. When the famous builder William Levitt began a new suburban development of lower-middle-class housing near Philadelpha, Gans moved into the community and remained there for two years. During that period, he explored the inhabitants' reasons for moving to the community and their attitudes after settling in. His book, **The Levit-towners,** is a result of that study.

Gans' findings are most notable for their refutation of the suburban myth. With few exceptions, the people who moved to Levittown found there what they had expected to find, and consequently the level of satisfaction was quite high. In the selection from his book reprinted below, Gans discusses some of the questions raised by the critics about the relationship between suburban living and mass society. He describes the features of the life-style that have been scrutinized and found wanting by outsiders and reports that, rather than annoying the residents of the community, these very features make the community attractive. In closing, however, Gans notes that one segment of the population— the adolescent group—is generally dissatisfied with suburbia. He warns the residents of suburban communities that some steps should be taken to relieve teen-age discontent in order to prevent an increasingly dangerous generation gap, which might lead to undesirable consequences.

Leading with their assumption of homogeneity and conformity, many critics see the culture of communities like Levittown—those features transcending social life—as marked by sameness, dullness, and blandness. The image of sameness derives from the mass-produced housing, and also from the prevalence of a national and equally mass-produced culture of consumer goods which is extended to characterize the consumers themselves. Part of the critique is tinged with political fear that the national culture and the deleterious effects of conformity may sap the strength of local organizations, which will in turn break down the community social structures that act as barriers between the individual and the state. According to theorists of the mass society, the individual then becomes submissive and subject to demagoguery that can incite mass hysteria and mob action, destroying the checks and balances of a democratic society. This hypothesis, developed originally by Ortega y Gasset, the Spanish conservative philosopher who feared popular democracy, gained prominence during the 1930s when Hitler and Stalin systematically eliminated local organizations to forestall opposition to their plans. In America, this analysis has flowered with the increasing centralization of the federal government, but suburbia is considered particularly susceptible to the dangers of mass society because of the rootlessness and absence of community strength supposedly induced by the large number of Transients.[1] Other observers, less fearful of mass society, stress the blandness of suburban life, which, they fear, is producing dull and apathetic individuals.[2]

These charges are serious and, if accurate, would suggest that suburbia is a danger to American democracy and culture. Most of them, however, are either inaccurate or, when accurate, without the negative consequences attributed to them. Levittown is very much a local community; if anything, it neglects its ties to the larger society more than it should. It is not rootless, even with its Transients, and it is not dull, except to its teenagers. The critics' conclusions stem in part from the previously mentioned class and cultural differences between them and the suburbanites. What they see as blandness and apathy is really a result of the invisibility and home-centeredness of lower middle class culture, and what they consider dullness derives from their cosmopolitan standard for judging communities, which condemns those lacking urban facilities—ranging from museums to ethnic districts—that are favored by the upper middle class.

They also look at suburbia as outsiders, who approach the community with a "tourist" perspective. The tourist wants visual interest, cultural diversity, entertainment, esthetic pleasure, variety (preferably exotic), and emotional stimulation. The resident, on the other hand, wants a comfortable, convenient, and socially satisfying place to live—esthetically pleasing, to be sure, but first and foremost functional for his daily needs. Much of the critique of suburbia as community reflects the critics' disappointment that the new suburbs do not satisfy their particular tourist requirements; that they are not places for wandering, that they lack the charm of a medieval village, the excitement of a metropolis, or the architectural variety of an upper-income suburb. Even so, tourism cuts across all classes. A neighbor, returning from a trip to Niagara Falls, complained bitterly about commercialization, using much the same language as the critics do about suburbia. What he felt about the Falls, however, he did not feel about Levittown.

---

[1] See, e.g., Fromm, pp. 154–163; and Stein, Chaps. 9 and 12.
[2] This charge is made by Keats and, in more qualified and muted tones, by Riesman (1957).

We are all tourists at one time or another, but most communities can serve both tourist and residential functions only with difficulty. For example, the crowding and nightlife that attract the tourist to Greenwich Village make it uncomfortable for the resident. Although the tourist perspective is understandable, and even justifiable, it is not by itself a proper criterion for evaluating a community, especially a purely residential one like Levittown. It must be judged first by the quality of community life and culture it offers its residents; the needs of the tourist are secondary.

THE NATIONAL CULTURE AND THE COMMUNITY

To the outside observer, Levittown appears to be a community on which the national American culture has been imprinted so totally as to leave little room for local individuality. The houses express the current national residential style: pseudo-Colonial fronts borrowed from the eighteenth century glued on a variety of single-family house styles developed between the eighteenth and twentieth centuries, and hiding twentieth century interiors. Schools are all contemporary, modular, one-story buildings that look like all other new schools. The shopping center is typical too, although the interior is more tastefully designed than most. It consists mainly of branches of large national chains, whose inventory is dominated by prepackaged national brands, and the small centers are no different. The old "Mom and Pop" grocery has been replaced by the "7 to 11" chain, which, as its name indicates, opens early and closes late, but sells only pre-packaged goods so that each store can be serviced by a single cashier-clerk. Even the Jewish and Italian foods sold at the "delis" are cut from the loaf of a "pan-ethnic" culture that is now nationally distributed.

A large, partially preplanned residential development must almost inevitably depend on national organizations, since these are the only ones that can afford the initial capital investment and the unprofitable hiatus before the community is large enough to support them properly. This is as true of stores in a new shopping center—which sometimes wait years before they show a profit—as it is of churches and voluntary organizations. In addition, Levittown itself is in some ways a national brand, for the size of Levitt's operation in an industry of small entrepreneurs has made his communities a national symbol of low-price suburbia. This has helped to attract national organizations, as well as Transients who work for large national corporations. When they move into a new metropolitan area, they usually do not know where to find housing, and having heard of Levittown, are likely to look there first. The brand name "Levittown" makes the housing more trustworthy than a small subdivision constructed by an unknown local builder.

Although Levittown would thus seem to be, as much as any community in America, an example of Big Culture, this is only superficially true, for the quality of life in Levittown retains a strictly local and often anti-national flavor, exploiting national bodies and resources for strictly local purposes whenever possible. To the visitor, the Levittown houses may look like all other pseudo-Colonial ones in South Jersey, but Levittowners can catalog the features that distinguish their houses from those in nearby subdivisions. The stores may be chains selling brand-name goods, but the managers become involved in local activities and enable local groups to hold bazaars and other fund-raising affairs, including bakesales which compete with store merchandise. The same patterns obtain in voluntary associations and churches. For example, the Boy Scouts are run by an intricate national bureaucracy which sets detailed rules for the activities of local troops. Since the organization must attract children, however, what actually goes on at troop meetings bears little resemblance to the rules, and the less the national office knows, the better for it and the troop leader.

The priority of local concerns is even more emphatic in government, for federal agencies and national party headquarters are viewed mainly as sources of funds and power to be used for local needs. A civil defense agency was set up in Levittown, not to satisfy national regulations, but because the county civil defense director was running for political office. The national program provided him with an opportunity to distribute some funds to local communities, which in turn enhanced his political fortunes. Federal funds which came to Levittown for civil defense were used for local police and fire needs as much as possible within the limits of the law. Similarly, when the Township Committee in 1960 invited both Nixon and Kennedy to campaign in Levittown, its purpose was not to support the national candidates of the two parties but to gain publicity for Levittown.

Many Levittowners work in branch offices or factories of national corporations, and their reports about their work and their employers suggest that national directives are often viewed as outlandish and unreasonable, to be sabotaged in favor of local priorities. However much a national corporation may give the appearance of a well-run and thoroughly centralized monolith, in actual fact it is often a shaky aggregate of local baronies. The result is considerable skepticism among Levittowners about the effectiveness and power of national corporations, a skepticism easily extended to all national agencies.

Generally speaking, Levittowners do not take much interest in the national society, and rarely even see its influence on their lives. As long as they are employed, healthy, and able to achieve a reasonable proportion of their personal goals, they have no need for the federal government or any other national agency, and being locals, they do not concern themselves with the world outside their community. Indeed, they might better be described as *sublocals*, for they are home-oriented rather than community-oriented. Although the lower middle class is sometimes said to reject bigness, the Levittowners do not share this feeling. They do not scorn big supermarkets and national brands as do the critics, and although they do not see the big society very clearly, it appears to them as an inept octopus which can only cope with the community through force or bribery. It is opposed not because of its size, but because it is an outsider. When a national service club organized a branch in Levittown, one of the Levittowners said, "They are big and they can help us, but we don't have to follow national policy. . . . National headquarters is only a racket that takes your money." The cultural orientation toward localism is supported by more pressing sociological factors; if a local branch of a national association is to succeed, it must adapt itself to local priorities in order to attract members, and national headquarters must be opposed if it refuses to go along. The most disliked outsider is not the national society, however, but the cosmopolitan with his "Brookline values."

All this does not, of course, imply that the national society and culture are powerless in Levittown. When industrial giants set administered prices for consumer goods sold in the local shopping center, or when Detroit engineers the annual style change in its automobiles, the individual purchaser can only express his discontent by refusal to buy, and when it comes to necessities, he lacks even that choice. In Levittown, however, the discontent and the lack of choice are minimized, for most people have enough money to pay administered prices and enough freedom to choose among products. In fact, they find themselves well served by the corporations who sell them their housing, food, furnishings, and transportation. However, Levittowners are less concerned with "consumption" than the critics. They care less about the things they buy and are less interested in asserting individuality through consumer behavior, for they do not use consumption to express class values as much as the upper middle class does. They may not like mass-produced bread as well as the local bakery product they perhaps ate in childhood, but they do not make an issue of it, and do not feel themselves to be mass men simply because they buy a mass-produced item. Goods are just not important enough. Only when they become tourists are they "materialistic"—and traditional. One of my neighbors who was once stationed in Japan was not at all concerned about the national prepackaged brands sold in Levittown, but talked frequently about the commercialization of Japanese culture and the unattractive goods he found in the souvenir shops.

The Mass Media

For Levittowners, probably the most enduring—and certainly the most frequent—tie to the national culture is through the mass media. Yet even this is filtered through a variety of personal predispositions so that not many messages reach the receiver intact. Few people are dominated by the mass media; they provide escape from boredom, fill up brief intervals, and (perhaps most important) occupy the children while the adults go about their business.

The most frequently used mass medium is television, with newspapers, magazines, and paperback novels following in that order. In working class homes in Levittown as elsewhere, the TV set is likely to be on all the time, even when company comes, for as one Levittowner explained, "If conversation lags, people can watch or it gives you something to talk about." This statement suggests more the fears that working class people have about their social skills than their practice, for conversation does not often lag, at least among friends.

Middle class people, surer of their social skills, use television more selectively. The children watch when they have come in from play; after they are put to bed the adults may turn on the set, for television fills the hours between 9 P.M. and bedtime, when there is not enough of a block of time for other activities. A few favorite programs may get rapt attention, but I doubt that television supplanted conversation among either middle or working class Levittowners. There is no indication that television-viewing increased after people moved to Levittown, for no one mentioned it when interviewed about changes in spare-time activities. I suspect that viewing had actually decreased somewhat, at least during the time of my study, when gardening was still a time-consuming novelty for many people.

Television viewing is also a much less passive activity than the critics of the mass media suspect.[3] Routine serials and situation comedies evoke little response, although Levittowners are sensitive to anachronisms in the plots and skeptical of advertising claims.[4] Dramatic programs may provoke spirited—and quite personal—reactions. For example, one evening my neighbors and I watched an hour-long drama which depicted the tragic career of an introverted girl who wanted desperately to become a serious actress but was forced to work as a rock-and-roll dancer, and finally decided to give up show business. One neighbor missed the tragedy altogether, and thought the girl should have kept on trying to become an actress. The other neighbor fastened on—and approved of—the ending (in which the actress returned to her husband and to the family restaurant in which she had been "discovered") and wondered, rightly, whether it was possible to go back to a mundane life after the glamor of the entertainment world.

People do not necessarily know what they want from the media, but they know what they do not want and trust their ability to choose correctly. A discussion of television critics one night revealed that Levittowners read their judgments, but do not necessarily accept them. "The critics see so much that they cannot give us much advice," said one. "They are too different in their interests from the audience, and cannot be reviewers for it," said another.

Forty per cent of the people interviewed said they were reading new magazines since moving to Levittown; general-interest periodicals—*Life*, *Look*, *Reader's Digest*, *Time*, and the *Saturday Evening Post*—led the list. Only 9 of the 52 magazines were house-and-garden types such as *American Home* and *Better Homes and Gardens*, but then 88 per cent of the people were already reading these, at least in the year they moved to Levittown. Although not a single person said these magazines had helped in the decision to buy a home in Levittown, 57 per cent reported that they had gotten ideas from the magazines to try out in their houses, primarily on the use of space, furniture, and shrubbery arrangements, what to do about pictures and drapes, and how to build shelves and patios. The magazines provided help on functional rather than esthetic problems of fixing up the new house. People rarely copied something directly from the magazines, however. Most often, their reading gave them ideas which they then altered

---

[3]This cannot be surmised either from inferences about media content or from sociological surveys, but becomes quite evident when one watches TV with other people, as I did with my neighbors.

[4]I had observed the same reactions among the working class Bostonians I studied previously, although they were more interested in the performers than the Levittowners. Gans (1962a), Chap. 9.

for their own use, sometimes after talking them over with the neighbors. Similarly, people who adopted new furniture styles after moving to Levittown got their inspiration from their neighbors rather than from magazines, although all who changed styles (but only 53 per cent who did not) said they had obtained some hints for the house from the home and garden magazines.

The media also provide "ideas" for community activities, but these are altered by local considerations and priorities. For example, a few days after the Nixon-Kennedy television debates in 1960, candidates for township offices were asked to participate in a similar debate in Levittown. Everyone liked the idea, but after a few innocuous questions by out-of-town reporters, the debate turned into the traditional candidates' night, in which politicians from both parties baited their opponents from the audience with prepared questions. Sometimes, local organizations put on versions of TV quiz games, and honored retiring officers with a "This Is Your Life" presentation. A few clubs, especially Jewish ones, held "beatnik" parties, but since most Levittowners had never seen a beatnik, the inspiration for their costumes came from the mass media.

The impact of the media is most apparent among children; they are easily impressed by television commercials, and mothers must often fight off their demands on shopping trips. But the adults are seldom touched deeply; media content is always secondary to more personal experience. For example, people talked about articles on child-rearing they had seen in popular magazines, but treated them as topics of conversation rather than as possible guides for their own behavior. A neighbor who had read that "permissive" child-rearing was going out of style after thirty years had never even heard of it before, even though she had gone to college. I remember discussing Cuba with another neighbor, an Air Force officer, shortly after Castro confiscated American property there. Although he had been telling me endless and angry stories about being exploited by his superiors and about corruption among high-ranking officers, he could not see the similarity between his position and that of the Cuban peasant under Batista, and argued strenuously that Castro should be overthrown. His opinions reflected those of the media, but their content did not interest him enough to relate it to his own experiences. He did, however, feel that Castro had insulted the United States—and him personally—and the media helped him belong to the national society in this way. Indeed, the media are a message from that society, which, like all others, remains separate from the more immediate realities of self, family, home, and friends. These messages really touch only the people who feel isolated from local groups or who, like the cosmopolitans, pay close attention to the printed word and the screen image.

Levittown and the Mass Society

The Levittowners' local orientation will not prevent them from becoming submissive tools of totalitarian demagogues if, according to the critics of mass society, the community is too weak to defy the power of the state. Social scientists concerned about the danger of dictatorship have often claimed, with DeTocqueville, that the voluntary association is the prime bulwark against it. For example, Wilensky writes: "In the absence of effective mediating ties, of meaningful participation in voluntary associations, the population becomes vulnerable to mass behavior, more susceptible to personality appeals in politics, more ready for the demagogues who exploit fanatical faiths of nation and race."[5]

If Wilensky is correct, Levittowners should be invulnerable to mass behavior, for they have started about a hundred voluntary associations and 73 per cent of the two interview samples belong to at least one. Levittown should also be more immune than other communities, for about half of both interview samples reported more organizational participation than in the former residence.[6] The way they participate, however, has little consequence for their relation to the national society. The handful of leaders and really active people become familiar with the mechanics of organizational and municipal politics, but the rank-and-file members, coming to meetings mainly for social and service reasons, are rarely involved in these matters. Yet not even the active participants are exposed to national issues and questions, and they learn little about the ways of coping with the manipulatory techniques feared by the critics of mass society.

Nor does participation necessarily provide democratic experience. Organizations with active membership are likely to have democratic politics, but when the membership is passive, they are often run by an individual or a clique and there is little demand for democratic procedure. Nothing in the nature of the voluntary association would, however, preclude mob behavior and mass hysteria when the members demand it. The ad hoc groups that arose during the school budget fight and in the controversies over liquor, nonresident doctors, and fluoridation, often acted in near-hysterical ways. Admittedly, these were temporary organizations; permanent ones, conscious of their image, are more likely to refrain from such behavior and, like political parties, often avoid taking stands on controversial issues. They do inhibit mob action—or, rather, they refuse to be associated with it, forcing it into temporary organizations. Yet if the majority of a permanent group's membership is angry about an issue, it can act out that anger and even put its organizational strength behind hysteria. At the time of racial integration, a sizeable faction in one of the men's groups was contemplating quasi-violent protest, and was restrained as much by pressure from the churches, the builder, and some government officials as by cooler heads within the group.

Mob action and mass hysteria are usually produced by intense clashes of interest between citizens and government agencies, especially if government is not responsive to citizens' demands. If an issue is especially threatening and other avenues for coping with it are blocked, irrational action is often the only solution. Under such conditions, voluntary associations can do little to quell it, partly because they have no direct role in the government, but mainly because their impact on their membership is, in Wilensky's terms, not meaningful enough to divert members from affil-

[5]Wilensky, p. 237. See also Kornhauser, Chap. 3, and Lipset, pp. 66–67.
[6]Fifty-six per cent of the random sample and 44 per cent of the city sample reported more participation than previously.

iating with violent protest groups. Even national officers of voluntary associations can rarely control irrational actions by local branches, especially since these rarely come to "national's" attention.

The other relationships of the individual Levittowners vis-à-vis the national society are so indirect that it would be hard to pinpoint where and how the two confront each other. It would be harder still to convince the average Levittowner, locally oriented as he is, to change his stance. Unlike the aristocrat or the intellectual, who was once able as an individual to influence the national society and still attempts to do so, the Levittowners come from a tradition—and from ancestors—too poor or too European even to conceive the possibility that they could affect their nation. And unlike the cosmopolitans of today, they have not yet learned that they ought to try. As a result, the Levittowner is not likely to act unless and until national issues impinge directly on his life. When this does happen, he is as frustrated as the cosmopolitan about how to be effective. All he can really do is voice his opinion at the ballot box, write letters to his congressman, or join protest groups. In times of crisis, none of these can change the situation quickly enough, and this of course exacerbates threat, hysteria, and the urge toward mob action or scapegoating.

The national society and the state have not impinged negatively on the average Levittowner, however; indeed, they have served him well, making him generally content with the status quo. The Congress is dominated by the localistic and other values of the white lower middle and working class population, and since the goods and services provided by the influential national corporations are designed largely for people like the Levittowners, they have little reason to question corporate behavior. The considerable similarity of interests between Levittowners and the nationally powerful agencies, private and public, makes it unnecessary for the Levittowners to concern themselves with the national society or to delude themselves about the sovereignty of the local community.[7]

What appears as apathy to the critics of suburban life is satisfaction with the way things are going, and what is interpreted as a "retreat" into localism and familism is just ahistorical thinking. Most lower middle and working class people have always been localistic and familistic; even during the Depression they joined unions only when personal economic difficulties gave them no other alternative, becoming inactive once these were resolved or when it was clear that political activity was fruitless.[8] Indeed, the alleged retreat is actually an advance, for the present generation, especially among working class people, is less isolated from the larger society than its parents, less suspicious, and more willing to believe that it can participate in the community and the larger society. The belief is fragile and rarely exercised, but people like the Levittowners confront the national society more rationally than their ancestors did, and if the signs of progress

---

[7] In this respect, the Levittowners differed significantly from the residents of Springdale, a rural community in New York State, who developed a set of illusions to hide their dependence on state and national political and economic forces. See Vidich and Bensman.

[8] Part of the difficulty is that critics compare the present generation to the previous generation, that of the Depression, which was an unusual period in American history and no baseline for historical comparisons of any kind.

are few, progress has nevertheless taken place. Whether there has been enough progress to prevent the emergence of dictatorship in a severe national crisis is hard to tell, but certainly the Levittowners and their community fit few of the prerequisites that would make them willing tools of totalitarian leaders today.

TRANSIENCE AND ROOTLESSNESS

Part of the fear of mass society theorists and suburban critics alike is the transience of the new suburban communities and the feelings of rootlessness that allegedly result. About 20 per cent of Levittown's first purchasers were Transients, who knew even when they came that their employers— national corporations or the armed services—would require them to move elsewhere some years hence. Their impermanency is reflected in residential turnover figures which showed that in 1964, 10 per cent of the houses were resold and another 5 per cent rented, and that annual turnover was likely to reach 20 per cent in the future.[9] Not all houses change hands that often, of course; a small proportion are sold and rented over and over again.[10] Much of the initial turnover resulted from job transfers—55 per cent in 1960, with another 10 per cent from job changes.[11]

Whether or not the 15 per cent turnover figure is "normal" is difficult to say. National estimates of mobility suggest that 20 per cent of the population moves annually, but this figure includes renters. Levittown's rate is probably high in comparison to older communities of home owners, fairly typical of newer ones, and low in comparison to apartment areas.[12]

[9]There is no secular trend in turnover, however, for between 1961 and 1964 the rate in the first neighborhood increased from 12 per cent to only 14 per cent, but the third and fourth neighborhoods both showed turnover rates of 19 per cent in 1964. Renting occurs primarily because the softness of the housing market makes it difficult for people to sell their houses without a considerable loss; they find it more profitable to rent them, with management turned over to the local realtors.

[10]According to a story in the October 21, 1957 issue of Long Island's *Newsday*, 27 per cent of the first 1880 families in Levittown, New York, were still living there ten years later.

[11]Another 10 per cent left because they were unhappy in the community; 7 per cent, for financial reasons; 5 per cent, because of an excessive journey to work; and 4 per cent, because of death, divorce, or other changes in the family. These figures were collected from real estate men and people selling their homes privately and may not be entirely reliable. Real estate men may not be told the real reasons for selling and private sellers may have been reluctant to mention financial problems. However, only about 1 per cent of the houses were foreclosed annually.

[12]In the mid-1950s, when Park Forest was seven years old, annual turnover of homes was 20 per cent. See Whyte (1956), p. 303. In Levittown, New York, a 1961 study reported an average annual rate of about 15 per cent. See Orzack and Sanders, p. 13. In Levittown, Pennsylvania, the rate varied from 12 to 15 per cent between 1952 and 1960. See Anderson and Settani. A study of a forty-year-old English new town reported an annual rate of 10 per cent the first ten years, which has now dropped to 1 per cent. See Willmott (1963), p. 20. A study of 30,000 apartments in 519 buildings all over the country, conducted by the Institute of Real Estate Management and reported in the *New York Times* of November 10, 1963, showed an annual turnover of 28 per cent, and 35 per cent for garden apartments.

Conventional standards of "normal" turnover are so old and communities like Levittown still so new on the American scene that it is impossible to determine a normal turnover rate. Indeed, the need to judge turnover stems from the assumption that it is undesirable; once there are sufficient data to test this assumption, the concept of normal turnover can perhaps be dismissed.

The crucial element in turnover is not its extent but the change in population composition and its consequences. If the departing Transients and Mobiles are replaced by Settlers, then turnover will of course be reduced. Early in the 1960s, the second buyers were, however, also Transients, who needed a house more quickly than the builder could supply it, as well as people of lower income (probably Settlers) who could not afford the down payment on a new house. If more of the latter come to Levittown over the years, the proportion of lower-status people in the community will increase, and there may be fears of status loss among those of higher status. Although such fears were rare during my time in the community, they existed on a few blocks and may account in part for the strong reactions to status-depriving governmental actions that I described earlier.

Despite the belief that Transients do not participate in community life, in Levittown they belonged to community organizations in considerably larger numbers than Settlers did, partly because of their higher status.[13] More of them also reported increased participation after moving to Levittown than did Settlers.[14] They were, however, likely to list fewer people with whom they visited frequently.[15] Their organizational activity is not surprising, for being used to transience, they are socially quite stable, usually gravitating to the same kinds of communities and joining the same kinds of organizations in them. In fact, their mobility has provided them with more organizational experience than other Levittowners have, enabling them to help found several groups in the community.

It has often been charged that modern transience and mobility deprive people of "roots." Because of the botanical analogy, the social conception of the word is difficult to define, but it generally refers to a variety of stable roles and relationships which are recognized by other residents. Traditionally, these roles were often defined by one's ancestors as well. Such roots are hard to maintain today and few people can resist the temptation of social or occupational mobility that requires a physical move. This does not mean, however, that the feeling of rootedness has disappeared. One way in which Transients maintain it is to preserve the term "home" for the place in which they grew up. When Levittowners talk of "going home," they mean trips to visit parents. People whose parents have

[13] Eighty-four per cent of the Transients reported organizational membership at the time of the second interview, as compared to 86 per cent of the Mobiles and only 44 per cent of the Settlers. Sixty-two per cent of the Transients belonged to organizations other than the church, compared to only 25 per cent of the Settlers.

[14] Seventy-five per cent of the Transients were more active than in their former residence, as compared to 60 per cent of the Settlers, and none of the Transients but 20 per cent of the Settlers said they were less active than before.

[15] The mean number of couples named by Transients was 2.75; by Mobiles, 3.25; and by Settlers, 3.3. Nineteen per cent of the Transients said they had no friends in Levittown, as compared to 8 per cent of the Settlers.

left the community in which they grew up may, however, feel homeless. I remember a discussion with a Levittowner who explained that he was going "home to Ohio" to visit his mother, and his wife said somewhat sadly, "My parents no longer live where I grew up, and I never lived with them where they live now. So I have only Sudberry Street in Levittown; I have no other home." Because they were Transients, she could not think of Levittown as home and, like many others, looked forward to the day when her husband's occupational transience would come to an end and they would settle down.

Such Transients obviously lack roots in an objective sense and may also have feelings of rootlessness. My impression is that these feelings are not intense or frequent. One way they are coped with is by moving to similar communities and putting down temporary roots; another, by joining organizations made up of fellow Transients.[16] Professionals who are transient often develop roots in their profession and its social groups. As Melvin Webber and others have argued, occupational or functional roots are replacing spatial roots for an ever increasing proportion of the population.[17] This kind of rootedness is easier for men to establish than for women, and wives, especially the wives of professionals, often suffer more from transience than their husbands. Some become attached to national voluntary associations—as men in nonprofessional occupations do—and develop roots within them. This is not entirely satisfactory, however, for it provides feelings of rootedness in only a single role, whereas spatial rootedness cuts across all roles, and rewards one for what one is rather than for what one does.

New communities like Levittown make it possible for residents, even Transients, to put down roots almost at once. People active in organizations become known quickly; thus they are able to feel part of the community. Despite Levittown's size, shopkeepers and local officials get to know people they see regularly, offering the feeling of being recognized to many. The ministers take special care to extend such recognition, and the churches appoint themselves to provide roots—and deliberately, for it attracts people to the church. Protestant denominations sought to define themselves as small-town churches with Colonial style buildings because these have been endowed with an image of rootedness.

Intergenerational rootedness is seldom found today in any suburban or urban community—or, for that matter, in most small towns—for it requires the kind of economic stability (and even stagnancy) characteristic only of depressed areas of the country. Moreover, the romanticizing of this type of rootedness ignores the fact that for many people it blocked progress, especially for low-status persons who were, by reason of residence and ancestry, permanently defined as "shiftless" or "good for nothing." Roots can strangle growth as well as encourage it.

Transience and mobility are something new in middle class American life, and like other innovations, they have been greeted by predictions of undesirable consequences, on family life, school performance, and mental health, for example. Interviews with school officials, doctors, and police-

[16]Whyte (1956), p. 289.
[17]Webber.

men indicated, however, that Transients appeared no more often as patients and police or school problems and delinquents than other Levittowners. Transience *can* create problems, but it has different effects for different people. For young men, a transfer usually includes a promotion or a raise; for older ones it may mean only another physical move or a transfer to a corporate "Siberia." If a Transient is attached to his home, but is asked to move by his company, he can say "no" only once or twice before being asked to resign or face relegation to the list of those who will not be promoted further. The move from one place to another is a pleasure for few families, but the emotional costs can easily be overestimated.[18] Because Transients move to and from similar types of communities, they have little difficulty adapting themselves to their new homes. In large corporations, they generally receive advice about where to look for housing, often going to areas already settled by colleagues who help them make the residential transition.

Frequent moving usually hurts other family members more than the breadwinner. Wives who had made good friends in Levittown were especially sad to go, and adolescents object strenuously to leaving their peers, so that parents generally try to settle down before their children enter high school. For wives and adolescents transience is essentially an involuntary move, which, like the forced relocation of slum dwellers under urban renewal, may result in depression and other deleterious effects.[19] Transience may also engender difficulties when problems of social mobility antedate or accompany it, as in the case of older corporate employees who must transfer without promotion, or suburbanites who move as a result of downward or extremely rapid upward social mobility.[20] Studies among children of Army personnel, who move more often than corporation Transients, have found that geographical mobility per se did not result in emotional experience,[21] except among children whose fathers had risen from working class origins to become officers.[22]

These findings would suggest that transience has its most serious effects on people with identity problems. The individual who lacks a fairly firm sense of his identity will have difficulties in coping with the new experiences he encounters in moving. He will also suffer most severely from rootlessness, for he will be hindered in developing the relationships and reference groups that strengthen one's identity. This might explain why adolescents find moving so difficult. Transients without roots in their community of origin or their jobs must rely on their family members in

[18] Gutman, p. 180.

[19] See, e.g., Fried.

[20] Gordon, Gordon, and Gunther. This study did not distinguish between residential and social mobility, but its case studies of disturbed suburbanites suggest the deleterious effects of the latter.

[21] Pederson and Sullivan.

[22] This study—by Gabower—came to other conclusions, but a close reading of her data shows that the strains of the long and arduous climb required of an enlisted man in the Navy who becomes an officer were passed on to the children. Conversely, children from middle class homes, whose fathers had graduated from Annapolis, rarely suffered emotionally from geographical mobility. Teenagers of both groups suffered from moving, however.

moments of stress. Sometimes, the family becomes more cohesive as a result, but since stresses on one family member are likely to affect all others, the family is not always a reliable source of support. If identity problems are also present, the individual may have no place to turn, and then transience can produce the *anomie* that critics have found rampant in the suburbs. But such people are a small minority in Levittown.

THE VITALITY OF LEVITTOWN: THE ADULT VIEW

When the Levittowners were asked whether they considered their community dull, just 20 per cent of the random sample said yes, and of Philadelphians (who might have been expected to find it dull after living in a big city), only 14 per cent.[23] Many respondents were surprised at the very question, for they thought there was a great deal to do in the community, and all that was needed was a desire to participate. "It's up to you," was a common reaction. "If a person is not the friendly type or does not become active, it's their own fault." "I don't think it's dull here," explained another, "there are so many organizations to join." Some people noted that Levittown was short of urban amusements, but it did not bother them. A former Philadelphian pointed out: "If Levittown is compared to city living, there are no taverns or teenage hangout places. Then it is dull. But we never had any of this in our own neighborhood and it's even better here. . . . We are perfectly content here, I'm afraid. Social life is enough for us; we are becoming fuddy-duddy." Nostalgia for urban places was not common; most people felt like the one who said, "We like quiet things . . . visiting, sitting out front in summer, having people dropping by." And if Levittown seemed quiet to some, it did not to others. "This is the wildest place I've ever been. Every weekend a party, barbecues, picnics, and things like that. I really enjoy it."[24] The only people who thought Levittown was indeed dull were the socially isolated, and upper middle class people who had tasted the town's organizational life and found it wanting.

What Levittowners who enjoy their community are saying is that they find vitality in other people and organizational activities; the community is less important. That community may be dull by conventional standards (which define vitality by urban social mixture and cultural riches) but Levittowners reject these standards; they do not want or need that kind of vitality or excitement. Mothers get their share of it from the daily adventures of their children and the men get it at work. The threshold for excitement is low, and for many, excitement is identified with conflict, crisis, and deprivation. Most Levittowners grew up in the Depression, and remembering the hard times of their childhood, they want to protect themselves and their children from stress.

[23] The question read: "Some people have said that communities like Levittown are pretty dull, without any excitement or interesting things to do. How do you feel about that? Do you agree or disagree?"

[24] This respondent was describing the extremely active social life of the Jewish community. Even so, Jews (particularly the better educated) were more likely than non-Jews to agree that Levittown was dull. Jews also seem to be more interested in city amusements.

Another difference in values between critics and Levittowners is at play here. The Italians who lived in the center city working class neighborhood I studied before Levittown were bored by "the country"—in which they included the suburbs—and so are critics of suburbia, albeit for different reasons. Many working class city dwellers enjoy street life and urban eating or drinking places; upper middle class critics like crowds and cosmopolitanism. The lower middle class and the kinds of working class people that came to Levittown had no interest in either. Even previous urbanites had made little if any use of the cultural facilities valued by the cosmopolitan, and had no need for them in the suburbs. And as the struggles over the liquor issue suggest, they want none of the vitality sought by the working class urbanite, for they are just escaping corner bars and the disadvantages of aging urban areas. What they do want is a kind of interpersonal vitality along with privacy and peace and quiet.[25] Vicarious excitement is something else again. Television provides programmed and highly predictable excitement, but it can get boring. A fire or accident, a fight at a municipal or school board meeting, and marital strife or minor misbehavior among neighbors involve real people and known ones. The excitement they provide is also vicarious, but it is not programmed and is therefore more rewarding.

The Blandness of Lower Middle Class Culture

Levittown's criteria for vitality may spell dullness to the critic and the visitor, partly because much of community life is invisible. Lower middle class life does not take place either on the street or in meetings and parties; it is home-centered and private. Once one penetrates behind the door, however, as does the participant-observer, people emerge as personalities and few are either dull or bland. But when all is said and done, something is different: less exuberance than is found in the working class, a more provincial outlook than in the upper middle class, and a somewhat greater concern with respectability than in either. In part, this is a function of religious background: being largely Protestant, the lower middle class is still affected by the Puritan ethos. It lacks the regular opportunity for confession that allows some Catholics to live somewhat more spiritedly, and has not adopted the sharp division into sacred and secular culture that reduces Jewish religiosity to observance of the High Holidays and permits Jews to express exuberance in their organizational, social, and cultural activities. But the difference is not entirely due to Puritanism, for

[25]Cosmopolitan friends often asked me if I did not find Levittown dull. As a participant-observer, I could not answer the question, for I was immersed in community life and strife and saw all of their vitality and excitement. Even the most routine event was interesting because I was trying to fit it into an overall picture of the community. As a resident, I enjoyed being with Levittowners, and the proportion of dull ones was certainly no higher than in academic or any other circles. Of course, Levittown lacked some of the urban facilities that I, as a city-lover, like to patronize. It was not dull, however—but then I would not make a public judgment about any community simply because it could not satisfy some of my personal preferences, particularly when the community seemed to satisfy the preferences of the majority of residents so well.

"restrictive" lower middle class culture appears also among Catholics who have moved "up," especially German and Irish ones, and even among Italians and among some Jews who have risen from working class origins.

If "blandness" is the word for this quality, it stems from the transition in which the lower middle class finds itself between the familial life of the working class and the cosmopolitanism of the upper middle class. The working class person need conform only within the family circle and the peer group, but these are tolerant of his other activities. Believing that the outside world is unalterably hostile and that little is to be gained from its approval, he can indulge in boisterousness that provides catharsis from the tensions generated in the family and peer circles. The upper middle class person, on the other hand, is lodged firmly in the world outside the home. At times he may have trouble reconciling the demands of home and outside world, but he has a secure footing in both.

Lower middle class people seem to me to be caught in the middle. Those whose origins were in the working class are no longer tied so strongly to the extended family, but although they have gone out into the larger society, they are by no means at ease in it. They do not share the norms of the cosmopolitans, but, unlike the working class, they cannot ignore them. As a result, they find themselves in a situation in which every neighbor is a potential friend or enemy and every community issue a source of conflict, producing a restraining and even inhibiting influence on them. Others, lower middle class for generations, have had to move from a rural or small-town social structure. They too are caught in the middle, for now they must cope with a larger and more heterogeneous society, for which their cultural and religious traditions have not equipped them.

If left to themselves, lower middle class people do what they have always done: put their energies into home and family, seeking to make life as comfortable as possible, and supporting, broadening, and varying it with friends, neighbors, church, and a voluntary association. Because this way of life is much like that of the small-town society or the urban neighborhood in which they grew up, they are able to maintain their optimistic belief that Judeo-Christian morality is a reliable guide to behavior. This world view (if one can endow it with so philosophical a name) is best seen in the pictures that amateur painters exhibited at PTA meetings in Levittown: bright, cheerful landscapes, or portraits of children and pets painted in primary colors, reflecting the wish that the world be hopeful, humorous, and above all, simple. Most important, their paintings insisted that life can be happy.

Of course, life is not really like this, for almost everyone must live with some disappointment: an unruly child, a poor student, an unsatisfied husband, a bored wife, a bad job, a chronic illness, or financial worry. These realities are accepted because they cannot be avoided; it is the norms of the larger society which frustrate. Partly desired and partly rejected, they produce an ambivalence which appears to the outsider as the blandness of lower middle class life. This ambivalence can be illustrated by the way Levittown women reacted to my wife's paintings. Since her studio was at home, they had an opportunity to see her work and talk to her about being a painter. The working class Italians with whom we had lived in Boston previously knew, by and large, how to deal with her activity. Unacquainted with "art," they could shrug off her activity and her abstract expressionist style to admire colors they liked or forms that reminded them of something in their own experience. Not knowing what it all meant, and not having to know, they concluded that painting was a good thing because it kept her out of trouble, preventing boredom and potentially troublesome consequences such as drinking or extramarital affairs.

The lower middle class Levittowners could not cope with her paintings as easily. They did not like her abstract expressionist style any more than the working class women, but they knew it was "art" and so could not ignore it. They responded with anxiety, some hostility, and particularly with envy of her ability to be "creative." But even this response was overlaid with ambivalence. As teenagers they had learned that creativity was desirable, and many had had some cursory training in drawing, piano, or needlework. Once they had learned to be wives and mothers and had enough sociability, the urge for creativity returned—but not the opportunity.

For working class women, keeping the family together and the bills paid is a full-time job. Upper middle class women are convinced that life ought to be more than raising a family, but lower middle class ones are not that sure. They want to venture into nonfamilial roles, but not so intensively as to engender role conflict and anxiety. As a result, they search for easy creativity, activities that do not require, as Levittowners put it, "upsetting the family and household." Serious artistic activity is difficult under such conditions, yet a compromise solution such as needlework or painting-by-numbers is not entirely satisfactory either, because, however rewarding, people know it is not really art. One Levittowner I met expressed the ambivalence between the familial role and artistic aspirations in an especially tortured way. She explained that she was very sensitive to paintings, but confessed that whenever she visited museums, she would begin to think about her family. She resolved the ambivalence by rejecting paintings that made her "think too much about art." For most people, however, the ambivalence is less intense.

A similarly ambivalent pattern is evident in government involvement. Many lower middle class people believe that the moral framework which governs their personal lives, the sort of relations they have with family members and friends, ought to govern organizational life and society as well. Any other type of behavior they call "politics," in and out of political life, and they try to avoid it as immoral. Working class people have the same perspective, but they are also realists and will exploit politics for their own ends, and upper middle class people believe in moral (reform) politics, but its norms are not borrowed from the family. Lower middle class citizens are once again caught between the standards of home and of the outside world, however, and the result is often political inaction. It is for them that politicians put on performances to show that their decisions are based on the standards of home and family and run election campaigns demonstrating the personal honesty of their candidates and the opposition candidates' immorality.

Of course, these are cultural propensities to act, and when personal interests are threatened, lower middle class people defend them as heartily as anyone else. Then, they identify their actions with morality—so much so that they lose sight of their self-interest and are easily hurt when others point out to them that they are selfishly motivated. Whereas working class people then become cynical, lower middle class people become hypocritical, often without being conscious of it. Blandness turns easily to bitterness, anger, and blind conflict—blind because every act of offense or self-defense is clothed in the terminology of personal morality.

What appears as blandness, then, to the outside observer is the outcome of conflict between self and society, and between what ought to be and what is. When and if a lower middle class person is secure, he appears bland, because he is not really willing to act within the larger society; when he is threatened, he is extremely angry, because his moral view of the world is upset. One target of his anger is the working class people who are less bothered by the moral dilemmas of the larger society; another is the upper middle class activitists who keep pressuring him to translate morality into action and to take a stand on community issues.

Many of these cultural predispositions seem to occur more among lower middle class women than among their husbands. If the men are employed in a bureaucracy, as most are, their work involves them not only in the larger society but also in office or factory political struggles which leave them little time to think about the ambivalence between the standards of home and outside world. The women, however, caught in a role that keeps them at home, are forever trying to break out of its confines, only to confront ambivalent situations. They respond with inhibiting blandness; it is they who are most concerned with respectability. Indeed, living with neighbors employed in large bureaucracies, I was struck over and over again by the feeling that if the men were "organization men," they were so only by necessity, not by inclination, and that if they were left alone, they would gravitate toward untrammeled creativity and individualism. Their wives, on the other hand, defended what Whyte called the Social Ethic, rejecting extreme actions and skeptical opinions, and tried to get their men to toe the line of lower middle class morality. If anything, their inclinations drove them toward being "organization women." But then, they had the job of maintaining the family's status image on the block, and they spent their days in the near-anarchy created by small children. Perhaps they were simply escaping *into* the order of lower middle class norms, while the men were escaping *from* the order imposed by their bureaucratic work.

LEVITTOWN IS "ENDSVILLE": THE ADOLESCENT VIEW

The adult conception of Levittown's vitality is not shared by its adolescents. Many consider it a dull place to which they have been brought involuntarily by their parents. Often there is no place to go and nothing to do after school. Although most adolescents have no trouble in their student role, many are bored after school and some are angry, expressing that anger through thinly veiled hostility to adults and vandalism against adult property. Their relationship to the adults is fraught with tension, which discourages community attempts to solve what is defined as their recreational problem.

Essays which students in grades 6–12 wrote for me early in 1961 suggest that most children are satisfied with Levittown until adolescence.[26] Sixty-eight per cent of the sixth-graders liked Levittown, but only 45 per cent of the eighth-graders, 37 per cent of the tenth-graders, and 39 per cent of the twelfth-graders did. In comparison, 85 per cent of the adults responded positively to a similar question.[27] Likes and dislikes reflect the state of recreational and social opportunities. Girls make little use of recreational facilities until they become adolescents, and before the tenth grade, they like Levittown better than the boys. Dislikes revolve around "nothing to do." The sixth- and eighth-grade boys say there are not enough gyms, playing fields, or hills, and no transportation for getting to existing facilities. Both sexes complain about the lack of neighborhood stores and that the houses are too small, lack privacy, and are poorly built. By the twelfth grade, disenchantment with the existing facilities has set in; those who like Levittown stress the newness and friendliness of the community, but references to the pool, the shopping center, and the bowling alley are negative.[28] As one twelfth-grader pointed out, "Either you have to pay a lot of money to go to the movies or the bowling alley, or you go to too many parties and that gets boring." Lack of facilities is reported most often by the older girls, for the boys at least have athletic programs put on by civic groups.[29]

But the commonest gripe is the shortage of ready transportation, which makes not only facilities but, more important, other teenagers inaccessible. One girl complained, "After school hours, you walk into an entirely different world. Everyone goes his own separate way, to start his homework, take a nap, or watch TV. That is the life of a vegetable, not a human being." A car, then, becomes in a way as essential to teenagers as to adults. Moreover, many small-town teenagers like to meet outside the community, for it is easier to "have fun" where one's parents and other known adults cannot disapprove. A high school senior who took a job to buy a car put it dramatically:

> I had no choice, it was either going to work or cracking up. I have
> another week of boring habits, then (when I get the car) I'll start living.
> I can get out of Levittown and go to other towns where I have many

[26] The students were asked what they liked and disliked about living in Levittown, and what they missed from their former residence. Since they were not asked to sign their names, and the questions were general, I believe the essays were honest responses. I purposely included no questions about the schools, and teachers were instructed not to give any guidance about how the questions should be answered. (One teacher did tell the children what to write, and these essays were not analyzed.) The data presented here are based on a sample of one sixth- and one eighth-grade class from each of the three elementary schools, and of all tenth- and twelfth-grade classes.

[27] The data are not strictly comparable, for the adults were asked outright whether they liked or disliked living in Levittown, whereas the teenagers' attitudes were inferred from the tone of the essays.

[28] Twenty-eight per cent of the boys liked the community's newness; 18 per cent, the friendly people. Among the girls, 34 per cent liked the people; 20 per cent, Levittown's newness.

[29] Twenty-five per cent of the tenth-graders and 50 per cent of the twelfth-graders say there is nothing to do, and 25 per cent and 46 per cent, respectively, mention the lack of recreational facilities. Among the twelfth-grade girls, 56 per cent mention it.

friends. . . . In plain words, a boy shouldn't live here if he is between
the ages of 14–17. At this age he is using his adult mind, and that
doesn't mean riding a bike or smoking his first cigarette. He wants to
be big and popular and go out and live it up. I am just starting the life
I want. I couldn't ask for more than being a senior in a brand new
high school, with the best of students and teachers, and my car on its
way.

Girls are less likely to have access to a car, and one explained, "We have
to walk, and the streets wind, and cause you to walk two miles instead of
one as the crow flies."

The adults have provided some facilities for teenage activities, but not
always successfully. One problem is that "teenage" is an adult tag; adolescents grade themselves by age. Older ones refused to attend dances with
the younger set, considering forced association with their juniors insult-
ing.[30] Some adolescents also found the adult chaperones oppressive. At
first, the chaperones interfered openly by urging strangers to dance with
each other in order to get everyone on the floor and to discourage intimate
dancing among couples. When the teenagers protested, they stopped, but
hovered uneasily in the background.[31]

Specifically, adolescent malcontent stems from two sources: Levittown
was not designed for them, and adults are reluctant to provide the recreational facilities and gathering places they want. Like most suburban communities, Levittown was planned for families with young children. The
bedrooms are too small to permit an adolescent to do anything but study
or sleep; they lack the privacy and soundproofing to allow him to invite
his friends over. Unfortunately, the community is equally inhospitable.
Shopping centers are intended for car-owning adults, and in accord with
the desire of property owners, are kept away from residential areas. Being
new, Levittown lacks low-rent shopping areas which can afford to subsist
on the marginal purchases made by adolescents. In 1961, a few luncheonettes in neighborhood shopping centers and a candy store and a bowling
alley in the big center were the only places for adolescents to congregate.[32]
Coming in droves, they overwhelmed those places and upset the merchants. Not only do teenagers occupy space without making significant
purchases, but they also discourage adult customers. Merchants faced with
high rent cannot subsist on teenage spending and complain to the police
if teenagers "hang out" at their places. Street corners are off limits, too,
for a clump of adolescents soon becomes noisy enough to provoke a call

[30] Similarly in the elementary schools, seventh- and eighth-graders complained about having
to go to school with "immature" and "childish" students; when they were moved to the
high school, the older students objected to their presence in the same terms.

[31] There was also a dispute over programming: the adults wanted slow music and the traditional dances they knew best; the teenagers wanted the latest best-selling records and
the newest dances. They signed petitions for the ouster of the man who chose the records,
but the adults refused to accept the petitions, arguing that they would be followed by
petitions to oust the school superintendent.

[32] Indeed, the existing teenage hangouts in little luncheonettes resulted from the lucky accident that the builder and the township planner were unable to regulate and limit the
number of small shopping centers which sprang up on the edge of the community.

to the police. Eventually they feel hounded and even defined as juvenile delinquents. Said one twelfth-grade girl, "I feel like a hood to be getting chased by the police for absolutely nothing."

The schools were not designed for after-hours use, except for adults and for student activities which entertain adults, such as varsity athletics. The auditoriums were made available for dances, although when these began, the school administration promptly complained about scuffed floors and damaged fixtures. Only at the swimming pool are teenagers not in the way of adult priorities, and during the day, when adults are not using it, it is their major gathering place. But even here, smoking and noisy activities are prohibited.

The design deficiencies cannot be altered, and should not be if they are a problem only for teenagers, but there is no inherent reason why teenage facilities cannot be provided. However, adults disagree on what is needed and, indeed, on the desirability of facilities, for reasons partly political, but fundamentally social and psychological. For one thing, adults are uncertain about how to treat teenagers; for another, they harbor a deep hostility toward them which is cultural and, at bottom, sexual in nature.

There are two adult views of the teenager, one permissive, the other restrictive. The former argues that a teenager is a responsible individual who should be allowed to run his own affairs with some adult help. The latter, subscribed to by the majority, considers him still a child who needs adult supervision and whose activities ought to be conducted by adult rules to integrate him into adult society. For example, when one of the community organizations set up teenage dances, there was some discussion about whether teenagers should run them. Not only was this idea rejected, but the adults then ran the dances on the basis of the "highest" standards.[33] Boys were required to wear ties and jackets, girls, dresses, on the assumption that this would encourage good behavior, whereas blue jeans, tee shirts, and sweaters somehow would not. The adults could not resist imposing their own norms of dress in exchange for providing dances.

The advocates of restriction also rejected the permissive point of view because they felt it wrong to give teenagers what they wanted. Believing that teenagers had it "too easy," they argued that "if you make them work for programs, they appreciate them more." Logically, they should, therefore, have let the teenagers set up their own activities, but their arguments were not guided by logic; they were, rather, rationalizations for their fear of teenagers. Although the "permissives" pointed out that teenagers might well set up stricter rules than adults, the "restrictives" feared catastrophes: fights, the "wrong crowd" taking over, pregnancies, and contraceptives found in or near the teenage facility. These fears accounted for the rules governing dances and inhibited the establishment of an adult-run teenage center, for the voluntary associations and the politicians were afraid that if violence or sexual activity occurred, they would be blamed for it.

---

[33]At one point adult-run dances failed to attract teenagers, and a group of teenage leaders were delegated to run the dances themselves. This foundered because other teenagers disagreed with the rules and program set up by these leaders, and since only one opportunity for dancing was provided, they could express their disagreement only by nonattendance.

The problem is twofold: restrictive adults want adolescents to be children preparing for adulthood, and are threatened by the teenage or youth culture they see around them. By now, adolescents are a cultural minority like any other, but whereas no Levittowners expect Italians to behave like Jews, most still expect teenagers to behave like children. They are supposed to participate in the family more than they do and, legally still under age, to subsume their own wishes to the adults'. The failure of teenagers to go along is blamed on the parents as well. If parents would only take more interest in their adolescent children, spend more time with them, be "pals" with them, and so on, then misbehavior—and even youth culture—would not develop. This argument is supported by the claim that delinquency is caused by broken homes or by both parents' holding full-time jobs.

Such views are espoused particularly by Catholics, who share traditional working class attitudes; the parochial school, with its emphasis on discipline to keep children out of trouble, is their embodiment. Even adult-devised programs are considered undesirable, for, as one Catholic working class father put it, "In summer, children should either work or be at home. Summer arts and crafts programs are a waste of time. My kid brought home dozens of pictures. What's he going to do with so many pictures?" The adolescents' social choices are also restricted. Adults active in youth programs frequently try to break up their groups, damning them as cliques or gangs, and even separating friends when athletic teams are chosen. Some teenagers react by minimizing contact with adults, pursuing their activities privately and becoming remarkably uncommunicative. In essence, they lead a separate life which frees them from undue parental control and gives an air of mystery to the teenager and his culture.

Among restrictive adults, the image of the teenager is of an irresponsible, parasitic individual, who attends school without studying, hangs out with his peers looking for fun and adventure, and gets into trouble—above all, over sex. There were rumors of teenage orgies in Levittown's school playgrounds, in shopping center parking lots, and on the remaining rural roads of the township. The most fantastic rumor had 44 girls in the senior class pregnant, with one boy singlehandedly responsible for six of them. Some inquiry on my part turned up the facts: two senior girls were pregnant and one of them was about to be married.

If the essays the students wrote for me have any validity, the gap between adult fantasy and adolescent reality is astonishing. Most teenagers do not even date; their social life takes place in groups. Judging by their comments about the friendliness of adult neighbors, they are quiet youngsters who get along well with adults and spend most of their time preparing themselves for adulthood. Needless to say, these essays would not have revealed delinquent activities of sex play. However, I doubt that more than 5 per cent of the older teenagers live up to anything like the adult image of them.

What, then, accounts for the discrepancy? For one thing, adults take little interest in their children's education; they want to be assured that their children are getting along in school, but not much more. The bond that might exist here is thus absent. Changes in education during the past two decades have been so great that even interested parents can do little to help their children with their school work. Consequently, adults focus on teenagers in their nonstudent roles, noting their absence from home, the intensity of their tie to friends and cliques, and their rebelliousness.

Second, there is the normal gap between the generations, enlarged by the recent flowering of youth culture, much of which is incomprehensible or unesthetic to adults. Despite the parents' belief that they should be responsible for their adolescents' behavior, they cannot participate in many joint activities or talk meaningfully with them about the experiences and problems of teenage life. This gap is exacerbated by a strange parental amnesia about their own—not so distant—adolescence. I recall a letter written by a twenty-one-year-old mother who wanted to help the Township Committee set up a delinquency prevention council because she was concerned about teenage misbehavior.

Third, there is enough teenage vandalism and delinquency to provide raw material for the adult image, although not enough to justify it. According to the police and the school superintendent, serious delinquency in Levittown was minimal; in 1961, about 50 adolescents accounted for most of it. Many were children from working class backgrounds who did poorly in school, or from disturbed middle class families. From 1959 to 1961, only 12 cases were serious enough to go to the county juvenile court, and some were repeaters. Vandalism is more prevalent. The first victim was the old Willingboro YMCA, which was wrecked twice before it was torn down. Schools have been defaced, windows broken, garbage thrown into the pools, flowerbeds destroyed, and bicycles "borrowed." The perpetrators are rarely caught, but those who are caught are teenagers, thus making it possible for adults to suspect all adolescents and maintain their image.

Finally, some adults seem to project their own desires for excitement and adventures onto the youngsters. For them, teenagers function locally as movie stars and beatniks do on the national scene—as exotic creatures reputed to live for sex and adventure. Manifestly, teenagers act as more prosaic entertainers: in varsity athletics, high school dramatic societies, and bands, but the girls are also expected to provide glamor. One of the first activities of the Junior Chamber of Commerce was a Miss Levittown contest, in which teenage girls competed for honors in evening gown, bathing suit, and talent contests—the "talent" usually involving love songs or covertly erotic dances. At such contests unattainable maidens show off their sexuality—often unconsciously—in order to win the nomination. Men in the audience comment *sotto voce* about the girls' attractiveness, wishing to sleep with them and speculating whether that privilege is available to the contest judges and boyfriends. From here, it is only a short step to the conviction that girls are promiscuous with their teenage friends, which heightens adult envy, fear, and the justification for restrictive measures. The sexual function of the teenager became apparent when the popularity of the Miss Levittown contest led to plans for a Mrs. Levittown contest. This plan was quickly dropped, however, for the idea of married women parading in bathing suits was thought to be in bad taste, especially by the women. Presumably, young mothers are potential sexual objects, whereas the teenagers are, like movie stars, unattainable, and can therefore serve as voyeuristic objects.

Although suburbia is often described as a hotbed of adultery in popular fiction, this is an urban fantasy. Levittown is quite monogamous, and

I am convinced that most suburbs are more so than most cities.[34] The desire for sexual relations with attractive neighbors may be ever present, but when life is lived in a goldfish bowl, adultery is impossible to hide from the neighbors—even if there were motels in Levittown and baby-sitters could be found for both parties. Occasionally such episodes do take place, after which the people involved often run off together or leave the community. There are also periodic stories of more bizarre sexual esca-pades, usually about community leaders. In one such story, a local poli-tician was driving down the dark roads of the township in a sports car with a naked young woman while his wife thought he was at a political meeting. If there was any roadside adultery, however, it remained unre-ported, for no cases ever appeared on the police blotters during the two years I saw them.[35] Similar stories made the rounds in Park Forest, the new town I studied in 1949, and one of them, which began after a party where some extramarital necking had taken place, soon reported the gath-ering as a wife-swapping orgy.

"The Juvenile Problem" and Its Solutions

The cultural differences between adults and adolescents have precipitated an undeclared and subconscious war between them, as pervasive as the class struggle, which prevents the adults from solving what they call "the juvenile problem." Indeed, putting it that way is part of the trouble, for much of the adult effort has been aimed at discouraging delinquency, providing recreational activities in the irrational belief that these could prevent it. Sports programs were supposed to exhaust the teenagers so that they would be too tired to get into trouble (harking back to the Victorian myth that a regimen of cold showers and sports would dampen sexual urges, although ironically, varsity athletes were also suspected of being stellar sexual performers); dances were to keep them off the street. When delinquency did not abate, a Youth Guidance Commission to deal with "the problem," and a Teenage Panel to punish delinquencies too minor for court actions, were set up. The police chief asked for a curfew to keep youngsters off the street at night, hoping to put pressure on parents to act as enforcing agents and to get his department out of the cross fire between teenagers, merchants, and home owners. Chasing the teenagers from shop-ping centers and street corners was useless, for having no other place to go they always returned the next night, particularly since they knew people would not swear out complaints against their neighbors' (or customers') children. The police chief also did not want "the kids to feel they are being bugged," for they would come to hate his men and create more trouble for

[34] A comparison of urban and suburban marriages indicated that extramarital affairs occur principally in older and well-educated populations, and that place of residence is irrelevant. Ubell. For another observer's skepticism about suburban adultery, see Whyte (1956), p. 355–357.

[35] Since the blotter listed adolescent promiscuity, adult suicide attempts, and even drunk-enness and family quarrels among community leaders, I assume it was not censored to exclude adultery.

them.[36] If he cracked down on them, they would retaliate; if he did not, the adults would accuse him of laxity. Although the curfew was strongly supported by parents who could not control their children, it was rejected as unenforceable.

Adult solutions to the juvenile problem were generally shaped by other institutional goals which took priority over adolescent needs. The organizations which scheduled dances wanted to advertise themselves and their community service inclinations, even competing for the right to hold them, and the churches set up youth groups to bring the teenagers into the church. Indeed, those who decide on adolescent programs either have vested interests in keeping teenagers in a childlike status (parents and educators, for example) or are charged with the protection of adult interests (police and politicians). The primacy of adult priorities was brought out by a 1961 PTA panel on "How Is Our Community Meeting the Needs of the Adolescents?" With one exception the panelists (chosen to represent the various adults responsible for teenagers) ignored these needs, talking only about what teenagers should do for *them*. For example, the parent on the panel said, "The needs of adolescents should first be met in the home and young energies should be guided into the proper normal channels." The teacher suggested that "parents should never undermine the authority of the teacher. Parents should help maintain the authority of the school over the child, and the school will in turn help maintain the authority of the parent over the child." The minister urged parents to "encourage youth leadership responsibilities within the church," and the police chief explained "the importance of teaching adolescents their proper relationship to the law and officers of the law."[37]

Political incentives for a municipal or even a semipublic recreation program were also absent. Not only were prospective sponsors afraid they would be held responsible for teenage misbehavior occurring under their auspices, but in 1961 not many Levittowners had adolescent children and not all of them favored a public program. Middle class parents either had no problems with their youngsters or objected to the working class advocacy of municipal recreation, and some working class parents felt that once children had reached adolescence they were on their own. The eventual clients of the program, the adolescents, had no political influence whatsoever. They were too young to vote, and although they might have persuaded their parents to demand facilities for them, they probably suspected that what their parents wanted for them was more of what had already been provided.

In the end, then, the adults got used to the little delinquency and vandalism that took place, and the teenagers became sullen and unhappy, complaining, "This place is Endsville," and wishing their parents would move back to communities which had facilities for them or pressuring them for cars to go to neighboring towns.

The best summary of what is wrong—and what should be done—was stated concisely by a twelfth-grade essayist: "I think the adults should

---

[36] Actually, since the police usually sided with the merchants against the teenagers, the latter did feel "bugged."

[37] "Panel Features Junior High P.T.A. Meeting," *Levittown Herald*, January 26, 1961.

spend less time watching for us to do something wrong and help us raise money for a community center. We're not asking for it, we only want their help." If one begins with the assumption that adolescents are rational and responsible human beings whose major "problem" is that they have become a distinctive minority subculture, it is not too difficult to suggest programs. What else the teenagers want in the way of recreation can be readily inferred from their essays: besides the center, a range of inexpensive coffeehouses and soda shops and other meeting places, bowling alleys, amusement arcades, places for dancing, ice and roller skating rinks, garages for mechanically inclined car owners (all within walking or bicycling distance or accessible by public transportation), and enough of each so that the various age groups and separate cliques have facilities they can call their own. Since adolescents are well supplied with spending money, many of these facilities can be set up commercially. Others may need public support. It would, for example, be possible to provide some municipal subsidies to luncheonette operators who are willing to make their businesses into teenage social centers.[38]

Recreational and social facilities are not enough, however. Part of the adolescents' dissatisfaction with the community—as with adult society in general—is their functionlessness outside of school. American society really has no use for them other than as students, and condemns them to spend most of their spare time in recreational pursuits. They are trying to learn to be adults, but since the community and the larger society want them to be children, they learn adulthood only at school—and there imperfectly. Yet many tasks in the community now go unfilled because of lack of public funds, for example, clerical, data-gathering, and other functions at city hall; and tutoring children, coaching their sports, and leading their recreational programs. These are meaningful duties, and I suspect many adolescents could fill them, either on a voluntary or a nominal wage basis. Finally, teenagers want to learn to be themselves and do for themselves. It should be possible to give them facilities of their own—or even land on which they could build—and let them organize, construct, and run their own centers and work places.

Needless to say, such autonomy would come up against the very real political difficulties that faced the more modest programs suggested in Levittown, and would surely be rejected by the community.[39] The ideal solution, therefore, is to plan for teenage needs outside the local adult decision-making structure, and perhaps even outside the community. It might be possible to establish Teenage Authorities that would play the same interstitial role in the governmental structure as other authorities set up in connection with intercommunity and regional planning functions. Perhaps the most feasible approach is to develop commercially profitable facilities, to be set up either by teenagers or by a private entrepreneur who would need to be less sensitive to political considerations than a public agency. If and when the "juvenile problem" becomes more serious in the

[38] A combination neighborhood store and social center has been proposed in the plan for the new town of Columbia, Maryland.

[39] In 1966, no teenage centers had yet been established in Levittown, and campaigning politicians were still arguing about the wisdom of doing so.

suburbs, federal funds may become available for facilities and for programs to create jobs, like those now being developed for urban teenagers. Most likely, this will only happen when "trouble" begins to mount.

References

Anderson, Judith, and Settani, Nicholas. "Resales in Levittown, Pennsylvania, 1952–1960." Unpublished paper, Department of City Planning, University of Pennsylvania, 1961.

Fried, Marc. "Grieving for a Lost Home," in Leonard J. Duhl, ed., *The Urban Condition.* New York: Basic Books, 1963, pp. 151–171.

Fromm, Erich. *The Sane Society.* New York: Holt, Rinehart and Winston, 1955.

Gabower, Genevieve. *Behavior Problems of Children in Navy Officers' Families as Related to Social Conditions of Navy Life.* Washington: Catholic University of America Press, 1959.

Gans, Herbert J. *The Urban Villagers: Group and Class in the Life of Italian-Americans.* New York: Free Press of Glencoe, 1962(a).

Gordon, R., Gordon, K., and Gunther, M. *The Split Level Trap.* New York: Geis, 1961.

Gutman, Robert. "Population Mobility in the American Middle Class," in Leonard J. Duhl, ed., *The Urban Condition.* New York: Basic Books, 1963, pp. 172–183.

Keats, John. *The Crack in the Picture Window.* Boston: Houghton-Mifflin, 1956 (Ballantine Books paperback, 1957).

Kornhauser, William. *Politics of Mass Society.* New York: Free Press of Glencoe, 1959.

Lipset, S. M. *Political Man.* Garden City: Doubleday, 1960.

Orzack, Louis H., and Sanders, Irwin T. *A Social Profile of Levittown, New York.* Ann Arbor: University Microfilms, O. P. 13438, 1961.

Pederson, Frank A., and Sullivan, Eugene. "Effects of Geographical Mobility and Parent Personality Factors on Emotional Disorders in Children." Washington: Walter Reed General Hospital, 1963, mimeographed.

Riesman, David (with N. Glazer and R. Denney). *The Lonely Crowd.* New Haven: Yale University Press, 1950.

Stein, Maurice. *The Eclipse of Community.* Princeton: Princeton University Press, 1960.

Ubell, Earl. "Marriage in the Suburbs." *New York Herald-Tribune,* January 4–8, 1959.

Vidich, Arthur J., and Bensman, Joseph. *Small Town in Mass Society.* Princeton: Princeton University Press, 1958.

Webber, Melvin M. "Order in Diversity: Community Without Propinquity," in Lowdon Wingo, Jr., ed., *Cities and Space: The Future Use of Urban Land.* Baltimore: Johns Hopkins University Press, 1963, pp. 23–54.

Whyte, William H., Jr. *The Organization Man.* New York: Simon & Schuster, 1956.

Wilensky, Harold L. "Life Cycle, Work Situation and Participation in Formal Associations," in Robert W. Kleemeier, ed., *Aging and Leisure*. New York: Oxford University Press, 1961, pp. 213–242.

Willmott, Peter. *The Evolution of a Community.* London: Routledge & Kegan Paul, 1963.

Counter-culture youth rejected many of mainstream America's values

The Counter-Culture

WILLIAM L. O'NEILL

If we use the term "culture" to refer to the way of life of a people, then American society from its very beginning has been made up of a variety of cultures. However, throughout our history a more or less prevailing culture has dominated or attempted to dominate competing or conflicting cultures. Over the years, attempts have been made to describe this dominant culture, and many studies have pointed out aspects of the culture that have had a tremendous success in creating certain attitudes, if not always in controlling behavior.

The idea of culture contains both attitudes and behavior, and the secret of successful studies of any culture derives from the ability of the scholar to ferret out the patterns of behavior that may, in fact, run counter to the overt attitudes of a group.

What interests us in the following selection, however, is not the conflict between attitude and behavior, but the conflict between the dominant culture and a deviant culture that has as its goal a deliberate attack on the dominant culture and an elimination of the gap between attitude and behavior—what the participants in this counter-culture call hypocrisy.

Ever since the founding of the Massachusetts Bay Colony, the body of New World society has contained deviant cultural elements. This description refers, not to such entirely foreign cultures as the American Indian or the African, but to those deviations from the dominant culture that were exhibited by the settlers themselves. The English settlers who danced with Indians around a Maypole at Merry Mount in the 1630s presented a challenge to the prevailing culture; such challenges persist to the present day. The dominant culture has usually had the power of public opinion or, when necessary, the power of police authority to subdue deviants in its midst. This power, however, is not always invoked. In the twentieth century, there has developed a tradition often referred to as "bohemian" culture, restricted almost entirely to a small number of artists, writers, and composers. These creative bohemians have not sought to foster their way of life—composed as it is of a freedom from what they call bourgeois morality—on the rest of America. They merely want to be left alone. And they usually are unless they become too flagrant in their violations of community norms.

In the 1960s, an extremely powerful challenge to the dominant culture came into being. The term counter-culture, rather than subculture, can correctly be applied to this movement because it saw itself as a frontal attack on what it called "straight" culture. It had a visionary purpose—to "turn on" the world. At the heart of the counter-culture was a contempt for all traditional forms of author-ity and, theoretically, an intent to replace them with the authority of inner expe-rience and interpersonal relationships. Since these new authorities were difficult to isolate and identify, much less obey, the counter-culture's adherents turned to all sorts of gurus (spiritual leaders) in an attempt to find their way into the brave new world they forecast.

In the chapter from his book on the 1960s reprinted below, William O'Neill, of Rutgers University, describes many facets of the counter-culture movement of the decade. He notes the critical importance of the mass media, which proved so influential in spreading the new gospel as well as in denigrating it. O'Neill rightly points out that the movement was not limited to the young but increasingly began to attract older people to certain aspects of the freedom it espoused. In his concluding paragraphs, the author renders what may be too harsh a judg-ment on the movement. A longer perspective is no doubt needed to evaluate accurately the impact of this flashy and furious attempt to find a more meaningful and more human life-style in the midst of what many saw as an inhuman and materialistic middle-class morality.

C ounter-culture as a term appeared rather late in the decade. It largely replaced the term "youth culture," which finally proved too limited. When the sixties began, youth culture meant the way adolescents lived. Its central institutions were the high school and the mass media. Its principal activities were consuming goods and enacting courtship rituals. Critics and students of the youth culture were chiefly interested in the status and value systems associated with it. As time went on, college enrollments increased to the point where colleges were nearly as influential as high schools in shaping the young. The molders of youthful opinion got more ambitious. Where once entertainers were content to amuse for profit, many began seeing themselves as moral philosophers. Music especially became a medium of propaganda, identifying the young as a distinct force in society with unique values and aspirations. This helped produce a kind of ideological struggle between the young and their elders called the "gen-

"The Counter-Culture." From *Coming Apart*, by William L. O'Neill. pp. 233–240, 248–256, 258–271. Copyright © 1971 by William L. O'Neill. Reprinted by permission of Times Books, a division of Quadrangle/The New York Times Book Co., Inc.

eration gap." It was the first time in American history that social conflict was understood to be a function of age. Yet the young were not all rebellious. Most in fact retained confidence in the "system" and its norms. Many older people joined the rebellion, whose progenitors were as often over thirty (where the generation gap was supposed to begin) as under it. The attack on accepted views and styles broadened so confusingly that "youth culture" no longer described it adequately. Counter-culture was a sufficiently vague and elastic substitute. It meant all things to all men and embraced everything new from clothing to politics. Some viewed the counter-culture as mankind's best, maybe only, hope; others saw it as a portent of civilization's imminent ruin. Few recalled the modest roots from which it sprang.

Even in the 1950's and very early sixties, when people still worried about conformity and the silent generation, there were different drummers to whose beat millions would one day march. The bohemians of that era (called "beatniks" or "beats") were only a handful, but they practiced free love, took drugs, repudiated the straight world, and generally showed which way the wind was blowing. They were highly publicized, so when the bohemian impulse strengthened, dropouts knew what was expected of them. While the beats showed their contempt for social norms mostly in physical ways, others did so intellectually. Norman Mailer, in "The White Negro," held up the sensual, lawless hipster as a model of behavior under oppressive capitalism. He believed, according to "The Time of Her Time," that sexual orgasm was the pinnacle of human experience, perhaps also an approach to ultimate truth. Norman O. Brown's *Life Against Death*, a psychoanalytic interpretation of history, was an underground classic which argued that cognition subverted intuition. Brown called for a return to "polymorphous perversity," man's natural estate. The popularity of Zen Buddhism demonstrated that others wished to slip the bonds of Western rationalism; so, from a different angle, did the vogue for black humor.

The most prophetic black humorist was Joseph Heller, whose novel *Catch-22* came out in 1960. Though set in World War II the book was even more appropriate to the Indochinese war. Later Heller said, "That was the war I had in mind; a war fought without military provocation, a war in which the real enemy is no longer the other side, but someone allegedly on your side. The ridiculous war I felt lurking in the future when I wrote the book." *Catch-22* was actually written during the Cold War, and sold well in the early sixties because it attacked the perceptions on which that war, like the Indochinese war that it fathered, grew. At the time reviewers didn't know what to make of *Catch-22*. World War II had been, as everyone knew, an absolutely straightforward case of good versus evil. Yet to Heller there was little moral difference between combatants. In fact all his characters are insane, or carry normal attributes to insane lengths. They belong to a bomber squadron in the Mediterranean. Terrified of combat, most hope for ground duty and are free to request it, but: "There was only one catch and that was Catch-22, which specified that a concern for one's own safety in the face of dangers that were real and immediate was the process of a rational mind. Orr was crazy and could be grounded. All he had to do was ask; and as soon as he did, he would no longer be crazy and would have to fly more missions. Orr would be crazy to fly more missions and sane if he didn't, but if he was sane he had to fly them. If he flew them he was crazy and didn't have to; but if he didn't want to he was sane and had to."

The squadron's success depends more on having a perfect bomb pattern than hitting the target. Milo Minderbinder is the key man in the Theater, though only a lieutenant, because he embodies the profit motive. He puts the entire war on a paying basis and hires the squadron out impartially to both sides. At the end Yossarian, the novel's hero, resolves his dilemma by setting out for neutral Sweden in a rubber raft. This was what hundreds of real deserters and draft evaders would be doing soon. It was also a perfect symbol for the masses of dropouts who sought utopian alternatives to the straight world. One day there would be hundreds of thousands of Yossarians, paddling away from the crazed society in frail crafts of their own devising. *Catch-22* was not just black comedy, nor even chiefly an anti-war novel, but a metaphor that helped shape the moral vision of an era.[1]

Although children and adolescents watched a great deal of television in the sixties, it seemed at first to have little effect. Surveys were always showing that youngsters spent fifty-four hours a week or whatever in front of the tube, yet what they saw was so bland or predictable as to make little difference. The exceptions were news programs, documentaries, and dramatic specials. Few watched them. What did influence the young was popular music, folk music first and then rock. Large-scale enthusiasm for folk music began in 1958 when the Kingston Trio recorded a song, "Tom Dooley," that sold two million records. This opened the way for less slickly commercial performers. Some, like Pete Seeger, who had been singing since the depression, were veteran performers. Others, like Joan Baez, were newcomers. It was conventional for folk songs to tell a story. Hence the idiom had always lent itself to propaganda. Seeger possessed an enormous repertoire of message songs that had gotten him blacklisted by the mass media years before. Joan Baez cared more for the message than the music, and after a few years devoted herself mainly to peace work. The folk-music vogue was an early stage in the politicalization of youth, a forerunner of the counter-culture. This was hardly apparent at the time. Folk music was not seen as morally reprehensible in the manner of rock and roll. It was a familiar genre. Folk was gentle music for the most part, and even when sung in protest did not offend many. Malvina Reynolds' "What Have They Done to the Rain?" complained of radioactive fallout which all detested. Pete Seeger's anti-war song "Where Have All the Flowers Gone?" was a favorite with both pacifists and the troops in Vietnam.

Bob Dylan was different. Where most folk singers were either clean-cut or homey looking, Dylan had wild long hair. He resembled a poor white dropout of questionable morals. His songs were hard-driving, powerful,

---

[1] Lenny Bruce was a more tragic harbinger of change. He was a successful night club comedian who created an obscene form of black comedy that involved more social criticism than humor. Bruce was first arrested for saying "motherfucker" on stage in 1962. Later he was busted for talking dirty about the Pope and many lesser offenses. He may have been insane. He died early from persecution and drug abuse, and then became an honored martyr in the anti-Establishment pantheon. He was one of the spiritual fathers of the Yippies.

intense. It was hard to be neutral about them. "The Times They Are a-Changing" was perhaps the first song to exploit the generation gap. Dylan's life was as controversial as his ideology. Later he dropped politics and got interested in rock music. At the Newport Jazz Festival in 1965 he was booed when he introduced a fusion of his own called "folk-rock." He went his own way after that, disowned by the politically minded but admired by a great cult following attracted as much, perhaps, by his independent life as by his music. He advanced the counter-culture in both ways and made money too. This also was an inspiration to those who came after him.

Another early expression, which coexisted with folk music, though quite unlike it, was the twist. Dance crazes were nothing new, but the twist was remarkable because it came to dominate social dancing. It used to be that dance fads were here today and gone tomorrow, while the two-step went on forever. Inexpert, that is to say most, social dancers had been loyal to it for generations. It played a key role in the traditional youth culture. Who could imagine a high school athletic event that did not end with couples clinging to one another on the dimly lit gym floor, while an amateur dance band plodded gamely on? When in 1961 the twist became popular, moralists were alarmed. It called for vigorous, exhibitionistic movements. Prurient men were reminded of the stripper's bumps and grinds. They felt the twist incited lust. Ministers denounced it. Yet in the twist (and its numerous descendants), bodies were not rubbed together as in the two-step, which had embarrassed millions of schoolboys. Millions more had suffered when through awkwardness they bumped or trod on others. The twist, by comparison, was easy and safe. No partner was bothered by the other's maladroitness. It aroused few passions. That was the practical reason for its success. But there was an ideological impulse behind it also. Amidst the noise and tumult each person danced alone, "doing his own thing," as would soon be said. But though alone, the dancer was surrounded by others doing their own thing in much the same manner. The twist celebrated both individuality and communality. This was to become a hallmark of the counter-culture, the right of everyone to be different in much the same way. The twist also foretold the dominance of rock, to which it was so well suited.

No group contributed more to the counter-culture than the Beatles, though, like folk music and the twist, their future significance was not at first apparent. Beatlemania began on October 13, 1963, when the quartet played at the London Palladium. The police, caught unawares, were hardly able to control the maddened throngs. On February 9, 1964, they appeared on U.S. television. The show received fifty thousand ticket requests for a theater that seated eight hundred. They were mobbed at the airport, besieged in their hotel, and adored everywhere. Even their soiled bed linen found a market. Their next recording, "Can't Buy Me Love," sold three million copies in advance of release, a new world's record. Their first movie, *A Hard Day's Night* (1964), was both a critical and a popular success. Some reviews compared them with the Marx brothers. They became millionaires overnight. The Queen decorated them for helping ease the balance-of-payments deficit. By 1966 they were so rich that they could afford to give up live performances.

For a time the Beatles seemed just another pop phenomenon, Elvis Presley multiplied by four. Few thought their music very distinguished. The reasons for its wide acceptance were hard to fathom. Most felt their showmanship was the key factor. They wore their hair longer than was fashionable, moved about a lot on stage, and avoided the class and racial identifications associated with earlier rock stars. Elvis had cultivated a proletarian image. Other rock stars had been black, or exploited the Negro rhythm-and-blues tradition. The Beatles were mostly working class in origin but sang with an American accent (like other English rock stars) and dressed in an elegant style, then popular in Britain, called "mod." The result was a deracinated, classless image of broad appeal.

The Beatles did not fade away as they were supposed to. Beatlemania continued for three years. Then the group went through several transformations that narrowed its audience to a smaller but intensely loyal cult following in the Dylan manner. The group became more self-consciously artistic. Their first long-playing record took one day to make and cost £400. "Sergeant Pepper's Lonely Hearts Club Band" took four months and cost £25,000. They were among the first to take advantage of new recording techniques that enabled multiple sound tracks to be played simultaneously. The Beatles learned new instruments and idioms too. The result was a complex music that attracted serious inquiry. Critics debated their contributions to musicology and argued over whether they were pathfinders or merely gifted entrepreneurs. In either case, they had come a long way aesthetically from their humble beginnings. Their music had a great effect on the young, so did their styles of life. They led the march of fashion away from mod and into the hairy, mustached, bearded, beaded, fringed, and embroidered costumes of the late sixties. For a time they followed the Maharishi, an Indian guru of some note. They married and divorced in progressively more striking ways. Some were arrested for smoking marijuana. In this too they were faithful to their clientele.

John Lennon went the farthest. He married Yoko Ono, best known as an author of happenings, and with her launched a bizarre campaign for world peace and goodness. Lennon returned his decoration to the Queen in protest against the human condition. Lennon and Ono hoped to visit America but were denied entry, which, to the bureaucratic mind, seemed a stroke for public order and morality. They staged a bed-in for peace all the same. They also formed a musical group of their own, the Plastic Ono Band, and circulated nude photographs and erotic drawings of themselves. This seemed an odd way to stop the war in Indochina, even to other Beatles. The group later broke up. By then they had made their mark, and, while strange, it was not a bad mark. Whatever lasting value their music may have, they set a good example to the young in most ways. Lennon's pacifism was nonviolent, even if wildly unorthodox. At a time when so many pacifists were imitating what they protested against, that was most desirable. They also worked hard at their respective arts and crafts, though others were dropping out and holding up laziness as a socially desirable trait. The Beatles showed that work was not merely an Establishment trick to keep the masses in subjection and the young out of trouble.

● ● ●

Beatlemania coincided with a more ominous development in the emerging counter-culture—the rise of the drug prophet Timothy Leary. He and Richard Alpert were scientific researchers at Harvard University who studied the effects of hallucinogenic drugs, notably a compound called LSD. As early as 1960 it was known that the two were propagandists as well as scientists. In 1961 the University Health Service made them promise not to use undergraduates in their experiments. Their violation of this pledge was the technical ground for firing them. A better one was that they had founded a drug cult. Earlier studies of LSD had failed, they said, because the researchers had not themselves taken the drug. In order to end this "authoritarian" practice, they "turned on" themselves. Their work was conducted in quarters designed to look like a bohemian residence instead of a laboratory. This was defended as a reconstruction of the natural environment in which social "acid-dropping" took place. They and many of their subjects became habitual users, not only of LSD but of marijuana and other drugs. They constructed an ideology of sorts around this practice. After they were fired the *Harvard Review* published an article of theirs praising the drug life: "Remember, man, a natural state is ecstatic wonder, ecstatic intuition, ecstatic accurate movement. Don't settle for less."

With some friends Leary and Alpert created the International Foundation for Internal Freedom (IF-IF) which published the *Psychedelic Review*. To advertise it a flyer was circulated that began, "Mescaline! Experimental Mysticism! Mushrooms! Ecstasy! LSD-25! Expansion of Consciousness! Phantastica! Transcendence! Hashish! Visionary Botany! Ololiuqui! Physiology of Religion! Internal Freedom! Morning Glory! Politics of the Nervous System!" Later the drug culture would generate a vast literature, but this was its essential message. The truth that made Western man free was only obtainable through hallucinogenic drugs. Truth was in the man, not the drug, yet the drug was necessary to uncover it. The natural state of man thus revealed was visionary, mystical, ecstatic. The heightened awareness stimulated by "consciousness-expanding" drugs brought undreamed-of sensual pleasures, according to Leary. Even better, drugs promoted peace, wisdom, and unity with the universe.

Alpert soon dropped from view. Leary went on to found his own sect, partly because once LSD was banned religious usage was the only ground left on which it could be defended, mostly because the drug cult *was* a religion. He wore long white robes and long blond hair. And he traveled about the country giving his liberating message (tune in, turn on, drop out) and having bizarre adventures. His personal following was never large, but drug use became commonplace among the young anyway. At advanced universities social smoking of marijuana was as acceptable as social drinking. More so, in a way, for it was better suited to the new ethic. One did not clutch one's solitary glass but shared one's "joint" with others. "Grass" made one gentle and pacific, not surly and hostile. As a forbidden pleasure it was all the more attractive to the thrill-seeking and the rebellious. And it helped further distinguish between the old world of grasping, combative, alcoholic adults and the turned-on, cooperative culture of the young. Leary was a bad prophet. Drug-based mystical religion was not the wave of the future. What the drug cult led to was a lot of dope-smoking and some hard drug-taking. When research suggested that LSD caused genetic damage, its use declined. But the effects of grass were hard to determine, so its consumption increased.

Sometimes "pot" smokers went on to other drugs—a deadly compound called "speed," and even heroin. These ruined many lives (though it was never clear that the lives were not already ruined to begin with). The popularity of drugs among the young induced panic in the old. States passed harsher and harsher laws that accomplished little. Campaigns against the drug traffic were launched periodically with similar results. When the flow of grass was interrupted, people turned to other drugs. Drug use seemed to go up either way. The generation gap widened. Young people thought marijuana less dangerous than alcohol, perhaps rightly. To proscribe the one and permit the other made no sense to them, except as still another example of adult hypocrisy and the hatred of youth. Leary had not meant all this to happen, but he was to blame for some of it all the same. No one did more to build the ideology that made pot-smoking a morally constructive act. But though a malign influence, no one deserved such legal persecution as he experienced before escaping to Algeria from a prison farm.

In Aldous Huxley's prophetic novel *Brave New World*, drug use was promoted by the state as a means of social control. During the sixties it remained a deviant practice and a source of great tension between the generations. Yet drugs did encourage conformity among the young. To "turn on and drop out" did not weaken the state. Quite the contrary, it drained off potentially subversive energies. The need for drugs gave society a lever should it ever decide to manipulate rather than repress users. Pharmacology and nervous strain had already combined to make many adult Americans dependent on drugs like alcohol and tranquilizers. Now the young were doing the same thing, if for different reasons. In a free country this meant only that individual problems increased. But should democracy fail, drug abuse among both the young and old was an instrument for control such as no dictator ever enjoyed. The young drug-takers thought to show contempt for a grasping, unfeeling society. In doing so they opened the door to a worse one. They scorned their elders for drinking and pill-taking, yet to outsiders their habits seemed little different, though ethically more pretentious. In both cases users were vulnerable and ineffective to the extent of their addiction. Of such ironies was the counter-culture built. . . .

The rebellion against traditional fashion went in two directions, though both were inspired by the young. The line of development just described emphasized brilliant or peculiar fabrics and designs. Here the emphasis was on costuming in a theatrical sense. People wore outfits that made them look like Mongols or cavaliers or whatever. These costumes, never cheap, were often very costly, though not more so than earlier styles. They were worn by others besides the young. What they owed to the emerging counter-culture was a certain freedom from constraint, and a degree of sensuality. Though the mini-skirt became a symbol of rebellious youth, it was so popular that wearing it was not an ideological statement, even if Middle Americans often thought so.

The other direction clothing took was more directly related to counter-cultural patterns. This mode had two seemingly incompatible elements—surplus military garments and handcrafted ones. Army and navy surplus clothing was the first style to be adopted by young people looking for a separate identity. Socially conscious youths began wearing army and navy jackets, shirts, and bell-bottom trousers in the early sixties. This was not meant to show centempt for the military, for anti-war sentiment was then at a low ebb, but as a mark of ostentatious frugality in the high-consumption society. As these garments become more in demand, the price went up and more expensive commercial imitations appeared. Wearing them accordingly meant less, but a certain flavor of austere noncomformity stuck to them all the same. They remained favorites of dissenting youths thereafter, even though worn by the merely fashionable too.

The hippies made handcrafted items popular. The implication here was that the wearer had made them, thus showing his independence and creativity. In the beginning this may often have been so. Soon, however, the market was so large and the people with skill and patience so limited that handcrafted items were commercially made and distributed, frequently by entrepreneurs among the young, sometimes through ordinary apparel channels. Bead shops and hippie boutiques became commonplace. Though their products were often quite costly, the vogue persisted among deviant youths anyway, partly because it was clear that whatever they wore would soon be imitated, partly because the message involved was too dear to abandon. Wearing beads, bangles, leather goods, fringes, colorful vests, and what all showed sympathy for American Indians, who inspired the most common designs, and fitted in with the popular back-to-nature ethic. When combined with military surplus garments they enabled the wearer to touch all the counter-cultural bases at once. Thus these fashions transmitted, however faintly, signals meaning peace, love, brotherhood, noble savagery, community, folk artistry, anti-capitalism and anti-militarism, and, later, revolutionary zeal.

This hippie *cum* military surplus mode also had a functional effect. It was a great leveler: when everyone wore the same bizarre costumes, everyone looked alike. Even better, it gave the ugly parity with the beautiful for the first time in modern history. Many of these costumes were pretty ghastly. A string of beads or an Indian headband did not redeem faded blue jeans and an army shirt. Long stringy hair or an untrimmed beard only aggravated the effect. Yet the young called such outfits beautiful. In effect, aesthetics were exchanged for ethics. Beauty was no longer related to appearance but to morality. To have the proper spirit, though homely, was to be beautiful. This was a great relief for the poorly endowed and a point in the counter-culture's favor. Yet it enraged adults. Once the association between beads, beards, and military surplus goods on the one hand, and radicalism and dope on the other, was established, Middle America declared war on the counter-culture's physical trappings. School systems everywhere waged a relentless struggle against long hair. To dress this way in many places was a hostile act which invited reprisals. The style became a chief symbol of the generation gap, clung to fanatically by youngsters the more they were persecuted for it, as fiercely resisted by their elders. The progress of the generational struggle could almost be measured by the spread of these fashions.

No doubt older people would have resented the new styles in any case, but the way they emerged made them doubly offensive. They were introduced by young bohemians, mainly in New York and San Francisco, whose deviant attributes were highly publicized. New York hippies were concentrated in a section called the East Village. (Greenwich Village, the traditional bohemian refuge, had gotten too commercial and expensive.) By the mid-sixties a sizable community of radicals, dropouts, youthful vagrants, unrecognized avant-garde artists, and others were assembling there and a variety of cults beginning to flourish. One of the odder was called Kerista. It was a religio-sexual movement that planned to establish a colony in the Caribbean. "Utopia Tomorrow for Swingers," its publication, the *Kerista Speeler*, proclaimed. Kerista invoked a murky, perfectionist theology revolving around sexual love. Sometimes the members engaged in bisexual gropes to advance the pleasure principle. This sounded like more fun than it actually was, according to visitors.

The mainstream of East Village cultural life was more formally political and artistic. The many activities of Ed Sanders suggest the range of enterprises generated there. He was editor and publisher of *Fuck You: A Magazine of the Arts.* A typical editorial in it begins: "Time is NOW for TOTAL ASSAULT ON THE MARIJUANA LAWS. It is CLEAR to us that the cockroach theory of grass smoking has to be abandoned. IN THE OPEN! ALL THOSE WHO SUCK UP THE BENEVOLENT NARCOTIC CANNABIS, TEENSHUN!! FORWARD, WITH MIND DIALS POINTED: ASSAULT! We have the facts! Cannabis is a nonaddictive gentle peace drug! The marijuana legislations were pushed through in the 1930's by the agents and goonsquads of the jan-sensisto-manichean fuckhaters' conspiracy. Certainly after 30 years of the blight, it is time to rise up for a bleep blop bleep assault on the social screen. . . . But we can't wait forever for you grass cadets to pull the takeover: grass-freak senators, labor leaders, presidents, etc.! The Goon Squads are few and we are many. We must spray our message into the million lobed American brain IMMEDIATELY!"

Sanders was also head of the East Village's most prominent rock group, The Fugs. They sang obscene songs of their own composition, and created equally obscene instruments for accompaniment (such as the erectophone, which appeared to be a long stick with bells on it). Among their better efforts were "What Are You Doing After the Orgy?" and the memorable "Kill for Peace." *The Fugs Song Book* described their music thusly:

> The Fug-songs seem to spurt into five areas of concentration:
> a) nouveau folk-freak
> b) sex rock and roll
> c) dope thrill chants
> d) horny cunt-hunger blues
> e) Total Assault on the Culture
>   (anti-war/anti-creep/anti-repression)
> . . . The meaning of the Fugs lies in the term BODY POETRY, to get at the frenzy of the thing, the grope-thing, The Body Poetry Formula is this:

The Head by way of the Big Beat to the genitals
The Genitals by way of Operation Brain Thrill to the Body Poetry.

In his spare time Sanders made pornographic movies. His most epic work, *Mongolian Cluster Fuck!*, was described in *Fuck You* as a "short but searing non-socially redeeming porn flick featuring 100 of the lower east side's finest, with musical background by Algernon Charles Swinburne & THE FUGS." Though more versatile and creative than most, Sanders was typical of the East Village's alienated young artists. Tiny papers like *Fuck You* were springing up everywhere. All tried to be obscene, provocative, and, it was thought, liberating. They despised form, caring only for the higher morality and aesthetics it was their duty to advance. Some were more political (porno-political usually) than others. Collectively they were soon to be known as the "underground press."

Several cuts above the underground press were the flourishing little magazines. They were avant garde in the traditional sense and aimed, in their way, for greatness. By 1966 there were at least 250 of these (as against sixty or so in the 1920's). The better financed (*Outsider, Steppenwolf*) were tastefully composed and printed; others were crudely photo-offset (*Kayak, Eventorium Muse*). The *Insect Trust Gazette,* an annual experiment, once published an issue in which the original manuscripts were simply photographed and printed without reduction. About a third of the "littles" were mimeographed. There was even a little magazine for scientists, the *Worm-Runners' Digest*, edited by a droll researcher at the University of Michigan for people of like taste.

Older cultural rebels contributed to the ferment. George Brecht's musical composition "Ladder" went as follows: "Paint a single straight ladder white/ Paint the bottom rung black/Distribute spectral colors on the rungs between." Even more to the point was "Laugh Piece" by John Lennon's future wife, Yoko Ono. It went "Keep laughing for a week." Nam June Paik composed a work known as "Young Penis Symphony." He was also an underground film producer and put on elaborate performances resembling the late happenings. One such was given at the Film-Makers Cinematheque using film, live music, and the cellist Charlotte Moorman. The audience saw short segments of a film by Robert Breer, alternating with views of Miss Moorman, silhouetted by backlighting behind the projection screen, playing short phrases of a Bach cello sonata. On completing each phrase she removed a garment. Another film clip would then be shown. This continued until she was lying on the floor, completely nude, playing her cello which was now atop her. Miss Moorman, "the Jeanne d'Arc of New Music," as she was called, appeared in other Paik compositions. She had been trained at the Juilliard School and was a member of Leopold Stokowski's American Symphony Orchestra.

As these few examples suggest, the East Village gained from its proximity to the New York avant garde. The mature counter-culture owed a lot to this relationship, but even in its early stages the East Village suffered from the influx of teenie-boppers and runaways who were to spoil both it and the Haight-Ashbury for serious cultural radicals. The people who were soon to be called hippies meant to build alternatives to the straight world. Against the hostile competitive, capitalistic values of bourgeois America they posed their own faith in nonviolence, love, and community. Drugs were important both as means to truth and advancers of the pleasure principle. The early hippies created institutions of sorts. Rock bands like the Jefferson Airplane, the Grateful Dead, Country Joe and the Fish flourished, as did communal societies, notably the Diggers. They were inspired by the seventeenth-century communists whose name they took. In practice they were a hip version of the Salvation Army.

Hippies lived together, in "tribes" or "families." Their golden rule was "Be nice to others, even when provoked, and they will be nice to you." In San Francisco their reservation was the Haight-Ashbury district near Golden Gate Park. They were much resented in the East Village by the natives, poor ethnics for the most part. In the Hashbury, on the other hand, they were welcome at first. Though peculiar, they were an improvement over the petty criminals they displaced. Even when freaked-out in public from drugs, a certain tolerance prevailed. After all, stepping over a drooling flower child on the street was better than getting mugged. Civic authorities were less open-minded. The drug traffic bothered them especially, and the Hashbury was loaded with "narks" (narcotics agents). Hunter S. Thompson wrote that "love is the password in the Haight-Ashbury, but paranoia is the style. Nobody wants to go to jail."

The fun-and-games era did not last long, perhaps only from 1965 to 1966. The hippie ethic was too fragile to withstand the combination of police surveillance and media exposure that soon afflicted it. The first hippies had a certain earnestness. But they were joined by masses of teen-age runaways. Nicholas von Hoffman observed that the Hashbury economy that began as a fraternal barter system quickly succumbed to the cash nexus. It became the first community in the world to revolve entirely around the buying and selling and taking of drugs. Marijuana and LSD were universal; less popular, but also commonplace, were LSD's more powerful relative STP, and amphetamines. "Speed kills" said the buttons and posters; speed freaks multiplied anyhow. To support themselves some hippies worked at casual labor or devised elaborate, usually unsuccessful schemes to make money out of hippie enterprises. Panhandling was popular, so was theft, disguised usually as communalism.

Bohemians invariably deplore monogamy, and the hippies were no exception. As one member of the Jefferson Airplane put it "The stage is our bed and the audience is our broad. We're not entertaining, we're making love." Though committed to sexual freedom on principle, and often promiscuous in fact, the hippies were not really very sexy. Timothy Leary notwithstanding, drugs seemed to dampen the sexual urge. And the hippies were too passive in any case for strenuous sex play. Conversely, the most ardent free lovers, like those in the Sexual Freedom League, had little interest in drugs. Among hippies the combination of bad diets, dope, communal living, and the struggle to survive made for a restricted sex life. Of course the hippies were always glad of chances to shock the bourgeoisie, which made them seem more depraved than they were. Then too, people expected them to be sexually perverse, and the more public-spirited hippies tried to oblige. Like good troupers they hated to let the public down, though willing to put it on.

Hippie relations with black people were worse than might have been supposed. Hippies owed blacks a lot. Their jargon was derived from the ghetto. They admired blacks, as certain whites always have, for being more emotional, sensual, and uninhibited. But there were very few black hippies. Superspade, a beloved Negro drug pusher, was an exception. Most hippies were frightened of blacks. "Spades are programmed for hate" was the way many put it. The Hashbury was periodically swept by rumors of impending black attacks. Some hippies looked to the motorcycle outlaws to protect them from black rage. This was not without a certain logic. Outlaws hated blacks and loved to fight. But they played their role as hippie militiamen uneasily. In truth they were more likely to destroy a hippie than defend him.

In the end it was neither the bikers nor the blacks but the media that destroyed hippiedom. The publicity given the summer of love attracted countless thousands of disturbed youngsters to the Hashbury and the East Village in 1967. San Francisco was not burdened with the vast numbers originally expected. But many did come, bringing in their train psychotics, drug peddlers, and all sorts of criminals. Drug poisoning, hepatitis (from infected needles), and various diseases resulting from malnutrition and exposure thinned their ranks. Rapes, muggings, and assaults became commonplace. Hippies had little money, but they were irresistibly easy marks. Hippie girls were safe to assault. They reacted passively, and as many were drug users and runaways they could not go to the police.

So the violence mounted. On the West Coast one drug peddler was stabbed to death and his right forearm removed. Superspade's body was found hanging from a cliff top. He had been stabbed, shot, and trussed in a sleeping bag. On October 8 the nude bodies of Linda Rea Fitzpatrick, eighteen, and James Leroy "Groovy" Hutchinson, twenty-one, were discovered in an East Village boiler room. They had been murdered while high on LSD. Though pregnant, Miss Fitzpatrick had also been raped. That was how the summer of love ended. Two days earlier the death and funeral of hippie had been ritually observed in San Francisco's Buena Vista Park. But the killing of Linda and Groovy marked its real end. The Hashbury deteriorated rapidly thereafter. Bad publicity drove the tourists away, and the hippie boutiques that serviced them closed. Some local rock groups dissolved; others, like the Jefferson Airplane and even the Grateful Dead, went commercial. The hippies and their institutions faded quietly away. The Hashbury regained something of its old character. The East Village, owing to its more diverse population and strategic location, changed less.

At its peak the hippie movement was the subject of much moralizing. Most often hippies were seen as degenerate and representative of all things godless and un-American. A minority accepted them as embodying a higher morality. The media viewed them as harmless, even amusing, freaks—which was probably closest to the truth. But before long it was clear that while the hippie movement was easily slain, the hippie style of life was not. Their habit of dressing up in costumes rather than outfits was widely imitated. So was their slang and their talk of peace, love, and beauty. The great popularity of ex-hippie rock groups was one sign of the cultural diffusion taking place, marijuana another. Weekend tripping spread to the suburbs. While the attempt to build parallel cultures on a large scale in places like the Hashbury failed, the hippies survived in many locales. Isolated farms, especially in New England and the Southwest, were particularly favored. And they thrived also on the fringes of colleges and universities, where the line between avant-garde student and alienated dropout was hard to draw. In tribes, families, and communes, the hippies lived on, despite considerable local harassment wherever they went.

Though few in number, hippies had a great effect on middle-class youth. Besides their sartorial influence, hippies made religion socially acceptable. Their interest in the supernatural was contagious. Some of the communes which sprang up in the late sixties were actually religious fellowships practicing a contemporary monasticism. One in western Massachusetts was called the Cathedral of the Spirit. Its forty members were led by a nineteen-year-old mystic who helped them prepare for the Second Coming and the new Aquarian Age when all men would be brothers. The Cathedral had rigid rules against alcohol, "sex without love," and, less typically, drugs. Members helped out neighboring farmers without pay, but the commune was essentially contemplative. Its sacred book was a fifty-seven-page typewritten manuscript composed by a middle-aged bus driver from Northfield, Massachusetts, which was thought to be divinely inspired. Another commune in Boston, called the Fort Hill Community, was more outward looking. Its sixty members hoped to spread their holy word through the mass media.

Some of the communes or brotherhoods sprang from traditional roots. In New York City a band of young Jews formed a Havurah (fellowship) to blend Jewish traditions with contemporary inspirations. They wanted to study subjects like "the prophetic mind; new forms of spirituality in the contemporary world; and readings from the Jewish mystical tradition." At the University of Massachusetts a hundred students celebrated Rosh Hashanah not in a synagogue but in a field where they danced and sang all night. Courses in religion multiplied. At Smith College the number of students taking them grew from 692 in 1954 to nearly 1,400 in 1969, though the student body remained constant at about 2,000. Columbia University had two hundred applicants for a graduate program in religion with only twenty openings.

Students saw traditional religion as a point of departure rather than a place for answers. Comparatively few joined the new fellowships, but large numbers were attracted to the concepts they embodied. Oriental theologies and the like grew more attractive, so did magic. At one Catholic university a coven of warlocks was discovered. They were given psychiatric attention (thereby missing a great chance. If only they had been exorcised instead, the Establishment would have shown its relevance). When a Canadian university gave the studentry a chance to recommend new courses they overwhelmingly asked for subjects like Zen, sorcery, and witchcraft. A work of classic Oriental magic, *I Ching*, or the *Book of Changes*, became popular. The best edition, a scholarly product of the Princeton University Press, used to sell a thousand copies a year. In 1968 fifty thousand copies were snapped up. Sometimes magic and mysticism were exploited more in fun than not. The Women's Liberation Movement had guerrilla theater troupes calling themselves WITCH (Women's International Terrorist Conspiracy from Hell). During the SDS sit-in at the University of Chicago they cursed the sociology department and put a hex on its chairman.

But there was a serious element to the vogue for magic. Teachers of philosophy and religion were struck by the anti-positivist, anti-science feelings of many students. Science was discredited as an agent of the military-industrial complex. It had failed to make life more attractive. Whole classes protested the epistemology of science as well as its intellectual dominion. Students believed the Establishment claimed to be rational, but showed that it was not. This supported one of the central truths of all religion, that man is more than a creature who reasons. Nor was it only the young who felt this way. Norman Mailer was something of a mystic, so was Timothy Leary. And the most ambitious academic effort to deal with these things, Theodore Roszak's *The Making of a Counter Culture*, ended with a strong appeal to faith. Like the alienated young, Roszak too rejected science and reason—"the myth of objective consciousness" as he called it. Instead of empiricism or the scientific method he wanted "the beauty of the fully illuminated personality" to be "our standard of truth." He liked magic as "a matter of communion with the forces of nature as if they were mindful, intentional presences." What he admired most in the New Left was its attempt, as he thought, to revive shamanism, to get back to the sanity and participatory democracy of prehistoric society. But he urged the left to give up its notion that violence and confrontation would change the world. What the left must do to influence the silent majority "was not simply to muster power against the misdeeds of society, but to transform the very sense men have of reality."

The anti-war movement was strongly affected by this new supernaturalism. On Moratorium Day in 1969 a University of Massachusetts student gave an emotional speech that brought the audience to its feet shouting, "The war is over." "He went into a dance, waving his arms," a campus minister said. "It was the essence of a revival meeting, where the audience makes a commitment to Christ at the end." The great peace demonstrations in 1969 were full of religious symbolism. In Boston 100,000 people gathered before a gigantic cross on the Common. In New York lighted candles were carried to the steps of St. Patrick's Cathedral. Candles were placed on the White House wall during the November mobilization. At other demonstrations the shofar, the ram's horn sounded by Jews at the beginning of each new year, was blown. Rock, the liturgical music of the young, was often played. So was folk music, which continued as a medium of moral expression after its popular decline.

. . . On its deepest level the counter-culture was the radical critique of Herbert Marcuse, Norman O. Brown, and even Paul Goodman. It also meant the New Left, communes and hippie farms, magic, hedonism, eroticism, and public nudity. And it included rock music, long hair, and miniskirts (or, alternatively, fatigue uniforms, used clothes, and the intentionally ugly or grotesque). Most attacks on the counter-culture were directed at its trivial aspects, pot and dress especially. Pot busts (police raids), often involving famous people or their children, became commonplace. The laws against pot were so punitive in some areas as to be almost unenforceable. Even President Nixon, spokesman for Middle American morality that he was, finally questioned them. Local fights against long hair, beards, and short skirts were beyond number. The American Civil Liberties Union began taking school systems to court for disciplining students on that account. New York City gave up trying to enforce dress codes. It was all the more difficult there as even the teachers were mod. At one school the principal ordered women teachers to wear smocks over their minis. They responded by buying mini-smocks.

Nor were athletics—the last bastion of orthodoxy, one might think— exempt, though coaches struggled to enforce yesterday's fashions. At Oregon State University one football player, the son of an Air Force officer, went hippie and dropped the sport. His coach said, "I recruited that boy thinking he was Jack Armstrong. I was wrong. He turned out to be a free-thinker." At the University of Pennsylvania a star defensive back showed up for summer practice with shoulder-length hair, sideburns down to the neck, beads, bells, thonged sandals, and a cloth sash round his waist. He was the only man on the team to bring a pet dog and a stereo set to the six-day camp. After a war of nerves culminating in an ultimatum from the coach, he grudgingly hacked a few inches off his mane. And so it went all over America.

Both sides in this struggle took fashion and style to be deadly serious matters, so political conflicts tended to become cultural wars. In the fall of 1969 the most important radical student group at New York University was called Transcendental Students. At a time when SDS could barely muster twenty-five members, five hundred or more belonged to TS. It began the previous semester when a group protesting overcrowding in the classroom staged a series of freak-outs in classrooms. This proved so attractive a custom that it was institutionalized. Rock, pot, and wine parties had obvious advantages over political action. The administration shrewdly made a former restaurant available to TS for a counter-cultural center. The students welcomed it as a haven for "guerrilla intellect" where the human spirit could breathe free. The administration saw it as just another recreational facility, which, of course, it was. And what dean would not rather have kids singing out in a restaurant than locking him in his office? Sometimes culture and politics were united. When the $12 million center for the performing arts opened in Milwaukee, Wisconsin, on September 18, 1969, six hundred students disrupted the inaugural concert. They rubbed balloons, blew bubble pipes, threw rolls of toilet paper, and demanded that 20 per cent of the seats be given free to welfare recipients.

The greatest event in counter-cultural history was the Woodstock Festival in Bethel, New York. It was organized on the pattern of other large rock festivals. Big-name groups were invited for several days of continuous entertaining in the open. A large crowd was expected, but nothing like the 300,000 or 400,000 youngsters who actually showed up on August 15, 1969. Everything fell apart in consequence. Tickets could not be collected nor services provided. There wasn't enough food or water. The roads were blocked with abandoned autos, and no one could get in or out for hours at a time. Surprisingly, there were no riots or disasters. The promoters chartered a fleet of helicopters to evacuate casualties (mostly from bad drug trips) and bring in essential supplies. Despite the rain and congestion, a good time was had by all (except the boy killed when a tractor accidentally drove over his sleeping bag). No one had ever seen so large and ruly a gathering before. People stripped down, smoked pot, and turned on with nary a discouraging word, so legend has it. Afterward the young generally agreed that it was a beautiful experience proving their superior morality. People were nicer to each other than ever before. Even the police were impressed by the public's order (a result of their wisely deciding not to enforce the drug laws).

But the counter-culture had its bad moments in 1969 also. Haight-Ashbury continued to decay. It was now mainly a slum where criminals preyed on helpless drug freaks. Worse still was the Battle of Berkeley, which put both the straight culture and the counter-culture in the worst possible light, especially the former. The University of California owned a number of vacant lots south of the campus. The land had been cleared in anticipation of buildings it was unable to construct. One block lay vacant for so long that the street people—hippies, students, dropouts, and others—transformed it into a People's Park. Pressure was brought on the University by the local power structure to block its use, which was done. On May 15 some six thousand students and street people held a rally on campus, then advanced on the park. County sheriffs, highway patrolmen, and the Berkeley police met them with a hail of gunfire. One person died of buckshot wounds, another was blinded. Many more were shot though few arrested. Those who were arrested were handled so brutally that the circuit court enjoined the sheriff to have his men stop beating and abusing them. Disorders continued. Governor Reagan declared a state of emergency and brought in the National Guard. Five days later one of its helicopters sprayed gas over the campus, thus making the educational process at Berkeley even more trying than usual.

Of course the Establishment was most to blame for Vietnamizing the cultural war. But the meretricious aspects of the counter-culture were evident too. If the police were really "fascist pigs," as the street people said, why goad and defy them? And especially why harass the National Guardsmen who didn't want to be in Berkeley anyhow? This was hardly on the same order as murdering people with shotguns. Yet such behavior was stupid, pointless, and self-defeating, like so much else in the counter-culture. The silent majority was not won over. Nor was the People's Park saved. A year later the area was still fenced in. (Though vacant, the University, having pretended to want it as a recreational area, tried to make it one. But as the students thought it stained with innocent blood, they avoided it.)

The rock festival at Altamount that winter was another disaster. It was a free concert that climaxed the Rolling Stones' whirlwind tour of the U.S. They called it their gift to the fans. Actually it was a clever promotion. The Stones had been impressed with the moneymaking potential of Woodstock. While Woodstock cost the promoters a fortune, they stood to recoup their losses with a film of the event. This inspired the Stones to do a Woodstock themselves. At the last minute they obtained the use of Dick Carter's Altamont Raceway. It had been doing poorly and the owner thought the publicity would help business. Little was done to prepare the site. The police didn't have enough notice to bring in reserves, so the Stones hired a band of Hell's Angels as security guards (for $500 worth of beer). The Stones did their thing and the Angels did theirs.

The result was best captured by a *Rolling Stone* magazine photograph showing Mick Jagger looking properly aghast while Angels beat a young Negro to death on stage. A musician who tried to stop them was knocked unconscious, and he was lucky at that. Before the day was over many more were beaten, though no others fatally. Sometimes the beatings were for aesthetic reasons. One very fat man took off his clothes in the approved rock festival manner. This offended the Angels who set on him with pool cues. No one knows how many were clubbed that day. The death count came to four. Apart from Meredith Hunter, who was stabbed and kicked to death, they mostly died by accident. A car drove off the road into a clump of people and killed two. A man, apparently high on drugs, slid into an irrigation canal and drowned. The drug freak-outs were more numerous than at Woodstock. The medical care was less adequate. Not that the physicians on hand didn't try; they just lacked the support provided at Woodstock, whose promoters had spared no expense to avert disaster. Oddly enough the press, normally so eager to exploit the counter-culture, missed the point of Altamont. Early accounts followed the customary rock festival line, acclaiming it as yet another triumph of youth. In the East it received little attention of any kind.

It remained for *Rolling Stone,* the rock world's most authoritative journal, to tell the whole story of what it called the Altamont Death Festival. The violence was quite bad enough, but what especially bothered *Rolling Stone* was the commercial cynicism behind it. That huge gathering was assembled by the Stones to make a lucrative film on the cheap. They could have hired legitimate security guards, but it cost less to use the Angels. (At Woodstock unarmed civilians trained by the Hog Farm commune kept order.) They were too rushed for the careful planning that went into Woodstock, too callous (and greedy) to pour in the emergency resources that had saved the day there. And, appropriately, they faked the moviemaking too so as to have a documentary of the event they intended, not the one they got. *Rolling Stone* said that a cameraman was recording a fat, naked girl freaking out backstage when the director stopped him. "Don't shoot that. That's ugly. We only want beautiful things." The cameraman made the obvious response. "How can you possibly say that? Everything here is so ugly."

Rolling Stone thought the star system at fault. Once a band got as big as the Stones they experienced delusions of grandeur, "ego trips" in the argot. And with so much money to be made by high-pressure promotions, "the hype" became inevitable. Others agreed. The *Los Angeles Free Press,* biggest of the underground papers, ran a full-page caricature of Mick Jagger with an Adolf Hitler mustache, arm draped around a Hell's Angel, while long-haired kids gave them the Nazi salute. Ralph Gleason of the *San Francisco Chronicle* explained Altamont this way: "The name of the game is money, power, and ego, and money is first as it brings power. The Stones didn't do it for free, they did it for money, only the tab was paid in a different way. Whoever goes to the movie paid for the Altamont religious assembly."[2] Quite so. But why did so many others go along with the Stones? The Jefferson Airplane, and especially the Grateful Dead, reputedly the most socially conscious rock bands, participated. So did counter-culture folk heroes like Emmet Grogan of the Diggers. Here the gullibility—innocence, perhaps—of the deviant young was responsible. Because the rock bandits smoked pot and talked a revolutionary game, they were supposed to be different from other entertainers. Even though they made fortunes and spent them ostentatiously, their virtue was always presumed. What Altamont showed was that the difference between a rock king and a robber baron was about six inches of hair.[3]

If Altamont exposed one face of the counter-culture, the Manson family revealed another. Late in 1969 Sharon Tate, a pregnant movie actress, and four of her jet-set friends were ritually murdered in the expensive Bel-Air district of Los Angeles. Though apparently senseless, their deaths were thought related to the rootless, thrill-oriented life style of the Beautiful People. But on December 1 policemen began arresting obscure hippies. Their leader, Charles Manson, was an ex-convict and seemingly deranged. Susan Atkins, a member of his "family," gave several cloudy versions of what had happened. On the strength of them Manson was indicted for murder. Though his guilt remained unproven, the basic facts about his past seemed clear. He was a neglected child who became a juvenile delinquent. In 1960 he was convicted of forgery and spent seven years in the penitentiary. On his release he went to the Hashbury and acquired a harem of young girls. After floating through the hippie underground for a time, he left the Hashbury with his family of nine girls and five boys early in 1968. They ended up at Spahn's Ranch in the Santa Susana Mountains, north of the San Fernando Valley. The owner was old and blind. Manson terrified him. But the girls took care of him so he let the family stay on. They spent a year at the ranch before the police suspected them of stealing cars. Then they camped out in the desert until arrested.

Life with the Manson family was a combination of hippieism and paranoia. Manson subscribed to the usual counter-cultural values. Inhibitions, the Establishment, regular employment, and other straight virtues were bad. Free love, nature, dope, rock, and mysticism were good. He believed a race war was coming (predicted in Beatle songs) and armed his family in anticipation of it. Some of the cars they stole were modified for

---

[2] Gleason was the best writer on popular music and the youth culture associated with it, which he once admired greatly. For an earlier assessment see his "Like a Rolling Stone," *American Scholar* (Autumn 1967).

[3] This is to criticize the singer, not the song. Whatever one might think of some performers, there is no doubt that rock itself was an exciting musical form. Adults rarely heard it because rock seldom was played on television, or even radio in most parts of the country. Rock artists appeared mainly in concerts and clubs, to which few over thirty went. Not knowing the music, there was little reason for them to buy the records that showed rock at its most complex and interesting. Like jazz, rock became more sophisticated with time and made greater demands on the artist's talent. Even more than jazz, rock produced an army of amateur and semi-professional players around the country. Though often making up in volume what they lacked in skill, their numbers alone guaranteed that rock would survive its exploiters.

use in the desert, where he meant to make his last stand. And, naturally, he tried to break into the rock music business. One reason why he allegedly murdered Miss Tate and her friends was that they were in a house previously occupied by a man who had broken a promise to advance Manson's career. The Manson family was thought to have killed other people even more capriciously. Yet after his arrest most of the girls remained loyal to Manson. Young, largely middle class, they were still "hypnotized" or "enslaved" by him. Those not arrested continued to hope for a family reunion. Of course hippies were not murderers usually. But the repressed hostility, authoritarianism, perversity, and mindless paranoia that underlay much of the hippie ethic were never displayed more clearly. The folkways of the flower children tended toward extremes. At one end they were natural victims; at the other, natural victimizers. The Manson family were both at once.

Taken together the varieties of life among deviant youths showed the counter-culture to be disintegrating. What was disturbing about it was not so much the surface expression as its tendency to mirror the culture it supposedly rejected. The young condemned adult hypocrisy while matching its contradictions with their own. The old were materialistic, hung up on big cars and ranch houses. The young were equally devoted to motorcycles, stereo sets, and electric guitars. The old sought power and wealth. So did the young as rock musicians, political leaders, and frequently as salesmen of counter-cultural goods and services. What distinguished reactionary capitalists from their avant-garde opposite numbers was often no more than a lack of moral pretense. While condemning the adult world's addiction to violence, the young admired third-world revolutionaries, Black Panthers, and even motorcycle outlaws. The rhetoric of the young got progressively meaner and more hostile. This was not so bad as butchering Vietnamese, but it was not very encouraging either. And where hate led, violence followed.

Adults pointed these inconsistencies out enough, with few good results. Usable perceptions are always self-perceptions, which made the *Rolling Stone* exposé of Altamont so valuable. This was a small but hopeful sign that the capacity for self-analysis was not totally submerged, despite the flood of self-congratulatory pieties with which the deviant young described themselves. The decline of the New Left was another. Once a buoyant and promising thing, it became poisoned by hate, failure, and romantic millennialism. Its diminished appeal offered hope of sobriety's return. So did the surge of student interest in environmental issues at the decade's end. These were not fake problems, like so many youthful obsessions, but real ones. They would take the best efforts of many generations to overcome. No doubt the young would lose interest in them after a while as usual. Still, it was better to save a forest or clean a river than to vandalize a campus. No amount of youthful nagging was likely to make adults give up their sinful ways. It was possible that the young and old together might salvage enough of the threatened environment to leave posterity something of lasting value. The generations yet unborn were not likely to care much whether ROTC was conducted on campus or off. But they will remember this age, for better or worse, with every breath they take.

One aspect of the counter-culture deserves special mention: its

assumption that hedonism was inevitably anti-capitalist. As James Hitchcock pointed out, the New Left identified capitalism with puritanism and
deferred gratifications. But this was true of capitalism only with respect
to work. Where consumption was concerned, it urged people to gratify
their slightest wish. It exploited sex shamelessly to that end, limited only
by law and custom. When the taboos against nudity were removed, merchants soon took advantage of their new freedom. Naked models, actors,
even waitresses were one result, pornographic flicks another. Who doubted
that if marijuana became legal the tobacco companies would soon put
Mexican gold in every vending machine? It was, after all, part of Aldous
Huxley's genius that he saw how sensual gratification could enslave men
more effectively than Hitler ever could. Victorian inhibitions, the Protestant Ethic itself were, though weakened, among the few remaining defenses against the market economy that Americans possessed. To destroy
them for freedom's sake would only make people more vulnerable to con-
sumerism than they already were. Which was not to say that sexual and
other freedoms were not good things in their own right. But there was no
assurance that behavioral liberty would not grow at the expense of political
freedom. It was one thing to say that sex promoted mental health, another
to say it advanced social justice. In confusing the two young deviants laid
themselves open to what Herbert Marcuse called "repressive de-sublimation," the means by which the socio-economic order was made more attractive, and hence more durable. Sex was no threat to the Establishment.
Panicky moralists found this hard to believe, so they kept trying to suppress
it. But the shrewder guardians of established relationships saw hedonism
for what it partially was, a valuable means of social control. What made
this hard to get across was that left and right agreed that sex was subversive. That was why the Filthy Speech Movement arose, and why the John
Birch Society and its front groups divided a host of communities in the
late sixties. They insisted that sex education was a communist plot to fray
the country's moral fiber. They could hardly have been more wrong. As
practiced in most schools, sex education was anything but erotic. In fact,
more students were probably turned off sex than on to it by such courses.
The Kremlin was hardly less orthodox than the Birch Society on sexual
matters, sexual denial being thought a trait of all serious revolutionaries.
But the sexual propaganda of the young confirmed John Birchers in their
delusions. As elsewhere, the misconceptions of each side reinforced one
another.

Still, the counter-culture's decline ought not to be celebrated prematurely. It outlasted the sixties. It had risen in the first place because of the
larger culture's defects. War, poverty, social and racial injustice were widespread. The universities were less human than they might have been. The
regulation of sexual conduct led to endless persecutions of the innocent or
the pathetic to no one's advantage. Young people had much to complain
of. Rebellious youth had thought to make things better. It was hardly their
fault that things got worse. They were, after all, products of the society
they meant to change, and marked by it as everyone was. Vanity and
ignorance made them think themselves free of the weaknesses they saw
so clearly in others. But adults were vain and ignorant too, and, what's
more, they had power as the young did not. When they erred, as in Viet-

nam, millions suffered. The young hated being powerless, but thanks to it they were spared the awful burden of guilt that adults bore. They would have power soon enough, and no doubt use it just as badly. In the meantime, though, people did well to keep them in perspective.

The dreary propaganda about youth's insurgent idealism continued into the seventies. So did attempts to make them look clean-cut. American society went on being obsessed with the young. But all popular manias are seasonal. Each era has its own preoccupations. The young and their counter-culture were a special feature of the 1960's and would probably not be regarded in the old way for very long afterward. And, demographically speaking, youth itself was on the wane. The median age of Americans had risen steadily in modern times, reaching a peak of thirty years of age in 1952. The baby boom reversed this trend, like so many others. In 1968 the median age was only 27.7 years. But as the birthrate fell the median age began to rise. By 1975 it would be over twenty-eight. By 1990 it should be back up to thirty again, putting half the population beyond the age of trust. Their disproportionate numbers was one reason why youth was so prominent in the sixties. It was reasonable to suppose they would become less so as their numbers declined in relation to older people.

Common sense suggested that work and the pleasure principle would both continue. Once life and work were thought to be guided by the same principles. In the twentieth century they had started to divide, with one set of rules for working and another for living. The complexities of a post-industrial economy would probably maintain that distinction. The discipline of work would prevail on the job. The tendency to "swing" off it would increase, and the dropout community too. The economy was already rich enough to support a substantial leisure class, as the hippies demonstrated. The movement toward guaranteed incomes would make idleness even more feasible. A large dependent population, in economic terms, was entirely practical—perhaps, given automation, even desirable. How utopian to have a society in which the decision to work was voluntary! Yet if economic growth continued and an effective welfare state was established, such a thing was not unimaginable, however repugnant to the Protestant Ethic. Perhaps that was what the unpleasant features of life in the sixties pointed toward. Later historians might think them merely the growing pains of this new order. A Brave New World indeed!

A further reason for taking this view was the rise of an adult counter-culture. Americans have always been attracted to cults and such. No enthusiasm, however bizarre, fails to gain some notice in so vast and restless a country. Crank scientists and religious eccentrics are especially welcomed. In the 1960's this was more true than ever, and there seemed to be more uniformity of belief among the cults than before. Perhaps also they were more respectable. The Esalen Institute in northern California was one of the most successful. It offered three-day seminars conducted by Dr. Frederick S. Perls, the founder of Gestalt therapy. When his book by that title was published in 1950 it won, as might have been expected, little attention. But in the sixties it flourished to the point where perhaps a hundred Gestalt therapists were in practice. As employed at Esalen, Gestalt therapy involved a series of individual encounters within a group context. Perls tried to cultivate moments of sudden insights that produced a strong awareness

of the present moment. Unlike psychoanalysis, Gestalt therapy was directive. The therapist diagnosed the ailment and organized its cure in short
bursts of intensive treatment. People were encouraged to act out dreams
so as to discover their hidden message. The emphasis was on sensuality,
spontaneity, and the reduction of language which was seen as more a
barrier to understanding than as a means of communication. There was
much role-playing, aggression-releasing exercises, and "unstructured
interaction." Esalen itself, with its hot sulphur baths where mixed nude
bathing was encouraged, combined the features of a hip spa, a mental
clinic, and a religious center. It brought social scientists and mystics together
in common enterprises. By 1967 Esalen grossed a million dollars a year.
Four thousand people attended its seminars. Twelve thousand used its
branch in San Francisco.

Though Esalen was the most celebrated center of "Third Force Psychiatry," it was hardly alone. Encounter groups, T-groups, sensitivity groups
all practiced variations of the same theme. So, in a more intense way, did
Synanon. Synanon was founded in 1958 by an ex-alcoholic named Charles
E. Dederich. It began as a way of reclaiming alcoholics, and especially
drug addicts, through communal living and group therapy. It aimed to
peel away the defenses that supported addiction. The cure was a drastic
one and the Synanon ethic extremely authoritarian, as a treatment based
not on clinical experience but actual street life would naturally be. Synanon's most popular feature was the Synanon game, a kind of encounter
group open to outsiders. From its modest beginning Synanon expanded
rapidly into a network of clinics and small businesses operated by members to support the therapeutic program. Already a corporation by the
decade's end, Dederich expected it to become a mass movement in time.
Others thought so too. Abraham Maslow of Brandeis University declared
that "Synanon is now in the process of torpedoing the entire world of
psychiatry and within ten years will completely replace psychiatry."

Esalen and Synanon got much publicity, but, though substantial efforts,
they were only the tip of the iceberg. Beneath them were literally thousands
of groups dedicated to better mental health through de-sublimation, often
sponsored by businesses and universities. In a sense what they did was
rationalize the counter-cultural ethic and bend it to fit the needs of middle-
class adults. For some, expanding their consciousness meant little more
than weekend tripping, with, or more commonly without, drugs. If most
didn't give up work in the hippie manner, they became more relaxed about
it. Some thought less about success and more about fun. Some found new
satisfaction in their work, or else more satisfying work. The range of individual response was great, but the overall effect was to promote sensuality,
and to diminish the Protestant Ethic. As with the counter-culture, an inflated
propaganda accompanied these efforts. Ultimate truth, complete harmony with self, undreamed-of pleasures, and the like were supposed to
result from conversion. De-sublimation did not mean license, of course.
As the Haight-Ashbury showed, without self-denial there is self-destruction. The cults tried to develop more agreeable mechanisms to replace the
fears and guilts undergirding the old morality. They wanted people to live
more rich and immediate social lives, but they didn't propose to do away
with restraint entirely. Mystic cults promoted self-discipline through var-

ious austere regimes. Psychiatric cults used the group as a control. One learned from his fellows what was appropriate to the liberated spirit.

The sensuality common to most of these groups was what the sexual revolution was all about. Properly speaking, of course, there was no sexual revolution. Easy divorce, relatively free access to contraceptives, and tolerated promiscuity were all well established by the 1920's. Insofar as the Kinsey and other reports are historically reliable, there had been little change since then in the rate of sexual deviance. What had changed was the attitude of many people toward it. In the 1960's deviance was not so much tolerated as applauded in many quarters. Before, college students having an affair used discretion. Later they were more likely to live together in well-advertised nonmarital bliss. Similarly, adults were not much more promiscuous in the sixties than in the forties or fifties, but they were more disposed to proclaim the merits of extra-marital sexuality. The sexualization of everyday life moved on. This was often desirable, or at least harmless, except for the frightening rise in the incidence of VD after the Pill made condoms seemingly obsolete.

Fornication, though illegal in most places, was not usually regarded as actionable. But there remained many laws against sexual behavior that were enforced, if erratically. Contraceptives were difficult to get in some places, especially for single women. Legal abortions were severely limited. Homosexuals were persecuted everywhere. Attempts to change these laws were part of the new moral permissiveness. Few legal reforms were actually secured in the sixties. Liberalized abortion laws were passed in Colorado and elsewhere to little effect. Abortions remained scarce and expensive. The overwhelming majority continued to be illegal. Contraceptive laws did not change much either, though in practice contraceptives became easier to get. Nor were the laws prohibiting homosexuality altered much. Here too, though, changes in practice eased conditions. The deliberate entrapment of homosexuals declined in some cities. Some police forces, as in San Francisco, made more of an effort to distinguish between harmless (as between consenting adults) and anti-social perversions.

More striking still was the willingness of sexual minorities to identify themselves. Male homosexuals were among the first to do so. In the Mattachine Society and later organizations they campaigned openly for an end to discriminatory laws and customs. The Daughters of Bilitis did the same for lesbians. Even the most exotic minorities, like the transvestites and transsexuals (men, usually, who wanted to change their sex surgically), became organized. The creation of homosexual churches, like the Metropolitan Community Church of Los Angeles, testified to that. They hoped mainly to be treated the same as heterosexuals. But in the Gay Liberation Front the sexual underground produced its own New Left organization. Its birth apparently dated from the night of June 28, 1969, when police raided a gay bar in Greenwich Village called the Stonewall Inn. Homosexuals usually accepted arrest passively. But for some reason that night it was different. They fought back, and for a week afterward continued to agitate, ending with a public march of some one thousand people.

More sober homosexuals greeted this event with mixed emotions. They were astonished to find such spirit among the so-called street queens, the poorest and most trouble-prone homosexuals of all. But they didn't really dig the violence. As one leader of the Mattachine Society (a sort of gay NAACP) put it: "I mean, people did try to set fire to the bar, and one drag queen, much to the amazement of the mob, just pounded the hell out of a Tactical Patrol Force cop! I don't know if battering TPF men is really the answer to our problem." In any event the Gay Liberation Front followed these events. Rather like a Homosexuals for a Democratic Society, the GLF participated in the next Hiroshima Day march that summer. It was the first time homosexuals ever participated in a peace action under their own colors. The "Pink Panthers" were mostly young, of course. But whether their movement flourished or, most probably, withered away, the mere fact of its existence said a lot about changing mores in America.

While it was difficult in 1969 to tell where the counter-culture would go, it was easy to see where it came from. Artists and bohemians had been demanding more freedom from social and artistic conventions for a long time. The romantic faith in nature, intuition, and spontaneity was equally old. What was striking about the sixties was that the revolt against discipline, even self-discipline, and authority spread so widely. Resistance to these tendencies largely collapsed in the arts. Soon the universities gave ground also. The rise of hedonism and the decline of work were obviously functions of increased prosperity, and also of effective merchandising. The consumer economy depended on advertising, which in turn leaned heavily on the pleasure principle. This had been true for fifty years at least, but not until television did it really work well. The generation that made the counter-culture was the first to be propagandized from infancy on behalf of the pleasure principle.

But though all of them were exposed to hucksterism, not all were convinced. Working-class youngsters especially soon learned that life was different from television. Limited incomes and uncertain futures put them in touch with reality earlier on. Middle-class children did not learn the facts of life until much later. Cushioned by higher family incomes, indulged in the same way as their peers on the screen, they were shocked to discover that the world was not what they had been taught it was. The pleasure orientation survived this discovery, the ideological packaging it came in often did not. All this had happened before, but in earlier years there was no large, institutionalized subculture for the alienated to turn to. In the sixties hippiedom provided one such, the universities another. The media publicized these alternatives and made famous the ideological leaders who promoted them. So the deviant young knew where to go for the answers they wanted, and how to behave when they got them. The media thus completed the cycle begun when they first turned youngsters to pleasure. That was done to encourage consumption. The message was still effective when young consumers rejected the products TV offered and discovered others more congenial to them.

Though much in the counter-culture was attractive and valuable, it was dangerous in three ways. First, self-indulgence led frequently to self-destruction. Second, the counter-culture increased social hostility. The generation gap was one example, but the class gap another. Working-class youngsters resented the counter-culture. They accepted adult values for the most part. They had to work whether they liked it or not. Beating up the long-haired and voting for George Wallace were only two ways they expressed these feelings. The counter-culture was geographical too. It flourished in cities and on campuses. Elsewhere, in Middle America especially, it was hated and feared. The result was a national division between the counter-culture and those adults who admired or tolerated it—upper-middle-class professionals and intellectuals in the Northeast particularly—and the silent majority of workers and Middle Americans who didn't. The tensions between these groups made solving social and political problems all the more difficult, and were, indeed, part of the problem.

Finally, the counter-culture was hell on standards. A handful of bohemians were no great threat to art and intellect. The problem was that a generation of students, the artists and intellectuals of the future, was infected with romanticism. Truth and beauty were in the eye of the beholder. They were discovered or created by the pure of heart. Formal education and training were not, therefore, merely redundant but dangerous for obstructing channels through which the spirit flowed. It was one thing for hippies to say this, romanticism being the natural religion of bohemia. It was quite another to hear it from graduate students. Those who did anguished over the future of scholarship, like the critics who worried that pop art meant the end of art. Those fears were doubtlessly overdrawn, but the pace of cultural change was so fast in the sixties that they were hardly absurd.

Logic seemed everywhere to be giving way to intuition, and self-discipline to impulse. Romanticism had never worked well in the past. It seemed to be doing as badly in the present. The hippies went from flower power to death-tripping in a few years. The New Left took only a little longer to move from participatory democracy to demolition. The counter-cultural ethic remained as beguiling as ever in theory. In practice, like most utopian dreams, human nature tended to defeat it. At the decade's end, young believers looked forward to the Age of Aquarius. Sensible men knew there would be no Aquarian age. What they didn't know was the sort of legacy the counter-culture would leave behind. Some feared that the straight world would go on as before, others that it wouldn't.

*Working men and women struggled hard to maintain
a decent standard of living*

Working Men and Women

LILLIAN BRESLOW RUBIN

Labor historians have been primarily concerned with men and industry. The long struggle of the worker in heavy industry to organize was finally ended during the mobilization for the Second World War. Although there continues to be conflict between unions and management over wages, conditions of work, and fringe benefits, both big business and big labor have come to agree that cooperation is a better tool than conflict in most labor disputes. Thus, if the economy does not deteriorate completely, continued improvement in wages and working conditions for organized industrial labor seems assured.

What is often not recognized, however, is the limited extent of union membership. The long-established and conservative craft unions, the newly arrived industrial unions, and the increasingly active white-collar and service unions still cover less than half of the American labor force. Women make up a disproportionate number of the unorganized workers, and most of these women are in the increasingly important service sector of the economy.

Recent legislation by the federal government prohibiting discrimination by gender in the labor market and the movement to amend the Constitution to grant equal rights to women in federal programs have focused national attention on working women. The history of women as a factor in the employed labor force began in the nineteenth century. Women had always worked, of course, in home, farm, and mill. But the same nineteenth-century urbanization that created the "cult of domesticity" for middle-class women forced working-class women (and their children) into the workplace so that their families could earn a survival income.

Today, any attempt to sustain the notion that women's sphere is limited to the home flies in the face of reality at all class levels. Over half of all women between the ages of eighteen and sixty-four are now in the labor force. Four out of ten working women are mothers, and 36 percent of these have children under the age of six. The persistence of the traditional division of labor in the home requires many working women, particularly in families with limited income, to hold two full-time jobs—one in the workplace and one in the home.

In the economically precarious times in which we live, all families except the very wealthy are feeling the strains of trying to make ends meet. For working-class families the attempt to maintain a decent standard of living is particularly stressful. Lillian Breslow Rubin, of the Institute for Scientific Analysis in San Francisco, has described working-class life in a remarkably perceptive and sympathetic fashion. Using interviewing techniques and applying her extensive knowledge of the scholarly literature on work and families, Rubin has created a masterpiece of social analysis.

There have been many studies in recent years that have described the attitudes of American workers toward their work. The boredom, alienation, and frustrations have been amply catalogued. What is new in Rubin's analysis of the work people do, as described in the chapter of her book reprinted here, is her account of the impact of work on domestic relations. What spillover does life on the job have on life in the home? What does it do to a man's image of himself if he has difficulty providing a good living for his household?

Perhaps the most important insights come in Rubin's description of what happens to the relationship between husband and wife when the wife goes to work. Even though most of the women interviewed worked only part-time, this apparent break with the traditional role differentiation of husband and wife often put an almost intolerable strain on the marriage. Not only was the authority of the husband threatened (an attitude the men described freely), but also the women experienced an exhilarating sense of independence when they had pay envelopes of their own, no matter how small. As increasing numbers of women continue to enter the work force, for whatever reasons, they are likely to continue to challenge male dominance both at home and in the workplace. If men fail to change their attitudes about the "proper" relationship between men and women, one can expect to see an increase in stressful family situations, which contribute heavily to the dis-ease of our society.

> *Tell me something about the work you do*
> *and how you feel about it.*

For the men, whose definition of self is so closely tied to work, it's a mixed bag—a complex picture of struggle, of achievements and disappointments, of successes and failures. In their early work life, most move restlessly from job to job seeking not only higher wages and better working

"Work and Its Meaning" (Editor's title: "Working Men and Women"). From *Worlds of Pain: Life in the Working-Class Family*, by Lillian Breslow Rubin. Copyright © 1976 by Lillian Breslow Rubin. Reprinted by permission of Basic Books, Inc., Publishers, New York.

conditions, but some kind of work in which they can find meaning, purpose, and dignity:

> God, I hated that assembly line. *I hated it.* I used to fall asleep on the job standing up and still keep doing my work. There's nothing more boring and more repetitious in the world. On top of it, you don't feel human. The machine's running you, you're not running it.
>
> [*Thirty-three-year-old mechanic.*]

Thus, by the time they're twenty-five, their post-school work life averages almost eight years, and half have held as many as six, eight, or ten jobs.

Generally, they start out as laborers, operatives in an oil refinery, assembly-line workers in the local canneries, automobile or parts plants, warehousemen, janitors, or gas station attendants—jobs in which worker dissatisfaction is well documented. Some move on and up—into jobs that require more skill, jobs that still demand plenty of hard work, but which at least leave one with a sense of mastery and competence:

> I'm proud of what I've done with my life. I come from humble origins, and I never even finished school; but I've gotten someplace. I work hard, but it's good work. It's challenging and never routine. When I finish a day's work, I know I've accomplished something. I'm damned good at what I do, too. Even the boss knows it.
>
> [*Thirty-six-year-old steam fitter.*]

But the reality of the modern work world is that there are fewer and fewer jobs calling for such traditional skills. So most job changes don't mean moving up, but only moving on:[1]

> When I first started, I kept moving around. I kept looking for a job I'd like. You know, a job where it wouldn't make you tired just to get up in the morning and have to go to work. [*With a heavy sigh.*] It took me a number of years to discover that there's not much difference—a job's a job. So now I do what I have to do, and maybe I can get my family a little security.
>
> [*Twenty-seven-year-old mail sorter.*]

For some, the job changes are involuntary—due to lay-offs:

> When I first got out of high school, I had a series of jobs and a series of lay-offs. The jobs lasted from three weeks to three months. Something always happened—like maybe the contract didn't come through—

---

[1] In his fine treatise on the nature of work in modern industrial society, Braverman (1974) argues that while short-term trends in rapidly growing industries may open the way for the advancement of a few, the lower skill requirements that characterize the largest majority of jobs mean that there are fewer and fewer opportunities to move into skilled work. This suggests even more serious limitations on upward mobility than the American society heretofore has known since, as Thernstrom (1972) persuasively argues, to the degree that upward mobility existed in the working class, it was *intra*stratum mobility—that is, men moving up within the class from less skilled to more skilled labor. If work itself has been and will continue to be stripped of skill requirements, then, as Braverman asserts, that avenue of upward mobility will be largely closed off. Cf., Aronowitz (1973) who also deals with this issue in his analysis of the forces that are shaping working-class consciousness in America.

> and since I was low man on the totem pole, I got laid off. A lot of
> times, the lay-offs lasted longer than the jobs.

. . . or industrial accidents—a common experience among men who work
in factories, warehouses, and on construction sites:

> I was working at the cannery about a week when my hand got caught
> in the belt. It got crushed, and I couldn't work for three months. When
> I got better, they wouldn't put me back on the job because they said I
> was accident-prone.

By the time they're thirty, about half are settled into jobs at which
they've worked for five years. With luck, they'll stay at them for many
more to come. Without it, like their fathers, they'll know the pain of periodic unemployment, the fear of their families doing without. For the other
half—those still floating from job to job—the future may be even more
problematic. Unprotected by seniority, with work histories that prospective
employers are likely to view as chaotic and unstable, they can expect little
security from the fluctuations and uncertainties of the labor market.

But all that tells us nothing about the quality of life on the job—what
it feels like to go to work at *that* particular job for most of a lifetime—an
experience that varies in blue-collar jobs just as it does in white-collar
ones. For just as there are elite jobs in the white-collar work force, so they
exist among blue-collar workers. Work that allows for freedom and autonomy on the job—these are the valued and high-status jobs, rare in either
world. For the blue-collar worker, that means a job where he can combine
skill with strength, where he can control the pace of his work and the order
of the tasks to be done, and where successful performance requires his
independent judgments. To working-class men holding such jobs—skilled
construction workers, skilled mechanics, truck drivers—the world of work
brings not only goods, but gratifications. The man who drives the long-
distance rig feels like a free agent once he gets out on the road. It's true,
there's a time recorder on the truck that clocks his stops. Still, compared
to jobs he's had before in factories and warehouses, on this one, he's the
guy who's in control. Sometimes the road's easy; sometimes it's tough.
Always it requires his strength and skill; always he's master of the machine:

> There's a good feeling when I'm out there on the road. There ain't
> nobody looking over your shoulder and watching what you're doing.
> When I worked in a warehouse, you'd be punching in and punching
> out, and bells ringing all the time. On those jobs, you're not thinking,
> you're just doing what they tell you. Sure, now I'm expected to bring
> her in on time, but a couple of hours one way or the other don't make
> no difference. And there ain't nobody but me to worry about how I
> get her there.
>
> [*Twenty-eight-year-old trucker.*]

The skilled construction worker, too, finds challenge and reward in
his work:

> I climb up on those beams every morning I'm working, and I like being
> way up there looking down at the world. It's a challenge up there, and
> the work's hardly ever routine. You have to pay attention and use your

head, too, otherwise you can get into plenty of trouble in the kind of work I do. I'm a good man, and everybody on the job knows it.

[*Thirty-one-year-old ironworker.*]

But most blue-collar men work at jobs that require less skill, that have less room for independent judgment—indeed, often expect that it will be suspended—and that leave their occupants with little freedom or autonomy. Such jobs have few intrinsic rewards and little status—either in the blue-collar world or the one outside—and offer few possibilities for experiencing oneself as a "good man." The men who hold these jobs often get through each day by doing their work and numbing themselves to the painful feelings of discontent—trying hard to avoid the question, "Is this what life is all about?" Unsuccessful in that struggle, one twenty-nine-year-old warehouseman burst out bitterly:

A lot of times I hate to go down there. I'm cooped up and hemmed in. I feel like I'm enclosed in a building forty hours a week, sometimes more. It seems like all there is to life is to go down there and work, collect your pay check, pay your bills, and get further in debt. It doesn't seem like the circle ever ends. Everyday it's the same thing; every week it's the same thing; every month it's the same thing.

Some others respond with resignation:

I guess you can't complain. You have to work to make a living, so what's the use.

[*Twenty-six-year-old garage man.*]

. . . some with boredom:

I've been in this business thirteen years and it bores me. It's enough.

[*Thirty-five-year-old machine operator.*]

. . . some with alienation:

The one thing I like is the hours. I work from seven to three-thirty in the afternoon so I get off early enough to have a lot of the day left.

[*Twenty-eight-year-old assembly-line worker.*]

All, in fact, probably feel some combination of all these feelings. For the men in such jobs, bitterness, alienation, resignation, and boredom are the defining features of the work experience. For them, work is something to do, not to talk about. "What's there to talk about?"—not really a question but an oft-repeated statement that says work is a requirement of life, hours to be gotten through until you can go home.[2]

---

[2]This is, of course, not a new finding. Dubin (1956) long ago argued that work is not a "central life interest" for most industrial workers. Chinoy (1955) studied automobile workers and found that success and gratification were defined primarily in non work-related terms. And Herzberg (1959) and Herzberg, et al. (1959) made essentially the same observation that I make here—that is, that most blue-collar workers are neither satisfied nor dissatisfied with their work. They do their jobs because they must and try to think as little as possible about whether they're happy, satisfied, or interested in their work.

Criticizing such work-satisfaction studies, Braverman (1974:28–29) argues that the appropriate matter for concern ought not to be with how workers feel about their jobs but

No big news this—at least not for readers of *The Wall Street Journal*
and *Fortune* magazine, both aimed at the leaders of the industrial world.
No big news either in the highest reaches of government where in 1972
the United States Senate sponsored a symposium on worker alienation.[3]
When absentee and turnover rates rise, when wildcat strikes occur with
increasing frequency—in short, when productivity falls off—the alienation
of workers becomes a focal concern for both industrial managers and
government. That concern increasingly is expressed both in the media and
in the work of industrial sociologists, psychologists, and labor relations
experts who more and more talk of plans for "job enrichment," "job
enlargement," and "the humanization of work."

Despite the talk, however, the history of industrialization shows that
as industry has become more capital intensive, the thrust has been toward
technological developments which consistently routinize work and require
less skill of the masses of workers. Today more than yesterday—because
technology has now caught up with work in the office as well as the
factory—most work continues to be steadily and systematically standard-
ized and routinized; the skills of the vast majority of workers have been
degraded. So profound is the trend that generally we are unaware that the
meaning of "skill" itself has been degraded as well.[4] This, too, is no new
phenomenon as even a casual glance at the historical record shows. For
whether in 1875 or 1975, most of those concerned with the organization
of work and with the qualities most desired in a work force talk not about
skill but about "discipline" and "responsibility."[5] The difference in these

---

with the nature of the work itself. He charges that by the methods they use (i.e., survey
research) and the questions they ask "sociologists [are] measuring not popular consciousness but their own." The sociologist, he asserts, shares with management the conviction that
the existing organization of the process of labor is necessary and inevitable. "This leaves to
sociology the function, which it shares with personnel administration, of assaying not the
nature of the work but the degree of adjustment of the worker. Clearly, for industrial sociology the problem does not appear with the degradation of work, but only with the overt
signs of dissatisfaction on the part of the worker."

[3] See U.S. Senate Committee on Labor and Public Welfare (1972) for the hearings on SB 3916,
a bill brought before the United States Senate whose purpose was: "To provide for research
for solutions to the problems of alienation among American workers in all occupations and
industries and technical assistance to those companies, unions, State and local governments
seeking to find ways to deal with the problem . . ." See also the U.S. Department of Health,
Education, and Welfare report entitled *Work in America* (1973). For other recent studies on
the consequences of alienation from work on life both on and off the job, see Levitan (1971);
Meissner (1971); Seashore and Barnowe (1972); Shepard (1970); Sheppard (1971); Sheppard
and Herrick (1972). For a more radical view of the alienation of American workers and
their developing class consciousness, see Aronowitz (1973) and Braverman (1974).

[4] See Aronowitz (1973) and Braverman (1974) for excellent recent discussions of this phenomenon and its consequences.

[5] See Blauner (1964:169) who comments that "the shift from skill to responsibility is the most
important historical trend in the evolution of blue-collar work." For an historical analysis
of continuity and change in the ideologies of management in the course of industrialization,
see Bendix (1963). Bremer (1970) presents a documentary history of the early reform movements in America and their view of the poor and working classes. Threaded throughout,
one finds expressions of concern about the unruliness of the masses and their consequent
unfitness for the world of work. Even a casual examination of such early documents leaves

hundred years in what is required of the mass of workers is one of degree not of kind. Advancing technology means that there is less need than before for skill, more for reliability—that means workers who appear punctually and regularly, who work hard, who don't sabotage the line, and who see their own interests as identical with the welfare of the company. These are the "skills" such capital-intensive industries need. And these are the skills toward which—today as yesterday—training programs of the unemployed and underemployed so often are directed.[6]

In fact, there is no argument among most students of work in America that most work—whether in the factory or in the office—requires less skill than before. Rather the argument is heard around the *meaning* of the trend in the lives of those affected by it. In the United States, at least, most analysts insist upon the inevitability of the process, arguing that where technology exists it will be used—as if it had a force or life of its own; where it doesn't exist, it will be invented. Human beings, such people argue, must invent their future; that is one essential meaning of being "human."[7]

That argument, however, fails to grapple with the fact that only a tiny minority of us ever are involved in inventing our present, let alone our future. Ordinary women and men—which means almost all of us—struggle along with received truths as well as received ways of being and doing. For such people, at least one half of the waking hours of each day are spent in doing work that is dull, routine, deadening—in a word, alienating and alienated labor. True, these analysts would say. But for those people, there are substitute gratifications to be found in the private sphere of life—that is, the family—and in their leisure hours.

But again, that formulation fails to deal with the degree to which the parts of human life are interrelated—each interacting with and acting upon the other—so that such a separation is nearly impossible. In fact, any five-year-old child knows when "daddy has had a bad day" at work. He comes home tired, grumpy, withdrawn, and uncommunicative. He wants to be left alone; wife and children in that moment are small comfort.

---

the clear impression that one important—if not explicitly articulated—goal of the reformers was to turn the masses into docile and disciplined Americans who could be counted on to work every day in the factories for which they were destined. Cf., Bendix (1963) who shows that Sunday schools were introduced in eighteenth-century England as a means of governing the poor and training them for what was considered their appropriately subordinate place. In his outstanding analysis of the origins of early school reform in Massachusetts, Katz (1968) argues that this was precisely the function of the developing public-school system and compulsory attendance regulations.

[6] Punctuality, regularity, cleanliness, and orderliness have long been the focus of training for the industrial work world. Cf., Greer (1972) and Katz (1968) for excellent analyses of the historical function of the schools in providing this training. More recently, national man-power-training programs and state programs sponsored by the Human Resources Development Agency also have focused heavily on training the poor, the unemployed, and the underemployed in those traits.

[7] See, for example, the publications of the Harvard University Program on Technology and Society established in 1964 by a grant from International Business Machines Corporation. Also Burke (1966); Theobald (1967); Torbert (1963). For a fine critique of the technology-as-progress view, see Ellul (1967).

When *every* working day is a "bad day," the family may even feel like the enemy at times. But for them, he may well think, he could leave the hated job, do something where he could feel human again instead of like a robot.

Over a century ago, in the early stages of industrialization, Karl Marx spoke to the profoundly important human consequences of alienation from work—of work that doesn't permit the development of skill, of a sense of mastery, of an understanding of the totality of the *process* of production, of a connectedness with its *product*. Those issues are no less real today. The overt brutalization of industrial workers is no longer with us. But the intensification of technological developments has given rise to dehumanization and alienation in the work world on a scale far greater than anything known before.

For the working-class men I met, these issues, while unarticulated in this way, are nevertheless real. Most are in a constant struggle to make some order and continuity out of the fragments of their lives. Thus, they come home after work and plunge into projects that offer the possibility for feeling useful, competent, whole again—fixing the car or truck, remodeling the kitchen, building something for the kids.[8] Others—those who seem already to have given up life and hope—collapse into a kind of numbed exhaustion from which they stir only to eat, drink, and watch television. Either way, the implications for family life are clear. Husbands and fathers are removed from active involvement—some because they are in a desperate struggle to retain some sense of their humanity, others because they have given it all up.

There are still a few who have fantasies of one day doing some other kind of work—owning a farm, a ranch, a small business are the most common of these dreams. No new phenomenon; for part of the American dream always has been to have a business of one's own. Rarely, however, are these dreams voiced spontaneously in the course of a discussion about work and their feelings about it. In that context, work tends to be seen as a given in life—more or less enjoyable, but ultimately unavoidable, thus not something to give much thought to. Only when the question itself has a dreamlike and unreal quality does it encourage and get a fantasy response:

> *Would you fantasy for a minute about what you'd do if you suddenly inherited a million dollars?*[9]

---

[8]Discussing the trivialization of labor in modern capitalist society, Aronowitz (1973:130) comments on the same point:

> Under modern conditions, the self is only realized in the world of leisure, which now becomes the location for autonomy rather than work . . . That is why, with few exceptions, workers expect nothing intrinsically meaningful in their labor, and satisfy their desire for craftsmanship in the so-called "private realm." For example, tens of thousands of young people have become "car freaks." The automobile is invested with much more than reified status or power. It has become a vital means for the realization of the frustrated need to make a direct link with the totality of production for youth who are condemned to either the fragmented labor of the factory or the office or the truncated learning of the school.

[9]For three decades now, a popular question used in surveys seeking to determine work satisfaction asks the respondent whether he would continue to work if he had enough money

Most working-class people—men and women—are stopped cold by the question. Most say at once, "I've never thought about it." One thirty-two-year-old man added in wonder:

> Most of my life I've been lucky to have ten dollars; thinking about a million—wow, that seems impossible.

When pushed to think of the question in terms of the work they'd like to do, slowly, thoughtfully, a few gave voice to their fantasies. But always the implicit understanding was there: both of us knew that *he knew* it was just a dream:

> Well, I guess if I had a million dollars, I'd buy me a cattle ranch in the mountains and go live in the country. I like to hunt and fish. I like the country. I like animals. And I'd sure like to be my own boss and to work when I want to work. Oh, I know I'd have to work hard on a ranch, but it would be *my* work, and it would be on *my* time, and with me deciding what needed doing and doing it.
> [*Thirty-three-year-old delivery man.*]

> Like I said, my job is tedious. I'd actually be glad to quit it. I don't mean I'd quit work; nobody should ever do that. I might buy a goat farm and raise goats and pigs—just something where I could do something a person could care about. You know, something that was mine and that wasn't so tedious.
> [*Twenty-nine-year-old postal clerk.*]

> I guess if I was going to have a fantasy about anything, it would be to have a little sporting-goods store in the neighborhood, a place where

---

to live comfortably without working. See, for example, Kaplan and Tausky (1972); Morse and Weiss (1955); Tausky (1969); Veroff and Feld (1970). The question I asked also was designed to tap attitudes about work. I chose the more ambiguous wording, however, in order that it might be more in the nature of a projective test which gives the respondent fewer cues toward which to direct an answer. The question, therefore, tapped not only attitudes toward work, but also gave me data on the issues that preoccupy the people in this study and their fantasied solutions.

In a challenge to attitude surveys and the traditional questions in work-satisfaction studies, Kaplan and Kruytbosch (1975) made a "behavioral test of the commitment to work" by studying lottery winners in New York and New Jersey. They found that while commitment to *work* was pervasive, commitment to one's *job* was not, and that the greater the amount of the winnings, the greater was the number of quits and job changes. The authors conclude:

> The most significant finding of this study is that many people when given a real opportunity to choose between keeping their present jobs and quitting or changing, choose the latter. When the economic necessity to work is removed [in fact, not in fantasy], as in the case of the millionaires, eight out of ten quit their jobs . . . If there are lessons to be learned from this research it is that attitudinal questions about satisficing states are intriguing but not necessarily conducive to an accurate interpretation of social reality. Asking workers whether they are satisfied with the work they do and finding that most say they are is like asking a horse that has always been fed hay if he likes his diet. The opportunities for a change of work or diet are closed, unknown or impractical . . . But when people had a chance, they knew what to do. They got out—not of *work* . . . but of their *jobs* which they viewed as dull, dirty and dead-end.

all the kids on the local teams could come to get outfitted. I would feel a lot of satisfaction to have a store like that, and I think it would be a terrific business to be in. But it's just a dream. I'll never get enough money together to do it, and you can be sure there's nobody going to leave me no thousand dollars, let alone a million.

[*Thirty-one-year-old night watchman.*]

One twenty-seven-year-old warehouseman, after talking at length about the business he hoped he'd have some day, took a mental step back from our conversation, observed himself thoughtfully and said:

After all that talk, I really doubt I'll ever make any change. I'll probably stay where I am forever. Once you've been on the job seven years, look what you'd have to give up—good money, good benefits, seniority. What if I tried my own business and it didn't work? Then I'd have to come back and start all over again. No. I don't think I'll ever take that chance.

Paradoxically, then, the "good money, good benefits, seniority" that come with long tenure on the job also serve to limit his choices—to bind him to it, trading the dream for this stagnant stability. Perhaps, in the long run, that makes sense given the failure rate of small, independent businesses in America. In the immediate moment, there's pain and pathos when, at twenty-seven, he already knows his life choices largely are over.

Imagine the consequences to the shape and form of that human life. Imagine, too, an environment in which the same paucity of choices is the reality of most lives—no friends or relatives around who see a future with plenty of possibilities stretching before them; no one who expects very much because experience has taught them that such expectations end painfully. Such is the fertile field in which the fatalism, passivity, and resignation of the working class grow—qualities so often remarked upon by professional middle-class investigators. But it is not these qualities that are responsible for their humble social status. That is the illusion with which so many middle-class observers attempt to palliate their guilt about the inequalities in American life—inequalities that are at such odds with our most cherished ideological myth of egalitarianism. Rather it is their social status from which these qualities stem. No, these are not personal failings, nor are they outgrowths of character or personality deficiencies. They are, instead, realistic responses to the social context in which most working-class men, women, and children live, grow, and come to define themselves, their expectations, and their relationship to the world around them.

Would you fantasy for a minute about what you'd do if you suddenly inherited a million dollars?

For a few of the men, answering the fantasy question is easier; they know just what they would do. These are the half dozen who have some natural skill or talent in music or drawing and painting—talents that are untutored and undeveloped, talents discovered accidentally:

I don't know how I know how to draw. I just know how. I guess I've been doing it since I was a little kid but nobody paid it any mind.

"Nobody paid it any mind"—unthinkable that such childhood demonstration of artistic abilities would go without attention and nurturance in most modern middle-class families. At the very least, such a boy would be encouraged to use those capabilities to become an architect, an engineer. But when you're one of ten children in a family where survival is the principal preoccupation, it seems quite natural that no one pays "any mind" to a boy who draws. No surprise, either, if you grow up without a family at all:

> I was about sixteen the first time I held a banjo in my hands, and I just played it. It was the same thing later, the first time I sat down at a piano. I just taught myself how to play. I've wondered before about how that happened, but I don't know. One thing I remember from when I was little was I was a quiet, unhappy kid. Every time I moved to a new foster home, I'd be scared all over again, and I got quieter and quieter. I think what kept me from being panicked out all the time was the music I had in my head. It was like it kept me company. I used to make up songs and sing them to myself. And I used to pretend I was playing music on a great big piano in front of a hundred people. [*Laughing.*] I thought that was a lot of people then.

For these men, without exception, some part of the million would be spent on training—perhaps on becoming professionals—in their particular creative endeavor.

Whether the men like their work or not, whether it offers more gratification or less, whether they have active fantasies about another way of life or they accept what is without allowing dreams to intrude upon reality, the work they do powerfully affects the quality of family life. What happens during the day on the job colors—if it doesn't actually dictate—what happens during the evening in the living room, perhaps later in the bedroom. And the size of the weekly pay check is importantly related to how men feel about themselves, their work, and their responsibilities. Probably men of all classes experience those responsibilities with heavy weariness at times, but they seem to be felt more keenly among the working class where the choices are narrower and the rewards slimmer.[10]

[10]For the last two decades, social scientists have argued about whether the work force has become increasingly proletarianized or increasingly middle class. Mills (1951), for example, argues for the increasing proletarianization of white-collar workers as their traditional status edge over blue-collarites disappears as office work requires less and less specialized skill and training. Wilensky (1964, 1966), one of the foremost proponents of the other side of the argument which rests on the diminution of observed lifestyle differences between the classes, developed the notion of the "middle mass" to reflect his view of the homogenization of the upper working class and the lower middle class. In recent years, Marxist theorists have developed a theory of the "new working class" which takes as its starting point the fact that not only are white-collar workers divorced from the means of production as are manual workers, but that they, too, have been systematically dispossessed of their skills, their status, their prestige, and their historical advantage in earnings over blue-collar workers. Aronowitz (1973); Braverman (1974); Smith (1974) persuasively develop and argue various facets of new working-class theory.

These provocative formulations, while pointing to some important core truths about the *process* of work in America, still leave us with some dilemmas about how to define

Even before 1975 and early 1976, when the national unemployment rate consistently stood at more than 8 percent, and the California rate at 10 percent, the vision of the American worker supporting his family with ease and style was a palpable distortion, visible to any observer not blinded by the prevailing myth of his affluence. For just below that apparent affluence, working-class families have always lived with the gnawing fear of unemployment and underemployment—always aware that any cutback in overtime, any lay-off would send them over the edge into disaster. For most, it takes the combined incomes of wife and husband, plus a heavy load of overtime for him, just to stay even. In fact, even with those conditions met, few manage to keep up with all their bills:

> Would you fantasy for a minute about what you'd do if you suddenly inherited a million dollars?

After the first surprised silence, both women and men answer with a regularity that quickly becomes predictable. "I'd pay off my bills," is the first thought that comes to 70 percent; for another 24 percent, it is the second thought. To the remaining few who don't give this evidence of financial stress, I remarked:

> Most people I've talked to say they'd pay off their bills, and I'm wondering why that doesn't occur to you?

The answer is simple: they have no bills. These are the few families who buy only when they have cash in hand—a rare phenomenon in American life at any class level.

There is no issue in which the class differences are more striking, none which tells more about how differently families in the professional middle class experience financial pressures. For not one woman or man in the middle-class families talked about paying off their bills if they were suddenly to come into a large inheritance. It is not that such families don't have bills; indeed, they have very large ones—mortgages on expensive homes; cars, boats, vacations bought on credit; the bills from monthly charge accounts. Rather their failure to mention them stems from the relatively secure knowledge that annual incomes are high and climbing, and that professionals generally get hit last and least in the crunch of economic hard times.[11] In their mid-thirties, these professional men stand

---

class in this advanced industrial society, and about the differences in life situation between what traditionally has been known as the working class and the middle class. While it is patently absurd to hold tenaciously to these traditional distinctions, there still remains an important difference between the mass of hourly workers and the mass of salaried workers in their vulnerability to economic fluctuations. Despite the fact that some white-collar occupations have been hard hit by the current recession, the burden of unemployment and underemployment still is carried most heavily by the hourly workers in the factories, the trades, and the service sector of the economy. In 1974, for example, the rate of unemployment among male professional and technical workers, age 25–44, was 1.5 percent compared to 5.3 percent for operatives and 4.5 percent for transport equipment operators (U.S. Department of Labor, *Handbook of Labor Statistics*, 1975).

[11] A recent article in the San Francisco *Chronicle* (December 25, 1975) reported the research of Eugene Hammel and Virginia Aldrich, who studied the job fate of 5,550 University of

on the lower rungs of their career ladders. Barring a national economic catastrophe, a long climb up with steadily increasing earnings is assured.

At the same age and stage of the life cycle, working-class men generally are at the top of their truncated career ladders. Increased earnings can be anticipated only insofar as union negotiations are successful or in routine cost-of-living increases, which at best keep them barely even with the inflationary spiral. Moreover, even in the event of economic disaster, most men in the professional middle class can count on holding jobs or getting them more readily than their less educated working-class brothers. Recall the depression of the 1930s when college graduates displaced those with only a high-school diploma behind the counters in major department stores and at the gas pumps.

> *Would you fantasy for a minute about what you'd do if you suddenly inherited a million dollars?*

Other interesting differences between the classes appear—differences that speak powerfully to their widely divergent early life experiences as well as to differences in their present life styles. Among the working-class families, for example, 34 percent said they would help their families:

> First of all, I'd fix up my parents and Bob's so that none of them would ever have to worry again. Then I'd buy my sister and brother-in-law a house.
>
> *[Thirty-year-old housewife.]*

> I'd be able to help my mother and father and set them up so they wouldn't have to worry about anything anymore.
>
> *[Twenty-seven-year-old carpenter's helper.]*

Almost identical words issuing from so many lips—"so they wouldn't have to worry anymore"—give testimony to the precariousness with which their parents and some of their siblings still live, to the continuing fragility of life in these families. Only one professional man exhibited a similar concern for his family—the only man from a working-class background. For the rest, there is no need to think about such things. Their parents can not only take care of themselves but usually can—and often do—help the children as well.

Finally, there are those—just over half and most often women—whose fantasies include buying some small services not now possible:

> I'd get the TV fixed. It's not working right, but right now, it's hard to take the money to have it fixed. There's so many bills that *have* to be paid right now.
>
> *[Thirty-six-year-old mother of four.]*

California, Berkeley, students who received the Ph.D. degree between 1967 and 1974. Expressing irritation at the press stories about Ph.D.'s who can't find work, Hammel said, "Sure, you can always find a taxi-driving physicist somewhere . . . but that just isn't typical." In fact, the research found that *at least* 97.6 percent of these women and men found work in their chosen fields, indicating an unemployment rate of "no higher than 2.4 percent and maybe as low as 1.1 percent." While it may be true that the job market is less favorable to professionals from less prestigious schools, it still is a far cry from the unemployment rate of, for example, automobile workers.

. . . getting some needed, but neglected, medical attention:

> I'd make sure the kids would have everything they needed. Then I'd
> go to the dentist and get me some teeth where I've got some missing.
> [*Twenty-nine-year-old father of two.*]

. . . or doing something special for the children—"special" usually defined
in such a way as to highlight the scarcity of comforts that are taken for
granted in most middle-class families:

> I think I'd buy each of the kids a dozen pair of shoes. Poor little things,
> they only have one pair of shoes at a time. They're lucky to get that.
> It's practically a holiday when we go out to buy shoes for one of the
> kids. They get so excited.
> [*Thirty-four-year-old mother of five.*]

> I'd spend a lot of it on giving the kids a good time. We hardly ever have
> anything extra to take them to Kiddieland or something like that. Once
> this year we did, and they were so happy and excited. It made both of
> us feel good to see them that way.
> [*Twenty-eight-year-old mother of three.*]

Under the pressures of these financial strains, 58 percent of the working-class wives work outside the home—most in part-time jobs.[12] Of those
who stay at home, about two-thirds are happy to do so, considering the
occupation of "housewife and mother" an important and gratifying job.
Some are glad to work only in the home because jobs held earlier were
experienced as dull and oppressive:

> I worked as a file clerk for Montgomery Ward's. I hated it. There was
> always somebody looking over your shoulder trying to catch you in
> mistakes. Besides, it was boring; you did the same thing all day long.
> Now I can stop when I don't feel like doing something and play with
> the children. We go for walks, or we work in the garden.

. . . some, because life outside seems frightening:

> No. I don't ever want to work again if I don't have to. It's really too
> hectic out there. Now when I'm home, I can go out to it when I want.
> I suppose it sounds like I'm hiding from something, or escaping from
> it. But I'm not. It's just that sometimes it's overwhelming.

. . . and some, just because they enjoy both the tasks and the freedom of
work in the home:

> I wouldn't work ever again if I didn't have to. I like staying home. I
> sew and take care of the house and kids. I go shopping. I'm my own
> boss. I like that. And I also like fixing up the house and making it look
> real nice. And I like cooking nice meals so Ralph is proud of me.

But few working-class wives are free to make the choice about working
inside or outside the home depending only on their own desires. Most often,

---

[12] In 1973, the labor force participation of all married women (husbands present), regardless
of class, with children under six was 32.7 percent; with children between six and seventeen,
it was 50.1 percent. (U.S. Bureau of the Census, 1974).

economic pressures dictate what they will do, and *even those who wish least to work outside the home probably will do so sometime in their lives.* Thus, for any given family, the wife is likely to move in and out of the labor force depending on the husband's job stability, on whether his overtime expands or contracts, on the exigencies of family life—a sick child, an aging parent.

The women I met work as beauticians, sales clerks, seamstresses, cashiers, waitresses, office clerks, typists, occasionally as secretaries and factory workers; and at a variety of odd jobs such as baby-sitters, school-crossing guards, and the like. Their work hours range from a few hours a week to a few—nine in all—who work full-time. Most—about three-quarters—work three or four days a week regularly.

Their attitudes toward their work are varied, but most find the work world a satisfying place—at least when compared to the world of the housewife. Therefore, although many of these women are pushed into the job market by economic necessity, they often stay in it for a variety of other reasons.

An anomaly, a reader might say. After all, hasn't it already been said that wives who hold jobs outside the home often are resentful because they also bear most of the burden of the work inside the home? Yet both are true. Women can feel angry and resentful because they are overburdened when trying to do both jobs almost single-handedly, while at the same time feeling that work outside the home provides satisfactions not otherwise available. Like men, they take pride in doing a good job, in feeling competent. They are glad to get some relief from the routines of housewifery and mothering small children. They are pleased to earn some money, to feel more independent, more as if they have some ability to control their own lives. Thus, they ask no more—indeed, a good deal less—than men do; the chance to do work that brings such rewards while at the same time having someone to share some of the burdens of home and family.

There is, perhaps, no greater testimony to the deadening and deadly quality of the tasks of the housewife than the fact that so many women find pleasure in working at jobs that by almost any definition would be called alienated labor—low-status, low-paying, dead-end work made up of dull, routine tasks; work that often is considered too menial for men who are less educated than these women. Nor is there greater testimony to the efficacy of the socialization process. Bored and discontented with the never-ending routine of household work, they seek stimulation in work outside the home. But a lifetime of preparation for housewifery and motherhood makes it possible to find gratification in jobs that require the same qualities—service, submission, and the suppression of intellectual development.[13]

[13] The literature on the socialization of women to "femininity" is vast. For some recent analyses of particular interest, see Bardwick and Douvan (1971); Bem and Bem (1972); Broverman, et al. (1972); Brun-Gulbrandsen (1971); Chafetz (1974); Chodorow (1971, 1977 forthcoming); Freeman (1974); Oakley (1972); Shainess (1972); Weisstein (1971); Weitzman, et al. (1972). Hoffman (1972) and Horner (1972) are particularly interesting on the issue of achievement-related conflicts in women. In a study of urban natives in Alaska, Jones (1975) also argues that one reason why native women adapt more readily than men to low-status demeaning jobs is because the women are so well socialized to passivity and subordination.

No accident either that these traits are the ideal complements for the needs of the economy for a cheap, supplemental labor pool that can be moved in and out of the labor force as the economy expands and contracts. Indeed, the sex-stereotyped family roles dovetail neatly with this requirement of our industrial economy. With each expansion, women are recruited into the labor force at the lowest levels. Because they are defined primarily in their family roles rather than as workers, they are glad to get whatever work is available. For the same reason, they are willing to work for wages considerably below those of men. When the economy contracts, women are expected to give up their jobs and to return quietly to the tasks of housewifery and mothering.[14] Should they resist, they are reminded with all the force that society can muster that they are derelict in their primary duties and that those they love most dearly will pay a heavy price for their selfishness.

Tell me something about the work you do and how you feel about it?

A thirty-one-year-old factory worker, mother of five children, replies:

> I really love going to work. I guess it's because it gets me away from home. It's not that I don't love my home; I do. But you get awfully tired of just keeping house and doing those housewifely things. Right now, I'm not working because I was laid off last month. I'm enjoying the lay-off because things get awfully hectic at work, but it's only a short time. I wouldn't like to be off for a long time. Anyhow, even now I'm not completely not working. I've been waiting tables at a coffee shop downtown. I like the people down there, and it's better than not doing anything.

> You know, when I was home, I was getting in real trouble. I had that old housewife's syndrome, where you either crawl in bed after the kids go to school or sit and watch TV by the hour. I was just dying of boredom and the more bored I got, the less and less I did. On top of it, I was getting fatter and fatter, too. I finally knew I had to do something about it, so I took this course in upholstery and got this job as an upholstery trimmer.

"It gets me away from home"—a major reason why working women of any class say they would continue to work even apart from financial necessity. For most, however, these feelings of wanting to flee from the boredom and drudgery of housewifery are ambivalently held as they struggle with their guilt about leaving young children in someone else's care.

For all women, the issues around being a "working mother" are complex, but there are some special ones among the working class that make it both harder and easier for women to leave their homes to work. It is harder because, historically, it has been a source of status in working-class communities for a woman to be able to say, "I don't *have* to work." Many men and women still feel keenly that it's his job to support the family,

---

[14]See Aronowitz (1973); Braverman (1974); Holter (1971); Sokoloff (1975); Zaretsky (1973) for discussion and analysis of the importance of women as a reserve labor force in the economy.

hers to stay home and take care of it.[15] For her to take a job outside the house would be, for such a family, tantamount to a public acknowledgment of his failure. Where such attitudes still are held strongly, sometimes the wife doesn't work even when it's necessary; sometimes she does. Either way, the choice is difficult and painful for both.

On the other hand, it's easier for the wives of working-class men to override their guilt about leaving the children because the financial necessity is often compelling. On one level, that economic reality is an unpleasant one. On another, it provides the sanction for leaving the home and makes it easier for working-class women to free themselves from the inner voices that charge, "You're self-indulgent," that cry, "What kind of mother are you?"—as this conversation with a twenty-five-year-old working mother of two shows:

How do you feel about working?

I enjoy it. It's good to get out of the house. Of course, I wouldn't want to work full-time; that would be being away from the kids too much.

Do you sometimes wish you could stay home with them more?

Yeah, I do.

What do you think your life would look like if you could?

Actually, I don't know. I guess I'd get kind of bored. I don't mean that I don't enjoy the kids; I do. But you know what I mean. It's kind of boring being with them day after day. Sometimes I feel bad because I feel like that. It's like my mind battles with itself all the time—like, "Stay home" and "Go to work."

So you feel guilty because you want to work and, at the same time, you feel like it would be hard for you to stay home all the time?

Yeah, that's right. Does it sound crazy?

No, it doesn't. A lot of women feel that way. I remember feeling that way when my children were young.

You, too, huh? That's interesting. What did you do?

Sometimes I went to work, and sometimes I stayed home. That's the way a lot of women resolve that conflict. Do you think you'd keep on working even if you didn't need the money at all?

I think about that because Ed says I could stop now. He says we can make it on his salary and that he wants me home with the kids. I keep saying no, because we still need this or that. That's true, too. It would be really hard. I'm not so sure we could do it without my salary. Sometimes I think he's not sure either. I've got to admit it, though, I don't really want to stay home. I wouldn't mind working three days instead of four, but that's about all. I guess I really work because I

---

[15] See Easton (1975, 1976) for a picture of the historical development of the woman's-place-is-in-the-home ideology and its relationship to the economic requirements of the burgeoning industrial society. Cf., also Lazerson (1975); Sokoloff (1975).

> enjoy it. I'm good at it, and I like that feeling. It's good to feel like you're competent.

> *So you find some real gratifications in your work. Do you also sometimes think life would be easier if you didn't work?*

> Sure, in some ways, but maybe not in others. Anyhow, who expects life to be easy? Maybe when I was a kid I thought about things like that, but not now.

Faced with such restlessness, women of any class live in a kind of unsteady oscillation between working and not working outside the home—each choice exacting its own costs, each conferring its own rewards. Another woman, thirty-two and with four children, chooses differently, at least for now:

> Working is hard for me. When I work, I feel like I want to be doing a real good job, and I want to be absolutely responsible. Then, if the little one gets a cold, I feel like I should be home with her. That causes complications because whatever you do isn't right. You're either at work feeling like you should be at home with your sick child, or you're at home feeling like you should be at work.

> *So right now, you're relieved at not having to go to work?*

> Yeah, but I miss it, too. The days go faster and they're more exciting when you work.

> *Do you think you'll go back to work, then?*

> Right now, we're sort of keeping up with the bills, so I probably won't. When we get behind a lot again, I guess I'll go back then.

Thus, the "work-not work" issue is a lively and complicated one for women—one whose consequences radiate throughout the marriage and around which important issues for both the individuals and the marital couple get played out. Even on the question of economic necessity, wives and husbands disagree in a significant minority of the families. For "necessity" is often a relative term, the definition ultimately resting on differences between wives and husbands on issues of value, lifestyle, sex-role definitions, and conjugal power. Thus, he says:

> She doesn't have to work. We can get by. Maybe we'll have to take it easy on spending, but that's okay with me. It's worth it to have her home where she belongs.

She says:

> My husband says I don't have to work but if I don't, we'll never get anywhere. I guess it's a matter of pride with him. It makes him feel bad, like he's not supporting us good enough. I understand how he feels, but I also know that, no matter what he says, if I stop working, when the taxes on the house have to be paid, there wouldn't be any money if we didn't have my salary.

In fact, both are true. The family *could* lower its living standard—live in an apartment instead of a house; have less, do less. On his income of about $11,500, they undoubtedly could survive. But with all his brave words about not wanting his wife to work, he is not without ambivalence about the consequences. He is neither eager to give up the few comforts her salary supports nor to do what he'd have to do in order to try to maintain them. She says:

> He talks about me not working, then right after I went back this time, he bought this big car. So now, I have to work or else who would make the payments?

He says:

> If she stops working, I'd just get a second job so we could keep up this place and all the bills and stuff.

> *How do you feel about having to do that?*

> Well, I wouldn't exactly love it. Working two jobs with hardly any time off for yourself isn't my idea of how to enjoy life. But if I had to, I'd do it.

> *What about the payments on the car? Wouldn't they get to be a big problem if she didn't work?*

> Yeah, that's what she says. I guess she's right. I don't want her to work; but even if I worked at night, too, I don't know how much I could make. She's right about if I work two jobs then I wouldn't have time to do anything with the family and see the kids. That's no life for any of us, I guess.

The choices, then, for this family, as for so many others, are difficult and often emotionally costly. In a society where people in all classes are trapped in frenetic striving to acquire goods, where a man's sense of worth and his definition of his manhood rest heavily on his ability to provide those goods, it is difficult for him to acknowledge that the family really does need his wife's income to live as they both would like. Yet, just beneath the surface of his denial is understanding—understanding that he sometimes experiences with pain, sometimes masks with anger. His wife understands his feelings. "It's a matter of pride with him," she says. "It makes him feel bad, like he's not supporting us good enough," she says. But she also knows that he, like she, wants the things her earnings buy.

It should be clear by now that for most women there are compensations in working outside the home that go beyond the material ones—a sense of being a useful and valued member of society:

> If you don't bring home a pay check, there's no gauge for whether you're a success or not a success. People pay you to work because you're doing something useful and you're good at it. But nobody pays a housewife because what difference does it make; nobody really cares.
>
> [*Thirty-four-year-old typist.*]

. . . of being competent:

> In my work at the salon, it's really like an ego trip. It feels good when
> people won't come in if you're not there. If I go away for two weeks,
> my customers will wait to have their hair done until I come back. I'm
> not always very secure, but when I think about that, it always makes
> me feel good about myself, like I'm really okay.
>
> [*Thirty-one-year-old beautician.*]

. . . of feeling important:

> I meet all kinds of interesting people at work, and they depend on me
> to keep the place nice. When I don't go in sometimes, the place gets
> to be a mess. Nobody sweeps up, and sometimes they don't even call
> to have a machine fixed. It makes me feel good—you know, impor-
> tant—when I come back and everybody is glad to see me because they
> know everything will be nice again.
>
> [*Twenty-nine-year-old manager
> of a self-service laundromat.*]

. . . and of gaining a small measure of independence from their husbands:

> I can't imagine not working. I like to get out of the house, and this
> money makes me feel more independent. Some men are funny. They
> think if you don't work, you ought to just be home every day, like a
> drudge around the house, and that they can come home and just say,
> "Do this," and "Do that," and "Why is that dish in the sink?" When you
> work and make some money, it's different. It makes me feel more
> equal to him. He can't just tell me what to do.

In fact, students of the family have produced a large literature on
intra-family power which shows that women who work outside the house
have more power inside the house.[16] Most of these studies rest on the
resource theory of marital power—a theory which uses the language of
economics to explain marital relations. Simply stated, resource theory con-
ceptualizes marriage as a set of exchange relations in which the balance
of power will be on the side of the partner who contributes the greater
resources to the marriage.[17] While not made explicit, the underlying

[16]For a comprehensive review of the literature on working mothers and family power along
with an extensive and up-to-date bibliography, see Hoffman and Nye (1974). Chapter 7,
written by Steven J. Bahr is of particular interest. For a fine critique of this literature and
its unspoken assumptions, see Gillespie (1972).

[17]For an early and comprehensive statement, see Blood and Wolfe (1960). In a more recent
formulation, Scanzoni (1972:66–70) writes:

> In simplified form, we may suggest that *the husband in modern society exchanges
> his status for marital solidarity.* If we accept as given that expressive satisfac-
> tions(companionship, physical affection, empathy) are the obvious goals of
> modern marriage, and that the major latent goal is status and economic well-
> being, then we may say that the latent goal influences the attainment of the
> manifest goal. *Specifically, the greater degree of the husband's integration into
> the opportunity system (the more his education, the higher hs job status, the
> greater his income), the more fully and extensively is the interlocking network*

assumption of this theory is that the material contributions of the husband are the "greater resource." The corollary, of course, is the implicit denigration and degradation of the functions which women traditionally perform in the household—not the least of them providing the life-support system, the comfort, and the respite from the outside world that enables men to go back into it each day.

So pervasive is the assumption of the greater importance of the male contribution to the family, that generations of social scientists have unthinkingly organized their research around this thesis. Unfortunately, however, it is not the social scientists alone who hold this view. For women as well too often accept these definitions of the value of their role in the family and do, in fact, feel more useful, more independent, more able to hold their own in a marital conflict when they are also working outside the home and contributing some share of the family income. Such is the impact of the social construction of reality[18]; for, as the old sociological axiom says: "If men define situations as real, they are real in their consequences."

Indeed, it is just this issue of her independence that is a source of conflict in some of the marriages where women work. Mostly, when women hold outside jobs, there is some sense of partnership in a joint enterprise—a sharing of the experience of two people working together for a common goal. But in well over one third of the families, husbands complain that their working wives "are getting too independent." Listen to this conversation with a thirty-three-year-old repairman:

> She just doesn't know how to be a real wife, you know, feminine and really womanly. She doesn't know how to give respect because she's too independent. She feels that she's a working woman and she puts in almost as many hours as I do and brings home a pay check, so there's no one person above the other. She doesn't want there to be a king in this household.

> *And you want to be a king?*

> No, I guess I don't really want to be a king. Well [*laughing*] who wouldn't want to be? But I know better. I just want to be recognized as an important individual. She needs to be more feminine. When she's able to come off more feminine than she is, then maybe we'll have something deeper in this marriage.

> *I'm not sure I know what you mean. Could you help me to understand what you want of her?*

---

of marital rights and duties performed in reciprocal fashion. The economic rewards he provides motivate the wife to respond positively to him, and her response to him in turn gives rise to a continuing cycle of rectitude and gratitude. [emphasis mine]

For other similar analyses, see Bahr (1972, 1974); Blood and Hamblin (1958); Heer (1958, 1962); Hoffman (1960).

[18]See Berger and Luckman (1967).

Look, I believe every woman has the right to be an individual, but I
just don't believe in it when it comes between two people. A man needs
a feminine woman. When it comes to two people living together, a
man is supposed to be a man and a woman is supposed to be a woman.

But just what does that mean to you?

I'd like to feel like I wear the pants in the family. Once my decision is
made, it should be made, and that's it. She should just carry it out.
But it doesn't work that way around here. Because she's working and
making money, she thinks she can argue back whenever she feels
like it.

Another man, one who has held eight jobs in his seven-year marriage,
speaks angrily:

I think our biggest problem is her working. She started working and
she started getting too independent. I never did want her to go to work,
but she did anyway. I don't think I had the say-so that I should have.

*It sounds as if you're feeling very much as if your authority has been
challenged on this issue of her working.*

You're damn right. I feel the man should do the work, and he should
bring home the money. And when he's over working, he should sit
down and rest for the rest of the day.

And you don't get to do that when she's working?

Yeah, I do it. But she's got a big mouth so it's always a big hassle and
fight. I should have put my foot down a long time ago and forced her
into doing things my way.

The women respond to these charges angrily and defensively. The men
are saying: be dependent, submissive, subordinate—mandates with which
all women are reared. But for most white working-class women—as for
many of their black sisters—there is a sharp distinction between the commandments of the culture and the imperatives of their experience.

The luxury of being able to depend on someone else is not to be theirs.
And often, they are as angry at their men for letting them down as the
men are at the women for not playing out their roles in the culturally
approved ways. A thirty-two-year-old mother of two speaks:

I wish I could be dependent on him like he says. But how can you
depend on someone who does the things he does. He quits a job just
because he gets mad. Or he does some dumb thing, so he gets fired.
If I didn't work, we wouldn't pay the rent, no matter what he says.

Another thirty-year-old mother of three says:

He complains that I don't trust him. Sure I don't. When I was pregnant
last time and couldn't work, he went out with his friends and blew
money around. I never know what he's going to do. By the time the
baby came, we were broke, and I had to go back to work before she
was three weeks old. It was that or welfare. Then he complains because
I'm too independent. Where would we be if I wasn't?

Thus are both women and men stuck in a painful bind, each blaming the other for failures to meet cultural fantasies—fantasies that have little relation to their needs, their experiences, or the socio-economic realities of the world they live in. She isn't the dependent, helpless, frivolous child-woman because it would be ludicrously inappropriate, given her life experiences. He isn't the independent, masterful, all-powerful provider, not because he does "dumb" or irresponsible things, but because the burdens he carries are too great for all but a few of the most privileged—burdens that are especially difficult to bear in a highly competitive economic system that doesn't grant every man and woman the right to work at a self-supporting and self-respecting wage as a matter of course.

For those who hold to traditional notions that men are entitled to power and respect by virtue of their position as head of—and provider for—the family, a working wife may, in fact, be a threat. When, as is the case among the working-class families, a woman working part-time earns almost one fourth of the total family income, there is a shift in the power relations in the family—a shift which may be slight but with which, nevertheless, men of any class in this culture are likely to be uncomfortable. The fact that the professional middle-class men I met did not express these negative feelings about their wives working may be less related to their liberated attitudes about sex roles than to the fact that the wives' earnings comprise only 9 percent of the family income—a proportion so insignificant that it poses no threat to the traditional balance of power within the family.[19]

No surprise this, in a culture where "money talks" is a phrase embedded deep in the folklore. No surprise either that working-class men often feel forced into an arbitrary authoritarianism as they seek to uphold their authority in the family and to insist upon their entitlement to respect. Sadly, probably no one is more aware than they are that the person who must insist upon respect for his status already has lost it. That fact alone is enough to account for the seemingly arbitrary and angry demands they sometimes make upon wives and children. Add to that the fact that, unlike their professional counterparts, the family is usually the only place where

[19]At the time of this study, the range of income among working-class women was $400 to $8,000 annually. Median income for part-time workers was $2,900; for full-time workers (only nine in number), $6,000, with those women who worked full-time found in the lower family income levels. Assuming even that the income in a family where the woman works full-time was at the median of $12,300, that woman would be contributing very close to half the total family income. In contrast, median wages of part-time women workers in the professional middle-class families was $2,000, or 9 percent of family income. Only one wife in those families worked full-time. With earnings of $15,000 a year, she still contributed only 27 percent of the total family income which was $54,000.

The literature which compares class differences in family power is slim, indeed. Still, what exists supports the argument I make here. Barh (1974) reviewed that literature and concluded that "Working-class wives gain more power through employment than middle-class wives." Cf., also Scanzoni (1972:66–70) who examines the tools for measuring family decision-making and shows that regardless of the methodology or the instrument used, "husbands are more powerful than wives in routine family decisions as well as in conflict resolution, and higher status husbands generally have the greatest amount of family authority." See also Note 17 above for a further statement of his argument.

working-class men have any chance of exercising authority, and their behavior—while often unpleasant—may no longer seem so unreasonable. Those realities of their husbands' lives also at least partly explain the apparent submissiveness of working-class wives who, understanding the source of their men's demands, often try to accede to them in a vain attempt to relieve their husbands' pain and restore their bruised egos.

Thus, in some families, husbands win the struggle to keep their wives from either working or going to school to prepare for a job. Sometimes the wife is compliant, as in this family:

> I want to go back to school, but he doesn't want me to. He thinks I should just stay home with the children. But you know, I just can't stay home with them forever. After all, what am I going to do when they get to junior high school?

> I always really wanted to be a teacher, and I thought now would be a good time to start. I could take classes while the children are in school and be home before they get back. I keep telling him that it wouldn't make any difference in the house. I'd still get all my work done. It wouldn't interfere with anything—not with the housework, or cooking the meals, or the kids, or anything. He wouldn't even know I was gone. By the time he'd get home, everything would be just like it always was.

> I don't know what he worries about. Just because I want to go to school doesn't mean I'm going to go out and do anything. I guess he just doesn't want me getting too independent. We know some couples where the wife works, and then they get into fights over who should keep her money or what to spend it on. I wouldn't do that, but I guess he really isn't sure.

> *That seems like a real issue between you. How do you resolve such a conflict?*

> I keep talking to him, but I'm not getting anywhere yet. I'll keep trying, and maybe in a few years, he'll see it my way. Sometimes I understand how he feels, but sometimes I get mad because it doesn't seem fair that he can tell me no. I say to him, "It's my life; why can't I do what I want." And he says, "It's my life, too, and I say no." Then I get mixed up and I don't know what to say, so I just wait, and I'll try to talk to him again sometime when he's in a good mood.

The husband:

> I don't want her to work, and I don't want her to go to school. What for? She doesn't have to. She's got plenty to keep her busy right here.

> *You feel strongly about that. Could you say why?*

> Mostly because of the kids. I think a mother should stay home with the kids. I told her when we first got married that I'd earn the money and she'd take care of the kids. I've never run across a family yet where the husband and wife work where there wasn't a lot of arguments and where the kids seem to grow up differently.

> *I understand that right now all she wants is to go to school.*

Yeah, for five years and then eventually do something I don't want her to do anyhow. I told her she can't. Anyhow, I don't think she'd go all the way with it. Becoming a teacher, I don't know how many years you'd have to go to college for that. She wouldn't be able to go through with it.

If that's so, wouldn't it be worth letting her try so that she could find out for herself either that she couldn't or didn't want to do it?

No, not really. It would cause arguments between us, and the kids would be growing up with baby-sitters, and stuff like that. No, she can't do it.

I wonder, how far do you think you'd be willing to hold this position? If it threatened your marriage, would you be willing to go along with her even if you don't like the idea?

No, I wouldn't. I'd say this is the way it's going to be; it's the way I want it. If I was to back down because I feel it's not worth risking what I've got, what good would it be? I wouldn't have that much. She wouldn't be the same girl I married, so what would I be giving up?

So far, the stress of this struggle is not evident in the marriage. The battle lines are drawn, but the rules of war in this household are those of gentlepeople.

In other families, the battle is far more devastating and the victory a pyrrhic one—as the story of this couple, married thirteen years and parents of four, shows. Before the first word is spoken, the senses give evidence of the chaos in which they live. The front yard is a weed-infested patch, the porch cluttered and unswept. Inside, the house is dirty and disordered. My hostess matches the house—unkempt and uncared for. When she starts to speak, however, I am surprised. For here is an extremely articulate woman—her eyes bright, her voice lively and energetic. With a wave of her hand, she apologizes:

I know it's a mess, but somehow I just can't ever seem to get things organized. I know it doesn't look like it, but I really do work hard around here. It's just that I'm so disorganized that I never finish anything I start. So there's always a million things piled on top of one another.

She talks easily and brightly about one subject after the other. Finally, we get to the issue of work. Her voice flat, she says:

No, I don't work. My husband doesn't like me to work. He thinks a wife ought to be home taking care of the children and her husband.

You sound as if you wish it were otherwise.

[*Wistfully.*] Yes, I really enjoyed working. I used to work down at the bank and I really enjoyed it. I was the best girl in the office, too. You know, it's funny, but I'm very organized when I work. I guess you wouldn't believe it, would you, but my desk was as neat as a pin. There was never a paper out of place. I even used to be more organized around the house when I was working.

Maybe it'll sound silly to you, but I still belong to the Business and Professional Women's Club here. When I get dressed to go to one of their meetings, it's the only time I feel like a whole individual. I'm not somebody's wife, or somebody's mother. I'm just Karen. I suppose that's why I liked working, too. When I'd be there, I could just be who I am—I mean, who I am inside me not just all those other things.

It seems as if you all pay a heavy price for your not working. Have you and your husband tried to reconcile that difference in some way that wouldn't be so costly to all of you?

We've tried, but we don't get anywhere. I understand his point, too. He wants me to be at home when he leaves and he wants me to be here when he comes home. It's because of his upbringing. He was sent from one foster home to another when he was growing up, and he has a pretty big thing about the family staying together and about mothers being home with their kids. I suppose I would, too, if my mother ran off and left me.

Here, then, we see expressed her yearnings for herself, her anger because she feels deprived of an important part of that self, and her insight into the source of her husband's unwillingness to compromise the issue. But while insight generates understanding, it does little to assuage the pain of deprivation she experiences every day of her life.

Her husband, a tall, thin man, with a shy, sensitive smile, also talks openly and easily, but with a great deal of bitterness about the state of the house:

I just don't understand. She works like a beaver around here and never gets anything done. [*Pointing to the litter of cans all over the kitchen.*] I don't know how to convince her that if you open a tin can, it's easier to put it right in the garbage instead of sticking it on the sink, then opening another one and putting it on top of the frig, then opening another one and putting it on the table. Eventually, you spend all your time cleaning up all the opened cans. I keep telling her, but I can't make a dent.

You sound very frustrated about that.

Sure, I hate to walk into the bathroom and try to shave with everything stacked up around me, or try to find a clean coffee cup, or try to find a place to sit down with junk all over everything, or to look in my drawer and not find any underwear for the fourth day in a row because it's still stacked up on a chair in the living room.

Karen says things were different around the house when she was working, that things were much more organized. Is that your recollection, too?

Oh yeah, when she's working, she's much better.

It sounds as if there might be a message in that for you. Don't you hear it?

Sure, I hear that message, but I'm a little stubborn myself. And from my background, I can't help wanting her home with my kids. Sometimes I think I'm nuts or something. I can't understand why a young woman who only wanted to get married can do such a poor job of being a housewife and such a good one at an occupation.

Since she does so much better a job at home when she's also working outside, maybe you could both get what you want if she felt free to do that.

[*Slamming his hand down on the table in anger.*] Dammit, no! A wife's got to learn to be number two. That's just the way it is, and that's what she better learn. She's not going to work. She's going to stay home and take care of the family like a wife's supposed to do.

And she does. But the wreckage of the struggle is strewn around the house, its fallout contaminating everything it touches—husband, wife, children, and the marriage.

Thus does work performed outside the house—the values associated with it and the stereotypic conceptions about who must do it—touch the core of life inside the house.[20] For the men, there is no real choice. Like it or not, they work—never seriously questioning how it came to be that way, why it must remain so. Despite the enormity of the burdens they carry, many men still feel they must do it alone if they are to fulfill their roles successfully. Often they cannot, as the soaring proportion of married women who work attests. For the working-class man, that often means yet another challenge to his already uncertain self-esteem—this time in the only place where he has been able to make his authority felt: the family. For his wife, it means yet another burden in the marriage—the need somehow to shore up her husband's bruised ego while maintaining some contact not only with her own desires but with family needs as well. For both wives and husbands, it means new adjustments, new ways of seeing themselves and their roles in the family—a transition that some make more successfully than others.

Who works? What kind of work do they do? Do they earn enough— either separately or together—to support the family in reasonable comfort? What are the objective conditions *and* the subjective experience of work? In the context of family life, these are the central questions around work and its meaning. The answers determine the quality not only of work but of leisure as well.

References

Aronowitz, Stanley. *False Promises*. New York: McGraw-Hill, 1973.

Bahr, Stephen J. "Comment on 'The Study of Family Power Structures: A Review 1960–1969.'" *Journal of Marriage and the Family* 34 (1972): 239–243.

Bahr, Stephen J. "Effects on Family Power and Division of Labor in the Family." In *Working Mothers*, edited by Lois W. Hoffman and F. Ivan Nye. San Francisco: Jossey-Bass, 1974.

[20]See Terkel (1974) for some compelling vignettes about the ways in which a person's work life, the social value placed on a particular kind of work, and the internalization of that value affect off-work life. Also Sennett and Cobb (1973) for an analysis of these issues.

Bardwick, Judith M., and Elizabeth Douvan. "Ambivalence: The Socialization of Women." In *Women in Sexist Society*, edited by Vivian Gornick and Barbara K. Moran. New York: Basic Books, 1971.

Bem, Sandra L., and Daryl J. Bem. "Training the Woman to Know Her Place." In *The Future of the Family*, edited by Louise Kapp Howe. New York: Simon and Schuster, 1972

Bendix, Reinhard. *Work and Authority in Industry*. New York: Harper Torchbooks, 1963.

Berger, Peter L., and Thomas Luckman. *The Social Construction of Reality*. Garden City, N.Y.: Anchor Books, 1967.

Blauner, Robert. *Alienation and Freedom*. Chicago: University of Chicago Press, 1964.

Blood, Robert O., Jr., and Robert M. Hamblin. "The Effect of the Wife's Employment on the Family Power Structure." *Social Forces* 36 (1958): 347–352.

Blood, Robert O., Jr., and Donald M. Wolfe. *Husbands and Wives: The Dynamics of Married Living*. New York: Free Press, 1960.

Braverman, Harry. *Labor and Monopoly Capitalism: The Degradation of Work in the Twentieth Century*. New York: Monthly Review Press, 1974.

Bremer, Robert H., ed. *Children and Youth in America*, vols. 1 and 2. Cambridge, Mass.: Harvard University Press, 1970.

Broverman, Inge K., et al. "Sex-Role Stereotypes: A Current Appraisal." *Journal of Social Issues* 28 (1972): 59–78.

Brun-Gulbrandsen, Sverre. "Sex Roles and the Socialization Process." In *The Changing Roles of Men and Women*, edited by Edmund Dahlström. Boston: Beacon Press, 1971.

Burke, John, ed. *The New Technology and Human Values*. Belmont, Calif.: Wadsworth Publishing, 1966.

Chafetz, Janet Saltzman. *Masculine/Feminine or Human?* Itasca, Ill.: F. E. Peacock, 1974.

Chinoy, Eli. *Automobile Workers and the American Dream*. New York: Random House, 1955.

Chodorow, Nancy. "Being and Doing: A Cross-Cultural Examination of the Socialization of Males and Females." In *Woman in Sexist Society*, edited by Vivian Gornick and Barbara K. Moran. New York: Basic Books, 1971.

Chodorow, Nancy. *The Reproduction of Mothering: Family Structure and Feminine Personality*. Berkeley: University of California Press (forthcoming, 1977).

Dubin, Robert. "Industrial Workers' World: A Study of the Central Life Interests of Industrial Workers." *Social Problems* 3 (1956): 131–141.

Easton, Barbara Leslie. "Industrialization and Femininity: A Case Study of Nineteenth Century New England." *Social Problems* 23 (forthcoming, 1976).

Easton, Barbara Leslie. "Women, Religion, and the Family: Revivalism as an Indicator of Social Change in Early New England." Ph.D. dissertation, University of California, Berkeley, 1975.

Ellul, Jacques. *The Technological Society*. New York: Vintage Books, 1967.

Freeman, Jo. "The Social Construction of the Second Sex." In *Intimacy, Family, and Society*, edited by Arlene Skolnick and Jerome Skolnick. Boston: Little, Brown, 1974.

Gillespie, Dair. "Who Has the Power? The Marital Struggle." In *Family, Marriage, and the Struggle of the Sexes*, edited by Hans P. Dreitzel. New York: Macmillan, 1972.

Greer, Colin. *The Great School Legend*. New York: Basic Books, 1972.

Heer, David M. "Dominance and the Working Wife." *Social Forces* 36 (1958): 341–347.

Heer, David M. "Husband and Wife Perceptions of Family Power Structure." *Marriage and Family Living* 24 (1962): 65–77.

Herzberg, Frederich. *Work and the Nature of Man*. Cleveland: World Publishing, 1966.

Herzberg, Frederich, et al. *The Motivation to Work*. New York: John Wiley, 1959.

Hoffman, Lois Wladis. "Early Childhood Experiences and Women's Achievement Motives." *Journal of Social Issues* 28 (1972): 129–155.

Hoffman, Lois Wladis. "Effects of Employment of Mothers on Parental Power Relations and the Division of Household Tasks." *Marriage and Family Living* 22 (1960): 27–35.

Hoffman, Lois Wladis, and F. Ivan Nye. *Working Mothers*. San Francisco: Jossey-Bass, 1974.

Holter, Harriet. "Sex Roles and Social Change." *Acta Sociologica* 14 (1971): 2–12.

Horner, Matina S. "Toward an Understanding of Achievement-Related Conflicts." *Journal of Social Issues* 28 (1972): 157–175.

Jones, Dorothy. *Urban Native Men and Women: Differences in Their Work Adaptations*. Publication of I.S.E.G.R., University of Alaska, Fairbanks, Alaska, 1975.

Kaplan, H. Roy, and Carlos Kruytbosch. "Sudden Riches and Work Behavior: A Behavioral Test of the Commitment to Work." Delivered at the Seventieth Annual Meeting of the American Sociological Association, San Francisco, California, August 25–29, 1975.

Kaplan, H. Roy, and Curt Tausky. "Work and the Welfare Cadillac: The Function of and Commitment to Work Among the Hard-Core Unemployed." *Social Problems* 19 (1972): 469–483.

Katz, Michael B. *The Irony of Early School Reform: Educational Innovation in Mid-Nineteenth Century Massachusetts*. Cambridge, Mass.: Harvard University Press, 1968.

Lazerson, Marvin. "Social Change and American Families: Some Historical Speculations." Xerox, 1975.

Levitan, Sar A., ed. *Blue Collar Workers: A Symposium on Middle America*. New York: McGraw-Hill, 1971.

Meissner, Martin. "The Long Arm of the Job: A Study of Work and Leisure." *Industrial Relations* 10 (1971): 239–260.

Mills, C. Wright. *White Collar*. New York: Oxford University Press, 1951.

Morse, Nancy C., and Robert S. Weiss. "The Function and Meaning of Work and the Job." *American Sociological Review* 20 (1955): 191–198.

Oakley, Ann. *Sex, Gender and Society*. New York: Harper Colophon, 1972.

Scanzoni, John H. *Sexual Bargaining: Power Politics in the American Marriage*. Englewood Cliffs, N.J.: Prentice-Hall, 1972.

Seashore, Stanley E., and Thad J. Barnowe. "Demographic and Job Factors Associated with the 'Blue Collar Blues.'" Mimeo, 1972.

Sennett, Richard, and Jonathan Cobb. *The Hidden Injuries of Class*. New York: Vintage Books, 1973.

Shainess, Natalie. "Toward a New Feminine Psychology." *Notre Dame Journal of Education* 2 (1972): 293–299.

Shepard, Jon M. "Functional Specialization, Alienation, and Job Satisfaction." *Industrial and Labor Relations Review* 23 (1970): 207–219.

Sheppard, Harold L. "Discontented Blue Collar Workers—A Case Study." *Labor Review* 94 (1971): 25–32.

Sheppard, Harold L., and Neal Herrick. *Where Have All the Robots Gone?* New York: Free Press, 1972.

Smith, David N. *Who Rules the Universities? An Essay in Class Analysis*. New York: Monthly Review Press, 1974.

Sokoloff, Natalie J. "A Description and Analysis of the Economic Position of Women in American Society." Xerox, 1975.

Tausky, Curt. "Meanings of Work Among Blue Collar Men." *Pacific Sociological Review* 12 (1969): 49–55.

Terkel, Studs. *Working*. New York: Avon Books, 1974.

Theobald, Robert, ed. *Dialogue on Technology*. Indianapolis: Bobbs-Merrill, 1967.

Thernstrom, Stephan. *Poverty and Progress: Social Mobility in a Nineteenth-Century City*. New York: Atheneum, 1972.

Torbet, William R. *Being for the Most Part Puppets*. Cambridge, Mass.: Schenkman Publishing, 1973.

United States Bureau of the Census. *Statistical Abstract of the United States: 1974*. 95th ed. Washington, D.C.: U.S. Government Printing Office, 1974.

United States Department of Health, Education, and Welfare. *Work in America*. Cambridge, Mass.: M.I.T. Press, 1973.

United States Department of Labor, Bureau of Labor Statistics. *Handbook of Labor Statistics—1975*. Washington, D.C.: U.S. Government Printing Office, 1975.

United States Senate Committee on Labor and Public Welfare. *Worker Alienation*. Hearings, Subcommittee on Employment, Manpower, and Poverty, July 25–26. Washington, D.C.: U.S. Government Printing Office, 1972.

Veroff, Joseph, and Sheila Feld. *Marriage and Work in America*. New York: Van Nostrand Reinhold, 1970.

Weisstein, Naomi. "Kinder, Küche, Kirche: Psychology Constructs the Female." In *Sisterhood Is Powerful*, edited by Robin Morgan. New York: Vintage Books, 1970.

Weitzman, Lenore J., et al. "Sex-Role Socialization in Picture Books for Preschool Children." *American Journal of Sociology* 77 (1972): 1125–1150.

Wilensky, Harold L. "Class, Class Consciousness, and American Workers." In *Labor in a Changing America*, edited by William Haber. New York: Basic Books, 1966.

Wilensky, Harold L. "Mass Society and Mass Culture: Interdependence or Independence." *American Sociological Review* 29 (1964): 173–197.

Zaretsky, Eli. "Capitalism, the Family, and Personal Life: Parts I and II." *Socialist Revolution* 3 (1976): 69–126, 19–70.

*A five-year-old girl watching "The Flintstones"
on Saturday morning television*

Television and the Perception of Social Reality

NATIONAL INSTITUTE OF MENTAL HEALTH

There has been an information explosion in our time. We are bombarded with data from a variety of sources: conversations, newspapers, magazines, billboards, placards, brochures, and, most significantly, from the electronic media—radio and television. Since there is more information available than most people have the time or the desire to sort out, we increasingly have turned to the most widespread and painless source—television.

More families in the United States have television sets than have cars or even bathtubs—the most tumbledown shack may boast a television antenna. Many Americans spend more hours watching the tube than they spend engaged in any other waking activity except school or the job, and there are exceptions even here. As a cultural pastime, television viewing is the single most important practice shared by the American people, regardless of class, gender, racial or ethnic group, or age. Television is the great leveler.

Throughout most of human history few people have had any awareness of the world outside the area of their own personal contacts. Their lives were focused on their own particular family, clan, tribe, village, or town, and their ignorance of the areas outside this sphere neither helped nor hindered them as they went about their daily tasks.

The invention of the printing press in the fifteenth century, however, led to an expansion of literacy and the beginnings of what we have come to call the mass media. Print and speech remained the primary means of transmitting information and ideas until the early years of this century. First radio, leaping into prominence in the 1920s, altered the leisure-time activities of many Americans in significant ways. During hours that had previously been spent in a variety of activities, families now gathered around the radio set seeking entertainment and/or information. Radio had the advantage of requiring only one of the senses, and people could still engage in other useful occupations, if they so chose, while listening.

Television was invented not long after radio, but its development was delayed by struggles over patents and the designation of appropriate transmission and merchandising techniques. The first commercially viable television productions were demonstrated at the New York World's Fair in 1939. The coming of the Second World War caused an interruption in the distribution of the new medium, however, and the expansion of the television industry had to await the end of hostilities. The immediacy of electronic media for the broadcasting of news events was proven during the war years as millions of Americans listened regularly to voices coming directly from the battlefronts of Europe.

After the war the major radio networks and broadcasting corporations decided that the future lay with television. They invested their immense profits from radio in the development of the new visual medium, and by the 1950s the big business of broadcasting had shifted almost entirely to television. A new era in mass media had arrived, but unfortunately, the vast amounts of money required to mount successful productions, combined with the cowardice and caution of Cold War America, led to programming aimed at the lowest common denominator. Nevertheless, people watched by the millions, first out of curiosity, and then out of habit.

The television viewing habits of Americans have become a cause for concern. Agencies of the federal government and, on occasion, private organizations have noted with alarm some of the implications of this practice. Since most people receive more information from television than any other medium, it seems reasonable to assume that it has a strong influence on their perceptions of the world around them. Questions about this influence are most often raised in connection with the amount of violence, both real and fictional, shown on the screen. But there are other, more subtle areas of perception in which television's simplified view of society—and individuals—may play a large role in the formation of attitudes. The National Institute of Mental Health has been sponsoring research into these questions for a number of years, and in 1982 it published a summary of its findings to date. Reprinted here is a section of that report that deals with the ways in which television distorts certain very basic aspects of American life. No one can say for certain how perceptions are influenced by endless hours of watching the small screen, but the research findings described here do suggest that something must be done to control the impact of this massest of all media.

People have to learn how to behave in different social situations and how to learn various social roles. They become socialized. During the first few years of life, children learn an incredible amount about living in the world with other people. Much of this learning comes from watching their parents and other adults, their brothers, sisters, friends, and later their teachers. Today's children also watch the characters who appear on television. The question is: Does television contribute to their socialization and to their learning of social roles?

Many of the studies of socialization are based on content analyses. As a result, detailed information is now available on the "demography" of television's fictional characters—their age, sex, race, occupation, socioeconomic status, and so on. In recent years, research has been trying to learn about the effects of these television portrayals on sex, age, race, and occupational and consumer roles.

"Social reality" is a term used to refer to the way a person thinks about the world, the person's cognitive system or frame of reference. It has been assumed that television has an effect on people's conceptions of the world around them. If television does indeed influence how people think and feel about the world, it could have far-reaching implications for culture and society. The accumulated evidence from research over the past decade seems to support the proposition that television, in some instances, does affect the "world view" of those who watch a great deal. In addition to demonstrating television's effects, recent analysis has turned to the question of how the construction of social reality occurs.

SEX-ROLE SOCIALIZATION

Sex and gender roles on television have been studied extensively since the 1950s, with a large amount of work taking place in the 1970s. All content analyses agree that the men characters greatly outnumber the women; the ratio is about 3 to 1.[1] In the early 1970s, the ratio was even higher in favor of men in leading roles, but at the end of the decade there was an increase in the number of women. The number of men and women varies with the kind of program: Situation comedies, family dramas, and soap operas have about the same number of men and women, but in action-adventure shows the men outnumber the women by a ratio of 5 to 1 and in the Saturday morning cartoons the ratio is 4 to 1.[2]

---

[1] Gerbner, G., and Signorielli, N. *Women and minorities.* Unpublished report, Annenberg School of Communications, University of Pennsylvania, Philadelphia, 1979.

Greenberg, B., Simmons, K., Hogan, L., and Atkin, C. *A three-season analysis of the demographic characteristics of fictional television characters.* Project CASTLE, Report No. 9, Department of Communication, Michigan State University, East Lansing, 1978.

Tedesco, N. Patterns in prime time. *Journal of Communication*, 1974, 24(1), 119–124.

[2] Katzman, N. Television soap operas: What's been going on anyway? *Public Opinion Quarterly*, 1972, *36*, 200–212.

"Television and the Perception of Social Reality." From *Television and Behavior: Ten Years of Scientific Progress and Implications for the Eighties*, Vol. I: Summary Report (Rockville, Md.: National Institute of Mental Health, 1982), pp. 54–62.

The analyses have looked at age, race, and occupation as related to sex roles.[3] Men characters on the average are older than the women. Most of the women are in their twenties or early thirties, and the men are about 10 years older. Black men appear far more often than black women; Hispanic men greatly outnumber Hispanic women (but the total number of Hispanic characters is very small). On television, the world of work is almost entirely the world of men. The number of women characters who do not have jobs has been set at 64 to 70 percent. Over 90 percent of the lawyers, ministers, storeowners, and doctors are men. The women are usually secretaries, nurses, entertainers, teachers, and journalists. There have been many more television men in law-related jobs, though a recent analysis shows an upward trend for women characters. Women are underrepresented as lawbreakers and overrepresented as victims. Men have a greater variety of jobs. On Saturday morning, for example, an analysis found men in 42 different jobs, women in only 9 different jobs.[4] Another study showed that twice as many women as men are in low-prestige jobs.[5] In a few of the new programs begun in the late 1970s, women do have difficult and daring jobs. These women are usually single, sophisticated, often divorced, and their work is glamorous and dangerous. Some observers say, however, that these new roles are not really so different from past roles because the women still usually depend on men, they are more emotional than men, and there is more concern for their safety.[6]

In interactions between men and women on television, the men ordinarily are more dominant.[7] Men give the orders, and their orders are more likely to be followed, except in situation comedies and family dramas. Typically, men issue their orders on "masculine" activities, such as business, law, and government. Women give orders on both masculine and feminine topics, but mainly on neutral ones. Women are more passive and less involved in problem solving. They ask for more psychological support and usually get it. Making plans differs between the sexes; men make most

[3]Dominick, J., and Rauch, G. The image of women in network TV commercials. *Journal of Broadcasting*, 1972, *16*, 259–265.

McGhee, P. *Television as a source of sex role stereotypes.* Paper presented at the meeting of the Society for Research in Child Development, Denver, 1975.

Seggar, J. Imagery of women in television drama: 1974. *Journal of Broadcasting*, 1975, *19*, 273–282.

[4]Busby, L. Defining the sex role standard in commercial network television programs directed toward children. *Journalism Quarterly*, 1974, *51*, 690–696.

[5]McNeil, J. Feminism, femininity, and the television series: a content analysis. *Journal of Broadcasting*, 1975, *19*, 259–269.

[6]Himmelweit, H. T., and Bell, N. Television as a sphere of influence on the child's learning about sexuality. In E. J. Roberts (Ed.). *Childhood sexual learning: The unwritten curriculum.* Cambridge, Mass.: Ballinger, 1980.

[7]Henderson, L., and Greenberg, B. S. Sex typing of common behaviors on television. In B. S. Greenberg (Ed.). *Life on television.* Norwood, N.J.: Ablex Press, 1980.

Lemon, J. Women and blacks on prime-time television. *Journal of Communications*, 1977, *27*(1), 70–74.

Seggar, J., 1975. Op. cit.

Turow, J. Advising and ordering: daytime, prime time. *Journal of Communication*, 1974, *24*(2), 138–141.

of the plans for themselves and others, and more of the plans made by men are successful.

According to a study on personal characteristics, the men on television are rational, ambitious, smart, competitive, powerful, stable, dominant, violent, and tolerant, while the women are sensitive, romantic, attractive, happy, warm, sociable, peaceful, fair, submissive, and timid.[8] Other studies show that women on television are more concerned with family, romance, and social relationships but are less competent than men.[9] Men are more interested in their professions and businesses. Various studies have compared the usual activities of televised men and women.[10] Entertaining, preparing food, and doing housework were all done by women; business phone calls, drinking and smoking, using firearms, and engaging in athletics characterized the men. Women often depend on men to solve their problems for them. If a man and woman on television have similar personalities or perform similar tasks, they are apt to have a relationship involving conflict and violence.[11]

On television, for men the emphasis is on strength, performance, and skill; for women, it is on attractiveness and desirability. Women characters are more likely than the men to use their bodies seductively, according to a survey of sexual behavior on prime time television.[12] Many of the plots and stories require erotically enticing costumes on the women, and the camera often focuses on particular parts of their bodies. Women are often treated as sex objects. But men also are sex objects, especially in the action-adventure stories where they must constantly be tough and strong. Like latter-day gladiators, they repeatedly prove their physical prowess.

Intimacy is rarely portrayed, and almost never does it appear on action-adventure shows. The characters seem to lead thrilling, rewarding, professional lives, but somewhat austere private lives without physical or verbal tenderness.[13] Most "close relationships" on television seem to be between partners who work together.[14] If displays of affection occur, they are usually in situation comedies.

Explicit erotic activity has not appeared on television—at least not yet—but there was an increase in flirtatious behavior and sexual innuendo

[8]McGhee, 1975. Op. cit.

[9]Donnagher, P. C., Poulos, R. W., Liebert, R. M., and Davidson, E. S. Race, sex, and social example: An analysis of character portrayals on inter-racial television entertainment. *Psychological Reports*, 1976, *38*, 3–14.

[10]Henderson, L., and Greenberg, B., 1980. Op. cit.

[11]Phelps, E. *Comparisons of the personality traits of television characters who are portrayed in amicable and violent relationships.* Unpublished paper based on analysis of the Cultural Indicators Project, Annenberg School of Communications, University of Pennsylvania, Philadelphia, 1976.

[12]Silverman, L. T., Sprafkin, J. N., and Rubinstein, E. A. Physical contact and sexual behavior on prime-time TV. *Journal of Communication*, 1979, *29*(1), 33–43.

[13]Franzblau, S., Sprafkin, J. N., and Rubinstein, E. A. Sex on TV: A content analysis. *Journal of Communication*, 1977, 27(2), 164–170.

[14]Gerbner, G. *A preliminary summary of the special analysis of television content.* Unpublished paper written for the Project on Human Sexual Development, Annenberg School of Communications, University of Pennsylvania, 1976.

in the 1970s.[15] On television, most sexual references, either verbal or implied by the action, are to extramarital sex; this occurs five times as often as references to sexual activity between married couples. References to intercourse with prostitutes is next in frequency. A total of about 70 percent of references to sexual activity are to extramarital sex or to prostitution. Sex is commonly linked with violence. On dramatic and action shows, discussions of sex are often in the context of rape or other sex crimes. Erotic relationships are seldom seen as warm, loving, or stable.

Marriage and family are not important to television's men. One study found that for 46 percent of the men it was not possible to tell whether or not they were married, in contrast to 11 percent of the women.[16] In another study, family life and romance were rated as important to 60 percent of the women and 40 percent of the men.[17] When husbands and "heroes" on Saturday morning shows were compared, the husbands came out not only as fat and quarrelsome but also as less intelligent, logical, and helpful than the heroes.[18]

On television, marriage and family belong to the women.[19] Most of the women are married. If they are single, divorced, or widowed, they are almost always looking for a husband. Few of the married women have outside jobs, but even in her home the woman does not have much authority. A character who is a successful working woman usually has problems with lover, husband, or children. Most women characters do not gain financial stability or social standing by earning it; they have it through marriage or family background.

Men, on the other hand, do not have much home life on television. Jobs come first, family life second.[20] Less than 20 percent of interactions of men are concerned with marital or family relationships. If they are married, however, men seem to have more successful marriages than the women. Men are less likely to be divorced. The television message to the viewer is that for women marriage is all consuming, but for men it is secondary.

These content analyses show that on television male and female sexuality is characterized by a double standard and by stereotyped definitions of masculine and feminine traits and roles. Television portrays a situation in which affection and intimacy are viewed as inappropriate to the real world. Sex is often seen as a dirty joke or an exciting and dangerous activity that frequently leads to trouble. While both male and female roles are stereotyped, there is more stereotyping in the female roles. Some of this difference may be attributed to the smaller number of female characters; if there were more females on television, the writers and producers could give them more varied characteristics.

[15]Franzblau, S., Sprafkin, J. N., and Rubinstein, E. A., 1977. Op. cit.

[16]McNeil, J., 1975. Op. cit.

[17]Gerbner, G., and Signorielli, N. Women and minorities on television. Unpublished report, Annenberg School of Communications, University of Pennsylvania, Philadelphia, 1979.

[18]Busby, L., 1974. Op. cit.

[19]Long, M., and Simon, R. The roles and statuses of women and children on family TV programs. Journalism Quarterly, 1974, 51, 107–110.

[20]McNeil, J., 1975, Op. cit.

Silverman, L. T., Sprafkin, J. N., and Rubinstein, E. A., 1979. Op. cit.

Research on television effects of sex-role socialization has been concerned mainly with sex-role stereotyping. In other words, does the viewer select roles for men and women that are like the stereotypes seen on television? The answer is "yes." One study asked 3- to 6-year-old children to indicate whether a man or woman would be in a certain occupation and found that the children who watched a great deal of television gave the more stereotyped answers.[21] Another study, in which youngsters were asked to say whether certain activities were more likely to be done by a man or a woman, also resulted in more sex-stereotyped replies from the heavy viewers.[22] The same investigator asked children whether a character in a story would be a man or a woman, and again, the heavy viewers gave the stereotyped answers.

But television can have the opposite effect, as shown in a study in which children did learn counterstereotyped roles from the same programs.[23] Five television characters were chosen; all were in nontypical occupational roles for women—two police officers, a park ranger, a television producer, and a school principal. The children who correctly identified the character and her occupation were compared with those who could not make the identification. The children who could identify them said that the occupation was appropriate for a woman. The exception was the role of the producer whose job did not seem to be understood by the children.

Children have been asked which television characters they prefer and which characters "you would like to be when you grow up." Boys pick more total characters than girls, and they always pick men. Girls sometimes pick women characters, but they too often pick the men. When asked the reasons for their choices, boys usually say it is physical aggressiveness, while girls say it is physical attractiveness.[24]

In general, television's effects seem to be that heavy viewing perpetuates sex stereotyping, that counterstereotypes presented in programs are accepted by children, and that males are seen as more desirable role models.

Finally, in recent years, entertainment television as a socializing force in the lives of children has become conspicuous in the area of sex education. Four characteristics of television make such education likely: Most programs watched by children are intended for adults; children have little experience to contradict or balance what they see on television; television is remarkably realistic; and television gives constant messages about sexuality.

A report on family life and sexual learning found that, of the 1,400 mothers and fathers who were interviewed, over 50 percent thought that their children learned more about sex from television than from any other

[21] Beuf, A. Doctor, lawyer, household drudge. *Journal of Communication*, 1974, 24(2), 142–145.

[22] McGhee, P., 1975. Op. cit.

[23] Miller, M., and Reeves, B. Dramatic TV content and children's sex-role stereotypes. *Journal of Broadcasting*, 1976, 20, 35–50.

[24] Miller, M., and Reeves, B., 1976. Op. cit.

Miller, M. *Television and sex-typing in children: A review of theory and research.* Unpublished report, Michigan State University, East Lansing, 1976.

source except themselves.[25] Mothers and fathers who were heavy viewers—between 27 to 35 hours a week—were most likely to give this opinion. Yet, most of the parents did not think that television is accurate or reliable in conveying knowledge about sex. A higher proportion of the heavy viewers, however, did think it is accurate.

For families in which there was heavy television viewing, the parents were not apt to talk about sexuality with their children. But these parents also believed that sexuality should not be discussed outside the family. Although television does not deliberately intend to educate children about sexuality, its characteristic and consistent messages, together with a typical lack of sexual discussion between parents and children, mean that entertainment television has become an important sex educator.[26]

AGE-ROLE SOCIALIZATION

Those who watch television most are young children and the elderly. Ironically, it is these ages that are seen the least on entertainment television.[27] According to one analysis, only 10 percent of television characters are under 19, but in census figures this age group accounts for one-third of the population.[28] At the other end of the spectrum, only a little over 2 percent of television characters are age 65 or over, but there are about 11 percent in real life, and the percentage is growing. Another analysis gives about the same percentages;[29] about 4 percent of characters are in the preteens; about 8 percent are teenagers; about one-third are age 20 to 34; about one-third are age 35 to 49; about 16 percent are in their fifties and early sixties; and about 3 percent are over 65.

In addition to counting the number of characters in various age groups, studies have noted the kinds of roles they play, programs in which they appear, and sex, race, and socioeconomic status in relation to age.[30] Young characters under 20 tend to appear in regular recurring roles, while older characters appear about equally in regular and in guest roles. On Saturday morning shows and in family dramas there are many characters under 20, but, as might be expected, there are few young people on the police-

[25] Roberts, E. J., Kline, D., and Gagnon, J. *Family life and sexual learning.* Cambridge, Mass.: Population Education, Inc. 1978.

[26] Roberts, E. J. *Social influences on sexual learning in childhood.* Manuscript in preparation, Population Education, Inc., Cambridge, Mass.

[27] Ansello, E. *Broadcast images: The older woman in television.* Paper presented at the meeting of the Gerontological Society, Dallas, 1978.

[28] Gerbner, G., Gross, L., Signorielli, N., and Morgan, M. Aging with television: Images on television drama and concepts of social reality. *Journal of Communication,* 1980, *30*(1), 37–47.

[29] Simmons, K., Greenberg, B., and Atkin, C., with Heeter, C. *The demography of fictional television characters in 1975–76.* Project CASTLE, Report No. 2, Department of Communication, Michigan State University, East Lansing, 1977.

[30] Gerbner, G., Gross, L., Signorielli, N., and Morgan, M., 1980. Op. cit.

Greenberg, B. S., Buerkel-Rothfuss, N., Neuendorf, K., and Atkin, C. Three seasons of television family role interactions. In B. S. Greenberg (Ed.), *Life on television.* Norwood, N.J.: Ablex Press, 1980.

detective shows. On crime shows, most of the characters are about 35 to 49 years old.

Almost half the women are between 20 and 34, and only a fourth of the men are in that age bracket.[31] The reverse is true for the age group 35 to 49. About 20 percent of the male characters and about 10 percent of the female characters are over 50. Elderly characters over age 65 are almost always men.[32]

Black characters are more likely than white characters to be portrayed as young, 38 percent of blacks versus 18 percent of whites in 1978. When white and black characters are in the same show, the blacks are younger. Blacks are also consistently underrepresented in the portrayal of older characters.[33]

As television characters become older, they attain a higher level job and higher socioeconomic status.[34] Few of the elderly are in service worker positions or in the lower social classes, and contrary to what might be expected, they are not depicted as poor. Older characters do not appear in any particular type of show. They are dispersed in small numbers over the whole range of prime time television. Saturday morning programs and family dramas, the kinds of programs most often watched by children, have a high count of characters under age 20 and few old people.

Content analyses of the portrayals of older people do not present a favorable picture. Old men are often cast in comic roles. One study done in 1974 is often cited;[35] it claimed that old people on television are ugly, toothless, sexless, senile, confused, and helpless. An analysis in 1979 found the elderly to be comical, treated with disrespect, and shown as stubborn, eccentric, and foolish.[36] In a fictional world where portrayals are generally favorable and most endings happy, less than half the old men and a smaller number of old women are seen as successful, happy, and good. When old people are characters on prime time programs, they often are either the villains or the victims. Men are the "good guys" when they are young and "bad guys" when they are old. If an old man fails, it appears that he does so because he is evil, but an old woman fails because she is old.

Despite all these unfavorable portrayals, there are a few bright spots.[37]

[31] Aronoff, C. Old age in prime time. *Journal of Communication*, 1974, 24(1), 86–87.

[32] Petersen, M. The visibility and image of old people on television. *Journalism Quarterly*, 1973, 50, 569–573.

[33] Greenberg, B., Buerkel-Rothfuss, N., Neuendorf, K., and Atkin, C. 1980. Op. cit.

[34] Gerbner, G., and Signorielli, N. *Women and minorities on television.* Unpublished report, Annenberg School of Communications, University of Pennsylvania, Philadelphia, 1979.

[35] Aronoff, C., 1974, Op. cit.

[36] Gerbner, G., Gross, L., and Signorielli, N., 1980. Op. cit.

[37] Ansello, E., 1978. Op. cit.

Barton, R. L. Soap operas provide meaningful communication for the elderly. *Feedback*, 1977, 19, 5–8.

Downing, M. Heroine of the daytime serial. *Journal of Communication*, 1974, 24(3), 130–137.

Harris, A., and Feinberg, J. Television and aging: Is what you see what you get? *Gerontologist*, 1977, 17, 464–468.

Ramsdell, M. The trauma of TV's troubled soap families. *Family Coordinator*, 1973, 22, 299–304.

Cassata, M., Anderson, P., and Skill, J. The older adult in daytime serial drama. *Journal of Communication*, 1980, 30(1), 48–49.

The elderly are rarely depicted as lonely, and they sometimes are portrayed as useful. Older men are relatively often seen as successful and held in high esteem by others. An important exception to the dismal picture of aging women is found in soap operas where an older woman is likely to be attractive, independent, sought after for advice, and employed in an important position.

One surprise in the content analyses is that old people are rather often shown engaging in moderate to high physical activity, such as energetic dancing, riding a motorcycle, or alluding to a vigorous sex life.[38] But these "reversed stereotypes" may do more harm than good for the image of the elderly, it is said, because they usually are interpreted as comical and inappropriate.

In addition to analyzing program content, researchers have surveyed the television-viewing habits of older people. Everyone agrees that television is very important in the lives of older people. Surveys going back to the early 1960s show that, when old people are asked to tell about their daily activities, the most frequently named activity is television.[39] In 1976, the average number of viewing hours per week for persons over age 50 was 35 hours.[40] This intensive viewing is found for all old people, whether they are living at home or in an institution, in the inner city or the suburbs, and regardless of their socioeconomic status. As with other adults, most of their viewing takes place in the late afternoon and evening, but their "prime time" is about an hour earlier than for younger adults.[41]

All studies show that the elderly prefer news, documentaries, and public affairs programs.[42] Older people, it is obvious, are turning to television for more than mere entertainment. Television provides them information about the world; it becomes a substitute for the many sources of information formerly available in the community or on the job. Next in order of popularity are variety shows, musicals, and travel films.[43] It is no surprise that Lawrence Welk emerges as a special favorite, along with some

[38]Kubey, R. W. Television and aging: Past, present, and future. *Gerontologist*, 1980, *20*, 16–35.

[39]Schramm, W. Aging and mass communication. In M. W. Riley, J. W. Riley Jr., and M. E. Johnson (Eds.) *Aging and society* (Vol. 2). *Aging and the professions*. New York: Sage Foundation, 1969.

[40]Nielsen, A. C. *Nielsen estimates: National audience demographics report*. Chicago: A. C. Nielsen Co., 1970, 1973, 1974, 1975.

[41]Davis, R. H. Television communication and the elderly. In D. S. Woodruff and J. E. Birren (Eds.), *Aging: Scientific perspectives and social issues*. New York: D. Van Nostrand, 1975.

[42]Bower, R. T. *Television and the public*. New York: Holt, Rinehart, and Winston, 1973.

   Korzenny, F., and Neuendorf, K. *TV and the aging: Exposure, functions, perceptions, and self concept*. Paper presented at the meeting of American Association for Public Opinion Research, Buck Hill Falls, Pa., 1979.

   Wenner, L. Functional analysis of TV viewing for older adults. *Journal of Broadcasting*, 1976, *20*, 77–88.

[43]Adams, M., and Groen, R. *Reaching the retired: A survey of the media habits, preferences, and needs of senior citizens in Metro Toronto*. Ottawa, Canada: Information Canada, 1974.

   Danowski, J. *Informational aging: Interpersonal and mass communication patterns in a retirement community*. Paper presented at the meeting of the Gerontological Society, Louisville, Ky., 1975.

of the other well-known "personalities," such as Bob Hope. The few programs with older characters in them are also particularly well liked by elderly viewers. Daytime soap operas provide a real contribution to the viewing pleasure of older people.[44]

Because the elderly often watch television no matter what is on and even when they do not like the programs, some gerontologists say that they may become too dependent on it.[45] But other experts on aging believe that television has many benefits. Television permits older people to stay involved with the world and to know what is going on outside their often restricted environments. Failing eyesight may make reading difficult, and hearing impairment may prevent listening to the radio, but television with its simultaneous presentation of visual and auditory stimuli may be more accessible than other media to the elderly.[46]

On both informational and entertainment programs, the elderly make many "friends" and have a large coterie of fictional companions.[47] Television personalities come to be loved by some elderly persons as attractive, safe, and nonthreatening friends. With its organized time schedules for programs and regularity of appearances by performers, television can give some structure and order to the otherwise empty and unstructured days of many old people. One report suggests that the reason some elderly people look at television is simply to "kill time"; it gives them something to do—something easy and often interesting—rather than sit all day doing nothing.[48]

What is the effect of television on the aging population and attitudes about the elderly? There has thus far been little research on the impact of television on the values and behavior of older people. One study has shown that negative opinions about aging are more likely to be held by the young and the old, rather than the middle aged; and it is, of course, the young and the old who watch the most television.[49] In contrast to this study, however, several studies have found that, as people grow older, their attitudes toward the elderly on television become more favorable.[50] Another survey reported that many viewers are dissatisfied with portrayals of old people on television.[51] Attitudes toward the elderly are reported to be

[44]Barton, R. L., 1977. Op. cit.

[45]Kubey, R. W., 1980. Op. cit.

[46]Doolittle, J. C. News media use by older adults. *Journalism Quarterly*, 1979, *56*, 311–317, 345.

[47]David, R. H., 1975. Op. cit.

[48]Christensen, R. M., and McWilliams, R. D. (Eds.) *Voice of the people: Readings in public opinion and propaganda.* New York: McGraw-Hill, 1967.

[49]Shinar, D., and Biber, A. *Images of aging among specific groups: The theater as a research framework.* Paper presented at the meeting of the International Gerontological Society, Jerusalem, 1978.

[50]Bower, R. T., 1973. Op. cit.

Davis, R. H. Television and the older adult. *Journal of Broadcasting*, 1971, *15*, 152–159.

Harris, L., and Associates. *The myth and reality of aging in America.* Washington: National Council on the Aging, 1975.

Korzenny, F., and Neuendorf, K., 1979. Op. cit.

[51]Hemming, R., and Ellis, K. How fair is TV's image of older Americans? *Retirement Living*, April 1976, 21–24.

related to the type of programming; viewers who looked at many fantasy-type programs perceived the elderly on television as "hindrances to society," but those who watched realistic programs held the opposite opinions.[52] Several studies agree that heavy viewing leads to inaccurate beliefs about old people, such as a belief that the number of old people is declining or that people are less healthy and do not live as long as they used to, or that old people are not open-minded and adaptable and not good at getting things done.

Probably the major fault in television with respect to aging is that it does not accurately portray real life in either the numbers of old people or in presentations of their attributes. According to the National Council on the Aging, television is the channel through which elimination of stereotypes about aging must occur. Finally, it is noteworthy that in the late 1970s the Committee on Aging of the House of Representatives held hearings on age stereotyping in the media.[53] And a recent review of prime time programs found that the number of older characters on television has increased and that television seems more willing to confront issues on aging as subject matter.[54]

RACE-ROLE SOCIALIZATION

For many Americans, television is a prime source of information about Black, Hispanic, Asian, and Native Americans. There have been several content analyses of programs depicting Blacks on television, but almost none of Hispanic, Asian, or native Americans except for frequency counts.

In the 1950's there were only a few black characters on television, all of whom were classic comic stereotypes, like *Amos and Andy* and *Beulah.* These programs were canceled as a result of organized protests. For the next 12 years, there were essentially no black characters on television, but then a few began to appear. By 1968, the proportion of black characters rose to about 10 percent, and it has remained at about that level ever since.[55] There are far fewer Hispanics, for example, only about 1.5 percent in 1975–77. During 1970–76, the percentage of Asian Americans was 2.5, and of native Americans it was less than half of 1 percent. For all minorities combined, there were about 12 percent in the period 1969–78, with a high of 18 percent in 1975.[56]

Black and Hispanic characters are both cast mainly in situation com-

[52]Korzenny, F., and Neuendorf, K., 1979. Op. cit.

[53]U.S. Senate. *Media portrayal of the elderly.* Hearing before the Select Committee on Aging, House of Representatives, April 26, 1980. Washington: U.S. Government Printing Office, 1980.

[54]Davis, R. H. *Television and the aging audience.* Los Angeles: Andrus Gerontology Center, University of Southern California, 1980.

[55]Dominick, J., and Greenberg, B. Three seasons of blacks on television. *Journal of Advertising Research*, 1970, *10*, 21–27.

[56]Gerbner, G., and Signorielli, N. *Women and minorities on television.* Unpublished report, Annenberg School of Communications, University of Pennsylvania, 1979.

edies.[57] About 41 percent of all black characters appear in only six shows. The same kind of clustering occurs with Hispanic characters; 50 percent are in just four shows. Blacks are less likely than whites to have a job, and if they are working, more likely to have a low prestige job.[58] Most Hispanic characters work in unskilled and semiskilled jobs. Many of them are cast either as comic characters or in law-breaking and law-enforcing roles.

A few studies have looked at what black characters do on television. Blacks dominate whites in situation comedies, but the reverse is true on crime shows.[59] On series with all black characters, the blacks have more personal and family problems and a lower social status than on series with both black and white characters. In the shows with both black and white characters, there was no difference between blacks and whites in giving orders or giving and receiving advice.[60]

Both black children and black adults are more likely than whites to watch programs with black characters in them. Black children usually pick white television characters as their favorites and as their models to imitate, but, unlike white children, they also choose some black characters. Compared with white children, the black children believe there are more black characters on television.[61] Black children also have more positive perceptions of black characters in terms of their activity, strength, and beauty than they have of white characters; moreover, they think the portrayals of blacks are realistic. In general, research has shown that black children exposed to a white-dominated medium do not develop destructive self-images.[62]

One line of research has studied the self-image of minority group children who have watched programs such as *Sesame Street*, *Carrascolendas*, and *Villa Alegre*. All three of these public television shows have had a favorable effect on cultural pride, self-confidence, and interpersonal cooperativeness of minority children.[63]

[57] Baptista-Fernandez, P., Greenberg, B. S., and Atkin, C. The context, characteristics, and communication behavior of blacks on television. In B. S. Greenberg (Ed.), *Life on television*. Norwood, N.J.: Ablex Press, 1980.

[58] Northcott, H., Seggar, J., and Hinton, J. Trends in TV portrayal of blacks and women. *Journalism Quarterly*, 1975, 52, 741–744.

Seggar, J., and Wheeler, P. World of work on TV: Ethnic and sex representation in TV drama. *Journal of Broadcasting*, 1973, 17, 201–214.

[59] Lemon, J. Women and blacks on prime-time television. *Journal of Communication*, 1977, 27(1), 70–74.

[60] Banks, C. *A content analysis of the treatment of black Americans on television.* (ERIC Document 115 576, 1975.)

[61] Greenberg, B., and Atkin, C. *Learning about minorities from television.* Paper presented at the UCLA Center for Afro-American Studies conference, Los Angeles, 1978.

[62] Atkin, C., Greenberg, B., and McDermott, S. *Television and radical socialization.* Paper presented at the meeting of the Association for Education in Journalism, Seattle, 1978.

[63] Filip, R., Miller, G., and Gillette, P. *The Sesame mother project: Final report.* Institute for Educational Development, El Segundo, Calif.: 1971.

Va Wart, G. *Carrascolendas: Evaluation of a Spanish/English educational television series within Region XIII. Final Report. Evaluation Component.* Education Service Center, Region 13, 1974.

Another line of research has investigated the impact of minority characters on the perceptions and attitudes of white children. Many white children throughout the country are dependent on television for their information about minorities. White children having the least direct experience with blacks said that television gave them information about the physical appearance, speech, and dress of blacks.[64] These children also had positive racial attitudes. Studies of *Sesame Street* give evidence of its favorable effect on racial attitudes. In one study, children who looked at *Sesame Street* for more than 2 years had more positive attitudes toward other races than children who had not been exposed to the program.[65]

Only a small amount of research has tested the effects of commercial programs. For example, in a study of adults it was found that with *All in the Family* and its many racial slurs, the impact on racial attitudes was directly related to the prejudices already held by the viewers.[66] In another study of *All in the Family*, the results showed that children did not seem to be influenced by the character's prejudices.[67] Finally, a different kind of program, the miniseries *Roots*, was demonstrated to have a positive impact on racial attitudes.[68]

OCCUPATIONAL ROLE SOCIALIZATION

The two main concerns of those who have investigated portrayals of occupations on television are the overrepresentation of high prestige jobs and of the "cops and robbers."

Fully one-third of television's "labor force" is in professional and managerial positions, about three times the number in real life.[69] In an analysis of soap operas, it was found that 62 percent of the women and 89 percent of the men were in the top three occupations categories, in contrast with 19 percent and 30 percent respectively in the actual labor force.[70] At the other end of the scale, a similar discrepancy exists for low status jobs. About 81 percent of women in real life hold low status jobs, but only 38

[64] Greenberg, B. Children's reactions to TV blacks. *Journalism Quarterly*, 1972, *49*, 5–14.

[65] Bogatz, G., and Ball, S. J. *The second year of Sesame Street: A continuing evaluation.* Princeton, N.J.: Educational Testing Service, 1971.

[66] Surlin, S., and Tate, E. All in the Family: Is Archie Funny? *Journal of Communication*, 1976, *26*(3), 61–68.

[67] Meyer, T. Impact of "All in the Family" on children. *Journal of Broadcasting*, 1976, *20*, 23–33.

[68] Surlin, S. "Roots" research: A summary of findings. *Journal of Broadcasting*, 1978, *20*, 309–320.

[69] Seggar, J., and Wheeler, P., 1973. Op. cit.

   Long, M., and Simon, R. The roles and statuses of women and children on family TV programs. *Journalism Quarterly*, 1974, *51*, 107–110.

   Greenberg, B., Simmons, K., Hogan, L., and Atkin, C. *A three-season analysis of the demographic characteristics of fictional television characters.* Project CASTLE (Report No. 9), Department of Communication, Michigan State University, East Lansing, 1978.

[70] Gade, E. Representations of the world of work in daytime serial television serials. *Journal of Employment Counseling*, March 1971, 37–42.

percent of television characters have these menial positions.[71] For men the gap is even greater with 12 percent on television and 63 percent in the labor force. Only two occupations rank about the same on television as in the census figures: female clerical workers and farmers.[72]

The range of different kinds of jobs on television is much narrower than in real life.[73] For white male characters, 30 percent are in just five different jobs, and for black characters, 50 percent are in only five kinds of jobs. For women, the job situation is even more homogeneous.

Concerning "cops and robbers"—actually all law-enforcement and law-breaking characters—there are many more law-related jobs in television's world of work than in the actual labor force, including not only the police, but also detectives, lawyers, judges, matrons, and wardens.[74] More of television's criminals are white than is indicated by FBI crime statistics. These criminals also are older on the average than real criminals.

What is the effect on viewers' perceptions of occupations as a result of this information coming from television? Since children ordinarily have rather limited knowledge about many occupations, it might be assumed that they obtain quite a bit of information about jobs from television. Research has borne out this assumption. When children were asked open-ended questions about various occupations, the responses were consistent with the depictions of the occupations on television.[75]

A field study in two cities was able to compare responses to two shows with characters in different occupations. The *Andy Griffith Show* had a barber and a sheriff, and *That Girl* had an actress and a magazine writer. Viewers and nonviewers, frequent and infrequent viewers, and current and noncurrent viewers among fourth, fifth, and sixth graders were compared. All three successful role models—the barber, sheriff, and magazine writer—favorably influenced the children's evaluations and perceptions of the rewards and physical requirements of the job. Neither frequency nor recency had an effect; apparently beliefs about occupations are retained for a long time.

CONSUMER ROLE SOCIALIZATION

In the study of television's effects on consumer roles, a small amount of work has been done on entertainment programs, game shows, and public service messages, but most of it has dealt with advertisements. And most of the research has been done with children.

[71]Gade, E., 1971. Op. cit.

[72]DeFleur, M. Occupational roles as portrayed on television. *Public Opinion Quarterly*, 1964, *28*, 57–74.

   Seggar, J., and Wheeler, P., 1973. Op. cit.

[73]Seggar, J., and Wheeler, P., 1973. Op. cit.

[74]Jeffries-Fox, S., and Signorielli, N. *Television and children's conceptions of occupations*. Paper presented at the Airlie House Telecommunications Conference, Warrenton, Va., 1978.

[75]Abel, J., Fontes, B., Greenberg, B., and Atkin, C. *The impact of television on children's occupational role learning*. Unpublished report, Michigan State University, East Lansing, 1981.

Young children say they enjoy advertisements, especially if they are humorous and entertaining.[76] Older children have mixed feelings about them, and adults often say that what they like least about television is the commercials. Acceptance of the truthfulness of advertisements also varies with age.[77] Young children usually believe the claims, but, by the time they are about 10 years old, about three-fourths of them have become more skeptical. Children's trust is related to the product being advertised. They are more distrustful of claims made about toys with which they are familiar than they are about medical or nutritional products. Children who are heavy viewers are more likely to believe advertisements than are light viewers.

Research has examined the effect of television on children's desire to have a product, requests that parents purchase it, and patterns of consumption. When black elementary school children were asked where they learned about a favorite toy, television was most often mentioned as a source of information.[78] Children told to list what they wanted for Christmas also named television as the most frequent source.[79] About a third of kindergarten children and more than half of third and sixth graders said that they heard about toys and snack foods on television.[80] Mothers of young children also cited television as their prime source of product information.[81]

When children were asked if they would like to have the things they saw advertised on television, two-thirds of the kindergarteners and half of the third and sixth graders answered, "yes."[82] For a group of children 5 to 12 years old, there was a high positive correlation between viewing commercials and liking frequently advertised foods.[83] Many of the children who saw an advertisement for a toy said that they would rather play with

---

[76]Atkin, C. *Effects of television advertising on children—Survey of children's and mother's responses to television commercials.* Technical report, Michigan State University, 1975.

    Robertson, T., and Rossiter, J. Children and commercial persuasion: An attribution theory analysis. *Journal of Consumer Research*, 1974, *1*, 13–20.

[77]Atkin, C., 1975. Op. cit.

    Bearden, W., Teel, J., and Wright, R. Family income effects on measurement of attitudes toward television commercials. *Journal of Consumer Research*, 1979, *6*, 308–311.

    Haefner, J., Leckenby, J., and Goldman, S. *The Measurement of advertisement impact on children.* Paper presented at the meeting of the American Psychological Association, Chicago, 1975.

    Rossiter, J. Reliability of a short test measuring children's attitudes toward commercials. *Journal of Consumer Research*, 1977, *3*, 179–184.

    Ward, S., Wackman, D., and Wartella, E. *How children learn to buy: The development of consumer information processing skills.* Beverly Hills: Sage, 1977.

[78]Donohue, T. Effects of commercials on black children. *Journal of Advertising Research*, 1975, *15*, 41–46.

[79]Caron, A., and Ward, S. Gift decision by kids and parents. *Journal of Advertising Research*, 1975, *15*, 12–20.

[80]Ward, S., Wackman, D., and Wartella, E., 1977. Op. cit.

[81]Barry, T., and Sheikh, A. Race as a dimension in children's TV advertising: The need for more research. *Journal of Advertising*, 1977, *6*, 5–10.

[82]Ward, S., Wackman, D., and Wartella, E., 1977. Op. cit.

[83]Atkin, C., Reeves, B., and Gibson, W. *Effects of television food advertising on children.* Paper presented at the meeting of the Association for Education in Journalism, Houston, 1979.

the toy than with a friend, and, in fact, they would rather play with a not-so-nice friend if he or she owned the toy than with a nice friend.[84]

Children not only say they want television-advertised products, but they urge their parents to buy them.[85] Children from 3 to 12 years old were asked how often they tried to have their parents buy an advertised toy, and 28 percent replied, "a lot," while 55 percent said, "sometimes." In a laboratory study, children were observed as they looked at television including the commercials.[86] When they later went to the supermarket, the children who had paid more attention to the commercials made more requests to buy the advertised products. Another study used a projective assessment technique.[87] Children were asked to finish a story in which a child saw advertisements for toys, food, and clothing. Ninety percent of the children said that the child in the story felt like asking for the products. Only three-fifths, however, said that the child would actually ask the parents to buy it.

The next question of course is whether or not children use or consume the product after they have it. All evidence is that they do. In a group of fourth to seventh graders, 49 percent of heavy viewers of a candy-bar advertisement ate the bar "a lot" versus 32 percent of the light viewers.[88]

A significant finding, especially for young children, is that they often take advertisements literally. When two cartoon characters, Fred Flintstone and Barney Rubble, said a cereal was "chocolately enough to make you smile," two-thirds of the children said a reason they wanted the cereal was the chocolate taste, three-fifths because it would make them smile, and over half because Fred and Barney liked it.[89] In another advertisement, wild vegetation was depicted as edible, and the children viewing it believed that they could eat a similar appearing but toxic plant.[90] After seeing a cereal advertisement with a circus strongman lifting a heavy weight, children thought that eating the cereal would make them strong.[91] Many children have great faith in the characters they see on television; they believe that Fred Flintstone and Barney and all their other television "friends" know what children should eat.

The impact of advertising on teenagers has been studied primarily by questionnaires. In most studies, total amount of viewing, rather than specific exposure to commercials, is measured, which means, of course, that

[84]Goldberg, M., and Gorn, G. Some unintended consequences of TV advertising to children. *Journal of Consumer Research*, 1978, 5, 22–29.

[85]Atkin, C., 1975. Op. cit.

[86]Galst, J., and White, M. The unhealthy persuader: The reinforcing value of television and children's purchase-influencing attempts at the supermarket. *Child Development*, 1976, 47, 1089–1096.

[87]Sheikh, A., and Moleski, L. Conflict in the family over commercials. *Journal of Communication*, 1977, 27(1), 152–157.

[88]Atkin, C., 1975. Op. cit.

[89]Atkin, C., and Gibson, W. *Children's nutrition learning from television advertising.* Unpublished manuscript, Michigan State University, 1978.

[90]Poulos, R. *Unintentional negative effects of food commercials on children: A case study.* Unpublished manuscript, Media Action Research Center, New York, 1975.

[91]Atkin, C., and Gibson, W., 1978. Op. cit.

the results show overall effects of television, not just the effects of commercials. In general, teenagers' awareness of brands and brand slogans does not seem to be related to the amount of television they watch. But a study, in which actual viewing of alcohol advertisements was measured, found that the teenagers did become aware of the brands, symbols, and content of the commercials.[92] In addition, according to other studies, teenagers who are heavy viewers tend to think that people need and use highly advertised products.[93]

Watching television is correlated to a small degree with "general materialism," defined as an attitude emphasizing the importance of material possessions and money as a means to personal satisfaction and social progress.[94] Buying and using the product are also somewhat related to seeing the advertisements.[95] These findings suggest that advertising does have some impact on the attitudes and behavior of teenagers, but it is not great. With adults, however, advertising is thought to have a strong influence on their knowledge of brand names and advertising claims.[96] Buying the product or service is, of course, the whole point; advertisements apparently do bring in more sales, sometimes to a high degree but often only to a small degree.[97]

Game shows with money and other prizes display explicit consumer behavior. The ecstasy of the winners and the studio audience's appreciative applause probably engender desires for consumer goods among the viewers. The upper-class lifestyles of characters in many dramas and situation comedies may have the same effect. Future research should move beyond advertising to explore the impact of television's information and entertainment messages on consumer behavior.

CONCEPTIONS OF VIOLENCE AND MISTRUST

Televised violence and its contribution to viewers' conceptions of social reality have been the concern of much research. For example, beliefs about the prevalence of violence in American life have been correlated with amount

[92]Atkin, C., Block, M., and Reid, L. *Advertising effects on alcohol brand images and preferences.* Paper presented at the meeting of the Association for Education in Journalism, Boston, 1980.

[93]Robertson, T., Rossiter, J., and Gleason, T. Children's receptivity to proprietary medicine advertising. *Journal of Consumer Research*, 1979, *6*, 247–255.

   Atkin, C. Effects of drug commercials on young viewers. *Journal of Communication*, 1978, *28*(4), 71–79.

[94]Atkin, C., 1975. Op. cit.

   Churchill, G., and Moschis, G. Television and interpersonal influences on adolescent consumer learning. *Journal of Consumer Research*, 1979, *6*, 23–35.

   Moschis, G., and Churchill, G. Consumer socialization: A theoretical and empirical analysis. *Journal of Marketing*, 1978, *15*, 599–609.

[95]Ward, R., and Robertson, T. Adolescent attitudes toward television. In E. A. Rubinstein, G. A. Comstock, and J. P. Murray. *Television and social behavior* (Vol. 4). *Television in day-to-day use.* Washington: U.S. Government Printing Office, 1972.

[96]Atkin, C., Block, M., and Reid, L., 1980. Op. cit.

[97]Ackoff, R., and Emshoff, J. Advertising research at Anheuser-Busch, Inc. *Sloan Management Review*, 1975, *17*, 1–15.

of television viewing. People are asked questions such as "What are your chances of being involved in some kind of violence?" "How many males work in law enforcement and crime detection?" "Does most fatal violence occur between strangers?" The answers that could be inferred from watching television are then compared with actual statistics from crime surveys and the census. The percentage of heavy viewers of television giving a television-biased answer minus the percentage of light viewers giving a television-biased answer has been called the "cultivation differential." Television, it is said, has "cultivated" the television-biased answers. Beginning in 1972, study after study in the United States has found a "cultivation differential" for prevalence of violence; people who look at a great deal of television tend to believe that there is more violence in the real world than do those who do not look at much television.[98] A possible disconfirmation comes from a study in England, but the discrepancy between the American and the English research may perhaps be explained by the fact that English television is much less violent than that in America and that heavy television viewers in England actually see less violence than do American light viewers.[99]

Exposure to televised violence has also been found to lead to mistrust, fearfulness of walking alone at night, a desire to have protective weapons, and alienation.[100]

Experimental studies have investigated changes in social reality. In one such project, undergraduate students were randomly assigned for 6 weeks to one of three television diets: light viewing; heavy viewing of programs with violence ending in justice; and heavy viewing with violence ending in injustice.[101] By the end of 6 weeks, both groups of heavy viewers became

[98]Gerbner, G., and Gross, L. Living with television. The violence profile. *Journal of Communication*, 1976, *26*(1), 173–199.

Gerbner, G., Gross, L., Eleey, M., Jackson-Beeck, M., Jeffries-Fox, S., and Signorielli, N. TV violence profile no. 8. *Journal of Communication*, 1977, 27(2), 171–180.

Gerbner, G., Gross, L., Eleey, M., Jackson-Beeck, M., Jeffries-Fox, S., and Signorielli, N. *Violence profile no. 8. Trends in network television drama and viewer conceptions of social reality 1967–1976.* Annenberg School of Communications, University of Pennsylvania, 1977.

Gerbner, G., Gross, L., Jackson-Beeck, M., Jeffries-Fox, S., and Signorielli, N. Cultural Indicators: Violence profile no. 9. *Journal of Communication*, 1978, *28*(3), 176–207.

Gerbner, G., Gross, L., Jackson-Beeck, M., Jeffries-Fox, S., and Signorielli, N. *Violence profile no. 9: Trends in network television drama and viewer conceptions of social reality 1967–1977.* Annenberg School of Communications, University of Pennsylvania, 1978.

Gerbner, G., Gross, L., Signorielli, N., Morgan, M. and Jackson-Beeck, M. *Violence profile no. 10: Trends in network television drama and viewer conceptions of social reality 1967–1978.* Annenberg School of Communications, University of Pennsylvania, 1979.

Gerbner, G., Gross, L., Morgan, M., and Signorielli, N. *Violence profile no. 11: Trends in network television drama and viewer conceptions of social reality 1967–1979.* Annenberg School of Communications, University of Pennsylvania, 1980.

[99]Wober, J. M. Televised violence and paranoid perception. The view from Great Britain. *Public Opinion Quarterly*, 1978, 42, 315–321.

[100]Gerbner, G., Gross, L., Jackson-Beeck, M., Jeffries-Fox, S., and Signorielli, N., 1978. Op. cit.

Gerbner, G., Gross, L., Signorielli, N., Morgan, M., and Jackson-Beeck, M., 1979. Op. cit.

[101]Bryant, J., Carveth, R., and Brown, D. Television viewing and anxiety: An experimental examination. *Journal of Communication*, 1981, *31*(1), 106–119.

more anxious and fearful. But there was a difference between those who saw the "just" endings and those who saw the "unjust" endings. The viewers of the programs ending in justice later chose to watch more violent television, and the viewers who saw the injustice later chose to watch fewer action-adventure programs. This finding suggests that there may be some kind of reciprocal effect in which television contributes to the formation of an attitude and then that attitude fosters looking at certain kinds of programs.

Processes and Conditions

The next question is "How does this 'cultivation effect' occur?" Or, more specifically, the questions are "Under what conditions does construction of social reality occur?" and "What are the psychological processes involved?"

The information-processing abilities of an individual may be important in construction of social reality. For example, ability to infer patterns from discrete events might be required for television programs to have an effect. Then perhaps viewer intelligence would be related to cultivation effects. Another approach might be based on the notion that children have less well-developed processing abilities than adults and therefore television's influences on them would be stronger. Young children's tendency to remember incidental information in programs might also suggest that they would be more influenced in constructions of social reality.

Viewers' attitudes toward television and how critically and attentively they view it may be significant in determining cultivation effects. Perhaps television has more impact on viewers who are inactive and passive. A relevant study here is one with soap opera fans who were attending a "soap opera convention."[102] They were compared with a random sample of women. The soap opera fans, who could be presumed to be involved and active viewers, were less influenced in their thinking by the soap operas than the other women.

Viewers' experience, including that with other media, friends, and family, as well as their already established beliefs may interact in some way with constructions of social reality. Three possible effects have been hypothesized: One is "confirmation" (or "resonance"), as when television's content is confirmed or validated by the real world.[103] A second is disconfirmation, which happens if information and experience in the world come from powerful or relied-on sources, and the messages from television then lose their effect and are disconfirmed. Third, there may be a "mainstreaming" effect: Heavy viewers from different social and cultural groups may share common concepts of social reality.[104]

The social groups around an individual could make a difference in television's effects. Two studies are relevant. In one of them, the investigator classified children according to whether their peer groups were co-

---

[102] Pingree, S., Starrett, S., and Hawkins, R. *Soap opera viewers and social reality.* Unpublished manuscript, Women's Studies Program, University of Wisconsin-Madison, 1979.

[103] Gerbner, G., Gross, L., Morgan, M., and Signorielli, N., 1980. Op. cit.

[104] Gerbner, G., Gross, L., Morgan, M., and Signorielli, N., 1980. Op. cit.

hesive or not cohesive.[105] A cohesive group was defined as one in which all the children nominated one another reciprocally as friends. The children were tested on their attitudes toward sex and gender, occupational aspirations, and interpersonal trust. Those in the cohesive group were less influenced by television. These findings suggest that the increased social interaction in groups provides alternate information which may counteract television's message.

Differences in the cultivation effect are related to family's patterns of watching television. In one study, families were described according to their tendency to restrict amount of viewing, the parents' perception of the usefulness or reality of television, conflict over television, and independence, or lack of restriction, in viewing.[106] In families that restricted use of television and in which there was little conflict, the children showed no cultivation effect for interpersonal mistrust but did show an effect for prevalence of violence. The students who could select programs as they pleased also had a higher prevalence-of-violence effect.

Finally, the specific programs watched may be related to construction of social reality. Viewing crime-adventure shows has been related both to attitudes about prevalence of violence and interpersonal mistrust, while viewing cartoons only to prevalence of violence.[107]

In summary, there is reasonably good evidence that television does contribute to viewers' conceptions of social reality, especially when they are related to violence and to feelings of mistrust. There also is evidence that television may contribute to attitudes about sex, age, and family structure.[108] Television may be only one of many influences playing a part in the shaping of social reality, but it has come to play a role that is generally regarded as significant.

[105] Rothschild, N. *Group as a mediating factor in the cultivation process among young children.* Unpublished master's thesis. Annenberg School of Communications, University of Pennsylvania, 1979.

[106] Gross, L., and Morgan, M. Television and enculturation. In J. Dominick and J. Fletcher (Eds.), *Broadcasting research methods*. Boston: Allyn and Bacon, in press.

[107] Hawkins, R., and Pingree, S. Some processes in the cultivation effect. *Communication Research*, 1980, 7, 193–226.

[108] Gerbner, G,, and Signorielli, N. *Women and minorities in television drama 1969–1978.* Annenberg School of Communications, University of Pennsylvania, 1979.

Morgan, M. *Longitudinal patterns of television viewing and adolescent role socialization.* Unpublished doctoral dissertation, University of Pennsylvania, 1980.

Morgan, M., and Harr-Mazer, H. *Television and adolescent's family life expectations.* Annenberg School of Communications, University of Pennsylvania, 1980.

Gonzalez, M. *Television and people's images of old age.* Unpublished master's thesis. Annenberg School of Communications, University of Pennsylvania, 1980.

Suggestions for Further Reading

A useful survey of the postwar years is found in Godfrey Hodgson, *America in Our Time: From World War II to Nixon, What Happened and Why** (Garden City, N.Y., 1976). The history of suburban development is found in Kenneth T. Jackson, "The Crabgrass Frontier: 150 Years of Suburban Growth in America," in *The Urban Experience: Themes in American History*,* edited by Raymond A. Mohl and James F. Richardson (Belmont, Cal., 1973). For works by critics of suburban life, see John Keats, *The Crack in the Picture Window* (Boston, 1956); William H. Whyte, Jr., *The Organization Man** (New York, 1956); and R. Gordon, K. Gordon, and M. Gunther, *The Split-Level Trap* (New York, 1961). The suburban myth developed by the critics was challenged by Herbert J. Gans, *The Levittowners** (New York, 1967), and Bennett M. Berger, *Working Class Suburb** (Berkeley, Cal., 1960). See also J. Seeley, R. Sim, and E. Loosley, *Crestwood Heights** (New York, 1956), a study of a Canadian suburb. An interesting study illustrating the suburbanization of small towns is found in Arthur J. Vidich and Joseph Bensman, *Small Town in Mass Society** (Princeton, N.J., 1958). A recent attempt to evaluate suburban life was made by Samuel Kaplan in *The Dream Deferred: People, Politics and Planning in Suburbia** (New York, 1976).

The problems of adolescents in the 1950s and early 1960s are critically explored in Paul Goodman, *Growing Up Absurd** (New York, 1960), and in two works by educational sociologist Edgar Z. Friedenberg, *The Vanishing Adolescent** (Boston, 1959), and *Coming of Age in America** (New York, 1965). For an interesting contrast, compare James S. Coleman's two works on young people, *The Adolescent Society** (Glencoe, Ill., 1961) and *Youth: Transition to Adulthood** (Chicago, 1974).

A good place to begin studying the youth of the counter-culture years is in two works by Kenneth Keniston that deal with nonhippie youth, *The Uncommitted: Alienated Youth in American Society** (New York, 1965) and *Young Radicals** (New York, 1968). A historian, Theodore Roszak, has written a sympathetic exploration of the reasons for the growth of the counter-culture in *The Making of a Counter-Culture** (New York, 1969). Many of the books that describe the cultural devel-

*Available in paperback edition.

opments of the late 1960s also advocate change. See, for example, Tom Wolfe, *The Electric Kool-Aid Acid Test** (New York, 1968); Charles Reich, *The Greening of America** (New York, 1960); and William Braden, *The Private Sea: LSD and the Search for God* (Chicago, 1967). Nicholas von Hoffman, a journalist, has explored the hippie phenomenon in *We Are the People Our Parents Warned Us Against** (Chicago, 1968). The adult counter-culture is described in Rasa Gustaitis, *Turning On** (New York, 1969). For events leading to the music explosion among the counter-culture, see the work of art historian Carl Belz, *The Story of Rock** (New York, 1968). Lawrence Veysey has written a fascinating history of communitarianism in America, including many counter-culture communes, in *The Communal Experience: Anarchist and Mystical Counter-Cultures in America* (New York, 1973). On the student political movement, see *SDS** (New York, 1973) by Kirkpatrick Sale. The impact of Eastern religions on the United States can be seen in Robert Ellwood, Jr., *Religious and Spiritual Groups in Modern America** (Englewood Cliffs, N.J., 1973), and Jacob Needleman, *The New Religions** (New York, 1970). Two science fiction works that had a great influence on the counter-culture are Robert Heinlein, *Stranger in a Strange Land** (New York, 1961), and Frank Herbert, *Dune** (Philadelphia, 1965).

Two recent books that evaluate the status of the American family in contrasting ways are Kenneth Keniston and the Carnegie Council on Children, *All Our Children: The American Family Under Pressure** (New York, 1977), and Mary Jo Bane, *Here to Stay: American Families in the Twentieth Century** (New York, 1976). The working-class family was insightfully examined directly by Mirra Komarovsky in *Blue Collar Marriage** (New York, 1964) and indirectly by Richard Sennett and Jonathan Cobb in *The Hidden Injuries of Class** (New York, 1973). An excellent collection of documents is found in *America's Working Women: A Documentary History—1600 to the Present** (New York, 1976), edited by Rosalyn Baxandall, Linda Gordon, and Susan Reverby. Ann Oakley's two books on housework are basic for an understanding of women in families: *The Sociology of Housework** (New York, 1975) and *Woman's Work: The Housewife, Past and Present** (New York, 1976).

The standard history of television is Erik Barnouw, *Tube of Plenty: The Evolution of American Television** (New York, 1975). Robert Sklar has explored the world of television in *Prime-Time America: Life On and Behind the Television Screen* (New York, 1980). Jeff Greenfield has written a popular history of the medium in *Television: The First Fifty Years* (New York, 1977). Critical studies of the impact of television are found in the following: the Report to the Surgeon General, *Television and Social Behavior*, 5 vols. (Rockville, Maryland, 1972); Horace Newcomb (ed.), *Television: The Critical View**, 2nd ed. (New York, 1979); George Comstock, *et al.*, *Television and Human Behavior** (New York, 1978); and Mariann P. Winick and Charles Winick, *The Television Experience: What Children See** (Beverly Hills, 1979).